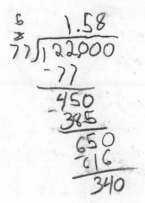

$$\begin{array}{r} 1.58 \\ 77\overline{)122.000} \\ -77 \\ \hline 450 \\ -385 \\ \hline 650 \\ -616 \\ \hline 340 \end{array}$$

$$\overline{39} \qquad 34$$

SCOTT, FORESMAN
SOCIAL STUDIES

Our World
Yesterday and Today

Teacher Consultants

Dyalthia DeFever
Amarillo Independent School
    District
Amarillo, Texas

Vidal M. Trevino
Laredo Independent School
    District
Laredo, Texas

Lillian D. Howard
Voorhees Township School
    District
Voorhees, New Jersey

Special Program Consultants

Africa
Donna Maier
University of Northern Iowa
Cedar Falls, Iowa

Asia
Linda S. Wojtan
Indiana University
Bloomington, Indiana

Bilingual Education
Lucia P. Hall, D. Psy.
Comprehensive Psychological
    Services
Albuquerque, New Mexico

Maria Guadalupe Ramos
Metz Elementary School
Austin Independent School
    District
Austin, Texas

Ricardo Romo
University of Texas at Austin
Austin, Texas

Computer Education
William Stepien
School District No. 300
Dundee, Illinois

Hispanic History
Felix D. Almaraz, Jr.
University of Texas at San
    Antonio
San Antonio, Texas

Latin America
Blanca G. Silvestrini
Center for Latin American
    Studies
University of Puerto Rico
Rio Piedras, Puerto Rico

Middle East
Henry E. Speck III
Abilene Christian University
Abilene, Texas

ISBN: 0-673-43059-6
Copyright © 1988, Scott, Foresman and Company, Glenview, Illinois. All Rights Reserved. Printed in the United States of America.
This publication is protected by Copyright and permission should be obtained from the publisher prior to any prohibited reproduction, storage in a retrieval system, or transmission in any form or by any means, electronic, mechanical, photocopying, recording, or otherwise. For information regarding permission, write to: Scott, Foresman and Company, 1900 East Lake Avenue, Glenview, Illinois 60025.

The Acknowledgments section on pages 577–578 is an extension of the copyright page.
    5678910RRW91908988

SCOTT, FORESMAN
SOCIAL STUDIES

Our World
Yesterday and Today

Book Authors

Dorothy Drummond
St. Mary-of-the-Woods
   College
Terre Haute, Indiana

Bruce Kraig
Roosevelt University
Chicago, Illinois

Program Authors

Pat Tanabe Endsley
Berkeley Unified School
   District
Berkeley, California

Geneva Gay
Purdue University
West Lafayette, Indiana

John J. Patrick
Indiana University
Bloomington, Indiana

Robert A. Pavlik
Cardinal Stritch College
Milwaukee, Wisconsin

Richard Remy
Mershon Center
Ohio State University
Columbus, Ohio

Joan Schreiber
Ball State University
Muncie, Indiana

Barbara J. Winston
Northeastern Illinois
   University
Chicago, Illinois

Lawrence Wolken
Texas A&M University
College Station, Texas

Scott, Foresman and Company

Editorial Offices: Glenview, Illinois

Regional Offices: Sunnyvale, California • Tucker, Georgia • Glenview, Illinois •
Oakland, New Jersey • Dallas, Texas

How to Use This Book

The **Contents** pages show the book's organization. Use the **Contents** pages to find page numbers for the parts of the book.

Introduction: Using Maps and Globes

This special section follows the **Contents** and has 10 lessons. These lessons will help you review map and globe skills you have learned before and preview new skills you will need this year.

Unit Organization

Our World Yesterday and Today is divided into 6 units. Each unit begins with a two-page introduction. The left-hand page has a map or a picture. The right-hand page tells you something about what will come in the unit.

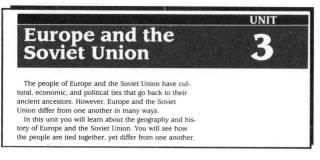

Each unit ends with a **Unit Review**. Answer the questions in the review to check your understanding of the unit. You also will find an essay question to help you tie together what you have learned.

Chapter Organization

Our World Yesterday and Today has 26 chapters. Each chapter begins with

a picture, an introduction, and a list of lessons in the chapter.

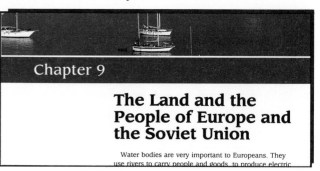

At the end of each chapter, you will find a **Chapter Review.** The review begins with a summary of the lessons in the chapter. Read this summary to remind yourself what the chapter was all about. Then answer the review questions to check your understanding of the chapter. You can apply what you have learned by doing the activities at the end of the review.

Lesson Organization

The chapters of the book are divided into lessons. Each lesson begins with a **Looking Ahead** box that lists the key words, people, and places in the lesson. Questions about the lesson's main ideas also are given.

The key words, which appear in **dark print** in **Looking Ahead,** also appear in

Lesson 1   Western Europe in the Nineteenth Century

LOOKING AHEAD As you read, look for—

Key words, people, and places:

nationalism
autocrat
kaiser

Giuseppe Mazzini
Count Camillo Cavour

Giuseppe Garibaldi
Otto von Bismarck
Sardinia
Sicily
Prussia

Answers to these questions about **main ideas:**

1. How did nationalism lead to the development of new nations in Western Europe?
2. How did the Italian states become unified as one nation?
3. How did the German states become unified as one nation?

dark print in the lesson. Every key word is defined when first used in the lesson.

Each map in a lesson has a **Map Study** caption, which asks questions to help you grasp the map's meaning and practice your map skills.

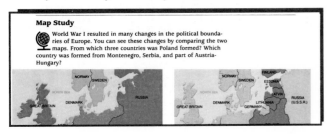

Also within lessons, large blue quotation marks set off diary entries, poems, and other special readings.

Each lesson ends with **Reviewing the Lesson**. Answer the questions in this section to check your understanding of the key words, people, and places and the main ideas in the lesson. Under the title **Thinking Things Over**, you will find one or two questions that ask you to think about the meaning of the lesson.

Special Features

Our World Yesterday and Today includes several kinds of special features that give you additional information and skills practice.

Linking Past and Present. This picture feature tells you about a topic that links history to life today.

Facts and Figures, Mystery in History, What's in a Name?, Someone to Know, By the Way. These features offer background information about interesting people and events.

Skills Workshop. Text and maps or other pictures in this feature teach you a new skill and give you practice in using that skill.

Biography. In this feature you will read about the achievements of an important person.

Geography: A Key to Our World. This feature explains how some part of geography has affected the lives of the world's people.

Resource Section

A helpful **Resource Section** begins on page 526. For more information about it, see page 527.

Contents

UNIT 2

Events That Shaped Our Modern World   100

UNIT **3**

Europe and the Soviet Union   206

xiii

Charts and Graphs

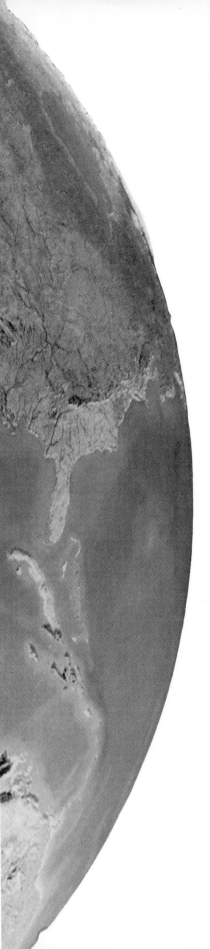

Using Maps and Globes

Think for a moment about times when you have used maps or globes. Perhaps you and your family have studied a road map before visiting friends or family in another community. Maybe you have used a globe to get a sense of what land and water features look like on our round earth.

Maps and globes serve many purposes if you know how to use them. For example, you need to know what map symbols mean and what directions are—north, south, east, west, and the directions in between. You need to know what "scale" is and how a map can show a huge area on earth on a small, flat piece of paper. As you study the pages that follow, you will find out about using maps and globes. The lessons in the section are listed below.

Lesson 1   Reviewing the Parts of a Map

Maps and globes show where places on earth are located. Globes are three-dimensional models of the earth. Maps are two-dimensional, flat drawings. They are drawings from above. Maps can show large areas, even the whole world, or small areas, such as part of a community or even a neighborhood. When you look at a map, you are looking down at an area. You can see all of the area's parts at once. You probably have used maps many times. Use the map of a school campus on page 3 to see how much you remember about maps.

First, look at the title. The title tells what information is shown on a map. The title is the best place to start when you study a map. What is the title of the map on page 3?

Second, look at the map key, also called the legend. The key shows what symbols are used on the map and what each symbol stands for. Check the map key to see what symbols are used.

The next thing to look at is the direction symbol. It shows where places are in relation to the North Pole. The letter N means "toward the North Pole." On this map and most others, north is at the top.

North (N), south (S), east (E), and west (W) are the cardinal, or main, directions. The letters NE, NW, SE, and SW, which may or may not be included in a map's direction symbol, stand for the intermediate directions. Intermediate means "in between" the cardinal directions. For example, NE stands for northeast—between north and east. What do the other letters stand for?

Another part of this map is the grid. A grid has two sets of lines. One set runs north and south. On this grid, the spaces between the north-south lines are labeled with numbers. The second set of lines runs east and west. Spaces between these lines are labeled with letters. The two sets of lines make squares that can be labeled as A-1, A-2, and so on. The grid squares are useful in describing exactly where something is located on the map. For example, the bleachers where fans watch baseball are in square C-3.

Skills Practice

1. How many symbols are listed in this map key? Describe the symbol used for the running track.
2. What direction does the front of the main building face?
3. What part of the school campus is farthest northwest?
4. What direction is the main building from the tennis court?
5. In what direction is the running track from the administration building?
6. If you walked from the southeast corner of the main building to the running track, in what direction would you be walking?
7. What is the grid location of the tennis court? In what direction is the parking lot from the tennis court?
8. What is the grid location of the baseball diamond? the ticket booth?
9. What part of the campus is mostly in grid locations B-1 and B-2?
10. Draw a map of your school and surrounding grounds. Be sure it is a proper map with all the parts to make it useful.

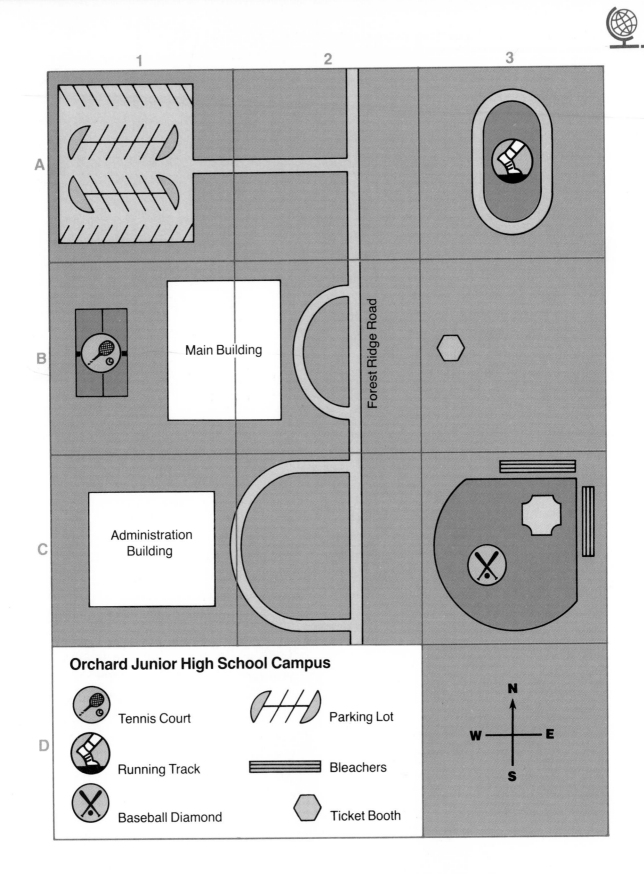

Orchard Junior High School Campus

Lesson 2   Comparing Maps and Satellite Images

As you have learned, maps are drawings that show what places on earth look like. Satellite images show what places look like too. Look at the satellite image on this page. It shows part of the boundary between the United States and Canada, and land on both sides of the boundary.

An orbiting satellite recorded the information for this image from the heat and light reflected from the earth's surface. The information then was sent back to earth. Here it was changed into an image that looked like a black and white photograph. Color was added, and the result is the satellite image you see.

Satellite images have many uses. Because certain features of land and water can change, maps sometimes need to be updated. Maybe winds and rain have eroded, or worn away, part of a lake's shoreline, for example. Perhaps heavy flooding has made a river or its tributaries change course. Perhaps new islands have risen from the ocean floor, or existing islands have been submerged by seawater and are no longer visible. Perhaps acres upon acres of trees have been lost to forest fires.

Land use may have changed—for example, with the planting of new trees or crops. Perhaps new dams have been built, creating artificial lakes. Maybe a desert has increased in area. Perhaps forces of the earth, such as earthquakes and volcanoes, have changed the shape of the land.

This satellite image, taken from an orbiting satellite in space, shows part of the earth. The image yields information for maps.

Satellite images can record the changes, and mapmakers can use the images to draw new maps. Why do you think it might be useful to show such changes on a map?

Look again at the satellite image. See if you can tell land from water. Try to find a river and a lake. Study the areas shown in a reddish color. Those are places where the land is rougher and higher than surrounding land.

Note that much of the lower half of the image is lighter in color than the upper half. The lighter-colored area shows cropland in Montana. The

4

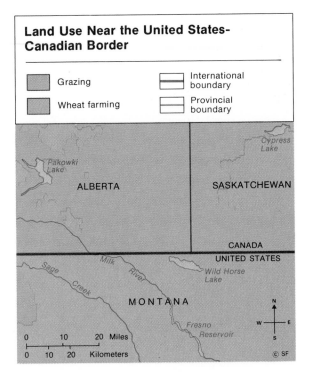

darker areas in the upper part of the picture represent grazing land in Canada. Because of these differences in land use, the boundary between the two nations is clearly shown on the image.

Compare the map on this page with the satellite image. Both illustrations show the same area. Notice how different they look, though.

One difference is that the map has labels to identify land and water features and places in the area. Without the labels on the map it would be almost impossible to know which part of the earth the satellite image showed. The labels tell you that you are looking at a part of Montana, as well as parts of the Canadian provinces of Alberta and Saskatchewan.

Another difference is that the map has a key to show ways that people use the land in the area. Use the key to identify the two kinds of land use in the area.

A third difference is that the map has a direction symbol. Because the map has a direction symbol, as well as labels and a key, you can locate real places in the area shown. You can say, for example, that Saskatchewan is east of the province of Alberta.

Skills Practice

For questions 1 through 4, decide whether you need the satellite image, the map, or both in order to answer.
1. Name a river and a lake in Alberta. Which illustration did you use?
2. Do any rivers in the area flow across the boundary between the two nations? Which illustration did you use?
3. What crop do farmers raise in the part of Montana shown? Which illustration did you use?
4. How is the land used in Canada just north of the boundary shown? Which illustration did you use?
5. Both the map and the satellite image use color. What differences do you see in their use of color?
6. Make up a statement based just on the map. Here is an example: Montana is south of Alberta and Saskatchewan.
7. Make up a statement based just on the satellite image. Here is an example: From above, some of the farms look like light-colored rectangles.
8. Suppose you wanted to make a map of an area showing changes in land use during the last few years. Why might you need several satellite images to help you make the map?

5

Lesson 3   Deciding Which Map Scale Is Best

The three maps on these pages show Paris, France. Paris is one of the world's great cities. It is located on the continent of Europe. The maps showing Paris are different, though, because each one is drawn to a different scale.

To draw or make anything to scale means to make a copy that is exactly like the real thing, except to shrink it down. A scale model of a city, for example, looks just like the city only it is much smaller. Similarly, mapmakers cannot use a piece of paper big enough to draw a whole city, so they have to draw it to scale.

To see how scale works, imagine a straight section of a road. The section is 100 miles from one point to another. Draw a line to represent the 100-mile section of the road, but make the line exactly 10 inches long. Your line is drawn to scale. One inch on the line represents 10 miles on the road.

Look at Map A. It is a close-up view of Paris. Find the bar scale on Map A. It shows that a certain distance on that map represents so many miles in Paris. Lay a piece of paper along the bar scale, and mark off where the scale begins and ends. Now line up the marks on your paper between any two points on the map. The real distance between those two points is 2 miles. Two bar-scale lengths represent 4 miles. Four bar-scale lengths represent 8 miles, and so on.

Look at Map B. It shows metropolitan Paris—Paris and some surrounding towns and cities in northern France.

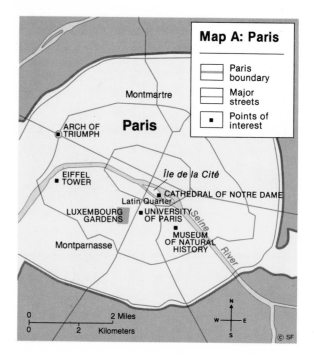

The bar scale on Map B tells you that a certain distance on the map represents 20 miles in France. Lay a piece of paper along the bar scale, and mark off where it begins and ends. Now lay your paper on the map to find 20 miles.

Now look at Map C. It shows all of France, including the city of Paris. It shows the bodies of water and countries around France also. Use the same procedure and mark a bar-scale length to show 200 miles in France.

Because the scales are different, Maps A, B, and C are useful for different kinds of information. To understand this point, think of a world map with a scale of perhaps 1 inch equal to 1,500 miles. Then think of how little detail the world map can show compared to Map A with its scale.

6

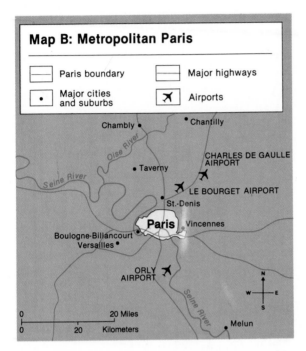

Map B: Metropolitan Paris

- ▭ Paris boundary
- ▭ Major highways
- • Major cities and suburbs
- ✈ Airports

Chambly •
• Chantilly
Taverny •
CHARLES DE GAULLE AIRPORT
✈ LE BOURGET AIRPORT
Oise River
Seine River
St.-Denis
Paris Vincennes
Boulogne-Billancourt
Versailles •
ORLY AIRPORT ✈
Seine River
Melun

0 ——— 20 Miles
0 ——— 20 Kilometers

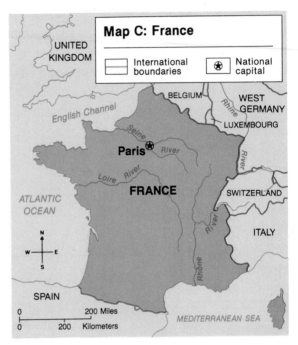

Map C: France

- ▭ International boundaries
- ⊛ National capital

UNITED KINGDOM
BELGIUM
WEST GERMANY
LUXEMBOURG
English Channel
Seine
Rhine
River
Paris ⊛ River
Loire River
ATLANTIC OCEAN
FRANCE
SWITZERLAND
Rhône River
ITALY
SPAIN
MEDITERRANEAN SEA

0 ——— 200 Miles
0 ——— 200 Kilometers

Skills Practice

Use the maps of Paris on these pages to answer questions 1–9.

1. a. Which map of Paris shows the largest land area?
  b. Which map shows the smallest land area?

2. a. What are the names of all the countries that surround France?
  b. Which map did you use?

3. a. Which place is closer to the Luxembourg Gardens—the University of Paris or the Museum of Natural History?
  b. Which map did you use?

4. a. About how far is the Eiffel Tower from the Arch of Triumph?
  b. Which map did you use?

5. a. Which map would you use to find the distance from Paris to Orly Airport?
  b. What is the distance?

6. a. What city is about 25 miles southeast of Paris?
  b. Which map did you use?

7. a. Which map would you use to find the distance from Paris to the boundary between France and Switzerland?
  b. What is the distance?

8. a. The center of Paris is on a little island called *Île de la Cité* (ēl də lä sē tā′)— the "island of the city." Which map would you use to find the distance between the Île de la Cité and the northern boundary of Paris?
  b. What is that distance?

9. a. What is the name of the river that flows through Paris?
  b. Is the answer to question 9a available from Map A, B, or C, or from all three maps?

10. Explain these statements in your own words:
  a. The smaller a map's land area is, the more details it can show.
  b. The smaller a map's scale, the larger the region it shows.

7

Lesson 4   Reading Road Maps

Perhaps you have used road maps for car trips. Road maps show how people can drive from one place to another. Look at the map of southern England below. Note that the key shows three different kinds of roads. What color is used for highways?

Now look at how the roads are numbered on the map. How are the expressways numbered differently from the two other kinds of roads? Find Highway 494 in grid squares A-2 and B-2. Through what national park does Highway 494 run?

In addition to showing what roads exist, road maps show road distances from place to place. What color are the numbers showing "Mileage between markers" in the map key? Now notice these mileage markers along the roads on the map. The numbers between the markers tell the road miles from one marker to the other. These are not the same as bar-scale distances, which are measured "as the crow flies." "As the crow flies" means that bar-scale distances are measured not along roads but rather are measured along a

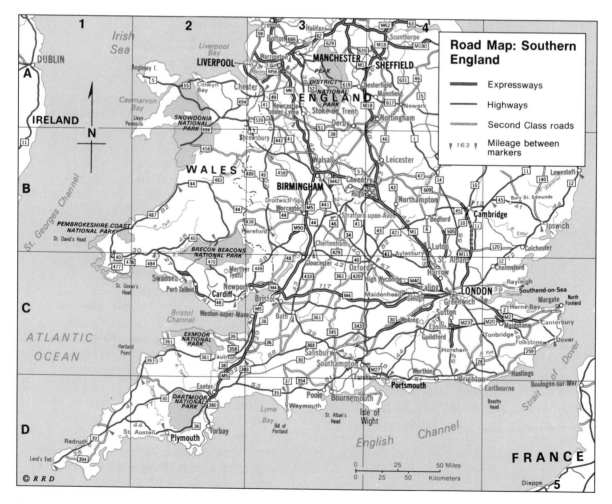

straight line from place to place. Find the markers for London and Oxford, which are both in grid square C-4. Oxford is northwest of London. The number between the two markers tells that the road distance is 57 miles between the cities of London and Oxford.

To figure out long distances you may need to add numbers together. For example, a trip from London to Oxford and then northwest to Stratford-upon-Avon (B-3), would be 97 miles altogether. Now use the bar scale to measure the distance between London and Stratford-upon-Avon. It is about 80 miles "as the crow flies."

Road distance often is a little longer than distance measured with a bar scale. Roads usually are not quite so direct as the "crow flies" routes.

A mileage chart such as the one at right is a quick way to find road distances between places. Road maps often include a mileage chart, which works like a grid. To use a mileage chart, follow these steps:

Find Manchester in the left-column list of cities on the chart. Place your left finger on the word *Manchester.* Then find Cambridge in the list across the top of the chart. Place your right finger on *Cambridge.* From Manchester move your finger along the row of numbers from left to right. From Cambridge move your finger down the row of numbers. The square where your two fingers meet shows the mileage (169 miles) between the two cities.

Mileage Chart Selected Cities

	Birmingham	Bristol	Cambridge	Liverpool	London	Manchester	Sheffield
Birmingham		96	115	94	121	83	87
Bristol	96		149	186	126	170	188
Cambridge	115	149		193	68	169	131
Liverpool	94	186	193		247	35	73
London	121	126	68	247		204	185
Manchester	83	170	169	35	204		38
Sheffield	87	188	131	73	185	38	

Skills Practice

1. What do the black numbers on the map on page 8 show? What do the red numbers show?
2. Of the three kinds of roads shown on the map, which kind is M5?
3. Which road is the most direct route between Worcester (B-3) and Gloucester (C-3)?
4. Find Portsmouth (D-4) and Brighton (C-4) in southeastern England. What is the road distance between them?
5. What is the road distance between Newport (C-3) and Swansea (C-2) in southwestern England? What is the approximate bar-scale distance between the two cities?
6. Use the mileage chart to give the road distance between each pair of cities:
   a. Liverpool and London
   b. Sheffield and Manchester
   c. Birmingham and Manchester
7. Suppose you are planning a trip from Birmingham to Liverpool. What road would you use for most of the way? What is the mileage between the two cities?

9

Lesson 5   Boundaries, Capitals, and Other Cities on Maps

Africa is a vast continent nearly four times as large as the United States. Use the Atlas map on pages 528-529 to find out where Africa is in relation to the other continents. In what direction is Africa from Europe?

Africa is not only a continent but a land of many countries. If you counted the African nations carefully on the Atlas map on page 529, you will find fifty-three of them. Some are so small

they are hard to see on the map. Now look at the map of northern Africa and the desert fringe countries below. Note that the countries look slightly larger here than on the two Atlas maps on pages 542 and 543. As you have read, maps are drawn to different scales. The map below shows a smaller land area, drawn to a larger scale, than the Atlas maps do. Therefore, the countries look larger, and you can see more details.

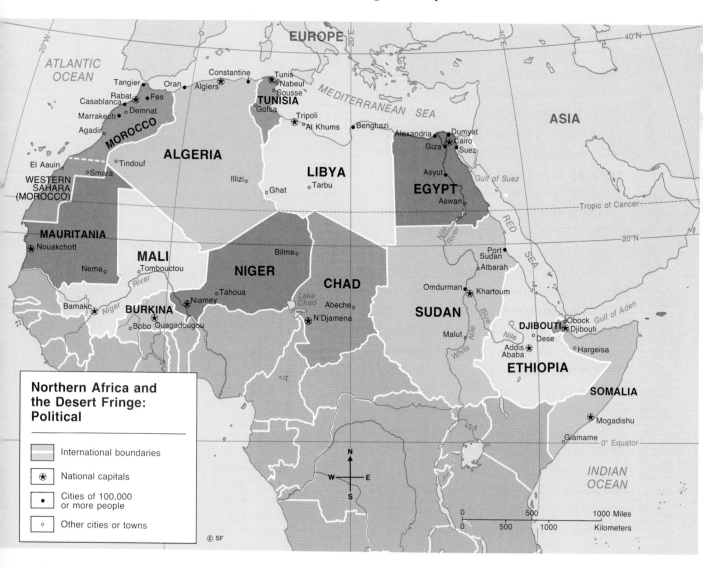

Count the number of African countries on the map on page 10. Use the map key to find out what symbol is used for the international boundaries. An international boundary is a border between countries. You should find fourteen countries. (Western Sahara is claimed by Morocco, although that claim has been disputed.)

Now look at some of the cities on the map. Note that national capitals are shown by a star. A national capital is the city from which each country runs its government. Each country has a national capital. Find the capitals of Tunisia and Mali. These cities are Tunis and Bamako.

Use the key to find what other kinds of cities are shown on the maps. For example, find Giza, Egypt. The key tells you that Giza is a large city but not the capital of Egypt. Find Demnat in Morocco. What does the key tell you about this city?

Notice the way the names of the countries and cities are printed on the map. The countries are all labeled in large, dark capital letters. The national capitals are labeled in small letters, and their labels are not as large or as dark as the country names. The names of the other cities are printed exactly like those of the capital cities. The different sizes and darknesses of letters are symbols used to help you gain information easily when you are reading the map.

In other words, labels often serve as symbols in themselves. That is, you can figure out what a label means just by the way it is shown. For example, suppose you did not know that Morocco is a country in Africa. If you know that Algeria, Libya, and other places are countries, you can figure out that Morocco is also a country. Its label is shown the same way as the labels of the other countries.

Skills Practice

1. Name all the African countries that border the Mediterranean Sea.
2. What countries border Libya?
3. What country borders Ethiopia on the west?
4. Name the national capitals of the following countries:
   a. Niger
   b. Sudan
   c. Egypt
   d. Ethiopia
   e. Somalia
5. Name a major city that is not a national capital in each of these countries:
   a. Libya
   b. Morocco
   c. Sudan
   d. Egypt
6. Which country and national capital have the same name?
7. What does the key tell you about the following three cities:
   Aswan, Egypt;
   Hargeisa, Somalia; and
   Tombouctou, Mali?
8. In general, where are most of the African cities shown on the map located?
9. What part of Africa shown on the map has the fewest cities?
10. Think about your answers to questions 8 and 9 above. What might be some reasons why there are more cities in one part of Africa—or anywhere—than in another?

Lesson 6   Land and Water on Maps

If you looked down on the earth from high above, you would see its swirling oceans and varied landforms all at once. In some ways your view would be like that shown by a physical map of the earth. A physical map shows the elevation, or height, of land compared to sea level. Sea level is the level of the ocean's surface. Most land on earth is well above sea level. Mountains are high above sea level.

Physical maps can tell you a great deal about elevation and other features of the land and water. On page 13 is another map of northern Africa and the desert fringe—a physical map. Notice the colors of the land areas. Look at the key to see what the colors mean. The dark green areas on the map represent land that is between sea level and 700 feet above. The light green areas show higher land, between 700 and 1,500 feet above sea level. What color is used to show the highest land on the map? These different colors are used to help you see different elevations easily.

If you cut the part of Africa shown on the map along a line from west to east, you would have a cross-section.

This picture shows one of the landforms found in Africa.

Look at the cross-section shown below the map. It shows some of Africa's land as it stretches from the Atlantic Ocean to the Gulf of Suez. Use the physical map and the cross-section to find the names of some of Africa's landforms.

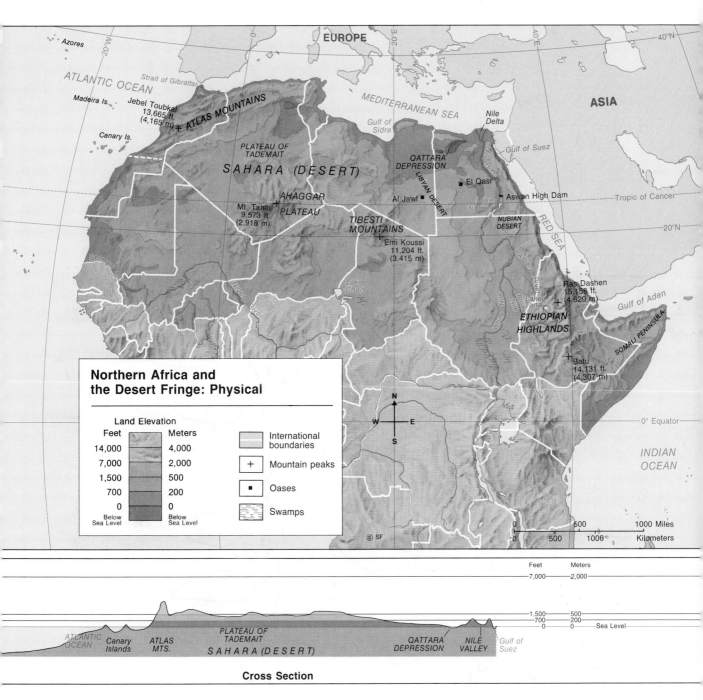

Northern Africa and the Desert Fringe: Physical

Land Elevation

Feet	Meters
14,000	4,000
7,000	2,000
1,500	500
700	200
0 Below Sea Level	0 Below Sea Level

International boundaries

+ Mountain peaks

Oases

Swamps

Cross Section

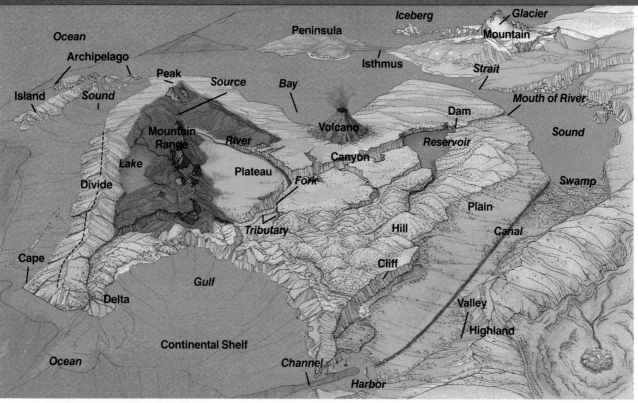

Land and Water Terms

archipelago, a group of many islands.

bay, a part of an ocean or lake extending into the land, usually smaller than a gulf.

canal, a waterway dug across land through which ships can pass.

canyon, a deep, narrow valley with high, steep sides.

cape, a point of land extending into a body of water.

channel, a narrow, deep waterway connecting two bodies of water; the deepest part of a river or waterway.

cliff, a steep slope of rock or soil.

continental shelf, a plateau beneath the ocean from which the continents rise.

dam, a wall built across a stream or river to hold back water.

delta, a triangular deposit of sand and soil that collects at the mouth of some rivers.

divide, a ridge of land between two regions drained by different river systems.

fork, the place where a stream or river joins another river.

glacier, a huge mass of ice that moves slowly down a mountain.

gulf, a part of an ocean extending into the land, usually larger than a bay.

harbor, a sheltered area of water where ships can anchor safely.

highland, an area of mountains, hills, or plateaus.

hill, a raised part of the earth's surface, with sloping sides—smaller than a mountain.

iceberg, a large mass of ice floating in the ocean.

island, an area of land completely surrounded by water.

isthmus, a narrow strip of land with water on both sides, connecting two larger areas of land.

lake, a large body of water surrounded by land.

mountain, a raised part of the earth's surface, with a pointed or rounded top—higher than a hill.

mountain range, a row of connected mountains.

mouth (of a river), the part of a river where its waters flow into another body of water.

ocean, the great body of salt water that covers almost three-fourths of the earth's surface; the sea.

peak, the pointed top of a mountain or hill.

peninsula, land surrounded by water on all sides but one.

plain, a broad and flat or gently rolling area, usually low in elevation.

plateau, a large and flat or gently rolling area high above sea level that may have deep canyons.

reservoir, a place where water is collected and stored.

river, a large stream of water that flows into a lake, ocean, or other body of water.

sound, 1. a narrow body of water separating a large island from the mainland. **2.** an inlet of the ocean.

source (of a river), the place where a river or stream begins.

strait, a narrow waterway connecting two large bodies of water.

swamp, low wetland on which grass and trees grow.

tributary, a stream or river that flows into a larger stream or river.

valley, lowland between hills or mountains.

volcano, an opening in the earth's crust through which steam, ashes, and lava are forced out.

14 Basin - Low area of
land on both sides
of a river

What is the approximate latitude of the cross section below the map?

Now look at the drawing on page 14. It does not picture a real place like a map does. It shows a closer view of some of the features shown on the map. It also shows additional features that you may find on other physical maps.

The "Land and Water Terms" list below the drawing defines each of the features shown in the picture. Find *peninsula* in the drawing and in the list. You should find that a peninsula is land surrounded by water on all sides but one. Now find *mouth* and *source* in the picture and in the list. Note that both terms have to do with rivers.

Find a hill and a mountain in the drawing on page 14. What is the difference between these two landforms? To find out, read the definitions of *hill* and *mountain* in the "Land and Water Terms" list. Notice that both a hill and a mountain are "a raised part of the earth's surface." The difference is that a hill is smaller than a mountain.

What is the difference between a mountain and a mountain range? Reading the definitions tells you that a mountain range is a row of connected mountains.

Review the map, cross-section, picture, and "Land and Water Terms" list. If necessary, check the list to find the meanings of the map symbols shown. Look at some of the labels on the map too. Note that many of the labels include terms in the list.

Skills Practice

1. How is the picture on page 14 like the map on page 13? What is the major difference between the picture and this map or any other map?

Refer to the maps on pages 10 and 13 for questions 2–6.

2. What is the elevation of most of the land in Sudan?
3. In general, which country has more lowland—Mauritania or Niger?
4. How many different levels of land does the map show for Libya? What is the highest of these levels?
5. Find the Nile River on the map. What are the two tributary rivers that join the Nile at Khartoum, Sudan?
6. Find the Nile Delta. According to the definition of *delta,* is the Nile Delta at the mouth or the source of the Nile River?
7. Review the river terms in the "Land and Water Terms" list and decide in which direction the Nile flows—from north to south or from south to north.
8. What oceans do some of Africa's coastal lowlands border?
9. What is the highest peak shown on the map?
10. Decide if the following statements are true or false. Base your answers on the map, the "Land and Water Terms" list, or both.
    a. An island is connected to a larger area of land.
    b. Mountains are not necessarily part of large mountain ranges.
    c. The entire Sahara is a plain.
    d. The Qattara Depression is about 500 feet above sea level.
    e. The Atlas Mountains in Morocco include a larger area of higher land than the Ethiopian Highlands.
11. What is the difference between a bay and a gulf?
12. Both a glacier and an iceberg are composed of ice. What is the difference between a glacier and an iceberg?
13. Does a peninsula or an isthmus have land on two sides of it?

Lesson 7 Mapping Temperature and Elevation

You probably have realized by now that map symbols come in many forms. A mapmaker can use symbols to show almost anything on a map. Isolines are an example of map symbols. Isolines are lines that show some characteristic, such as temperature or elevation, that is the same throughout an area. The word *isoline* comes from the Greek word *iso,* which means "equal."

Look at the temperature map of Asia below. Each line represents a certain average January temperature in degrees Fahrenheit. Each place located along a line has the same average temperature in January. Find the isoline that crosses the southern tip of India. Use the Atlas map on page 529 to help you locate India if necessary. The isoline indicates that southern India has an average January temperature of 80°F. Note that the same isoline goes through parts of southeast Asia too.

Find the coldest temperature on the map. The isolines indicate that average January temperatures reach −50°F in the northeastern part of the Soviet Union. Notice what a wide temperature range Asia has. How many degrees of difference are there between average temperatures in January?

Isolines can show elevation too. We usually call such lines contour lines. The elevation map in the previous lesson used color to symbolize elevation. Turn back to that map, on page 13. If that map had contour lines, each colored land area would have been separated by a line labeled with so many feet—700, for example.

The drawing and map on the next page show how contour lines work. Look at the drawing of Sugar Hill. It is a side view of the hill, drawn as if you were standing next to it. The base, or bottom, of the hill is at sea level, or

Asia: Average January Temperatures (°F)

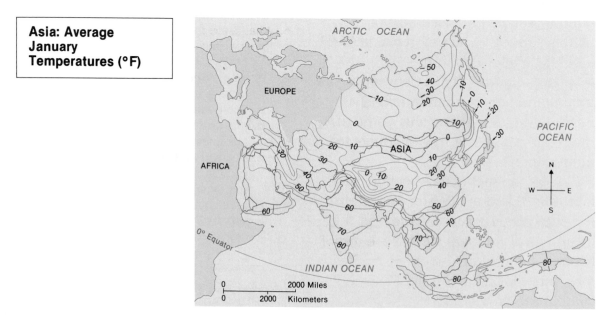

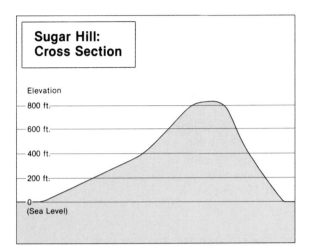

Sugar Hill: Cross Section

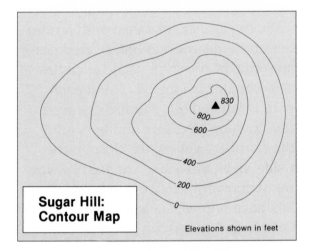

Sugar Hill: Contour Map

Elevations shown in feet

Top: Drawing of Sugar Hill showing elevation.
Bottom: Contour map of Sugar Hill.

0 feet. Find the contour line labeled 200 feet. It connects all the points on the hill with an elevation of 200 feet above sea level. Another contour line is drawn to connect points with an elevation of 400 feet, and so on. Since a contour line is drawn for every 200 feet of elevation you can tell that the top of the hill is more than 800 feet, but less than 1,000 feet.

Now look at the contour map. It too shows Sugar Hill, but this time as if you were directly above it. Find the contour lines labeled 200, 400, and 600 feet. The map shows the exact elevation for the very top of the hill. How high is Sugar Hill?

Skills Practice

For questions 1-4 use the temperature map on page 16 and the Atlas map of Asia on page 540 for reference.

1. What is the range of average January temperatures in India?
2. Give a general description of the area in Asia where average January temperatures are 10 degrees Fahrenheit.
3. What is Japan's highest average January temperature?
4. The isoline showing what average January temperature cuts through the following area: central Japan, the southern tip of South Korea, central China, and the southwestern Soviet Union near the edge of the Caspian Sea?
5. How do contour lines differ from isolines showing temperature?
6. What is the lowest elevation shown by the contour lines on the map of Sugar Hill?
7. Look at the area between the contour lines labeled 400 feet and 600 feet on the contour map of Sugar Hill. Give a statement describing the elevation of this land.
8. Look at the diagram of the side of Bald Mountain below. Use the diagram to draw a contour map of Bald Mountain. Estimate the elevation of the peak and give your map a title.

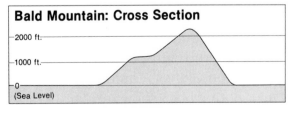

Bald Mountain: Cross Section

Lesson 8 Understanding Latitude and Longitude

Suppose you had to tell someone where the city of Tokyo is. You might describe Tokyo's location in different ways. You might say that Tokyo is in Japan, a country in Asia. You might say that Tokyo is west of the United States, far across the Pacific Ocean. You also might point to Tokyo on a world map or a globe.

All these ways of describing Tokyo's location are helpful, but they are not exact. Did you know that maps and globes have a "world address" system that can help people locate places quickly, easily, and exactly? If you understand how to use special lines that appear on maps and globes, you can understand this address system. Then you can describe Tokyo's location, or the location of any other place in the world, in more exact terms.

Here is how the address system works. Many maps and globes show a set of east-west lines called parallels. Parallels are lines that never meet. They remain at an equal distance from one another as they circle the globe completely.

The Equator is one of these parallels. It is the imaginary east-west line that circles the earth halfway between the North and South poles. The Equator divides the earth into two hemispheres, or half spheres. Everything north of the Equator is in the Northern Hemisphere. Everything south of the Equator is in the Southern Hemisphere. Find the Equator on Globes A and B on this page. Both globes show the Northern

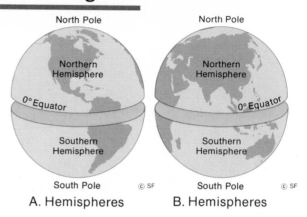

A. Hemispheres   B. Hemispheres

and Southern hemispheres from different viewpoints.

Every parallel is labeled with a number and a degree symbol (°). Degrees are units of measure used for circles. The Equator is labeled 0° and each pole is labeled 90°. Parallels nearest the Equator have low numbers, and the numbers get higher close to the poles. Look at Globe C to see how the numbers work. Notice that some parallels have names, such as the Tropic of Cancer and the Arctic Circle.

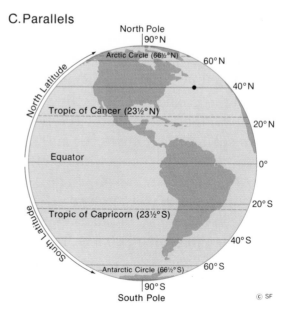

C. Parallels

18

Notice too that some parallels on Globe C are labeled *N* and some are labeled *S*. The letter *N* means the parallel is in the Northern Hemisphere, north of the Equator. What do you think *S* means?

Latitude is another word used to describe location north or south of the Equator. To find the latitude of a place, find the parallel on which it is located. Find the dot on Globe C. Its latitude is forty degrees north (40°N).

Meridians are the second set of lines that appear on many maps and globes. Meridians are north-south lines running halfway around the globe, from pole to pole. The Prime Meridian divides the earth into halves—the Eastern and Western hemispheres. Find the Prime Meridian on Globe D. The Prime Meridian is labeled 0°, and meridians on either side of it are labeled with numbers that go up to 180°. Notice that meridians that are in the Eastern

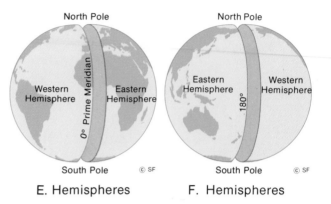

E. Hemispheres   F. Hemispheres

Hemisphere—east of the Prime Meridian—are labeled with *E* for east. What do you think *W* means? Globes E and F show the Eastern and Western hemispheres from different views.

Another word used to describe location east or west of the Prime Meridian is longitude. Find the dot on Globe D. Its longitude is 20° degrees east (20°E).

The Prime Meridian (0°) runs through the middle of this observatory in Greenwich, England.

D. Meridians

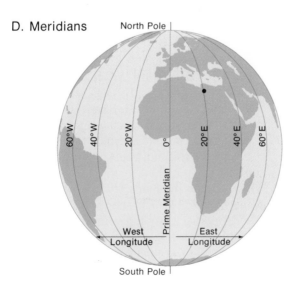

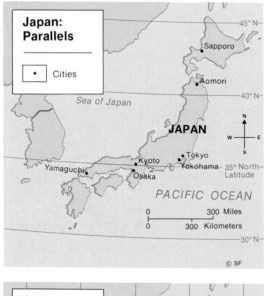

Japan: Parallels

- • Cities

Sea of Japan

JAPAN

Sapporo
Aomori
Kyoto • Tokyo
Yamaguchi• Yokohama — 35° North Latitude
Osaka

PACIFIC OCEAN

45°N
40°N
30°N

| 0 | 300 Miles |
| 0 | 300 Kilometers |

© SF

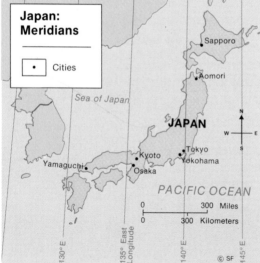

Japan: Meridians

- • Cities

Sea of Japan

JAPAN

Sapporo
Aomori
Kyoto • Tokyo
Yamaguchi• Yokohama
Osaka

PACIFIC OCEAN

| 0 | 300 Miles |
| 0 | 300 Kilometers |

130° E   135° East Longitude   140° E   145° E

© SF

Look at the two maps of Japan. The first map shows parallels, which allow you to describe the locations of the cities shown on the map by their latitude. Note that Tokyo is at about 35 degrees north latitude. The second map shows meridians. Tokyo is at about 140 degrees east. Name the locations of other cities on the maps according to their latitude and longitude.

20

Skills Practice

1. What point on earth is 90 degrees north of the Equator?
2. What point on earth is 90 degrees south of the Equator?
3. Describe the locations of points A, B, C, D, E, and F on the globes below by their latitude or longitude. State each location properly—10 degrees north latitude or 10°N, for example.

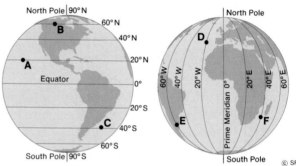

© SF

4. Arrange the following points from closest to the Equator to farthest from the Equator. Explain your answer.
   a. 30° north latitude
   b. 10° north latitude
   c. 50° south latitude
   d. 42° south latitude
5. Arrange the points from closest to the Prime Meridian to farthest from the Prime Meridian. Explain your answer.
   a. 60° east longitude
   b. 65° west longitude
   c. 25° east longitude
   d. 30° west longitude

Use the maps of Japan on this page to answer questions 6-9.

6. Is Japan located in the Northern or the Southern Hemisphere? How do you know?
7. Is Japan located in the Eastern Hemisphere or the Western Hemisphere? How do you know?
8. Which city on the maps of Japan is closest to the Equator? Which one is closest to the Prime Meridian? Explain your answers.
9. Give the approximate latitude of the following cities in Japan:
   a. Osaka
   b. Sapporo

Together, parallels and meridians form a global grid. To give the exact location of a place on earth, you need to know both the latitude and the longitude. With this information you can find any city on a map or globe.

Practice using latitude and longitude together on the map of Australia. Note that not every parallel and meridian is shown on this map or on most others, or on globes. The lines would crowd the maps and globes too much.

Find Melbourne. It falls exactly on the 145° east meridian. What is its latitude? You have to estimate this becuase Melbourne falls between two parallels on the map—35° and 40° south. The city seems to be about halfway between the two parallels—about 38° south. Melbourne's location, then, is 38° south latitude and 145° east longitude. You can write this as 38°S, 145°E. When writing location, always state latitude first.

Now locate Canberra, Australia's capital. Canberra's latitude is about 35° south and its longitude is about 149° east—35°S, 149°E.

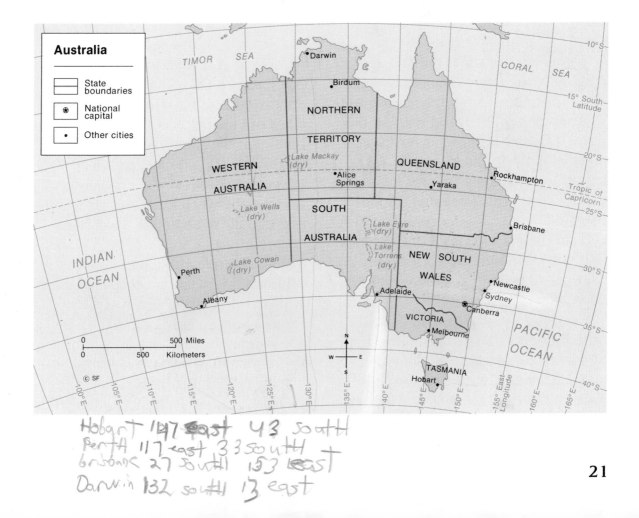

Hobart 147 east 43 south
Perth 117 east 33 south
brisbane 27 south 153 east
Darwin 132 south 13 east

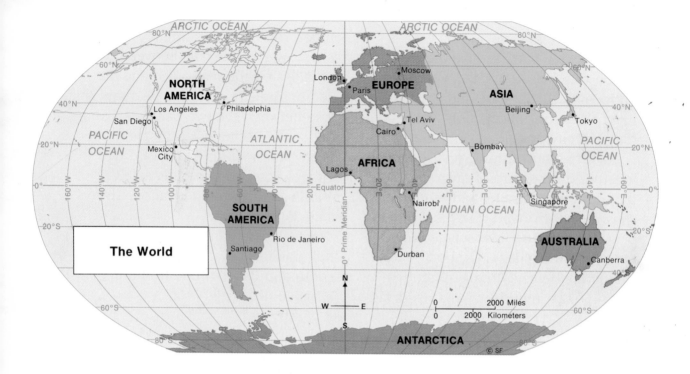

In general, the larger the area shown on a map, the larger the spacing between degrees of latitude and longitude shown. Look at the world map on this page. Note that it shows every 20 degrees of latitude and longitude. No matter what degrees are shown, however, you still can estimate locations using the latitude and longitude grid. Look at the map to check Tokyo's location one more time. See if it agrees with previous findings—35°N, 140°E. It does agree.

Now locate Rio de Janeiro in South America and estimate its latitude and longitude. Rio de Janeiro's latitude is about 23° south and its longitude is about 42° west—23°S, 42°W. Find the city located at about 30°S, 30°E. If you found Durban, you are correct.

Looking at the world map again, can you find two cities that are located on approximately the same parallel? The cities of Philadelphia and Beijing are both near the same parallel. What is that parallel? Both cities are near 40°N.

Now locate the continent that stretches between 40°N and 40°S and between 20°W and 60°E. That continent is Africa.

What latitude and longitude does the continent of Australia occupy? Looking at the world map, you can see that Australia occupies a latitude between approximately 10°S and 40°S. It occupies a longitude between approximately 110°E and 160°E.

Finally, locate a city with a longitude of 0°. It is London.

Skills Practice

1. Give the latitude and longitude of points A, B, and C on the globe below. Write the locations correctly—20°S, 40°E, for example.

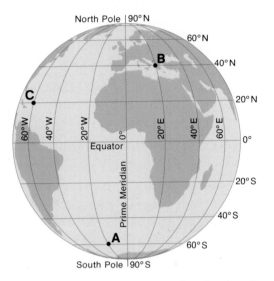

2. Give the latitude and longitude of points D, E, and F on the globe below. Write the locations correctly.

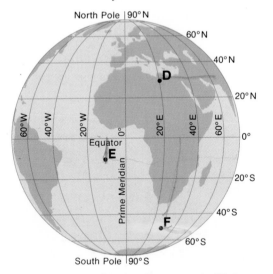

3. Use the map of Australia on page 21 to estimate the latitude and longitude of each of the following cities:
   a. Adelaide
   b. Darwin
   c. Sydney

4. Use the map of Australia to name the lake that is located nearest each of these points of latitude and longitude:
   a. 22°S, 128°E
   b. 28°S, 137°E
   c. 33°S, 122°E

5. Use the map on page 22 to estimate the latitude and longitude of these cities:
   a. Bombay
   b. Moscow
   c. Philadelphia
   d. Mexico City

6. Use the world map on page 22 to estimate the location of your community. Then estimate your community's latitude and longitude.

7. Name the cities located at these points of latitude and longitude on the map on page 22:
   a. 33°S, 70°W
   b. 1°S, 36°E
   c. 30°N, 31°E
   d. 39°N, 116°E

8. Atlases and other references often list the latitude and longitude of selected cities. Sometimes you may want to double-check your estimates against such a list. Below are the locations for some of the cities shown on the map on page 22.

PLACE	Lat.	Long.
Los Angeles..........	33°N	118°W
Singapore	1°N	104°E
Lagos.....................	6°N	3°E
Tel Aviv	32°N	34°E

   a. Place paper over the latitude and longitude of each city listed. Estimate the location of each city by looking at the map on page 22.
   b. Look at the map on page 22 to see which city has the latitude and longitude listed. Then see if your answer agrees with the list.

Lesson 10   Day, Night, and Seasons

The earth is constantly rotating, or spinning, in space. Because the earth rotates, we have day and night. When North America faces toward the sun, we have day. When North America faces away from the sun, we have night. It takes 24 hours for earth to make one complete rotation. From midnight to noon is 12 hours. From noon to midnight is another 12 hours.

Place a globe on a table. Rotate it until North America is facing you. Now pretend you are the sun. You, "the sun," are shining on the United States. It is day here, but it is night on the other side of the earth.

Now rotate the globe until North America is on the side away from you, "the sun." Now it is night in North America and day on the other side of the earth. Rotate the globe another half turn. Once more, when North America faces you, it is day all over again. The pictures on this page can help you see

how the earth's rotation causes day and night.

The earth moves in another way as well. The earth revolves, or moves, around the sun. It takes about 365 days—or one year—for the earth to make a complete revolution, or orbit, around the sun.

The diagram on the next page shows the earth revolving around the sun as the earth rotates. Note that the earth is always tilted in the same direction. We say that the earth is tilted on its axis—an imaginary line running through the center of the earth from pole to pole.

Because the earth revolves, and also because it remains tilted the same way on its axis, the earth has different seasons—summer, fall, winter, and spring. Study the diagram showing revolution. Note that the sun's direct rays strike the earth above or below the Equator at different times of the year.

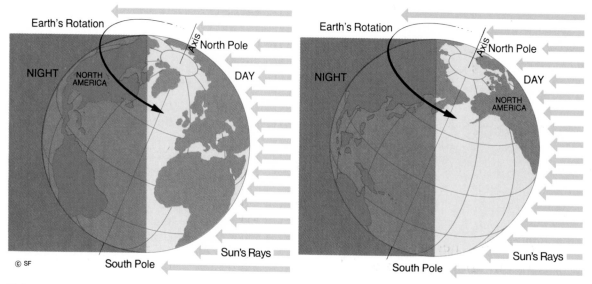

24

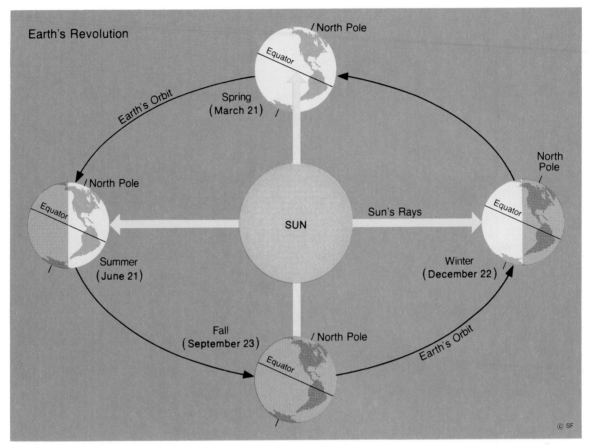

Earth's Revolution

In June, when the North Pole is tilted toward the sun, the Northern Hemisphere begins to have summer. Notice that in June the Southern Hemisphere tilts away from the sun. In June the Southern Hemisphere begins its winter.

Six months later the earth has revolved halfway around the sun. By December the North Pole is tilted away from the sun, but the South Pole is tilted toward it. The Northern Hemisphere begins its winter, while the Southern Hemisphere begins summer.

In March and September, the tilt of the North Pole is neither toward nor away from the sun. Spring and fall begin in the Northern Hemisphere at these times. Spring and fall are "in between" seasons when the Northern Hemisphere is moving toward summer or winter. The Southern Hemisphere is moving toward winter or summer.

Skills Practice

1. When it is night in most of North America, is it night or day in most of Asia and Africa? Explain your answer.
2. When it is night in South America, is it day or night in North America? Explain your answer.
3. When does fall begin in the Southern Hemisphere? Toward what season is the Northern Hemisphere moving at this time?

25

UNIT 1

The Geography of Our World

Caucasoid
features-
1. light-colored skin
2. straight, fine hair
(light to very dark)

Imagine you are an explorer. You have just discovered a new island in the middle of the ocean. As you start to send news of your discovery back home, you suddenly realize you do not know what to say. You ask yourself, "What kinds of information would people want to know about this place?"

You begin to make a list of the questions you think people back home will ask. Your list might look something like this: What does the land look like? Does the island have mountains, hills, rivers, or lakes? What kind of plants grow there? What kind of weather occurs in different seasons of the year? Does the island have anything valuable on it, such as gold, oil, or diamonds? Do any people live on the island? What are the religion, laws, and games of the island's people?

As you read this unit, you truly will be an explorer. You will explore the entire world and learn the answers to many of your questions. You will learn much about the world where you live. You also will get to know many of the people who share the earth with you.

Before You Go On

Preview the unit. This unit is about the geography of the world. Read the chapter titles below. What do you study in geography?

Study the picture. The picture shows a special room in Boston where people can view a globe from the inside. Describe the details you see in the picture.

Chapter 1 **Our World: Landforms, Climate, and Resources**

Chapter 2 **The People of Our World**

Chapter 3 **Ways of Living in Our World**

Our World: Landforms, Climate, and Resources

The earth's surface and the air above it form patterns. You can see some of these patterns by looking at pictures taken from space. If you look carefully at the picture, you can see certain land, water, and cloud patterns.

As you read this chapter, you will learn about the earth's land and water. You also will learn about the world's patterns of rainfall and temperature and how these patterns affect plant life. Then, you will study the causes of rainfall and temperature. Finally, you will discover which materials people use from the earth. The lessons in this chapter are listed below.

Lesson 1   Land and Water

Lesson 2   Climate and Vegetation Regions

Lesson 3   The Causes of Climate

Lesson 4   The Resources of the Earth

Lesson 1   Land and Water

 LOOKING AHEAD As you read, look for—

Key words, people, and **places:**

landform	Ural Mountains
elevation	Caucasus Mountains
	Himalayas
	North European Plain
	Plateau of Tibet
	Lake Superior
	Nile River

Answers to these questions about **main ideas:**

1. What are the seven continents of the earth?
2. What are the four major landform regions of the earth?
3. What kinds of bodies of water are found on the earth?

You can get an astronaut's view of the world by looking at a globe. As you spin the globe, notice its color patterns. You can see landmasses separated by large, blue oceans. If you have a physical globe, you probably can make out mountain ranges. You can clearly see the lowland areas, too.

Your mission in this lesson is to take a much closer look at the earth's natural features. If you need to, look back at the information on page 14 as you read the lesson. That information will help you fulfill your mission.

Continents

The seven large landmasses on the earth's surface are called continents. From largest to smallest, the continents are Asia, Africa, North America, South America, Antarctica, Europe, and Australia. Find these continents on the map on pages 32-33. Which continents are in the Southern Hemisphere?

Asia and Europe. Because they actually are part of one landmass, Asia and Europe sometimes are viewed as one continent called Eurasia. Looking at the map, you can see that Eurasia stretches from the Atlantic Ocean to the Pacific Ocean. The United States could fit into this area five times.

Although Eurasia could be called one continent, certain physical features do separate Asia from Europe. In the north, the Ural Mountains divide Asia and Europe. In the south, the Caspian Sea, the Black Sea, and the Caucasus Mountains divide the two continents. Look at the map on pages 32-33. With your finger, trace the physical boundary between Asia and Europe.

Africa. The continent of Africa makes up 20 percent of the world's land. Only Asia has more land area than Africa. The Atlantic Ocean lies to the west of Africa, and the Indian Ocean lies to the east. Look at the map on pages 32-33. What body of water separates Africa from Europe?

North and South America. On the map on pages 32-33, notice that North America stretches from the Arctic Ocean in the north to the Caribbean

Sea in the south. North America covers more than 15 percent of the world's land. The land area of South America is a little more than two-thirds the size of North America. Both North and South America are bordered by the Atlantic Ocean in the east and the Pacific Ocean in the west.

Antarctica and Australia. Although Antarctica makes up 9 percent of the world's land, little land can be seen. A huge icecap covers most of the continent. In some places, this icecap is more than a mile thick.

Australia sits in the Southern Hemisphere, surrounded by the Pacific and Indian oceans. Find Australia on the map on pages 32-33. How does the size of Australia compare with the sizes of the other continents?

Landform Regions

Geographers use the word **landform** to describe a surface feature of the earth. The major kinds of landforms are mountains, hills, plateaus, and plains. Geographers divide land into landform regions based on what kind of landform occurs most often in an area. The map on pages 32-33 shows the world's major landform regions.

Mountain and Hill Regions. Mountains and hills are raised parts of the earth's surface with sloping sides. The main difference between mountains and hills is their **elevation**—their height above sea level. Mountains rise 2,000 or more feet above sea level. Hills are lower than 2,000 feet.

The highest mountains in the world are in central Asia. One of central

This plateau once was flat like a table. However, water and wind have cut deep, narrow valleys into the land.

Only a few people live in the Himalayas, where peaks rise higher than 20,000 feet above sea level. How is the land where this village sits different from the land around it?

Asia's mountain ranges, the Himalayas (him′ə lā′əz), has the two hundred highest peaks in the world.

Fewer people live in mountain and hill regions than on flatter land. People who do live in mountain and hill regions often make their homes in the valleys between the mountains or hills.

Plains Regions. Plains are flat or gently rolling areas that are close to sea level in elevation. Plains often are heavily populated. Plains make up only 40 percent of the land's surface, but they are home to over 80 percent of the earth's people. Railroads, highway systems, and large cities usually have been built on plains. In addition, some plains regions have thick, fertile soil that is good for farming.

The world's largest plain—the North European Plain—stretches for over 1,000 miles. It runs from the Ural Mountains to the western coast of France. Find the North European Plain on the map on pages 32-33.

Plateau Regions. Plateaus, like plains, are flat or gently rolling areas. However, unlike plains, plateaus are high above sea level. A plateau also may be cut with deep, narrow valleys, giving it a rugged look. Plateaus rise at least 2,000 feet above sea level. Some plateaus reach much higher elevations. For example, the world's highest plateau—the Plateau of Tibet—has an elevation of 20,000 feet above sea level.

Bodies of Water

Land makes up only a small part of the earth's surface. Water is far more widespread, covering about 70 percent of the earth's surface.

31

The World: Landform Regions

Legend:
- Mountains
- Hills
- Plateaus
- Plains
- Ice-covered land
- International boundaries

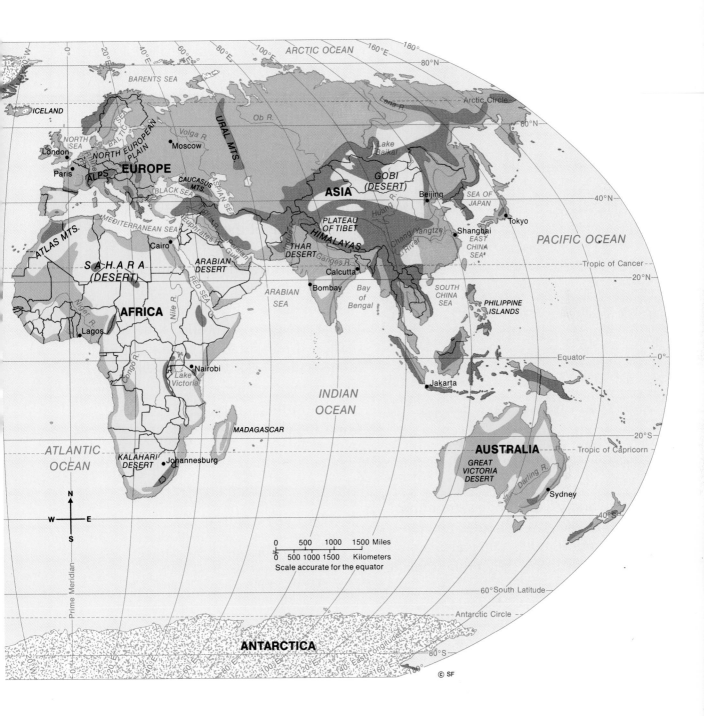

Map Study

The map shows where the major landform regions of the world are located. Which continent has a greater area of plateaus than any other landform? Which two continents have mountains running almost the entire length of their western coasts? What landform region borders the Arctic Ocean in Asia?

33

The Nile River provides a highway of water for the people of Egypt.

The world's water bodies are important to people. Water bodies provide transportation routes. They also are a source of food, and they bring water to animals and people.

Oceans. The four oceans of the world are really one body of water. Only the names change as you move from one part of the globe to another. On the map on pages 32-33, trace with your finger the connections among the Pacific, the Indian, the Atlantic, and the Arctic oceans.

Seas and Lakes. Most seas are bodies of salt water that are smaller than oceans. Actually, seas are extensions of oceans, partly surrounded by land. A sea may be linked to the ocean by a narrow channel of water called a strait. For example, the Strait of Gibraltar connects the Mediterranean Sea and the Atlantic Ocean. Find a strait in the picture on page 14.

Lakes are large bodies of water completely surrounded by land. Most lakes contain fresh water. The largest freshwater lake in the world is Lake Superior. It is one of the five Great Lakes of North America.

Rivers. A river is a stream of water that usually flows into an ocean, a lake, or some other body of water. The longest river in the world is the Nile in Africa. It measures 4,145 miles from its source near Lake Victoria to where it enters the Mediterranean Sea. On the landform map on pages 32-33, use your finger to follow the course of the Nile River.

Reviewing the Lesson

Recalling Key Words, People, and Places
1. Identify the key words defined below:
    a. a surface feature of the earth
    b. height above sea level
2. Tell where each place is located:
    a. Ural Mountains
    b. North European Plain
    c. Lake Superior
    d. Nile River

Remembering Main Ideas
1. Explain why the continents of Europe and Asia sometimes are called Eurasia.
2. What is the difference between mountains and hills?
3. What are the differences among oceans, seas, and lakes?

Thinking Things Over
Why do you think large cities usually have been built in plains regions?

34

Lesson 2   Climate and Vegetation Regions

LOOKING AHEAD As you read, look for—

Key words, people, and **places:**

weather
climate
precipitation
natural vegetation
tropics

rainforest
scrub
deciduous
tundra

Answers to these questions about **main ideas:**

1. What are the main types of climate and natural vegetation?
2. What kinds of natural vegetation are found in hot climate regions?
3. Where are warm climates usually found?
4. What kinds of natural vegetation are found in the cool climate regions?
5. Where do cold climates occur?

What is the weather like today? Is it raining? Is the sun shining? Is the wind blowing? Is it cold or warm? Is this a good day to play baseball or a good day to go ice-skating? All these questions concern the conditions around you today.

The word **weather** describes the daily conditions of the air around and above us. In most places the weather changes from day to day. However, every place has a pattern of weather that occurs over a long time. This pattern of weather is called **climate.**

Climate has two main parts. The first part is **temperature**—how hot or cold the air gets. The second part is **precipitation**—moisture that falls to the ground as rain or snow. Other things, such as air pressure and the usual strength and direction of the wind, also play a part in the climate of a place.

In parts of Asia, a season of heavy rains occurs each year. This weather pattern is part of the climate of the region.

World Climate and Vegetation Regions

In this lesson you will learn about the major climate types found throughout the world. You also will learn about the different kinds of natural vegetation that are found in the various climate regions. **Natural vegetation** is plant life that is native to a region and grows without the help of people. The kind of natural vegetation in a place mostly depends on its climate.

The map below shows where the world's major climate types are found. Look at the map and its key and note that the climate regions of the world can be put into five groups: hot, warm, cool, cold, and high mountains.

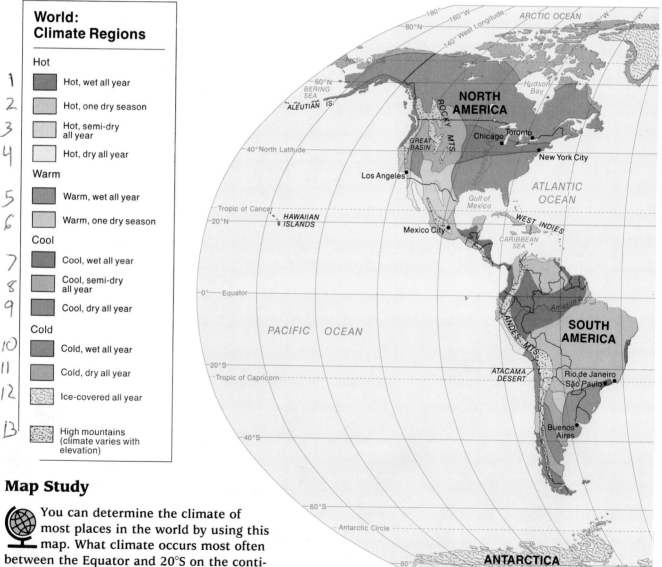

World: Climate Regions

Hot
1.   Hot, wet all year
2.   Hot, one dry season
3.   Hot, semi-dry all year
4.   Hot, dry all year

Warm
5.   Warm, wet all year
6.   Warm, one dry season

Cool
7.   Cool, wet all year
8.   Cool, semi-dry all year
9.   Cool, dry all year

Cold
10.   Cold, wet all year
11.   Cold, dry all year
12.   Ice-covered all year
13.   High mountains (climate varies with elevation)

Map Study

You can determine the climate of most places in the world by using this map. What climate occurs most often between the Equator and 20°S on the continents of Africa and South America?

The map on pages 38-39 shows the world's natural vegetation regions. Notice the six main groups of natural vegetation: forest, grassland, desert, tundra, ice-covered land, and high mountains. As you read, check and compare these maps to note the locations of and the relationships between climate regions and natural vegetation regions.

Hot Climate Regions

For the most part, hot climates occur in the parts of the world between the Tropic of Cancer and the Tropic of Capricorn. The Tropic of Cancer is the parallel 23½ degrees north of the Equator, and the Tropic of Capricorn is the parallel 23½ degrees south of the Equator. The area between these two

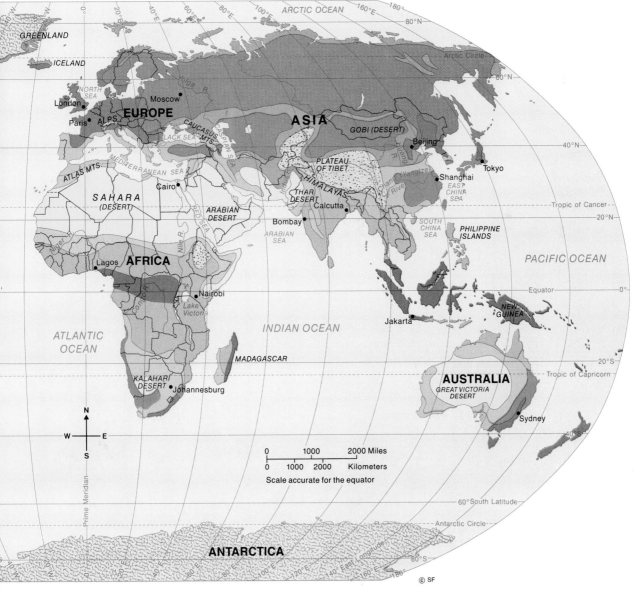

parallels often is called the **tropics.** The climates and natural vegetation in the tropics sometimes are called *tropical.* Temperatures in the hot climates usually are high all through the year. However, rainfall in hot climates varies.

One kind of hot climate has heavy rains throughout the year. This kind of climate can be found in much of Africa around the Equator, the area around the Amazon River in South America, and the islands of Southeast Asia. **Rainforests,** as the name suggests, grow in these areas of heavy rainfall. Moisture and strong sunlight create thick, fast-growing forests. Most trees in the rainforests keep their broad, shiny leaves all year long.

A second kind of hot climate has one dry season. On the map on pages

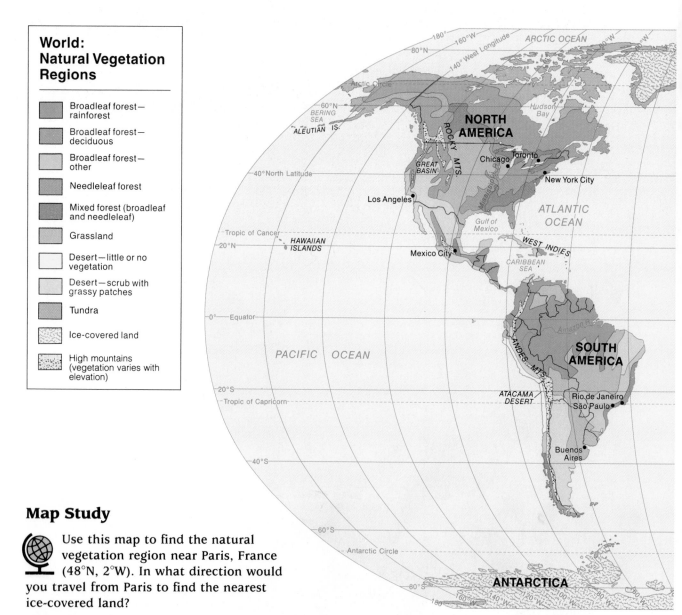

Map Study

Use this map to find the natural vegetation region near Paris, France (48°N, 2°W). In what direction would you travel from Paris to find the nearest ice-covered land?

38

36-37, find the areas that have a climate that is hot with one dry season. The natural vegetation in this climate region depends on the amount of rainfall. Heavy rainfall produces rainforests. However, in areas that receive less rain, tall, thick grasslands are found.

3 Grasslands also grow in a third type of hot climate, which is semi-dry all year. Areas with this type of climate receive only a little rain—less than 2 inches each month. Therefore, the grasses in these areas are shorter and less thick than those in wetter regions.

4 A fourth kind of hot climate is dry all year. It usually receives less than ½ inch of rain per month. These regions, called deserts, are so dry that only the most hardy plants can survive. A kind

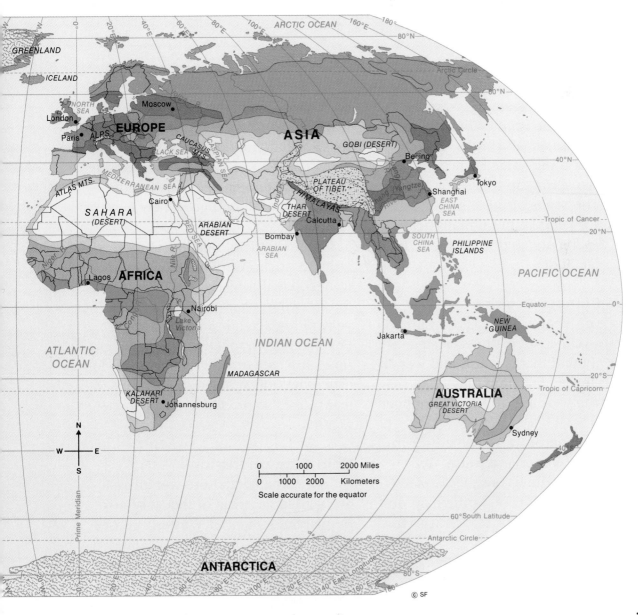

© SF

Facts and Figures

The Sahara is the largest and one of the hottest deserts in the world. *Sahara* means "desert region" in Arabic. The Sahara covers an area in northern Africa equal to the entire area of the continent of Australia. The greatest distance from east to west in the Sahara is about 3,200 miles. This is greater than the distance from New York to San Francisco.

In some parts of the Sahara, daytime temperatures can reach 120°F. in the summer. However, when the sun sets, the desert cools off quickly. The difference between daytime and nighttime temperatures can be more than 50°F. In winter even daytime in the Sahara cools off. Average winter temperatures range between 50°F. and 60°F. Frosts and light snowfall occur in some of the high areas of the Sahara in the winter months.

of vegetation called **scrub** grows in some deserts. Scrub includes patches of hardy grass, small shrubs, and cactuses. After a rain, small flowering plants also spring up to live for a few weeks. The seeds of these plants can survive for years until rain falls again. Other deserts are so dry they have little or no vegetation.

Warm Climate Regions

Much of Japan, southeastern China, and the southeastern United States have a climate that is warm and wet all year. In these areas rain falls in all seasons of the year and winters do not get very cold.

Another kind of warm climate—with its mild, wet winter and warm, dry summer—sometimes is called a Mediterranean climate. Look at the map on pages 36-37 and find a reason why this climate got its name.

Most warm climate regions receive enough rain—more than 20 inches each year—for forests to grow. Broadleaf deciduous forests grow where rain falls regularly and winters are not very cold. These forests are called **deciduous** because their trees shed their leaves each fall and grow new leaves in spring.

Certain kinds of needleleaf forests grow in warm, wet climates. The trees in needleleaf forests shed their leaves too. However, new needles grow all year to replace the ones that are lost. For this reason, needleleaf trees sometimes are called evergreens. Mixed forests of broadleaf deciduous and needleleaf trees also grow in warm climate regions.

Cool Climate Regions

Cool climates that are wet all year occur in large areas of the Northern Hemisphere. Most of Western Europe and large parts of the United States have this climate. This type of climate has warm summers and cool or cold

40

winters. On the map on pages 36-37, find the areas in the Southern Hemisphere that have a cool, wet climate. The natural vegetation found in this climate region mostly consists of broadleaf deciduous and mixed forests. However, some regions with this climate contain grasslands.

A small part of the plains and plateau regions of North America, South America, and Eurasia have a cool climate that is semi-dry all year. Rainfall in these places averages less than 20 inches a year. These cool, semi-dry climate regions usually are made up of grasslands.

Central Asia, southern Africa, South America, and the United States contain areas with a climate that is cool and dry all year. These areas receive very little precipitation and usually have cold winters. These areas contain scrub or else have little or no vegetation.

Cold Climate Regions

The far northern United States, much of Canada, and parts of northern Europe and the Soviet Union are cold and wet all year. Summers in these places are cool. Winters, which can last for four or five months or more, are cold. For the most part, the natural vegetation of these places consists of needleleaf forests.

In regions that are cold and dry all year, small amounts of precipitation fall as snow. Temperatures are always low, so the snow remains on the ground for many months. On the map on pages 36-37, notice that there is a cold and dry climate region along the shores of the Arctic Ocean.

Vegetation grows thickly in the climate of the rainforest (left). However, few plants survive the cold tundra (right).

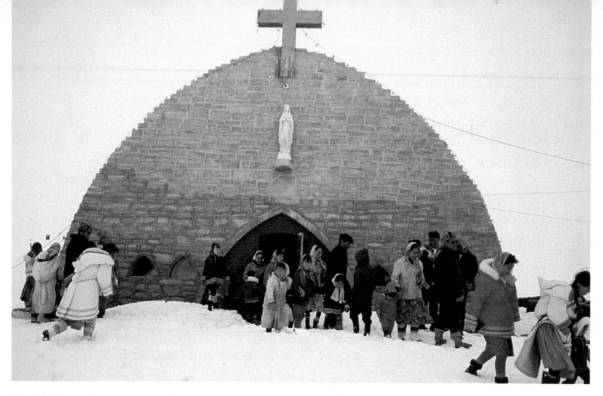

People live almost everywhere, even in the worst climates. These Eskimos live in the cold climate north of the Arctic Circle.

The natural vegetation of cold and dry regions consists mostly of mosses and short, hardy grasses. The area where this type of natural vegetation grows is called **tundra.**

The temperatures in ice-covered regions average below 32°F. all year long. The snow and the ice in these areas never melt. No vegetation grows in these areas. Notice that both the climate map and the natural vegetation map show Antarctica and most of Greenland as areas that are ice-covered all year.

The mountain areas of the world have many different climates and many different types of natural vegetation. Because of this, mountain areas are a separate climate and natural vegetation region. In mountain areas natural vegetation and climate vary with elevation. In fact, elevation is a very important influence on climate. In the next lesson, you will learn how elevation and other factors affect the climate of a place.

Reviewing the Lesson

Recalling Key Words, People, and Places
Identify the key words defined below:
1. the kind of weather that occurs regularly in one place over a long period of time
2. natural vegetation that includes patches of hardy grass, small shrubs, and cactuses
3. an area of natural vegetation consisting mostly of mosses and short, hardy grasses

Remembering Main Ideas
1. What are the five main climate types?
2. Where do rainforests grow?
3. What type of climate is found in most areas around the Mediterranean Sea?
4. What vegetation grows in cool, semi-dry climate regions?
5. Where are the coldest places on earth?

Thinking Things Over
In which climate region do you live? Describe your region's climate, and then explain how climate affects the activities of the people.

42

Lesson 3   The Causes of Climate

LOOKING AHEAD As you read, look for—

Key words, people, and **places:**

latitude   windward
ocean current   leeward
altitude

Answers to these questions about **main ideas:**

1. How does latitude affect climate?
2. How does nearness to large bodies of water affect climate?
3. In what ways do landforms affect climate?

You have read that the word *climate* describes the kind of weather that occurs regularly in one place over a long period of time. However, you also need to know what causes climate. In this lesson you will learn that the three most important causes of a place's climate are its latitude, its nearness to water, and its landforms.

Latitude

You have learned that **latitude** is location north or south of the Equator. The Equator at 0° latitude is an imaginary line midway between the earth's poles. The North Pole is 90° north latitude, and the South Pole is 90° south latitude.

The map on this page divides the earth into three latitude zones: the low latitudes, the middle latitudes, and the high latitudes. Notice that the latitude zones in the Southern Hemisphere are a mirror image of those in the Northern Hemisphere.

The low latitudes—also known as the tropics—are those close to the Equator. As you can see on the map, the low latitudes extend from the Equator to 23½°N and 23½°S.

Climates within the tropics tend to be hotter year-round than climates in the middle and high latitudes. This is because the sun's rays shine more directly in the low latitudes than they do in the middle and high latitudes.

The middle latitudes extend from 23½° to 66½° north and south of the Equator. The sun's rays in the middle

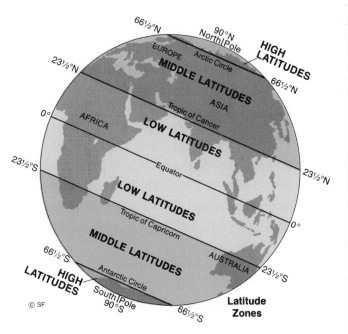

Latitude Zones

Map Study

Which continent is mostly in the low latitudes? In what latitude zone is Asia?

43

Florida (left) is warm in the winter and Alaska (right) is cool in spring. How does latitude affect the climate of these places?

latitudes are nearly direct in the summer and quite indirect in the winter. This difference causes the weather to change with the seasons.

The high latitudes extend from 66½°N to the North Pole and 66½°S to the South Pole. The high latitudes never receive direct rays from the sun. Every place in the high latitudes has at least one day a year when the sun never rises. At the North and South poles, the sun is not even visible for half the year. Because of this, lands in the high latitudes have very cold winters and quite cold summers.

Look again at the map on page 43. Notice how most of Europe is in the middle latitudes. This is a main reason why Europe is neither very hot nor very cold. Asia is so large that it sits in all three latitude zones. Those parts of Asia in the high latitudes have long, cold winters. In contrast, the parts of Asia in the tropics are hot all year.

Nearness to Water

Latitude is not the only cause of a place's climate. The climate of a place near a large body of water tends to be warmer in winter and cooler in summer than the climate of other places at the same latitude. There are two reasons for this difference.

First, water heats up and cools down more slowly than large landmasses do. Thus, water temperatures tend to stay more even than do land temperatures. When winds pass over water, they are affected by the temperature of the water. As a result, winds blowing off large bodies of water keep the land nearby from getting too hot or too cold. In winter the winds warm the land. In summer they cool the land.

Second, ocean currents affect climate. An **ocean current** is a flow of water through the ocean. Ocean currents are something like rivers. However, an ocean current carries many times more water than even the largest river.

Look at the map of ocean currents below. Warm currents tend to raise the temperature of nearby land that otherwise would be cool or cold. For example, temperatures in Tokyo, on the eastern coast of Japan, would be much lower if it were not for the warm Japan current. The east coast of North America also is warmed by an ocean current. Find this current on the map.

What is the name of this current?

Cold currents, on the other hand, have a cooling effect on land. On the map, find the cold ocean current that runs along the west coast of South America. This ocean current carries more water than any other current. What is the name of this cold ocean current?

Landforms

Landforms affect climate in two ways. First, the elevation of a landform has an important effect on climate. Elevation is height above sea level. Another word for elevation is **altitude.**

Map Study

This map shows the world's major ocean currents. In which direction does the current called the North Atlantic Drift flow? Is the North Atlantic Drift a cold current or a warm current? Which current moves north along the southwestern coast of Africa?

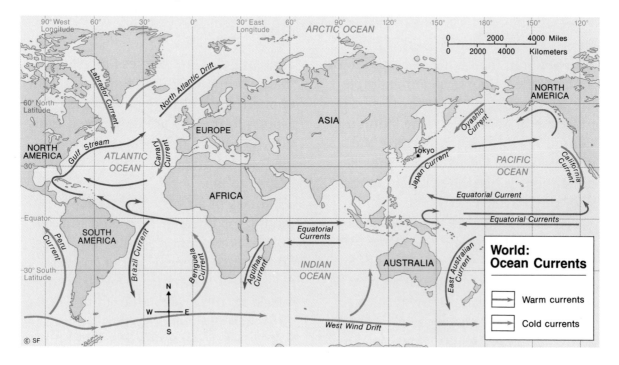

45

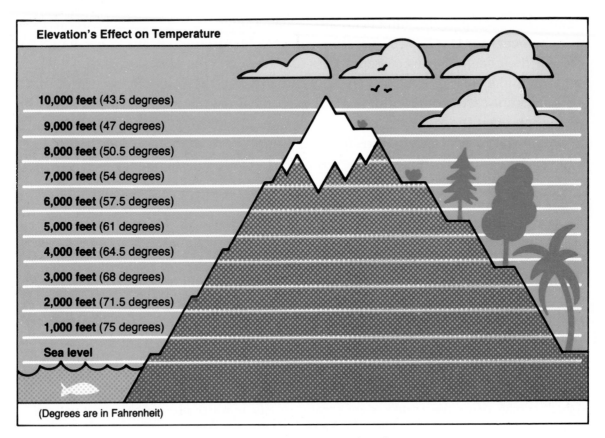

Elevation's Effect on Temperature

10,000 feet (43.5 degrees)

9,000 feet (47 degrees)

8,000 feet (50.5 degrees)

7,000 feet (54 degrees)

6,000 feet (57.5 degrees)

5,000 feet (61 degrees)

4,000 feet (64.5 degrees)

3,000 feet (68 degrees)

2,000 feet (71.5 degrees)

1,000 feet (75 degrees)

Sea level

(Degrees are in Fahrenheit)

Use the diagram to solve this problem: The temperature is 55°F. at an altitude of 1,000 feet above sea level. What is the temperature at 7,000 feet above sea level?

In general, the higher the altitude of a place, the colder it is. For example, the Himalayas and the Thar Desert in India are at about the same latitude in Central Asia. However, because the desert has a lower elevation, the climate there is hot. The climate in the high Himalayas is cold. The diagram above shows that, on the average, temperatures fall 3° to 4°F. for every 1,000 feet of altitude.

Landforms also affect the amount of precipitation a place receives. A mass of air picks up moisture as it moves across a body of water. However, air can hold only so much moisture,

and cool air can hold less moisture than warm air. When the air gets cold enough, the moisture condenses. Clouds in the sky are condensed moisture. When a cloud becomes overloaded with moisture, rain or snow begins to fall.

A mass of air becomes cooler as mountains or other high land force it to rise. For example, moist air moves off the Pacific Ocean in the southern part of South America. The air is forced to rise by the Andes Mountains. As the air rises and cools, moisture condenses and falls as rain or snow on Chile. The air that moves down the eastern slopes

These South American mountains are in the tropics. How is this picture like the diagram on page 46? What vegetation might you expect to see if you traveled farther down the mountains?

of the Andes toward Patagonia in Argentina is dry. Look at the map on pages 36-37. What types of climate occur in the southern part of South America?

Chile is to the windward side of the Andes. The **windward** side of a mountain or other landform faces the usual direction of the wind. Patagonia is on the **leeward** side—that is, the side away from the wind. The windward side of the Andes receives more than 60 inches of rain each year. However, the yearly rainfall in Patagonia measures less than 10 inches. Deserts sometimes are found on the leeward side of high mountain ranges.

Reviewing the Lesson

Recalling Key Words, People, and Places
Identify the key words defined below:
1. a large amount of water flowing through the ocean, like a river
2. height above sea level
3. the side of a mountain or other landform on the side toward the wind

Remembering Main Ideas
1. What kind of climate do lands in high latitudes have?
2. How do ocean currents affect the temperature of a place?
3. How do landforms affect the precipitation of a place?

Thinking Things Over
What are the most important influences on the climate of the area where you live? Give reasons for your answer.

Lesson 4   The Resources of the Earth

LOOKING AHEAD As you read, look for—

Key words, people, and **places:**

natural resource
mineral
technology
pollution

Answers to these questions about **main ideas:**

1. What are the life-giving natural resources?
2. How are minerals distributed across the earth?
3. For what purposes are coal, oil, and natural gas used?
4. Why is it important to manage the world's resources carefully?

Did you ever think of the earth as a treasure house of gifts? You may wonder what gifts the earth offers you. The earth gives you, for instance, air to breathe, food to eat, and water to drink. It provides gifts of materials for clothes and buildings and sources of energy. These gifts, called natural resources, make life possible.

A **natural resource** is anything in, on, or above the earth that people use to meet their needs. Some natural resources, such as air, are found almost everywhere. Others, like water, are unevenly distributed over the earth. Also, some areas of the world have many different kinds of natural resources, while other areas have few.

Life-giving Resources

The earth's most important natural resources are air, water, soil, and sunlight. People tend to take them for granted, but these resources make it possible for life on earth to exist.

Water, for instance, is used for drinking, cooking, and washing. Without

How many ways can you think of that people use the materials they get from trees?

48

This factory is located next to the Dead Sea in the country of Israel. The factory processes salt and other minerals from the water. Salt is a mineral with many uses.

water, farmers could not grow food. People also use water as a means of transportation. They even use water to produce energy.

Land on which crops can be grown is one of the earth's most important life-giving resources. Only about 10 percent of the earth has climate and soil suitable for farming. However, this small part of the earth's surface can produce enough food to feed the world's people.

Minerals from the Earth

Minerals from beneath the earth's surface also are valuable natural resources. **Minerals** are nonliving substances that people obtain through mining, or digging in the earth. Gold, silver, copper, tin, iron ore, salt, diamonds, and different kinds of stone all are minerals. Other minerals include coal, oil (petroleum), and natural gas.

Minerals have a variety of uses. For example, the electrical wiring and some of the pipes in your home are made of the mineral copper. Much of your food has the mineral salt in it. Salt even was used to make the windows in your home.

Minerals are unevenly distributed across the earth. Some minerals, such as iron ore, have been found in all the continents except Antarctica. Other minerals, such as diamonds, have been found in only a few places.

Some countries have little mineral wealth. Other countries, such as the United States, the Soviet Union, and South Africa, have a wide variety of minerals. However, no country has all the minerals it needs. The map below shows the distribution of a few major minerals—coal, iron ore, and oil. What map symbol is used to represent oil? Which continent has the most oil symbols?

People find ways to use minerals and other natural resources through technology. **Technology** refers to all the knowledge, skills, tools, and methods people use to meet their needs. Thousands of years ago, technology was very limited. For example, people used different kinds of stones to make simple tools.

The knowledge, skills, tools, and methods used by people advanced tremendously over time. For example, people found ways to take minerals such as copper, tin, and iron ore from the earth. They also found ways to combine certain minerals to form harder materials and better tools. With each change in technology, people found different uses for minerals.

Map Study

Coal and iron ore are the most important minerals needed for making steel. Europe was the first steel-making center in the world. Point to a place in Africa that might be a good place for making steel. Does Australia have the natural resources needed for making steel?

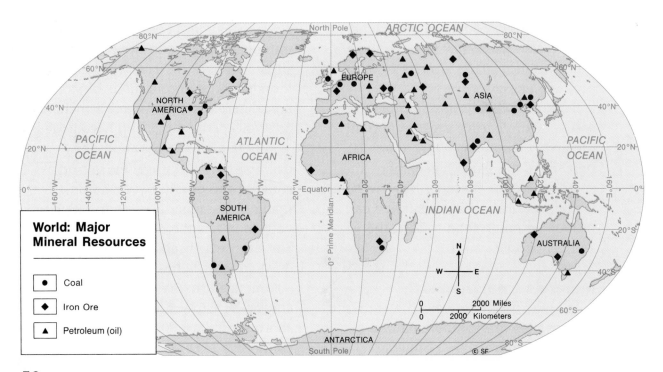

World: Major Mineral Resources

- • Coal
- ◆ Iron Ore
- ▲ Petroleum (oil)

In the port of Dalian, China, burning fuel dirties the air. Dirty air can result when people use minerals unwisely.

Minerals for Energy

Coal, oil, and natural gas are special kinds of mineral resources. They provide energy to heat homes and power vehicles and other kinds of machinery. Coal, oil, and natural gas come from the remains of plants and animals. Over millions of years, these remains were covered by deposits of mud, sand, and rock. The pressure from the deposits changed the remains to form coal, oil, and natural gas.

Coal became a very important mineral about two hundred years ago, when the steam engine was invented. People burned coal to heat water to make the steam that ran the engine. Later, with the development of new technology, oil, natural gas, and electricity replaced coal for many uses. However, even today coal has many energy uses. It often fuels generators that produce electricity, and it provides the energy for many of the world's industries.

The use of oil and natural gas has increased greatly during the 1900s. The oil industry grew rapidly after the invention of the automobile, which was designed to use gasoline. Gasoline is made from oil. Most of today's trains, ships, and airplanes are powered by fuels made from oil. Oil, as well as coal, fuels the generators that produce electricity. Natural gas is widely used for heating homes.

Managing the World's Resources

Some of the world's resources are renewable. Such resources, if used correctly, always will be available because nature replaces what people use. The life-giving resources—such as air, water, sunlight, and soil—are renewable. Other resources are nonrenewable. Once these resources are used, they will be gone forever. All minerals, including fuels, are nonrenewable.

In recent years people all over the world have become concerned about the danger of harming or using up natural resources. The world's population is growing rapidly. If the needs of future generations are to be met, the world's resources must be managed carefully.

Renewable Resources. The main danger to renewable resources is **pollution,** which is the dirtying of any part of the air, water, or soil. Laws have been passed in many countries to reduce automobile and industrial pollution of the air. The dumping of waste materials on the land and in the water now is closely watched. However, air and water pollution remain major problems in some countries.

Nonrenewable Resources. A very different problem faces the earth's nonrenewable resources. If people continue to use these minerals at the present rates, the supplies of some minerals may be used up. To keep from running out of these minerals, scientists are looking for new deposits of minerals and are trying to develop more careful ways of using known sources of minerals.

Linking Past and Present

An Old Source for New Energy

One of the world's newest sources of energy—the windmill—also is one of the oldest. Windmills, such as those you see on the left, were built as long ago as the year 1200 in the Netherlands. They powered pumps that removed ocean water from fields that lay below sea level. The land the windmills drained became productive farmland.

The windmills on the right do not power pumps. They produce electricity for the United States. Winds move the blades, which are connected to a giant magnet. The moving magnet causes an electrical current to flow in wires that are coiled around the magnet. Power lines carry this electrical energy to homes, farms, factories, and offices throughout the country.

The energy that powers windmills—moving air—is a renewable energy source. As more and more windmills are built, they can help save more of our limited supply of nonrenewable fuels.

World Energy Sources

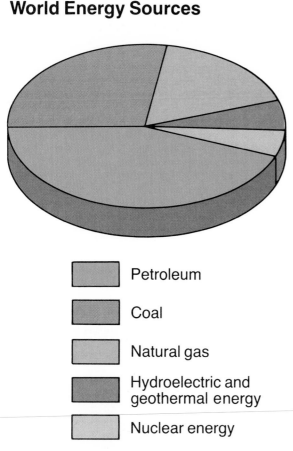

- Petroleum
- Coal
- Natural gas
- Hydroelectric and geothermal energy
- Nuclear energy

Most of the world's energy comes from coal, oil, and natural gas.

New Energy Resources. The supplies of coal, oil, and natural gas are limited. For this reason, scientists have been searching for other sources of energy. At one time they hoped nuclear energy would be a good replacement for other energy resources. Nuclear energy is produced by splitting atoms of uranium. Only a small amount of uranium is needed to produce huge amounts of energy.

However, using nuclear energy presents many problems. Harmful radiation is given off when nuclear energy is produced. This radiation continues for thousands of years when wastes from nuclear energy are stored. Also, accidents can occur at nuclear power plants, resulting in the release of radiation into the air. The cost of making nuclear energy safe to use has made it expensive. Some countries, however, such as France and the Soviet Union, depend heavily on nuclear energy.

Many other sources of energy can be used. Hydroelectric plants use falling water to produce power. Use of solar power includes capturing energy from the sun's rays. Geothermal energy comes from heat within the earth's crust. In some countries people even are attempting to use the power produced by the winds and the tides.

However, all these other sources of energy account for only a small part of the energy produced today. The circle graph on this page shows that nonrenewable fuels continue to be the world's major source of energy.

Reviewing the Lesson

Recalling Key Words, People, and Places
Identify the key words defined below:
1. anything in, on, or above the earth that people use to meet their needs
2. any dirtying of any part of the air, water, or soil

Remembering Main Ideas
1. Explain how water is important to life.
2. How has technology influenced the way people use minerals?
3. Why has the use of oil and natural gas increased greatly during the 1900s?
4. What problem is connected with the use of the earth's nonrenewable resources?

Thinking Things Over
What do you think is the most important challenge involving the use of natural resources that faces the world? Explain your answer.

Comparing Different Kinds of Maps

Many factors, including temperature and precipitation, greatly affect the natural vegetation that grows in a region. If you compare maps of rainfall (one kind of precipitation) and vegetation patterns, you can more clearly see just how closely rainfall and vegetation are related.

Rainfall and Vegetation in China

China is the third-largest country, in area, in the world. Because China is so huge, climates—including rainfall amounts—vary in different parts of the country. Read the map key for the map on this page. Notice that some regions of China average less than 10 inches of rain per year. Notice also that other regions receive more than 80 inches of rain per year. Find the capital of China on the map. According to the map key, how much rain does the capital receive? Actually, Beijing averages about 25 inches of rain per year. Occasionally, northern China even has snow, although such snowfalls are light.

The map on page 55 shows China's natural vegetation regions. Use the key to find an example of each kind of vegetation on the map. Actually, much of the vegetation of China has been greatly changed because of centuries of farming. For instance, much of

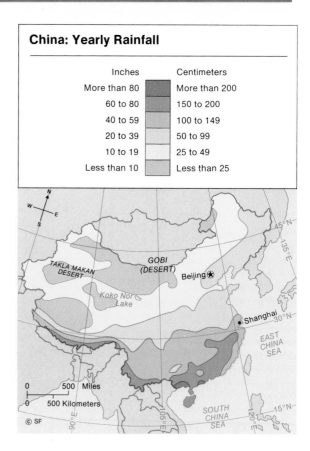

China: Yearly Rainfall

Inches		Centimeters
More than 80		More than 200
60 to 80		150 to 200
40 to 59		100 to 149
20 to 39		50 to 99
10 to 19		25 to 49
Less than 10		Less than 25

southern China once had forests of broadleaf trees, as shown on the map. Most of these trees have been cleared away to raise crops through the years.

Comparing a Rainfall Map and Vegetation Map

On the rainfall map of China, put your finger on the large region that receives the least rainfall per year. The map key tells you that this region receives less than 10 inches of rain in a year. What kind of natural vegetation would you predict this region has?

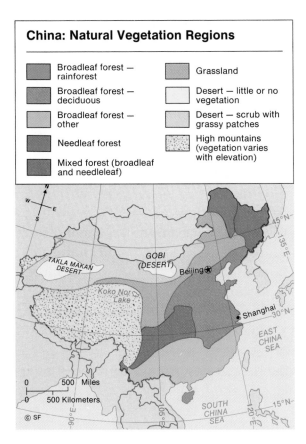

China: Natural Vegetation Regions

- Broadleaf forest — rainforest
- Broadleaf forest — deciduous
- Broadleaf forest — other
- Needleaf forest
- Mixed forest (broadleaf and needleleaf)
- Grassland
- Desert — little or no vegetation
- Desert — scrub with grassy patches
- High mountains (vegetation varies with elevation)

TAKLA MAKAN DESERT

GOBI (DESERT)

Beijing

Koko Nor Lake

Shanghai

EAST CHINA SEA

SOUTH CHINA SEA

45°N
135°E
30°N
15°N
90°E
105°E
120°E

0   500   Miles
0   500 Kilometers

© SF

How much rainfall do you think this area of China receives?

Why? To find whether your prediction is correct, keep your finger on this region of the rainfall map and look at the same general area on the vegetation map. Notice that both maps show a region of roughly the same size and shape. Looking at the vegetation map key, you see that this dry region has either desert scrub vegetation or little or no vegetation at all. Does this match your prediction? You have just demonstrated the relationship between the vegetation of an area and its rainfall by comparing two maps.

Skills Practice

Use the maps on these pages to answer the questions.

1. What is the vegetation in the Takla Makan and Gobi deserts? How much rain falls yearly in these deserts?
2. What are the rainfall and vegetation in the area around Shanghai?
3. You can see that the vegetation regions do not match the rainfall regions exactly. Why do you suppose this is so?
4. What statement can you make about how rainfall and natural vegetation regions are related?

55

Chapter 1 Review

Chapter Summary

Lesson 1   Land and Water—Earth is made up of seven continents separated by oceans. The major kinds of landforms on the continents are mountains, hills, plateaus, and plains. About 70 percent of the earth's surface is covered by water—oceans, seas, lakes, and rivers.

Lesson 2   Climate and Vegetation Regions—Temperature and precipitation are the two main parts of climate. Five major climate types are found in the world. They help determine the natural vegetation, or plant life, in a region. The five climate types are: hot, warm, cool, cold, and high mountains. The six main groups of natural vegetation are forest, grassland, desert, tundra, ice-covered land, and high mountains.

Lesson 3   The Causes of Climate—A region's climate is determined largely by the place's latitude (location north or south of the Equator), its nearness to water, and its landforms. For example, climates in the low latitudes tend to be hotter than other climates.

Lesson 4   The Resources of the Earth—Our most important natural resources are air, water, soil, and sunlight, which are renewable if used carefully. Minerals, which are unevenly distributed across the earth, also are valuable natural resources. Some minerals are used for energy. Minerals are not renewable, and eventually some may be used up.

Write your answers on a separate sheet of paper.

Testing Key Words, People, and Places

Part A

Give the definition of each key word.

1. **landform**
2. **elevation**
3. **weather**
4. **climate**
5. **precipitation**
6. **natural vegetation**
7. **tropics**
8. **rainforest**
9. **scrub**
10. **deciduous**
11. **tundra**
12. **latitude**
13. **ocean current**
14. **altitude**
15. **leeward**
16. **windward**
17. **natural resource**
18. **mineral**
19. **technology**
20. **pollution**

Part B

Match each description with the correct place in the list.

1. the world's largest plain
2. the world's longest river
3. the world's highest plateau
4. the world's highest mountains
5. one of the five Great Lakes
   a. Himalayas
   b. North European Plain
   c. Plateau of Tibet
   d. Lake Superior
   e. Nile River

Testing Main Ideas

Answer these questions.
1. What is a continent?
2. What is the difference between a plateau and a plain?
3. How do oceans and lakes differ?

4. In which kind of climate might you find scrub growing?

5. Where might you find a climate that is cold and dry, with tundra?

6. Why do climates near the Equator tend to be hotter than climates farther away?

7. What does the climate near a large body of water tend to be like?

8. How does the elevation of a landform affect its temperature?

9. Which natural resources are found almost everywhere?

10. Which minerals are used for energy?

Testing Skills

1. Comparing maps. Write the letters a through d on your paper. Read the questions that follow. Next to each letter, write *yes* if you could expect to get an answer to the question by comparing a rainfall map and a vegetation map of the same area. Write *no* if you could *not* expect to answer the question by comparing those maps.

  a. How many people live in the area?

  b. What kind of plant life grows in the places that receive over 30 inches of rain each year?

  c. Are the driest places grasslands or deserts?

  d. Is the area a plateau?

2. Locating continents and bodies of water on a map. Write the letters A through E on your paper. Write the name of the correct continent or ocean shown on the map next to each letter.

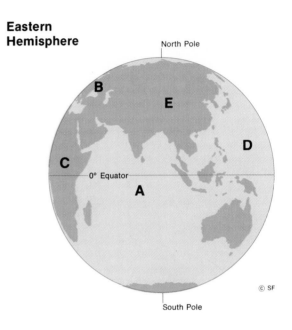

Eastern Hemisphere

Activities

1. On a separate sheet of paper, trace North and South America from the map on pages 36–37. Use colored pencils to indicate the climate regions on the two continents.

2. Find one of Jack London's books in your library—*The Call of the Wild, White Fang,* or any of his other novels set in Alaska or northern Canada. Look for descriptions of the intense cold found in the far north. Try rewriting one of the descriptions in your own words.

Chapter 2

The People of Our World

Every person living on the earth is an individual. Each one differs from all the others. However, the people of the world have some things in common. For example, everyone needs a place to live. Nearly half the people in the world live in cities. The picture shows a busy street scene in a large city in Europe.

As you read this chapter, you will learn about the population patterns in the world today. In addition, you will learn how people use the land to meet their needs. Finally, you will find out about the ways that people in different countries are linked together. The lessons in the chapter are listed below.

Lesson 1 Patterns of Population

Lesson 2 How People Use the Land

Lesson 3 Linkages: Transportation, Communication, and Trade

Lesson 1 Patterns of Population

LOOKING AHEAD As you read, look for—

Key words, people, and **places:**

demographer   **suburb**
migration   **rural area**
population distribution   Mexico City
urban area

Answers to these questions about **main ideas:**

1. What do people study about population?
2. Why do people live in certain places?
3. Why has the world's population grown?
4. What are some important population trends?

What kinds of people make up your class? For example, how many boys and how many girls do you count? How old are they? How many were born in your community, and how many moved to your community from somewhere else? The answers to these questions tell you facts about the population of your class. *Population* refers to the people in a place at a certain time.

Studying Population

We learn about population through the work of demographers. **Demographers** are people who study human populations. To determine population patterns, demographers ask themselves many questions as they do their work. These questions include: How many babies were born in a certain year? How many people died in a certain year? Another question demographers ask concerns **migration**—how many people came to a place or left that place during a particular time.

The answers to these questions tell about the population growth rate—how the number of people in a population is changing. You can see how births and deaths affect population growth. Migration plays an important part in population growth too. For example, between 1890 and 1920, the population of the United States grew by about 43 million people. During that period about 18 million people migrated to the United States from other countries. The country's population would have grown much more slowly during that period without migration.

Demographers also are interested in where people live. The way in which people are spread out over the earth is called **population distribution.** The world's population is not evenly distributed across the earth.

The map on page 60 clearly shows this uneven distribution of population. This map tells a story with dots. In some places on the map, the dots are so close to one another that they run together. These parts of the world have many people—that is, they are crowded. In other places on the map, you see few or no dots. These areas of the world have few people. On the map, locate two crowded areas in Asia.

59

Why People Live Where They Live

Why are some parts of the world crowded while other parts contain few people? You can find some answers to this question by comparing the population distribution map on this page with some of the maps in Chapter 1.

Look at the landform map on pages 32-33 and the climate regions map on pages 36-37. Notice that few people live where it is very mountainous, very dry, or very cold. On the other hand, people usually crowd into plains or low hill areas that have warm or cool climates. One reason is that such areas usually are good for growing food.

A closer look at the map below shows another population pattern. Notice that the map shows many dots around the urban, or city, areas on the map. **Urban areas** consist of a central city surrounded by smaller cities and towns called **suburbs.**

Rural areas are areas made up of farms, villages, and small towns. Generally, rural areas have few people. However, some rural areas are quite crowded. You can locate some of these crowded rural areas in India and eastern China.

In the past most people lived in rural areas. However, since about 1800 the

Map Study

Almost three out of every four people in the world live in five crowded areas. Use this map and the Atlas map on pages 528-529 to name some countries in each area. The five areas are: East Asia, South Asia, Southeast Asia, Europe, and the northeastern coast of North America.

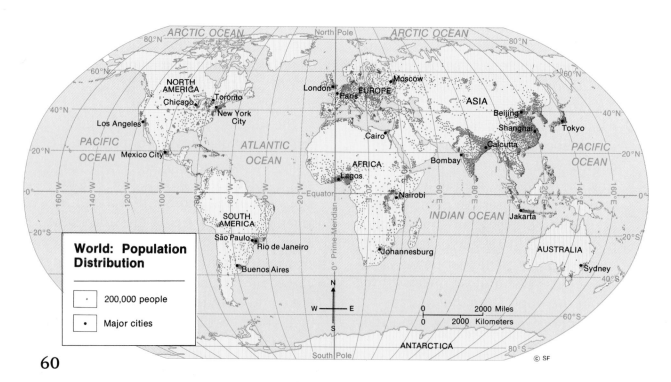

World: Population Distribution

· 200,000 people

• Major cities

© SF

number of people living in urban areas has grown rapidly. For example, in 1800 only about 3 percent of the world's people lived in urban areas. Today more than 40 percent of the people in the world live in urban areas.

World Population Growth

Until about three hundred years ago, world population growth was very slow. Growth was slow because the number of deaths almost equaled the number of births each year. Birth rates were very high. Some families had ten or fifteen children. However, death rates were very high too. In the late 1600s, for example, about two of every five babies died before they were one year old. Adults rarely lived beyond the age of fifty.

The way people lived contributed to these high death rates. First, living conditions for most people were poor. Drinking water often was polluted and homes in cold climates were not heated. Diseases spread very quickly.

Second, health care was poor. Doctors knew little about the causes of disease and so could do little to prevent or cure disease. Finally, food was not always plentiful. Many people might die when crop failures occurred.

Advances in medicine and technology helped solve these problems in most parts of the world. Such advances allowed people to live longer and more children to survive. However, the number of births continued to be high. The combination of low death rates and high birth rates caused world population to grow.

In 1796, an English doctor, Edward Jenner, developed the first vaccine. The vaccine prevented smallpox.

Identifying Population Trends

Demographers look for population trends. A trend is the general direction or course being followed. Trends are important. Once trends have been identified, they can be used to project what might happen in the future.

One important trend is that world population is growing at a rapid rate. Since 1960, world population has "exploded," growing from 3 billion to about 5 billion. During this time world population has increased by about 2 percent each year.

Population growth rates have not been the same in all parts of the world. For example, populations in Western Europe and North America have been growing at a rate of about 1 percent each year. However, the rate of growth has been over 2½ percent in Africa, Asia, and Latin America. If these rates do not slow down, more than 8 billion people will live in the world by the

Ten Largest Urban Areas in 1950, 1980, 2000*

1950	Population (in millions)	1980	Population (in millions)	2000	Population* (in millions)
1. New York	12.4	1. Tokyo	20.0	1. Mexico City	27.6
2. London	10.4	2. New York	17.7	2. Shanghai	25.9
3. Essen/Dusseldorf	6.9	3. Mexico City	15.1	3. Tokyo	23.8
4. Tokyo	6.7	4. Shanghai	15.0	4. Beijing	22.8
5. Shanghai	5.8	5. São Paulo	12.6	5. São Paulo	21.5
6. Paris	5.5	6. Beijing	12.0	6. New York	19.5
7. Buenos Aires	5.3	7. Los Angeles	10.1	7. Bombay	16.3
8. Chicago	5.0	8. Buenos Aires	10.1	8. Calcutta	15.9
9. Moscow	4.8	9. London	10.0	9. Djakarta	14.3
10. Calcutta	4.7	10. Paris	9.7	10. Rio de Janeiro	14.2

*Estimated.

Cities everywhere continue to grow in size. The largest gains in population, however, will be in Asia, Africa, and Latin America.

year 2025. Almost 7 billion of these people will live in Africa, Asia, and Latin America.

A second trend is that urban population is growing very quickly. In recent years the greatest growth in urban population has come in certain countries of Asia and Latin America.

Look at the chart showing the world's ten largest urban areas above. Notice that Mexico City is expected to be the largest urban area in the world by the year 2000. Mexico City was not on the list at all in 1950. Migration has played a major part in the rapid growth of Mexico City. Every day hundreds of people leave the countryside of Mexico and move to Mexico City in search of a better life. People who live in the city call the newcomers paracaidistas (pä-rä kī dēs'täs) because they seem to fall out of the sky. *Paracaidista* means "parachutist" in Spanish.

Many world leaders worry about rapid population growth. In particular, they worry about the growing number of people in places where food shortages now exist. In these places, such as parts of Asia, Africa, and South and Central America, dealing with population growth is a major challenge for the future.

Reviewing the Lesson

Recalling Key Words, People, and Places
1. Identify the key words defined below:
   a. the movement of people from one place to another place
   b. a central city surrounded by smaller cities and towns
2. Tell how Mexico City shows an important population trend.

Remembering Main Ideas
1. Give two examples of the kinds of questions that demographers ask.
2. Give an example of how landforms and climate influence where people live.
3. What effect did the drop in death rates have on world population?
4. In which areas of the world are population growth rates the highest?

Thinking Things Over
Why do you think people live in the area where you live?

Lesson 2 How People Use the Land

LOOKING AHEAD As you read, look for—

Key words, people, and **places:**

subsistence farming
commercial farming
gross national product

Answers to these questions about **main ideas:**

1. How do people use the land throughout the world?
2. What three kinds of work do people do?
3. How are technology and land use related?
4. What are the three major characteristics of countries with developing economies?

Thousands of years ago, people met their needs by hunting animals, gathering wild fruits and vegetables, and fishing. Their simple tools were made of stones, animal bones, and wood. They made clothing and shelters from animal skins. Today few people meet their needs in these ways.

Ways of Using the Land

The map on pages 64-65 shows the different ways that people use the land throughout the world today. The type of land use you just read about is called hunting, fishing, and gathering. Today only a few groups of people in rainforests and in tundra areas practice this type of land use. Find these hunting, fishing, and gathering areas on the map.

Some hunters, fishers and gatherers use methods that have not changed for thousands of years. For example, some Indians of the South American rainforest still hunt with blowguns, darts, and spears.

Nomadic herding is another kind of land use. *Nomad* means "wanderer." Nomadic herders follow their animals, wandering from place to place in search of grazing land. Like hunters, fishers, and gatherers, nomadic herders follow a way of life that has changed little over thousands of years. On which continents is nomadic herding practiced, according to the map on pages 64-65?

Farming is the most widespread form of land use. Two main kinds of farming are practiced. One kind—subsistence farming—is practiced in parts of Africa, Asia, and Latin America. The word *subsistence* means "keeping alive." **Subsistence farming** produces only about enough crops for farmers and their families to meet their basic needs. In **commercial farming** people produce more than enough crops to meet their needs. Commercial farmers sell most or all of the crops they grow. The farming areas of Canada, the United States, and Europe are used mostly for commercial farming.

Ranching is done in grassland areas that are too dry for farming. Unlike nomadic herders, ranchers graze their animals in one place. Ranchers sell most

63

of the cattle, sheep, and other animals they raise.

Lumbering is another kind of land use. Compare the land use map below with the natural vegetation map on pages 38-39. Notice that the major areas for lumbering are found in the needleleaf forests of the Northern Hemisphere. On the land use map, use your finger to trace the land in the Northern Hemisphere used for lumbering.

Mining is one kind of land use found in almost all parts of the world. Notice on the land use map that mining occurs on land that is also used for other purposes. Find the symbol used for mining in the map key. What other kinds of land use are practiced in the mining areas of Australia?

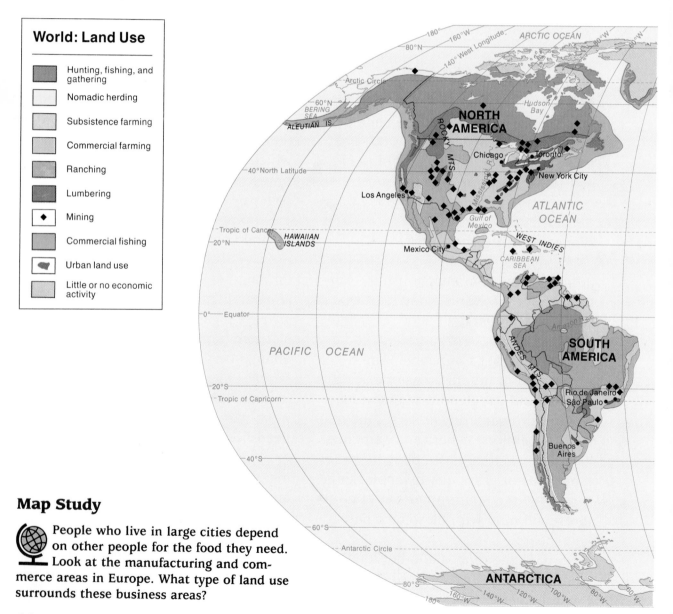

World: Land Use

- Hunting, fishing, and gathering
- Nomadic herding
- Subsistence farming
- Commercial farming
- Ranching
- Lumbering
- ◆ Mining
- Commercial fishing
- Urban land use
- Little or no economic activity

Map Study

People who live in large cities depend on other people for the food they need. Look at the manufacturing and commerce areas in Europe. What type of land use surrounds these business areas?

64

One type of land use—commercial fishing—actually uses the water rather than the land. You can see from the land use map that the world's oceans and seas support commercial fishing.

Manufacturing and commerce (business) are the most important land uses in the world's urban areas. The total amount of land used for manufacturing and commerce is very small compared to other land uses. Land in urban areas also is used for housing and roads.

Three Kinds of Work

Using the land to meet needs always involves work. People do three main kinds of work. The first kind involves using the earth's natural resources in a direct way. For example, farmers use

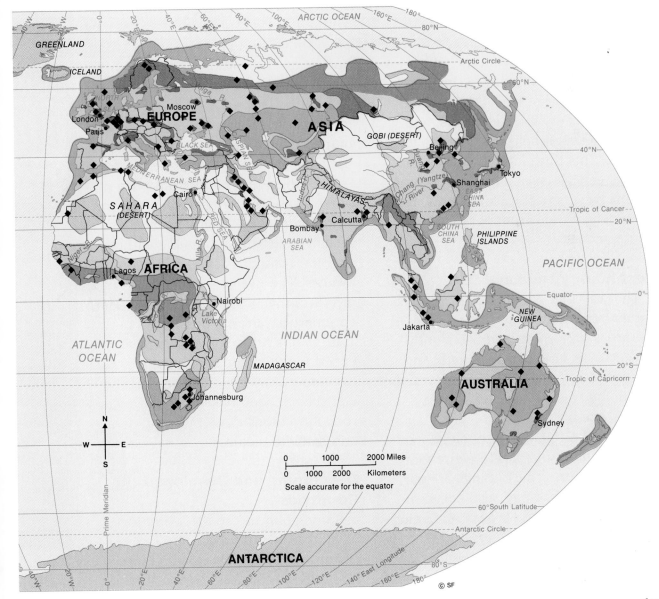

the soil to grow crops, and miners take minerals from below the earth's surface. Fishing and lumbering also use resources directly. More than half the world's people do this kind of work. Most of them are farmers.

The second kind of work changes the earth's natural resources into useful goods. This kind of work often is called manufacturing and processing. Examples include producing iron and steel; making cars; constructing buildings; and food processing, such as canning and bottling.

The third kind of work includes moving goods from factories to the people who buy and use them. Automobile dealers, grocery store checkers, and truck drivers all help move goods to buyers. This third kind of work also includes service tasks. People who provide services include bank clerks, religious leaders, newspaper reporters, and teachers.

Technology and Land Use

The way that people use the land varies from one country to another. A country's pattern of land use is influenced by its landforms, climate, and natural resources. A country's level of technology also influences the way land is used.

When you think of technology, you probably think of space travel, robots, and computers. These things are part of modern technology, also called industrial technology. Modern technology makes use of the latest scientific knowledge and most up-to-date tools. However, people in many parts of the world depend on traditional technology. Their tools and ways of using them have been handed down from generation to generation, changing little over time.

Hunters, fishers, and gatherers and nomadic herders follow ways of life that have changed little in recent years. Some farmers also follow traditional ways. For example, many farmers of the Nile River Valley in Egypt use traditional methods to irrigate (supply water to) their fields. The picture on the next page shows an Egyptian farmer using a bucket on the end of a pole to bring water to his land. New methods of irrigating the land have been introduced in Egypt in recent years. However, many Egyptian farmers still use traditional ways.

Technology influences land use in other ways too. For example, the construction of large buildings in urban areas would not be possible without such inventions as steel girders and elevators. The use of fertilizers and modern farm machines help make modern commercial farming possible.

In recent years computers have influenced land use too. For example, decisions to mine in certain areas of the world have been based on studies of rock formations done by computers and satellite pictures.

Developing and Developed Countries

Some countries in the world are wealthy. Most of the people in these countries use and produce a large amount of goods and services. Other

Many Egyptian farmers use the shadoof to water their fields. The shadoof is an example of traditional technology.

A country's level of economic development depends partly on the technology that the country uses. For example, people in developing countries tend to use traditional technology. People in developed countries tend to use modern technology. Of course, modern technology can cost a great deal of money. Developing countries—because they are poor—cannot always afford to buy the modern technology they want.

Countries with developing economies have three major characteristics. First, developing countries have a low gross national product compared with the size of their population. **Gross national product** (GNP) is the value of all goods and services produced by a country in a given year.

The map on page 68 shows GNP per person throughout the world. GNP per person is found by dividing a country's GNP by that country's population. GNP per person is the average value of goods and services available for each person in a country in a given year. The map labels the countries with a GNP per person of over two thousand dollars as developed. Countries with a GNP per person of less than two thousand dollars are labeled as developing.

The second characteristic of countries with developing economies is that most people work as farmers. Much of the farming in developing countries is subsistence farming. In contrast, most people in developed countries work in manufacturing and service jobs.

countries are poor. Most of their people use and produce few goods and services. Wealthy countries have developed economies—that is, a high level of economic development. Poor countries have developing economies—that is, a low level of economic development.

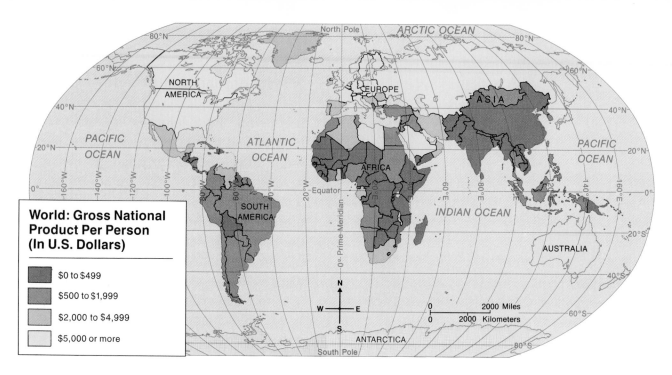

World: Gross National Product Per Person (In U.S. Dollars)

- $0 to $499
- $500 to $1,999
- $2,000 to $4,999
- $5,000 or more

Map Study

Use the Atlas map on pages 528–529 to find these countries that export oil: Venezuela, Saudi Arabia, and Libya. How do these countries differ from the countries surrounding them?

The third characteristic of developing countries is that most have rapidly growing populations. As you have read, the populations of Africa, Asia, and Latin America are growing at a yearly rate of about 2½ percent. Each year in these areas, the limited amounts of goods and services must be shared among more and more people.

A developing country must produce more goods and services if it is to become developed. However, the use of traditional technology tends to keep production, and therefore GNP per person, low. Some developing countries have made a great deal of economic progress. However, economic growth in the developing countries remains a challenge for the future.

Reviewing the Lesson

Recalling Key Words, People, and Places

Identify the key words defined below:
1. farming that produces only enough crops to meet the needs of farmers and their families
2. the value of all the goods and services produced by a country in a given year

Remembering Main Ideas
1. What is the most widespread form of land use in the world?
2. Give two examples of manufacturing and processing work.
3. Give an example of how technology influences land use.
4. Compare the major kinds of work done in developing countries with the major kinds of work done in developed countries.

Thinking Things Over
1. How is the land used in the area where you live? Why do you think the land is used in this way?
2. Give examples of the kinds of service workers you come into contact with every day.

Lesson 3 Linkages: Transportation, Communication, and Trade

LOOKING AHEAD As you read, look for—

Key words, people, and **places:**

import
export

Answers to these questions about **main ideas:**

1. What kinds of transportation networks are found throughout the world?
2. What kinds of communication networks are found throughout the world?
3. How do linkages help trade?

The stores in your community probably are well stocked with goods from all over the world. In the grocery store, you might find fruits and vegetables from some Caribbean countries. You also might find canned meat from Argentina and cheeses from France or the Netherlands. Televisions and stereos from Japan probably line the shelves of the appliance store.

A system of linkages makes it possible for you to buy goods from all over the world at your local stores. Linkages are the transportation and communication networks that allow the exchange of goods, information, and ideas.

Transportation Networks

A transportation network consists of the vehicles and routes that allow movement of people and goods from one place to another. Vehicles range from the traditional and simple to the highly modern and complex. In some developing countries, many people get around by riding on animals, such as horses, donkeys, or oxen, or by using

the animals to pull carts or wagons. In other developing countries, such as India, the bicycle is the most common form of transportation.

Developed countries use vehicles built with modern technology. For

Farmers in the African country of Tunisia transport their cabbages to market by donkey cart.

69

Facts and Figures

There are two kinds of communications satellites. A passive satellite simply reflects signals that are sent to it back to receiving stations on earth. Some passive satellites are just large balloons covered with metal. An active satellite receives signals, strengthens them, and then sends them back to earth. Today most communications satellites are active.

One of the first active satellites was *Early Bird,* which sent signals between Europe and North America. Today communications satellites are organized into networks that send signals to one another as well as back to earth. The largest network is *INTELSTAT.* In this system 18 satellites send messages to about 600 receiving stations in 140 countries.

example, they use such modern vehicles as automobiles, ocean-going ships, jet airplanes, and even spaceships. These vehicles are a familiar sight to people in the United States and other developed countries.

Developments in technology continually change transportation networks. Many years ago certain natural features, such as mountain ranges and wide rivers, blocked transportation routes. However, new methods of road and rail construction introduced in the late 1800s allowed highways and railroads to cross very high mountains. Bridges made of iron or steel eased the problem of transportation over wide rivers.

Technological changes also have affected the kinds of vehicles people use. For example, from the late 1800s until the mid-1900s, people traveled across the oceans in large passenger ships. Today most people fly over the oceans in jet airplanes. Some people think space travel will become very common in the next century.

Communication Networks

Information and ideas, like people and goods, can be moved from one place to another. A communication network carries information and ideas. Two people talking together is the simplest form of communication. One of the most complex forms involves sending radio, television, or telephone signals from one place on earth to an orbiting communications satellite. The satellite, in turn, sends the signals back to other places on earth.

The developed countries of the world have very complex communication networks. Letters, newspapers, telephones, radios, and televisions keep people in these countries well-informed. They are aware of what is going on in their community, in their country, and in the rest of the world.

Radio, television, and the telephone make up the telecommunications network. This network links together all parts of the world. For example, you probably can call nearly every country in the world from the telephone in

People all over the world trade goods with one another. These people are buying and selling gold in the city of Hong Kong.

your home. Television broadcasts of major world events are watched by millions of people in many of the world's countries. People see these events even as they take place.

The most important thing about the telecommunications network is the speed with which it carries information. For example, your television can show you an incident as it happens, even if the incident is taking place thousands of miles away. Communications satellites make such great speed possible.

Technological developments continually improve telecommunications. One such recent development is the computer. Using a computer, people can organize, store, recall, and send information very quickly. Jobs that once took many hours or days now can be done in minutes. Information that once filled a library now can be stored on small computer disks. Already computers are widely used in business. Some people believe almost all business will be conducted through computers in the near future.

Linkages and Trade

Individuals cannot produce all the goods and services they need. They must exchange some of what they have for some of what they cannot produce for themselves. In other words, they need to trade. In the past people used a form of direct trade called barter. For example, farmers might trade grain to shoemakers for shoes. Potters might trade pots to fishers for fish. However, most trade today involves money. People sell the goods and services they produce for money. In turn, people use this money to buy goods and services.

Trade can take place between countries as well as individuals. The buying and selling that takes place between countries is called international trade. This kind of trade involves imports and exports. The goods that one country buys from other countries are called **imports. Exports** are the goods one country sells to other countries. Because so much international trade takes place, the countries of the world have become interdependent. That is, countries depend on one another for certain goods and services.

Linkages play a major part in trade, especially international trade. A look at something familiar—a bicycle—will help show this. The materials used to make the bicycle might come from various countries. For example, the rubber used to make the tires might come from Malaysia in Southeast Asia. Find Malaysia on the Atlas map, page 540.

Ships transport rubber from Malaysia across the Pacific Ocean to one of the west coast ports of the United States. From there, a truck or train takes the rubber to a tire factory. Later, a truck

Map Study

Oil and oil products account for much of the cargo carried over ocean trade routes. Find Ras Tanura on the map in Southwest Asia near the beginning of the widest line. With your finger, trace all the paths an oil tanker could take from this oil and pipeline center to reach Europe. Using the width of the lines as a guide, list the world's busiest seaports by continent.

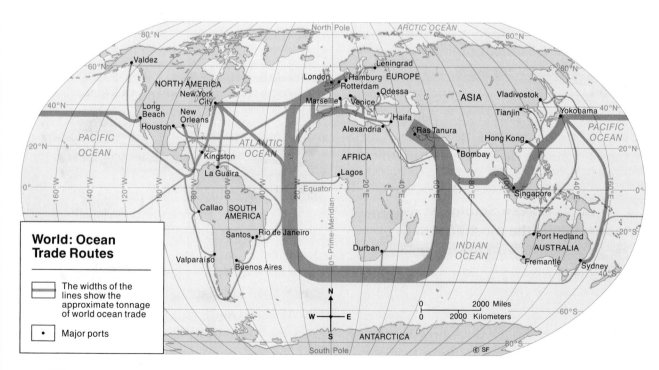

World: Ocean Trade Routes

The widths of the lines show the approximate tonnage of world ocean trade

• Major ports

or train transports the finished tires to the bicycle factory.

The mineral bauxite, used to make the aluminum for the bicycle frame, might come from Jamaica in the Caribbean Sea. Locate Jamaica on the Atlas map on page 534. Ships carry bauxite to such ports as New Orleans or Galveston. From there, a truck or train moves the bauxite to a processing factory where aluminum is made. The aluminum is then transported to the bicycle factory. Later, a truck or train transports the finished bicycle to a warehouse and then to the store, where it is sold.

Communication linkages also play a part in the story of the bicycle. The factories must place orders for rubber, tires, or aluminum. Most likely these orders are placed by telephone, and a record of these orders is entered on computer disks. The store owner trying to sell the bicycle may place an advertisement in a newspaper or on television or radio. Without linkages, trade would be almost impossible.

The red lines on the map on page 72 show the world's ocean trade routes. Notice that some lines are wider than others. The wider the line, the greater the amount of goods carried on that route. One of the widest lines on the map runs between Southwest Asia and Europe. Oil is the most important of the goods carried on this route.

Transportation, communication, and trade connect you with your community, your country, and the world. Because of linkages, the boundaries of your world are almost limitless.

A ship delivers goods from many distant countries. From where do the boxes on this dock come?

Reviewing the Lesson

Recalling Key Words, People, and Places
Identify the key words defined below:
1. a good that one country buys from another country
2. a good that one country sells to another country

Remembering Main Ideas
1. How has technology improved transportation networks?
2. What makes up the telecommunications network?
3. Tell how linkages play a part in international trade.

Thinking Things Over
Describe how linkages might have been involved in the production and sale of something you own.

Finding Directions on Special Maps

Many maps are drawn with north at the top. On some maps, however, north is not at the top. For this reason, you need to look closely at any map's direction symbol.

Using a Direction Symbol

The map on this page shows part of the city of Seoul, Korea. Look at the direction symbol for the map. Place your finger on the corner of the map where north is. Now use another finger to trace down the Han-gang River. This river runs in a mostly intermediate direction, from northwest to southeast.

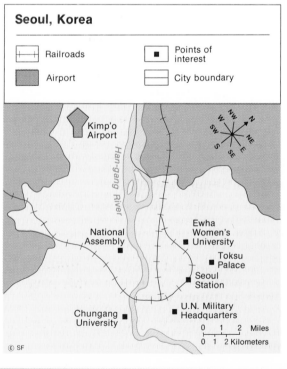

Seoul, Korea

┼┼┼ Railroads	■ Points of interest
▓ Airport	▭ City boundary

Kimp'o Airport

Han-gang River

National Assembly ■

Ewha Women's University ■

Toksu Palace ■

Seoul Station ■

Chungang University ■

U.N. Military Headquarters ■

0   1   2   Miles
0   1   2 Kilometers

© SF

Notice that Toksu Palace, the Seoul Railroad Station, and Chungang University are all roughly in line, in a cardinal direction, from north to south.

Finding Directions on a Polar Map

A polar map is a map that is centered on either the North Pole or the South Pole. On such a map, you find directions in a different way than on other maps. The polar map on page 75 shows the North Pole in the center of the map, with meridians running outward from the pole like spokes of a wheel. **Meridians** are imaginary lines that run halfway around the earth, from pole to pole. The location of a place east or west of the Prime Meridian (0°) is its **longitude.** On the map, you also can see parallels circling the North Pole. **Parallels** are imaginary lines that run from east to west around the earth. The location of a place north or south of the Equator (0°) is its **latitude.** The North Pole is at 90° north latitude (90°N). On the map, find the meridians labeled 0°, 180°, 90°E, and 90°W. Find the parallels labeled 40°N, 60°N, 80°N, and 90°N.

Now place your finger on any one of the meridians at the outer edge of the map. Move your finger along the meridian as far as the North Pole. Since north is always toward the North Pole, you were moving your finger north. If you place your finger on the North Pole and move it along any

Polar Region: North

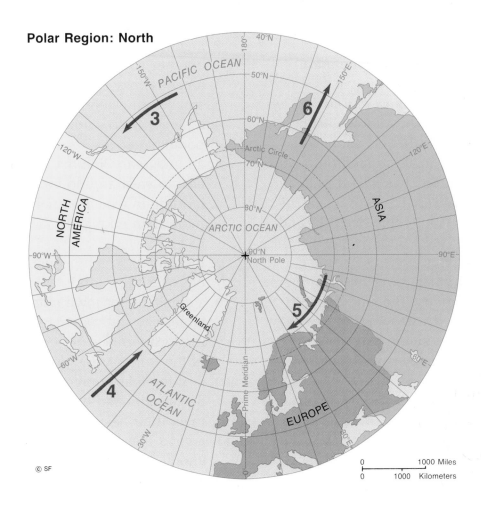

meridian toward the edge of the map, you will be moving your finger south. South is always away from the North Pole.

Now place your finger on the Prime Meridian at the point where the 50°N parallel crosses it. Trace the 50°N parallel all the way around the map, going counterclockwise. You will have circled the map going east. If you start at the same point and move your finger clockwise, you will circle the map going west.

Skills Practice

Use the map of Seoul, Korea, on page 74 to answer questions 1 and 2.

1. What direction is Kimp'o Airport from Seoul Station?

2. What direction is Ewha Women's University from the National Assembly?

Finish numbering your paper from 3 to 6. Look at the polar map on this page. Beside each number, write the direction toward which the numbered arrow points.

Chapter Summary

Lesson 1 Patterns of Population— Demographers study human populations, including why people live where they do. They know people tend to live in places that do not have extremes in climate or landforms. Also, world population has grown as death rates have lowered.

Lesson 2 How People Use the Land— Throughout the world, people use the land for such activities as farming, mining, manufacturing, and commerce. The way they use the land depends partly on their technology. Technology also helps determine whether a country's economy is developed or developing.

Lesson 3 Linkages: Transportation, Communication, and Trade— Linkages are the transportation and communication networks that allow exchanges of goods, information, and ideas. Transportation ranges from wagons to cars, ships, and airplanes. Communication networks include telephones, radios, and televisions. Linkages help make trade possible.

Write your answers on a separate sheet of paper.

Testing Key Words, People, and Places

Match each definition with the correct key word in the list.

1. an area of farms, villages, and small towns
2. a good that one country buys from another country
3. a central city surrounded by smaller cities and towns
4. a person who studies human populations
5. an imaginary line that runs from east to west around the earth
6. farming in which farmers produce more than enough to meet their needs
7. the way in which people are spread out over the earth
8. a small city or town outside a larger city
9. the location of a place east or west of the Prime Meridian
10. farming that produces only enough for farmers and their families to meet their basic needs
11. a good that one country sells to another country
12. an imaginary line that runs halfway around the earth, from pole to pole
13. the total value of goods and services produced by a country in a given year
14. the movement of people from one place to another

a. demographer
b. migration
c. population distribution
d. urban area
e. suburb
f. rural area
g. subsistence farming
h. commercial farming
i. gross national product
j. import
k. export
l. meridian
m. longitude
n. parallel

Testing Main Ideas

Answer these questions.

1. What do demographers do?
2. What is one reason many people live in plains areas?
3. Why was world population growth so slow in the past and why is rapid growth a problem today?
4. What are four kinds of land use and where are they found?
5. What is the difference between modern and traditional technology?
6. What are two characteristics of countries with developing economies?
7. What makes up a transportation network? a communications network?
8. How do linkages help trade expand throughout the world?

Testing Skills

1. **Finding directions on a map.** Study the map of Washington, D.C. on this page. Then answer the questions.
   a. Is north toward the top of the map? How do you know?
   b. In what direction is the Washington Monument from the Lincoln Memorial? from the White House?
   c. In what direction is the Jefferson Memorial from the Lincoln Memorial?
2. **Classifying.** Write the following headings on your paper. Then write each job under the correct heading.
   A. Using Resources Directly

Washington, D.C.: Points of Interest

B. Turning Resources into Finished Goods
C. Moving Finished Goods from Factories to Buyers

furniture maker	coal miner
truck driver	farm worker
grocery store clerk	baker

Activities

1. Make a scrapbook of ways of using the land. Cut out pictures that show different kinds of land use from old magazines and newspapers. Under each picture write the kind of land use shown.
2. In your library find one or more books on transportation and read about the development of the train, automobile, subway, and airplane. How did each development change people's lives?

Chapter 3

Ways of Living in Our World

Food
Education
{Rec + Sports}
Clothes
Technology
Language
Economic System
Housing
Religion
(Art)
Music

As you have learned, the people of our world live in many different places. People also have very different ways of living. However, all people do have certain things in common. The picture shows a family from Thailand eating dinner. What similarities do you see between the family in the picture and your family? What differences do you see?

As you read this chapter, you will learn about the ways of living the people of the world have developed. Also, you will take a close look at the ways of life of two families, including the one shown in the picture. The lessons in the chapter are listed below.

monotheism - one God
polytheism - many Gods
aetheism - no God
agnostic - belief in God if proven
Paganism - worship idols
satanism - worship the devil

78

Lesson 1   Society and Culture

📖 **LOOKING AHEAD** As you read, look for—

Key words, people, and **places:**

society
culture
norm
custom
mores
value

extended family
reincarnation
caste system

Chhatara
Delhi

Answers to these questions about **main ideas:**

1. How does a society and its culture help people meet their needs?
2. What are seven important characteristics of culture?
3. How does life in Chhatara illustrate the characteristics of culture?

When you eat dinner, you probably use a knife, a fork, and a spoon. People in China and Japan usually use chopsticks when eating. Many people in India eat using the fingers of their right hand, scooping up the food with bread or rice. These ways of eating are neither right nor wrong. They simply are the accepted behavior at dinner time in different countries. Accepted behavior differs from place to place throughout the world. However, you can see certain patterns in the ways people behave.

Society and Culture

All people need food, shelter, and safety. Since earliest times people have joined together in groups to help one another meet these and other needs and wants. A group of people who have common goals—helping one another make a living, for example—is called a **society.**

The way of life a society develops to reach its common goals is called a **culture.** Culture is the total way of life, including ways of thinking and behaving,

Nomadic herders, such as this Laplander of northern Europe, follow a traditional way of life.

79

The traditional culture of Japan has been influenced by other cultures. What evidence of this influence do you see?

that people in a society share. All people have a culture. It includes all parts of people's lives.

Today the world has many different cultures. Your culture, for example, uses modern technology for most daily activities. Also, most people in our society earn a living from manufacturing jobs or by providing services. Other cultures, such as that of the Laplanders who live in the northern regions of Europe, follow a way of life that is very different. The Laplanders use traditional technology, and people earn a living by nomadic herding. In this book you are going to read about many people with cultures different than your own.

The Characteristics of Culture

All cultures have a number of common characteristics. Seven important characteristics are listed below. As you read about these characteristics, think about how they apply to the way you lead your life.

Work and Rewards. All cultures have a system of work and rewards through which needs and wants can be met. That is, members of a society have jobs to do and, in return, they receive a share of the goods and services produced. The way that goods and services are produced, distributed, and used in a culture is called its economic system.

Organized Groups. All cultures have organized groups that are part of the culture. These organized groups include governments and groups for work and play. Families are one of a culture's most important organized groups. Families prepare children for life in the society and give support for both parents and children.

Norms. All cultures have standards of behavior, or rules by which members of the society are supposed to live. These standards of behavior are called **norms.** People accept some of these norms simply as the normal way to behave. For example, people in the United States consider eating with a knife and a fork normal behavior. The common way of doing something in a society is called a **custom.**

Certain other norms establish the morally right or wrong thing to do in a society. These norms are called **mores.** For example, the mores of your culture require you to obey some adults, such as your parents and teachers. However, in some other cultures, the mores require young people to obey the commands of all adults, even strangers. Many mores and other rules about right and wrong are written into laws. Members of a society who break laws usually are punished.

Values. All cultures have values. A **value** is an object, idea, or belief that a culture considers very important. For example, your culture holds such values as the beliefs in democracy, freedom, and minority rights.

Religion. All cultures have a set of beliefs about the cause and nature of the universe. When these beliefs involve the worship of one or more gods, they are called a religion.

Linking Past and Present

Passing Through a Shinto Gate

The structure you see in the picture is a gate. It marks the entrance to a shrine (holy place) for followers of the Shinto religion. Why do you think this Shinto gate stands in the empty ocean?

The Shinto religion, like all major religions, is very old. It developed in Japan almost 2,500 years ago. Although the religion has changed since its beginning, it still is a central part of Japanese culture.

Followers of Shinto worship nature. They believe that being close to nature will result in being close to the true spirit of life. The shrine in the picture is the ocean and the mountains beyond. Shinto gates also are found near places such as waterfalls, rivers, and forests.

People in every culture must do certain jobs to meet their needs. The women of Chhatara come to the well once a day.

Religious beliefs are very important to a culture. Religion provides many of the norms that people follow in a culture and influences a culture's values. Religion also gives meaning to the way people lead their lives.

A Body of Knowledge. Cultures possess a body of knowledge and have ways to pass this knowledge on to all members of the society. People learn this knowledge from their families, friends, teachers, and neighbors. Some knowledge is gained informally, by listening to and watching other people. Other knowledge is learned in schools. Language serves as one of the most important ways of passing on knowledge in society.

Art Forms. All cultures also have art forms through which members of the society make statements about their feelings and experiences. These art forms can include painting, sculpture, writing, and music.

Life in Chhatara

A close look at the way of life of one society can help you understand culture more fully. Let's look at the way of life in Chhatara (chut'ə rə), a farming village in northern India. Find India on the Atlas map on page 540.

Work and Rewards. In Chhatara the people are farmers. They grow corn, wheat, soybeans, and sugar cane. They also raise cattle for the milk.

One custom in Chhatara is that men and women do different kinds of work. The men of the village do most of the field work. The hardest work comes during the planting and the harvesting seasons. The men also maintain the irrigation canal that runs from a nearby river.

The women of Chhatara stay in or near the village to do their work. They milk the cows, churn butter, and grind flour from wheat grown in the fields. Also, they make oplas (ôp'läs), cakes of cow dung (waste) to be used for fuel. At least once a day, the women go to one of the village wells to get water.

The women also prepare the food. One important food is a flat wheat bread called chappati (chə pat'ē). The villagers also eat rice, corn, and beans. They drink milk and tea.

Chhatara's people trade with people from other parts of India to make their economic system work. The villagers sell their extra corn, wheat, and sugar cane in nearby Delhi (del'ē). They use the money they receive to buy rice, spices, cloth, and farm tools. Some of the goods they buy come from the United States and other parts of the world.

Organized Groups. In Chhatara a family includes not only parents and children but also grandparents, uncles, aunts, and cousins. Such a family is called an **extended family.** Each family lives in a two- or three-room house.

Norms. In Chhatara a governing group called the Panchayat (pun'chə-yät) makes decisions that affect the entire village. The adults of the village elect the members of the Panchayat. The Panchayat makes laws, settles arguments, and decides punishments for lawbreakers.

In Chhatara, a person can be punished for violating mores, even though he or she has not violated any written laws. For example, a man who fails to work in the fields and allows his family to go hungry might be punished. People who have committed serious crimes may be forced to leave Chhatara. Because the village is the most important place in the world to the people of Chhatara, this is a severe punishment.

Values. The well-being of the family comes before that of the individual in the culture of Chhatara. Family members cooperate for the good of all. They share food and other belongings, and they take care of each other.

Indian villagers dry their grain by spreading it on the ground. They dry the grain evenly by turning it over with their feet.

83

The golden cow shows the respect that Hindus have for all animals.

Religion. In Chhatara the villagers practice the religion called Hinduism. Hindus believe in **reincarnation,** or the rebirth of the soul in a new body. According to the Hindu religion, a soul needs many lifetimes to become pure enough to join Brahman—the Hindu god. Hindus believe that after death their soul will live again in another body.

Hindus follow a **caste system.** This system divides people into groups based on the caste of their parents. A person's caste determines his or her place in society. People in different castes do different jobs and have different norms. People stay in one caste all their lives.

Although the people of Chhatara have many cattle, they do not eat meat. Hinduism forbids the killing of animals for food. Hindus believe that animals have souls, as humans do.

A Body of Knowledge. The people of Chhatara speak and write a language called Hindi (hin′dē). They learn to read and write the language in the village school. Hindi is one of about 180 languages spoken in India.

Art Forms. Few of Chhatara's villagers are artists. However, the villagers share in the art of all the Hindu people. Hindus weave colorful fabrics. They decorate their buildings with paintings. They also write stories and compose music.

The culture of Chhatara is very old. It has changed very little over hundreds of years. However, this culture still helps each individual get what he or she needs. It is easy to see why the people of Chhatara do what they can to make village life run smoothly.

Reviewing the Lesson

Recalling Key Words, People, and Places
Identify the key words defined below:
1. the way of life a society develops to meet a common goal
2. norms that establish what is morally right and wrong
3. a family that includes parents, children, grandparents, uncles, aunts, and cousins

Remembering Main Ideas
1. For what purpose do groups of people form societies?
2. What different kinds of norms do all cultures have?
3. Explain how the people of Chhatara meet their need for food.

Thinking Things Over
1. For each of the seven characteristics of a culture, give a specific example from American culture.
2. Compare your culture with the culture of Chhatara.

84

Lesson 2   A Family of Southeast Asia

LOOKING AHEAD As you read, look for—

Key words, people, and **places:**

monastery   San Tan Bong
                               Chiang Mai
Tasanee Engaew

Answers to these questions about **main ideas:**

1. How does Tasanee Engaew spend her day?
2. What kinds of work do the members of Tasanee's family do?
3. How does religion affect the culture of San Tan
   Bong?

Tasanee Engaew (tä′sä nē əng ga′ů) lives in the village of San Tan Bong in northern Thailand (tī′land). Thailand is a country in Southeast Asia. Find Thailand on the Atlas map on page 540. Name four countries that border the country of Thailand.

The way of life that Tasanee leads is much the same as that followed by most young people who live in rural Thailand. This way of life reflects Thailand's culture.

Tasanee's Day

San Tan Bong is a village of fifty families. The houses sit in two rows on each side of a narrow road. Behind the houses, green rice fields stretch almost as far as the eye can see. The houses are made of wood and brick. Wooden columns raise the houses off the ground.

Tasanee lives in one of these houses with her extended family. It includes her parents, grandparents, older sister, and two cousins. Tasanee's other relatives live in the ten houses east of her house and the five houses west of her house.

On most mornings Tasanee wakes a little after 5:00 A.M. She sleeps on a mat that rests on the floor of her room. A net protects her from the mosquitoes that thrive in the hot, wet climate of Thailand.

Tasanee Engaew

85

Tasanee's mother prepares breakfast. Breakfast almost always includes rice and tea. Rice is eaten with nearly every meal in Thailand. In fact, Thai people say "Come over for rice" when they invite friends for a meal. Most often the Thais serve curry with their rice. Curry consists of spices mixed with fish or meat and vegetables. Tasanee loves curry made with coconut milk.

After breakfast Tasanee straightens out her blankets and puts away her mosquito net. She then goes out to the water tank in the yard. An electric pump brings water up into the tank. This is where the family washing is done. Tasanee does her washing on Wednesday and Sunday mornings. Like all Thai family members, Tasanee helps out with many household chores.

Tasanee goes to school in Chiang Mai (chyäng′ mī′), the second largest city in Thailand. To get to school, Tasanee rides a motor scooter to a nearby town. From there she takes a bus to Chiang Mai. Tasanee studies English, French, health, social studies, science, mathematics, and religion. Tasanee likes French best of all. She wants to be a tour guide when she leaves school, and knowing French will be very useful.

In the evenings or whenever Tasanee has some free time, she likes to play badminton, ride her motor scooter, or do embroidery. Sometimes she watches television at a cousin's house. Tasanee likes to watch news of Thailand's royal family. Because she and her family rise so early, Tasanee is in bed by 9:00 P.M.

Work and Rewards in Tasanee's Culture

While Tasanee is at school, her mother works in the house and in the fields. Tasanee's father spends most of his time in the fields. In addition, he is in charge of the village water pump. Heavy rains fall from June to November, which is the rice-growing season. However, during the dry season, fields must be irrigated. Each family has a certain time to use the pump to water their vegetable gardens or their fields of peanuts, beans, and chili peppers.

Tasanee's grandparents have duties too. Twice a day her grandfather feeds the family chickens. He also sweeps

Tasanee does many household chores such as washing clothes.

the bare earth underneath the house to keep it free of insects. In addition, he checks on the rice storehouse to make sure the rice is clean and dry. Tasanee's grandmother helps with the cooking and the housecleaning. She also collects mangoes and other fruits from the fruit trees in the yard.

School is out at the end of May. At about this time of year, rice planting begins. When the heavy rains begin to fall in June, all the people who are old enough and fit enough go out into the fields. Buffaloes usually are used to pull plows over the ground, but sometimes the villagers rent a small tractor to do some of the plowing. Then the villagers begin planting. This is hard work, because they must bend over time and again to plant the rice seedlings in the soft mud. Later in the year, when the rice is ready to be picked, nearly all the villagers help with the harvest.

Tasanee's relatives own their land. They work the land together and then share the crops. They produce enough rice each year for their own needs and have some left over to sell.

Religion in Tasanee's Culture

Buddhism is the religion of most people in Thailand. Buddhism came from India and is similar to Hinduism,

Tasanee checks her family's crops (left). Later in the day, she pauses to chat with a friend (right).

Tasanee and members of her family offer a gift of food to a Buddhist monk. The gift honors the monk for his wisdom.

the religion practiced by the people of Chhatara. Both Buddhists and Hindus believe in the reincarnation of the soul. However, Buddhists believe that people are equal and do not have a caste system.

A major goal of Buddhism is to reach a state of wisdom through meditation. Buddhists meditate by thinking hard about religious ideas, such as the meaning of life. Buddhist monks lead the people during religious celebrations.

On special occasions the people of San Tan Bong walk to the Buddhist monastery in the center of the village. A **monastery** is a group of buildings where the monks live and work. Once a month religious services are held at the monastery. In addition, local festivals are held on or near the monastery grounds. Sometimes these festivals last all day.

The monks spend their time studying Buddhist writings and meditating. The people of the village honor the monks for their wisdom. When problems need to be settled, the village leaders often go to the monks for advice. The villagers give the monks rice and other food in return for the help the monks provide them.

Reviewing the Lesson

Recalling Key Words, People, and Places
1. What is a group of buildings where religious men called monks live and work?
2. Where does Chiang Mai rank in size among Thai cities?

Remembering Main Ideas
1. What subjects does Tasanee study in school?
2. What types of work do Tasanee's grandparents perform?
3. How do the villagers pay the Buddhist monks for their help in settling problems?

Thinking Things Over
How is Tasanee's culture like your own? How is it different?

Lesson 3   A Family of Western Europe

LOOKING AHEAD As you read, look for—

Key words, people, and **places:**

nuclear family

Helmut Sassman

Hamburg

Answers to these questions about **main ideas:**

1. How does Helmut Sassman spend his day?
2. What are some of the organized groups in Helmut's culture?
3. What are the important bodies of knowledge in Helmut's culture?

Helmut Sassman lives in Hamburg, the second largest city in West Germany. More than 1,500,000 people live in the city of Hamburg. It is located on the Elbe (el'bə) River about seventy miles from the North Sea. Find West Germany in the "Facts About the Countries of the World" section starting on page 546. What is the capital of West Germany?

The needs of Helmut's family are much the same as those of Tasanee's family. However, you will see that Helmut's way of life, which reflects the culture of West Germany, is different from Tasanee's.

Helmut's Day

Helmut lives with his mother and father. The Sassmans live in a rented apartment. It is in one of the new brick and glass apartment buildings that line the broad streets of the city. Most of the Sassmans' friends and relatives live in similar apartments or in small townhouses on the edge of the city. Few West Germans live in single-family houses because such houses are very expensive.

Helmut and his parents like their apartment. It has two bedrooms, a living room, and a large kitchen with a dining area. Outside, the streets are wide and clean. Nearby are parks and playing fields for everyone to enjoy.

Helmut Sassman lives with his family in Hamburg, West Germany.

89

What's in a Name?

As you might suspect, hamburgers are named for the city of Hamburg. Long ago, people in Germany made a food out of chopped beef mixed with bread crumbs. They cooked the mixture and topped it with fried onions. Germans who came to the United States in the 1800s brought this food with them. Many of them sailed from Hamburg.

When a world's fair was held in St. Louis in 1904, someone thought up the idea of putting the "hamburger" on a bun. This made it easier for people to eat while walking around the fairgrounds. Thus, the modern hamburger was born.

Many of Hamburg's buildings have been built in the last forty years. Hamburg was heavily bombed during World War II, and much of the city was rebuilt after the war.

Helmut starts his day at about 6:00 A.M. He and his parents eat a breakfast of rolls, cheese, sausage, and coffee mixed with a lot of milk. Helmut walks down the street to the bakery each day to buy the rolls. He loves to go there because of the delicious smells.

During the week and on two Saturdays a month, Helmut walks to school. He must be there by 8:00 A.M. He does not take a lunch, because school is over by 1:00 P.M. After school Helmut goes home to study. He usually has about three hours of homework each school day.

When he finishes his homework, Helmut does other things. Like most boys and girls in West Germany, he likes to play soccer. Helmut dreams of playing for the Hamburg professional soccer team some day.

Playing soccer is fun, but the city also has other fun things to do. When cousins or family friends from out of town visit Hamburg, Helmut and his parents take them on a tour of the city. The best way to see the city is on a tour boat that travels along the Elbe River. Many canals run through the city and into the river, and the tour boats explore all of them. One canal runs by the big, old Lutheran church that Helmut and his parents attend. The church is one of the few buildings that survived the wartime bombing.

During Christmas vacation and often during the summer, Helmut goes to the Hamburger Dom. This is a huge amusement park near the center of the city. Helmut's parents think the Dom has the best sausages in Hamburg. However, Helmut prefers the food specialty from America. It is called the hamburger!

Organized Groups in Helmut's Culture

Helmut's culture contains many organized groups. Some of these groups help the Sassmans make a living. Other groups provide services that

Helmut and his family need. Finally, the Sassmans belong to organized groups that allow them to participate in activities they enjoy.

Helmut's father and mother both work in organized business groups related to shipping. Trade, shipping, and shipbuilding make Hamburg one of the largest and most important seaports in Europe. A seaport is a city with a harbor that ships can reach from the ocean. Helmut's father works as an electrician for a company that builds and repairs ships in Hamburg's large shipyards. Helmut's mother is a bookkeeper for a company that imports and exports cloth. Helmut's mother keeps track of the money that her company takes in and pays out.

Most family groups in Helmut's culture are **nuclear families.** They include only the parents and their children. The children in a nuclear family usually leave home when they become adults and form their own households. Nuclear families are typical in industrialized cities.

Helmut and his family choose to belong to some groups. For example, Helmut has joined a sports club because he enjoys playing soccer. This club is not part of school, but instead is a private group organized to play various sports. Helmut plays soccer for his club team.

Knowledge in Helmut's Culture

Helmut's culture depends on modern technology. This technology requires Helmut and other young people in his culture to spend many years in school.

Schools teach them the special body of knowledge they need to live in their society.

Helmut studies hard because he has important tests coming up soon. At the age of eleven, all students in West Germany take a test that determines the kind of high school they will enter. If Helmut does well on his test, he will enter the over-school. This type of school will prepare him for college. If he does less well, he will go to either the middle school or the ordinary high school. In either of these schools, Helmut would begin to learn a trade.

Helmut also is learning another body of knowledge. However, he never will be tested about this knowledge. He is learning about his culture. Helmut— like people everywhere—needs to learn the norms and values of his culture. He gains this knowledge from his family, friends, and teachers. All his daily activities add to this body of knowledge.

Reviewing the Lesson

Recalling Key Words, People, and Places
1. What is a family made up of two parents and their children?
2. Tell where the city of Hamburg is located.

Remembering Main Ideas
1. Describe Helmut's house and the neighborhood in which he lives.
2. To what organized groups do Helmut and his family belong?
3. What is the difference between an over-school and an ordinary high school in Helmut's culture?

Thinking Things Over
1. Compare Helmut's way of life with your own.
2. Which is more like your way of life, Helmut's or Tasanee's way of life? Explain your answer.

Understanding Time Zones

When it is 5:00 P.M. on Saturday in New York, Tasanee Engaew is waking up at 5:00 A.M. on Sunday in her country, Thailand. Why are the times different?

What Time Zones Are

The earth's movement causes the difference in times. You know that the earth rotates, or spins, constantly. It rotates on its axis, an imaginary slanted line that runs through the earth from the North Pole to the South Pole. The earth makes one complete rotation every twenty-four hours. It is daytime on the side of the earth turned toward the sun. It is nighttime on the side turned away from the sun.

The exact time in any place is measured from noon, the time of day when the sun is directly overhead. Noon occurs at exactly the same moment at every place along a particular meridian. Each meridian has its own noon and therefore its own time. Thus, sun time, or actual time, is slightly different every few miles as you move east or west on the earth.

Instead of sun time, however, most countries use standard time. The **standard time** system divides the earth into twenty-four regions called time zones, one for each hour of the day.

All places within a given **time zone** use the same time. As you cross from one time zone to another, you must change the time on your watch. If you travel west, you "gain" time. That is, you move your watch back one hour. If you travel east, you "lose" time by moving your watch ahead one hour.

Each day has twelve hours before noon and twelve hours after noon. The hours before noon are called *ante meridiem,* which is Latin for "before noon." The abbreviation for *ante meridiem* is A.M. *Post meridiem,* or P.M., means "after noon."

What a Time Zone Map Shows

The map on page 93 shows the world's twenty-four time zones. Notice that the zones have jagged shapes. These adjustments allow all the people in a city, state, or small country to have the same time. Some large countries have several time zones. Count the time zones in Australia, for instance. Notice that one zone in Australia is called *irregular.* The time in an irregular zone usually differs from time in an adjoining zone by only half an hour rather than a full hour.

The meridian passing through Greenwich, England, just outside London, is the starting line for measuring the world's time zones. You have learned that this line, at 0° longitude, is called the Prime Meridian. Find the Prime Meridian on the map.

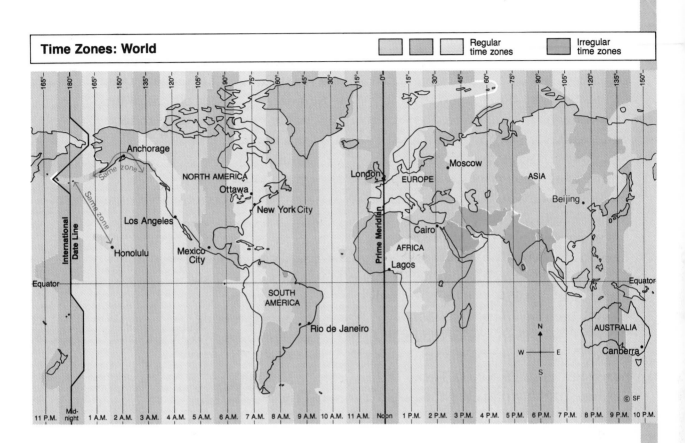

Time Zones: World

Regular time zones | Irregular time zones

The map shows that each time zone covers about 15° longitude, east or west of the Prime Meridian. Every fifteen degrees, standard time changes by one hour.

Now find the International Date Line, at 180°, on the map. The International Date Line is the ending line for measuring time zones. When you cross the International Date Line, the day of the week changes. If you travel west approaching the International Date Line on Sunday, it is Monday after you cross the line. If you travel east on Sunday, it is Saturday after you cross the line.

Skills Practice

1. At noon in London, what time is it in the following cities? Label your answers A.M. or P.M.
   a. Ottawa
   b. Beijing
   c. Canberra

2. When it is 4:00 P.M. in Los Angeles, it is 9:00 P.M. in what other city on the map?

3. How many hours' difference is there between the time in Los Angeles and the time in Rio de Janeiro?

4. What time is it in London when it is 3:00 P.M. in New York? (Use A.M. or P.M.)

Chapter Summary

Lesson 1   Society and Culture—A group of people who have common goals is called a society. The total way of life a society develops to reach its common goals is called a culture. All cultures have common characteristics: work and rewards, organized groups, norms (standards of behavior), values, religion, a body of knowledge, and art forms. Life in Chhatara, a village in India, shows these characteristics.

Lesson 2   A Family of Southeast Asia—Tasanee Engaew and her family live in a village in Thailand. Tasanee spends her day going to school and doing chores. Everyone in the family works, including planting and harvesting rice. Like most Thais, Tasanee's family practices the Buddhist religion.

Lesson 3   A Family of Western Europe—Helmut Sassman and his family live in West Germany. Helmut goes to school and plays soccer for his club team. The team is one of the many organized groups in Helmut's culture. Helmut studies hard to learn the technological body of knowledge he needs.

Write your answers on a separate sheet of paper.

Testing Key Words, People, and Places

Part A

Use each key word in a sentence.

1. society
2. culture
3. norm
4. custom
5. mores
6. value
7. extended family
8. reincarnation
9. caste system
10. monastery
11. nuclear family
12. standard time
13. time zone

Part B

Match each description with the correct place.

1. a city in West Germany
2. a village in northern India
3. a village in Thailand
   a. Chhatara
   b. San Tan Bong
   c. Hamburg

Testing Main Ideas

Choose the answer that best completes each sentence.

1. All cultures have
   a. a caste system.
   b. ways of farming.
   c. norms and values.
2. One of the most important ways of passing on knowledge is
   a. language.
   b. money.
   c. work.
3. In Chhatara's culture
   a. men and women do the same work.
   b. lawbreakers are not punished for crimes.
   c. family members cooperate for the good of all.

4. Tasanee Engaew
   a. goes to school in San Tan Bong.
   b. goes to school in a large city.
   c. does not go to school.

5. Most people in San Tan Bong
   a. plant and harvest rice.
   b. have jobs in a nearby city.
   c. constantly move from place to place.

6. Buddhists like those in San Tan Bong
   a. believe people are equal.
   b. believe the soul dies when the body does.
   c. believe in a caste system.

7. Helmut Sassman
   a. lives in a suburban house.
   b. plays baseball for a club team.
   c. goes to school on some Saturdays.

8. Helmut Sassman's parents
   a. drive to work by car.
   b. work in businesses related to shipping.
   c. live with many relatives.

Testing Skills

1. Understanding time zones. Study the map on this page. It shows the time zones in the main part of the United States. Then answer the questions.
   a. When it is noon at point W, what time is it on the west coast? *9:00 A.M.*
   b. If it is 2 P.M. at point X, what time is it on the east coast? *3:00 P.M.*
   c. What time is it at point Y when it is 5 P.M. at point Z? *6:00 P.M.*

United States: Time Zones

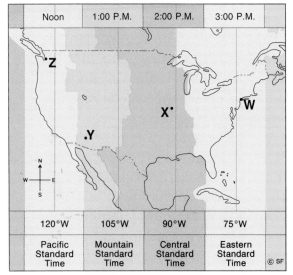

Noon	1:00 P.M.	2:00 P.M.	3:00 P.M.	
120°W	105°W	90°W	75°W	
Pacific Standard Time	Mountain Standard Time	Central Standard Time	Eastern Standard Time	© SF

2. Practicing narrative writing. Write a description of how an American your age might spend his or her day. Use words and phrases that will help the reader understand the order of the day's events.

Activities

1. Make a bulletin-board display on culture. Set aside one section of the board for each of the characteristics of culture. Arrange pictures you have cut out or drawn that show the characteristics.

2. Imagine you are visiting a family in another country of your choice. Write a letter to your own family, describing what you have seen about the culture. If you need to, do some research into the country at your library.

Biography Mother Teresa

In 1910 Agnes Bojaxhiu (ôg′nes boi yä′jü) was born to Albanian parents who owned a grocery store in present-day Yugoslavia. That baby girl grew to be loved and respected throughout the world as Mother Teresa.

By the time she was twelve, Agnes knew she wanted to "go out and give the love of Christ." When she was eighteen, she began training to become a Roman Catholic nun, joining other nuns who were working in Calcutta, India. There, Sister Teresa, as she was now known, began teaching geography at St. Mary's High School. Outside the walls of the school, however, Sister Teresa saw people living in cardboard boxes and even in gutters. She began to feel she had to contribute more directly to the community.

Deciding to give up her interest in teaching, Sister Teresa trained to be a nurse. At the age of 38, she put on a rough sari (a robelike dress worn by Indian women) and went barefoot and alone into the streets of Calcutta. When she saw people who were hungry, she begged for food for them. When she saw children who had no schools, she taught them outside, between huts. Because they had no books or paper, she scratched letters of the alphabet in the earth with a stick. When she found sick people, she persistently asked doctors for medical supplies.

In 1950 she began a new order, a society, of nuns: the Missionaries of Charity. Soon other women joined Sister Teresa, who became known as Mother Teresa. Mother Teresa and the Missionaries of Charity nursed and fed abandoned babies and built homes for children, women, and sick, old, and handicapped people. Mother Teresa once said, "We must love each other . . . [which involves] making people feel they are wanted." In time, her missionary order, which depends entirely on private donations, spread to fifty cities in India and to thirty other countries.

Mother Teresa has won many international honors, including the Nobel Prize for Peace in 1979. She said, "Personally, I am unworthy. I accept in the name of the poor, ..." She used the money from the award to build more homes for people in need.

Questions to Think About

1. What was one thing Sister Teresa did for the good of the community?
2. How would you explain the willingness of someone like Mother Teresa to devote her or his life to helping the poor?

Arable Land—The Key to Growing Food

Because the United States has so much rich farmland, we tend to take it—and the food it grows—for granted. Yet, as the map shows, only about one-third of the earth's land area is **arable**—suitable for growing crops.

What makes land suitable for growing crops? First, the land must be fairly flat. Otherwise, rain will quickly run off, leaving crops without water. Also, rain tends to erode, or wear away, the soil on sloping land. Second, the soil itself must have certain nutrients needed for crops to grow and must be easy to break up by plowing. Rocky soil, for example, makes poor farmland. Third, the land must be in a climate that provides a certain amount of rain. The climate also must provide a long enough growing season—a period of time without frost. Most crops need a growing season of at least ninety days.

Climate also helps determine the type of crop a farmer can grow. Rice, for example, only grows in hot or warm climates with plentiful rainfall.

Using Your Geography Skills

1. Look at the map on this page. Why is the land across the northern part of Europe and Asia not suitable for growing crops? Use the climate map on pages 36–37 to explain your answer.
2. Compare the map on this page with the population distribution map on page 60. How does the location of arable land seem to affect the number of people who live in an area?

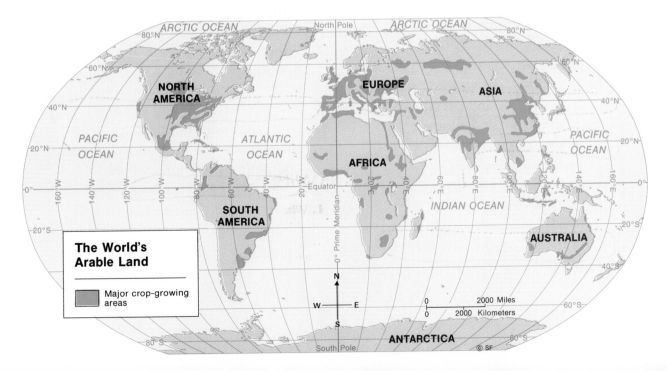

The World's Arable Land

Major crop-growing areas

Unit 1 Review

Write your answers on a separate sheet of paper.

Key Words
Give the definition of each key word.

1. landform
2. climate
3. natural vegetation
4. latitude.
5. natural resource –h
6. technology
7. demographer–d
8. urban area
9. gross national product –g
10. export
11. longitude –f
12. culture– c
13. norm –a
14. custom– b
15. time zone – e

Main Ideas
Choose the answer that best completes each sentence.

1. Mountains, hills, plateaus, and plains are the major kinds of
   a. grasslands.
   b. landforms.
   c. natural vegetation.
2. The two main parts of a place's climate are
   a. oceans and latitude.
   b. landforms and vegetation.
   c. temperature and precipitation.
3. Hot climates mostly occur
   a. in the tropics.
   b. near the poles.
   c. in the United States.
4. Needleleaf trees
   a. shed their leaves each fall.
   b. constantly grow new leaves.
   c. are the same as broadleaf trees.

5. The higher the altitude of a place,
   a. the hotter it is.
   b. the colder it is.
   c. the less precipitation it receives.
6. Coal, oil, and natural gas
   a. are nonmineral resources.
   b. are evenly distributed across the earth.
   c. are minerals used for producing energy.
7. It is important to use minerals wisely because
   a. they are not renewable.
   b. they are harmed by pollution.
   c. they are renewable resources.
8. World population growth is rapid because
   a. death rates are low while birth rates are high.
   b. health care is poor while food is plentiful.
   c. people die younger than in the past.
9. The kind of land use practiced in urban areas is
   a. nomadic herding.
   b. commercial farming.
   c. manufacturing and commerce.
10. Low gross national product, subsistence farming, and a growing population are characteristics of
    a. developing countries.
    b. developed countries.
    c. the United States only.

98

11. Vehicles and routes that allow movement of people and goods make up a
  a. transportation network.
  b. communication network.
  c. trade network.

12. Families are an example of
  a. customs.
  b. organized groups.
  c. work and rewards.

13. The women of Chhatara
  a. work in or near the village.
  b. do most of the fieldwork.
  c. work in a nearby city.

14. In San Tan Bong, most of the men
  a. are Buddhist monks.
  b. plant and harvest rice.
  c. hunt and fish for a living.

15. In Hamburg, both of Helmut's parents work
  a. in the shipping industry.
  b. at a telephone company.
  c. for the government.

Skills

1. Comparing sun time and standard time. If you took a plane from New York City to Cleveland, Ohio, you would remain in the same time zone. Therefore, your watch would tell you the correct standard time when you landed. However, the sun time would be different. Would this sun time be earlier or later than the time your watch shows? Explain your answer.

2. Locating continents and countries on a map. Write the letters A through C and then the numbers 1 through 3 on your paper. The letters on the map below mark the locations of Europe, Australia, and Asia. Write the name of the correct continent next to each letter. The numbers on the map mark the locations of Thailand, West Germany, and India. Write the name of the correct country next to each number on your paper.

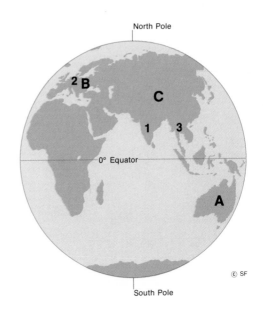

Essay

Imagine that a person from another country wants to know what American culture is like. Write an essay that explains how American culture shows the seven characteristics of cultures.

Events That Shaped Our Modern World

Did you know that people settled in cities thousands of years ago? They set up governments. They developed religions and found ways to write and keep records. They traded, traveled, and spread knowledge. In short, they created civilization. Some important figures of the earliest civilizations of Asia, Africa, and Europe are pictured at left. In this unit you will learn about civilizations and how they grew over centuries.

Before You Go On

Preview the unit. Read the chapter titles below. In which chapter do you think you will read about the earliest civilization in history?

Study the time line. How many years does the time line show? What does it tell you about the Roman Empire?

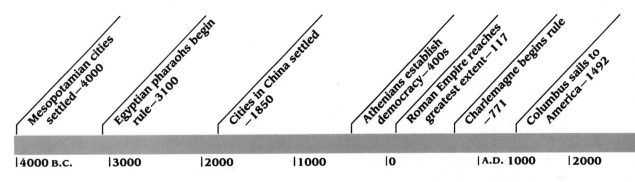

Mesopotamian cities settled—4000

Egyptian pharaohs begin rule—3100

Cities in China settled —1850

Athenians establish democracy—400s

Roman Empire reaches greatest extent—117

Charlemagne begins rule —771

Columbus sails to America—1492

| 4000 B.C. | 3000 | 2000 | 1000 | 0 | A.D. 1000 | 2000 |

Chapter 4

The Beginnings of Civilization

For tens of thousands of years, human beings survived by gathering wild plants and by hunting and fishing. Their way of life started to change when they began to farm and settle into villages. Over several thousand years, villagers living in major river valleys in Asia and in northern Africa developed new ways of living that we call civilization. The picture shows a wall painting from Sumer, an ancient civilization in Mesopotamia.

In this chapter you will discover the contributions of the first ancient civilization in Mesopotamia; the later civilizations of the Babylonians, Phoenicians, and Hebrews; two civilizations of the Nile River; and civilizations in India and China. The lessons in the chapter are listed below.

Lesson 1 Early Civilization in Mesopotamia

Lesson 2 Babylonians, Phoenicians, and Hebrews

Lesson 3 Civilization Along the Nile

Lesson 4 Early Indian and Chinese Civilizations

Lesson 1   Early Civilization in Mesopotamia

LOOKING AHEAD As you read, look for—

Key words, people, and **places:**

archaeologist
civilization
specialization
cuneiform

Sumerian

Mesopotamia
Euphrates River
Tigris River

Answers to these questions about **main ideas:**

1. Why is Mesopotamian culture considered a civilization?
2. How did the first cities develop in Mesopotamia, between the Tigris and Euphrates rivers?
3. What were the main features of Sumerian cities?

Pretend you are flying over the country of Iraq. Iraq is in Southwest Asia, as you can see from the Atlas map on page 540. Looking down from the window of the airplane, you see a vast desert that looks as if it has been bleached white by the hot sun. In the distance are blue-gray mountains. Just beneath the airplane you see a river that looks like a ribbon of green cutting through the dry white land. This river is called the Euphrates (yü frā′tēz). Not far away is the Tigris (tī′gris) River.

For many years the land you are looking at was called Mesopotamia (mes′ə pə tā′mē ə). *Mesopotamia* means "the land between the rivers." Find the Tigris and Euphrates rivers on the map on page 104. Notice that the shape of Mesopotamia closely follows the area outlined by the rivers.

As your airplane flies closer to the ground, you notice large white and tan mounds on either side of the Euphrates River. These mounds are the remains of ancient settlements begun more than seven thousand years ago.

Early Mesopotamian Civilization

How do we know that the mounds are places where Mesopotamians once lived? Scientists called **archaeologists** (är′kē ol′ə jists) study the people, customs, and life of ancient—very old—times. The archaeologists have dug into the mounds and found the ruins the ancient Mesopotamians left behind. Walls, temples, and ordinary houses lie in crumpled piles. Sometimes diggers have found clay tablets with writing on them. By studying the objects and writing, archaeologists and historians have been able to piece together the story of an ancient civilization.

Civilizations are advanced cultures usually based on city living. Mesopotamian city life had all the characteristics of a civilization:

- a well-organized government
- variety in people's jobs
- social classes based on wealth or family position
- ways of keeping records
- a highly organized religious life

Of course, Mesopotamian cities did not just suddenly appear. Like many

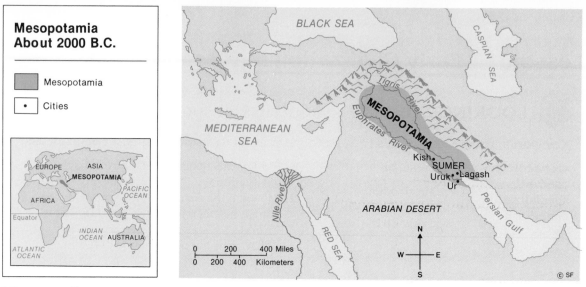

Map Study

Both maps show Mesopotamia. Which map is better for describing Mesopotamia's location in relation to continents? If you want to estimate Mesopotamia's size, which map is better? About how many miles did Mesopotamia extend northwest from the Persian Gulf?

developments in history, the cities formed gradually. As the cities developed, Mesopotamian civilization took shape.

How the First Cities Developed

About ten thousand years ago, some groups of people in the hilly parts of Southwest Asia settled down into villages to farm. As the village populations grew larger, the farmers needed more and better land to feed the people. The search for new land led the farmers from the hills of Mesopotamia into the land between the Tigris and Euphrates rivers around 6000 B.C. It was here that Mesopotamian civilization developed. Look at the map above. In what direction, mostly, would the farmers have traveled from the hills into the valley?

Actually the land in Mesopotamia was dry much of the year. With careful irrigation, however, the soil became highly productive. The farmers dug channels from the rivers to their fields so the river water could reach the crops. Using this method the farmers were able to produce more food than they needed for their families.

The increase in food production brought a number of changes to Mesopotamian society. First, some people gave up farming. Many people could spend their time at other jobs instead. They could make products, for example—things such as metal tools, pottery, and leather goods. We call a situation in which each person does only one kind of job **specialization.** Second, since the farmers and other workers now could sell surplus food and other goods to other villagers, trade began to grow.

Third, as trade increased, social classes became important. Certain people began to direct the trade. They kept records of goods bought and sold and made laws about buying and selling products. These directors became permanent leaders of Mesopotamian society. In later years leaders would become the kings and priests to whom the people looked for law and order.

By about 5000 B.C. large villages could be found throughout Mesopotamia. More and more people came to live in the large villages. Some villages became centers for manufacturing and trade. These villages—with growing populations, trade, and specialization of jobs—were the earliest cities. By about 4000 B.C., the largest Mesopotamian villages were true cities.

Sumerian Cities

The earliest Mesopotamian civilization we know about is Sumer. Sumer was an advanced civilization that developed in southeastern Mesopotamia near the Persian Gulf. The Sumerians built several cities. The largest one was Ur, which had a city population of about 25,000 in 3000 B.C. Find the names of three other Sumerian cities on the map on page 104. Which city was farthest south?

All the Sumerian cities had at least one major temple as well as many small temples. Most Sumerians believed in many gods. The largest temple in each city was built in honor of the god who was believed to protect that city. Powerful priests ran the temples. Because religion was so important to the Sumerians, the priests often had a say in running the cities too.

Archaeologists and teams of helpers worked for years to find the ruins of ancient Sumer.

Trade was another important part of Sumerian city life. Local workers sold their pottery, tools, cloth, and other goods in small marketplaces throughout the city. Trade on a larger scale took place in the city's central market, which was located near the main temple in most cities. Each day farmers from outside the city and traders from distant lands came to the central market to buy and sell. Priests and government officers kept track of the goods that came into the city.

With so many people living in one place and so much trade going on, city people needed ways to keep order. Thus, kings and priests made laws. The laws helped people live together safely, and they helped trade go smoothly. Officials of the king and the priests enforced the laws. People thought that the royal laws were also the laws of the gods. If the laws were broken, angry gods might destroy the world.

Kings and priests kept order partly by recording things that went on in the city. The Sumerians kept records in writing. The idea of making notes on clay, stone, or wood was very old when the first cities developed. However, Sumerian city dwellers developed the first complete writing system. This system, called **cuneiform,** consisted of thousands of small pictures. Each picture stood for a different word.

Many features of Sumerian civilization passed down through time to the modern world. These features include not only writing but the very idea of city life as people moved from a simple farming way of life.

This Sumerian medical tablet lists fifteen cures for illnesses.

Reviewing the Lesson

Recalling Key Words, People, and Places
1. Identify the key words defined below:
   a. scientist who studies ancient cultures
   b. the first complete writing system, with thousands of small pictures
2. Tell where each is located in relation to the others:
   a. Mesopotamia
   b. Euphrates River
   c. Tigris River

Remembering Main Ideas
1. Name two characteristics of Mesopotamian civilization.
2. How did specialization of jobs develop in Mesopotamia as cities began to develop there?
3. What role did kings and priests play in Sumerian cities?

Thinking Things Over
If you had to choose one characteristic as the most important for a civilization, which one would you choose? Give reasons to support your answer.

Lesson 2 Babylonians, Phoenicians, and Hebrews

LOOKING AHEAD As you read, look for—

Key words, people, and **places:**

empire
colony
monotheism

Babylonian
Phoenician
Hebrew
Hammurabi

Answers to these questions about **main ideas:**

1. What were the main accomplishments of the Babylonians?
2. What were the major accomplishments of the Phoenicians?
3. What was the major difference in religious belief between the Hebrews and other people in Southwest Asia?

The people of Sumer created the world's first civilization about six thousand years ago. Their form of civilized life passed down through the centuries to later groups of people in the Middle East. Three of these groups were the Babylonians, the Phoenicians, and the Hebrews. All three groups had important roles to play in the development of later civilizations, including our own.

The Babylonians

Look at the map on page 108. Note that the city of Babylon (bab′ a lən) was located in Mesopotamia. About how far from Ur was Babylon? Babylon was founded about 1900 B.C. on an important trade route near the Euphrates River. Partly because of its location, the city became the center of the Babylonian kingdom in Mesopotamia.

Hammurabi. Babylon's rise to power happened in the late 1700s B.C. At this time a great king named Hammurabi (ham′ủ rä′bē) formed a strong army with which he conquered lower Mesopotamia. Because of his power and

fame, the government Hammurabi set up was followed by later rulers in the area. Hammurabi ruled for nearly fifty years and created an **empire.** That is, he controlled land in Mesopotamia far beyond Babylon itself.

The king appointed governors to help rule these lands and had the governors report back to him. The army and the governors protected the empire's trade and farming from invaders. They also made sure the conquered people paid taxes of some kind to support the king, the officials, and the army. Taxing conquered people was not a new idea in Mesopotamia, but Hammurabi used it over a wider area than ever before.

Hammurabi is most famous for a set of laws called Hammurabi's Code. The king had the laws carved on large stone pillars in the marketplace of cities all over the empire. Hammurabi acted as judge when people disagreed over matters. Suppose, for example, a carpenter and a customer disagreed over the cost of a job. Hammurabi would make a decision and then have

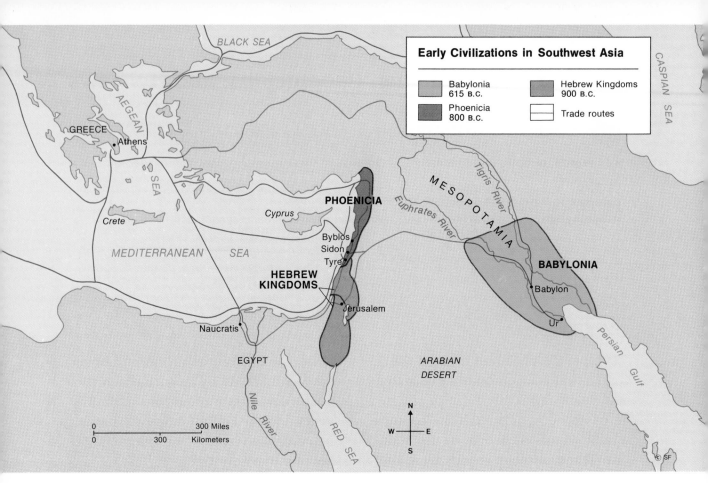

Map Study

Was the trade route the shortest distance between Jerusalem and Babylon? Use the bar scale to compare the trade-route distance and the most direct distance between the cities.

the decision written down for future reference. The king's decision became a law for similar cases.

Other laws in the code came from earlier Mesopotamian rulers. The code is the most complete set of early laws ever discovered.

Babylonian Culture. The Babylonians did a great deal of work in science and medicine. By watching the sun, moon, and stars, they worked out a calendar that still is used today. The Babylonians invented a system of astrology by watching the sun, moon, and stars to try to predict the future. In later years astrology became a basis for modern astronomy, the science that deals with stars and planets. Babylonian doctors did complex surgery and cured some diseases with medicines made from plants. People still use some of these methods today.

Babylonian officials also used writing widely. They recorded business contracts and other legal matters on clay tablets. The tablets were stored in central offices or in the king's palace. Hammurabi and later rulers in Southwest Asia kept large libraries filled with government records, poetry, and other literature. These collections were the world's first major libraries.

Babylonians preserved many of the writings of ancient Mesopotamia. When archaeologists found the ancient libraries, the modern world began to learn about these ancient people of Mesopotamia. For example, we know the Babylonians spoke one of the Semitic languages. The Semitic languages still exist today. The main ones are Arabic and Hebrew. Most people in the Middle East and North Africa speak Arabic. Hebrew is the language of Israel. Language is a way that ancient cultures were passed down through the centuries.

After Hammurabi's death, control of Babylonia passed to other groups of people. Not for several centuries did the empire achieve the fame and greatness that Hammurabi brought.

The Phoenicians

About five hundred years after Hammurabi ruled in Babylonia, people called Phoenicians (fe nish′əns), who lived in cities on the eastern shore of the Mediterranean Sea, became

Linking Past and Present

Hammurabi's Code

In 1901 archaeologists found one of the stone pillars that contains Hammurabi's Code. The pillar, shown in part at right, is more than seven feet high and contains nearly three hundred laws. Hammurabi's laws are decisions about what would happen *if*—if someone were hurt, robbed, or cheated, for example.

Some of the laws tell the punishment for certain crimes. We use the phrase "an eye for an eye" to describe these laws. For example, the code states that "if a man destroy the eye of another man, they [the government] shall destroy his eye." In other words, people received punishments similar to their crimes. Most of the laws in Hammurabi's code cover property rights, wages, taxes, debts, and business arrangements. The laws are concerned with the fair treatment of people. Hammurabi saw himself as a fair leader and a protector of the weak.

By the Way

Have you ever heard of the word *phonetics* (fə net′iks)? It refers to the sounds of a language.

The English alphabet is phonetic because letters stand for sounds, not for things or ideas. The Phoenician alphabet was phonetic also. In fact, the Phoenician and English alphabets have some similarities. Compare the Phoenician and English letters shown in the picture. Now cover the English letters and see if you can identify the Phoenician letters.

Although the English alphabet is not based directly on the Phoenician letters, there are certain links. The Phoenicians had contacts with the early Greeks, who did influence our alphabet more directly. Then another people, the Romans, made changes in the Greek alphabet and produced letters very much like our own.

powerful. Like the Babylonians, the Phoenicians shared in much of Mesopotamian culture. They were also great sailors and traders.

If you look at the map on page 108, you will see that the Mediterranean's eastern shore is well located for trade. Phoenicians traded with Mesopotamia and with Mediterranean cities. So skilled were the Phoenician sailors that they made a voyage all around Africa. European explorers did not repeat this accomplishment for two thousand more years.

Between 1000 and 580 B.C., the Phoenicians enjoyed great power. They established colonies along the coast of northern Africa. **Colonies** are places controlled by distant governments. Some of these colonies, such as Carthage, became powerful cities in their own right in later years.

Perhaps the most important thing handed down by the Phoenicians is their alphabet. Phoenicians took the old Sumerian writing system and made it simpler. In Sumerian cuneiform, every word had a picture symbol. In an alphabet, one written symbol, or letter, stands for a sound. Many different words can be made by putting letters together in various ways.

Using the Phoenician alphabet, someone who wanted to write did not have to learn thousands of different symbols. Instead, the person needed only to learn twenty-two letters. The Phoenicians took their new writing system with them as they traveled all over the known world. All European and American writing today comes from this Phoenician invention.

The Hebrews

The Hebrews were a third important people in the ancient Middle East. The Hebrews lived near the Phoenician cities, as you can see from the map on page 108. Some Hebrews had fled slavery in Egypt. By about 1000 B.C., the

This painting shows the Hebrew leader Moses receiving the Ten Commandments from God.

Hebrews had set up two kingdoms where Israel is today. It was not a great empire that made the Hebrews important for modern civilization, however. Instead, it was the Hebrews' ideas about religion that made them important. These ideas influenced today's major religions in Europe, the Middle East, the Americas, and Australia.

The religious ideas of the Hebrews are recorded in their holy book, the Torah, also called the Old Testament. The Torah tells about the Hebrews' belief in only one God. Belief in one God is called **monotheism.** This belief was the major difference between the Hebrews and other people of the time, who believed in many gods. The Hebrews believed they had an agreement with God. They would obey His laws. In return, God would protect them as His chosen people. God was seen as a judge who punished wrongdoers. However, God also gave mercy to those who admitted their wrongs.

One important idea in the Hebrew faith is that all people are equal in the sight of God. Another important idea is that God's laws could not be overruled by kings. Later these ideas would spread over much of the world.

The Hebrews, Babylonians, and Phoenicians all were connected with the earliest Mesopotamian civilization. Hebrews, for example, believed they were descended from a man named Abraham who came from the early Mesopotamian city of Ur on the Euphrates River. Old Mesopotamian ideas were kept alive by these later people, who passed on their culture from one generation to the next.

Reviewing the Lesson

Recalling Key Words, People, and Places
1. Identify the key words defined below:
    a. a group of lands ruled by one leader
    b. a place, such as a city, controlled by a distant government
    c. belief in only one God
2. Tell why it is important to remember:
    a. Phoenicians
    b. Hebrews

Remembering Main Ideas
1. For what accomplishment is the Babylonian king Hammurabi most famous?
2. Why is the Phoenicians' writing system considered one of their most important accomplishments?
3. Tell one way the Hebrew faith was different from the belief of other people in Southwest Asia.

Thinking Things Over
Choose one contribution of the Babylonians, Phoenicians, or Hebrews. Tell how you think our civilization might be different today without this contribution.

Lesson 3   Civilization Along the Nile

📖 LOOKING AHEAD As you read, look for—

Key words, people, and **places:**

pharaoh   Kush
hieroglyph   Meroe

Answers to these questions about **main ideas:**

1. How did the pharaohs probably rise to power in Egypt?
2. What were the major characteristics of ancient Egyptian civilization?
3. What was the Kushite civilization like?

In northern Africa, civilization first grew up along the banks of the Nile River in Egypt. Find ancient Egypt on the map on page 113. Then find modern Egypt on the Atlas map on page 542. Like Mesopotamia, Egypt is mostly desert land. In both places rivers bring life to the dry land.

The Rise of Pharaohs in Egypt

Egypt today is mostly a land of farming villages. This fact has not changed much for the last eight thousand years. The earliest Egyptian farm villages probably developed between 6000 and 5000 B.C. Some villages grew into small towns with chiefs and priests in control of them.

By about 3100 B.C., a major change had taken place. Kings called **pharaohs** came to rule over Egypt. Historians are not sure exactly what brought on the rule of pharaohs. It is likely that some village chiefs and their families gained more and more power. The richest of the chiefs became nobles and kings. Then one family of kings conquered all of Egypt and united the country under its rule. From this point on, a series of royal families, known as dynasties, ruled Egypt.

The pharaohs ruled Egypt as if it were their own property. Egyptians believed that each pharaoh was a living god on earth. They thought the pharaoh was all-powerful. He was said to cause the Nile to flood and so bring life-giving water to the land. The pharaoh could make any laws that he wished.

Egyptian Civilization

Ancient Egypt had many small villages and market towns. Egypt had some cities, too, but they were different from the busy Mesopotamian trading centers you read about earlier. Archaeologists believe cities in Egypt served mainly as centers for government and religion. Although the Egyptians did trade with outside people, trade was not as important in Egypt as it was in Mesopotamia and the eastern Mediterranean region. Most Egyptians were simple farmers and most villages could provide for their own needs.

Egyptian civilization had social classes. At the top were the pharaoh, government officials, and nobles. These groups owned most of the land and wealth. Next was a small group of traders and craft workers. Farmers made up a large group in the lowest social classes. People from the lowest ranks of Egyptian society could rise to the top, however, through service in the army or through special schools for scribes. Scribes were people who learned how to write.

Writing was another characteristic of Egyptian civilization. The Egyptians may have borrowed the idea of writing from the Mesopotamians. However, they did not usually write on clay as the Mesopotamians had. Instead, Egyptians made a kind of paper from the papyrus (pə pī′rəs) reed, a tall marsh plant. Writers painted symbols called **hieroglyphs** on the papyrus. The hieroglyphs were small pictures and signs that stood for words.

Few people in ancient Egypt knew how to write. Like cuneiform, the hieroglyphs took years of study to learn.

Religion had a central place in Egyptian life. The ancient Egyptians believed in many gods. The pharaoh was the most important god. Two others were Ra, the sun god, and Osiris (ō-sī′ris), the god of the afterlife. Every village and town had its own gods also.

The people of Egypt worked hard to please the gods. Working for the pharaoh, for example, was considered a form of worship. The Egyptians honored the pharaoh by building him a huge palace. Officials brought the pharaoh food and treasure from throughout the kingdom.

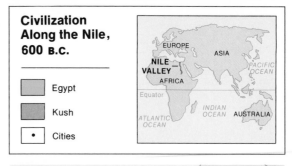

Civilization Along the Nile, 600 B.C.

- Egypt
- Kush
- • Cities

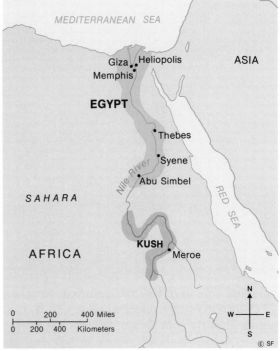

Map Study

What do the locations of all the cities shown on the map have in common?

Even in death, the pharaoh had to have a splendid house. The ancient Egyptians believed the soul of a person lived on after death. Therefore, they built the pharaohs' tombs to be like their palaces and to make their next life comfortable.

The elaborate tombs were known as pyramids. Workers labored for years to build the huge stone structures that have fascinated later generations.

113

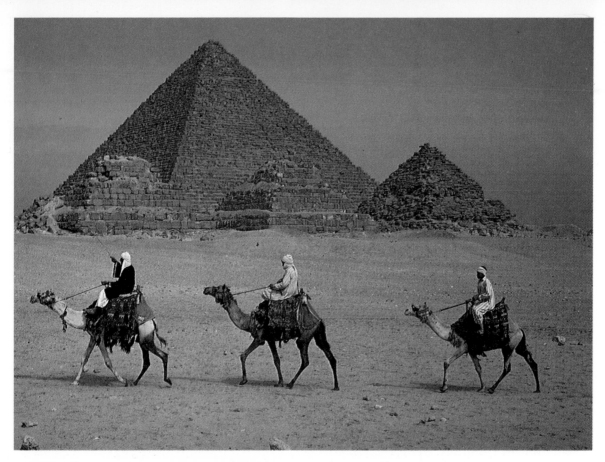

Imagine you were able to explore inside the pyramids! Actually, many of their treasures have been stolen. Still, the structures themselves remind us of the wonders of ancient Egypt.

Imagine the excitement of archaeologist Howard Carter when he first found the tomb of the young Egyptian pharaoh Tutankhamen (tü′tängk ä′men) in 1922. Carter excavated and wrote about Egyptian tombs.

❝ Surely never before in the whole history of excavation had such an amazing sight been seen as . . . we looked down from our spy-hole in the blocked doorway, casting the beam of light from our torch—the first light that had pierced the darkness of the chamber for three thousand years . . . [There were] exquisitely painted and inlaid caskets; alabaster vases . . . strange black shrines, from the open door of one a great gilt snake peeping out . . . chairs beautifully carved; a golden inlaid throne . . . a confused pile of overturned chariots, glistening with gold and inlay; and peeping from behind them another portrait of a king. **❞**

Kushite Civilization

Ancient Egypt shared the Nile River valley with another early civilization, Kush, to the south. Kush was centered around the city of Meroe (mër′ō ē). Today the region is in the country of

Sudan. Find Kush on the map on page 113. What similarity between Egypt and Kush do you see?

Kush and Egypt had close contact. In fact, the Egyptians ruled Kush for about five hundred years, between 1500 and 1000 B.C. The Kushites adopted many Egyptian ways during this time. Still, Kush had its own characteristics. The Egyptians did not completely overshadow their southern neighbors.

The Kushite language was probably the ancient language of the region. It was quite different from Egyptian. After gaining independence in 1000 B.C., Kush created its own writing system. This system had some Egyptian hieroglyphs, but archaeologists have never been able to understand Kushite writing completely.

Kush shared some gods with the Egyptians, but the Kushites had their own gods as well. Archaeologists know Kush had powerful priests. As in other ancient civilizations, priests were powerful because religion was very important to the people.

Women seem to have had more power in Kush than in many other early civilizations, including Egypt. In fact, queens ruled Kush at one point. We know little else about Kushite rulers, however. If Kushite writing could be read, more would be known about the kings and queens. More would also be known about how Kushite civilization ended.

We do know Meroe was a famous ironworking center from about 500 B.C., when the people learned how to

Look at the hieroglyphs on this Kushite tomb painting. The bird was an important symbol in Kush.

make iron from iron ore. Iron brought great wealth from trade. The Kushites traded their iron tools and weapons with people elsewhere in Africa and beyond. Because of its trade and wealth, Kush prospered as a civilization for several hundred years after gaining independence from Egypt.

Reviewing the Lesson

Recalling Key Words, People, and Places
1. Identify the key words defined below:
   a. ancient Egyptian king
   b. ancient Egyptian writing symbol
2. Describe the locations of the following places:
   a. Kush
   b. Meroe

Remembering Main Ideas
1. How did the government of Egypt change about 3100 B.C.?
2. What were some characteristics of ancient Egyptian religion?
3. Why was ironworking important to the civilization of Kush?

Thinking Things Over
How do civilizations spread their culture to other lands? Give as many examples as you can.

115

Lesson 4   Early Indian and Chinese Civilization

LOOKING AHEAD As you read, look for—

Key words, people, and **places:**

ancestor worship

Aryan
Shang Dynasty

Indus River
Hwang Ho

Answers to these questions about **main ideas:**

1. What facts are known about the earliest Indian civilization?
2. What was Aryan society like?
3. How did the earliest Chinese people live?
4. What were the major characteristics of life under the Shang Dynasty?

River valleys were good places for early civilizations to begin. For one thing, people could travel up and down the rivers. Boats could carry many goods for trade. Also, farming usually was good along rivers. With irrigation, many crops could thrive in the river valleys. Not all civilizations grew up along rivers, of course. Some of the most important ones in the ancient world did though. Two of these were in the Indus River valley, where Pakistan is today, and in the Hwang Ho valley of China. *Hwang Ho* means "yellow river." Find both civilizations on the map on page 117.

Early Indian Civilization

Like all other early civilizations, that of the Indus valley was based on farming. Look at the map on page 117. To the north and west of the Indus there are hills, and beyond them are mountains. Archaeologists think the first farming villages in southern Asia began in the hills before 5000 B.C. The villages eventually grew in size, and peo- ple started to leave the hills in search of more productive land for the growing population. The farmers found good conditions in the Indus valley. The land was fertile, farm animals did well, and the river was full of fish. Villages developed in the Indus valley.

Sometime around 3000 B.C., town and city life began in the Indus valley. The towns and cities spread up and down the valley for about a thousand miles. One of the cities, Mohenjo-Daro (mō hen′jō dä′rō) probably had about forty thousand people in it at one point. Find Mohenjo-Daro on the map on page 117. Mohenjo-Daro was an orderly, planned city, just as the other Indus valley cities were. You can visit the ruins today and still see the even pattern made by the streets.

By 2400 B.C., and perhaps earlier, Indus people traded with Mesopotamia. Ships traveled the 1,200 miles between these two places. Use the map on page 541 and with your finger trace the route the ships probably followed. Indus valley ships carried goods such as precious gems, ivory, dyes, and fine cotton cloth. In what direction did ships travel from the Indus valley to Mesopotamia?

Mesopotamians named the land of the Indus River valley, Meluhha. We do not know what the Indus people called themselves, however. In fact, much about Indus valley life is unknown. We do not know exactly who the Indus valley people were or what language they spoke. We do not know how they ran their governments. So much is unknown because no one has learned how to read the written language of the Indus people. Archaeologists have found thousands of clay markings, but no one knows what they say.

By 1500 B.C. the Indus River had flooded the nearby towns and farmland. Many people went south to find better conditions, and the Indus civilization weakened. At about the same time, a new people began entering the valley from the northwest. These people, called Aryans (er′ē ənz), ruled the Indus valley by 1000 B.C.

The Aryans

We know something about the Aryans from their writing. The oldest book of religious writing in India, the *Rig-Veda,* is theirs. Through the *Rig-Veda,* we learn that the Aryans used bronze weapons, rode horses, and

Map Study

Both early Asian civilizations were located near mountains, as well as along rivers. Did the mountains protect the Indus civilization from the Aryan migrations?

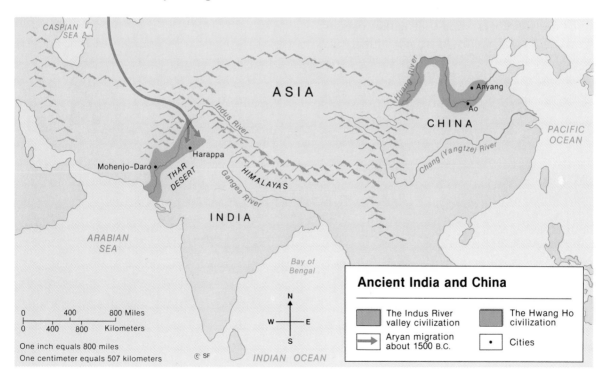

Ancient India and China

- The Indus River valley civilization
- Aryan migration about 1500 B.C.
- The Hwang Ho civilization
- Cities

One inch equals 800 miles
One centimeter equals 507 kilometers

© SF

117

drove chariots. Chariots are wheeled carts pulled by horses.

Aryan society had four social groups. At the top were the nobles and warriors. They had most of the cattle, gold, and other wealth. Next came the priests. Then there were the ordinary people who herded cattle, raised crops, and made goods. At the very bottom of society were the slaves—mostly conquered, non-Aryan people.

Many of the Aryan people who came to the Indus valley intermarried with the people they found there. Aryan culture adapted to the new homeland, and the old Indus people changed, too, over several hundred years.

Early China

Far to the east of the Indus valley, another civilization took form in China.

Find the Hwang Ho civilization near the Huang River on the map on page 117. What two cities are shown there?

If we could go back in time to about 8000 B.C., we would not see many people in the Hwang Ho valley. In the nearby hill country, though, small groups of people made their living by hunting small animals and gathering grain.

By about 5000 B.C., early Chinese people had developed farming villages. Farmers grew a grain called millet. They also knew how to use the cocoons of a certain moth to make silk. You may have seen some of the beautiful silk clothing made in China and Japan today. The method of making silk has not really changed for more than seven thousand years. By about 2000 B.C. the farming villages had spread down into the river valley.

Early Chinese women roll out newly woven silk. Special silkworms produce the silk fibers when they make cocoons.

The Shang Dynasty

By about 1850 B.C., cities had developed in the Hwang Ho valley. They were different from the cities of Mesopotamia and Phoenicia though. Ancient Chinese cities were mainly government centers. Most people lived in villages outside the cities. The city of Ao (ou), which is modern Cheng Chou (jung' jō'), had a palace at its center. A wall of pounded earth surrounded the palace. From this center, the king controlled nearby land and villages. Some villages had only metal workers, some only potters. Other villages were for farmers and their families.

One family of kings who ruled part of the Hwang Ho valley was named Shang. The Shang Dynasty seems to have begun between 1800 and 1500 B.C. With this dynasty came the first major civilization in China's Hwang Ho valley.

Shang kings surrounded themselves with nobles who led the armies and ruled over local villages. The kings also had scribes and priests who kept records. Like societies in Mesopotamia, Egypt, and the Indus valley, early Chinese society had social classes. The king and the nobles, priests, and scribes were at the top. Farmers and craft workers were at the bottom. The lower classes lived simple lives in the villages. The upper classes lived in great luxury. This is the pattern Chinese civilization would follow for hundreds of years.

People in Shang times believed the king had godlike powers. They also believed the king was in contact with the spirits of his dead ancestors. When members of upper-class families died, the people believed their spirits stayed close to home. The spirits were thought to be so powerful that families practiced **ancestor worship** by honoring the dead and bringing gifts to their tombs. In 1928 archaeologists found treasures in the royal tombs at the Shang city of Anyang (än'yäng'). The treasures were there to make the afterlife more comfortable for the dead.

The Shang Dynasty controlled only a small area of the Hwang Ho valley. However, Shang culture spread over larger areas. The Shang Dynasty was overthrown in 1027 B.C. Then a new dynasty of kings arose and spread its rule over larger areas of China.

Reviewing the Lesson

Recalling Key Words, People, and Places
1. Tell what the term **ancestor worship** means.
2. Tell why it is important to remember:
   a. Aryans
   b. Shang Dynasty
   c. Indus River
   d. Hwang Ho

Remembering Main Ideas
1. How did town and city life develop in the earliest Indian civilization?
2. What does the *Rig-Veda* tell us about Aryan society?
3. What special skill did the earliest Chinese farmers practice?
4. How were class differences and religious beliefs connected during the Shang Dynasty's rule in China?

Thinking Things Over
If the language of an ancient civilization cannot be understood, what other clues might be used to find out about the people? Think of as many examples as you can.

Reading and Making Time Lines

The beginnings of civilization described in this chapter took place over thousands of years. The time line on this page highlights some of these events and developments in Mesopotamia and the Mediterranean world. The time line can help you better understand the order in which the events occurred.

How to Read a Time Line

The time line below covers a period of 4,000 years, beginning in 4000 B.C. You read the time line from left to right. The earlier events appear toward the left. Later events appear toward the right. For example, pharaohs ruled Egypt before Babylon was founded. The Hebrews set up two kingdoms after Ur grew to a population of 25,000

people. Would Hammurabi have been able to use metal weapons when he conquered Mesopotamia? Reading the time line shows you that he could have used metal weapons.

How many years passed between the development of cuneiform writing and the Phoenician alphabet? Looking at the time line, you see that cuneiform writing developed about 3500 B.C. The Phoenician alphabet was in wide use by 500 B.C. Subtracting these two dates, 500 from 3500, tells you 3,000 years passed between the development of the two ways of writing.

How to Make a Time Line

To make a time line, you first need to decide the period your time line will include. Once you know the beginning and ending dates, you mark off your line in equal sections.

Each large section of the time line below stands for 1,000 years. Each smaller section stands for 250 years. Put your finger on the mark that stands

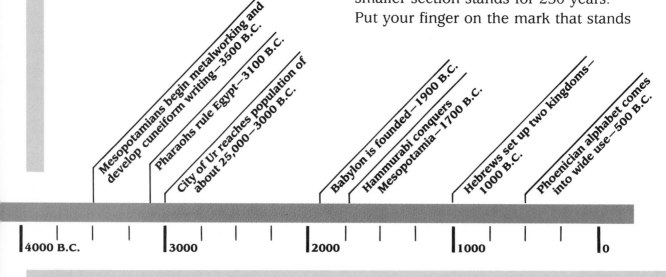

Mesopotamians begin metalworking and develop cuneiform writing—3500 B.C.

Pharaohs rule Egypt—3100 B.C.

City of Ur reaches population of about 25,000—3000 B.C.

Babylon is founded—1900 B.C.

Hammurabi conquers Mesopotamia—1700 B.C.

Hebrews set up two kingdoms—1000 B.C.

Phoenician alphabet comes into wide use—500 B.C.

4000 B.C.   3000   2000   1000   0

for the year 3000 B.C. The next mark to the left of your finger stands for the year 3250 B.C. The pharaohs ruled Egypt beginning in the year 3100 B.C. The entry for 3100 B.C., therefore, falls between 3250 B.C. and 3000 B.C. If you were making this time line, you would need to estimate where 3100 falls between 3250 and 3000.

Many time lines are made to be read from left to right. However, time lines also can be made to be read from top to bottom. The time line below reads from top to bottom. The earlier events are toward the top, beginning with 6000 B.C. Later events are farther down, closer to A.D. 1000.

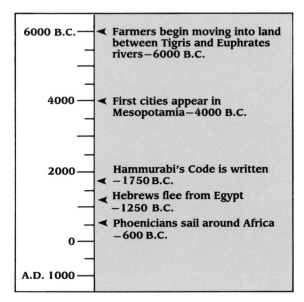

6000 B.C. — ◀ **Farmers begin moving into land between Tigris and Euphrates rivers—6000 B.C.**

4000 — ◀ **First cities appear in Mesopotamia—4000 B.C.**

2000 — ◀ **Hammurabi's Code is written —1750 B.C.**
◀ **Hebrews flee from Egypt —1250 B.C.**
◀ **Phoenicians sail around Africa —600 B.C.**
0 —

A.D. 1000 —

Skills Practice

Use the time line at left below to answer questions 1 and 2.

1. How many years are included between the small marks on the time line?
2. About how many years passed between Hammurabi's Code and the Phoenicians' sailing?

Now make a new time line. First, copy the time line at the bottom of this page. Write the events listed on the time line at left in the correct places below your time line. Next write the following events in the correct places above your time line.

3000 B.C. Hieroglyphics in use in Egypt
2600 B.C. Egyptians begin building pyramids
1339 B.C. Tutankhamen, pharaoh of Egypt, dies

Use your new time line to answer questions 3–5.

3. Were Egyptians writing before or after Mesopotamian cities first appeared?
4. Was Hammurabi's Code written before or after Tutankhamen died?
5. Had the Egyptians begun building pyramids by the time the Phoenicians sailed around Africa?

| 6000 B.C. | 5000 B.C. | 4000 B.C. | 3000 B.C. | 2000 B.C. | 1000 B.C. | 0 | A.D. 1000 |

Chapter 4 Review

Chapter Summary

Lesson 1   Early Civilization in Mesopotamia—By 4000 B.C. ancient Mesopotamia had the characteristics of a civilization, including well-organized government and social classes. Mesopotamian cities developed as farmers produced surpluses, people took up other jobs, and trade increased.

Lesson 2   Babylonians, Phoenicians, and Hebrews—In the late 1700s B.C. King Hammurabi built a powerful empire centered in the city of Babylon in Mesopotamia. Great sailors and traders, the nearby Phoenicians also developed an alphabet. Their neighbors, the Hebrews, differed from other people of the time in that they believed in only one God.

Lesson 3   Civilization Along the Nile—By 3100 B.C. kings called pharaohs had come to rule ancient Egypt. In Egyptian civilization religion held a central place. Farther south, the Kushite civilization prospered by trading its iron tools with other people.

Lesson 4   Early Indian and Chinese Civilizations—The earliest Indian civilization, located in the Indus valley, had cities and trade around 3000 B.C. As the Indus people moved south to escape floods, Aryans from the north moved in. In early China, people in the Hwang Ho valley lived in farming villages. Under the Shang dynasty, which began around 1800 B.C., Chinese civilization developed.

Write your answers on a separate sheet of paper.

Testing Key Words, People, and Places

Part A

Match each definition with the correct key word in the list.

1. a belief in only one God
2. an advanced culture based on city living
3. the king of Egypt in ancient times
4. a picture or sign that stands for a word
5. a situation in which each person does only one kind of job
6. a writing system with thousands of small pictures
7. a place controlled by a distant government
8. a group of lands ruled by one leader
9. scientist who studies the people, customs, and life of ancient times
10. the practice of honoring dead family members

a. **archaeologist**
b. **civilization**
c. **specialization**
d. **cuneiform**
e. **empire**
f. **colony**
g. **monotheism**
h. **pharaoh**
i. **hieroglyph**
j. **ancestor worship**

Part B

In a sentence, tell why each person or place is important.

1. Mesopotamia
2. Hammurabi
3. Kush
4. Aryan
5. Indus River
6. Hwang Ho

Testing Main Ideas

Choose the answer that best completes each sentence.

1. Mesopotamian civilization developed
   a. as farmers produced less and less.
   b. as farming came to an end.
   c. as farmers produced a surplus.
2. In Sumerian cities, trade took place
   a. in temples.
   b. in marketplaces.
   c. at the king's palace.
3. The Babylonians are well known for
   a. their system of astrology.
   b. their lack of laws.
   c. their refusal to tax people.
4. The Phoenicians
   a. used cuneiform.
   b. invented the alphabet.
   c. were great hunters.
5. What set the Hebrews apart was
   a. their belief in one God.
   b. their great empire.
   c. their writing system.
6. The Egyptian pharaohs
   a. were in the middle social class.
   b. had very little power.
   c. were honored in death as well as life.
7. The Aryans who came into the Indus valley
   a. came from the southeast.
   b. rode horses and drove chariots.
   c. were a very peaceful people.
8. The first major civilization in China began under
   a. the Shang dynasty.
   b. the pharaoh.
   c. Hammurabi.

Testing Skills

1. **Making a time line.** Make a time line that includes the following events in their correct positions.
   4000 B.C. Mesopotamian villages are true cities
   1000 B.C. Phoenicians have greatest power
   1900 B.C. Babylon is founded
   3100 B.C. Pharaohs come to rule Egypt
   1500 B.C. Indus valley civilization weakens
2. **Identifying cause-effect relationships.** Match each cause with the correct effect.
   Causes
   A. Farmers irrigate in Mesopotamia.
   B. Sumerian city people need ways to keep order.
   C. Phoenicians travel over the known world.
   D. Egyptians worship the pharaohs.
   Effects
   a. The pyramids are built.
   b. Kings and priests make laws.
   c. The alphabet spreads.
   d. A surplus of food is produced.

Activities

1. Try developing your own system of cuneiform or hieroglyphs. For example, design a picture to stand for each of your favorite sports.
2. Learn more about the work of archaeologists. If you can, visit a museum or historic site that has archaeological exhibits.

Chapter 5

The Civilization of Greece

Many of the ways we think about the world come from ancient Greece. Democratic government is rooted in Greek tradition. Greek poetry and plays form a basis for much of our modern literature. Buildings still are constructed in the Greek style. The picture shows the Parthenon (pär′thə non), a Greek temple.

In this chapter you will meet the ancestors of the Greeks. You will see how Greek civilization developed and how it reached great heights in the city-state of Athens. You also will see how Greek civilization spread throughout much of the Mediterranean world. The lessons in the chapter are listed below.

Lesson 1   Old Europe and the Indo-Europeans

LOOKING AHEAD As you read, look for—

Key words, people, and **places:**

deity	Old European
tribe	Indo-European

Answers to these questions about **main ideas:**

1. How did farming spread throughout Europe?
2. What was Old European civilization like?
3. What allowed the Indo-Europeans to leave their homeland and where did they go?
4. How did Indo-European languages develop?
5. What was Indo-European society like?

If you look at the Atlas map on pages 528-529, you will see that Southwest Asia is very close to southeastern Europe. Even in hunting and gathering times, people traveled between the two continents. They traded shells for jewelry. They also traded tools and ideas. One important idea was farming. Since the remains of the earliest known farming villages have been found in Southwest Asia, most archaeologists believe the idea of farm villages spread from there to Europe.

Farming Becomes Established in Europe

The earliest European farm villages date from before 7000 B.C. These villages were in southeastern Europe, where Greece and Bulgaria are today. Gradually farming became established and the farming villages grew in number. Villages sent out people to settle the fertile lands nearby. Then, between 7000 and 5000 B.C., farmers migrated farther. That is, they moved to various regions of Europe, where they settled onto new lands. Look at the map on page 126. Use your finger to trace the spread of farming from Southwest Asia to the points the farmers had reached by 5000 B.C. In what general direction did the farmers migrate?

Wherever they migrated, the farmers took their ideas to the hunting and gathering people. The early farmers cut the trees of the European forests to plant their fields. In this way they were very much like the pioneers in North America who migrated westward. The farmers burned the trees they cut down. The ashes made the soil fertile for a few years. After the soil gave out, the farmers would keep moving on. Use the map on page 126 to find what areas the farmers had reached by 4200 B.C.

Old European Civilization

During the time the farmers migrated across Europe, the older farming villages grew larger. Eventually the people of these villages formed a civilization we call Old Europe. Find the area of Old European civilization on the map on page 126.

125

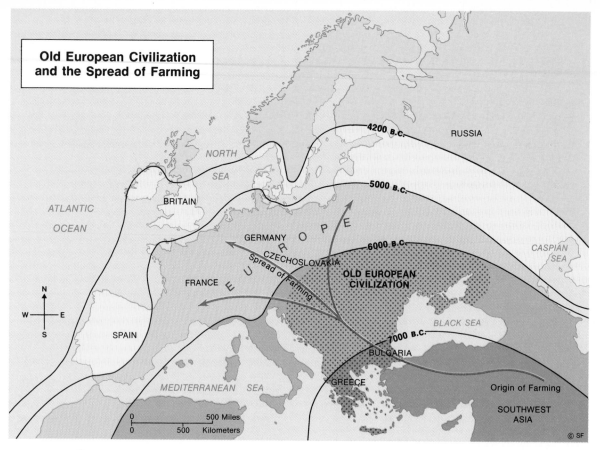

Old European Civilization and the Spread of Farming

Map Study

Farming spread gradually throughout Europe from Southwest Asia, or the Middle East. About how many years did it take for farming to spread from Greece to Spain? Find the location of the Old European civilization on the map. During what years did farming become established there?

Old European towns usually had between one thousand and five thousand people. The people made their houses out of packed mud or out of wood. The insides often were painted with beautiful spiral and geometric designs. The houses had several rooms, each with different purposes.

Religion was well organized in Old Europe by 5000 B.C. Archaeologists have found small temples with wall paintings in the Old European villages. Many small statues of gods, goddesses, and animals also have been found. A mother goddess probably was the most important deity among Old Europeans. A **deity** is a god or goddess worshiped by the people. The people believed the mother goddess was the source of all life. Statues of her have been found by the thousands.

Most Old Europeans were farmers. They used wooden plows and grew many kinds of crops. Some people specialized in crafts, making pottery, jewelry, or metal tools. The Old Europeans traded their goods in their own villages and with outsiders as well. In general, life among the Old Europeans was peaceful. However, changes were coming, starting around 3500 B.C., when the Indo-Europeans began to arrive.

The Indo-Europeans Leave Their Homeland

On the eastern edge of Europe lived a group of people who followed a way of life different from that of the Old Europeans. We call these people Indo-Europeans. The Aryans were one group of Indo-Europeans. As you have read, the Aryans moved into the Indus River valley about 1500 B.C. Thousands of years before that, the earliest Indo-Europeans were living in the forests and steppes of southwestern Russia. They lived here in tribes. A **tribe** is a group of people related by common ancestors and a common way of life. A chief or group of older tribe members governed each tribe.

The earliest Indo-Europeans lived by hunting and farming. Then, around 4500 B.C. or perhaps before, the Indo-Europeans tamed the horse. They were the first people to tame the horse, and they changed their way of life by doing so. Now the Indo-Europeans could travel long distances fairly quickly. Indo-Europeans also invented the chariot. Riding horses or driving chariots, the Indo-Europeans began moving out of Russia. They gave up the settled life of farming and became herders.

Archaeologists think the Indo-Europeans moved in tribal groups for thousands of years, between 4500 and 1500 B.C. Most of them went west into Europe. Other tribes moved east, entering present-day Iran and India. The map below shows the directions in which the Indo-Europeans migrated. The heritage of horse riding and herding was to last in some places right up

Map Study

The Indo-Europeans migrated throughout Europe and Asia. Use the Atlas maps on pages 538 and 540 to name one European and one Asian country they reached.

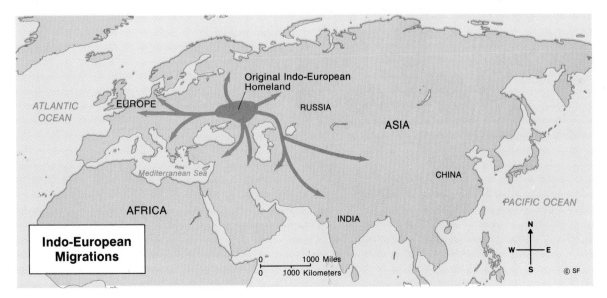

Indo-European Migrations

ATLANTIC OCEAN

EUROPE

Original Indo-European Homeland

RUSSIA

ASIA

Mediterranean Sea

CHINA

AFRICA

INDIA

PACIFIC OCEAN

0 1000 Miles
0 1000 Kilometers

N
W — E
S

© SF

to the present day. The modern herders of Mongolia—just north of China—
still live in some of the same ways as
the ancient Indo-Europeans.

Indo-European Languages

In addition to describing these ancient people, the word *Indo-European*
refers to a group of languages spoken
in many parts of Europe and Asia.

The chart on page 129 shows that
many modern languages came from
the ancient Indo-European language
and so are related to one another. Of
course, these languages also are different. Someone who speaks only English
cannot understand Greek or German.
Indo-European tribes moved from

place to place for many years. When
people live apart from one another, the
language they once had in common
begins to change in different ways.

Another reason the ancient Indo-
European language became many languages was that the tribes met new
people as they moved. Often the migrating Indo-Europeans settled down
and married into the group of people
they found. Thus, over centuries new
languages developed. In spite of
changes, though, all Indo-European
languages share some similar words.

Indo-European Society

We know much about the Indo-
Europeans from their writing. We

Today's Mongolians, descendants of the Indo-Europeans

Indo-European Languages						
Baltic	**Slavic**	**Germanic**	**Celtic**	**Italic**	**Hellenic**	**Indo-Iranian**
Lithuanian Latvian	Polish Czech Serbo- Croatian Russian	German Scandinavian Dutch English	Irish (Gaelic) Welsh	Latin (no longer spoken)	Greek	Persian Hindi Urdu
				French		
				Spanish		
				Italian		
				Portuguese		
				Romanian		

What are the seven major Indo-European language families? Is English in the same family as German or as Spanish and French?

know, for example, that they were a warlike people who took control of the areas they entered. They were led by chiefs or older tribal members and, later, kings. The leaders collected wealth in the forms of cattle, gold, bronze objects, and jewelry.

Like other societies you have read about, Indo-European society was layered. At the top were the royal family and nobles. Beneath this group were ordinary people such as herders and craft workers. At the bottom were slaves, usually people captured in war.

The tribal chief or king made the laws. He also was a judge and a warrior. A group of older men advised the chief in decisions. The older men remembered all the laws and old traditions. The people gathered at times to hear what the king and his advisers had to say.

Indo-Europeans began to enter Old Europe around 3500 B.C. They intermarried with the Old Europeans and formed new cultures. The blending of Indo-European and Old European ways of life formed the basis for all later cultures of Europe. One of these cultures, as you will see, was that of ancient Greece.

Reviewing the Lesson

Recalling Key Words, People, and Places
1. Identify the key words defined below:
   a. a god or goddess worshiped by people
   b. a group of people with common ancestors and a common way of life
2. Tell why it is important to remember
   a. Old Europeans
   b. Indo-Europeans

Remembering Main Ideas
1. How did the migrating farmers of ancient Europe make the soil fertile?
2. What do we know about the religion of the Old European civilization?
3. How did taming the horse change the lives of the Indo-Europeans?
4. Why are today's Indo-European languages different from one another?
5. How was Indo-European society governed?

Thinking Things Over
How do you think migrations of people might bring changes in history? Think of as many examples as you can.

129

Lesson 2   The Rise of Greece

LOOKING AHEAD As you read, look for—

Key words, people, and **places:**

city-state
barbarian
aristocracy
citizen

Minoan
Mycenaean

Greece
Crete

Answers to these questions about **main ideas:**

1. What was Minoan civilization like?
2. What is known about the Mycenaean period in Greek history?
3. How did Greek government change after the rise of the city-states?

The Greek peninsula juts into the Mediterranean Sea, surrounded by many islands, large and small. Look at the Atlas map on pages 528-529. See if you can figure out where Greece is in relation to Mesopotamia.

The Indo-Europeans began entering Greece around 2800 B.C. From the gradual blending of Old and Indo-European ways grew one of the most important civilizations of the ancient world, that of Greece. Meanwhile, in the nearby Mediterranean, another civilization developed alongside that of early Greece. This was the Minoan (mi-nō'ən) civilization on the island of Crete. Find Crete on the Atlas map on page 538. What direction is Crete from Greece?

Minoan Civilization

People from Southwest Asia settled Crete as early as 6000 B.C., archaeologists believe. By 2000 B.C. the Minoan civilization was flourishing on the island. Minoan civilization is named after a legendary king of Crete, King Minos.

The Minoans were skilled sailors and traders. They traded goods such as oils, perfumes, and pottery to other people of the Mediterranean area in return for gold, silver, copper, ivory, and other goods. Minoan craft workers turned these materials into many beautiful works of art.

The ruins of a beautiful Minoan palace stand at Knossos (nos'əs) on Crete.

Wall paintings of ancient Crete show people leaping over bulls. According to legend, King Minos kept a Minotaur (min′ə tôr), a monster that was half human and half bull.

Trade was controlled by kings who lived in magnificent palaces. Scribes, officials, and craft workers lived and worked at the palaces under royal direction. The king also was a priest and led religious ceremonies. Religion seems to have been very important to the Minoans. The people worshiped a mother goddess who was thought to rule the universe.

Minoan civilization began to decline after 1600 B.C. By this time an Indo-European people we call Mycenaeans (mī sə nē′ənz) had established a civilization in Greece. The Mycenaeans eventually took over Mediterranean trade from the Minoans. They began capturing some of the Minoan cities on Crete in the 1400s B.C.

Mycenaean Greece

While Minoan civilization had been flourishing, Greek culture was slowly taking shape in other areas. The Indo-Europeans brought the Greek language and other customs to Old European Greece. Greek religion showed the mixture of Old European and Indo-European beliefs. For example, the Greeks believed in both the Indo-European sky god Zeus and the Old European mother goddess.

By 1600 B.C. the Mycenaeans had developed a more complex Greek culture. Mycenaean civilization is named after one of its important cities, Mycenae (mī sē′nē). Mycenaean rule went far beyond Mycenae, however. Much of the Greek mainland and the islands in

131

Some of the most interesting glimpses of Mycenaean Greece come to us from the poet Homer. Homer created two long poems, called epics, the *Iliad* (il'ē əd) and the *Odyssey* (od'ə sē) about the Trojan War of the Mycenaean period. In Homer's time poets sang or recited their works. Eventually the *Iliad* and the *Odyssey* were written down and preserved for later generations.

According to Greek legend, the Trojan War was fought between Greece and Troy, a city on the eastern shore of the Aegean Sea.

The Greeks were fighting for the return of Helen, the beautiful wife of a Greek king. Helen had been kidnapped and carried off to Troy. Both epics are filled with adventures. The *Iliad* tells of some of the battles in the war. The picture shows a scene from the *Iliad*. The *Odyssey* describes the journey of a Greek warrior named Odysseus on his way home from the war.

For a long time, there was doubt that Homer really existed. Today many scholars agree the poems are too fine to be just a hodgepodge of legends. Whoever he was, Homer created some of the finest literature of ancient Greece.

---

the nearby Mediterranean all became part of Mycenaean Greece. Find this area on the map on page 133.

What do we know of the Mycenaean years of Greek history? Archaeologists have found evidence of a warlike society. Many kings and nobles ruled from different parts of Greece at this time. The Mycenaean kings often fought with one another. Probably much of this warfare was for control of scarce resources such as copper and tin or for cattle and sheep.

The Mycenaeans were accomplished sailors and traders. Craft workers made jewelry and weapons from gold, silver, and bronze for the leaders. Many of the methods they used were borrowed from the Minoans. The people of Mycenaean Greece had a written language, and they knew about mathematics and medicine.

By the 1100s B.C., warfare among the Mycenaean kings had grown intense. At the same time, another group of herding Indo-Europeans, the Dorians, migrated into Greece. The newcomers destroyed some Mycenaean cities. Dorian culture was not as advanced as that of the Mycenaeans. Most of Greece returned to a life of simple farming villages. This period, from about 1100 to 800 B.C., often is called the "dark age" of Greece.

The Greek City-States

The end of the Greek dark age is marked by the growth of trade among Greek towns. By 800 B.C. towns such as Athens, Sparta, Thebes, and Corinth were becoming important. They were known as **city-states.** Each city and the surrounding land was like a little nation all its own. People in other city-states were thought of as foreigners, even though they spoke the same language and shared the same customs. People who did not speak Greek were called **barbarians,** after the Greek word meaning "to babble." Find the Greek city-states on the map below. Where is Athens in relation to Sparta?

From about 800 to 600 B.C., upper-class families governed Greek society.

Greeks called this group the **aristocracy.** Aristocrats ruled through a council of elders. Elders were the older men who headed the most important families. They passed on power through their families, much like royalty. Aristocrats made most of the important decisions for Greece during these years.

An assembly of ordinary citizens took part in the government too. As members of the city-state, **citizens** had rights and responsibilities. Citizens rarely made important decisions before 600 B.C., though.

Map Study

Because Greek soil was not very fertile, the Greeks had trouble feeding their growing population. The solution was for each town to send out groups of settlers to form colonies in other parts of the world. How far were the colonies on the island of Cyprus from the city state of Athens?

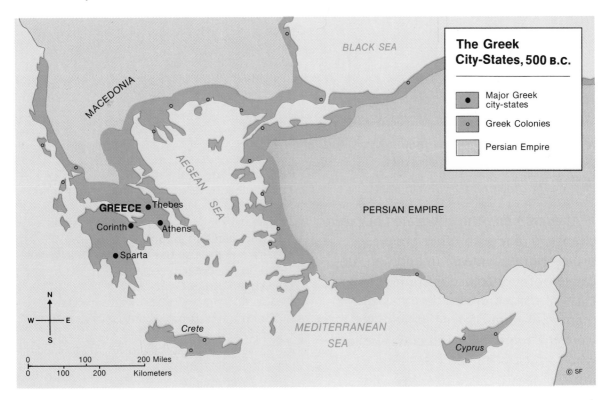

133

A great wall with a famous "lion gate" guarded Mycenae in ancient Greece.

After 600 B.C. the city-states began to change. Trade with other people brought in new ideas. In addition, because of the increase in trade, a new class of individuals came into being in many city-states. These individuals were the merchants and craft workers who formed a middle class. The Greek middle class banded together and

began to change politics, society, and culture in many of the city-states throughout Greece.

The most important of these changes were in government. As middle-class people gained wealth, they also wanted more say about their government. Middle-class people joined with farmers to take political power from the aristocrats. Sometimes they chose a single leader and sometimes a small group of leaders took control of a city-state. In some places, such as Athens, government came into the hands of the people, as you will see in the next lesson.

Reviewing the Lesson

Recalling Key Words, People, and Places
1. Identify the key words defined below:
    a. a city with its surrounding land, which acts like a nation
    b. an upper class of people who ruled in ancient Greece
    c. a member of a state or nation, having certain rights and responsibilities
2. Tell why it is important to remember:
    a. Minoan
    b. Mycenaean
3. Describe the location of the following places:
    a. Greece
    b. Crete

Remembering Main Ideas
1. Describe the role of the Minoan king in ancient Crete's civilization.
2. How did the Mycenaean period in Greek history come to an end?
3. Why was the rise of the middle class important to the Greek city-states?

Thinking Things Over
1. How do wars and invasions cause change? Use examples from what you have read to support your ideas.
2. Why do you think the growing middle class in the Greek city-states wanted more say in the government?

134

Lesson 3   The Glory of Athens

LOOKING AHEAD As you read, look for—

Key words, people, and **places:**

democracy
philosopher

Pericles

Athens
Sparta

Answers to these questions about **main ideas:**

1. How did the Athenians govern their city-state?
2. What was the cultural life of Athens like?
3. How did wars affect Athens?

Greece's "golden age" took place in the 400s B.C. During this time the Greeks developed ideas about government, art, science, and learning that would influence the world for centuries to come. Athens was the most important Greek city-state of the golden age. It was here that ancient Greek civilization flowered.

Democracy in Athens

Many ancient Greeks took a great interest in government. They thought of their city-state as a community in which all citizens took part, much like a large family.

In a **democracy,** government is run by the citizens who live under it. The people may rule directly, through meetings that all attend, or indirectly, through elected representatives. Shortly after 600 B.C. in Athens, an assembly of all the citizens began to make decisions about running their city. Small groups of assembly members, called councils, ran everyday affairs. They took care of trade, taxes, and other concerns of government. Citizens either were elected to the councils or chosen by lot. Citizens also ran the court system. Since there were no lawyers or professional judges, citizens acted as judges in law cases.

All Athenian citizens were expected to take part in running their government. They went to assembly meetings, talked about the problems of government, and voted on what to do. Almost every citizen worked on one of the assembly councils at one time or another. All citizens had equal rights and equal responsibilities.

While democracy was a fine ideal, most people living in Athens could not take part in it. Only a small number of adult men were citizens. Slaves and foreign-born men were not citizens. Women also could not take part in government.

Because so few Athenians could be citizens, many people have wondered whether ancient Athens should be called a democracy. For the citizens it was a true democracy, because all the citizens took part in it directly. However, if we consider all the people living in Athens, then it was not a true democracy. Still, democracy was an important ideal for many Greeks and for the future. We might not have democratic governments today if it were not for the example of Athens.

135

The Athenians took great pride in their city. Standing proudly above Athens, the Acropolis (above) symbolized the public spirit of the city, which was named for the goddess Athena (right).

Athens as a Cultural Center

Imagine you are back in Athens in the 400s B.C. You will see and hear the best of ancient Greek culture. Standing above the city you see a plateau called the Acropolis (ə krop′ə lis), meaning "high city." It was once the fortress of the city but later became a religious and cultural center.

The Acropolis is crowded with splendid buildings. The largest one is the great temple to the goddess Athena. This temple is the Parthenon pictured on page 124. Athena is worshiped as the city's protector. Inside the temple is a huge statue of the goddess made out of ivory and white stone. Around the temple's porch and on the outside are magnificent sculptures. The sculptures were made by a team of artists led by the great artist Phidias. Another statue

of Athena, fifty feet tall, stands next to the temple. You can see it from the harbor, about five miles away.

At the foot of the Acropolis, you walk through the Athenian marketplace. The people come here to buy and sell goods and to socialize. The marketplace is the real center of life in all Greek cities. The major government buildings are located around this center. In the marketplace you might hear a poet or other writer reciting literature. In ancient times poems and books were "published" this way. That is, they were "made public" in the town marketplace. The first historian, Herodotus (hə rod′ə təs), spoke his popular books here.

Nearby you visit the theater of Dionysus (dī ə nī′səs), the god of festivals. During the annual festival season, Athenians see plays performed in the theater. The plays are so popular that tickets are hard to get. Playwrights from all over Greece compete to have their plays performed, but only one writer wins the great honor each year. Most of the plays are tragedies, about human struggle and suffering. They are based on ancient myths and poems that are familiar to the audience. However, comedies and plays about current events also are performed.

In Athens you might visit the schools run by **philosophers.** The word *philosopher* comes from the Greek word

Greek philosophers held long discussions about life, truth, and many other issues.

meaning "love of wisdom." These people study everything having to do with nature and human beings, and they pass on what they have learned to their students. The philosopher Socrates (sok′rə tēz′) might be speaking about truth and how to find it. Plato (plā′to) is in the audience. One day he will start his own school and write many books. Plato will be very important to later European thinkers, as will Aristotle (ar′ə stot′l), one of Plato's students.

Aristotle will become one of the first great scientific thinkers. He will observe the natural world very closely and then form ideas about the world based on the facts he has collected. His work will help lay the foundation of modern science.

As you leave Athens, you know you have visited one of the great ancient civilizations.

Wars Affect Athens

Athens was not always at peace. To the east of Greece, the Persian Empire was a growing threat in the late 500s B.C. Find this empire of Southwest Asia on the map on page 133. How does the part of the empire shown compare with Greece in land area?

Several Greek cities on the eastern Aegean shore came under Persian rule. Starting in 490 B.C., Persia invaded the Greek mainland. At one point the invaders attacked Athens and destroyed much of the city. The Greek city-states banded together to fight off the Persians. Finally, the Greeks defeated the

Linking Past and Present

The Olympics

Did you know that one of our popular sporting events today has its roots in ancient Greece? The first Olympic games were held in 776 B.C. at Olympia, a valley in western Greece.

The athletic-minded Greeks celebrated their games as religious festivals. They viewed competition and fitness as tributes to their gods and goddesses. Every four years Greek athletes competed in the Olympics, which were held for several centuries. Then, for hundreds of years, the valley lay flooded.

After a group of archaeologists discovered the original Olympic stadium in 1875, the games that we know today

were revived. Since 1896 men and women from nearly every country have competed in Olympic athletic events. A scene from the 1984 summer games is shown in the picture above.

Persians in a sea battle, and the Persian Wars came to an end in 479 B.C.

The end of the Persian Wars brought a period of peace and prosperity to Athens. A leader named Pericles (per′ə-klēz′) rose to power in 460 B.C. Pericles was president of a board of generals elected by the Athenian assembly.

Pericles was a popular leader. His thirty-year rule often is called the golden age of Athens. Democratic government as practiced in Greece flourished, and the Athenians built some of their most famous buildings on the Acropolis during this time. Pericles was the force behind much of the public spirit in Athens at this time. He once summed up his view of government as follows:

> Our constitution is called a democracy because power is in the hands not of a minority but of the whole people. When it is a question of settling private disputes, everyone is equal before the law; when it is a question of putting one person before another in positions of public responsibility, what counts is not membership of a particular class, but the actual ability which the man possesses. . . .
>
> Here each individual is interested not only in his own affairs but in the affairs of the state as well . . . we do not say that a man who takes no interest in politics is a man who minds his own business; we say that he has no business here at all.

How did the other Greek city-states view Athens? They had some reason to be resentful. During the Persian Wars, Athens considered itself chief defender of all Greek city-states. As such, Athens demanded taxes from other areas in return for protection. After the Persian threat ended, however, the other city-states no longer wanted to pay for protection.

In addition, Athens was expanding in land area, and the other city-states watched suspiciously. Finally, a war broke out in 431 B.C. Another powerful city-state, Sparta, led the war against Athens. For more than twenty-five years, the Peloponnesian (pel′ə pə-nē′shən) War, as it was called, raged in Greece. When it was finally over, in 404 B.C., Athens had been defeated. Much of Greece lay weakened and divided. The golden age was over.

Reviewing the Lesson

Recalling Key Words, People, and Places
1. Identify the key words defined below:
   a. a government run by its citizens
   b. a person who loves wisdom and studies nature and human beings
2. Tell why it is important to remember:
   a. Pericles
   b. Athens
   c. Sparta

Remembering Main Ideas
1. What role did Athenian citizens play in their government?
2. How did the marketplace function as part of Athenian culture?
3. How did the Persian Wars affect the relationship of Athens with other city-states in Greece?

Thinking Things Over
Compare Athenian democracy with democracy in the United States. Tell how they are alike and different.

Lesson 4 The Spread of Greek Ideas

LOOKING AHEAD As you read, look for—

Key words, people, and **places:**

Philip II (of Macedonia)   Macedonia
Alexander the Great   Alexandria

Answers to these questions about main ideas:

1. How did Philip II and his son Alexander try to spread Greek culture?
2. What were the characteristics of the Hellenistic Age?

The defeat of Athens in the Peloponnesian War did not end conflict among Greek city-states. A long series of wars broke out again after 399 B.C. Gradually, the Greek cities grew weaker and weaker through war. Many people thought the Greeks could never unite or make peace. The time was right for a powerful leader to step in and take advantage of the situation.

The Conquests of Philip II and Alexander

Just north of Greece was a land called Macedonia (mas′ə dō′nē ə). Today most of this land is in Yugoslavia. The Macedonians were a Greek-speaking people. However, their culture was different from that of the Greek city-states to the south. Find Macedonia on the map on page 133 and the map

Philip II's son Alexander became one of the most famous generals in history. He extended Macedonian rule thousands of miles.

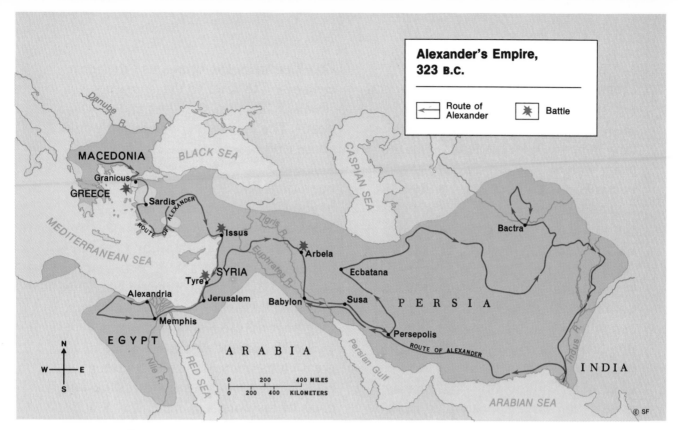

Map Study

The Macedonian leader Alexander the Great conquered a vast empire in ten years. Where was the first battle fought? Which area was conquered first, Egypt or most of Persia? Alexander conquered lands once part of early river-valley civilizations. Find four rivers that locate these civilizations.

above. Why do you think the area looks different in size on the two maps?

In 359 B.C. a young king named Philip II came to the Macedonian throne. Philip loved things Greek, and he believed in the idea of a united Greek people. If united, the Greeks would be powerful, he believed. They could attack and overthrow their old enemy, the Persian Empire. Maybe Greeks could even take over the entire world in time. After all, thought Philip, was not Greek culture superior to all others?

Philip made himself ready for battle. He built a powerful army and began to conquer Greek city-states. In 338 B.C. most of the remaining city-states opposed him in one final battle. Philip won. His eighteen-year-old son Alexander led the cavalry—soldiers on horseback—to victory. At last, all of Greece was united into one kingdom.

Philip was about to invade Persia when he was murdered by one of his own nobles who had a personal grudge. At age twenty-one, Alexander became king. We now know him as Alexander the Great.

141

Alexander followed his father's dream of Greek culture taking over others. In 333 B.C. he set out with an army of Macedonians and Greeks to attack Persia. Under his leadership the army won victory after victory over the Persians. In ten long years of fighting, Alexander conquered all of the Persian Empire, from Egypt to parts of India. Look at the map on page 141 and trace Alexander's route with your finger, beginning in Macedonia. At about what point was Alexander farthest from Macedonia? When his soldiers finally said they would go no farther, the king turned back toward home. Had the soldiers been willing, they might have gone as far as China. Stopping in Babylon on the journey home, Alexander died suddenly of fever in 323 B.C. He was only thirty-three years old at this time.

The Hellenistic Age

After Alexander's death, the empire he created was split up among several generals. There were three main kingdoms and a number of smaller states. The main kingdoms were Macedonia, Egypt, and a united Syria and Persia. Macedonia had some control over Greece.

Alexander deliberately had tried to spread Greek civilization to the places he conquered. The king had married a Persian princess and made three hundred of his officers marry Persian women also. This action was meant to unify Greeks and Persians into a new kingdom. The people who ruled after Alexander's death also tried to spread

Greek culture. Historians use the term *Hellenistic* to refer to the spread of Greek civilization after Alexander's death. The Hellenistic Age lasted until about 200 B.C.

Trade flowed between the Mediterranean area and Southwest Asia—and beyond—during the Hellenistic Age. Merchants traded such goods as grain, paper, glass, and cloth among the kingdoms. Indians sent spices, and from faraway China came precious silk. This trade would last for hundreds of years, long beyond the Hellenistic Age.

The Hellenistic Age was an age of great cities. Alexander had fourteen new Greek-style cities built in different parts of his empire. One of the new cities was Alexandria in Egypt. Find Alexandria on the map on page 141. Alexandria was the greatest city of the age. It was the capital of the rich kingdom of Egypt and had about one million people.

The rulers of Egypt had splendid buildings made for their city. One building was a lighthouse more than 350 feet high that stood in the city's harbor. This lighthouse was considered one of the seven wonders of the ancient world.

Alexandria was an important center of learning. The famous library in the city held hundreds of thousands of books. Scholars and scientists came to the library to study and write. One scientist in Alexandria invented a steam engine. Another discovered the way the planets moved and even determined the size of the earth fairly accurately. One of the world's most famous

By the Way

As long ago as the second century B.C., a mathematician named Eratosthenes (er ə tos′thə nēz), pictured at right, knew the earth was round. He scientifically estimated the circumference—the distance around—the earth.

Eratosthenes observed that the noon sun was directly overhead at the Egyptian town Syene (present-day Aswan) on the day of the summer solstice. The summer solstice is the longest "day" of the year. It takes place in June in the Northern Hemisphere. Syene was south of Alexandria, and Eratosthenes assumed that the cities were on about the same meridian.

Eratosthenes measured the angle at which the sun's rays struck Alexandria at noon on the summer solstice. He found that this angle was about 1/50th of a full circle. Next he reasoned that the distance between the two cities should be about 1/50th of the earth's circumference. Using these figures, Eratosthenes determined the earth's circumference to be about 24,000 miles. The actual circumference of the earth is 24,860 miles.

mathematicians, Euclid (yü′klid), lived and worked in Alexandria. In fact, many things that later scientists would "discover" actually were first discovered in Alexandria.

The rulers of the other Hellenistic kingdoms also built great buildings. In fact, each ruler tried to outdo the others in collecting art and contributing to learning.

The Hellenistic kingdoms rarely lived in peace. Leaders fought each other for control of land and trade. Fortunes were spent on armies and navies. Eventually the Hellenistic kingdoms ran out of money to pay for the military. The kingdoms grew weaker. After 200 B.C. they were taken over by two new powers. One of these powers was a new Persian Empire in the east. The other one was the great empire of Rome.

Although the Greek kingdoms declined, Hellenistic culture lived on. The Romans adopted almost all of Greek culture, including styles of art, literature, learning, and parts of language. In this way Greek culture was preserved.

Reviewing the Lesson

Recalling Key Words, People, and Places

Tell why it is important to remember:
1. Philip II (of Macedonia)
2. Alexander the Great
3. Macedonia
4. Alexandria

Remembering Main Ideas

1. Describe the conquests of Philip II and Alexander the Great.
2. What was the city of Alexandria like during the Hellenistic Age?

Thinking Things Over

Think about Philip and Alexander's dream of spreading Greek civilization. What possible good and bad results might their dream have had for the people they conquered?

143

Identifying Points of View

How many times have you and your friends disagreed about something? Maybe you have argued over the rules of a game. Perhaps you have not been able to agree on what to do for an afternoon. You probably have discussed more important issues too and found you have different opinions. These issues might have included topics in the news or events in your school or community.

People always have had differences of opinion on matters. If you study any issue carefully, you will find that disagreements often stem from people's different points of view.

You have read, for example, how the ancient Greeks disagreed about paying Athens to protect the city-states from a Persian invasion. Chances are that most Athenians favored the payments, while non-Athenians opposed them. The chart below compares possible points of view on the subject.

Study the chart. Try to think of other statements you might add to either side's point of view. Remember that the Athenian is speaking as one whose city receives the money. The non-Athenian has to pay the money to Athens.

You can break down almost any issue according to point of view. Consider citizenship in ancient Athens, for example. Only a small percentage of the people in ancient Athens were citizens, and this fact may have influenced points of view about issues. If you were a citizen in Athens, you were a member of the government and someone who helped make decisions for the city.

Noncitizens in ancient Athens, however, did not have the power to make such decisions. Which group do you think probably had more ideas about how the city should be run? Most likely, the citizens did. As decision makers, their point of view was different from that of the noncitizens.

Issue: Should Athens be paid money to protect the Greek city-states from invasion?		
Person	*Answer*	*Point of View*
Athenian	Yes	Athens is the leading city-state and deserves the money. Also, the Persians need to know that Athens is strong and able to protect Greece.
Non-Athenian	No	Athens is being unfair and greedy. The other city-states really receive no benefit because there probably is no Persian threat anymore.

Skills Practice

1. Pericles said, "Here each individual is interested not only in his own affairs but in the affairs of the state as well. . . ." What point of view might a woman or a slave have had about that statement? Give reasons for your answer.

2. Suppose a general in ancient Athens had this idea: "Everyone over the age of ten should serve in the army to help fight the Persians." What would be your point of view about this issue if you were a twelve-year-old living in ancient Athens?

3. Choose one of the issues listed below. Fill in a chart showing possible points of view of various people who might be concerned about the issue. Copy the chart at the right. Then fill it in.
   a. whether teachers should be forbidden from assigning homework
   b. whether all schools in the country should be closed at noon
   c. whether children in the United States should be made to go to school at all
   d. whether the government should give everyone under the age of fifteen an allowance of $100 each week

Person or Group	Answers (Yes or No)	Point of View

4. Make a chart for this issue: "Should the town library be closed for the summer to save money?" Then fill in your chart listing possible points of view for the following people.
   a. parents of school-age children
   b. parents whose children have finished school
   c. people who work in the library
   d. you and your friends

5. Think of an issue that interests you, perhaps one that involves current events in our country or the world. What is your point of view on this issue? What are some other points of view you have heard other people state? Explain these points of view in a paragraph.

Chapter Summary

Lesson 1   Old Europe and the Indo-Europeans—By 5000 B.C. farming villages had spread throughout much of Europe. The people formed a civilization known as Old Europe. By 3500 B.C. Indo-Europeans began to arrive in Europe from Russia.

Lesson 2   The Rise of Greece—By 1600 B.C. Mycenaeans had established Greek civilization. By 800 B.C. Greek city-states such as Athens and Sparta were thriving. Here democracy developed after 600 B.C.

Lesson 3   The Glory of Athens—Greek civilization reached its height in Athens in the 400s B.C. Great advances occurred in philosophy and the arts. However, wars brought the golden age of Athens to an end.

Lesson 4   The Spread of Greek Ideas—Philip II and Alexander of Macedonia conquered large areas, spreading Greek culture. After Alexander's death in 323 B.C., Greek culture continued to spread in the Hellenistic Age.

Write your answers on a separate sheet of paper.

Testing Key Words, People, and Places

Part A
Give the definition of each key word.

1. **deity**
2. **tribe**
3. **city-state**
4. **barbarian**
5. **aristocracy**
6. **citizen**
7. **democracy**
8. **philosopher**

Part B
In a sentence, tell why each person or place is important.

1. Indo-European
2. Mycenaean
3. Crete
4. Pericles
5. Athens
6. Sparta
7. Alexander the Great

Testing Main Ideas

Choose the best answer for each question.

1. When groups from southeastern Europe moved west, what did they spread?
   a. the idea of farming
   b. the idea of religion
   c. the knowledge of hunting
2. What allowed the Indo-Europeans to move to new places quickly?
   a. canoes and sailboats
   b. horses and chariots
   c. stagecoaches and paved roads
3. French, German, and Spanish all have their roots in what language?
   a. Indo-European
   b. Egyptian
   c. Greek
4. In Minoan civilization, who controlled trade?
   a. priests
   b. scribes
   c. kings
5. What was a characteristic of the Mycenaean period in Greek history?
   a. warfare
   b. the spread of Christianity
   c. a lack of trade

6. What kind of government did Athens have in the 400s B.C.?
a. an aristocracy
b. a true democracy
c. a form of democracy

7. What happened under Pericles?
a. Kings and queens ruled Greece.
b. Some of the most famous buildings on the Acropolis were built.
c. Athens fought in the Persian Wars.

8. Why were the conquests of Philip II and Alexander important?
a. They caused the fall of Athens.
b. They did away with slavery.
c. They spread Greek ideas to other parts of the world.

9. What marked the Hellenistic Age?
a. the rise of great cities
b. the rule of Alexander the Great
c. a slowdown in science and learning

a. What large island is southeast of Greece?
b. What country is north of Greece?
c. In which direction from Greece is the Persian Empire?
d. What direction is Corinth from Athens?

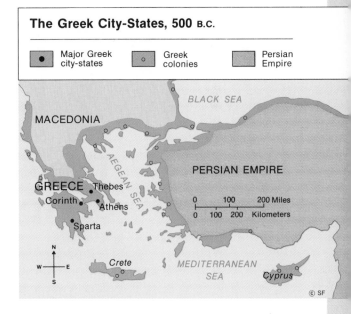

The Greek City-States, 500 B.C.

Testing Skills

1. Identifying points of view. Tell what you think each person's point of view was about the spread of Greek culture.
a. Alexander the Great
b. a soldier in Alexander's army
c. a citizen in one of the Greek city-states conquered by the Macedonians
d. a farmer in the Persian Empire

2. Finding relative locations of places. Study the map on this page and answer the questions.

Activities

1. Make a drawing or a model of the lighthouse at Alexandria. You also might draw or create models of some or all of the other six wonders of the ancient world. Consult an encyclopedia for information.

2. Read *Greek Everyday Life* by Roger Nichols and Sarah Nichols (Aspects of Greek Life Series, Longman, 1978). Report to the class on what new things you learned by reading the book.

147

The Civilization of Rome

Suppose you are living in Italy in the first century A.D. You live within the Roman Empire, a land that stretches from Britain in the west to Southwest Asia in the east. One day your parents decide to visit the capital city Rome. Traveling along the main road from the south, the Appian Way, you arrive at the immense walled city of Rome. You enter the city and soon come to the Forum. The Forum is the center from which Rome's vast empire is governed. You can see the ruins of the Forum above.

Roman government affected millions of people throughout the Mediterranean world and beyond. In this chapter you will see how early Rome developed into one of the mightiest empires of the ancient world. You also will see how the rise of Christianity affected Western Europe. The lessons in the chapter are listed below.

Lesson 1   The Roman Republic and Empire

Lesson 2   Christianity and a Changing Rome

Lesson 1   The Roman Republic and Empire

LOOKING AHEAD As you read, look for—

Key words, people, and **places:**

senate	Julius Caesar
patrician	Augustus
plebeian	
republic	
veto	

Answers to these questions about **main ideas:**

1. How was early Rome governed?
2. What were the main features of Roman government under the republic?
3. How did Rome extend its rule during the years of the republic?
4. What led to the end of the republic and the beginning of rule by emperors?

Early Romans had a myth, or story, about the beginning of their city. They believed that a hero named Romulus (rom′yə ləs) founded Rome. The story goes that Romulus and his brother Remus (rē′məs) were the sons of the war god Mars. They were born to a princess of a small city near the future Rome. The children's evil uncle wanted to rule the city, and he tried to kill the brothers. The princess put her sons in a basket and sent the basket down a river. According to the myth, here is what happened next:

> 66 As the helpless little beings lay crying, a kindly she-wolf came by, and, taking pity on them, carried them back to her lair [den], where she tended them as if they had been her own cubs. . . . The two royal babies, . . . grew up tall and strong, and were adopted by a shepherd and his wife. . . . Born with a natural gift of leadership, they placed themselves at the head of a band of young shepherds, and after a time drove [their uncle] from the throne which he had usurped [seized], . . .

> They then decided to found a city on the spot where they had spent their miraculous childhood, and a dispute arose between them which had a tragic end. Remus criticized the plans suggested by his . . . brother . . . Romulus became furious, and in his fury slew his . . . brother.

> Romulus, having decided to call his new city Rome—after himself—now offered a place of refuge there to any outcasts or fugitives from justice who might care to join him. 99

The people of Rome always believed that the gods, especially Mars, favored them. Romans often called themselves children of the wolf.

Early Rome

In reality, Rome was a small village in Italy founded by an Indo-European people called Latins about 1100 B.C. Find Italy and Rome on the Atlas map

Conquered people did not necessarily welcome Roman rule. Some groups rebelled against Rome. The leader of one rebellion was Boudicca (bü di'kə), queen of a British tribe in the first century A.D.

Roman rule was already established in Britain by the middle of the first century A.D. Boudicca led her tribe against the Romans when they tried to seize even more of her tribe's land and wealth in A.D. 61.

The queen's forces overcame thousands of Romans at first. Boudicca is shown in the picture at left. What kind of vehicle is she driving into battle? Only after reinforcements were rushed in were the Romans able to put down the uprising. Boudicca then drank poison rather than surrender.

The rebellion was very costly to the Romans. It also presented a threat to their rule. Historians believe that, in order to avoid more uprisings, the Romans treated the people of Britain better after Boudicca's rebellion.

on page 538. How would you describe Italy's location in relation to that of Greece?

Most early Latins farmed for a living. Others were traders. Trade with the Greeks was well established in early Rome. As with other Indo-European people, including the Greeks, early Latin society was ruled by the oldest men in the tribe.

In the 600s B.C. a powerful people known as Etruscans (i trus'kənz) conquered the Latins and took over Rome. Under the Etruscans Roman government developed in important ways. Latin tribal leaders elected the Etruscan kings. The kings ruled with the help of a group of advisers known as a **senate.** Senate members usually were rich landowners known as **patricians.** Ordinary people in Rome were called **plebeians.**

The Romans Establish a Republic

In 509 B.C. the Roman senate overthrew a hated Etruscan king. Rather than work with another king, the senators set up a republic instead. A **republic** is a government in which the citizens elect representatives to lead them. Under the republic, patricians elected members to the Roman senate. Plebeians elected members to an assembly.

Romans of the republic believed strongly in their laws. They also believed strongly in the rights of ordinary citizens. By the 300s B.C. the plebeian assembly had grown greatly in power. Elected plebeian representatives called tribunes could stop the senate from passing laws. Tribunes could **veto**—overturn—laws they did not think were in the best interest of the Roman people. In the Latin language, *veto* means "I forbid."

150

The Republic Expands

After 350 B.C. the Romans began to extend their rule beyond their city. The Roman government wanted riches and it wanted to test its power. First, the Romans conquered Italy. By the early 300s B.C., Rome controlled all of what today is Italy. From this point on, we use the term *Rome* to mean more than a small city in Italy and its surrounding villages. Rome was becoming a growing power in the Mediterranean.

Next, Rome turned its attention to powerful Carthage on the coast of northern Africa. As you have read, Carthage had been founded as a Phoenician colony. Over the centuries Carthage had become a major Mediterranean power in its own right. By the 200s B.C., Carthage controlled much of the northern African coast as well as present-day Spain and Portugal. Find Carthage on the map below. About how far and in what direction was Carthage from Rome?

Between 264 and 146 B.C., Rome fought three bitter wars, called the Punic Wars, against Carthage. By the

Map Study

The Roman Empire circled the Mediterranean by the first century A.D. Tell which areas of the empire were farthest north, south, east, and west in A.D. 50.

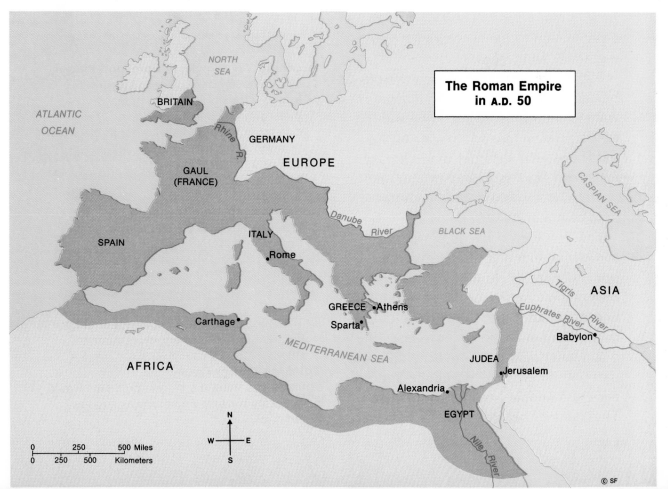

The Roman Empire in A.D. 50

© SF

end of the third war, Carthage lay in ruins. Rome now controlled the lands that Carthage once held.

Then, Rome attacked the Hellenistic kingdoms in the eastern Mediterranean region. By the 130s B.C., the Roman government ruled much of the Mediterranean area. Treasure poured into the city of Rome, making it a wealthy city and the center of a new empire.

Emperors Come to Power

During the wars the republican form of government had weakened in Rome as the plebeians lost power. The army was made up of plebeian men, and while they were away fighting, rich senators took away their lands.

After the wars, poor landless people flocked to the city of Rome. The poor had no real voice in the government. They looked to the senators for housing, food, and wages.

Fighting broke out between the plebeians and patricians. The plebeians wanted their lands back. They wanted to limit the wealth and power of the patricians. The disorder made it easy for strong leaders to step in and take power. They could do this with the help of the army.

The first leader whose power was something like that of an emperor was Julius Caesar. In 48 B.C. he and his followers took control of the government. Caesar realized that the empire had to be well organized in order to last. The new leader next organized the different parts of the empire. All middle and upper-class people became "Romanized." That is, they became citizens who were subject to Roman laws. They served in the army and the government. Meanwhile, Caesar weakened the power of the senate.

After Caesar's death in 44 B.C., a series of emperors came to rule. The first emperor was Augustus. He had roads built throughout the empire, making transportation and communication among different parts of the empire easier. Under Augustus the army controlled the empire and kept the peace. Government officials made sure that affairs ran smoothly. With the rule of Augustus came a period of general peace that lasted for about two hundred years. Look at the map of the Roman Empire on page 151. To what three continents did the empire extend in A.D. 50?

Reviewing the Lesson

Recalling Key Words, People, and Places
1. Identify the key words defined below:
   a. a wealthy landowner in Rome
   b. an ordinary person in Rome
   c. a government in which citizens elect representatives to lead them
2. Tell who these people were:
   a. Julius Caesar
   b. Augustus

Remembering Main Ideas
1. Describe Etruscan government in early Rome.
2. What power did the plebeian assembly have by the 300s B.C. under the republic?
3. How did Rome come to control Carthage's lands?
4. What weakened the republican form of government in Rome as emperors came to rule?

Thinking Things Over
What do you think the biggest problems would have been governing an empire as large as Rome was?

Lesson 2   Christianity and a Changing Rome

 LOOKING AHEAD As you read, look for—

Key words, people, and **places:**

Jesus   Constantine

Answers to these questions about **main ideas:**

1. Why is Roman civilization noted for its law and its cities?
2. What led to the end of the original Roman Empire?
3. How did Christianity develop?

By the early A.D. 100s, the Roman Empire was vast. It stretched over two thousand miles from east to west and contained up to one hundred million people. Roman rulers kept peace throughout their empire by running an orderly government.

Roman Civilization

Romans placed great value on the idea of order in the world. They believed one way to achieve this order was to extend rights to conquered people. Romans always believed that government was created by the people who lived in it. Even when emperors ruled, local government run by citizens was fairly strong. Moreover, Romans believed in rule by law—again even though an emperor ruled. Rule by law means that governments and rulers are supposed to obey the laws of the empire just as ordinary citizens are.

Roman law recognized property rights. It upheld contracts—written agreements between people. Perhaps most important, Roman law said that in legal cases people were innocent until proven guilty. Part of modern law and government in the United States and other countries is based on Roman ideas.

Cities were another important feature of Roman civilization. As with earlier civilizations you have read about, Roman cities were centers for trade, government, manufacturing, and culture. Roman cities had magnificent buildings, waterworks, and roads. The cities were linked by road systems that crisscrossed the empire. Some of these roads were built so well that they still are used today. Roman-built pipelines called aqueducts (ak′wə dukts) carried water to the cities from distant sources.

This Roman-built aqueduct still carries water to Segovia, Spain. Note how it towers over the city.

The aqueducts often were built atop high stone bridges. You can see a Roman aqueduct in the picture on page 153. Like Roman roads, some of the aqueducts still are used in places throughout Europe today.

Trouble in the Empire

Despite its strengths the Roman Empire suffered a growing weakness in government after A.D. 200. The empire had depended on its armies from the beginning. Armed forces kept the peace and protected the long borders from invasion. However, by the A.D. 300s, Roman leaders were having great difficulty finding people to be soldiers. No one knows exactly why, but the population in the empire dropped at this time. Maybe the drop was due to widespread disease. Without strong armies, the borders could not be defended, and emperors could not enforce their rule in all places of the empire.

By the end of the A.D. 300s, no one emperor could govern the entire empire. In A.D. 395 the Roman Empire was divided into two parts—the Eastern Empire and the Western Empire. Look at the map on page 155. Trace the dividing line between the parts of the empire with your finger. Were the parts of the empire about equal in size or not?

The Romans hired outsiders to protect the borders from invasion. In the western part of the empire, these protectors were German tribe members led by chiefs. The Germans were descendants of Indo-European people who came from areas east of the Rhine River.

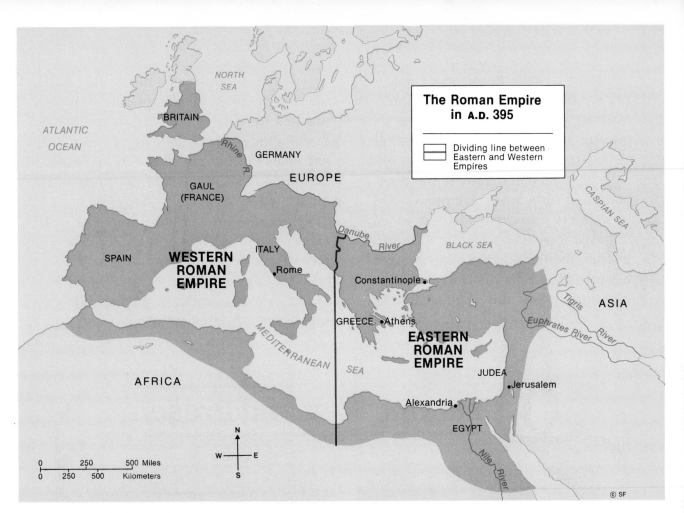

The Roman Empire
in A.D. 395

Dividing line between
Eastern and Western
Empires

Map Study

Compare this map with the one on page 151. How did the original Roman Empire change in size between A.D. 50 and A.D. 395? Give a general description of the areas that became part of the Western Roman Empire and those that became part of the Eastern Roman Empire.

Gradually the Germans took over areas of the Western Empire. By the late A.D. 400s, many parts of the Western Empire were divided into German kingdoms. Once this happened, the original Roman Empire no longer really existed. The eastern part of the empire continued, however. It became known as the Byzantine (bi′zan tēn) Empire. The Byzantine Empire lasted for hundreds of years and carried on much of Roman and Greek culture.

The Rise of Christianity

In the first century A.D., a new religion arose in Judea. Use the map above to find Judea. Here, a Jew named Jesus began Christianity. Like other Jews, Jesus believed in one God. He taught that people should be good to one another. He said that people should love their neighbors as much as they love themselves. He said that by being kind to others, people might become closer to God.

155

Jesus also said that people would be better able to lead good lives if they lived simply. He told his followers to give up all riches. Jesus explained his beliefs through stories called parables.

Jesus preached mainly to the poor people in rural areas. Around A.D. 30 he came to Jerusalem, a city in Judea. As Jesus traveled and spoke to more people, the Roman government grew alarmed. The Romans feared Jesus might try to set himself up as a political leader who would try to overthrow the government.

Jewish authorities also became alarmed by Jesus' teachings. He mocked the religious leaders who made a big show of their prayer and sacrifices but did not reach out to help people in need. His teachings threatened the Jewish leaders' authority. They and the Roman government viewed Jesus as an enemy. A Roman governor ordered Jesus put to death in A.D. 33.

The New Testament of the Bible tells how Jesus appeared to his followers after his death and promised eternal

Linking Past and Present

The Roman Arch

Many buildings, bridges, and other structures today have graceful, curved features known as arches. Did you know that the Romans made the arch famous? Arches can support the great weight of buildings without solid walls. Arched doorways and windows are not only purposeful, but very beautiful.

Note how similar the two colosseums (kol'ə sē'əms) shown in the pictures are. Colosseums are sports stadiums. The one at left above is the ancient Roman Colosseum. The other colosseum is in Los Angeles, California. Notice how the arches in the colosseums function as windows and doors. Why do you think so many doors are useful in a large stadium?

Try noticing the arches in other buildings you see around you. As you do, think of the Romans and how they improved architecture.

life to those who believed in him and followed his teachings. Jesus' followers traveled to major cities to spread his teachings. They called themselves Christians from the Greek word *Christos,* which means "savior."

At first Christianity had few members. However, under the leadership of several great preachers, it began to grow. Sometimes Roman leaders punished Christians, because they viewed them as enemies of the government. Some Christians would not go to war when ordered to do so. Nor would the Christians pray to the many gods of Rome.

Christianity grew more popular, even though it usually was against the law to be a Christian. Poor people were especially drawn to the new religion because it taught that all people were equal in the sight of God. Jesus had said that if people followed his teachings they would go to heaven. Heaven was the Christian place of reward after death.

By the A.D. 300s, the Christians had many churches and had become well organized. Perhaps one-tenth of the people in the Roman Empire were Christian by then. Even the Roman government eventually accepted Christianity. In A.D. 313 the Emperor Constantine made Christianity legal. Later it became the official religion of the empire. Gradually most people in the empire accepted the new faith, and Christianity became the major religion that it is today.

After the Roman Empire was divided, the Christian church helped keep

Jesus and two followers, also called apostles

Roman culture alive in the western part of the empire. Monasteries—places where people went to live quiet, holy lives—had vast libraries. There scribes read and copied Roman writings. The church kept the Latin language alive. In addition, the church adopted Roman architecture and used it for centuries in its buildings. In these ways and others, the heritage of the Roman Empire lived on for centuries.

Reviewing the Lesson

Recalling Key Words, People, and Places
Tell why these people were important:
1. Jesus
2. Constantine

Remembering Main Ideas
1. Describe one of the features of law under Roman civilization.
2. How did the Germans come to rule the western part of the original Roman Empire?
3. What ideas did Christianity teach?

Thinking Things Over
Why do you think the Roman government was not able to stop the spread of Christianity?

157

Using Primary and Secondary Sources

People today can learn much about the ancient Romans from the aqueducts, roads, and temple ruins that still stand. You also can learn about Roman history from a variety of written materials.

Recognizing Primary and Secondary Sources

A written primary source comes directly from the time when and the place where it was written. You can think of primary sources as firsthand sources. Many poems, stories, government documents, and letters written by people living in the Roman Empire still exist. These primary sources are extremely valuable to historians and to others who want to learn about Rome.

A written secondary source describes people, situations, or events of a past time or a distant place. The writer of a secondary source may gain information from primary sources or from other secondary sources. Most of the material in this textbook is a secondary source. In their own way, secondary sources also are valuable to historians and students.

Evaluating Sources

When working with written source materials, a historian tries to answer a number of questions. If the source is a firsthand account, the historian asks whether the writer was well qualified to make an accurate report. If the source is a secondhand account, the historian asks whether the writer did careful research.

For all materials, whether secondary or primary, a historian asks questions such as these: Are the writer's facts true and accurate? Did the writer have a particular point of view that might have affected the way he or she presented the facts? Is the writer's order of events correct? Once the answers to such questions are decided, the historian is ready to put together as accurate and complete a picture as possible.

In A.D. 79, Mt. Vesuvius, a volcano on the eastern shore of the Bay of Naples in the Roman Empire, erupted. The eruption killed many people as it destroyed Pompeii [pom pā'] and two other Roman cities near the foot of the mountain. When modern archaeologists uncovered Pompeii, they found the remains of a city brought to a sudden standstill at midday. Homes were just as the owners left them. Tracks of carts were still visible in the streets. Loaves of bread were still in the oven of a bakery. Following are two accounts of the disaster.

This account of the eruption of Mt. Vesuvius appeared in a book written in the 1980s. The book tells the story of an imaginary Roman youth who was studying medicine under a doctor who lived near Mt. Vesuvius in A.D. 79.

66 The ground shook and the mountain gave a muffled roar. . . . Then the ground lurched, and there was a tremendous explosion, a sound so enormous that it battered the world like a hurricane's winds. The darkness was lanced [pierced] with a frightful spray of light coming from the crest [peak] of Vesuvius, and a gigantic cloud, much the shape of a soft round pillow, soared into the sky, hideously lit by the brilliant cascades of fire that now fountained from the mouth of Vesuvius. Then, with one unimaginable surge, the volcano seemed to lift itself . . . as lava [melted rock] emerged and spilled over the cone, sliding down the southern front of Vesuvius. For close to an hour, cinders and ash fell. . . . 99

On the day Mt. Vesuvius erupted, a Roman youth named Pliny [plin′ē] was visiting his uncle. The uncle was in command of some Roman ships stationed at a coastal town not far from Pompeii. The following paragraph is from a letter Pliny wrote to a friend, describing what he saw on that day.

66 [A cloud of unusual size and appearance was coming from Vesuvius.] My uncle launched warships to save many people [who] lived along [the] coast. . . . The ashes which fell upon the ships grew hotter and thicker the nearer he approached. . . . The sea suddenly drew back and landslides from the mountain blocked the shore. . . . [My uncle then headed toward the household of a friend.] The house was tottering with frequent violent quakings and seemed to sway back and forth. . . . Outdoors there was the fall of [lightweight volcanic stones] to fear, but the family preferred this to the dangers indoors. . . . They tied pillows on their heads with towels to protect them from the downfall. 99

Skills Practice

1. Which of the two accounts is a secondary source, Pliny's letter or the 1980s book?
2. Which writer seems more interested in giving a colorful description? Why do you say as you do?
3. Do the two accounts agree or disagree about falling fragments in the air? about the ground shaking? Explain your answers.
4. Overall, how would you rate the accuracy of each account? Give reasons for your answer.

Chapter 6 Review

Chapter Summary

Lesson 1   The Roman Republic and Empire—The city of Rome was founded by Indo-Europeans called Latins about 1100 B.C. They were conquered in the 600s B.C. by the Etruscans, who established a government with kings who ruled with the help of a group of advisers called the senate. In 509 B.C. the senate overthrew the Etruscan king and set up a republic. The Romans extended their rule throughout much of the Mediterranean area. In time the republic weakened and a series of emperors ruled Rome.

Lesson 2   Christianity and a Changing Rome—The people of the Roman Empire benefited from Roman law and order. The Romans also built great cities with magnificent buildings, waterworks, and roads. In A.D. 395 the empire was divided into two parts. In the first century A.D., a Jew named Jesus began Christianity. He was put to death, but Christianity slowly gained strength.

Write your answers on a separate sheet of paper.

Testing Key Words, People, and Places

Part A

Choose the key word from the list that best answers each question.

1. What was a rich landowner in ancient Rome called?

2. In what kind of government do citizens elect representatives to lead them?

3. How could a plebeian representative stop the Roman senate from passing laws?

4. What was the Roman group of government advisers, usually patricians, called?

5. Who was an ordinary person in Rome?
   - **a.** senate
   - **b.** patrician
   - **c.** plebeian
   - **d.** republic
   - **e.** veto

Part B

Match each description with the correct person in the list.

1. the Jewish preacher who began Christianity

2. the first leader of Rome whose power was like that of an emperor

3. the emperor who made Christianity legal in the Roman Empire

4. the first emperor of Rome
   - **a.** Julius Caesar
   - **b.** Augustus
   - **c.** Jesus
   - **d.** Constantine

Testing Main Ideas

Choose the answer that best completes each sentence.

1. Under the Roman republic,
   - **a.** plebeian representatives could stop the patrician senate from passing laws.
   - **b.** the patrician senate held all power.
   - **c.** the emperor worked with the plebeians against the patricians.

160

2. Rome's wars with Carthage were called
  a. the Peloponnesian Wars.
  b. the Germanic Wars.
  c. the Punic Wars.

3. Roman civilization is noted for
  a. its belief in rule by law and its great cities.
  b. its refusal to conquer other people.
  c. its central marketplaces.

4. The people who came to rule the western part of the Roman Empire were
  a. the Persians.
  b. the Germans.
  c. the Greeks.

5. As Jesus traveled and spoke to more people, the Roman government
  a. decided to legalize Christianity.
  b. punished the Jewish authorities because they supported Jesus.
  c. grew alarmed that Jesus would try to overthrow the government.

Testing Skills

1. Using primary and secondary sources. In 58 B.C., Julius Caesar began an invasion of Gaul (present-day France). The war there became known as the Gallic War. Much has been written about this war. Each of the following sentences has an error. Tell why each sentence is incorrect and then rewrite the sentence to make it correct.
  a. *The Decline and Fall of the Roman Empire* by Edward Gibbon, first published between 1776 and 1788, is a primary source.
  b. *Commentaries on the Gallic War* by Julius Caesar is a secondary source.

2. Putting events in order. Put the following events in correct order.
  • The Roman Empire divided into parts—A.D. 395
  • The Etruscans conquer Rome— 600s B.C.
  • Rome defeats Carthage—146 B.C.
  • Christianity legalized in Rome— A.D. 313
  • Julius Caesar dies—44 B.C.
  • Jesus put to death—A.D. 33

Activities

1. Choose a short paragraph from one of your textbooks or a book you have read for fun. Use a dictionary to look up the origins of the words. How many words are of Latin origin? of Greek origin? of other origins? Show the original form for each word.

2. Read the chapter on ancient Rome in Hendrik W. van Loon's *The Story of Mankind* (Liveright, 1984). Write a brief report telling what van Loon thinks of the Romans and how he compares them with the Greeks.

3. Research some ancient Roman buildings such as the Colosseum and the Forum. What were they like in Roman times, and what are they like today?

Chapter 7

The Rise of European Civilization

Eleven hundred years ago, most Europeans lived by farming. Some cities existed, but they only had a few thousand people in and around them. From these beginnings modern Europe grew. Florence, Italy, shown above, became one of the first important cities of modern Europe.

In this chapter you will read about European life during the Middle Ages. You will follow the story of a powerful new faith called Islam and see how Islam affected Europe. You will see how the Renaissance and the Reformation changed European culture and religion. Finally, you will learn about the strong nations that formed in Europe after the Middle Ages. The lessons in the chapter are listed below.

162

Lesson 1 Europe's Middle Ages

LOOKING AHEAD As you read, look for—

Key words, people, and places:

medieval	Charlemagne
feudalism	
knight	
peasant	
serf	
crusade	
guild	

Answers to these questions about **main ideas:**

1. How did the Franks govern medieval Europe?
2. What troubles did Western Europe suffer after the death of Charlemagne?
3. What was feudal society like?
4. What role did the church and the popes have during the Middle Ages?
5. What effects did increased food production and population growth have in the later Middle Ages?

Have you ever heard or read stories of knights in shining armor? If so, you know a little bit about European life during the Middle Ages. The Middle Ages is the name we give the period of European history from about A.D. 500 to 1350. Another word that refers to the Middle Ages is **medieval.** During medieval times most Europeans were not knights. They were poor farmers. They lived on the lands of powerful kings or nobles who ruled after the Roman Empire broke down in Europe.

Early Medieval Government

As you have read, German tribes moved into Western European territory in the A.D. 300s. The Franks were one of these German tribes. They set up the most important kingdom in early medieval Europe.

Early German society was very much like that of other Indo-European people. A chief or king ruled with the advice of the oldest men in the tribe. The king depended on an army to fight for him and the tribe. Laws were simple, and life was centered in villages. When the Franks entered Roman lands, they kept many of their old customs but adopted some Roman ones as well. A new society emerged in Europe. It included a mixture of German and Roman ways.

The greatest of the Frankish kings was Charlemagne (shar'lə mān). He was a huge man, perhaps seven feet tall. He conquered large parts of Western Europe, including much of Italy.

Charlemagne saw himself as the rebuilder of the Roman Empire in the west. He was a strong supporter of Christianity as well. Charlemagne had monasteries and churches built. The monasteries often had schools, for Charlemagne wanted to spread education too. Usually priests were in charge of the schools. Some monastery priests were scribes who copied thousands of Roman writings that we know today. With Charlemagne's support, priests helped keep learning alive during the early Middle Ages.

163

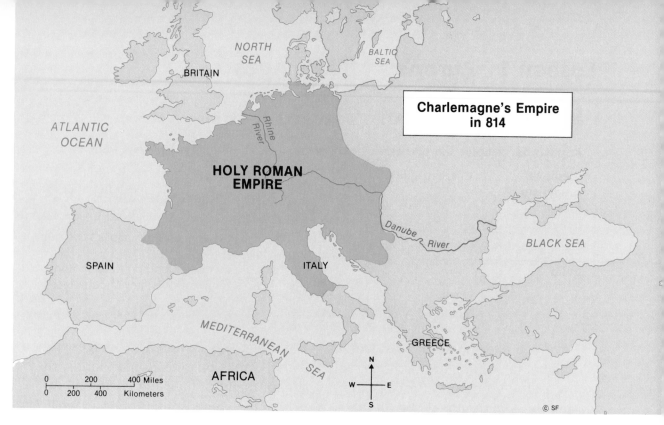

Map Study

What bodies of water bordered Charlemagne's empire? Use the map on page 155 to tell whether Charlemagne's empire was larger or smaller than the Western Roman Empire.

In 800 Charlemagne named himself Holy Roman Emperor. Find Charlemagne's empire on the map above. What was the empire called?

Trouble in Europe

When Charlemagne died in 814, no strong leader took his place. Charlemagne's three grandsons divided his empire among themselves in 843. These kings and those who followed them fought each other for land and power. To gain support, each king gave away land to the nobles. By the early 900s, the kings had lost so much land and power that their kingdoms really were controlled by nobles.

To add to the confusion and violence, raiders from the north and east attacked Western Europe in the 1000s and 1100s. The raiders from the east were nomads from central Asia called Magyars. Most present-day Hungarians are descended from the Magyars. From the north came the Vikings, also known as the Norse. People in present-day Denmark, Sweden, and Norway are descended from the Vikings. The Vikings sailed in magnificent ships, each decorated with a carved dragon head. They raided throughout Europe and many places beyond, collecting treasure.

The Rise of Feudalism

As central government broke down in Western Europe, a new system took its place. This system is called feudalism. **Feudalism** was a system in which a number of powerful nobles, also known as lords, controlled their own areas of land. The lords divided parts of their land among other, less powerful nobles in return for military service and money. Thus, most nobles controlled some land and owed service to a lord. The lands the lords controlled were called fiefs (fēfs) and usually included at least one village.

The organization of feudal society was like a pyramid. At the top were the lords. Further down the scale were lesser nobles. The lesser nobles were the famous **knights**—warriors—of the Middle Ages. At the bottom of medieval society were the peasants. **Peasants** were farmers who lived in and around the villages of a noble's fief.

The poorest peasants were **serfs.** The serfs were a little like slaves. They rented land from a lord and had to work for the lord. For example, serfs had to plant the lord's grain and harvest it. Serfs could not leave the land, and they had to receive the lord's permission to marry. For the lord's part, he acted as the village judge and protected the peasants in time of war or other trouble. Nor could the lord take the serf's land away.

Medieval knights practiced their battle skills in contests called jousts. Jousting knights tried to topple each other from their horses. The contests were popular spectator sports for the noble classes of the Middle Ages.

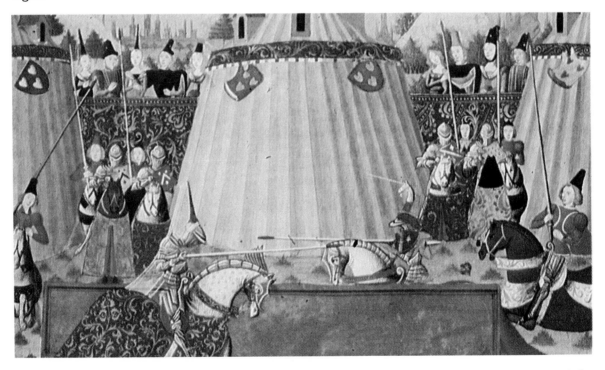

The Church and the Popes

During the Middle Ages, Christianity became a powerful force in the lives of Europeans. By the 900s most Europeans were Christians. A leader known as the Pope headed the Christian church and lived in Rome. By the 1000s the Pope had become as powerful as the great nobles. Medieval people were deeply religious. They believed the Pope and the church were carrying out God's will on earth.

The Pope controlled vast lands that the church owned. The Pope could even raise armies to fight for the church. In 1095 Pope Urban II declared a crusade against non-Christians in western Asia. **Crusades** are wars fought over religion, and several of them occurred in the Middle Ages. Many thousands of Europeans left their homes to fight in the Crusades.

The Later Middle Ages

After the year 1000, life in Europe began to change once more. As you can see from the graph on this page, the European population began to grow rapidly. Many historians think the growth took place because the Europeans began to produce more food. Farmers began to use more iron plows and iron harvesting tools. They could plow more land and harvest more food than before. Increased food production and population growth had two important effects in the Middle Ages: trade began to grow and so did towns.

The Growth of Trade. During feudal times Europeans carried on some local trade. Farmers sold their extra food in the villages. This kind of trade began to increase as farmers grew more food.

Another sort of trade was carried out over long distances. Europeans began to trade with Asia, including faraway India and China. The Europeans sent leather, furs, salt, grain, iron, and timber to the east. In return they got spices, fine cloth, oranges, almonds, raisins, figs, and more. Eventually people in Europe came to depend on the goods from long-distance trade.

The Growth of Towns. Some small towns and cities existed throughout the feudal years in Europe. As trade grew and population growth continued, more people came to live in the towns.

By about how much did Europe's population grow between the years 600 and 1200?

Population Growth in Medieval Europe
(France, Germany, Italy, and the British Isles)

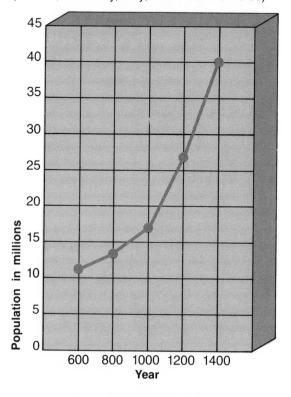

Medieval markets offered a variety of goods to townspeople.

Also, new towns formed. Many of the new townspeople had been peasants on manors. They moved to the towns to find jobs.

As towns and cities grew, feudal organization weakened. A new class of people arose in Europe—a middle class made up mainly of urban people. Some city people came to have more power and wealth than others. At the top of the middle class were rich merchants. They controlled much of the sea trade, and they ran the city governments. They lived in large houses very much as the lords did.

Craft workers had less wealth and power. They lived in small houses above or behind their shops. Craft workers banded together in guilds. The **guilds** were organizations that controlled the quality of goods produced. The guilds also trained young workers in the crafts. Craft workers took great care and pride in the things they made.

Least powerful among the city people were workers who did odd jobs of all kinds. They had no guilds. Often they rioted against the rich people who ran the cities. City society in Europe remained the same throughout the later Middle Ages and long afterward.

Reviewing the Lesson

Recalling Key Words, People, and Places

1. Identify the key words defined below:
   a. a system in which powerful nobles controlled their own areas of land
   b. one of the poorest farmers who lived somewhat like slaves in medieval times
   c. a war fought over religion
   d. a craft organization that controlled the quality of goods and trained young craft workers
2. Tell why Charlemagne was important.

Remembering Main Ideas

1. Describe the Frankish king Charlemagne's rule in medieval Europe.
2. What made Europe a confused and violent place after Charlemagne's death?
3. Where did each of these groups rank in feudal society: lords, knights, serfs?
4. Why were the Popes so powerful during the Middle Ages?
5. Describe the growth of towns and cities during the later Middle Ages.

Thinking Things Over

In medieval times a popular saying was, "City air makes one free." How would you explain this saying? Base your answer on what you know about the life of peasants on the manor and the growth of towns.

Lesson 2   The Islamic Challenge to Europe

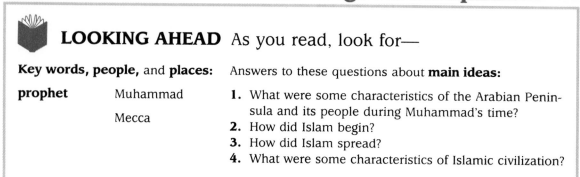

LOOKING AHEAD As you read, look for—

Key words, people, and **places:**

prophet   Muhammad

Mecca

Answers to these questions about **main ideas:**

1. What were some characteristics of the Arabian Peninsula and its people during Muhammad's time?
2. How did Islam begin?
3. How did Islam spread?
4. What were some characteristics of Islamic civilization?

Religion always has played an important part in history. You have read about the Hebrews and the Christians. By 800, people called Muslims controlled much of the Mediterranean land that was once part of the original Roman Empire. Muslims were, and are, followers of a religion called Islam. A leader named Muhammad (mü-ham'əd) founded Islam, which—like Judaism and Christianity—is based on belief in one God.

The Arabian Peninsula

Muhammad was an Arab. That is, he spoke the Arabic language and lived on the Arabian Peninsula, as Arabs still do today. Find the Arabian Peninsula on the map on page 169. Most of this land is desert, just as it was in Muhammad's time. Since farming land was very scarce, most of the people who lived in the interior parts of Arabia were nomads. Called Bedouins (bed'ü əns), these people moved from place to place to graze their sheep. Bedouins lived in tribes headed by chiefs. The tribal people often were warlike and raided each other's settlements.

Some important towns and cities sat near the edges of the Arabian Peninsula. Places such as Mecca and Medina were important trading centers. Mecca was a religious center as well. Before the development of Islam, Arab people came there often to worship their many gods. It was in this city, Mecca, that Muhammad was born about 570.

The Beginning of Islam

Muhammad came from one of the most important families in Mecca. He was a merchant in his young adulthood, but religion always had interested him. As a boy he had learned about his Arab religion. He learned about Christianity and Judaism also. Muhammad met Christians and Jews on his trading trips, and their ideas influenced him.

Muhammad often went into the hills near Mecca to pray. He began to have dreams and visions in which an angel spoke to him. Eventually Muhammad came to believe that God—Allah in Arabic—had chosen Muhammad to be his prophet. A **prophet** is a religious leader who claims to be God's messenger. As

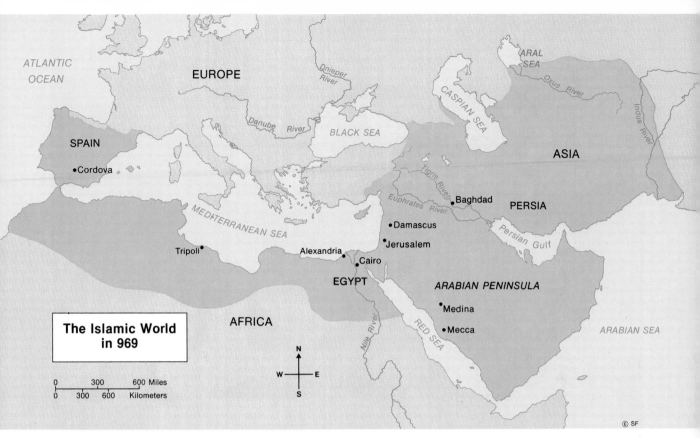

The Islamic World
in 969

0   300   600 Miles
0 300 600 Kilometers

Map Study

By 969 the Islamic world included parts of the old Roman Empire, the Persian Empire, and the empire of Alexander the Great. To what three continents did the Islamic world extend? With your finger, trace a route from Cordova, Spain, to the Indus River. Through what Islamic cities might you pass?

in Hebrew and Christian belief, Muhammad preached that there is only one true God.

Muhammad began to tell people about his visions. Word of his experiences started to spread through Mecca, and Muhammad began to attract followers. His followers wrote down his teachings in the Koran, the holy book of Islam. All those who accepted Muhammad's teachings were called Muslims. The faith was called *Islam,* meaning "submission to the will of God."

Muhammad taught that God was good and all powerful. Muhammad

believed in life after death and in the idea that God—Allah—would judge who would go to heaven. Muhammad said that all Muslims were united in one community and that all believers were equal. Thus, all Muslims were brothers and sisters in the sight of God.

The Spread of Islam

By the time of his death in 632, Muhammad had converted many of the people of southern Arabia to Islam. He had told followers to spread the faith to all people, using military force if it were necessary.

169

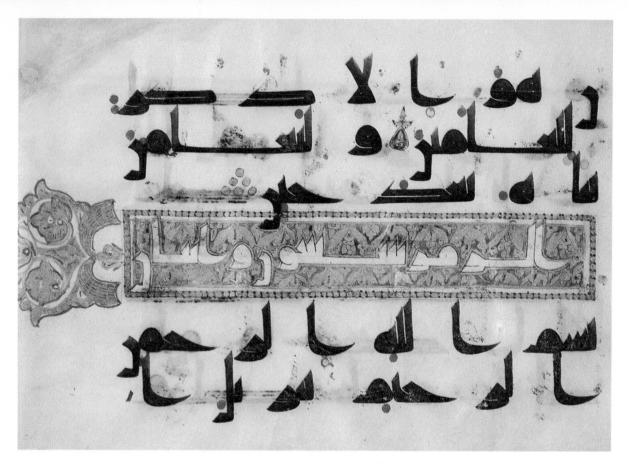

Muslims developed a beautiful style of writing known as calligraphy (kə lig′rə fē). A page from the Koran is shown above.

As it happened, the two major powers in Southwest Asia—Persia and the Byzantine Empire—had fought a long series of wars and had become very weak. Also, many people in both empires were unhappy with their governments. Beginning in 630, Muslim armies attacked these two powers.

By 660, Muslim armies had taken Egypt and much of North Africa, and almost the entire Persian Empire. By 711, Muslim armies had landed in Spain and soon had most of it under their control. At the same time, the armies captured parts of northern India and set up rule there. Look at the map on page 169. In what directions from Mecca had Islam spread by 969?

How did Islam affect Europe? Europeans feared the new religion and its power. Christian Europe fought against Islam. As you have read, several Crusades were organized during the Middle Ages. The Crusades were wars against Islam. During the Crusades European knights tried to take the Holy Land from Islamic rule. The Holy Land included Judea, or Palestine, where Jesus had lived. Thousands of people died in the Crusades, and the Europeans never held the Holy Land for any length of time.

The Crusades did have a positive side, though. Thousands of Crusaders were introduced to Southwest Asia just as European cities were growing. The

Arab astronomers located the stars with instruments they invented.

Crusaders brought back new goods and helped open up trade between Europe and Asia.

Islamic Civilization

Many people whom the Muslims conquered had highly developed cultures. The Arabs found cities active with trade and skilled craft workers. They also found art and books of philosophy and science. The Muslims learned much from the people they conquered. They protected the art, and they translated the writings of Greeks,

Romans, and Persians into Arabic. They collected the works in libraries, where Muslim thinkers could work and write.

The Arabs came up with new ideas as well, in medicine, mathematics, astronomy, and other sciences. They also wrote books on geography and history.

Trade always had been an important part of Arab life. Under Islam, trade became even more important. In addition to Western Europe, traders went to Russia, East Asia, and central Africa. The traders carried ideas as well as goods. For example, Muslims learned about the numbers 1 through 9 in India. The Arabs passed on these "Arabic numerals," along with the idea of zero, to Western Europe. As you will read later, Muslim influence became important in many other parts of Asia and in Africa as well.

Reviewing the Lesson

Recalling Key Words, People, and Places
1. What is a religious leader who claims to be God's messenger?
2. Tell why it is important to remember:
   a. Muhammad
   b. Mecca

Remembering Main Ideas
1. Why were cities important on the Arabian Peninsula in Muhammad's time?
2. Name two ideas that Muhammad taught through Islam.
3. How did Europeans react to the spread of Islam?
4. How did the Muslims both preserve and contribute to civilization as the Islamic religion spread?

Thinking Things Over
How were the early histories of Islam and Christianity alike? How were they different? Support your answer with information from this lesson and previous lessons.

171

Lesson 3 The Renaissance and Reformation

📖 **LOOKING AHEAD** As you read, look for—

Key words, people, and **places:**

renaissance
reform

Michelangelo
Leonardo da Vinci
William Shakespeare
Martin Luther
John Calvin

Answers to these questions about **main ideas:**

1. What were some of the accomplishments of the Renaissance?
2. What caused the Reformation?

By the 1300s many changes were taking place in Europe. As you have read, towns and cities were growing. Wealth from trade flowed into the cities. The Italian cities, especially, grew rich and important. They were closest to the Asian trade routes. Cities such as Venice and Florence became exciting places to live and work in the 1300s.

The Renaissance

Wealthy Italians took a great interest in art and learning in the 1300s. They could afford to support art and scholarship by donating money to artists and writers. With these donations, the artists and writers could afford to do their work. Soon Italy became famous as a center of art and learning. We use the word *Renaissance* to describe the heightened interest in art and learning that began in Italy in the 1300s. *Renaissance* means "rebirth" in French. A **renaissance** is a period of new interest in something.

Artists and scholars of the Renaissance took great interest in the accomplishments of ancient Greek and

Roman civilization. They built on these accomplishments. They developed new ideas of their own too—new styles of art, for example. Artists painted and sculpted realistic portraits of people. They invented landscape, or scenery, painting also.

The *Mona Lisa* is Leonardo da Vinci's best-known painting.

172

This painting by Brueghel shows a winter scene in Belgium. Can you describe the activities shown in the picture?

One of the greatest artists of the Renaissance was Michelangelo (mī′kə lan′-jə lō). Michelangelo made lifelike sculptures and painted elaborate frescoes, which are paintings on wet plaster, in famous churches. Leonardo da Vinci (lē ə när′dō də vin′chē) was another great artist. Besides being a painter and sculptor, Leonardo was an architect, inventor, and engineer. Leonardo made designs for flying machines, submarines, and engines that would be developed centuries later. You can see an example of the work of Leonardo on page 172.

News of the Renaissance spread beyond Italy. By the 1400s other places in Western Europe also enjoyed a new artistic spirit. This movement often is called the Northern Renaissance. Northern Renaissance artists are known for their paintings of everyday life. Look at the painting by Pieter Brueghel (pē′tər broi′gəl). It gives a glimpse of what life was like for the ordinary people in Western Europe in the 1500s.

Late Renaissance poet and playwright William Shakespeare of England is considered one of the greatest writers of all time. Shakespeare wrote nearly forty plays. These famous works still are performed today.

The Reformation

The excitement of the Renaissance was not limited to art. New ideas developed too. Scholars and others began to question old ways of doing things. Advances in printing helped spread their ideas. Some of these ideas involved religion.

As you have read, religion was very powerful during the Middle Ages. Christianity was unified in Western Europe at that time. There was one "church"—the Roman Catholic Church. The word *catholic* means "including all."

In the 1500s the Roman Catholic Church became deeply divided, though the Christian faith remained as strong as ever among the people. The changes that divided the Roman Catholic Church made up the movement known as the Reformation (ref ər mā′shən). The word *Reformation* comes from the word *reform*. People who were critics of the church wanted to **reform**—to improve or change—the church. The Reformation led to the establishment of new Christian churches throughout much of western Europe.

What led to the division of the Roman Catholic Church? In general, critics were unhappy with the church's

Linking Past and Present

The Printed Word

Have you ever wondered what the world would be like if printing presses had not been invented? Think of all the books, newspapers, magazines, advertisements, and other printed pieces we are so used to seeing.

Printing presses came into use during the 1400s in Western Europe. A German printer named Johannes Gutenberg developed a printing press that used movable type. Before movable type, printers carved the words for a whole page of a book on a wooden block. With movable type, all the letters were on separate metal blocks. They could be used over and over again for new pages. Movable type made printing much faster than it had been before.

Actually the Chinese had invented both paper and printing hundreds of years before Gutenberg's time. They had never used printing widely, however. Gutenberg developed printing to the point that he soon was able to print

three hundred books a day. He became best known for printing the Gutenberg Bibles.

The printing process has changed greatly since Gutenberg's day. Gutenberg developed a basic technology, however, that later printers improved upon. Look at the newspaper press above. How do newspapers and other forms of printing help people communicate with one another?

wealth and power. Often Popes acted like kings and emperors. They gathered great wealth for the glory of the church. Many Europeans felt that this was not the right thing for the church to do. They recalled Jesus' example of a simple, humble life as best. Moreover, city people and small landowners did not like paying taxes to a wealthy church. In addition, stronger rulers were emerging in Western Europe at this time. They did not like the power the church had over their land and kingdoms.

In 1517 a German priest named Martin Luther posted a list of complaints about the church and the Pope. Luther believed that people could communicate with God directly; they did not need priests or a powerful church to help them. He said that simply by having faith in God, men and women could lead holy lives. Luther broke away from the Roman Catholic Church and organized his own church.

Luther's ideas spread rapidly through Europe. Many other people protested and broke away from the Catholic Church as well. They became known as Protestants. Among these people was John Calvin. Calvin set up a new church in Geneva, a city in present-day Switzerland. Calvin stressed hard work as a way of showing religious faith.

New Christian churches continued to form. The division left the Catholic Church weakened but still standing. Often Catholics and Protestants became bitter enemies. The Reformation would have long-lasting effects in Europe and the world beyond.

When Martin Luther called for changes in Christian practices, he set the Reformation in motion.

Reviewing the Lesson

Recalling Key Words, People, and Places
1. Identify the key words defined below:
   a. a rebirth of interest in something, such as art or learning
   b. to improve or change something for the better
2. Tell who these people were:
   a. Michelangelo
   b. John Calvin

Remembering Main Ideas
1. Describe Leonardo da Vinci's and William Shakespeare's contributions to the Renaissance period.
2. Why did the priest Martin Luther start a new Christian church in the 1500s, the time of the Reformation?

Thinking Things Over
Today we sometimes use the term *Renaissance man* or *Renaissance woman* to refer to a person of many talents. What person in this lesson do you think was the original Renaissance man? Describe what a Renaissance person of today might be like.

175

Lesson 4   The Growth of Nations

 LOOKING AHEAD As you read, look for—

Key words, people, and **places:**

nation
monarchy
absolute monarchy
limited monarchy
constitution

Louis XIV
Philip II (of Spain)

Answers to these questions about **main ideas:**

1. How did kings form nations in Western Europe beginning in the later medieval period?
2. What was France's monarchy like?
3. What was Spain's monarchy like?
4. How was England's monarchy different from those in France and Spain?

Look at the Atlas map of Europe on page 538. How many countries do you count? Each country is independent of the others. Each one of them is a nation. The countries of Europe did not always exist in their present forms. How did countries such as France, Spain, and England come to be? The word *nation* gives a hint as to how it happened.

Nations Develop

A **nation** is a large group of people who live in a specific territory under one government. They usually share a language and certain customs, though not everyone in the nation has to be just the same.

In early medieval times, Europeans did not have a strong sense of belonging to a nation. They might know they were part of a large group of people who shared a language, customs, and maybe even a king. Most people did not feel strongly tied to a large national group, however. Their strongest ties were to the village, town, or small local region in which they lived.

Nations began to form as kings gained more power. After Charlemagne the great nobles held almost all the power in much of Western Europe. However, even under feudalism many nobles still owed some service and support to a king. Gradually, some kings were able to reduce the power of the nobles and form strong central governments beginning in the 1100s. The kings eventually set up clear national borders. Once that happened, everyone within the borders belonged to a national group. Those outside were thought of as foreigners.

Eventually people within a nation became more loyal to it than to their local lords. Strong monarchies developed in France, Spain, and England. A **monarchy** is a government ruled by a king or queen. In France and Spain the monarch—king or queen—had total control over the government. This kind of government is an **absolute monarchy.** In England the monarch's power was limited by law and custom. Thus, the English government was a **limited monarchy.**

176

France: Absolute Monarchy

If a ruler wants to have absolute control of a country, he or she must control the army, the laws and courts, and the taxes. If a king or queen controls the army, then no one—not even the greatest noble—can go against his or her wishes. If a king or queen controls the laws and courts, all justice comes from him or her. Finally, all governments need money. If a monarch controls all taxes, he or she has the money to govern.

In France a series of kings and their chief assistants got control of these parts of government between the late 1500s and the mid-1600s. Starting with King Henry IV in 1589, the French monarchs built a very powerful army. With it, they crushed the power of the great nobles. They used the army to destroy the nobles' castles. The monarchs ordered disobedient nobles to be arrested and executed (killed).

The French monarchy was strongest under King Louis XIV. Called the "Sun King" for his grand way of life, Louis built a vast palace at Versailles (ver sī'), near the city of Paris. He forced all the important nobles to live at Versailles so he could keep an eye on them. The nobles spent their days watching plays, operas, and concerts. They wore fine clothes and spent much of their time gossiping. Thus, the nobles had little time to think about politics.

Spain: Absolute Monarchy

Spain was an absolute monarchy that formed in 1479. Before that time Spain consisted of four kingdoms.

The clothing of King Louis XIV reflected a grand way of life.

Aragon and Castile (ka stēl') were the largest. In 1469 Prince Ferdinand of Aragon and Princess Isabella of Castile married. Ten years later they joined their kingdoms.

The nation grew rich in the 1500s as vast amounts of treasure poured in from the Spanish colonies. Spain conquered large parts of the Americas and mined gold and other valuable minerals there. With this wealth Spain built a powerful army and navy.

Under Philip II, Ferdinand and Isabella's grandson, Spain became the strongest military power in Europe in the 1500s. Philip had many trained

The French and English had been at war for nearly one hundred years when a peasant girl named Joan of Arc, pictured at left, was born in France in 1412. In 1429, with the countries still at war, Joan convinced the French king to let her lead French troops in battle. Joan claimed that voices from heaven told her to help the French. The king agreed to Joan's aid since he was deeply religious and France was desperate for a victory.

Joan won several battles and raised the hopes and spirits of the French people. However, she was captured in 1430 and later put to death by the English. Eventually, France won its war against the English—the Hundred Years' War—and France became a strong nation. Joan of Arc still is remembered for her role in the victory. Centuries after Joan's death, the Roman Catholic Church made her a saint.

officials who collected taxes, supervised the army, and otherwise ran the nation. Philip's agents sought out anyone who disagreed with the king. Such people could be imprisoned or even put to death. Philip controlled his kingdom tightly.

The Spanish Armada was the world's strongest navy in the early 1500s.

England: Limited Monarchy

England developed a government different from those in France and Spain. In 1215 powerful English nobles made King John I promise them certain rights. They had the king sign the *Magna Carta,* a Latin term for "great charter." The Magna Carta was an agreement in which the king promised not to take the nobles' property or money. Also, the agreement promised justice to the people of England. It said that no one could be imprisoned without cause. It also said that the government could not delay or deny justice to the English people.

The Magna Carta guaranteed fair court trials in England. Most important, it put limits on the monarch's power. King John and later rulers could not rule as absolute monarchs.

Parliament. In the late 1200s, a governmental body called Parliament formed in England. Parliament was a council of advisers to the monarch,

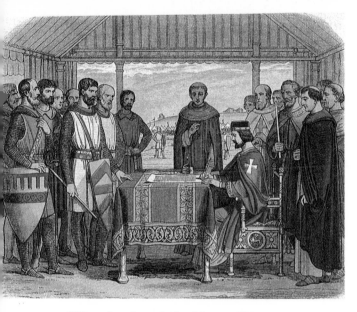

When he signed the Magna Carta, King John did away with some of the rights of absolute rulers.

made up partly of middle-class people who were elected to office. People eventually began to believe that Parliament should make the laws and the monarch should govern according to these laws.

The English called this system constitutional monarchy. A **constitution** is a set of rules used in governing a nation. Some nations, such as the United States, have a written constitution. England to this day never has had a written constitution.

English kings did not always agree with the idea of a constitution. In the early 1600s, for example, King James I declared that God alone gives monarchs the right to rule. He said all people in a nation must do as the king or queen says since monarchs rule by "divine right."

The Bill of Rights. England's Parliament never liked the idea of divine right. In the late 1600s, Parliament forced a new king, William I, to agree to a list of rules known as the Bill of Rights. The rights put further limits on the monarch's power. The limits included the following:

- Parliament makes the laws and the monarch cannot change them.
- People can speak without fear of being punished.
- Judges cannot be controlled by the monarch.
- The monarch cannot keep his or her own permanent army.

These rules marked the beginning of the modern constitutional monarchy that Great Britain has today.

Reviewing the Lesson

Recalling Key Words, People, and Places
1. Identify the key words defined below:
   a. a large group of people who live in a specific territory under one government
   b. a government ruled by a king or a queen
   c. a set of rules used in governing a nation
2. Tell why it is important to remember:
   a. Louis XIV
   b. Philip II (of Spain)

Remembering Main Ideas
1. Why were national borders important in forming nations?
2. How did King Henry IV and those who followed him use their power to build and keep absolute monarchy in France?
3. Why was wealth important to Spain's absolute monarchy in the 1500s?
4. Name two ways in which the English monarchy was limited between the 1200s and the 1600s.

Thinking Things Over
The French and Spanish absolute monarchies did not last. England's limited monarchy has lasted to the present day. Why do you think this may be so? Give reasons for your answer.

SKILLS WORKSHOP

Summarizing Information from a Special-Purpose Map

You learned in this chapter that the Crusaders returned home with new goods that interested the people of Europe. The Crusaders bought these goods at busy marketplaces in the Islamic lands at the eastern end of the Mediterranean Sea.

Most of the goods originally had come from more eastern points of Asia.

Merchant ships loaded with European goods sailed to the eastern Mediterranean. There Arab merchants exchanged Europe's trade items for Asian and African goods.

Some of the goods exchanged were silk, ivory, gold, furs, leather, grain, cloth, sugar, and spices. These and other goods came from many places, including Lübeck, Alexandria, Baghdad, and Peking (today called Beijing). Trade routes crossed hundreds of miles of land and water.

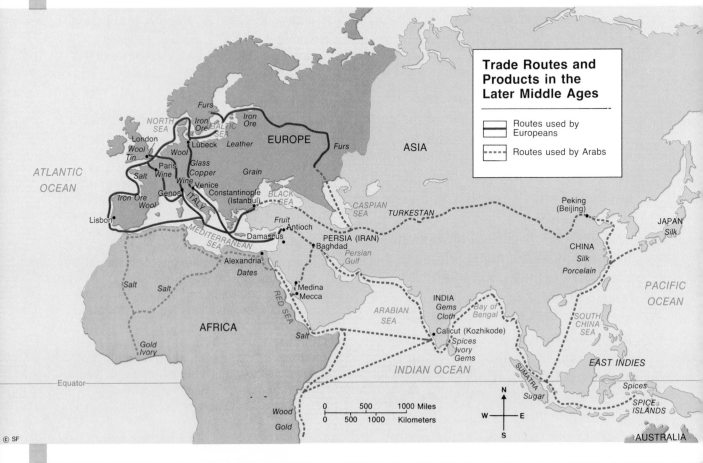

© SF

Using Special-Purpose Maps

The map on page 180 is an example of a special-purpose map. A special-purpose map does not show many different kinds of information, such as country boundaries, state boundaries, cities, lakes, and rivers. Instead, special-purpose maps focus on one or two particular features, such as precipitation, population, products, or trade routes. Most or all of the information on a special-purpose map is related to the one or two features. Special-purpose maps often use colors and special symbols to present information. For instance, how are trade routes presented on the special-purpose map on page 180?

Summarizing Information

By now you probably are familiar with summarizing. You summarize when you tell a friend about a movie you saw or a story you read. You summarize when someone asks, "What did you learn in school today?" You summarize every time your teacher asks you to tell the main ideas of a lesson or chapter you are studying.

A summary is a short statement that gives the highlights, or main ideas, of something you have read, seen, heard, or experienced. A summary skips details. Instead, a summary contains only the most important points. Summarizing information can help you remember important facts from your reading, for instance.

Information also can be summarized from a map such as the one on page 180. Summarizing information from a map can help you understand the map and remember the main ideas presented on the map.

Skills Practice

1. Write a summary sentence explaining what the special-purpose map on page 180 shows.
2. Europe was one of four main places involved in trading. Use the map on page 180 to list three other main places.
3. What cities were exchange points?
4. Near what body of water did most of the trade routes of the Arabs and Europeans meet?
5. Were the longest trade routes east or west of Damascus?
6. Copy and complete the chart below to summarize information about the products shown on the map.

Products by Place of Origin			
Europe	**Africa**	**Asia**	**East Indies**

Chapter 7 Review

Chapter Summary

Lesson 1   Europe's Middle Ages—In 800, Charlemagne, king of the Franks, named himself Holy Roman Emperor over much of Western Europe. After his death, European nobles gained power and outsiders raided Western Europe repeatedly. Most Europeans were Christians, and the church was very powerful. After 1000, increased food production led to growth of population, trade, and towns.

Lesson 2   The Islamic Challenge to Europe—An Arab named Muhammad founded the religion of Islam in the early 600s. Muslim armies conquered large areas of the Mediterranean. European Christians organized the Crusades against Islam. The Crusades failed but brought trade and new ideas to Europe from Islamic civilization.

Lesson 3   The Renaissance and Reformation—By the 1300s Italy became a center of art and learning. Painters and sculptors created masterpieces. The Renaissance also spread north. Advances in printing helped spread new ideas. The Reformation, led by Martin Luther in 1517, brought the Protestant branch of Christianity into being.

Lesson 4   The Growth of Nations— Beginning in the 1100s, some kings gained more power and were able to establish lasting national borders. The king of France and the king of Spain had absolute power. Parliament limited the king of England's power.

Write your answers on a separate sheet of paper.

Testing Key Words, People, and Places

Part A

Use each key word in a sentence.

1. medieval
2. feudalism
3. knight
4. peasant
5. serf
6. crusade
7. guild
8. prophet
9. renaissance
10. reform
11. nation
12. monarchy
13. absolute monarchy
14. limited monarchy
15. constitution

Part B

Match each description with the correct person in the list.

1. started his own church in the 1500s
2. the greatest king of the Franks
3. the "Sun King" of France
4. a Renaissance artist, inventor, and engineer
5. founded Islam

   a. Charlemagne
   b. Muhammad
   c. Leonardo da Vinci
   d. Martin Luther
   e. Louis XIV

Testing Main Ideas

Choose the answer that best completes each sentence.

1. After Charlemagne died, Western Europe was
   a. calm and peaceful.
   b. conquered by the Romans.
   c. attacked by Magyars and Vikings.

2. Popes were able to be powerful during the Middle Ages because
 a. people worshiped many gods.
 b. people were deeply religious.
 c. the Popes controlled the fiefs.

3. The class that arose as towns and cities grew was the
 a. peasant class.
 b. middle class.
 c. aristocracy.

4. Muhammad believed
 a. that Muslims were unequal in the sight of God.
 b. that Islam should only be spread by peaceful means.
 c. that God is good and all powerful.

5. The greatest playwright of the Renaissance was
 a. William Shakespeare.
 b. Michelangelo.
 c. Pieter Brueghel.

6. Critics of the Roman Catholic Church
 a. were unhappy with the church's wealth and power.
 b. thought the church should collect higher taxes.
 c. believed the Pope should take over more land.

7. Modern nations began to form
 a. when kings took power away from the nobles.
 b. when the peasants revolted.
 c. by order of the Pope.

8. The monarchies of France and Spain
 a. were weak.
 b. were absolute.
 c. followed constitutions.

Testing Skills

1. Summarizing information from a map. Answer the questions about the map below.
 a. What bodies of water bordered the Holy Roman Empire?
 b. What areas of Europe were *not* part of the Holy Roman Empire?

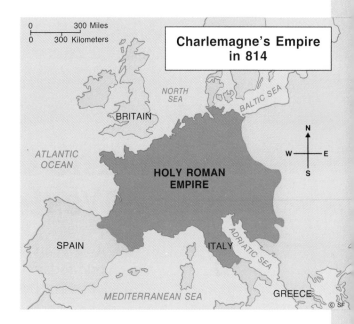

2. Making inferences. Why do you suppose Charlemagne never tried to conquer Britain? What clue does the map give?

Activities

1. Choose three pictures in this chapter. In your own words, explain what each picture tells you about the people or events of the time.

2. To learn more about Charlemagne, read *Stories of Charlemagne* by Jennifer Westwood (Phillips, 1976).

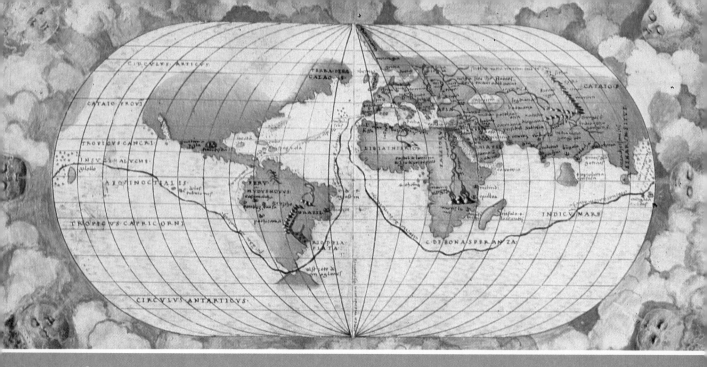

Chapter 8

The Global Spread of Western Civilization

European languages are the most widely spoken in the world today. Many governments are based on European types, too. How did European civilization spread? The picture above shows a map used by Europeans in the 1500s to set sail across the world's oceans. They spread their culture and created a civilization we call Western.

As you read this chapter, you will learn the answers to these questions: Why did European exploration begin when it did? What brought about the American and French revolutions and what effects did they have? What was the Industrial Revolution and what did it have to do with the spread of Western civilization? The lessons in the chapter are listed below.

Lesson 1   Exploring the World

Lesson 2   An Age of Revolutions

Lesson 3   The Industrial Revolution

Lesson 1   Exploring the World

LOOKING AHEAD As you read, look for—

Key words, people, and **places:**

conquistador   Christopher Columbus
Vasco da Gama
Ferdinand Magellan
Hernando Cortés
John Cabot
Jacques Cartier

Answers to these questions about **main ideas:**

1. What factors made European exploration possible in the late 1400s?
2. Why did the Europeans want to search for new trade routes to Asia beginning in the late 1400s?
3. What lands did the Europeans arrive at and what did they find there?

"In fourteen hundred and ninety-two, Columbus sailed the ocean blue." You probably know this rhyme, and you may know that Christopher Columbus was an Italian explorer who sailed west across the Atlantic Ocean in the service of Spain. By the 1500s the nations of Portugal, Spain, France, and England had begun to sail the oceans of the world. They were looking for new trade routes to Asia. What they found were lands they had not even known existed—a new world. The *New World* was the European term for North and South America.

What Made Exploration Possible?

Why did the European explorers set sail when they did? The first reason had to do with the growth of trade and cities during the Middle Ages. Without a growing population that wanted trade goods, without merchants and middle-class people, Europeans would have had no reason to set sail. They might have continued farming the land as they had for thousands of years. Even

This old cartoon shows Queen Isabella and King Ferdinand of Spain seeing ships off to the New World.

185

the feudal system might have continued. However, life changed as Europe developed and grew.

Another factor that allowed Europeans to explore was technology. By the 1500s they had the knowledge and tools for ocean navigation (sailing) that made worldwide exploration possible. For example, from the Arabs, Europeans had learned ways of using triangular sails to move ships quickly. European sailors also had learned to use compasses and to steer accurately using the sun, moon, and stars as guides. They were aided by new charts and maps as well.

New weapons made the Europeans more daring than ever too. Ironworkers in Europe had begun making guns. Gunpowder actually had been invented in China, but the Europeans put it to widespread use by the middle of the 1400s. Thus, European ships set sail protected against possible enemies by powerful guns.

Finally, there was the printing press. Before the printing press, books were handwritten and very expensive. After about 1450, when the printing press came into use in Europe, books became cheaper. Cheaper printed books and pamphlets meant ideas could travel much faster through all of Europe. New ideas and new information about inventions and travel spread rapidly. For example, Columbus's voyages were written about as soon as he returned. Reports of the voyages spurred more exploration. The first maps of the lands Columbus had seen appeared soon afterwards.

The Search for Trade Routes

Christopher Columbus was not looking for a place to settle when he came upon the islands off North America. He was looking for spices.

As you have read, Europeans in the Middle Ages wanted spices such as pepper and cinnamon. Spices were grown in Asia. The spices were picked, dried, and then carried by ship as well as overland all the way to Europe. Many merchants handled the spices along the way, and each one got some payment for handling them. By the time the spices reached Western Europe, the money paid out to all those people made the spices very expensive.

Someone who could find a way to bring spices to Europe more directly by ship could become wealthy. All the extra time and payments getting the spices to Europe would be cut out. Nations that controlled the new trade routes would become wealthy too. They could use the wealth to build powerful armies to defend themselves and conquer new lands.

The Explorers and Where They Went

Portuguese sailors were the first Western Europeans to search for new ocean trade routes in the 1400s. They ventured south, mainly to Africa. In 1488 Bartolomeu Dias rounded the southern tip of Africa. Ten years later Vasco da Gama sailed all the way around Africa and then east to India. Portugal claimed this route to India, leaving other countries' explorers to sail elsewhere.

Mystery in History

Did you know that America is named for the Italian explorer Amerigo Vespucci (ve spü′chē), pictured at right? Actually, there is a mystery about Vespucci. Many historians do not believe he set sail when he first said he did. How, then, did he get two continents named after him?

Vespucci wrote a letter in 1502. In it he said he had sailed to a "new world" in 1497. A few years later, Vespucci's letter was published, and soon everyone knew what he had said. Vespucci became known as the first explorer to realize he had reached the New World.

A mapmaker printed *America* on a New World map in honor of Amerigo Vespucci. Soon other mapmakers did the same. Vespucci holds one of these early maps in the picture.

Was Vespucci telling the truth? There is no proof of his 1497 voyage, though he did make later voyages to the New World. Who, then, *was* the first explorer to realize the Americas existed—and when?

Sailing for Spain, Columbus believed that it might be faster to sail west to India. He thought that the earth was smaller than it was. He also had no idea that North and South America lay between Europe and Asia. Thinking that he had reached islands near India in 1493, Columbus wrote the following:

> 66 Española [Columbus's name for the Caribbean island now known as Hispaniola] is a wonder. Its mountains and plains, and meadows and fields, are so beautiful and rich for planting and sowing, and rearing cattle of all kinds, and for building towns and villages. The harbors on the coast and the number and size and wholesomeness of the rivers, most of them bearing gold, surpass anything that would be believed by one who had not seen them. 99

Columbus also found people in "Española." Thinking that he had reached India, Columbus called these people "Indians." We still use the term *Indian* for the native, or first, people who lived in the Americas.

Look at the map on page 188 and use your finger to trace Columbus's route to the New World. In what general direction did Columbus sail?

Columbus most likely never knew that he had come to the New World. However, by the 1500s Europe knew about the New World. Knowledge of geography had grown, and explorers proved that the two "new" continents were part of the world. In 1519 Ferdinand Magellan (mə jel′ən) began the first successful sailing trip around the whole earth. Nations raced to stake claims for empire as they continued to search for new ocean routes to Asia.

187

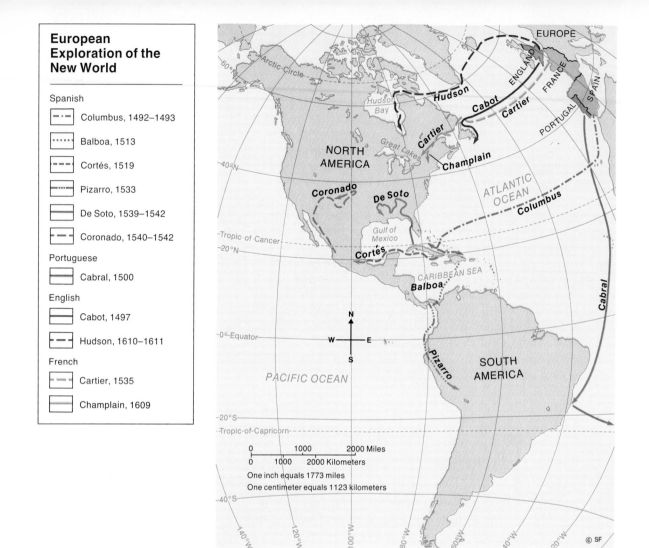

Map Study

Note that most of the explorers sailed north of the Equator. Which explorer reached farthest west and to about what degree of longitude? What was the northernmost latitude, approximately, that Henry Hudson reached on the North American mainland?

Hernando Cortés (kôr tez′) and other conquistadors conquered an empire for Spain in the Americas. The **conquistadors** were the Spanish conquerors of the 1500s. Many came to the New World in search of gold. They claimed the gold for Spain and subjected the Indians to Spanish rule, which lasted until the 1800s.

Explorers for England and France set their sights farther north in North America. Many of them searched unsuccessfully for the Northwest Passage to Asia. The Northwest Passage was a water route to Asia along the northern coast of North America that Europeans believed must exist. Explorers such as John Cabot and Jacques Cartier (zhäk′ kär tyā′) reached present-day Canada

Here is how one artist imagined the meeting between Jacques Cartier's expedition and the Indians of Canada.

and claimed large parts of North America for England and France. Look at the map on page 188. Name another explorer who sailed for England. Name one who sailed for France.

The lands these explorers found were rich in fish and furs. Later, the rich farmland would become valuable for trade and wealth. The North American Indians were skilled trappers and fishers. They became valued contacts for French and English traders in North America.

Their empires in the New World affected the European nations in several ways. The empires made some nations wealthy. Having empires affected European thinking also. As Europeans sailed to various parts of the world, they began to think they had the right to rule other people. Such thinking lingered for centuries.

Reviewing the Lesson

Recalling Key Words, People, and Places
1. What is the name for a Spanish conqueror who came to the New World in search of gold?
2. Tell why it is important to remember:
   a. Christopher Columbus
   b. Vasco da Gama
   c. Ferdinand Magellan

Remembering Main Ideas
1. How had European sailing technology improved enough for exploration by the late 1400s?
2. Why would direct ocean trade routes to Asia have made trading more profitable for Europeans starting in the late 1400s?
3. What did Columbus say he found on the island of Hispaniola?

Thinking Things Over
Do you think it is accurate to say that European explorers *discovered* the New World? Explain your answer.

189

Lesson 2 An Age of Revolutions

LOOKING AHEAD As you read, look for—

Key words, people, and **places:**

revolution   John Locke
liberalism   Napoleon Bonaparte

Answers to these questions about **main ideas:**

1. How did the liberal ideas of John Locke influence views on government in America and Europe?
2. What were the causes and results of the American Revolution?
3. What were the causes and results of the French Revolution?

As the nations of Europe developed, new ideas about society and government began to grow. Some of these ideas led to revolutions in the Western world in the 1700s. A **revolution** is a major change that makes a difference in the lives of many people. Political revolutions often involve the overthrow of a government and replacement of it with another. The political revolutions of the 1700s were based on ideas of democratic government.

The first of these revolutions took place in North America. The first European one happened in France. The ideas that appeared in these revolutions eventually spread all over Europe and, later, much of the world.

Liberal Ideas

In several important ways, the American and French revolutions were based on the ideas of John Locke. Locke was an English philosopher of the 1600s who wrote about government. He wrote that people were born with certain rights, mainly life, liberty,

and property. When people set up a government, Locke said, they gave it the power to protect those rights. If a government failed to do this, it could be overthrown. Locke said all human beings were created free and equal. These beliefs made up the philosophy of **liberalism.**

The United States Constitution is the oldest written plan of government still in use today. It reflects some of Locke's ideas.

Locke's ideas influenced people in Europe and America. Phrases in the American Declaration of Independence echo Locke. For example, the Declaration states that among people's rights are "life, liberty, and the pursuit of happiness."

The American Revolution

The American Revolution occurred in the English colonies in North America. As you have read, England had explored and claimed large sections of North America. In the early 1600s, English people began to settle in North America and form colonies. Some settlers went to the colonies to find religious freedom. Others went to see if they could make a better living.

By the mid-1700s more than one million people lived in the English colonies in North America. By this time many American colonists had become unhappy with English rule. This feeling grew over time as liberal ideas spread among the colonists. Revolution broke out in 1775 because the colonists felt the English government did not care about their rights.

Between 1689 and 1763 England and France had fought a series of four wars for control of North America. England had won with much help from the colonists. The cost of war and the cost of defending the colonies were very great, however. King George III and Parliament passed a number of taxes to pay these costs. The colonists complained because they had not been given a voice in Parliament. They had not voted on whether to be taxed.

Some colonists said they only wanted to keep their rights as English citizens. Others said they wanted to form a new government along liberal ideas. In any case Americans won their freedom and set up a new government. In 1789 the new United States Constitution went into effect. It set up a government that was both a republic and a democracy. The Bill of Rights was soon added, promising many freedoms that English people had and that liberals wanted. Two of these freedoms are freedom of speech and religion.

The French Revolution

The French Revolution broke out in 1789. At that time most of the French people were very poor. A tiny fraction of people, the aristocrats and nobles, owned most of the land and wealth and paid few taxes. They lived in great luxury while many ordinary people were starving and owed heavy taxes. Middle-class French people felt this situation was most unfair. Liberal ideas and the example of the Americans became popular in France. Revolution was brewing.

In 1788 droughts and hailstorms destroyed much of France's crops. With little food and money, the poor people's plight grew even worse. The king, Louis XVI, was weak and unable to help. Louis's government itself had little money. Much of it had been spent by the nobles.

In desperation by 1789, Louis called a meeting in Paris of various groups of people from throughout France. Aristocrats, church officials, and middle-class people attended. The king soon lost control of the meeting, however, and the middle-class people decided to form their own National Assembly.

The National Assembly issued a Declaration of the Rights of Man. Here are some of the things the Declaration said: (1) All human beings are free and equal and may form any government they wish. (2) Governments are formed to protect people's liberty and property. (3) The law protects freedom to speak, write, and think what one wishes. (4) In court cases all people are innocent until proven guilty. These ideas became the basis of the French Revolution.

While the National Assembly was meeting, the poor people of Paris grew impatient. Riots broke out and disorder spread quickly. Eventually the National Assembly set up a constitutional monarchy and forced the king to accept it. The revolution did not end peacefully, however. The new government did not hold, and disorder and mob violence lasted into the 1790s. New leaders took over France. They had the king and

Linking Past and Present

Bastille Day

The French people have a holiday something like our Fourth of July. On July 14 France celebrates Bastille (ba-stēl') Day.

On that day in 1789, French crowds attacked the Bastille—a famous prison in Paris—and began tearing it down. The French Revolution was just beginning that summer. People hated the prison because their cruel government could and did lock men and women in there with little reason. The picture at left above shows the crowds storming the Bastille.

Today on Bastille Day, French citizens celebrate with music, dancing, and parades. You can see a modern Bastille Day celebration in the picture at right above. By celebrating Bastille Day, the French people remember the revolution and give thanks for their freedom.

French crowds burn symbols of their royal government in this 1793 scene. Leaders tried to adopt a new constitution that year, but it did not survive the violent revolution.

queen executed along with forty thousand other people. France had entered a "reign of terror."

Meanwhile, France was at war in Europe also. The war gave a popular young army general named Napoleon Bonaparte (bō′nə pärt) a chance to gain fame. In 1799 Napoleon seized power in France and set up his own government.

Napoleon's government was not really democratic. Nevertheless, the ideals of the French Revolution inspired many people in various countries. Middle-class people entered governments. Democratic ideas became popular. Belief in equality of opportunity, even for the poorest citizen, spread widely. These and other ideals led to more revolutions. By the twentieth century, many nations would have constitutional governments.

Reviewing the Lesson

Recalling Key Words, People, and Places

1. Identify the key words defined below:
   a. a major change that makes a difference in the lives of many people
   b. a popular eighteenth-century philosophy holding that people are born with freedom and equality, and that a government could be overthrown if it did not protect people's rights
2. Tell why these people were important:
   a. John Locke
   b. Napoleon Bonaparte

Remembering Main Ideas

1. How does the Declaration of Independence show the influence of Locke's liberalism?
2. What causes did the English colonists in North America have to be unhappy with their government in the 1700s?
3. What was the role of the National Assembly in the French Revolution?

Thinking Things Over

How were the American and French revolutions different? Were they alike in any ways? If so, in what ways? Support your answer with facts from this lesson.

Lesson 3   The Industrial Revolution

📖 **LOOKING AHEAD** As you read, look for—

Key words, people, and **places:**

imperialism
James Watt
Robert Fulton

Answers to these questions about **main ideas:**

1. How did the Industrial Revolution begin?
2. How did the Industrial Revolution grow?
3. How did the Industrial Revolution help lead to the growth of European imperialism?

If you had been born in England in 1760 and lived until the 1840s, you would have seen great changes in the ways people lived. In this period people began to switch from handmade to machine-made goods. Now goods could be made faster than before. Factories sprang up to meet the ever increasing demand for goods. People left rural areas by the thousands to seek jobs in the factories. Cities grew faster than ever before. In other words, changes in manufacturing caused people's lives to change. We say the changes in manufacturing were part of a kind of revolution in human history, the Industrial Revolution. If you think about it, you could say the Industrial Revolution still goes on today.

The Industrial Revolution Begins

Europeans had been making and using some kinds of machines since the 900s. Among the early machines were waterwheels and windmills. The force of the wind and water could grind grain and do other tasks. Later, in the 1300s, clocks were invented. Then came the printing press in the 1400s and many other inventions. However, most of the goods people used—cloth and furniture, for example—still were made by hand. In eighteenth-century England, this began to change.

The Industrial Revolution began in the textile industry. *Textile* is another word for cloth. In the early 1700s, textiles were produced mostly by farm families. Usually, women and children worked at spinning wheels and hand looms to make cloth. Merchants paid the families for each finished piece. Textile production was slow.

Europe's population continued to rise, so there was an increasing demand for clothing. Merchants wanted to speed up the cloth-making process. Inventions such as the flying shuttle and the spinning jenny helped.

The flying shuttle was a large loom, or weaving machine, that people used to weave yarns into cloth. The shuttle was a small, flat piece of wood that pulled a yarn through other rows of yarn, weaving cloth. The water-powered machine "threw" the shuttle faster than workers could guide it along by hand. The spinning jenny was a machine that spun several yarns at once from cotton or flax fibers. Earlier,

Women run powerful machines that spin yarns for textiles in this English factory scene of the 1700s.

hand-driven spinning wheels could spin only one yarn at a time.

These inventions helped bring about the factory system. It was easier to house the large new machines in factories and pay the workers to use the machines there. Under one roof, people now worked at huge water-powered machines for hours on end. The picture above shows these machines. By the late 1700s, England was producing and exporting large amounts of textiles.

Fast-flowing water to power the mills was not always available. By 1769 a Scottish scientist named James Watt had perfected a steam engine to help solve the problem of power for machines. Fueled by burning coal or wood, this engine used the steam of boiling water to drive other machines. By the late 1700s, steam engines were used widely in textile factories.

Steam engines soon were put to other uses. In 1807 an American named Robert Fulton built the first usable steamboat. In England in 1825, George Stephenson invented a practical steam locomotive, an engine used to pull trains. By 1829 the world's first railroad line joined the English factory towns of Manchester and Liverpool.

The Industrial Revolution Grows

England was the first industrial nation in the world and the most powerful in the 1800s. Because steam-powered factories could be built anywhere, they were set up in towns all over England. More and more people came to work in these towns.

Other nations wanted to industrialize as well. At first English factory owners did not tell other people how their machines worked. Industrial secrets were hard to keep, however. Some workers

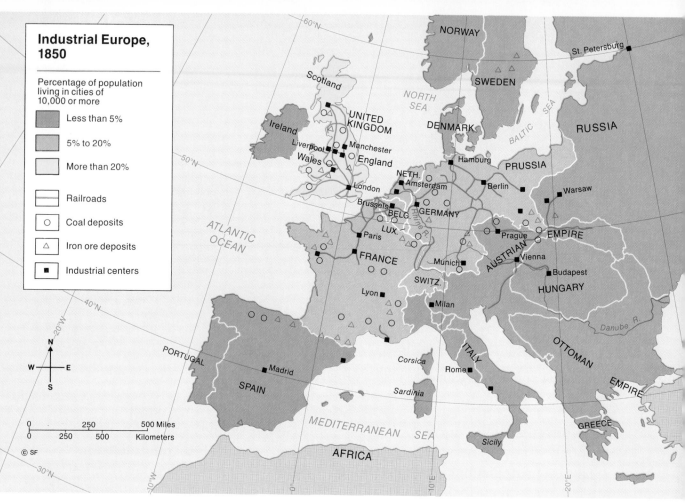

Industrial Europe, 1850

Percentage of population living in cities of 10,000 or more

- Less than 5%
- 5% to 20%
- More than 20%

	Railroads
O	Coal deposits
△	Iron ore deposits
■	Industrial centers

Map Study

In which European country did more than 20 percent of the population live in cities of 10,000 or more by 1850? What percentage of the population lived in such cities in Spain, Germany, and Italy? Now find the symbols besides color that the map uses. Did industrial centers usually have railroads?

left England and set up factories in other countries.

By 1850 the Industrial Revolution had reached the United States, France, Belgium, the Netherlands, Germany, and Switzerland. Rich reserves of iron ore and coal in these countries led to the growth of important steelmaking industries. Look at the map above. England still was the leading industrial nation at this time. What connection can you make between urban population and industrialization?

Up to the 1870s, industrial production was limited to a few fields such as textiles. After the 1870s greater changes took place. The first electric generating plant was built in England in 1881. Now electricity could be used to power factory machines. The internal combustion engine was invented in 1876, using fuel oil rather than steam.

Early railroads connected factory towns in England. Why do you think transportation was important to the Industrial Revolution?

It opened up new possibilities in transportation. In fact, the first automobile appeared in 1885. The possibilities for more inventions seemed endless. Meanwhile, the Industrial Revolution affected the way European governments acted in the world.

The Growth of European Empires

As you have read, Europeans began claiming overseas empires in the 1500s. Industrialization led to further expansion overseas. Industries needed lots of raw materials to turn into manufactured goods. Also, industries needed markets—opportunities for selling goods. European governments thought getting control of overseas places was the best way to help their industries. We call the control of a country's political and economic life by another country **imperialism.**

One way to get control of areas of the world was by setting up colonies. By the 1800s English colonies included India, Australia, New Zealand, large parts of Africa, and pieces of China.

France quickly followed England's lead in Africa and Asia, while the Netherlands took control of Indonesia and its rich sources of raw materials. Other European nations did the same. By the early 1900s, large parts of the world were colonies of industrial nations.

Reviewing the Lesson

Recalling Key Words, People, and Places
1. Tell what the word **imperialism** means.
2. Tell what contribution each of the following two people made to the Industrial Revolution:
   a. James Watt
   b. Robert Fulton

Remembering Main Ideas
1. How did such machines as the flying shuttle and the spinning jenny help bring about the Industrial Revolution?
2. What happened to England's towns as the Industrial Revolution grew?
3. How could imperialism help Europe's industries?

Thinking Things Over
Suppose you lived in England in the 1700s. You left a farm to take a factory job in a city. Tell how you think your life would have been changed by the move. Consider such things as your daily schedule, housing, and work.

Understanding Distortion on Maps

Europeans of the 1500s made maps of the lands that explorers visited in the New World. Like modern mapmakers, the mapmakers of the past needed a great deal of knowledge and skill to make their maps. Why is this true?

Problems with Flat Maps of the Round Earth

The earth is round like a ball. Any round object is a sphere. Because a globe also is a sphere, it can show the surface of the earth accurately. On globes, the shapes and sizes of land and water areas are accurate. Distances (to scale) and directions also are accurate.

An important fact about a sphere is that its surface cannot be perfectly flattened out. You can perform an experiment to prove this. Cut an orange in half and remove the peel. If you try to flatten out one of the half peels, part of it will stretch or break.

Mapmakers have a similar problem. No matter how hard they try, they cannot make true likenesses of the round earth on a flat sheet of paper—that is, on a map. They have to "stretch" and "cut" their maps just as you have to stretch and break an orange peel to make it lie flat.

When just a small part of the earth's surface is shown on a flat map, the map can be almost as accurate as a globe. However, when a large country, a continent, or the whole earth is shown on a flat map, distortion results. One or more of the following features will be distorted: size, shape, direction, or distance. Any flat map that shows parallels and meridians is called a **map projection.** Different kinds of projections can be drawn to show different features accurately. Each kind of projection shows at least one feature of the earth accurately.

Understanding the Mercator Projection

A Flemish mapmaker named Gerardus Mercator [jə rär′dəs mər-kā′tər] developed the Mercator projection during the 1500s. A Mercator projection shows the correct shape of land and water areas and the true, straight-line direction between any two places. Such maps can be useful for air and sea navigation even today, even though latitudes and longitudes are longer than they should be as you move away from the Equator.

On Mercator maps, therefore, some distances are distorted. For instance, lands far from the Equator appear much larger than they really are. Compare the sizes of Greenland and

Mercator Projection

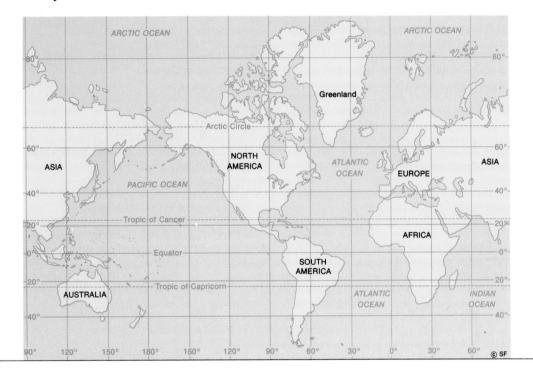

South America on the Mercator projection on this page with their undistorted sizes on a globe. You will see that on the Mercator projection, Greenland looks larger than South America. On a globe, however, you see that Greenland really is about one-eighth the size of South America.

A good map reader compares a map with a globe to see how the map distorts reality. Another good way to check distortion is to study the map's arrangement of parallels and meridians. Keep the following rules in mind.

On a globe (with no distortions):
1. All meridians meet at the poles.
2. All parallels are exactly parallel to one another.
3. Parallels vary in length.
4. All meridians are the same length.

Skills Practice

Apply the rules above to the Mercator map. Number your paper from 1 to 4. If the Mercator map breaks a rule, write *distortion* beside the number. If the map does not break a rule, write *no distortion*.

Chapter 8 Review

Chapter Summary

Lesson 1 Exploring the World—
Spurred by desire for trade goods and by improvements in ocean navigation, European explorers set sail in the 1500s. Spain claimed riches in southern North America. England and France settled areas farther north.

Lesson 2 An Age of Revolutions—
New liberal ideas about society and government were largely responsible for the American and French revolutions of the 1700s. American colonists won their war and set up a new government under the Constitution. A "reign of terror" resulted in Napoleon Bonaparte seizing power in France in 1799.

Lesson 3 The Industrial Revolution—
The Industrial Revolution began in the textile industry in England in the 1700s. Large factories were built and people moved from rural areas to work in them. To obtain raw materials and markets for goods, European countries took control of large parts of Africa and Asia.

Write your answers on a separate sheet of paper.

Testing Key Words, People, and Places

Part A
Give the definition of each key word.
1. **conquistador**
2. **revolution**
3. **liberalism**
4. **imperialism**
5. **map projection**

Part B
In a sentence, tell why each person is important.
1. Christopher Columbus
2. Ferdinand Magellan
3. John Cabot
4. Jacques Cartier
5. Napoleon Bonaparte
6. James Watt
7. Robert Fulton

Testing Main Ideas

Choose the answer that best completes each sentence.
1. In the 1500s Europeans could sail to faraway lands because of
   a. ships made of iron.
   b. new navigation tools.
   c. new maps of Columbus's routes east of Europe.
2. Europeans wanted to find sea routes to Asia so they could
   a. control trade and thus become wealthy.
   b. prove that there was no land route to Asia.
   c. force the Asians out of Asia.
3. The American and French revolutions were based on the ideas of
   a. Napoleon Bonaparte.
   b. Jacques Cartier.
   c. John Locke.
4. One effect of the French Revolution in other countries was that
   a. democratic ideas became popular.
   b. more upper-class people entered governments.
   c. belief in inequality grew popular.

5. The Industrial Revolution grew when factories began to use
   a. horsepower.
   b. human muscle power.
   c. steam power.
6. Industrialization led to
   a. European towns growing into large cities.
   b. farm families doing more cloth production.
   c. less interest in controlling places overseas.

Testing Skills

1. Understanding distortion on maps. Write a paragraph comparing the Mercator map (right) with the corresponding part of a globe. Which features—size, shape, direction, or distance—are distorted on the map? Which are not?
2. Making a chart. Make a chart that shows, for each explorer you read about in this chapter, the country for which the explorer sailed, when the explorer sailed, and what lands he explored. Use information from your textbook, from encyclopedias, and from other sources as necessary.

Activities

1. Report to the class on the life of James Watt. Ask your librarian for help in finding information about him. Find or draw a picture of his steam engine to include in your report.

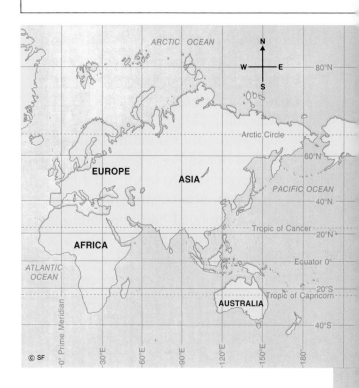

Mercator Projection

2. Read *Growing Up During the Industrial Revolution* by Penny Clarke (David and Charles, 1980). Write a paragraph on one of these two topics:
   • "Why I would like to have lived during the Industrial Revolution."
   • "Why I would not like to have lived during the Industrial Revolution."

Biography — Queen Elizabeth I

"I have desired to have the obedience of my subjects by love and not by compulsion [force]," Queen Elizabeth I once said. Guns boomed, church bells rang, people cheered, and children threw flowers before her as she traveled to the palace in London to become Queen of England in 1558.

Indeed her subjects grew to love her. She laughed loudly when someone amused her. She became furious when someone annoyed her. She shouted at bishops, threw slippers at diplomats, and even slapped an adviser.

Queen Elizabeth could dance all night and hunt all day, yet she spent hours and hours ruling her country.

Elizabeth was very intelligent and loved to learn. She spoke not only English but also Italian, Spanish, and French. She wrote Latin and Greek in beautiful handwriting.

When Elizabeth became queen in 1558 at the age of twenty–five, England had many problems. England was at war with France, there was not enough money in the royal treasury to run the country, and people were arguing over whether England should be a Roman Catholic or a Protestant country. Elizabeth ended the war, got England's finances back in order, and established the Church of England, making England primarily a Protestant country.

In 1588 the king of Spain decided to invade England and conquer the country. He sent a huge fleet of great warships, called the Spanish Armada, into the English Channel. However, Elizabeth's navy had faster and better-armed ships and defeated the Spanish.

Under Elizabeth's rule, England became the strongest country in the world and began building a colonial empire. England also became the Northern Renaissance center for poetry, music, writing, and learning.

Good Queen Bess, as her subjects sometimes called her, died in 1603. She had become one of the most famous rulers, and the most successful woman ruler, in history. She had done so much and was so admired that the 1500s became known as the Elizabethan Age.

Questions to Think About

1. How did Queen Elizabeth's strong leadership result in success for England?
2. How, do you think, did Queen Elizabeth help the growth of England as a nation?

202

The Search for the Northwest Passage

Beginning in the late 1490s, the Dutch, French, and English began their search for a sea passage through North America. This passage was called the Northwest Passage. As the map shows, such a passage does exist. However, nobody succeeded in sailing from one end of the passage to the other until 1906. Why is this so?

First, explorers faced a large, un-mapped maze of bays, straits, and is-lands. Many of the waterways turned out to be dead ends. For example, trace the route of Henry Hudson on the map below. Where did his route end? Did Hudson find the waterway that led to the Pacific Ocean?

Second, many explorers died in the cold climate of the far north. Much of the land is frozen year round. Ice floes, large sheets of floating ice, block the waters and prevent the passage of ships. In winter, many explorers were trapped when the water froze around their ships. As late as 1847, the men led by the English explorer, Sir John Franklin, died from the bitter cold and the lack of warm clothing.

Using Your Geography Skills

1. Look at the map below. What strait marks the end of Amundsen's route through the Northwest Passage?
2. Near which island did Franklin's journey come to an end?
3. Which explorer looked for the Northwest Passage south of the Arctic Circle?

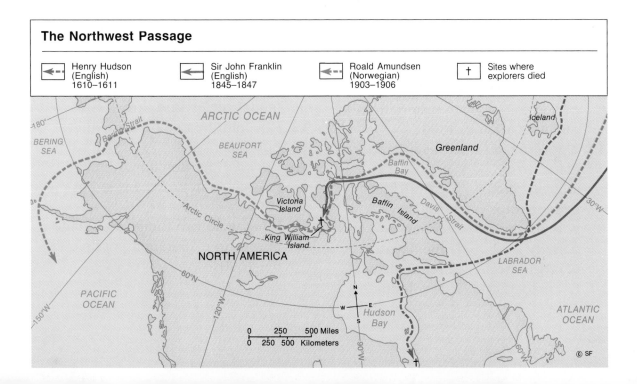

The Northwest Passage

Henry Hudson (English) 1610–1611

Sir John Franklin (English) 1845–1847

Roald Amundsen (Norwegian) 1903–1906

† Sites where explorers died

ARCTIC OCEAN   Iceland

BERING SEA   Bering Strait   BEAUFORT SEA   Baffin Bay   Greenland

Victoria Island   Baffin Island   Davis Strait

Arctic Circle   King William Island

NORTH AMERICA   LABRADOR SEA

PACIFIC OCEAN   60°N   Hudson Bay   ATLANTIC OCEAN

0 250 500 Miles
0 250 500 Kilometers

© SF

Unit 2 Review

Write your answers on a separate sheet of paper.

Key Words
Match each definition with the correct key word in the list.

1. a government run by the citizens who live under it
2. a writing system with thousands of small pictures
3. a belief in only one God
4. a government in which citizens elect representatives to lead them
5. a period of new interest in something, such as art and learning
6. a city and its surrounding land, which act together as a nation
7. an advanced culture based on city living
8. a major change that makes a difference in the lives of many people
9. a god or goddess
10. a group of government advisers
11. a word for the Middle Ages, the period of European history from about A.D. 500 to 1350
12. a government ruled by an upper class

a. civilization	g. democracy
b. cuneiform	h. senate
c. monotheism	i. republic
d. deity	j. medieval
e. city-state	k. renaissance
f. aristocracy	l. revolution

Main Ideas
Answer these questions.

1. How did the increase in food production affect early Mesopotamian society?
2. What was one accomplishment of the Babylonians? the Phoenicians?
3. What was ancient Egyptian religion like?
4. What things are known about the Indus valley civilization? What things are not known?
5. How was Indo-European society layered?
6. What characterized the Greek culture developed by the Mycenaeans?
7. What might a person see and hear at the Acropolis in Athens in the 400s B.C.?
8. What lands did Alexander the Great conquer?
9. How did the government of the Roman Republic work?
10. What ideas did Jesus teach?
11. What was the organization of feudal society in Europe like?
12. How did the rise of Islam affect Europe?
13. How did the Roman Catholic Church come to be divided in the 1500s?
14. What were two things that made European exploration possible in the 1500s?

15. How were the American and French revolutions alike and different?

16. How did the Industrial Revolution lead to the growth of imperialism?

Skills

1. **Using primary and secondary sources.** Which of the following is a primary source? a secondary source? Give reasons for your answers.
   a. Sumerian clay tablets with cuneiform
   b. Hammurabi's Code, translated into English
   c. a newspaper article about an Egyptian pharaoh
   d. the *Rig-Veda*

2. **Remembering main ideas.** Early civilizations followed a similar pattern of development. Put the events below in order in a chart to show the pattern of development from the earliest stage to the latest stage. Give your chart a title.
   - Farming villages develop in river valleys.
   - People live by hunting, fishing, and gathering.
   - City populations develop a form of government and a writing system and organize into social classes.
   - Villages grow, and people begin to specialize in different jobs.
   - Farming begins.

3. **Using latitude and longitude.** Write the letters A through F on your paper. Give the approximate latitude and longitude of each of the points shown on the globe below. Write the locations correctly—20°S, 40°E, for example.

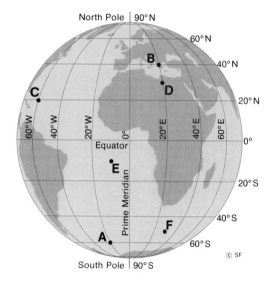

Essay

Review the characteristics of a civilization. Then choose one of the groups below. Write an essay that tells why the culture of this group can be called a civilization.

Sumerians   Egyptians
Babylonians   Greeks
Phoenicians   Romans

Europe and the Soviet Union Political

International boundaries
⊛ National capitals
• Other cities

1,000 Miles
Kilometers
1,000
500
500
0

© SF

Europe and the Soviet Union

The people of Europe and the Soviet Union have cultural, economic, and political ties that go back to their ancient ancestors. However, Europe and the Soviet Union differ from one another in many ways.

In this unit you will learn about the geography and history of Europe and the Soviet Union. You will see how the people are tied together, yet differ from one another.

Before You Go On

Preview the unit. Without looking at the map, how many European countries can you name?

Study the map. How does the size of the Soviet Union compare with the size of the other countries on the map?

Chapter 9   **The Land and the People of Europe and the Soviet Union**

Chapter 10   **From Past to Present in Europe and the Soviet Union**

Chapter 11   **The Countries of Western Europe Today**

Chapter 12   **The Countries of Eastern Europe Today**

Chapter 13   **The Soviet Union Today**

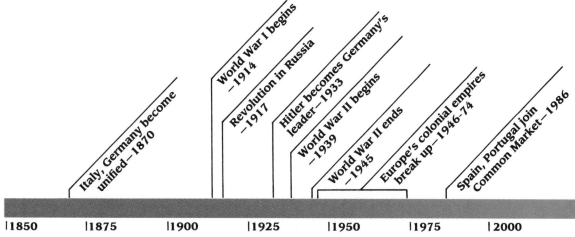

Italy, Germany become unified—1870

World War I begins —1914

Revolution in Russia —1917

Hitler becomes Germany's leader—1933

World War II begins —1939

World War II ends —1945

Europe's colonial empires break up—1946-74

Spain, Portugal join Common Market—1986

|1850 |1875 |1900 |1925 |1950 |1975 |2000

The Land and the People of Europe and the Soviet Union

Water bodies are very important to Europeans. They use rivers to carry people and goods, to produce electric power, and to bring water to factories and fields. The picture shows one way that seas and oceans have helped Europeans. They have provided excellent harbors.

As you read this chapter, you will learn about the water, land, climate, and vegetation of Europe and the Soviet Union. You will learn about the region's natural resources and land use. You also will learn about the people. The lessons in the chapter are listed below.

Lesson 1 The Natural Environment of Europe and the Soviet Union

Lesson 2 Resources and Land Use in Europe and the Soviet Union

Lesson 3 The People of Europe and the Soviet Union

Lesson 1 The Natural Environment of Europe and the Soviet Union

LOOKING AHEAD As you read, look for—

Key words, people, and **places:**

natural environment
peninsula
erosion
permafrost
steppe

Scandinavian Peninsula
Iberian Peninsula
Apennines
Pyrenees
Alps
West Siberian Plain
Siberia
Carpathian Mountains

Answers to these questions about **main ideas:**

1. What are the main landforms and water bodies of Western Europe?
2. What are Western Europe's climate and vegetation like?
3. What are the main landforms and water bodies of Eastern Europe and the Soviet Union?
4. What are the climate and vegetation of Eastern Europe and the Soviet Union like?

The physical setting of a place is called its **natural environment.** Landforms, climate, natural vegetation, and natural resources are the four main parts of a place's natural environment. Partly because of the continent's natural environment, European countries have become some of the wealthiest and most powerful in the world.

Land and Water of Western Europe

The Eurasian landmass is enormous. At the western end of this landmass is Europe. By looking at the map on this page, you can see that Europe can be divided into three regions: Western Europe, Eastern Europe, and the European part of the Soviet Union. Name the countries of Eastern Europe, using the map on page 206.

The official name for the Soviet Union is the Union of Soviet Socialist Republics (USSR). Part of the USSR lies in Asia. The Asian part of the Soviet Union stretches across the entire length of that continent.

Map Study

The map shows the three regions of Europe. Which covers more land, Western or Eastern Europe?

Europe: Three Regions

209

Five pieces of Western Europe's land are surrounded by water on all sides but one. These pieces of land are called **peninsulas.** One of the largest peninsulas is the Scandinavian Peninsula. Norway and Sweden are on it. Spain and Portugal make up a second peninsula called the Iberian (ī bir′ē ən) Peninsula. A third peninsula—the Apennine (ap′ə nīn) Peninsula—contains the country of Italy. This peninsula gets its name from the Apennines, a mountain range that runs down the center of the peninsula. The other two peninsulas are small. Denmark occupies one peninsula and Greece the other. Find these five peninsulas on the map on these pages.

Islands also are a part of Western Europe. Great Britain, Ireland, and Iceland are the three largest islands. Look again at the map on these pages. Name some of Western Europe's other islands. Most of these islands are in the Mediterranean Sea.

One of Europe's most striking features is the North European Plain. On the map on these pages, trace this plains region from France all the way to the Soviet Union.

Plateau and hill regions are found in central Spain, southern France, and parts of West Germany. The Pyrenees (pir′ə nēz′), a mountain range, separate Spain from France. The beautiful Alps, Europe's highest mountains, run from eastern France through Switzerland, southern West Germany, Austria, and northern Italy.

Most of the great rivers of Western Europe begin in the plateau or

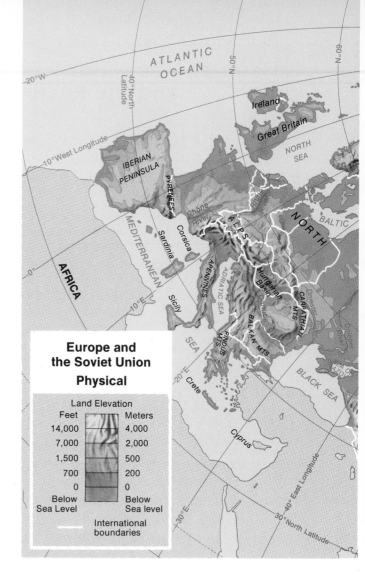

Europe and the Soviet Union Physical

Land Elevation

Feet		Meters
14,000		4,000
7,000		2,000
1,500		500
700		200
0		0
Below Sea Level		Below Sea level

International boundaries

mountain regions. On the map on these pages, use your finger to trace such great rivers as the Rhine, the Danube, and the Rhone.

Climate and Vegetation of Western Europe

Most Western European countries have warmer climates than do places in North America at the same latitudes. The warmer climates result from the North Atlantic Drift, a huge current of ocean water. This current brings warmth from the tropics to the coasts

Map Study

Landforms and water bodies in Europe and the Soviet Union include peninsulas, islands, seas, and rivers. Find the Iberian, Scandinavian, and Kola peninsulas. Which is largest? Find 10°W. Moving east, to what degree of longitude does Eastern Europe extend?

of Europe. Locate the North Atlantic Drift on the map on page 45.

Look at the climate map on pages 36–37. Notice that almost all of Western Europe has a cool, wet climate. Compare the natural vegetation map on pages 38–39 with the climate map. Which two types of forests occur in the cool, wet climate region of Western Europe? Today large areas of forest are found mainly on mountains. In lower areas people have cut down trees over the centuries to clear the land for farming and cities.

The warmest European climate is near the Mediterranean Sea. Almost all the trees in this region, which has one dry season, have been cut down. Trees hold moisture in the soil with their roots. When trees were cut from the Mediterranean hillsides, winter rains washed away part of the topsoil. The wearing away of land by water, wind, or ice is called **erosion.** Near the Mediterranean Sea, erosion has made the soil poorer for farming.

Smaller climate regions in Western Europe include the climate of northern Italy, which is warm and wet all year. The Alps have a high mountain climate, and most of the Scandinavian Peninsula and Finland have cold, wet climates.

The coast of Norway curves into many deep harbors. How many boats can you find in the picture?

Land and Water of Eastern Europe and the Soviet Union

Plains make up more than half the land of Eastern Europe and the Soviet Union. Land in East Germany, Poland, and the western part of the Soviet Union is part of the North European Plain. East of the Ural Mountains, which divide the European part from the Asian part of the Soviet Union, lies the West Siberian Plain. It is part of a vast area called Siberia. Plains also cover much of Hungary, northern Yugoslavia, and eastern Romania.

Three great rivers cut into the plain of the Soviet Union west of the Ural Mountains. These three rivers are the Don, the Dnieper (nē′pər), and the Volga. East of the Urals, the main rivers are the Ob, the Yenisey (yen′ə sā′) and the Lena.

Hills and mountains cover parts of Eastern Europe and the Soviet Union. The Carpathian Mountains run across Romania and part of Czechoslovakia (chek′ə slō vä′kē ə). Southern Yugoslavia, Albania, and Bulgaria are also hilly or mountainous.

Other mountains, as well as hills and plateaus, lie farther east in Asia. Look at the map on pages 210–211. Notice that the southern border of the Soviet Union is framed by a series of mountain ranges.

The Soviet Union has thousands of miles of coastline. However, most of the coastline is above the Arctic Circle, along icebound waters. The coasts of the Black Sea and the Baltic Sea—which are not icebound—have most of the Soviet Union's seaports.

What's in a Name?

The names and nicknames of many places in Europe tell you something about their geography. For example, Ireland is known as the "Emerald Isle" because it has abundant rainfall and so the grass is bright green. Does the picure of Ireland remind you of the color of emeralds?

The Black Forest in West Germany contains millions of pine trees that stand close together. As a result, the forest floor is dark and gloomy.

People call northern Norway the "Land of the Midnight Sun." In this area far above the Arctic Circle, the sun shines 24 hours a day during May, June, and July.

Climate and Vegetation of Eastern Europe and the Soviet Union

The southern part of Eastern Europe has a warm climate with one dry season. Most other parts of Eastern Europe have cool climates that are wet all year. Broadleaf deciduous and mixed forests are the natural vegetation within most of Eastern Europe.

The climate region farthest north in the Soviet Union is cold and dry all year. Its vegetation is tundra. In the summer the surface of the frozen earth thaws. A few feet down, though, the land remains frozen. This frozen layer of land is called **permafrost.**

Just south of the cold, dry climate in the Soviet Union is a climate that is cold and wet all year. In this climate the winters are cold. The summers are usually cool, but in some places, summers are warm. The natural vegetation consists mostly of needleleaf forests. At the southern edge of the cold climate region, grasses or mixed forests grow.

South of the cold climates in the Soviet Union are two cool climate regions. One cool climate is semi-dry. Its vegetation is mainly short grasses. This region is called the **steppe.** South of the steppe, around the Caspian Sea, the climate is drier still. This is a region of desert vegetation.

Reviewing the Lesson

Recalling Key Words, People, and Places
1. Identify the key words defined below:
   a. a piece of land surrounded by water on all sides but one
   b. the wearing away of the land by water, wind, or ice
   c. land, a few feet below the surface, that is always frozen
2. Tell where each place is located:
   a. Apennines
   b. West Siberian Plain

Remembering Main Ideas
1. Where do mountain ranges occur in Western Europe?
2. Why do most Western European countries have warmer climates than places in North America at the same latitudes?
3. Why are most seaports in the Soviet Union found along the coasts of the Black Sea and the Baltic Sea?
4. What are the main climate regions in the Soviet Union?

Thinking Things Over
Which landforms and rivers are found in both Western and Eastern Europe?

213

Lesson 2   Resources and Land Use in Europe and the Soviet Union

LOOKING AHEAD As you read, look for—

Key words, people, and **places:**

Hungarian Basin
Fertile Triangle

Answers to these questions about **main ideas:**

1. What crops and animals do farmers raise in Western Europe?
2. How do Western Europeans use their forests, mines, and fishing grounds?
3. What crops and animals do farmers raise in Eastern Europe and the Soviet Union?
4. Besides farming, how else do the people of Eastern Europe and the Soviet Union use their land?

Until the 1800s, most people in Europe were farmers living in small villages. Most of the land was farmland or forests. Today much farmland and some forests can still be found, but cities and suburbs have increased in size and importance.

Farming in Western Europe

Look back to the map on pages 64–65. Notice that Western Europeans use their land mostly for two kinds of economic activity. One of these activities is manufacturing and commerce. The other major economic activity is commercial farming. The amount of land used for farming and the kinds of crops and animals raised vary from place to place in Western Europe.

In southeastern Great Britain, where the land is mostly flat, farmers raise wheat and other crops. In the north and west of Britain, where the land is hilly, farmers raise grazing animals such as sheep and dairy cattle. If you were to drive through this part of Britain, you would see flocks of sheep, often herded by black-and-white dogs. Ireland is much the same, and wool is an important product of that country.

The Scandinavian Peninsula and Switzerland have little good farmland and short growing seasons. In these areas farmers raise sheep and dairy cattle. Norway manufactures woolen clothing. Switzerland is famous for its cheese.

On the European mainland, the best farmland is on the North European Plain. France is the main agricultural producer in the area. However, Denmark is famous for its dairy products and bacon. Dutch farmers produce flower bulbs, seeds, and garden plants. The farmers of West Germany grow grain, potatoes, and sugar beets.

Near the Mediterranean Sea, people grow such farm crops as olives and grapes. Olive oil is one of the area's most important products. Goats and sheep are the animals most often raised for both cheese and meat.

Forests, Mines, and Fisheries in Western Europe

Forests cover many of the mountains of Western Europe. For example, about seven-tenths of the Scandinavian Peninsula and Finland are forested. In these areas, lumbering is very important. Much of the world's timber and wood pulp come from Sweden and Finland.

Mining also is important in Western Europe. Great Britain and part of West Germany and eastern France produce large amounts of coal. Oil from the North Sea has become a major product of Great Britain and Norway.

The seas that border Western Europe have long been harvested for their fish. These seas have fed Europeans for many centuries. Some of the fish caught in these waters is exported around the world. Check your supermarket and you probably will find frozen fish from Iceland, for example.

Farming in Eastern Europe and the Soviet Union

As in Western Europe, Eastern Europe's best farmland is on its plains regions. Poland's part of the North European Plain has mainly sandy soil in which rye and potatoes are grown. Farther south, the Hungarian Basin is the plains region with the best cropland in Eastern Europe. Corn, wheat, and vegetables grow well in Hungary's rich soil.

Linking Past and Present

Cleaning Up the Ruhr Valley

One of the ugliest places on earth used to be the Ruhr Valley in the eastern part of West Germany. The sky was gray, filled with soot and smoke. Children who lived there got lung and bone diseases because of the dirty air. As one steel-plant manager said, "You can taste the Ruhr air." The river was even more polluted than the air. Almost no fish could live in the Ruhr River.

Finally, the people of the Ruhr Valley decided to make the valley look the way it had before the Industrial Revolution. As you can see in the picture, their clean-up job was a success. Today, people boat, fish, and swim in the Ruhr

River. Green parks and new housing developments lie along the riverbanks. Blue skies once again are part of the Ruhr Valley.

Eastern Europe's mountains are used for grazing. Sheep are raised at higher altitudes. Cattle are raised lower down the slopes.

Most people in the Soviet Union live in an area called the Fertile Triangle. Find this area on the map on page 206 by tracing a triangle with your finger. Start from Leningrad in the north and trace a line to Odessa in the southwest. Then move your finger to Novosibirsk (nō′vō sə bersk′) in Siberia and back to Leningrad. Most Soviet farmland is found in this Fertile Triangle. Farmers here grow mostly wheat, corn, beets, barley, and sunflowers.

To the north and east of the Fertile Triangle, nomadic herding is important. To the south of the Fertile Triangle are ranches and small farms. Farms in this area need irrigation. Near the Black Sea, where the climate is warm and rainfall is plentiful, farmers grow oranges, lemons, grapes, and other fruits.

Other Land Use in Eastern Europe and the Soviet Union

The people of Eastern Europe and the Soviet Union make use of many natural resources other than farmland. Coal mining is a major economic activity in East Germany, Czechoslovakia, and part of Poland. Romania has one of the world's largest oil fields. Yugoslavia uses its forests to make wood products.

The Soviet Union has by far the largest amount of mineral resources among the nations of Eurasia. Vast coal and iron deposits are found there. So are rarer minerals such as chromium—

Steel is turned into trucks at a factory in the Soviet Union.

used for making high-quality steel—and diamonds.

Mineral deposits are one reason the Soviet Union has become a leading industrial nation in this century. Drawing on the nation's vast natural resources, Soviet factories today turn out steel, chemicals, heavy machinery, clothing, and many other products. Only the United States produces more manufactured goods.

Reviewing the Lesson

Recalling Key Words, People, and Places
Tell why it is important to remember:
1. Hungarian Basin
2. Fertile Triangle

Remembering Main Ideas
1. What crops and animal products do farmers on the North European Plain produce?
2. What two main products do Western Europeans get from the North Sea?
3. What do farmers in the Soviet Union's Fertile Triangle grow?
4. What resources helped the Soviet Union industrialize?

Thinking Things Over
What kinds of occupations do you think most Europeans have? Give reasons for your answer.

Lesson 3   The People of Europe and the Soviet Union

LOOKING AHEAD As you read, look for—

Key words, people, and **places:**

tradition   Slavs
language family
ethnic group

Answers to these questions about **main ideas:**

1. How are people from various Western European countries alike and different?
2. How are the ethnic groups in Eastern Europe and the Soviet Union alike and different from each other?

If you were to travel through Europe and the Soviet Union, you would see that Europeans share many things. Everywhere you would find large cities with tall buildings. Television antennas rise from rooftops, and people go to movies and ball games. Many young people wear blue jeans.

However, each European nation has a different culture from the others. Also, a single nation may have different cultural groups within it. The cultural differences among Europeans are based partly on **traditions**—beliefs and customs handed down from generation to generation.

The People of Western Europe

People in Western Europe have many things in common. For example, most of them speak languages based on the ancient Indo-European language. Many of the words in Western European languages are the same, even though some of the letters might be different. Languages that have a common ancestor belong to the same **language family.**

Most Western Europeans are Christians. In general, they follow one of two different forms of that faith. In southern Europe, most people are Roman Catholic. In northern areas most people are Protestant. The map on page 218 shows where Catholicism and Protestantism are most common. It also shows where members of two smaller religious groups—the Eastern Orthodox Christians and the Jews—are located. Compare the map with the map on page 206. In what country do many members of the Eastern Orthodox Church live?

In addition to language and religion, most people in Western Europe have similar art forms. For example, a piece of music or painting from any country of Western Europe could not be mistaken for music or painting from China. Literature and architecture also are much the same. All these arts tend to tie Western Europeans together.

At the same time, not everyone who lives in Western Europe does things the same way. In earlier centuries, before modern means of transportation

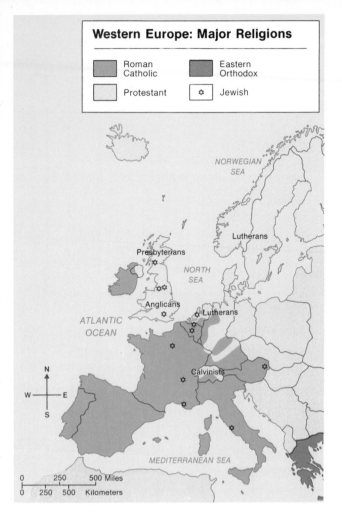

Western Europe: Major Religions

- Roman Catholic
- Eastern Orthodox
- Protestant
- Jewish

NORWEGIAN SEA

Lutherans

Presbyterians

NORTH SEA

Anglicans

Lutherans

ATLANTIC OCEAN

Calvinists

MEDITERRANEAN SEA

0   250   500 Miles
0   250   500 Kilometers

Map Study

What religion do most people in Western Europe follow? Compare this map with the map on page 206 to name the countries where Judaism is practiced.

and communication were invented, people were more isolated from one another. Thus, they developed different traditions. Favorite foods are one tradition that remains different in various parts of Western Europe. Celebrating different national holidays is another way in which Western Europeans differ from one another.

The People of Eastern Europe and the Soviet Union

Most people of Eastern Europe and the European part of the Soviet Union belong to the large ethnic group called Slavs. An **ethnic group** is a group whose members share the same cultural or racial background.

Various smaller ethnic groups make up the Slavs. The strongest link among different Slavs is language. Each Slavic group has its own language, but the speakers of one language often can understand the speakers of another. The Slavic language group is part of the Indo-European language family.

One difference among Slavic groups is their religion. The Slavs were converted to Christianity about a thousand years ago. About nine hundred years ago, the Catholic Church split in two. Western Slavs remained part of the Roman Catholic Church, headed by the Pope in Rome. Eastern Slavs became part of the Eastern Orthodox Church, which does not recognize the Pope as head of the church.

The Russians, who are a Slavic group, are the largest ethnic group in the Soviet Union. They make up more than half the population. Other Slavic groups make up an additional one-fifth of the Soviet population. Non-Slavic ethnic groups make up a little more than one-fourth of the population.

In the European part of the Soviet Union, non-Slavic ethnic groups live along the Baltic Sea in the east and near the Caucasus Mountains in the south. Each group uses its own

People from many different ethnic groups live in the Soviet Union.
These people from Soviet Central Asia speak different languages than
do Slavs in the Soviet Union.

language. The Baltic people mostly follow the Roman Catholic religion. In the
region of the Caucasus Mountains,
some groups have their own Eastern
Orthodox churches. The people of a
few ethnic groups are Muslims.

Far to the east, across the Urals, live
the various people of Soviet Central
Asia. They include many non-Slavic
ethnic groups. Most people in these
groups do not speak languages from
the Indo-European family, and Islam is
their religion. Their faith often makes
these people feel closer to Muslim
countries than to the rest of the Soviet
Union.

Reviewing the Lesson

Recalling Key Words, People, and Places
1. Identify the key words defined below:
   a. belief or custom handed down from generation to generation
   b. a group of languages with a common
   ancestor
   c. a group whose members share the same
   cultural or racial background
2. In what part of Europe do the Slavs live?

Remembering Main Ideas
1. What are the main religious groups in Western Europe?
2. What is the strongest link among different
   Slavic groups in Eastern Europe and the Soviet Union?

Thinking Things Over
Why might the Soviet Union be described as "a
world" rather than a country?

Making Generalizations from a Map

When you find a number of facts or examples that have something in common, you may be able to form a generalization about them. A generalization is a broad statement or rule that applies to many examples. As you study social studies, you can combine facts from different maps and from your reading to make generalizations.

Identifying Valid Generalizations

Look at the population distribution map of Europe below. Europe is the most densely populated continent in the world. When you look at the map, however, you can see that the population is not evenly distributed. Look at the key. What does each red dot symbolize? Some areas have so many people that the dots run together. Other areas have no dots. That means that fewer than 100,000 people live there.

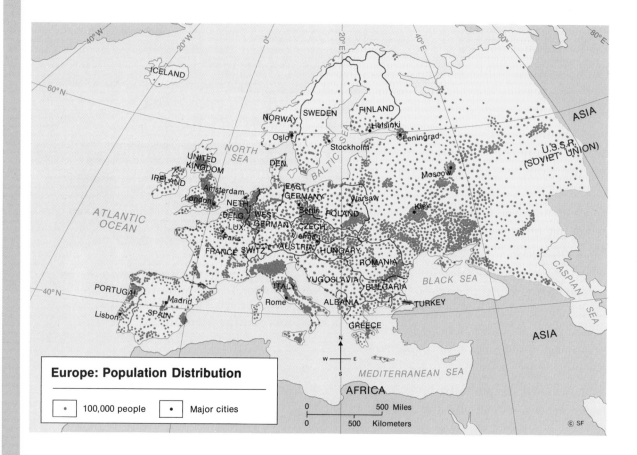

Europe: Population Distribution

| · | 100,000 people | • | Major cities |

Now let's look at some facts that you know about climate. You know that latitude affects climate. In general, climate becomes cooler the farther north or south of the Equator you go. Use these facts and what you see on the population distribution map to decide which of the following generalizations is valid.

A. No people live in the cold areas of Europe.

B. All Europeans choose to live in warm climates.

C. More Europeans choose to live in warm and cool climates than in cold climates.

Did you choose generalization C? C is the valid generalization. That is, it is the generalization that is best supported by the facts. Generalizations A and B are not valid because they use the words *no* and *all*. When you make generalizations of your own, you should avoid words such as *all, none, everyone,* and *always.* Instead, use words such as *more, often, generally,* and *usually.* By using such words, you make a generalization that can take into account the exceptions that most rules have.

Forming Generalizations

Now you are ready to make your own generalizations about why people choose to live where they do. Think about the following facts you learned about transportation in Europe:

1. Western Europe's coast provides it with many good harbors.
2. Europeans use rivers to carry people and goods, to manufacture electric power, and to supply water.

Look at the population distribution along Europe's coasts. Now look at the population distribution along the Rhine River. What generalization might you make that takes into account what you see? Your generalization might read something like this: More people choose to live in areas where nearby water can be used to provide transportation, to manufacture power, and to supply water.

Skills Practice

Number a separate sheet of paper from 1–3. Use the facts below and the population distribution map to make three generalizations about where people choose to live.

1. Erosion of the topsoil in the region near the Mediterranean Sea has left the land poor for farming. The soil in this area also is stony.
2. The Scandinavian Peninsula is covered by mountains. The Pyrenees Mountains separate Spain from France.
3. Great Britain, where the Industrial Revolution began, is highly industrialized. West Germany and France also have many industries.

Chapter Summary

Lesson 1   The Natural Environment of Europe and the Soviet Union—Partly because of the natural environment, Europe is wealthy and powerful. It lies at the western end of Eurasia, with a temperate climate. The European part of the Soviet Union borders Eastern Europe; the Asian part extends across Asia to the Pacific Ocean. Climates in the Soviet Union vary greatly.

Lesson 2   Resources and Land Use in Europe and the Soviet Union—Commercial farming, mining, and industry are important in Western Europe. The Soviet Union is rich in mineral resources and is a leading industrial nation.

Lesson 3   The People of Europe and the Soviet Union—Each country in Europe has its own distinct culture. Most languages are based on Indo-European. Most of the people practice Christianity. Most people in the Soviet Union are Slavs. Non-Slavs predominate in Soviet Central Asia, and most of them are Muslims.

Write your answers on a separate sheet of paper.

Testing Key Words, People, and Places

Part A

Match each definition with the correct key word in the list.

1. a group whose members share the same cultural or racial background

2. a cool climate region that is semi-dry with vegetation made up mainly of short grasses

3. land surrounded by water on all sides but one

4. a custom or way of doing things—literature, architecture, foods, national holidays—common to a people

5. the four main parts of a place consisting of landforms, climate, natural vegetation, and natural resources

6. a group of languages that have a common ancestor

7. the frozen layer of land a few feet below the surface

8. the wearing away of land by water, wind, or ice

   a. **natural environment**
   b. **peninsula**
   c. **erosion**
   d. **permafrost**
   e. **steppe**
   f. **tradition**
   g. **language family**
   h. **ethnic group**

Part B

In a sentence, tell why each person or place is important.

1. Scandinavian Peninsula
2. Iberian Peninsula
3. Apennines
4. Pyrenees
5. Alps
6. West Siberian Plain
7. Siberia
8. Carpathian Mountains
9. Hungarian Basin
10. Fertile Triangle
11. Slavs

Testing Main Ideas

Choose the answer that best completes each sentence.

1. Most people in Europe and the Soviet Union speak
   a. English.
   b. French.
   c. an Indo-European language.
2. Almost all countries of Western Europe have a
   a. cool, wet climate.
   b. hot, dry climate.
   c. tropical climate.
3. The warmest European climate is
   a. in France.
   b. in West Germany.
   c. by the Mediterranean Sea.
4. Most of the Scandinavian Peninsula is covered with
   a. grassland.
   b. forest.
   c. tundra.
5. Most of the Slavs in Europe live in
   a. Western Europe.
   b. Eastern Europe and the Soviet Union.
   c. the Iberian Peninsula.

Testing Skills

1. **Making generalizations from a map.** Based on the map on this page and what you have learned in the chapter, answer these questions.
   a. What parts of Western Europe have the most dense population?
   b. Why do you think people have chosen to live in these places?

Western Europe: Population Distribution

· 100,000 people

2. **Using latitude and longitude.** Give the definition of each term.
   a. Prime Meridian
   b. latitude and longitude

Activities

1. Write a letter to a friend describing what Siberia is like.
2. List the lands and cities through which either the Rhine River or the Danube River passes.

Chapter 10

From Past to Present in Europe and the Soviet Union

Europe and the Soviet Union have undergone great changes in the past. As you read this chapter, you will learn how several Western European nations formed in the 1800s. The picture shows a parade that celebrated the formation of Italy. You also will learn how boundaries in Eastern Europe changed in the 1800s and about the two world wars and the Russian Revolution of the 1900s. The lessons in the chapter are listed below.

Lesson 1 **Western Europe in the Nineteenth Century**

Lesson 2 **Eastern Europe and Russia in the Nineteenth Century**

Lesson 3 **Conflict and Change in the Twentieth Century**

Lesson 1   Western Europe in the Nineteenth Century

LOOKING AHEAD As you read, look for—

Key words, people, and **places:**

nationalism
autocrat
kaiser

Giuseppe Mazzini
Count Camillo Cavour

Giuseppe Garibaldi
Otto von Bismarck

Sardinia
Sicily
Prussia

Answers to these questions about **main ideas:**

1. How did nationalism lead to the development of new nations in Western Europe?
2. How did the Italian states become unified as one nation?
3. How did the German states become unified as one nation?

As you have read, the 1700s and 1800s were a time of great change in Europe. Revolutions and warfare were common. Also, the new technology of the Industrial Revolution began to change the way people lived and worked.

The Rise of Nationalism

As governments, jobs, and living conditions changed, people's ideas about the world changed also. In particular, three new ideas became very important in nineteenth-century Western Europe: liberalism, democracy, and nationalism. You learned about two of these ideas in Chapter 8. Liberalism was the idea that people were born with certain rights and should be free. In a democracy, the average person has a voice in the government.

The most powerful new idea spreading through Europe, however, was nationalism. **Nationalism** is the idea that people who are united by a common language, history, and tradition should form their own country. Nationalism is also the strong feeling of loyalty that people have toward their country.

The feeling of nationalism was especially strong among the Italian-speaking and German-speaking people of Western Europe. Much of their land was divided into small states, which were ruled by princes and kings. The boundaries of these states changed often. The rulers were **autocrats.** That is, they governed by themselves, without the consent of anyone else. In many small states, the rulers knew nothing of the language, history, or traditions of the people they ruled.

The Unification of Italy

In 1858 what is now Italy was a collection of small states. Local princes governed some of these states. Other states were ruled by the Roman Catholic Church. A foreign country, Austria, ran the government of several states in the northern part of the Apennine Peninsula. No nation of "Italy" existed.

Italian unity resulted mainly from the efforts of three leaders: Giuseppe Mazzini (jü zep'ā mät sē'nē), Count Camillo Cavour (kä mē'lō kä vür'), and Giuseppe Garibaldi (gar'ə bôl'dē). Mazzini was a writer whose works inspired young Italians to band together to try to form a unified, democratic nation.

Cavour was the leader of one of the most powerful states, Sardinia. Find Sardinia, an island off Italy's western coast, on the map on page 206. Sardinia took the lead in unifying Italy. Cavour obtained help from France and in 1859 defeated Austria in a war. In the peace treaty that followed, Austria agreed to allow one of its Italian states to unite with Sardinia. The remaining northern Italian states then successfully revolted against Austria and formed a union with Sardinia.

At this point Garibaldi came on the scene. He had already spent twelve years in South America, where he had fought for the independence of Uruguay from Spain. Garibaldi set out to defeat the Italian state called The Kingdom of the Two Sicilies. In May, 1860, Garibaldi anounced to his army of about 1,100 soldiers:

> I offer neither pay, nor quarters [housing], nor provisions [food]; I offer hunger, thirst, forced marches, battles and death. Let him who loves his country in his heart and not with his lips only, follow me.

Garibaldi conquered Sicily. Later, he joined forces with Cavour. They declared the Kingdom of the Two Sicilies united with the states ruled by Cavour. The next year, 1861, the Kingdom of Italy was organized. Its first monarch was the king of Sardinia. By 1870 all the states on the Apennine Peninsula had become part of the new nation of Italy.

The Unification of Germany

In the early 1800s, the future country of Germany was divided among thirty-nine states. The strongest of these states was Prussia. It had a powerful army and was feared by many of its neighbors.

Many Germans were nationalists, but the rulers of the German states were not willing to unite. That was left to the leader of Prussia, Otto von Bismarck. Bismarck did not like democracy. He believed in order and obedience to the authority of the government. Bismarck wanted to unify the German states, but he also wanted power for Prussia. He saw he could get that power by unifying the German states under Prussia's leadership.

With its powerful army, Prussia first drove out all the rulers of the northern German states. By 1867, all the states of northern Germany were united with Prussia.

Bismarck next turned his attention to the small states of southern Germany. Bismarck knew that many of these states were afraid of Prussia's power, but they were more afraid of France. So he made up a plan to force the southern German states into joining together with Prussia.

Bismarck's plan went like this: First, he would start a war with France. The

Bismarck unified Germany in a war with France.

war would put the southern states of Germany between two powerful armies. Bismarck figured that the southern states of Germany would rather choose to unite with Prussia than risk defeat by France.

In 1870 Bismarck carried out his plan, and it worked perfectly. The war between France and Prussia lasted only six months. Prussia won easily. All the remaining German states joined Prussia to form the German Empire. At its head was the emperor called the **kaiser**. The real builder of the new nation, however, was Bismarck.

Reviewing the Lesson

Recalling Key Words, People, and Places

1. Identify the key words defined below:
    a. the strong feeling of loyalty to a nation
    b. the title of Germany's emperor
2. Tell why it is important to remember:
    a. Giuseppe Garibaldi
    b. Otto von Bismarck

Remembering Main Ideas

1. What three ideas helped bring about changes in Western Europe in the 1800s?
2. How did Camillo Cavour help build the Italian nation?
3. How did wars result in the unification of Germany?

Thinking Things Over

Do you think nationalism is important in the United States today? Explain your answer.

Lesson 2   Eastern Europe and Russia in the Nineteenth Century

> **LOOKING AHEAD** As you read, look for—
>
> **Key words, people, and places:**
>
> | | |
> |---|---|
> | **tsar** | Mongols |
> | **exile** | Ivan the Great |
> | **socialism** | Alexander II |
> | **communism** | Alexander III |
> | | Karl Marx |
> | Magyars | |
> | Genghis Khan | Balkans |
>
> Answers to these questions about **main ideas:**
>
> 1. How did nationalism affect the Austrian Empire in the 1800s?
> 2. How did nationalism affect the Ottoman Empire in the 1800s?
> 3. What were the government and economy of the Russian Empire like in the 1800s?

Nationalism affected Eastern Europe as well as Western Europe. During the 1800s the eastern part of Europe was ruled by three large empires. These three empires were the Austrian Empire, the Ottoman Empire, and the Russian Empire.

The Austrian Empire

The Austrian Empire covered areas of both Western and Eastern Europe. The western part of this vast empire included lands that later became part of Italy and Germany. To the east, Austria reached to within 200 miles of the Black Sea. The emperor and other government officials of Austria spoke German. The empire itself, however, contained many groups. Each one had its own language and history.

Austria lost wars to both Italy and Prussia between 1859 and 1866. After these defeats, one ethnic group within Austria—the Magyars of the east—revolted against the emperor. The next year, Austria agreed to change the way the country was ruled. The Austrian emperor would still rule the country. However, the eastern part of the nation would be called Hungary. It would have its own official language and make some of its own laws. This satisfied the Magyars.

Many other groups within the empire were unhappy. They too wanted to be free. For instance, the Slavs in eastern Austria—Hungary—did not like being ruled by the Magyars any better than they liked being governed by the Austrians.

The Ottoman Empire

The Ottoman Empire was centered in Asia, where Turkey now stands. The empire's presence in Europe dated from the late 1400s, when Turks who had migrated from central Asia conquered the people of southeastern Europe. The area of Europe conquered by the Ottomans usually is called the Balkans because of the mountains nearby. Find the Balkan Mountains on the map on pages 210–211.

228

Like the Austrian Empire, the Ottoman Empire had many different ethnic groups within its borders. Many of these groups wanted to be independent of Turkish rule. The Greeks were the first group to win complete independence. After much bloodshed and help from other European countries, the independent country of Greece was formed in 1829.

With Greece as an example, other Balkan people began a long struggle for nationhood and freedom. Revolts against the Ottomans broke out all over the Balkans. By 1878, three new nations—Serbia, Romania, and Montenegro (mon′tə nē′grō)—won their independence from the Ottomans.

Problems in the Balkans continued, however. Nationalism led to several more wars in the region. Some of the wars were fought against the Turks, but sometimes the wars were between the different ethnic groups in the area. By 1914 the situation was so tense that the Balkans were known as "the powder keg of Europe." Everyone waited for the keg to explode.

The Russian Empire

A thousand years ago, only the people living in and around the city of Kiev called themselves Russians. Find Kiev, which sits near the Dnieper River, on the map on page 206.

In the 1200s Genghis Khan (jeng′gis kän′) led the Mongols into Russia and Eastern Europe. The Mongols were a warlike people who came from central Asia. Genghis Khan and the Mongols defeated the Russians in a brief but

Parades and festivals show Austrians' pride in their heritage.

bloody war. After the war, the Mongols allowed the local Russian princes to continue to rule their territories. However, the princes had to give a certain amount of their wealth to the Mongols each year.

In 1480, after more than 200 years of paying the Mongols, the Russians refused to pay any longer. The Mongols sent an army to Moscow. A Russian prince in that town, who later became known as Ivan the Great, defeated the Mongols. By the 1500s, the Russians finally had driven the Mongols out of Russia.

229

The Russians became the most powerful rulers in the area after they defeated the Mongols. Gradually, the Russian rulers, who now were known as **tsars,** began to conquer neighboring areas. By the 1600s, Russia had conquered much of Siberia. Over the next two centuries, the Russian Empire grew to include most of what is now the Soviet Union.

Autocracy in Russia. The Russian government was very autocratic. The tsar had absolute power over the country. He controlled all parts of government. He also used secret police to spy on the people. Anyone who openly disagreed with the tsar was killed or **exiled**—sent out of the country. Even the church and the wealthy landowners were under royal control. The Russian peasants were mainly serfs, like those of Western Europe during the Middle Ages. That is, they owned no land, had few rights, and were forced to work for wealthy landowners.

One tsar, Alexander II, admired the ideas of the French Revolution. He wanted to make Russia a freer nation and so avoid a revolution in the future. He said, "It is better to begin to abolish [do away with] serfdom from above than to wait for it to abolish itself from below." His many reforms included freeing the serfs from forced labor.

However, his son, Alexander III, who ruled from 1881 to 1894, was very autocratic. He crushed all political opponents. He ordered everyone, including the minority ethnic groups, to speak only Russian and to follow the Russian form of the Eastern Orthodox religion.

The Rise of Industry. Russia began to industrialize during the reigns of Alexander II and his son. Russia built many iron and steel plants, railroads, and oil refineries. By 1900 Russia was the world's fourth-largest iron and steel producer. It also produced half the world's oil.

Socialism and Communism. New ideas were influencing the Russian people in the 1800s and early 1900s. Many of these new ideas came from Western Europe. One idea was **socialism,** a theory about how the government and the economy should operate. Socialists believed that the government

Nicholas II, son of Alexander III, was the last tsar of Russia. He ruled from 1894 to 1917. With him are his wife and children.

should run the factories. The government also should decide how goods and services are distributed among the people. Socialists felt the government could best run the economy for the benefit of the workers and the country as a whole.

Socialists often split over how to achieve their goals. One small group of socialists followed the ideas of Karl Marx, a nineteenth-century German philospher. These ideas were known as **communism.** Most socialists believed democratic elections were the right way to carry out their ideas. The communists, however, believed the only way to bring about socialism was through violent revolution. Marx stated his views this way:

> 66 The Communists do not hide their views and aims. They openly declare that their ends can be attained only by the forcible overthrow of all existing social conditions. Let the ruling classes tremble at a Communist revolution. The proletarians [workers] have nothing to lose but their chains. They have a world to win. 99

A small number of Russians turned communist. They thought that communism was the best way to end the autocratic rule of the tsars. These communists began writing and organizing to overthrow the Russian government.

Reviewing the Lesson

Recalling Key Words, People, and Places
1. Identify the key words defined below:
   a. the title given to the ruler of the Russian Empire
   b. a philosophy that says socialism can come about only as a result of revolution
2. Tell why it is important to remember:
   a. Mongols
   b. Karl Marx

Remembering Main Ideas
1. What events led Austria to allow the Magyars to have their own government?
2. How did Greece become independent of the Ottoman Empire?
3. How did Alexander III rule Russia?

Thinking Things Over
How might the histories of the Austrian and Ottoman empires have been different if everyone in the empires had belonged to the same ethnic group?

231

Lesson 3   Conflict and Change in the Twentieth Century

LOOKING AHEAD As you read, look for—

Key words, people, and **places:**

military alliance
assassinate
soviet
depression
totalitarian
genocide

Bolshevik
Vladimir Lenin
Joseph Stalin
Adolf Hitler

Answers to these questions about **main ideas:**

1. How did World War I begin and end?
2. What happened in the Russian Revolution?
3. Where and how did totalitarian governments arise after World War I?
4. What were the major events of World War II?
5. How did Europe become divided after World War II?

The twentieth century has been a period of great political change in Europe and the Soviet Union. The 1900s have seen two world wars and a number of revolutions. Countries that were friends with one another became enemies and later became friends once again. This century also has seen the invention of atomic weapons. All these events have affected the way the people of Europe and the world live and think.

World War I

Between 1870 and 1914, the major countries of Europe struggled with each other for wealth and power. Outside of Europe, the European powers scrambled for territory. Belgium, France, Germany, Great Britain, and Italy took large areas of Africa and Asia as colonies. The Europeans gained control of these areas mainly by military force.

The European powers made **military alliances** among themselves. That is,

they each agreed to side with certain of the others in case of war. Germany, Austria, and the Ottoman Empire were on one side. They were known as the Central Powers. Great Britain, France, and Russia were on the other side. They were known as the Allied Powers. The smaller nations joined one side or the other. In 1914 the two groups became involved in a bloody war.

World War I began with a murder. Archduke Francis Ferdinand, the man who was to be the next Austrian emperor, was **assassinated**—killed for political reasons. The assassination took place in Sarajevo (sär′ə yä′vō), which was the capital of an Austrian province. Ferdinand's assassin was Gavrilo Princip, a young man who had lived in the Balkan country of Serbia. Austria blamed Serbia for the murder. Germany backed Austria. Russia supported Serbia. France supported Russia. The powder keg of the Balkans finally had exploded. Five weeks after the assassination, the two military alliances were at war.

The war lasted for four years. Millions of soldiers fought, and over 10 million died. In 1917 the United States entered the war, tipping the balance of power against Germany and its allies. By November, 1918, the war was over.

The winning countries punished Germany and Austria by taking large chunks of land away from them. Several new countries were carved from this land. Some of the territory for these new countries came from the Soviet Union, which had withdrawn from the war in 1917. Look at the maps below and see how borders changed after World War I. Which new countries were formed after the war?

The Russian Revolution

While World War I was going on, a revolution took place in Russia. The poor farm workers wanted land of their own. Factory workers wanted better pay. Educated people wanted some democracy. In addition, communists within Russia were pushing for violent change.

By 1917 life had become very hard for many people. They suffered from food shortages caused by World War I. Also, the Russian government did not seem to care about its people. For example, troops fighting in the war were not given enough weapons. As a result, the Russian army lost many battles,

Map Study

World War I resulted in many changes in the political boundaries of Europe. You can see these changes by comparing the two maps. From which three countries was Poland formed? Which country was formed from Montenegro, Serbia, and part of Austria-Hungary?

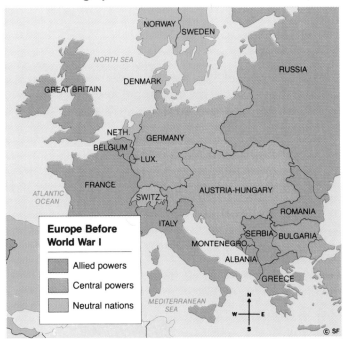

233

Soldiers attacked the tsar's police in Petrograd, now Leningrad, in the first days of the Russian Revolution.

and hundreds of thousands of soldiers were killed.

The Russian Revolution began in March, 1917, with riots by factory workers against the tsar's rule. The riots weakened the government. Some revolutionaries formed councils called **soviets** and took over parts of the government. They were joined by soldiers from the army. Soon the tsar was forced to step down as ruler of Russia.

For about eight months, the Russian government was in a state of confusion. Then, a small group called Bolsheviks (bōl′shə viks) seized power. The Bolsheviks were communists. Their leader was Vladimir Lenin. He demanded that people be given land, peace, and bread. By November, 1917, Lenin and the Bolsheviks controlled Russia. They were the people who changed the name of Russia to the Union of Soviet Socialist Republics.

Totalitarian Governments Arise in Europe

The peace that followed World War I did not bring security to the people of Europe. Although many new countries had been formed, some groups still were not happy with the borders that were drawn. Also, the countries that lost World War I were bitter about the peace terms. Germans, in particular, were angry because large parts of their country were taken away from them. The Allied Powers also forced Germany to pay money to the winning countries, and Germany was not allowed to have an army.

In 1929 an event occurred which hurt the chances for continued peace in Europe. The world entered a period of low economic activity known as a **depression.** Factories and banks closed. People lost both their jobs and their savings. In Great Britain, for example, one out of four workers was out of work. In Germany, two out of five were without jobs. People could not afford to buy goods, which led to the closing of even more businesses.

Partly as a result of these problems, a new kind of government spread throughout Europe in the 1920s and 1930s. This kind of government is called **totalitarian.** In totalitarianism, the government tries to control every area of life—even the books people read, the music they hear, and the art they see.

In a totalitarian government, one leader or a small group of leaders makes all political decisions. The leader rules through the army and usually has a secret police. Totalitarians use terror to enforce their rule. Any critic of the government can be arrested, jailed, or killed.

The Russian government of the tsars was an example of a totalitarian government. Lenin's Bolshevik government was totalitarian too. Lenin described his totalitarian government this way. "[It] is power, based directly upon force, and unrestricted by any laws."

The Soviet Union. Totalitarianism was not new to the Soviet people. The Soviet people, unfortunately, never had had much political freedom. The tsars had used terror and a secret police for centuries. However, the government of the Soviet Union became even more totalitarian in 1924 when Lenin died.

Joseph Stalin (stä′lin) seized power after Lenin's death. Stalin had most of his political rivals killed. Under Stalin the government completely controlled the country's economy. All who disagreed with Stalin or who tried to resist were killed or sent to prison. Millions died under Stalin's terror.

Italy. Italy became totalitarian under Benito Mussolini (bā nē′tō mü̇s′ə lē′-nē). His supporters were known as Fascists (fash′ists). The Fascists were very nationalistic. They wanted to make Italy a strong military power. Anyone who was not in favor of strengthening the country through warfare was jailed.

Germany. Germany became totalitarian under Adolf Hitler. Hitler was the leader of a German political party called the National Socialists, or Nazi (nä′tsē) Party. Hitler was a good speaker. He promised to solve Germany's economic problems. He also said that the Germans were members of a "master race." All non-Germans, he said, were inferior creatures who should be made slaves or killed. Hitler especially hated Jews, Slavs, and Gypsies. He called on Germans to remember their past glories. Germany's pride had been hurt badly by losing World War I, and so Hitler's message appealed to many Germans.

By 1933 the Nazis had taken power in Germany with Hitler as their leader. Germany quickly built up its military forces. Germany then began to seize land from neighboring European countries. In 1938 the Nazi army marched

Like millions of other Jews during World War II, Jews in Warsaw, Poland, were arrested by the Nazis and sent to death camps.

into Austria and united it with Germany. In early 1939 the Germans took over Czechoslovakia. When Hitler attacked Poland in September, 1939, France and Great Britain declared war on Germany. World War II had begun.

World War II

Germany quickly conquered Poland, Denmark, Norway, Belgium, the Netherlands, France, Greece, and Yugoslavia. Germany tried to bomb Great Britain into surrender but did not succeed.

In the summer of 1941, German troops invaded the Soviet Union. Now the Soviets and Great Britain were allies. By the end of 1941, the United States joined them. Japan, an ally of Germany, had attacked the United

States Navy at Pearl Harbor, Hawaii, in December, 1941.

For most of 1942, Germany and its allies, known as the Axis Powers, were successful. They conquered much of the Soviet Union. Japan took over much of China, as well as parts of the British, Dutch, and French territory in Asia.

During the course of the war, the Nazis forced conquered people to work for them in factories and on farms. More than 3 million Polish and Russian slave laborers died because of overwork and lack of food.

Part of the Nazi plan was to kill the people they did not like. Death camps were set up in which men, women, and children were killed. Jews were singled out for **genocide,** which is the deliberate killing of a cultural or racial group. Of the 12 million people killed in the Nazi death camps, about 6 million were Jews.

By late 1942 and early 1943, the tide began to turn against Germany, Italy, and Japan. The Soviets won major battles and drove the Germans back. The United States, Great Britain, and the other Allies invaded Italy and forced it to surrender. German cities came under daily attack from British and American bombers. In 1944 the Allies invaded France and pushed the Germans out. By May, 1945, Germany had been overrun from both the east and the west. Hitler committed suicide, and the war in Europe ended.

Meanwhile, the United States and the Allies were defeating Japan in the Pacific area and Asia. World War II came to an end in August, 1945, after the United States used a new weapon on Japan, the atomic bomb.

Postwar Europe

Since 1945, the nations of Europe have not fought a world war. However, conflict between the countries of Europe has continued. The main conflict has been between communist and noncommunist nations.

During the Nazi invasion of World War II, about 26 million Soviet people were killed. After the war, Soviet leaders wanted to make sure the countries on its border would be friendly in the future. The Soviets also wanted to spread their form of government. As a result, they helped many European communists take control of governments in their countries.

The United States and other Western European nations feared the spread of communism and opposed it. Warfare began in Greece and almost broke out in such places as Turkey and Germany.

At the present time, most of the nations of Europe belong to one of two groups. Most nations of Western Europe are part of an alliance called the North Atlantic Treaty Organization (NATO). The United States and Canada also belong to NATO. Most of the communist nations of Eastern Europe are allied with the Soviet Union under the Warsaw Pact. The struggle between the countries of NATO and the Warsaw Pact countries for influence around the world is known as the Cold War.

Reviewing the Lesson

Recalling Key Words, People, and Places
1. Identify the key words defined below:
   a. a joining together of countries that agree to support each other in case of war
   b. having to do with a government that tries to control every area of life
   c. the deliberate killing of a cultural or racial group
2. Tell why it is important to remember:
   a. Vladimir Lenin
   b. Adolf Hitler

Remembering Main Ideas
1. How did alliances among European countries lead to the start of World War I?
2. How did Bolsheviks take control of Russia?
3. Name three totalitarian governments in Europe after World War I.
4. Describe how Germany was defeated in World War II.
5. What two alliances are involved in the Cold War in Europe today?

Thinking Things Over
Do you think that it would be possible for a person such as Hitler to gain control of the United States today? Explain your answer.

Judging the News Media

How do you find out about world and national news events? Most people listen to news shows on television and radio or read about news events in newspapers or magazines. These news media communicate to the mass of people around the world. The news media are all parts of the field of mass communications.

Reporting the Facts

The news media often send reporters directly to newsworthy events so they can interview people and see events firsthand. Are their reports exactly the same? In some ways, yes.

For example, in 1986, President Ronald Reagan of the United States and General Secretary Mikhail Gorbachev (gôr′bə chôf′) of the Soviet Union held a summit meeting to talk about arms (weapons) control and peace. (A summit meeting is one held by the highest government leaders.) After several talks, the meeting ended suddenly and unexpectedly. The two leaders disagreed on how to achieve peace. Gorbachev wanted President Reagan to give up plans to build a defense system called the Strategic Defense Initiative (SDI) or Star Wars. President Reagan said, "No."

These events of the summit meeting were covered thoroughly on radio and television, in newspapers, and in news magazines. Many of the facts about the meeting were repeated from story to story, such as:

- FACT: The meeting took place in Reykjavik (Rā′kyə vēk′), Iceland.
- FACT: Experts from both sides met in all-night discussions.
- FACT: The two leaders left the meeting without coming to any firm decision about controlling the growth of arms.

Reporting More Than the Facts

News coverage can vary, however, in small ways from one newspaper to another or from one television station to another. People who report on and write about the news have differing points of view. Sometimes, these points of view come out in the words they choose to tell about an event or in the details they leave in or out of the news story.

In reporting about the meeting in Iceland, for example, some news reports used words such as "failure," "collapse," and "folly." Headlines such as the following suggested that President Reagan's Star Wars policies were at fault.

- "Sunk by Star Wars"
- "Star Wars Proved Fatal to Summit"
- "SDI Dream Beat Out Arms Control"

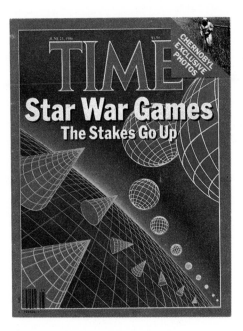

Other reports seemed more optimistic, or hopeful, about the meeting. Some suggested support for President Reagan's stand as well.

- "Hopeful Outlook on Arms"
- "Superpower Arms Accord [agreement]: Quite Close?"
- "It Was the President's Finest Hour"

The next time you hear or read a news report, listen or read carefully. See if you can tell the difference between facts being given and opinions or points of view being suggested.

Skills Practice

Read each of the following reports of the Iceland summit meeting, based on articles from different news media. Answer the questions that follow each report.

1. "The meeting took place against the backdrop of cold, gray Reykjavik Sound. Reagan, the optimist and dreamer, natural leader of great popularity, faced his opponent. This was Gorbachev, the vigorous new Soviet leader once complimented for his 'nice smile and iron teeth.' "

   a. What words has the writer used to describe Reagan? Do you think these words give a favorable or unfavorable view of Reagan? Explain your answer.

   b. What does the description "nice smile and iron teeth" suggest about Gorbachev?

2. "A poll taken among Americans after the Iceland talks shows that sixty-four percent of the people thought Reagan handled the summit well and twenty-two percent disapproved.

   Any considerations of this poll should recognize certain points. One is that nationwide polls taken right after a national crisis, such as the Iceland talks, always show that people support their President, at least at first. Also, these results may have been affected by the Reagan administration's work, since the meeting."

   a. How do you think this writer feels about the poll? Why do you think so?

   b. How do you think the writer feels about Reagan's handling of the summit? Give reasons for your answer.

Chapter 10 Review

Chapter Summary

Lesson 1   Western Europe in the Nineteenth Century—A spirit of nationalism spread across Western Europe in the 1800s. The thirty-nine German states were united largely by the Prussian leader Bismarck, who installed the kaiser as emperor of a united Germany.

Lesson 2   Eastern Europe and Russia in the Nineteenth Century—Nationalist revolutions in Eastern Europe gained some success against the Austrian, Ottoman, and Russian empires. Alexander II freed the serfs in Russia in the 1860s and began Russian industry on a large scale.

Lesson 3   Conflict and Change in the Twentieth Century—In World War I, the Allies opposed the Central Powers. The Central Powers surrendered in 1918. In World War II, the German war machine conquered most of Europe. Japan attacked the United States and conquered much of Southeast Asia. Germany and Japan surrendered in 1945.

Write your answers on a separate sheet of paper.

Testing Key Words, People, and Places

Part A

Choose the key word from the list that best completes each sentence.

1. A period of low economic activity is known as a _____.

2. An _____ rules alone, without the consent of anyone else.

3. After the defeat of the Mongols, a Russian ruler was known as the _____.

4. To _____ someone means to kill the person for political reasons.

5. People disagreeing with the tsar were killed or sent into _____.

6. The idea that the government could best run the economy for a country is _____.

7. During the Russian Revolution, workers formed councils known as _____.

8. A government that tries to control every area of life is _____.

9. During World War I, each power formed a _____, agreeing to side with other countries in case of war.

10. The emperor of Prussia in the late 1800s was called the _____.

11. The idea that people united by common traditions should form their own country is _____.

12. The murder of a people is called _____.

13. The idea that socialism can be brought about only by violent revolution is _____.

a. nationalism
b. autocrat
c. kaiser
d. tsar
e. exile
f. socialism
g. communism
h. military alliance
i. assassinate
j. soviets
k. depression
l. totalitarian
m. genocide

Part B

Match each description with the correct person in the list.

1. leader whose government took complete control of the Soviet Union after Lenin's death.
2. a strong influence on Russian political thought
3. ordered his subjects to speak only Russian
4. helped to unite the Italian states
5. Prussian leader who united Germany
6. leader of Bolsheviks in 1917
7. leader of Nazi Germany during World War II
8. freed the Russian serfs
9. leader of the Mongols of central Asia who defeated the Russians in the 1200s

a. Giuseppe Garibaldi	**f.** Karl Marx
b. Otto von Bismarck	**g.** Vladimir Lenin
	h. Joseph Stalin
	i. Adolf Hitler
c. Genghis Khan	
d. Alexander II	
e. Alexander III	

Testing Main Ideas

Answer these questions.

1. How did liberalism affect changes in Europe?
2. Why do you think the ideas of Karl Marx appealed to Russians living under the tsar?
3. How did the depression of 1929 hurt chances for continuing peace?
4. What is the North Atlantic Treaty Organization?

Testing Skills

1. **Using and judging the mass media.** Find newspaper and magazine accounts of the Soviet Union nuclear disaster at Chernobyl in 1986. How do the writers' assumptions, emotions, attitudes, and points of view differ?
   a. What would be primary and what would be secondary source material on this subject?
   b. How might accounts published in the Soviet Union differ from reports by the United States media?

2. **Making a time line.** Make a time line that covers the twenty-year period from 1929 to 1949. Put the following events in order and add them to your time line.
   a. Germans march into Austria, 1938
   b. World War II ends, 1945
   c. NATO begins, 1949
   d. Hitler becomes German dictator, 1933
   e. Great Depression begins, 1929
   f. Allies defeat Germans in France, 1944

Activities

1. Read *Nazi Germany,* by Richard Tames (David and Charles, Inc., 1985). Report to the class on new information you found in the book.
2. Draw and color the flags of the countries of Europe, including the Soviet Union.

Chapter 11

The Countries of Western Europe Today

The people of Western Europe and the people of the United States have many things in common. For example, the people of Western Europe live in countries with modern industries. Their countries also have democratic governments in which citizens vote.

As you read this chapter, you will learn about the location and resources of the countries of Western Europe. You will learn how the people—like the people of West Germany shown in the picture—earn a living and trade with one another. You also will learn about Western European governments and histories. The lessons in the chapter are listed below.

Lesson 1 The British Isles and Scandinavia

Lesson 2 The Continental Countries

Lesson 3 The Mediterranean Countries

Lesson 1   The British Isles and Scandinavia

 LOOKING AHEAD As you read, look for—

Key words, people, and **places:**

standard of living
direct democracy
representative democracy
parliament
prime minister

Celts
Anglo-Saxons
Vikings
Normans

Answers to these questions about **main ideas:**

1. What are the main characteristics of the land and the people of the British Isles and Scandinavia?
2. Why is Great Britain divided into several parts?
3. How has the history of Ireland been unique in the British Isles?
4. What kinds of industries help Scandinavians enjoy a high standard of living?
5. How do the governments in Great Britain and the Scandinavian countries work?

Western Europe is a region with many countries. Each country has its own language, government, laws, and traditions. For centuries these countries were often at war with one another. In recent years, however, they have begun to cooperate with one another more and more.

Land and People

The map of Western Europe on page 245 shows that the British Isles are made up of two main islands and some smaller ones. The large islands are Great Britain and Ireland. Look at the map and locate each of these smaller groups of islands: the Hebrides (heb′-rə dēz′), the Shetlands, and the Orkneys.

Two separate countries are located in the British Isles. One country, The United Kingdom of Great Britain and Northern Ireland, includes England, Scotland, Wales, and Northern Ireland. This nation is often called Great Britain.

The other country in the British Isles occupies five-sixths of the island from which it gets its name-—Ireland.

Scandinavia sometimes is called Northern Europe. It includes five countries: Norway, Sweden, Denmark, Finland, and Iceland. Look again at the map on page 245. Which Scandinavian nation is an island?

The people of the British Isles and Scandinavia are linked by history. Measure how far apart Norway is from Great Britain by using the map scale on page 245. Throughout history, people have sailed ships across the North Sea between the two areas.

The people of the British Isles and Scandinavia are among the best educated in the world. Almost everyone knows how to read and write. Their governments also have seen to it that their people receive excellent health care. Because of this, the life expectancy for Scandinavians is the longest in the world. On the average, Scandinavian men live about 73 years, and women live about 79 years.

Great Britain

Americans have many ties with Great Britain. Remember that the United States was once a colony of the British Empire. Our language and many of our ideas about government come from Great Britain.

History. Until about A.D. 400, Britain was part of the Roman Empire. However, the people of Britain were not Romans but Celts (selts). After the Romans left Britain, people known as Anglo-Saxons migrated to the islands from the western coast of the continent and pushed the Celts to the north and west. Within a few hundred years, Britain was divided into an Anglo-Saxon part and the land of the Celts. The Anglo-Saxon part became England, and the Celtic part became Wales, Scotland, and Ireland.

In 793 a group known as Vikings from the present-day countries of Norway and Denmark invaded the British Isles. The Vikings had developed a way of life based on sea travel. Some Vikings were traders. Others were pirates and conquerors. In their dragon-headed ships, the Vikings sailed to the British Isles. They conquered the eastern part of England and settled there.

In 1066 a group of people from present-day France, the Normans, invaded and conquered England. The Normans combined their way of life with the Anglo-Saxons and became known as the English.

Over hundreds of years, the English took over the Celtic parts of the British Isles. Today the English culture, including the English language, is common throughout all parts of Great Britain. However, the proud people of Wales, Scotland, and Northern Ireland still hold on to some of their ancient Celtic traditions.

Economy. The major products of Great Britain are manufactured goods. Great Britain has several great manufacturing centers. Two of these are Manchester and Birmingham. These two cities are among the world leaders in producing such goods as machine tools, automobiles, steel, silverware, and textiles. Point to Manchester and Birmingham on the map on page 245.

London, one of the world's largest cities, is the capital of Great Britain. It is a center of trade and education. London also is a major banking center. It is one of the oldest cities in the world and is rich in history. Today many millions of tourists visit London each year to enjoy its museums, theaters, and historic places.

Map Study

The map on the next page shows the countries of Western Europe. Which country is at 50°N and 10°E? Which countries have land along the Mediterranean Sea?

Western Europe: Political

International boundaries

⊛ **National capitals**

• **Other cities**

ARCTIC OCEAN

ATLANTIC OCEAN

NORWEGIAN SEA

ICELAND
Reykjavik

Faeroe Is. (Den.)

Shetland Is. (U.K.)

Hebrides Is. (U.K.)

Orkney Is. (U.K.)

SCOTLAND
Glasgow

NORTHERN IRELAND • Belfast

UNITED KINGDOM

Dublin

REPUBLIC OF IRELAND

ENGLAND
Manchester

WALES
Birmingham
London

NORTH SEA

NORWAY
Bergen
Oslo

SWEDEN
Stockholm
Orust I. (Sweden)

FINLAND
Helsinki

DENMARK Copenhagen

BALTIC SEA

Stockholm River

Vistula River

UNION OF SOVIET SOCIALIST REPUBLICS (SOVIET UNION)

Volga River

Hamburg

NETHERLANDS
The Hague ⊛ Amsterdam

Essen • Dortmund
Dusseldorf • Cologne
Bonn

Brussels ⊛
BELGIUM
LUXEMBOURG
Luxembourg

EAST GERMANY

Elbe

Oder River

POLAND

Dnieper River

WEST GERMANY

CZECHOSLOVAKIA

Dniester River

Paris ⊛

FRANCE

Loire River

Seine River

Rhine River

Zurich •
Bern ⊛
SWITZERLAND

LIECHTENSTEIN
Vaduz

Munich •
Vienna ⊛

AUSTRIA

HUNGARY

Danube River

ROMANIA

Dniester River

BLACK SEA

Bordeaux •

Garonne River

Rhône River

Lyon •

Milan •
Po River
Turin •
Genoa •

SAN MARINO
San Marino ⊛

YUGOSLAVIA

Danube River

BULGARIA

Marseille •
Monaco
MONACO

PORTUGAL

Madrid ⊛

SPAIN

Tagus River

Lisbon ⊛

Guadalquivir River
Córdoba •

Gibraltar (U.K.)

Andorra la Vella
ANDORRA

Barcelona •

Ebro River

Bay of Biscay

Corsica (Fr.)

ITALY

VATICAN CITY ⊛ Rome

Naples •

Sardinia (It.)

Balearic Is. (Sp.)

ALBANIA

GREECE

TURKEY

Istanbul •

ASIA

Athens ⊛

Palermo •

Sicily (It.)

MALTA ⊛ Valletta

Crete (Gr.)

Nicosia ⊛

CYPRUS

MEDITERRANEAN SEA

AFRICA

Arctic Circle

30°W   20°W   10°W   0°   10°E   20°E   30°E   40°E   50°E

70°N   60°N   50°North Latitude   40°N   30°N

10°West Longitude

N
W   E
S

0   200   400 Miles
0   200   400 Kilometers

245

© SF

Ireland

The history of Ireland differs from the other Celtic lands in the British Isles. The English conquered Wales in 1536 after two centuries of fighting. Since then, the English and the Welsh—as the people of Wales are called—have managed to get along with each other. The oldest son of the British monarch even is called the Prince of Wales. The Scots likewise fought against the English for many years. Then, the king of Scotland became king of England in 1603, and the two nations were united.

The English, however, never could control the Irish. The struggle between them went on for eight hundred years. At last, in 1922, Ireland broke away from England and became independent.

Some fighting still continues in Northern Ireland, which is part of Great Britain. The Protestants of Northern Ireland have ties to England and wish to remain part of Great Britain. The Catholics have ties to the Republic of Ireland and want Northern Ireland to join the Irish nation. The conflict between the Protestants and Catholics is economic, too. Catholics often have trouble finding good jobs in Northern Ireland, while most Protestants do not. Many Catholics protest that they are being treated unfairly.

In the 1840s, Ireland had about 7 million people. Ireland today has only $3\frac{1}{2}$ million people. The reason for this drop in population was a great disaster that occurred in the 1840s—the potato famine. For several years in a row, the potato crop failed. Over 750,000 people died and millions were forced to leave Ireland. Many Irish continued to migrate from the country in large numbers, even after the famine.

Since Ireland gained its independence, farming has become less important to the Irish economy. Manufacturing has grown, and fewer people are leaving the country. The leading industries are chemicals and machinery. The country is better known, however, for its handmade items. These include dishes, cut glass, and knitted wool sweaters. Ireland's largest city is its capital, Dublin.

Scandinavia

During the Viking period, Scandinavians lived in small groups ruled by local lords. At the end of the Viking period, about A.D. 1100, kings took control of Scandinavia, and countries began to form. In the Middle Ages, Denmark was the most powerful Scandinavian country. In the 1600s Sweden became an important power too. By the 1900s the countries of Scandinavia—which had been united in various combinations throughout their history—were independent.

Fish, wood products, dairy products, and oil are important Scandinavian exports. Denmark, for example, is famous for its dairy products.

Scandinavian factories are often small. All the nations in this part of Europe, however, are highly industrialized. Sweden is the most highly industrialized of all. It produces cars, machinery, engines, planes, and ships that are known for their high quality.

Vikings sailed in dragon-headed ships like the one shown.

The Scandinavian countries all enjoy a high **standard of living,** or quality of life. The people in these countries have a large amount of high-quality goods and services available to them. The Scandinavian people have used their wealth to create strong social security systems. In the Scandinavian social security systems, the people pay high taxes. In exchange, their governments provide complete medical care, generous payments when people retire, and other services.

Representative Democracy

The countries of the British Isles and Scandinavia have a long tradition of democracy. In all democracies, government is run by the citizens. Citizens have the right to vote, to think, to speak, and to write freely. Citizens also have the right to select the leaders of their government.

Not all democracies are the same, however. For instance, under a **direct democracy,** the citizens themselves make political decisions, often through meetings that all attend. Ancient Athens, for example, was a direct democracy. This type of government works best in small groups and is practiced in some small towns today.

In a **representative democracy,** citizens elect people to make political decisions for them. All Western European nations, as well as the United States, have representative democracies.

The representative democracies of the countries in the British Isles and Scandinavia work differently than the representative democracy of the United States. Voters cast ballots only for members of the legislature, or lawmaking body, called the **parliament.** They do not vote for a president or any other government officers. Once the election is over, the members of the parliament choose the executive leader of the country. This leader is called the **prime minister.** The prime minister has powers and duties similar to the powers and duties of the President of the United States. However, some differences do exist between a prime minister and a president.

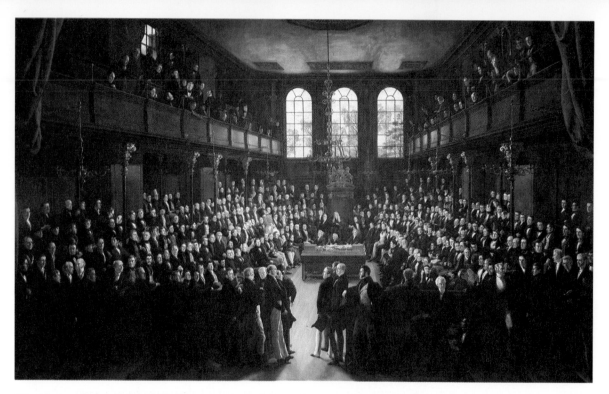

Members of the British Parliament meet in London, as shown in this early painting. In Britain and the Scandinavian countries, members of Parliament are chosen by the people. Parliament elects a prime minister, whose job is similar to that of the American President.

A prime minister must sit in the Parliament. He or she must answer questions and take part in debates. If a majority of the Parliament does not like a prime minister's actions, they can vote to remove the prime minister from office. Then, the Parliament will choose a new prime minister or call for a new election for members of Parliament.

The governments of Britain and the Scandinavian countries are different from the United States form of government. However, all are representative democracies. Their people are free to criticize government decisions. They also are free to form political groups to help make the changes they want. These same liberties are found in all the nations of Western Europe.

Reviewing the Lesson

Recalling Key Words, People, and Places

1. Identify the key words defined below:
   a. the quality of life enjoyed by the people of a country
   b. a government in which citizens vote for leaders to make decisions for them
   c. the executive leader of a country chosen by the Parliament

Remembering Main Ideas

1. Name the countries in the British Isles and Scandinavia.
2. What parts of Great Britain have a Celtic tradition?
3. What event caused many people to leave Ireland in the 1840s?
4. How does the social security system operate in Scandinavian countries?
5. What is the difference between the way a United States President and a prime minister are elected?

Thinking Things Over

What do Great Britain, Ireland, and the Scandinavian nations have in common?

Lesson 2   The Continental Countries

LOOKING AHEAD As you read, look for—

Key words, people, and **places:**

neutrality   Ruhr Valley
polder   Amsterdam
tariff

Answers to these questions about **main ideas:**

1. What are the main characteristics of the land and people of the continental countries?
2. Where does much of West Germany's and Austria's manufacturing take place?
3. What are the products of France and Switzerland?
4. What are the major economic activities of the Low Countries?
5. What are the goals of the European Communities?

South of Scandinavia and the British Isles lie the countries of Western Europe known as the continental countries. They are Belgium, the Netherlands, West Germany, Luxembourg, Liechtenstein, Switzerland, France, and Austria. With your finger, trace the outline of these countries on the map on page 245.

Land and People

Belgium and the Netherlands are located on a flat coast along the North Sea. Farther south and east lie the broad plains and hill regions of France, Luxembourg, West Germany, and Austria. Switzerland and Liechtenstein lie entirely in the tall, snowcapped Alps.

The climate in this part of Europe is classified as cool and wet all year. Most areas have cool winters and warm summers. The western coastal areas are somewhat warmer and wetter in winter than the inland areas.

Most people in the continental countries live in cities and work in manufacturing and commerce. Although farm-ing is important, especially in France and the Netherlands, industry forms the base of each country's wealth.

West Germany and Austria

Each of the continental countries has had a different history. You learned how the country of Germany was formed in the last chapter. At the end of World War II, it was divided into West Germany and East Germany.

West Germany is one of the world's strongest industrial powers. Much of its industry is located in the Ruhr Valley. Here the cities of Dortmund, Dussel-dorf, and Essen make up a major manufacturing center. These cities have the advantage of being near both coal fields and rivers. Thus, raw materials are easily brought into the factories, manufactured into goods, and shipped out.

Austria, like West Germany, is a country that relies on manufacturing and trade. The greatest number of factories are located near Vienna, the capital city. Austrian industries produce

Freighters dock near oil tanks at Rotterdam, in the Netherlands.

metals, chemicals, and processed foods. Small workshops throughout the country turn out jewelry, woodcarvings, and other handcrafted items.

Tourism is an important source of income in Austria. Over ten million people a year visit Austria. Most of these people come from West Germany. One reason why people come to Austria is the lovely mountains that cover the southern part of the country.

France and Switzerland

France and Switzerland were once part of the Roman Empire. Beginning in the fourth century, German tribes settled in this region. One tribe, the Franks, gave its name to France.

France has always been one of Europe's great nations. From the Middle Ages to this century, it has been one of the main centers of European art, music, and learning.

Good farmland is France's most important natural resource. Over nine-tenths of France's land can be used for growing crops. French farmers produce and export many kinds of grains, vegetables, and animal products. Although many French people work in agriculture, 80 percent of France's 55 million people live in urban areas. Most of these city dwellers work in manufacturing and commerce.

Most French manufacturing takes place near the capital city of Paris. France produces steel, machinery, chemicals, and textiles. It also has one of the world's largest automobile plants. This plant employs about 500,000 workers and produces about 3 million cars a year. The products for which France is best known, however, are luxury goods such as perfumes, fine wines, and expensive clothes.

Beginning in the 1200s, the Swiss began a series of wars for their independence. Over a period of three hundred years, the Swiss fought the Austrians, Germans, and the French. In 1515 the Swiss army lost badly to the French army in a war in northern Italy. Since that time, the Swiss have taken a position of **neutrality.** That is, they refuse to take sides in conflicts among other countries. Today Switzerland is a peaceful country that has not fought a war since being invaded by Napoleon in 1815.

Switzerland relies on manufacturing, banking, and tourism for most of its income. The Swiss are famous for the quality of their manufactured products. Skilled workers turn raw materials into products such as watches, machine tools, and electrical equipment.

The Low Countries and Liechtenstein

Belgium, the Netherlands, and Luxembourg are often called the Low Countries because of their low elevation. In fact, part of the Netherlands is below sea level. For hundreds of years, the people of the Netherlands—the Dutch—have worked to recover land from under the sea. Today, this land, which is called **polder,** is some of the best farmland in Europe.

The Low Countries almost always were under foreign rule through most of the 1500s. At that time Spain controlled the area. In 1581 the Dutch broke away from Spain and formed the Dutch Republic. It soon became a great sea power with colonies all over the world. New York City, for example, was once a Dutch colony. Belgium became an independent nation in 1830 and it, too, had colonies.

Today Belgium and the Netherlands are trading nations. They have important industries, such as chemicals, petroleum products, automobiles, and machinery. The Dutch cities of Amsterdam and Rotterdam are among Europe's greatest seaports. Amsterdam, in fact, is Europe's busiest port. Look at

Linking Past and Present

The Vienna State Opera House

Vienna is the capital of Austria. Some people also consider Vienna the capital of Western European music. Many of the world's greatest composers lived and worked in this city along the "beautiful blue Danube." The composers of Vienna have included such greats as Haydn, Mozart, Brahms, Shubert, Beethoven, Strauss, and Mahler.

The theater you see in the picture is the Vienna State Opera House. During World War II, the Vienna State Opera House was almost completely destroyed by bombing. After the war, the Austrians decided to build the opera house the way it had been before. The restored theater reopened in 1955. Since then, music has been performed in this theater almost every day for ten months out of every year.

the Atlas maps on pages 538 and 539. Why is Amsterdam a good location for a seaport?

Two of the world's smallest nations are Luxembourg and Liechtenstein. Luxembourg is only 1,034 square miles in area and has about 370,000 people. However, Luxembourg's iron and steel production give it one of the highest standards of living in all Europe.

Liechtenstein is about 62 square miles with a population of only 27,000 people. Liechtenstein is closely tied to Switzerland. The Swiss even operate part of Liechtenstein's government. This tiny rural country earns a great deal of money by putting out beautiful postage stamps that collectors love to buy.

The European Communities

For centuries, European countries competed with one another in industry and trade. They levied, or charged, taxes called **tariffs** on goods that they imported. In many cases, the competition for wealth and territory led to war. After the terrible destruction of World War II, Western Europeans began to think differently about one another. Why not be partners in trade?

Six European countries decided to do exactly that. In 1958 France, Belgium, West Germany, Italy, the Netherlands, and Luxembourg formed a trade organization. Later Great Britain, Denmark, Greece, and Ireland joined in. The organization then became known as the European Communities (EC). Portugal and Spain became members of the EC in 1986.

The most important part of the EC usually is called the Common Market. Its purpose is to break down trade barriers among member nations. The Common Market also works to improve the industries and economies of all its members. The Common Market has been a success. The flow of goods among member nations has increased greatly. Many businesses, industrial workers, and farmers have been helped.

In addition to the Common Market, the European Communities includes a Council of Ministers, a European Parliament, and a Court of Justice. The goal of these organizations is to unite all the democratic countries of Western Europe. Some people hope that someday the European Communities will become the United States of Europe.

Reviewing the Lesson

Recalling Key Words, People, and Places
1. Identify the key words defined below:
   a. a refusal to take sides in conflicts among other countries
   b. a tax on imports or exports
2. Tell why it is important to remember:
   a. Ruhr Valley
   b. Amsterdam

Remembering Main Ideas
1. What kind of climate is found throughout all the continental countries?
2. Why is much of West Germany's industry located in the Ruhr Valley?
3. How much of France's land can be used for producing crops?
4. What are the major economic activities in the Netherlands?
5. What has been one result of the Common Market?

Thinking Things Over
In the future, do you think the continental countries will cooperate more with one another or less? What makes you think so?

252

Lesson 3   The Mediterranean Countries

LOOKING AHEAD As you read, look for—

Key words, people, and **places:**

dictator

Moors

Vatican City

Answers to these questions about **main ideas:**

1. How have the land and climate of the Mediterranean countries affected the way people live?
2. What are the most important industries in Greece and Italy?
3. What are the main economic activities in Spain and Portugal?
4. How have the Mediterranean countries struggled to form democratic governments?

Four of the countries of Western Europe sit on three peninsulas that extend into the Mediterranean Sea. For this reason, they are called the Mediterranean countries. These countries are Greece, Italy, Spain, and Portugal. Find these countries on the map on page 245.

Land and People

The ancient philosopher Plato once said that his fellow Greeks lived at the edge of the sea "like frogs around a pond." Plato's description still fits life in the Mediterranean countries. Most people live near the coast. The sea has always been a means of transportation for them.

The Mediterranean countries have a warm climate with dry summers. Because of the warm climate, the people of the Mediterranean countries spend much of their lives in the open. If you walked through a city anywhere in the area, you would see open-air markets and many people sitting outside in restaurants.

For centuries most people of the area were poor farmers. Many farms were located on the stony Mediterranean hillsides. The plants grown on these dry, steep fields, such as olive trees and grapevines, have deep roots. Only recently has industry begun to take hold in the region. Membership in the Common Market has helped all four countries improve their industries.

Greece and Italy

Greece has the poorest land for farming of any Mediterranean country. It also has few major resources and not much manufacturing. However, Greece has a large shipping industry. Greek ships carry goods to and from all parts of the world. Greece also has a large tourist industry. People like to visit Greece because of its climate and to see the treasures from its glorious past. Athens, the capital, is the center of trade and tourism. One-third of all the Greek people live in Athens.

Partly because of its good farmland, Italy is the richest Mediterranean country. Italy also has busy industrial centers. Most industries are in the northern part of Italy, where water power can be used to make electricity. Factories in the cities of Milan and Turin turn out automobiles, bicycles, farm machinery, and textiles. Many of these products are exported from the port of Genoa, the seaport in which Christopher Columbus grew up. Find Milan, Turin, and Genoa on the map on page 245.

In addition to being a major manufacturing center, Milan is Italy's major banking center. In the southern part of Italy, the city of Naples is a busy port. It exports food products such as spaghetti, olive oil, and wines.

Italy also has a large tourist industry. Millions of people visit the cities of Florence and Rome because of their beautiful architecture and art. Tourists in Venice ride in boats on the city's canals, which serve in place of streets almost everywhere.

Europe's tiniest country—Vatican City—is located within the borders of Italy, in downtown Rome. The Vatican is the home of the Pope who heads the Roman Catholic Church. The church controlled over 16,000 square miles of land with a population of over 3 million people in the middle of the 1800s. However, the church lost all its land in 1871, after Italy was united. In 1929 the Roman Catholic Church signed a treaty with Mussolini making Vatican City an independent country. Vatican City is only 108 acres in size, with a population of about 1,000.

An open-air market on Mallorca (mä lyôr′kä), one of Spain's Balearic Islands.

Spain and Portugal

Spain's history is one of much conflict. After the fall of the Roman Empire, it was ruled by German tribes. Then, in the early 700s, it was conquered by Muslims from North Africa known as Moors. The Moors set up a brilliant civilization. Art and medicine flourished. The Christians of northern Spain, however, wanted the Moors out of Europe. They fought a long war against the Moors. At last, in 1492, the Spanish drove the Moors out of Europe. Thus, all of Spain was united into one Roman Catholic nation.

Portugal has been an independent country since the 1200s. Portugal is famous for its explorers, who sailed the Atlantic beginning in 1415. They explored the African coasts and were the first Europeans to sail around Africa's southern tip. They set the stage for European world expansion.

Spain and Portugal have some of the same problems as Greece. Much of the soil is poor. The hillsides are good only for growing olives and grapes. Citrus fruits and some grains can be grown on the plains. Raising cattle and sheep is important. Spain has been trying to develop its industries. New steel plants have been built, and Spanish shoes and textiles are sold all over the world. Portugal has some new small industries. However, a very large part of Portugal's workers are farmers.

Portugal and Spain joined the EC in 1986. The two countries hope that being trading partners with the other European countries will improve their economies.

A Struggle for Democracy

All four of the large Mediterranean countries are representative democracies. All have parliamentary systems like that of Great Britain. However, all four nations had to struggle with totalitarian governments in the recent past.

You have read about Benito Mussolini and his totalitarian government in Italy. Mussolini was a **dictator.** That is, he ruled his country with absolute authority. His fascist government ended after Italy's defeat in World War II.

In Greece, military dictators ran totalitarian governments from 1967 to 1974. Then, the Greek people successfully rebelled. Portugal was governed by a dictator between 1932 and 1968. It became a democracy in 1974.

General Francisco Franco (fran-sēs′co frang′kō) became dictator of Spain in 1939 after a long civil war. Hitler and Mussolini helped Franco gain power. Franco ruled Spain with an iron hand for thirty-six years. After his death in 1975, Spain become democratic. It held its first free election in over forty years in 1977.

Reviewing the Lesson

Recalling Key Words, People, and Places
1. What is the name for a leader who rules with absolute authority?
2. What Mediterranean country once was ruled by the Moors?
3. Where is Vatican City located?

Remembering Main Ideas
1. Describe the climate found in the Mediterranean countries.
2. Why do tourists like to visit Greece and Italy?
3. What benefits do Spain and Portugal hope to receive by joining the European Communities?
4. What changes in governments occurred in the Mediterranean countries in the 1900s?

Thinking Things Over
What do the four leading Mediterranean countries have in common? Name some things about the natural environment, economy, and government.

Predicting Consequences

You have learned that European countries competed with one another in industry and trade for centuries. One aspect of this competition involved tariffs on imports.

Countries collected tariffs on imports to protect their own industries. However, the consequences, or results, of high tariffs were damaging. To avoid the tariffs, people often bought products made in their own country that were not as good as imported ones. Tariffs also hurt each country's industries by limiting foreign markets and so cutting down on the number of goods that the industries could sell.

In Lesson 2, you learned that six European countries formed the European Economic Community, now called the European Communities (EC). By examining the effects that high tariffs had on their economies, experts from these countries were able to predict, or forecast, what might happen if the tariffs were eliminated. Based on these predictions, the countries of the EC decided to eliminate most tariffs on imports from one another.

Strategy for Making Predictions

Predicting consequences is something you do all the time, usually without realizing it. For example, imagine that you drop a jar of pickles.

European Communities meeting

What is the first thing that comes to your mind? Did you think, "It's going to break"? If so, you were predicting the consequence of dropping a breakable object. Think about what you did. First, you examined a fact: the jar fell. Next, you thought about past experiences: glass can break when dropped. Then, you made your prediction.

Different things can happen when you make a prediction. Your prediction may turn out to be correct. (The jar does break.) However, your prediction may turn out to be wrong. (The jar does not break.) If your prediction turns out to be wrong, you need to think about why it was wrong. You may have missed an important clue. For example, the jar may have been made from plastic instead of glass. Another possibility is that something unexpected happened. The jar may have fallen into the wastebasket, which cushioned the jar and prevented it from breaking.

When you read about social studies or other topics, you also make predictions—again, perhaps without realizing it. When you read about history, many of your predictions can be checked. When you read about a topic set in the present, you might not be able to check your predictions right away. However, even if you cannot check your predictions, making predictions can help you learn more from your reading. Here is a strategy to use to make predictions as you read.

- Examine the facts you are given in your reading.
- Think about what you know from experience or what you have read.
- Make several predictions about what might happen. Decide which is most likely to happen.
- If you are reading about a historical event, read on to see if your prediction is correct. If it is not correct, go back to see if you missed any important facts. Also see if new information was added that made an accurate prediction possible.

Skills Practice

Read the following situations and follow the directions for each. Use the steps you have learned to make your predictions.

1. The country of France grows more wheat than its people eat. Most other European countries need to import wheat. However, France has trouble selling wheat to other European countries because wheat from the United States, Canada, and Argentina costs less than French wheat. The EC wants to solve this problem. Predict two possible consequences of each action listed below.
   a. The EC raises tariffs on U.S., Canadian, and Argentine wheat.
   b. The EC asks France to reduce wheat production.
   c. The EC does nothing.
2. Five countries in the EC—Great Britain, Ireland, Denmark, Belgium, and France—have large herds of dairy cattle. Recently, a very large amount of milk, cheese, and butter has been produced. As a result, the prices for these products have been falling. The EC wants to solve this problem. Predict two possible consequences of each action listed below.
   a. The EC asks all five countries to reduce the sizes of their dairy herds.
   b. The EC asks only Great Britain to cut the amount of milk, cheese, and butter it produces in half.
   c. The EC does nothing.

Chapter Summary

Lesson 1 The British Isles and Scandinavia—The United Kingdom and the Republic of Ireland make up the British Isles. Great Britain is a major manufacturing nation. The Irish long resisted British rule. Scandinavia includes five countries. Like Great Britain, Scandinavian countries are industrialized democracies.

Lesson 2 The Continental Countries—The eight continental countries are Belgium, the Netherlands, West Germany, France, Luxembourg, Liechtenstein, Switzerland, and Austria. Farming and industry are prosperous there. Six countries formed the European Communities (EC). Later six more countries joined.

Lesson 3 The Mediterranean Countries—These countries are Greece, Italy, Spain, and Portugal. They share a warm climate with dry summers. Greece has a large shipping industry, Italy has developed industry on a vast scale, and Spain is beginning to do so.

Write your answers on a separate sheet of paper.

Testing Key Words, People, and Places

Part A

Choose the key word from the list that best answers each question.

1. What is a tax on imported goods called?

2. Citizens who rule directly through meetings that all attend have what kind of government?

3. In refusing to take sides in conflicts, the Swiss have taken what position?

4. What is the legislature called in Scandinavia and the British Isles?

5. People who enjoy a large amount of high-quality goods and services are said to have a high what?

6. What is the new land that the people of the Netherlands have reclaimed from the sea called?

7. Citizens who elect people to make political decisions have what kind of government?

8. What is the title of the executive leader in the British Isles and Scandinavia?

9. What is the term for someone who rules a country with absolute authority?

   a. standard of living
   b. direct democracy
   c. representative democracy
   d. parliament
   e. prime minister
   f. neutrality
   g. polder
   h. tariff
   i. dictator

Part B

In a sentence, tell why each person or place is important.

1. Celts   **4.** Ruhr Valley
2. Vikings   **5.** Amsterdam
3. Normans   **6.** Vatican City

Testing Main Ideas

Answer these questions.

1. What four countries combined to form Great Britain?
2. What are the countries of Scandinavia?
3. How has the United States been influenced by ideas and traditions from Great Britain?
4. The people of Northern Ireland belong to what two religions?
5. What type of democracy do all Western European nations have?
6. Which European countries are often called the Low Countries?
7. What kind of climate do the Mediterranean countries share?

Testing Skills

1. **Predicting consequences.** Since 1945 the European countries have enjoyed one of their longest periods of peace ever. One result has been the European Communities.
   a. What other results of this peace might be expected?
   b. Do you think a United States of Europe might be possible? Why or why not?
2. **Understanding time zones.** Study the map on this page and answer the questions.
   a. When it is noon in London, what time is it in Paris?
   b. When it is midnight in Paris, what time is it in Rome?
   c. How many hours later is it in Moscow than in London?

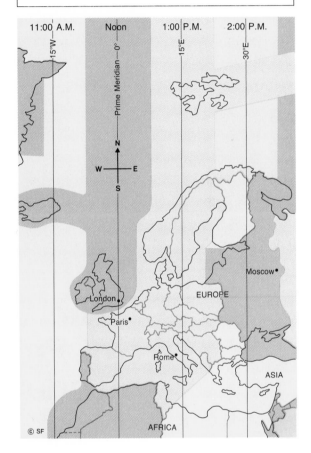

Time Zones: Europe

Regular time zones

Activities

1. Read *Netherlands* by Dennis B. Fradin (Childrens Press, 1983) to find out about life in the Netherlands. What kinds of things do you think you might like and dislike about living there?
2. Research the relations between the United States and Europe since World War I. Tell about some events that changed U.S.—European relations.

Chapter 12

The Countries of Eastern Europe Today

The countries of Eastern Europe are related by geography, culture, and history. These ties go back many centuries. Today, another tie among these countries is communism. The picture shows photographs of communist leaders displayed during a parade in Czechoslovakia.

All communist countries, however, are not alike. As you read this chapter, you will see how the different people of Eastern Europe live under their political and economic systems. The lessons in the chapter are listed below.

Lesson 1   Northern Countries of Eastern Europe

> **LOOKING AHEAD** As you read, look for—
>
> **Key words, people,** and **places:**
>
> **command economy**   Czechs
> **collective**   Slovaks
> **market economy**
>   Berlin
>
> Answers to these questions about **main ideas:**
>
> 1. What are the land and people in the northern countries of Eastern Europe like?
> 2. How does the economy of East Germany operate?
> 3. What are the two main ethnic groups in Czechoslovakia?
> 4. How has the way that farming is organized changed in Poland?
> 5. What happened in the Czech revolt of 1968?

The northern countries of Eastern Europe are East Germany, Poland, and Czechoslovakia. Look at the map on page 262. What countries and water bodies surround these three northern countries of Eastern Europe?

Land and People

Much of the land of East Germany, Poland, and Czechoslovakia lies on the North European Plain. As a result, this part of Europe has good farmland. The climate is cool and wet all year.

Three large rivers flow northward across East Germany and Poland. Look at the map on page 262 and name these rivers. Into what sea do they empty?

All three nations are urbanized, with more than half the population living in cities. Almost everyone knows how to read and write.

The people in this region have many links, including trade, with one another. However, the people have often been in conflict. For example, the land of East Germany once was held by Slavs. In the Middle Ages, Germans conquered the area and settled in it. Since then, Slavs and Germans have fought many battles. The boundaries of the northern countries of Eastern Europe often have changed as a result of war.

East Germany

The official name of East Germany is the German Democratic Republic. Like West Germany, East Germany was formed when Germany was divided after its defeat in World War II. At that time, the Soviets took control of the eastern part of the country. The British, French, and Americans took control of the western part. As a result of the Cold War between the western countries and the Soviet Union, Germany was not reunited. Each part of Germany became a separate country.

The city of Berlin also was divided. East Berlin is now the capital of East Germany. West Berlin is part of West Germany even though it lies about a

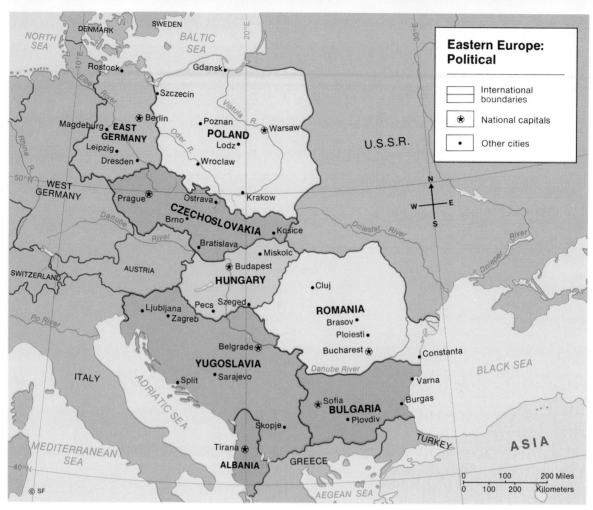

Map Study

This map shows the countries of Eastern Europe. Eastern Europe can be divided into northern countries and southern countries. Looking at the map and your text, give the names of the northern countries of Eastern Europe. Then name the capitals of the northern countries of Eastern Europe.

hundred miles inside the East German border.

East Germany was mostly farm country until after World War II. Then, it gradually became industrialized. Following the example of the Soviet Union, the communist government of East Germany set up a **command economy.** Under this system, the government decides how the economy of the country is to be run.

In a command economy, the government owns the factories, mines, railroads, restaurants, stores, banks, and everything else. Government planners decide what will be produced, where, how, and by whom. The planners pass those decisions on to the managers of the government-owned businesses. The manager of a steel mill, for instance, is told how much steel to produce. The manager is told how many workers to

In 1961 East German soldiers and police built the Berlin Wall to prevent East Germans from fleeing to West Germany.

use and how much to pay them. The government also sets the price at which the products of the steel mill will be sold.

East Germany today is Eastern Europe's major steel producer. As well as using its own minerals, East Germany gets iron ore and coal for making steel from Poland and Czechoslovakia. Workers in East Germany today have the highest standard of living in Eastern Europe.

Czechoslovakia

Czechoslovakia is named after its two main ethnic groups, the Czechs and the Slovaks. Both Czech and Slovak are official national languages. Fortunately, the two are so much alike that Czechs and Slovaks have little trouble understanding each other.

Czechoslovakia is a country that was created from the old Austrian Empire after World War I. As you have read, Nazi Germany took control of the country in 1939. The Germans were driven out at the end of World War II. Three years later, in 1948, communists came to power. They have run the country ever since.

Czechoslovakia has been an industrial nation since the late 1800s. Today only about 10 percent of the people of Czechoslovakia are farmers. Major Czech industries include iron and steel, machinery, and automobiles.

Poland

Poland was once a powerful country. From the 1300s to the 1600s, it controlled large parts of Eastern Europe. In the 1700s the Polish kingdom grew

weak, and it was divided between Russia, Prussia, and Austria. Only after World War I did Poland become an independent country once again.

During World War II, the western part of Poland was taken over by Nazi Germany, while the eastern part was taken over by the Soviet Union. Later, Soviet armies drove out the Nazis. In 1947 a communist government gained power in Poland and has remained in power ever since.

Many Poles do not like the kind of communist rule under which they live. Since the 1950s, strikes by workers and other protests against the government have occurred in Poland. In the 1980s a workers' movement called Solidarity began. It wants free elections and better living conditions for the Polish people. However, the Polish government has not given in to the demands of this movement.

In the area of farming, however, the Polish government has made some changes. Following the example of the Soviet Union, communists took land away from the big landowners. However, they took land away from the small farmers as well. Large farms called collectives were formed. On a **collective,** a group of families works the land together. Each family is paid according to the work that family members have done on the farm. The government tells the collective how much and what kind of crops to grow. It also sets the prices that will be paid for the crops.

Many of the small farmers in Poland did not like having their land taken away. They did not like collective farms at all. They wanted to keep the land that their families had lived on for many generations. They wanted a **market economy** like the economies of Western Europe. In a market economy, businesses, including farms, have the freedom to produce what they choose. They also can sell their products for whatever price they can get in the marketplace.

In the 1950s the Polish government agreed to some of the farmers' demands. Many collective farms were broken up and given back to the small farmers. Today, much of Poland's farmland is held by individual families.

However, the country still has a command economy. For the most part, farmers must grow crops the government wants and sell most of what they produce to the government at fixed prices. The government then sells the crops to the people.

More than one-fourth of Poland's workers are in farming. Farm products such as ham are one of the nation's leading exports.

Putting Down a Revolt

Most governments in Eastern Europe are not only communist but also very friendly to the Soviet Union. They are members of the Warsaw Pact. The armies of the Warsaw Pact countries have been used to put down rebellions against communist rule. That is what happened in Czechoslovakia in 1968.

During the 1960s Czechoslovakia began to move away from the Soviet Union. Citizens were given more freedom. They could even criticize their government. Czechoslovakia also grew friendlier toward the West.

Leaders of the Soviet Union and some Eastern European countries worried that the changes would weaken communist control in Czechoslovakia. They feared that people in other communist countries might want such changes too. As a result, the countries of the Warsaw Pact sent troops into Czechoslovakia to bring back the communist way of doing things. The troops replaced the president of Czechoslovakia with a new leader. Since then, Czechoslovakia usually has done whatever the Soviet Union has wanted.

Warsaw Pact tanks roll through the streets of Prague, Czechoslovakia.

Reviewing the Lesson

Recalling Key Words, People, and Places
1. Identify the key words defined below:
    a. a system in which the government decides how the economy is to be run
    b. a farm worked by a large group of people and directed by the government
2. Why has Berlin stayed divided?

Remembering Main Ideas
1. Why have the boundaries between the northern countries of Eastern Europe changed so often?
2. Describe how a steel mill in East Germany operates.
3. How do most Czechoslovakians earn a living?
4. What is farming in Poland like today?
5. What did Warsaw Pact armies do in Czechoslovakia in 1968?

Thinking Things Over
Compare the command economies of Eastern Europe with the market economy of the United States.

Lesson 2   Southern Countries of Eastern Europe

LOOKING AHEAD As you read, look for—

Key words, people, and **places:**

guerrilla

Bulgars
Josip Broz Tito

Answers to these questions about **main ideas:**

1. What are the land and people of the southern countries of Eastern Europe like?
2. What are the main economic activities in Yugoslavia and Albania?
3. How do the people of Bulgaria and Romania make a living?
4. What was the result of the 1956 Hungarian revolt?
5. How do the countries of Yugoslavia and Hungary differ from most other communist countries?

The southern countries of Eastern Europe include Yugoslavia, Albania, Bulgaria, Romania, and Hungary. Find these countries on the map on page 262. Which two countries have coasts on the Adriatic Sea? Which other two countries border the Black Sea?

All these countries, except Hungary, are located in the Balkans—the area once known as the "powder keg of Europe."

Land and People

As you have read, one reason why the Balkans were so explosive was the number of different ethnic groups living in the area. The southern countries of Eastern Europe still contain many ethnic groups. Yugoslavia, for example, has six major ethnic groups and eighteen smaller ones within its borders.

The landforms, soils, and climates of each of the southern countries of Eastern Europe differ. Yugoslavia, for example, has a long coast on the Adriatic Sea. Fishing and tourism are important

there. On the other hand, most of the land in Albania is mountainous with poor soil. The steep slopes and poor soil are two reasons why Albania is the poorest country in Europe.

Romania also contains mountains. They include the Transylvanian Alps, which extend through the central part of the country. However, fertile plains along the Danube River give Romania a large amount of good farmland. Bulgaria and Hungary also have fertile plains. Bulgaria raises and exports fruits and vegetables to the rest of Eastern Europe. Hungary, as you have read, contains the Hungarian Basin, Eastern Europe's richest farming area.

Climates in the southern part of Eastern Europe also vary. The coasts of the Black Sea and the Adriatic Sea generally have warm climates with one dry season. One part of Bulgaria's Black Sea coast, however, has a warm climate that is wet all year. Most places away from the coasts have cool climates that are wet all year.

Yugoslavia and Albania

Yugoslavia was formed after World War I. The countries of Serbia and Montenegro, along with part of the Austrian Empire, were combined to form Yugoslavia.

Since World War II Yugoslavia has built many industries. Today it produces steel, wood products, cement, and textiles. Yugoslavia even makes automobiles, some of which are sold in the United States.

Albania's communist government keeps very tight control over the country. Few people are allowed into Albania or out of it. It is one of the world's most totalitarian countries. The government outlawed all churches, mosques, and public worship in 1967. Before the ban on religions, most Albanians were Muslims. More than three out of every five people in Albania work on farms. All farms are owned by the government.

Bulgaria and Romania

Bulgaria was founded by nomadic people from central Asia, the Bulgars, who took control of the area in the A.D. 600s. The Bulgars mixed with the

Linking Past and Present

Castle Dracula

The Translyvanian Alps cut through northern Romania. Among the castles scattered through these mountains is the one you see in the picture—Castle Dracula.

Castle Dracula was built in the 1400s by a prince named Vlad Tepes. Tepes was a great soldier who successfully defended his region against the Ottoman Turks. At the same time, he was a man of terrible temper and great cruelty. He murdered many hundreds of the peasants under his control.

After Tepes died, the peasants in the mountains began to tell stories about him. The stories combined his wicked actions with vampire legends. The fictional vampire is a dead person that comes to life at night and attacks innocent people.

In 1897 English novelist Bram Stoker published his novel *Dracula*. It was

based on the life of and legends about Vlad Tepes. Since Stoker's book was published, the Dracula legend has been turned into various movies and television programs. Thousands of tourists come to Romania each year to see Castle Dracula. They walk around its stone walls and look through its narrow windows. What do you suppose they expect to see?

local people. The Ottoman Turks conquered the area in the 1300s and ruled for more than 500 years. With the help of the Russians, Bulgaria broke away from the Ottoman Empire in the 1870s.

Bulgaria, with its rich soil, is an important agricultural country. Farmlands cover over half the country. Such grains as wheat and corn are the leading crops. More than 90 percent of Bulgaria's farmland is owned and operated by the government.

Since World War II, industry has expanded in Bulgaria. Today almost two-thirds of Bulgarians work in manufacturing or service jobs and live in urban areas. Bulgaria's major industrial products are chemicals, metal products, and textiles.

The area of present-day Romania was conquered by the Romans in A.D. 106. Since that time, the area has been invaded from every direction. Magyars and Slavs invaded from the west and Mongols came from Asia in the east. From the north came Russians and, in the 1400s, the Ottoman Turks invaded from the south. Romania finally became independent in 1878.

Romania still is mainly an agricultural country. About two out of every five workers are farmers. Over 90 percent of the farms and all businesses in Romania are owned and operated by the government.

The Romanian government is trying hard to improve the country's industries. Romania's major industry is making machines for factories, mines, and farms. Romania's capital city, Bucharest, is the main industrial center.

Hungary

Nomadic, horse-riding people from central Asia—the Magyars—settled Hungary in the 800s. For many years, part of Hungary was ruled by the Ottoman Turks. Then, it became part of the Austrian Empire. Hungary gained its independence when the Austrian Empire broke up after World War I.

The main goods produced in Hungary are iron and steel, machinery, and communications equipment. Hungary exports agricultural goods such as grain, vegetables, and dairy products.

Hungarians revolted against their communist leaders in 1956. The Hungarian government, with the help of 200,000 Soviet soldiers and 2,500 Soviet tanks, quickly stopped the revolution. The Soviet Union would not allow a communist government to be overthrown. More than 200,000 Hungarians then fled the country to the United States.

Different Ways of Being Communist

All the southern countries of Eastern Europe are communist. Yet, they have different ways of doing things. Yugoslavia and Hungary are good examples of differences in communist systems.

During World War II, many Yugoslavs fought as **guerrillas**—fighters who are not part of a regular army. They fought against the Nazi Germans who had conquered their country. The main group of guerrillas were communists led by Josip Broz Tito (tē′tō). After the war, Tito and his followers took control of the country. Like every other communist government, Tito's

Hungary has many privately owned farms as well as collectives.

did not allow noncommunists to take part in the government. However, Tito also wanted to be independent of the Soviet Union. He threatened to fight if Soviet troops entered his country.

Yugoslavia has refused to take sides in the Cold War. It does not belong to the Warsaw Pact. Yugoslavia remains friends with both western countries and the Soviet Union.

Hungary has followed a different path. It is a member of the Warsaw Pact. Hungarian troops joined with Soviet troops to invade Czechoslovakia in 1968. Hungary, however, differs from the Soviet Union in its economy.

Visitors to Hungarian cities notice that markets are always full of fresh fruits, vegetables, and meat. These items are sometimes hard to get in other communist countries. In those countries, buyers sometimes have to wait hours in line to buy groceries.

In Hungary, a large part of the food comes from privately owned farms rather than from collective farms. However, Hungary is most different from other communist countries because many of its small businesses are privately owned. These private businesses compete with government-owned businesses.

Even in government-owned businesses, decisions about what and how much to produce are usually made by local managers rather than by the central government. These managers make many decisions based on what they think buyers want.

Hungary trades with western as well as communist countries. For example, a Hungarian factory has an agreement with an American manufacturer of blue jeans to make jeans in Hungary. Hungarian jeans are sold all over Europe.

Reviewing the Lesson

Recalling Key Words, People, and Places
1. What is the name given to a fighter who is not part of a regular army?
2. Tell what is important to remember about Josip Broz Tito.

Remembering Main Ideas
1. Name two kinds of climates found in the southern countries of Eastern Europe.
2. How do most Albanians earn a living?
3. Who owns almost all of the farmland in Romania and Bulgaria?
4. Why did so many Hungarians flee their country after 1956?
5. How is Hungary's economy different from that of most other communist countries?

Thinking Things Over
Are private businesses or government-owned businesses more likely to give buyers what they want? Base your answer on Hungary's experience.

Interpreting Political Cartoons

If you are like most people, you probably enjoy cartoons. A cartoon takes but a moment to read. What you read usually makes you laugh.

Some cartoons also make you think. These are the political cartoons that appear in newspapers and magazines. Such cartoons comment on political issues or people of the times. A political cartoon always expresses a point of view.

A Point of View About the Cold War

Look at the cartoon below.

"Handshake." A British view of Khrushchev and Eisenhower during the Cold War era.

This cartoon appeared in the mid-1950s. In order to understand it, you need to know what was going on in the world then. Here are some facts to help:

- During the 1950s, an ongoing, nonmilitary conflict known as the *Cold War* took place between communist countries and noncommunist countries.
- The communist countries were led by the Soviet Union, under General Secretary Nikita S. Khrushchev.
- The noncommunist countries were led by the United States, under President Dwight D. Eisenhower.
- In 1955, these two leaders met to try to solve their problems and put an end to the Cold War.

The cartoon expresses a point of view about this meeting. Read its title. What does a handshake between two people usually indicate? Now look at the picture of Khrushchev (on the left) and Eisenhower (on the right). What are the two men doing? Why do people sometimes arm wrestle? What does the cartoonist think about the Khrushchev-Eisenhower meeting?

A Point of View About Life in the Soviet Union

The cartoon you just looked at uses a single picture and a caption to express a point of view. On the next page is a different kind of political cartoon.

"And so, Comrades, rush right down to your local commissary and buy a box without delay."

Dana Fradon

This cartoon has two frames, or pictures, with a quotation below the first one. Look at the first frame, and read the quotation. Can you tell who is speaking? Look at the second frame. How do the people respond?

In order to understand the point of this cartoon, you need to know who the people are. The cartoonist provided clues. Notice the word *Comrades*. *Comrade* is a term that members of the Communist Party use for one another. Notice the clothes the people are wearing. The clothes go along with the mental picture that many Americans have of the Russian peasant. Along with the cartoonist's words, the clothes help us to identify the people as Soviet citizens.

How do the Soviet citizens respond to the commercial that they are watching on TV? Like all good Soviets, they do exactly as they are told to do. Notice too that they are told to go to a commissary—a kind of supply store usually found in places such as army camps. This cartoonist is expressing a point of view about life in the Soviet Union. How would you state that point of view?

Skills Practice

Find three political cartoons in a newspaper or magazine. Then do the following for each one.
1. Identify the characters.
2. Describe the issue being shown.
3. Tell the cartoonist's point of view.

271

Chapter Summary

Lesson 1 Northern Countries of Eastern Europe—Much of East Germany, Poland, and Czechoslovakia lies on the North European Plain and has good farmland. All three nations have communist governments and similar kinds of economies. East Germany and Czechoslovakia are both industrial nations. In Poland, more than one-fourth of the workers are in farming.

Lesson 2 Southern Countries of Eastern Europe—This region includes many different ethnic groups and varying kinds of land, soil, and climate. Major industrial products in the region include steel, textiles, and machinery. Farming is important in Albania, Bulgaria, Romania, and Hungary. All countries in the region are communist and all except Yugoslavia have close ties with the Soviet Union. In economic matters, however, Hungary is fairly independent.

Write your answers on a separate sheet of paper.

Testing Key Words, People, and Places

Part A

Choose the key word from the list that best completes each sentence.

1. Businesses have the freedom to produce whatever they choose in a _____.

2. The government decides how a country's economy is to be run under a _____.

3. A fighter who is part of a group that is not part of a regular army is a _____.

4. On a _____, a group of families works the land together.
   a. command economy
   b. collective
   c. market economy
   d. guerrilla

Part B

Match each description with the correct person or ethnic group in the list.

1. broke away from the Ottoman Empire
2. an ethnic group in Czechoslovakia
3. led Yugoslavia after World War II
   a. Czechs   **c.** Josep Broz Tito
   b. Bulgars

Testing Main Ideas

Choose the answer that best completes each sentence.

1. In the northern countries of Eastern Europe, most people live
   a. in rural areas.
   b. in cities.
   c. on collectives.
2. East Germany's government has a
   a. command economy.
   b. collective economy.
   c. market economy.
3. When the communists came to power in Poland,
   a. they did away with collectives.
   b. they formed collectives.
   c. they gave land to small farmers.

4. In 1968 the Soviet Union and its allies crushed a rebellion in
  a. East Germany.
  b. Yugoslavia.
  c. Czechoslovakia.

5. Under the government of Albania,
  a. religion is banned.
  b. people worship as they please.
  c. all people must work on farms.

6. The Soviet Union invaded Hungary in 1956 because
  a. Hungary invaded Bulgaria.
  b. Hungary traded goods with western countries.
  c. Hungarians tried to overthrow the government.

7. Hungary differs from other East European countries in that many of its small businesses are
  a. privately owned.
  b. owned by the government.
  c. going bankrupt.

The marvels of Soviet technology come to Hungary

Testing Skills

1. Interpreting political cartoons. The political cartoon at right above was published in American newspapers after leaders of the 1956 Hungarian revolution were executed by the Soviets. Study the cartoon. Then answer the questions.
  a. What country is represented by the man in the cartoon?
  b. How are the airplanes and the rope similar in meaning?
  c. Do you think the artist approved or disapproved of the executions? Explain your answer.

2. Classifying. For each country, write an *I* if the country is mainly industrialized. Write an *A* if the country is mainly agricultural.
  a. East Germany   **c.** Romania
  b. Czechoslovakia   **d.** Albania

Activities

1. Trace a map of Eastern Europe, including national boundaries, and show the location of each country's capital.

2. Find out why Lech Walesa of Poland won the Nobel Peace Prize in 1983.

273

Chapter 13

The Soviet Union Today

The Communist Party is the only political party allowed to exist in the Soviet Union. This makes the Communist Party very different from political parties in Western Europe or the United States. The picture shows a Communist Party leader addressing party members in the Soviet Union.

In this chapter, you will learn how the Soviet communist system works. You also will learn about Soviet life. The lessons in the chapter are listed below.

Lesson 1   The Communist System of Government

Lesson 2   Life in the Soviet Union

Lesson 1　The Communist System of Government

📖 **LOOKING AHEAD**　As you read, look for—

Key words, people, and **places:**

general secretary　　　Kremlin
premier
oligarchy

Answers to these questions about **main ideas:**

1. How is the Communist Party organized in the Soviet Union?
2. How does the government operate in the Soviet Union?
3. How does a person become a Communist Party member in the Soviet Union?

In some ways the Soviet Union looks like a republic. Voters elect representatives to a national legislature. An executive branch carries out the laws. In reality, though, voters in the Soviet Union have no choice of candidates, nor does the lawmaking branch of government have any real power. All important decisions are made by a few leaders of the Communist Party.

The Soviet Union reports that 99.9 percent of its people cast their ballots in every election (left). However, it is the Communist Party leaders (right) who make the important decisions in the Soviet Union. They control practically all phases of government and life.

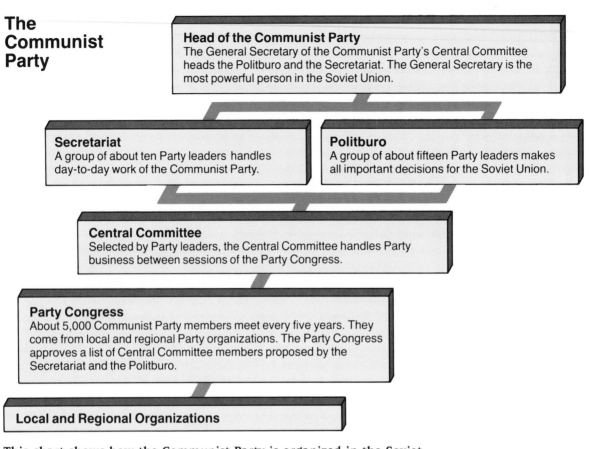

The Communist Party

Head of the Communist Party
The General Secretary of the Communist Party's Central Committee heads the Politburo and the Secretariat. The General Secretary is the most powerful person in the Soviet Union.

Secretariat
A group of about ten Party leaders handles day-to-day work of the Communist Party.

Politburo
A group of about fifteen Party leaders makes all important decisions for the Soviet Union.

Central Committee
Selected by Party leaders, the Central Committee handles Party business between sessions of the Party Congress.

Party Congress
About 5,000 Communist Party members meet every five years. They come from local and regional Party organizations. The Party Congress approves a list of Central Committee members proposed by the Secretariat and the Politburo.

Local and Regional Organizations

This chart shows how the Communist Party is organized in the Soviet Union today. What is the title of the most powerful person in the Soviet Union? Who chooses members of the Central Committee?

How the Communist Party Is Organized

Look at the organization chart of the Communist Party on this page. At the lowest level are more than 320,000 local and regional organizations. Local and regional organizations are found at every school, factory, office, and farm. Every five years, about 5,000 members from these organizations attend the Party Congress. Find the Party Congress on the chart.

Near the top of the chart are two small groups, the Politburo and the Secretariat. The Politburo makes all important decisions about running the country. These decisions include all important matters about the government, economy, Communist Party, army, and police. The Secretariat makes sure these decisions are carried out. You can see from the chart that the head of the Communist Party is called the **general secretary**.

During the 1930s and 1940s, Joseph Stalin was the general secretary of the Communist Party's Central Committee. Check your library to find out who is the present general secretary if you do not know.

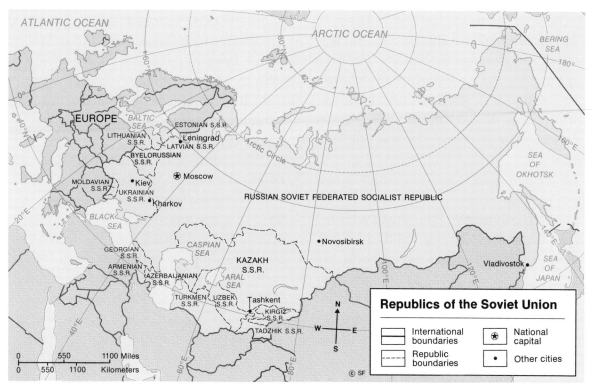

ATLANTIC OCEAN

ARCTIC OCEAN

BERING SEA

EUROPE

BALTIC SEA

ESTONIAN S.S.R.

LITHUANIAN S.S.R.

Leningrad

LATVIAN S.S.R.

BYELORUSSIAN S.S.R.

Arctic Circle

SEA OF OKHOTSK

MOLDAVIAN S.S.R.

Kiev

Moscow

UKRAINIAN S.S.R.

Kharkov

RUSSIAN SOVIET FEDERATED SOCIALIST REPUBLIC

BLACK SEA

CASPIAN SEA

Novosibirsk

Vladivostok

SEA OF JAPAN

GEORGIAN S.S.R.

KAZAKH S.S.R.

ARMENIAN S.S.R.

AZERBAIJANIAN S.S.R.

ARAL SEA

TURKMEN S.S.R.

UZBEK S.S.R.

Tashkent

KIRGIZ S.S.R.

TADZHIK S.S.R.

N W E S

0   550   1100 Miles
0   550   1100 Kilometers

© SF

Republics of the Soviet Union

International boundaries

National capital

Republic boundaries

Other cities

Map Study

This map shows the republics that make up the Soviet Union. Look at the map key. How are international boundaries shown on the map? How are the boundaries of the republics of the Soviet Union shown? Look at the map itself. How are the names of the republics shown?

How the Government Works

The national lawmaking body of the Soviet Union is called the Supreme Soviet. Like the United States Congress, the Supreme Soviet is made up of two houses. One house is elected according to population. The other house has representatives from the different republics that make up the Soviet Union. Look at the map on this page. Which Soviet republic covers the greatest amount of land?

The Supreme Soviet meets twice a year. Its only duty is to approve laws suggested by the Politburo. The Supreme Soviet never rejects a law that party leaders want.

The executive branch of the government is headed by a Council of Ministers. The Council of Ministers is like a cabinet. The chairman of the council is called the **premier**.

The national government of the Soviet Union is located in the capital of Moscow. Both the Supreme Soviet and the Council of Ministers meet in the ancient fortress of the city called the Kremlin.

The real leader of the Soviet Union is not the premier but the general secretary of the Communist Party's Central Committee. He is similar to an American President or a British prime minister. Citizens do not vote for the general secretary. He is chosen by the Politburo.

A type of government in which a few people have all the ruling power is called an **oligarchy**. The Soviet Union is an oligarchy, and the Politburo is its ruling body. Under the Soviet political system, the real debate about major issues takes place among the few members of the Politburo. The Politburo holds debates in secret.

As you have learned, the members of the Politburo tell the Supreme Soviet which laws to pass. They also decide who the one candidate for each major public office will be. Soviet citizens simply vote their approval of the party's choice.

Discussion of important political and economic issues often does take place within the many thousands of local party organizations. Elections for local offices, for example, may be hotly contested among several candidates. These candidates, of course, are all Communist Party members. Very often, however, each one will voice different ideas about how the country should be run.

Linking Past and Present

The Kremlin

The Kremlin—the place you see in the picture—and the government of the Soviet Union have been closely connected for almost 700 years. A *kremlin* is an area within a city protected by high walls. Moscow's first Kremlin was made of logs and earth. It was built in the 1300s, when Russia was ruled by the Mongols. The stone walls that surround the present-day Kremlin were built in the late 1400s by Ivan the Great, the tsar who drove the Mongols out of Russia.

From the time of Ivan the Great, the tsars lived in one of the palaces inside the Kremlin. In addition to palaces, the Kremlin contains more than a dozen churches and other buildings. Because they were constructed at different times, the buildings look different.

Many have tall towers with onion-shaped domes on top.

In 1955 the communists, who also rule from the Kremlin, turned some of the Kremlin's buildings into a national museum. Today the Soviet people go there to look at the crowns, clothing, and jewels that the tsars wore long ago.

General Secretary Mikhail Gorbachev's wife, Raisa, can shop abroad for the latest fashions. She is shown here with French president François Mitterand.

Who Party Members Are

Only about one of every sixteen Soviet people belongs to the Communist Party. To join, a person must be eighteen years old and be recommended by three party members. Members usually come from the Young Communist League, one organization that the Communist Party runs for young people.

At age eight, children can join the Octoberites. The Octoberites are named for the month in which Lenin and the Bolsheviks seized power in Russia. At age ten, children can join the Young Pioneers. At age fourteen, they are ready for the Young Communist League. In all three organizations, young persons play together, help out their communities, learn about their country, and learn about communism.

Soviet citizens join the Communist Party for several reasons. Some believe in communism. Also, party membership helps people get better jobs and better places to live. Children of party members have a good chance of going to special schools. A good school, in turn, helps them get the jobs they want. Important party members also can get goods such as washing machines and cars. These items are hard to get in the Soviet Union. Party members can also help relatives and friends get jobs and goods.

Many Soviet citizens dislike the fact that party members are given privileges. However, people do not criticize the Communist Party in public. They know that doing so will get them in trouble. People who speak against the government often are exiled to Siberia.

Reviewing the Lesson

Recalling Key Words, People, and Places
1. Identify the key words defined below:
   a. the head of the Soviet Communist Party
   b. the chairman of the executive branch of the Soviet government
   c. a government in which a few people have all the ruling power
2. Tell why it is important to remember the Kremlin.

Remembering Main Ideas
1. Which two groups in the Communist Party make and carry out decisions?
2. What is the role of the Supreme Soviet in government?
3. Why do people want to be members of the Soviet Communist Party?

Thinking Things Over
In what ways are the Soviet communist government and West European parliamentary governments different?

Lesson 2   Life in the Soviet Union

LOOKING AHEAD As you read, look for—

Key words, people, and **places:**

strike   Red Square
cooperative

Answers to these questions about **main ideas:**

1. What jobs do members of the Popov family have?
2. What is school like in the Soviet Union?
3. What kind of housing is available in Moscow?
4. What kinds of sports and entertainment does Ludya Popov like?

If you visited the Soviet Union, you would see much that looks like the rest of Europe. You also would see many things that are different from Western Europe. By visiting a family in the Soviet Union, you can learn a little about what life there is like.

A Soviet Family

Ludmilla (Ludya for short) Ivanovna Popov lives in Moscow. If you asked Ludya about her name, she would tell you that *Ivanovna* comes from her father's first name and means "daughter of Ivan." All Russians bear their father's first name in their middle name.

Ludya's father works for the trade union organization of the Soviet Union. All workers belong to a trade union, and all trade unions are run by the government. Mr. Popov translates articles from German and English newspapers. The Soviet government wants to know what trade unions in other countries are doing. Because he speaks several languages, Mr. Popov takes visiting unionists from other nations on tours of Moscow. Ludya has met many people from Western Europe.

Unlike most trade unions in Western Europe, Soviet unions are not allowed to **strike**—stop work to try to get better wages and working conditions. The government, which runs all trade unions and businesses, does not allow strikes. It claims to represent the interests of all the people. Going on strike in the Soviet Union, the Soviet government tells its workers, would be like striking against oneself.

Ludya's mother works as a nurse in a large hospital. Like all Soviet hospitals, it is owned by the government. Very few men work at the hospital. Most of the Soviet Union's doctors and nurses are women. Almost all Soviet women work outside the home.

No one but the very top leaders in the Soviet Union is paid much money. However, many things that people buy in the United States are provided by the government. For example, medical care is free. Vacations in resorts are paid for by Mr. Popov's union. Housing takes only a small portion of the Popovs' income.

The Popovs do not belong to a church or synagogue. The Soviet

280

government tries to discourage religion. As a member of the Communist Party, Mr. Popov does not want to act against the wishes of his government.

Going to School

When Ludya was little, she stayed with her grandmother during the day. Many children go to nursery schools operated by the Soviet government. Since these are often overcrowded, the Popovs were lucky to have Ludya's grandmother nearby.

Ludya began regular school at the age of six. The students who do best in elementary school go to high schools that prepare them for the university. Other students go to trade schools.

Ludya has worked hard at school. She has studied mathematics, sciences, and foreign languages. Since she is a good student, she sits in the front row of her class. The class is divided into five rows of seven students each. The row that has done best the previous week sits in front. The students who have done poorly sit in the back. Each row competes with the others. Students help each other so that they can keep their row ahead of the others. Students criticize each other so that they will improve. This kind of teamwork is part of the Soviet idea that people should learn and work together.

The Soviet government believes that the work students do should benefit the country. Students study a great deal of math and science to benefit their country. The government says that training scientists and engineers will help the country grow stronger.

Most people in Moscow live in apartment buildings. Different families may share a bathroom and kitchen.

281

These children in Moscow enjoy chess.

Living Conditions

The Popovs live in one of the newer parts of Moscow. Like most people in Moscow, the family lives in an apartment building owned and run by the government. Their apartment has one bedroom, a living room, a bathroom, and a kitchen. Ludya sleeps on a pull-out bed in the living room.

One day, if they can save enough money, the Popovs hope to buy a larger apartment in a **cooperative,** which is a building owned and operated by the people who live there. The Popovs also hope to buy a car. Not many Soviet people have their own cars. Being a member of the Communist Party will help Mr. Popov get a car if the family can save enough money.

Ludya's grandmother says that the Popovs are lucky to have such a nice apartment. Many families have to live in one room. They share a kitchen and bathroom with other families.

Grandmother also says that people should be happy to have so much good food to eat. She remembers the days during World War II—which the Soviets call "The Great Patriotic War"—when people were hungry all the time, and millions died. The Soviet people have never forgotten this terrible war in which more than one out of every ten Soviet people was killed.

Having Fun

Ludya and her family enjoy many of the same things that families in Western European nations do. On weekends they like to visit the park or the zoo. Sometimes they go to Red Square. This is the center of the city visited by tourists from all over the Soviet Union and the world. One of the main attractions in Red Square is Lenin's tomb. People stand in line for hours to get a glimpse of Lenin's preserved body.

The world-famous Bolshoi Theater Ballet of Moscow performs "Swan Lake" for appreciative Soviet audiences.

On weekends in the spring, the Popovs sometimes take trips to the country. They rent a little cottage in a small village about fifty miles from the city. During a part of each summer, Ludya goes to a government-owned camp. At summer camp Russian children learn crafts, boating, swimming, hiking, and camping. They also learn about a special topic each summer. When Ludya was eleven, she learned about Soviet ethnic groups. Ludya says she is proud to be Russian. However, she also likes to meet Soviet people from other ethnic groups, who speak different languages and do things in different ways.

Games and sports are an important part of Ludya's life. She does gymnastics and likes to watch the Olympic gymnasts when they perform in the Sports Palace in Moscow. She also likes to play chess, which is a major sport in the Soviet Union.

For a special treat, the Popovs get tickets to the ballet. These are hard to get because ballet is very popular in the Soviet Union. Watching the ballerinas glide and soar across the stage in "Swan Lake," Ludya wishes she were talented enough to be so graceful.

Reviewing the Lesson

Recalling Key Words, People, and Places
1. Identify the key words defined below:
   a. to stop work for the purpose of getting better wages or working conditions
   b. an apartment building owned and run by the people who live in it
2. Tell why Red Square is important.

Remembering Main Ideas
1. What work do Ludya's parents do?
2. Why does Ludya sit in the front row of her class?
3. In what kind of housing do the Popovs live?
4. Describe Ludya's summer camp.

Thinking Things Over
In what ways is Ludya's life different from yours? How is it similar?

Using a Map to Make Comparisons

The Soviet Union is the world's largest country, in area. It occupies more than one-seventh of the world's total land area. How did the Soviet Union grow to become so large?

Maps can show many things, including expansion, or growth, of countries. The map on these pages shows how the country that is now called the Soviet Union expanded from

1462 to 1917, the year of the Russian Revolution. During this time, the country was known as Russia. You can use this map to compare the size of Russia's territory at different times.

The Map Key Is the "Key"

The key to making comparisons on a map such as this is, in fact, the map key. Look at that key now. Notice that it includes six colored squares. The first square is pink and is labeled "Before 1462." Now find the area on

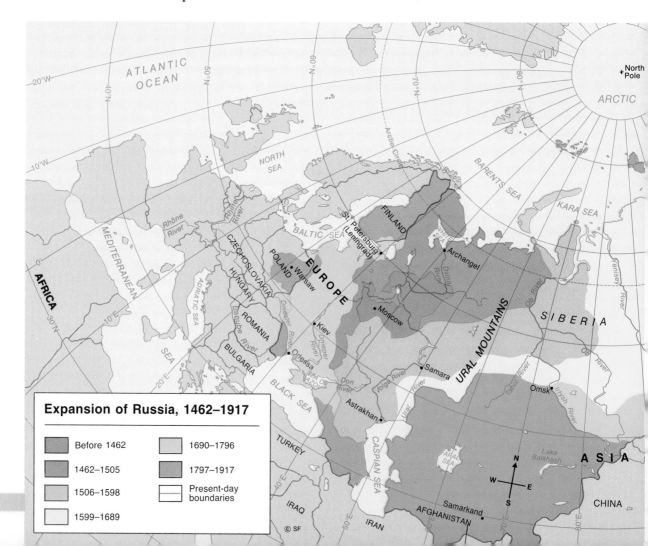

Expansion of Russia, 1462–1917

- Before 1462
- 1462–1505
- 1506–1598
- 1599–1689
- 1690–1796
- 1797–1917
- Present-day boundaries

© SF

the map that is that same color pink. It is the rather small area around the city of Moscow.

To understand how the country expanded over the years, here is what to do. Look at the next color square, and read the dates to the right of it. What is the first date? the second date? Then find the brown area on the map itself. The brown represents the expansion of Russia from 1462 to 1505. Continue in the same way with the rest of the key.

Making Comparisons

Now that you know how to read the map, you can use it to make comparisons. What comparison can you make between the size of Russia before 1462 and its size in 1917? Russia was over one hundred times larger in 1917 than before 1462. It extended to two continents. It included ports that Russia did not have before 1462.

Look again at Russia before 1462 and Russia of 1917. In which direction was expansion greatest: to the east or to the west? What do you suppose limited the westward expansion of this mighty country?

Now look at the present-day boundaries of the Soviet Union. Have any lands been lost since 1917? Where are those lands?

Skills Practice

1. During which period of expansion after 1462 did Russia increase its territory the most? the least?
2. Describe in your own words the territorial expansion that took place from 1462 to 1505. Use the names of features labeled on the map in your description. Also use latitude and longitude. Now describe Russian expansion between 1506 and 1598. How do the two compare?
3. How is the expansion that occurred from 1599 to 1689 different from that of the 1506–1598 period?

Chapter Summary

Lesson 1 The Communist System of Government—Although people in the Soviet Union elect representatives to a national legislature, all important decisions about running the country are made by the Politburo of the Communist Party. The duty of the Supreme Soviet, the Soviet Union's national law-making body, is to approve laws suggested by the Politburo. To join the Communist Party, a person must be eighteen years old and be recommended by three Party members.

Lesson 2 Life in the Soviet Union—Ludmilla Ivanova Popov lives in Moscow with her parents. Her father works for the trade union organization of the Soviet Union. Her mother is a nurse. In school, Ludmilla has studied mathematics, science, and foreign languages. The Popovs live in an apartment in Moscow. The Popovs like to visit the park or the zoo, or Red Square, or take a trip to the country. Ludmilla enjoys gymnastics and playing chess.

Write your answers on a separate sheet of paper.

Testing Key Words, People, and Places

Part A

Give the definition of each key word.

1. strike
2. cooperative
3. general secretary
4. premier
5. oligarchy

Part B

Choose the place that best completes each sentence.

1. The ancient fortress in the city of Moscow, shown on page 287, is called the _____.
2. In the center of Moscow is the _____.

   a. Red Square   **b.** Kremlin

Testing Main Ideas

Answer these questions.

1. What is the function of the Secretariat of the Communist Party?
2. What is the role of the general secretary?
3. What are the Octoberites?
4. How do trade unions in the Soviet Union differ from most trade unions in Western Europe?
5. Why do Soviet students study a great deal of science and math?
6. How could the Popovs living conditions be described?
7. What do Russian children study when they attend camp?

Testing Skills

1. **Making comparisons from maps.** Read the list of map titles. Then choose the two maps you would compare to decide whether each lettered statement is true or false.

   The Soviet Union: Population Distribution

   The Soviet Union: Climate Regions

   The Soviet Union: Natural Vegetation Regions

The Soviet Union: Major Cities
The Soviet Union: Land Use

a. Few people in the Soviet Union live in places that are cold and wet or ice-covered all year.

b. Needleleaf forests cover much of the land in the Soviet Union where the climate is cold and wet all year.

c. Population is more heavily distributed around Moscow than around Irkutsk.

d. The city of Tashkent has a climate that is cool and semi-dry all year.

e. Nomadic herding takes place on land in the Soviet Union where the climate is cold and wet all year.

2. **Practicing narrative writing.** Write a paragraph that answers the following questions.

a. Why does Ludmilla Popov sit in the front row of her class?

b. Who sits in the back row?

c. Why do the students in each row help and criticize each other?

d. What is your opinion of the seating arrangement at Ludmilla's school?

Activities

1. Imagine that you live in Moscow. Write four diary entries describing your day-to-day life. Include information about your parents' jobs and your schoolwork and future career plans.

2. Make a chart that shows differences between the Soviet government and the governments of Western European countries. List at least three differences in your chart. Give your chart a title.

3. Make a bulletin-board display of news stories about the Soviet Union. Check the daily newspaper every day for ten days. Clip or photocopy articles that deal with the Soviet Union. Post the articles on the bulletin board in the order in which they appeared in the paper.

Biography Anne Frank

Her family sometimes called her "Tender One." In 1947 the world came to know her name, Anne Frank. That was the year her diary was published. Since then *The Diary of Anne Frank* has become a symbol of courage and peace. After reading her diary, which is full of affection and caring, people who never met Anne Frank also knew her as "Tender One."

It is not unusual for a teenage girl to keep a diary, but Frank's diary was out of the ordinary. She wrote about the two years from 1942 to 1944, when her family and four other people had to hide in a tiny hidden part of an office in Amsterdam. These people had to hide because they were Jewish. The Nazis who had invaded the Netherlands were arresting and, in many cases, killing any Jewish people they could find.

Frank and the other Jews in hiding were helped by friends who were not Jewish. It was dangerous to help Jews then, but many people helped Jews because they did not approve of the Nazis.

Frank showed her concern for others through her writing. Although it was very difficult to hide and live in constant fear, Frank was aware of how much worse it was for the Jews who had no place to hide.

When the Nazis found Frank and the others in 1944, they were sent away to places called concentration camps, where many people died or were killed by the Nazis. Even there Frank showed courage. Witnesses said that when she saw others starving, she dared to ask for food for them. She was considered a leader by the others in the camp.

Sadly, though, Frank could not fight the sickness and starvation of the camp. She died in March, 1945, at the age of sixteen.

Back in Amsterdam, Frank's diary was discovered in its hiding place by a family friend. In her diary Anne Frank expressed hope that the world would improve. "I still believe, in spite of everything, that people are really good at heart," she wrote.

The Amsterdam hiding place is now a museum, called the Anne Frank House. It is also a meeting place for young people who want to promote world peace.

Questions to Think About

1. Was Anne Frank brave, even though she was called "Tender One"? Why do you think as you do?
2. Why do you suppose Anne Frank still believed that people are good?

Climate—the Silent Weapon

In 1812, a weapon more powerful than rifles or cannons helped defeat Napoleon Bonaparte's army. In 1941, the same weapon helped defeat the army of Adolph Hitler. That weapon was the climate of Russia, or the Soviet Union. Napoleon, trying to force the Russians to obey a trade agreement, invaded Russia in June, 1812. Over 100 years later, Hitler chose the same month to invade Russia during World War II. Both invasions were disasters.

Climate played a key role in both defeats, especially the bitter winter. Neither Napoleon nor Hitler planned to be fighting in winter. By invading in June, they thought their powerful armies could quickly capture Moscow, Russia's most important city. In both invasions, however, the Russian army fought the invaders along the way, staging ambushes and hit-and-run attacks. The climate also prevented the invaders from quickly reaching their goal. Summer, fall, and winter each took its toll.

In summer the soldiers were exhausted by marching hundreds of miles on hot and dusty unpaved roads. Travel also was hard on equipment. In 1812 many of Napoleon's wagons and cannons became stuck in loose sand. In 1941 dust and grit ruined the engines of Hitler's tanks.

In fall the invaders faced a new problem—rain. Downpours turned dusty roads and fields into seas of mud. Rivers that were easy to cross in summer were now cold and swollen.

Then, in early November, winter struck. None of the invading soldiers were ready for the freezing cold and heavy snow. In the summer heat, many of Napoleon's soldiers had simply dropped their winter coats by the wayside. In contrast, Hitler's soldiers never were equipped with winter coats or boots. Both Napoleon and Hitler lost more men to cold than to fighting.

Using Your Geography Skills

1. Why do you think the Russian climate was harder on the invading armies than on the Russian army?
2. Use the map on pages 36–37 to tell how the climate of the Soviet Union differs from the climate of western Europe.

Write your answers on a separate sheet of paper.

Key Words
Give the definition of each key word.

1. permafrost
2. nationalism
3. autocrat
4. socialism
5. communism
6. soviet
7. totalitarian
8. genocide
9. representative democracy
10. prime minister
11. command economy

Main Ideas
Choose the answer that best completes each sentence.

1. Europe's highest mountains are
   a. the Pyrenees.
   b. the Alps.
   c. the Apennines.
2. The North Atlantic Drift affects the climate of
   a. Western Europe.   c. Siberia.
   b. the Soviet Union.
3. More than half the land in Eastern Europe and the Soviet Union is
   a. plains.   c. hills.
   b. mountains.
4. The Fertile Triangle is located in
   a. Eastern Europe.
   b. Western Europe.
   c. the Soviet Union.
5. The Eurasian nation with the largest amount of mineral resources is
   a. Romania.
   b. the Soviet Union.
   c. Yugoslavia.

6. Most people in southern Europe are
   a. Eastern Orthodox.
   b. Roman Catholic.
   c. Protestant.
7. The prime minister of Sardinia who led the effort to unify Italy was
   a. Count Camillo Cavour.
   b. Giuseppe Mazzini.
   c. Giuseppe Garibaldi.
8. To force the southern German states into uniting with Prussia, Otto von Bismarck started a war between
   a. Prussia and the southern German states.
   b. Italy and France.
   c. France and Prussia.
9. Greece, Serbia, and Romania won independence from the
   a. Ottoman Empire.
   b. Russian Empire.
   c. Austrian Empire.
10. The Allied Powers included
   a. the Ottoman Empire, France, and Germany.
   b. Russia and Great Britain.
   c. Great Britain, France, and Russia.
11. The leader of the Bolsheviks was
   a. Alexander II.
   b. Vladimir Lenin.
   c. Joseph Stalin.

12. Hitler's takeover of Poland and Czechoslovakia took place
  a. after World War II began.
  b. after Germany invaded the Soviet Union.
  c. before World War II began.

13. The Catholics of Northern Ireland want Northern Ireland to
  a. join the Republic of Ireland.
  b. remain part of Great Britain.
  c. become an independent country.

14. Under the representative democracies of Great Britain and Scandinavia, people elect
  a. members of the parliament.
  b. a president.
  c. a prime minister.

15. Dortmund, Dusseldorf, and Essen are major industrial cities of
  a. Switzerland.
  b. West Germany.
  c. France.

16. The goal of the European Communities is to
  a. levy tariffs on goods.
  b. unite all the democratic countries of Europe.
  c. establish a Common Market.

17. The richest Mediterranean country is
  a. Italy.
  b. Greece.
  c. Spain.

18. East Germany and Poland have
  a. market economies.
  b. command economies.
  c. democratic governments.

19. The countries of Serbia and Montenegro were combined to form
  a. Yugoslavia.
  b. Bulgaria.
  c. Romania.

20. The General Secretary of the Communist Party is chosen by
  a. the Supreme Soviet.
  b. the Politburo.
  c. the Soviet voters.

Skills

1. Judging the news media. Read the headlines below. Write *F* if the headline gives a fact. Write *P* if the headline gives a point of view.
  a. U.S.–Soviet Summit Ends; Leaders Reach Arms Agreement
  b. President Triumphs at Summit
  c. Summit Results: Will They Last?
  d. President Calls Summit a Success

2. Using graphs.
  a. Which shows the parts of a whole, a circle graph or a line graph?
  b. Which shows change over time, a circle graph or a line graph?

Essay

Choose one of the events below. Then write an essay that describes three causes of the event.

1. Totalitarian governments arise in Europe.

2. World War II begins.

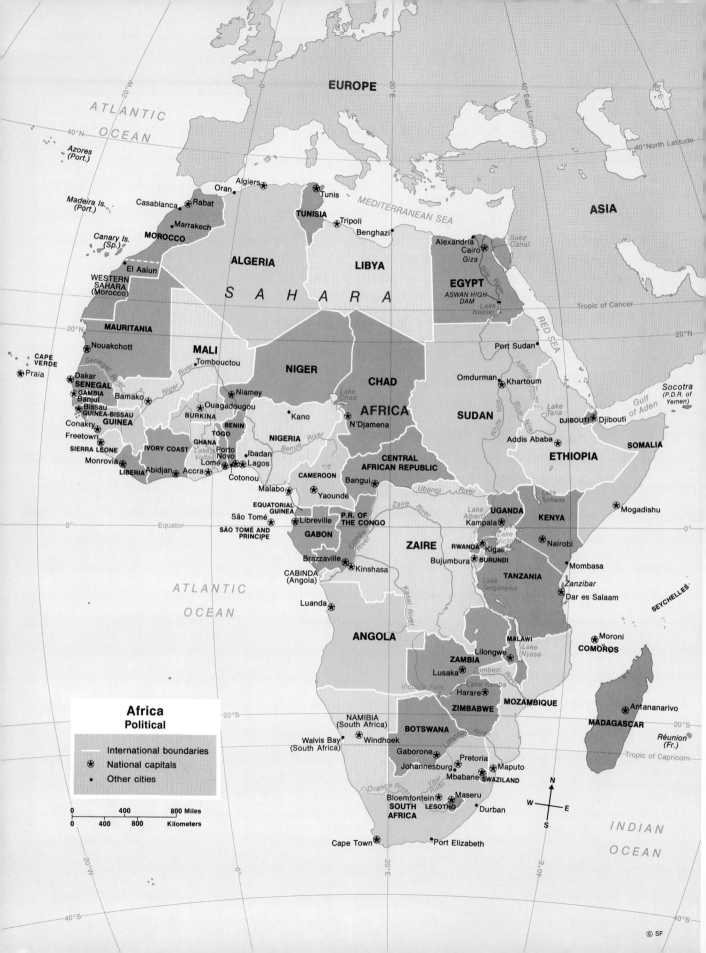

Africa

Africa is a huge and diverse continent. This is how John Gunther, an American travel writer, described Africa:

66 You could drop the continental United States into Africa four times and the edges would scarcely touch. And of course it is infinitely . . . complex. . . . Morocco differs from Swaziland more than Iceland differs from Peru. 99

In this unit you will learn about the geography and history of Africa. You also will learn about the ways that the African people live today.

Before You Go On

Preview the unit. Look at the chapter titles below and at the map on the left. What do you think is the major physical feature of northern Africa?

Study the map. Where are most of Africa's major cities located? What reason can you give for this?

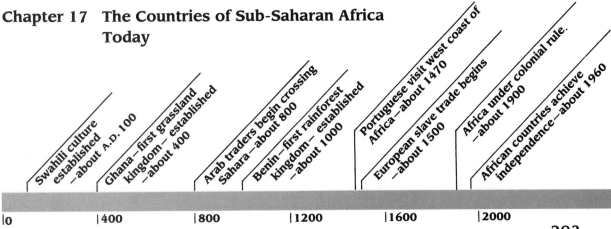

Swahili culture established –about A.D. 100

Ghana–first grassland kingdom–established –about 400

Arab traders begin crossing Sahara–about 800

Benin–first rainforest kingdom–established –about 1000

Portuguese visit west coast of Africa–about 1470

European slave trade begins –about 1500

Africa under colonial rule. –about 1900

African countries achieve independence–about 1960

|0 |400 |800 |1200 |1600 |2000

Chapter 14

The Land and the People of Africa

66 On the plains vast herds of zebra . . . graze the dry grasses, with gazelles and giraffes in smaller bands amongst them. In the forest . . . are buffalo and elephant, in the lakes hippopotamus and crocodile. 99

This is how a writer described one feature of Africa—its wildlife. The picture shows wildebeest grazing.

As you read this chapter, you will learn about the landforms, climate, and vegetation of Africa. You also will learn about natural resources and land use in Africa. Finally, you will learn about Africa's people. The lessons in the chapter are listed below.

Lesson 1   The Natural Environment of Africa

Lesson 2   Resources and Land Use in Africa

Lesson 3   The People of Africa

Lesson 1 The Natural Environment of Africa

 LOOKING AHEAD As you read, look for—

Key words, people, and **places:**

escarpment
cataract
oasis
savanna

Drakensberg Mountains
Atlas Mountains
Mount Kilimanjaro
Mount Kenya
Great Rift Valley

Lake Nyasa
Lake Tanganyika
Lake Victoria
Niger River
Congo River
Zambezi River
Victoria Falls
Sahara
Sahel

Answers to these questions about **main ideas:**

1. What kinds of landforms does Africa have, and where are they located?
2. What important bodies of water are found in Africa?
3. What are the patterns in Africa's climate and vegetation?
4. Into what five regions can Africa be divided?

The Egyptians knew that Africa was completely surrounded by water in 600 B.C. They had sailed around the continent. Over time, Europeans and Asians learned a great deal about the coasts of Africa but very little about its interior. Africa's mountains, rivers, forests, and deserts made travel in the interior difficult. As you read this lesson, you will learn why.

Africa's Landforms

Look back at the landform regions map on pages 32-33. Notice that much of the interior of Africa is a plateau. However, the elevation of this plateau differs from place to place. In general, the plateau in the southern part of Africa is higher than the plateau in northern Africa.

A band of lowlands—a coastal plain—surrounds much of the interior plateau. In many places the land rises sharply from the coastal plain to the plateau. These steep slopes between plain and

plateau are called **escarpments.** The escarpment of the Drakensberg Mountains in southern Africa rises sharply to as much as 10,000 feet above the coastal plain. Find the Drakensberg Mountains on the map on page 296.

On the map, notice that a number of other mountain ranges rise above the plateau. The longest mountain range in Africa—the Atlas Mountains—stands in the northwest. The Atlas Mountains have a number of peaks over 13,000 feet high.

Africa's highest mountains are in the eastern part of the continent. The two tallest are Mt. Kilimanjaro, at 19,340 feet, and Mt. Kenya, at 17,058 feet. Find these two mountains on the map on page 296. Both these mountains are volcanoes that are extinct, which means they are no longer active.

Both Mt. Kilimanjaro and Mt. Kenya rise above the Great Rift Valley. This is one of the longest and deepest valley systems in the world. Movements

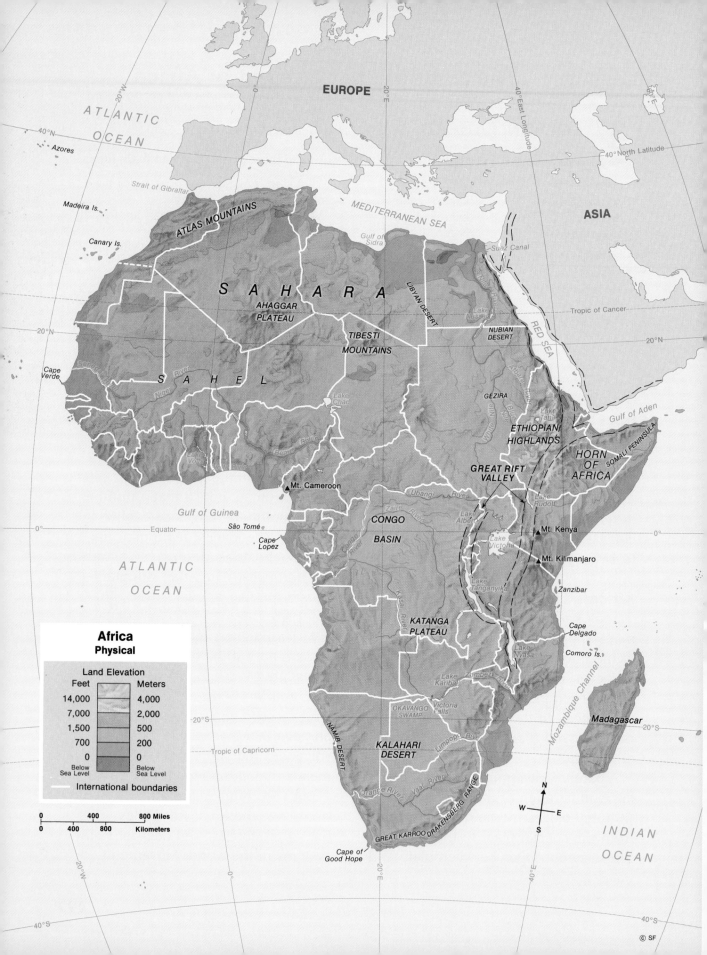

EUROPE

ATLANTIC
OCEAN

ASIA

40°N
40°N North Latitude

Azores

MEDITERRANEAN SEA

Madeira Is.
Strait of Gibraltar
Gulf of
Sidra

Suez Canal

Canary Is.
ATLAS MOUNTAINS

S A H A R A

LIBYAN DESERT

RED SEA

Tropic of Cancer
20°N

20°N
AHAGGAR
PLATEAU

NUBIAN
DESERT

Gulf of Aden

TIBESTI
MOUNTAINS

Lake
Nasser

Nile River

SOMALI PENINSULA

Cape
Verde

S A H E L

Niger River

Senegal River

Lake
Chad

GEZIRA

Blue Nile River

Lake
Tana

ETHIOPIAN
HIGHLANDS

HORN
OF
AFRICA

Mt. Cameroon

Benue River

Volta

GREAT RIFT
VALLEY

White Nile River

Lake
Rudolf

Gulf of Guinea

Ubangi River

CONGO

Zaire River

BASIN

Lake
Albert

Mt. Kenya

Equator
0°

São Tomé

Cape
Lopez

Congo River

Lake
Victoria

Mt. Kilimanjaro

Zanzibar

ATLANTIC

Kasai River

Lake
Tanganyika

Cape
Delgado

OCEAN

KATANGA
PLATEAU

Comoro Is.

Africa
Physical

Lake
Nyasa

Madagascar
20°S

Land Elevation

Mozambique Channel

Feet		Meters
14,000		4,000
7,000		2,000
1,500		500
700		200
0		0
Below Sea Level		Below Sea Level

Lake
Kariba

Zambezi River

OKAVANGO
SWAMP

Victoria
Falls

International boundaries

NAMIB DESERT

KALAHARI
DESERT

Limpopo River

20°S
Tropic of Capricorn

0   400   800 Miles

0   400   800
Kilometers

Orange River

Vaal River

N
W   E
S

GREAT KARROO

DRAKENSBERG RANGE

INDIAN

OCEAN

Cape of
Good Hope

40°S

© SF

under the earth's crust, which began millions of years ago, formed the Great Rift Valley. The valley runs for about 4,000 miles from Lake Nyasa (nī as′ə) in southeastern Africa north into Southwest Asia. The broken lines on the map on page 296 show the location of the Great Rift Valley. With your finger, trace its path from south to north.

Africa's Bodies of Water

Some important bodies of water sit in the Great Rift Valley. For example, the Red Sea, which forms the northeastern boundary of Africa, is part of the Great Rift Valley. The valley also is the location of two long lakes, Lake Tanganyika (tang′gə nyē′kə) and Lake Nyasa. At 450 miles long, Lake Tanganyika is the longest freshwater lake in the world. Lake Victoria, which is not part of the Great Rift Valley, is Africa's largest lake in area.

Africa has four major rivers—the Nile, the Niger, the Congo, and the Zambezi. The Nile flows into the Mediterranean Sea, the Niger and the Congo flow into the Atlantic Ocean, and the Zambezi flows into the Indian Ocean. Find these rivers on the map on page 296.

Traveling from the sea to the middle of the continent along Africa's rivers is

Victoria Falls is one of many huge African waterfalls.

difficult. Most of Africa's rivers plunge from the interior plateau to the coastal plain within a fairly short distance. For example, the Nile descends from the plateau in a series of six large waterfalls called **cataracts.**

The waterfalls on some of Africa's rivers are spectacular. The picture above shows Victoria Falls on the Zambezi River. These falls are about a mile wide and about 350 feet high at their highest point.

Map Study

This map shows the elevation of Africa's land. It also gives a general idea of the shape of the land. Locate two places in northern Africa that lie below sea level. About how high are the mountains in Madagasgar? Do you think the mountains in the Ethiopian Highlands have steep, rugged slopes? Why?

297

Africa's Climate and Vegetation

The climate regions of Africa stretch in great bands across the continent. The natural vegetation regions follow a similar pattern. You can see these patterns on the maps below and on page 299. Compare these two maps as you read.

The northwestern edge of the African continent—just north of the Atlas Mountains—has a warm climate with one dry season. This kind of climate has warm and dry summers and winters that are wet and somewhat cooler. The vegetation in this region consists of shrubs and small broadleaf trees that are green all year.

Most of northern Africa is a hot climate region that is dry all year. This region contains the huge desert called

---

Map Study

Locate Lagos—near the Niger River in Nigeria—and Kinshasa—on the Congo River in Zaire. Now imagine that you were going to travel from Lagos to Kinshasa. In which direction would you travel? How far would you have to go? Describe how the climate would change as you made your journey.

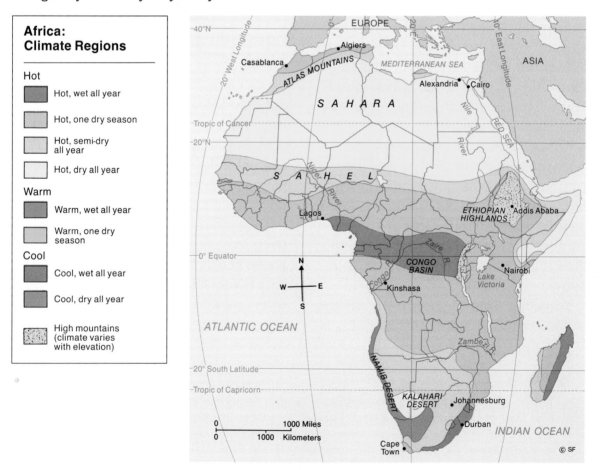

Africa: Climate Regions

Hot
- Hot, wet all year
- Hot, one dry season
- Hot, semi-dry all year
- Hot, dry all year

Warm
- Warm, wet all year
- Warm, one dry season

Cool
- Cool, wet all year
- Cool, dry all year
- High mountains (climate varies with elevation)

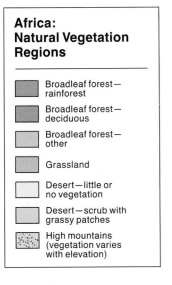

**Africa:
Natural Vegetation
Regions**

- Broadleaf forest—rainforest
- Broadleaf forest—deciduous
- Broadleaf forest—other
- Grassland
- Desert—little or no vegetation
- Desert—scrub with grassy patches
- High mountains (vegetation varies with elevation)

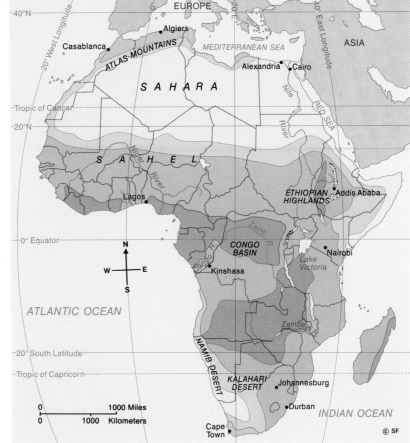

Map Study

Find the city of Nairobi, Kenya, on the map. What is the approximate latitude and longitude of Nairobi? What two bodies of water are closest to Nairobi? What is the natural vegetation in the region around Nairobi? Using the map on page 298, describe Nairobi's climate.

the Sahara. Little vegetation grows in the hot Sahara, except along the Nile River and in an occasional oasis. An **oasis** is a fertile spot in the desert where there is water and some vegetation.

A broad belt of grassland called **savanna** lies south of the Sahara. Near the desert the grasses are short and grow in patches. Moving southward the climate changes from hot and semi-dry all year to hot with one dry season.

With the change in climate, the grasses grow thicker and taller. Some small trees also grow in the areas of tall grasses.

In the center of Africa around the Equator, the climate changes to hot and wet all year. In this type of climate, temperatures average about 80°F. throughout the year, and rain falls nearly every afternoon. Thick rainforests grow in this climate.

Find the climate region that is hot and wet all year on the climate map on page 298. With your finger, trace a line from that climate region to the southern tip of Africa. As you move your finger, notice how the climate bands south of the hot and wet climate region are similar to those to the north. On the natural vegetation map on page 299, notice that the vegetation bands south of the Equator also are similar to those north of the Equator.

The Five Regions of Africa

Taking into account its landforms, climate, and vegetation, Africa can be divided into five regions. They are northern Africa, the desert fringe, western and central Africa, eastern Africa,

and southern Africa. Find these regions on the map below.

Northern Africa is made up of the lands bordering the Mediterranean Sea and the northern part of the vast Sahara. The desert fringe consists of the southern part of the Sahara and the semi-dry lands immediately south of the Sahara. The western part of the desert fringe also is called the Sahel (sä-hel'), which means "shore" in Arabic.

Western and central Africa contains the hot, wet lands around the Equator. Eastern Africa includes the areas east of where the Great Rift Valley begins. Finally, southern Africa occupies the southern tip of the continent. Later you will read about the countries in each of these five regions.

Map Study

Which two regions of Africa border on both the Atlantic and Indian oceans? What is the distance across Africa, from east to west, at the Equator?

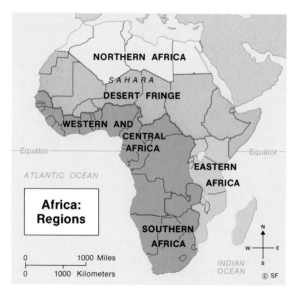

Africa: Regions

Reviewing the Lesson

Recalling Key Words, People, and Places
1. Identify the key words defined below:
    a. a steep slope
    b. a place in the desert where there is water and some vegetation
2. Tell where each place is located:
    a. Atlas Mountains
    b. Mt. Kilimanjaro
    c. Niger River

Understanding Main Ideas
1. What kind of landform makes up most of the interior of Africa?
2. Name two bodies of water located in the Great Rift Valley.
3. What type of natural vegetation is found directly south of the Sahara?
4. What is another name for the western part of the desert fringe region of Africa?

Thinking Things Over
Imagine you are traveling into the interior of Africa along the Zambezi River. Describe the scenery and natural obstacles you might encounter on your journey.

Lesson 2   Resources and Land Use in Africa

📖 **LOOKING AHEAD** As you read, look for—

Key words, people, and **places:**

shifting cultivation
plantation
Cape Town

Lagos
Alexandria
Lubumbashi
Johannesburg

Answers to these questions about **main ideas:**

1. What are Africa's major natural resources?
2. In what ways do Africans use the land?

66 We flew over the 'Big Hole' at Kimberley . . . it is three-quarters of a mile wide and 1,400 feet deep, and is supposed to be the largest hole on the earth's surface ever made by man. Out of it in less than half a century came something like fifteen million carats (over 6,000 pounds) of diamonds . . . 99

This is how a travel writer described a visit in the early 1950s to the Kimberley diamond mine in southern Africa. Diamonds are just one of the important resources found on the African continent.

Africa's Natural Resources

The map on page 302 shows Africa's rich mineral resources. One large area of minerals stretches south from Lake Victoria nearly all the way to the southern coast. From this area come large supplies of copper, gold, diamonds, silver, tin, uranium, and zinc. Find this area, which produces more than half the world's supply of diamonds and gold, on the map. What minerals besides those listed above are mined there?

A second belt of minerals occurs in western and central Africa. Such minerals as bauxite—aluminum ore—diamonds, and manganese come from this area. In addition, production of oil has been important since the 1960s.

A third area of minerals stretches from the Atlas Mountains in the northwest to the Red Sea. The Atlas Mountains have many kinds of minerals. Iron ore and phosphates are the most plentiful. Large supplies of oil and natural gas occur in the lands east of the Atlas Mountains. Compare the mineral resources map with the political map of Africa on page 292. Which countries in northern Africa have supplies of oil?

You have read that most of Africa's rivers have large waterfalls. Each of these waterfalls can be an important source of hydroelectricity. In fact, Africa has about 40 percent of the world's possible water-power resources. More than thirty African countries have built dams that produce hydroelectric power. Some countries produce more power than they need and sell the electricity to their neighbors. However, there are still places where dams could be built.

Some parts of Africa have plenty of water for farming. However, Africa's water resources are not distributed evenly, and much of the continent lacks the water it needs for growing crops.

Africa's plant and animal life are another important natural resource. The rainforests around the Equator provide timber for many uses. Tourists from all over the world come to Africa to see lions, elephants, giraffes, and rhinoceroses in their natural environment.

Using the Land

The people of Africa use the resources of their continent in many ways. These ways often involve traditional methods of doing things that have changed little over hundreds of

Map Study

Locate the flame symbol in the map key. What is the meaning of this symbol? Where in Africa can you find the mineral represented by the flame symbol? Deposits of petroleum often are found near deposits of natural gas. Where do you see this on the map?

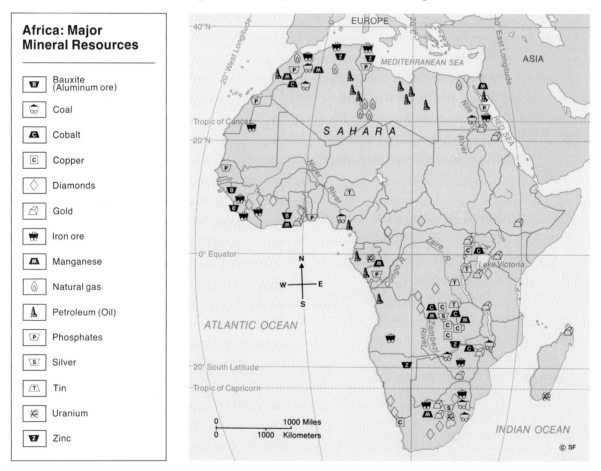

Africa: Major Mineral Resources

B	Bauxite (Aluminum ore)
	Coal
G	Cobalt
C	Copper
◇	Diamonds
	Gold
	Iron ore
M	Manganese
◊	Natural gas
A	Petroleum (Oil)
P	Phosphates
S	Silver
T	Tin
⚛	Uranium
Z	Zinc

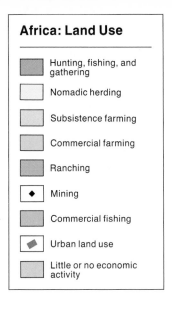

Africa: Land Use

Hunting, fishing, and gathering

Nomadic herding

Subsistence farming

Commercial farming

Ranching

◆ Mining

Commercial fishing

Urban land use

Little or no economic activity

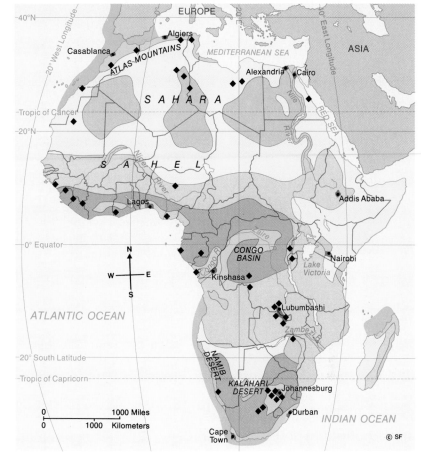

Map Study

Use this map to find two areas south of Lake Victoria where a large amount of mining takes place. What other way—besides mining—do people in these areas use their land? Now, find the areas in northern Africa where little or no economic activity takes place. Why don't people use this land?

years. The map above shows the kinds of land use practiced in Africa.

Hunting and Herding. Find the broad area of hunting, fishing, and gathering around the Equator in western and central Africa on the land-use map. What type of vegetation grows in this area? Check your answer with the natural vegetation map on page 299.

People in parts of northern Africa, the desert fringe, eastern Africa, and southern Africa use the land for nomadic herding. The herders follow their cattle, sheep, or goats from place to place in search of grazing land. Many of the herders in northern Africa are the descendants of the traders who carried goods across the desert a thousand years ago.

Nomadic herding causes problems in some parts of the desert fringe. During very dry periods in the desert fringe, large herds eat all the vegetation down to its roots. Without roots to hold the

303

People in some parts of Africa cannot raise certain animals because of an insect called the tsetse (tset′sē) fly. The tsetse fly carries a disease that causes death in large domestic animals such as cattle. When this disease strikes people, it is called sleeping sickness.

The tsetse fly lives in areas where the climate is hot and wet. Therefore, in much of western and central Africa, people cannot keep cattle, horses, or oxen. Subsistence farmers in other places often use these animals to pull plows to prepare soil for planting. The absence of these animals in western and central Africa means that the farmers must do their planting by hand using hoes.

soil in place, much of the soil can be blown away. Only desert scrub can live in the areas without topsoil. Such overgrazing of the southern fringe of the Sahara helped cause the desert to spread 60 miles south during the 1960s and 1970s.

Farming and Ranching. Much of the grassland and forest areas of Africa, as well as irrigated areas in the desert, are used for farming. Most farmers in Africa are subsistence farmers. These farmers grow only about enough to meet the needs of their families. Most subsistence farmers practice **shifting cultivation.** In this kind of farming, the farmers burn the natural vegetation of an area and use the ashes for fertilizer. The farmers farm the plot of land until the soil is no longer fertile enough to grow crops. The farmers then shift to another plot of land. They leave the first plot empty for as long as ten years, until it regains its fertility.

In the grassland areas, subsistence farmers grow a grain called millet. In the rainforest, farmers grow root crops such as manioc and sweet potatoes. The potatolike manioc is the main food for many Africans. Subsistence farmers also grow a variety of other vegetables.

Small areas of commercial farming can be found in all the regions of Africa. In a few places in western and central Africa, large farms called **plantations** grow crops for export. The crops grown for export include cotton, coffee, peanuts, and cacao (kə kā′ō), used in making cocoa and chocolate. Plantations in eastern Africa produce coffee, tea, cashews, peanuts, vanilla beans, and sisal (sis′əl). Sisal is a strong fiber used to make rope. On small farms on the Mediterranean coast and along the Nile River, farmers grow citrus fruits, cotton, olives, and some grains for export.

The largest area of commercial farming is in southern Africa. Along the coasts, the farmers grow fruits and grains such as wheat. In the dry plateau areas, ranchers raise sheep and

Workers near Lubumbashi, Zaire, mine copper—a valuable mineral resource. The country of Zaire depends on mineral resources, such as copper and cobalt, for much of its wealth.

cattle. Find these ranching areas on the map on page 303.

Urban Land Use. A number of African cities serve as manufacturing and commercial centers. Some of these cities are seaports. Cities such as Cape Town, Lagos (lä′gōs), and Alexandria handle the many imports and exports that are so important to Africa's economy. Some manufacturing and commerce centers also are mining areas. For example, some of the business activity in Lubumbashi (lü′büm bä′shē) depends on the many copper mines in the area. Compare the mineral resources map on page 302 with the land-use map. What precious stone do you think might be bought and sold in Johannesburg?

Reviewing the Lesson

Recalling Key Words, People, and Places
1. Identify the key words defined below:
   a. a type of farming where farmers use a plot of land until the soil is no longer fertile
   b. a large farm where crops are grown for sale
2. Tell the importance of:
   a. Lubumbashi
   b. Lagos

Remembering Main Ideas
1. What minerals are found in western and central Africa?
2. What kinds of crops are grown for export in eastern Africa?

Thinking Things Over
1. Do you think most countries in Africa have developed economies or developing economies? Give reasons for your answer.
2. How do you think shifting cultivation affects the land? Explain your answer.

305

Lesson 3   The People of Africa

LOOKING AHEAD As you read, look for—

Key words, people, and **places:**

drought
famine
official language
missionary

Gilene Gokana
Martin Kamau

Kounzoulou
Brazzaville
Nairobi

Answers to these questions about **main ideas:**

1. How is the population of Africa distributed over the continent?
2. What are some of the major languages and religions of Africa?
3. How have conflicts between ethnic groups arisen in some parts of Africa?
4. How do the lives of the Gokana family and the Kamau family differ?

66 A long time ago both Thunder and Lightning lived on Earth. . . . Thunder was an old mother sheep, and Lightning was her son.

When anybody made Lightning angry, he would fly into a rage and begin burning down huts and corn bins. . . . As soon as his mother knew he was behaving in this way, she would shout as loudly as she could.

Naturally, all the neighbors were upset, first at the damage . . . and then by the unbearable noise. . . . The villagers complained to the king until at last he sent Thunder and Lightning to live in the wild bush. **99**

This is part of a story African people have passed down from generation to generation. In this lesson you will learn more about the people of Africa.

The Population of Africa

The map on page 307 shows that Africa's population is very unevenly distributed over the continent. Less than 10 percent of all African people live in northern Africa and the desert fringe. Most of the Sahara has few or no people. Small groups of people do live around desert oases in the Sahara, and nomadic herders follow their animals from oasis to oasis in search of grazing land.

Most of Africa's people live south of the desert fringe. Notice on the map that most of the crowded areas are near water. Find the places where many people live along the coast of western Africa, around the lakes of eastern Africa, and along the southeastern coast. Notice also that there is a crowded area inland in southern Africa. Compare the population distribution map with the land-use map on page 303. Why do you suppose so many people live in this area?

In 1986, about 586 million people lived in Africa. Its population has been growing by about 3 percent each year. At this rate, Africa's population will double between 1986 and 2010.

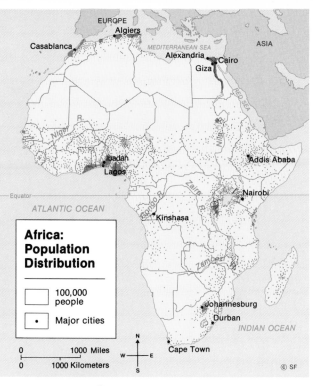

Africa: Population Distribution

☐ 100,000 people

• Major cities

0   1000 Miles
0   1000 Kilometers

© SF

Map Study

Use this map to locate the areas in Africa where few people live. Why don't people choose to live in these areas?

Rapid population growth has caused many problems in Africa. For example, the production of food has not kept up with the growth in population. In recent years this problem has been made worse by long periods without rain called **drought.** In some parts of Africa, millions of people face starvation, also known as **famine.** Providing enough food for the growing population has become a major challenge for many African countries.

Most people in Africa—about 70 percent of the population—live in rural areas. However, many people are leaving Africa's countryside to live and work in the cities. Because of this, some of Africa's larger cities have grown rapidly.

Languages and Religions

More than eight hundred different languages are spoken in Africa. Some of them are spoken by only a few hundred people. Most Africans, however, speak one of the thirty major African languages.

The many languages of Africa create problems when people of different groups must deal with one another. To understand one another, these groups must have a common language. For this reason, many African countries have adopted an official language. An **official language** is the language of business and government in a country. In much of northern Africa, people use Arabic as the official language. Swahili (swä hē′lē) is the official language of parts of eastern Africa. Other countries use French, Portuguese, or English as the official language.

Most people in Africa practice one of the traditional African religions, Islam, or Christianity. About 40 percent of Africans practice traditional religions. These religions are very widespread in western and central Africa. Most traditional religions teach that a faraway supreme being created the universe. Less powerful spirits or gods are believed to control the weather, harvests, a person's health, and other aspects of life on earth. People pray to the lesser spirits for help in their everyday lives.

Islam is the major religion in northern Africa and the desert fringe. Islam spread to both these regions through

Many Christians in northern Africa are Copts, or members of the Coptic Church. The word *Copt* comes from a Greek word that means "Egyptian." The Copts are the descendants of Egyptians who converted to Christianity in the A.D. 200s.

The Copts were the first Christians to set up monasteries. Coptic monks were powerful leaders among the early Christians. The picture shows a monk outside a Coptic monastery in Egypt today.

A disagreement over certain beliefs led to a break between the Copts and other Christians in A.D. 451. However, the Copts have very similar beliefs to other Christians. Today there are about 7 million Copts in northern Africa and Ethiopia.

Map Study

Compare this map with the map on page 299. Which ethnic groups live in the rainforest? Which groups live in the desert?

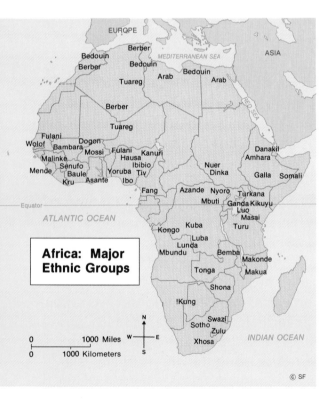

Africa: Major Ethnic Groups

conquests and trade during the A.D. 600s. About 30 percent of all Africans practice Islam.

Christians live in nearly every country in Africa. About 30 percent of the people in Africa practice Christianity. Many Africans were converted to the Christian religion by European or American missionaries. A **missionary** is a person sent by a church to teach others about the church's beliefs.

Ethnic Differences

Religion and language are important characteristics of ethnic groups. As you have learned, the word *ethnic* refers to a person's cultural and/or racial background. Africa is a land of many ethnic groups. The map on this page shows the major ethnic groups of Africa. Hundreds of smaller ethnic groups do not appear on the map. Notice that most of Africa's ethnic groups live south of the Sahara.

When the Europeans colonized Africa during the late 1800s, they did not consider the territories of African ethnic groups when they formed the borders of their colonies. Boundaries between some colonies split some ethnic groups. In other cases, borders brought together groups that were enemies.

When the colonies gained independence, the borders often remained the same. Conflicts arose over the way some ethnic groups were split apart and others were brought together. The Somalis (sə mä′lēz), for example, were split among a number of countries. The Somalis want to be part of the same country. A war was fought between the countries of Somalia and Ethiopia during the 1960s and 1970s over this conflict.

A different type of ethnic problem arose in Nigeria. A civil war was fought during the 1960s between the Ibo and the Hausa groups within the country of Nigeria. These two groups wanted to control Nigeria. Neither group wanted to share power. African leaders today are trying to find ways to allow the many ethnic groups of their countries to maintain their differences while living together in peace.

Two Families of Africa

A close look at the way some people of Africa live can help you see the cultural richness and differences of Africa. Let's look at two African families, one from the People's Republic of the Congo and one from Kenya.

A Family of the Congo. Gilene Gokana (gō ko′nə) lives with her parents, two brothers, and two sisters in the village of Kounzoulou (kün zû′lü), in the People's Republic of the Congo. About seven hundred people live in Kounzoulou. The village is on the Congo River,

Gilene, at right, with her two sisters and a brother

about 150 miles north of the country's capital, Brazzaville. Find the People's Republic of the Congo and Brazzaville on the map on page 292.

The People's Republic of the Congo was once a French colony, and French is the country's official language. Gilene studies French in school, but all the people in the village speak an African language as well. The village has a small Roman Catholic church. However, Gilene's family, like most in the village, practices a traditional African religion.

Kounzoulou looks like many other villages on the Congo River. Gilene's house is very small. It is made of woven branches plastered over with mud. The roof is made of reeds woven together to make a waterproof cover. Because the climate is hot, most activities take place outside.

Most of the village people are farmers. The Gokanas have fields along the river two miles from the village. The family grows manioc, peanuts, and bananas. Gilene's mother and father use a canoe to get to their fields. Sometimes, people from Kounzoulou go by riverboat to Brazzaville. There they buy tools and clothing. However, the villagers grow most of things they need or buy them at the village store.

Kounzoulou has a medical clinic. Gilene wants to be a nurse and work at the clinic when she is older. Most medical care is given by nurses because of the shortage of doctors in the country. After training, Gilene will be able to care for wounds and broken bones and to give medicines.

A Family of Kenya. Martin Kamau (k mou′) lives with his parents and two sisters in the city of Nairobi (nī rō′bē), the capital of Kenya. Find Kenya and Nairobi on the map on page 292. Nairobi is a pleasant place to live because the climate is not terribly hot, even though Kenya is on the Equator. The reason is that the city is on a plateau more than 5,000 feet above sea level.

The Kamau family lives in an apartment in a new section of Nairobi. Martin's father is the manager of a company that makes plastic dinner plates. Martin's mother works in a laboratory in a large hospital. Both his parents tell Martin that they got their jobs because they were lucky enough to have a good education.

Martin's father's parents were farmers in a small village several hundred miles from Nairobi. They came to the city when Martin's father was very young. By working hard and saving, they were able to send Martin's father through school and to the university. Most people in Kenya can afford to send their children to elementary school only.

Martin knows that he must do well in school, and so he studies very hard. Martin's lessons are given in Swahili, the official language of Kenya. However, Martin and his family also speak English.

Sometimes on the weekends, Martin goes with his parents to downtown Nairobi to shop at the many large stores. On special occasions Martin and his family visit Nairobi's art museum or

The Kamaus sit outside their home in the industrial city of Nairobi, Kenya.

one of the art galleries. The oldest works on display are beautifully carved wooden objects. The family also goes to the National Theater to see a play or to a movie theater.

Martin and his family are proud to be citizens of Kenya, but they never forget their own ethnic group's traditions. The Kamau family keeps in touch by visiting the small village from which Martin's grandparents came. On special occasions, such as weddings, lots of good food is served. Everyone takes part in traditional dances and songs.

The Kamau relatives are always glad to see Martin, his sisters, and his parents. The relatives say they are proud that members of their family have done so well in the city.

Reviewing the Lesson

Recalling Key Words, People, and Places
1. Identify the key words defined below:
   a. a long time with little or no rainfall
   b. the language used in business and the government of a country
2. Tell why it is important to remember:
   a. Brazzaville
   b. Nairobi

Remembering Main Ideas
1. Where do most of the people of Africa live?
2. What do most traditional African religions teach?
3. How did the colonization of Africa create ethnic conflicts?
4. How do the Gokana and Kamau families meet their needs?

Thinking Things Over
Whose way of life is most like your own: Gilene Gokana's or Martin Kamau's? Explain your answer.

Making Inferences from Maps

The maps in this chapter helped you see where the people of Africa live, how they use the land, and how they work with their natural environments. The three maps on these two pages focus on the region of northern Africa.

What an Inference Is

When you begin looking at a map, you first read its title and study its key. The title and key tell you what kind of information you will find on the map. After you have become familiar with the information on a map, you sometimes can make inferences about additional information that the map does not specifically show. An inference is a meaning you find by thinking about something you already know or have learned. An inference is a guess, but it is not a wild guess. The more information you have, the more accurate your inferences will be.

An inference from a map should begin with facts found on the map. Then, you apply other facts or information that you have read about or know to be true. Finally, you may be able to check your inference by looking at another map or referring to information found elsewhere in your book.

Kinds of Inferences Made from Maps

You have learned that nomadic herding is a common way of life in desert areas. Look at the land-use map below. Find the areas of nomadic herding and little or no economic activity. What might you infer, or guess, about the climate of these areas? You probably would infer that these areas have mostly a desert climate—hot and dry all year. Looking at the climate map on page 313, you find that your inference is correct.

Use information from the land-use and climate maps to make an

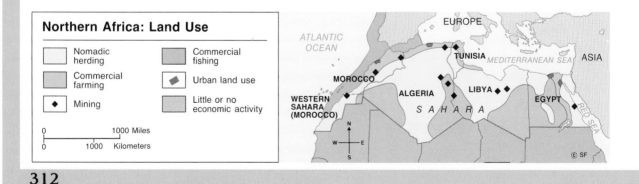

Northern Africa: Land Use

- Nomadic herding
- Commercial farming
- ◆ Mining
- Commercial fishing
- Urban land use
- Little or no economic activity

0 — 1000 Miles
0 — 1000 Kilometers

ATLANTIC OCEAN
EUROPE
TUNISIA
MEDITERRANEAN SEA
ASIA
MOROCCO
ALGERIA
LIBYA
EGYPT
WESTERN SAHARA (MOROCCO)
S A H A R A
RED SEA
N W E S
© SF

inference about population distribution in the areas used for nomadic herding and little or no economic activity. Would you infer that many people or few people live in these areas? Looking at the population distribution map at the bottom of this page, you see that few people live in these areas.

Skills Practice

1. On the land-use map, find the economic activities of Algeria.
   a. Without looking at the climate map, give an inference comparing the climate of coastal Algeria with that of southern Algeria.
   b. Find Algeria on the climate map.

Use information from the climate map key to tell whether your inference was correct.

2. On the population map, find the crowded area that runs mostly north and south through Egypt.
   a. Look at the climate map. In what kind of climate region does this crowded area lie?
   b. Look at the land-use map. How do people use land in this area?
   c. Make an inference that accounts for the crowded area and the kind of land use in this area.
   d. Use an Atlas map to check your inference. Write the page number on which you found the map.

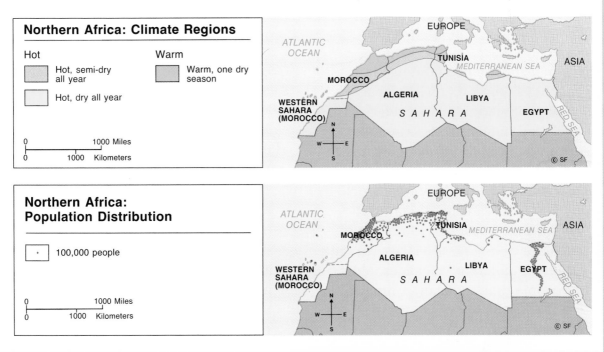

Northern Africa: Climate Regions

Hot
- Hot, semi-dry all year
- Hot, dry all year

Warm
- Warm, one dry season

0   1000 Miles
0   1000   Kilometers

Northern Africa: Population Distribution

· 100,000 people

0   1000 Miles
0   1000   Kilometers

Chapter Summary

Lesson 1   The Natural Environment of Africa—Much of Africa is an interior plateau surrounded by coastal plains. The interior also includes several mountain ranges and the Great Rift Valley. Africa's bodies of water include three large lakes—Tanganyika, Nyasa, and Victoria—and four major rivers—the Nile, Niger, Congo, and Zambesi. Africa's climate regions and natural vegetation regions stretch in great bands across the continent. The continent's five regions are: northern Africa, the desert fringe, western and central Africa, eastern Africa, and southern Africa.

Lesson 2   Resources and Land Use in Africa—Africa is rich in mineral resources, including copper, gold, diamonds, tin, silver, uranium, zinc, bauxite, iron ore, manganese, and phosphates. Oil and natural gas also are important resources. Hunting, herding, subsistence farming, and ranching support many Africans. Commercial farming has been developed in all regions. A number of African cities serve as manufacturing and export centers.

Lesson 3   The People of Africa—Nine out of ten Africans live south of the desert fringe, most of them along the seacoasts or around the lakes. Africans speak 800 different languages. Most of the people practice Islam, Christianity, or one of the traditional African religions.

Write your answers on a separate sheet of paper.

Testing Key Words, People, and Places
Part A
Use each key word in a sentence.

1. escarpment
2. cataract
3. oasis
4. savanna
5. shifting cultivation
6. plantation
7. drought
8. famine
9. official language
10. missionary

Part B
In a sentence, tell why each person or place is important.

1. Mount Kilimanjaro
2. Lake Tanganyika
3. Lubumbashi
4. Gilene Gokana
5. Brazzaville
6. Nairobi

Testing Main Ideas
Choose the answer that best completes each sentence.

1. Much of Africa's interior is a
   a. plateau.
   b. coastal plain.
   c. valley.
2. The Nile River flows into the
   a. Atlantic Ocean.
   b. Indian Ocean.
   c. Mediterranean Sea.
3. The climate of the Sahara is
   a. hot with one dry season.
   b. hot and dry all year.
   c. warm.

4. Iron ore and phosphates are the most plentiful minerals in the
   a. Red Sea.
   b. Great Rift Valley.
   c. Atlas Mountains.
5. Africa's largest area of commercial farming is in
   a. western and central Africa.
   b. the desert fringe.
   c. southern Africa.
6. Most people in Africa live in
   a. urban areas.
   b. rural areas.
   c. the desert fringe.
7. Missionaries converted many Africans to
   a. Christianity.
   b. Islam.
   c. Ibo.
8. Kenya's official language is
   a. French.
   b. English.
   c. Swahili.

Testing Skills

1. Making inferences from a map.
   Study the map at right above. Then complete the following.
   a. Where in Africa is the greatest amount of land where few or no people live?
   b. Based on what you already know about Africa's climate and vegetation, make an inference that accounts for the low population distribution in this area.

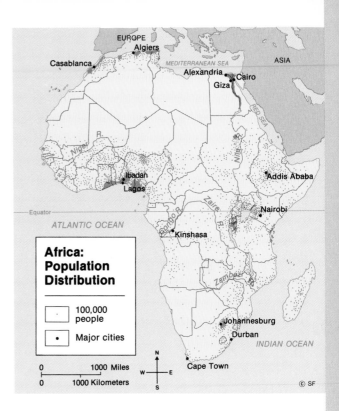

2. Summarizing data from a map. Use the map above to write a short summary of where most people in Africa live.

Activities

1. Read *Nomads of the World* edited by David J. Crump (National Geographic, 1971). Write a brief summary of the living conditions of African nomadic herders.
2. Make a list of African exports and decide which ones may be used in some form by your family.

315

Chapter 15

From Past to Present in Africa

Some early African civilizations controlled territory the size of the Roman Empire. However, as the old map—with its drawing of a Portuguese fort—shows, Africa began to change when Europeans began to trade and conquer there.

As you read this chapter, you will learn about the history of Africa, beginning with the great kingdoms of the past. You also will learn about the arrival of Europeans in Africa. Finally, you will learn about the movement toward independence in Africa. The lessons in the chapter are listed below.

Lesson 1   Early African Kingdoms

Lesson 2   European Influence in Africa

Lesson 3   African Countries Achieve Independence

Lesson 1 Early African Kingdoms

LOOKING AHEAD As you read, look for—

Key words, people, and **places:**

Mansa Musa   Songhai
Askia the Great   Kilwa
                   Zimbabwe
Tombouctou   Benin
Ghana   Kongo
Mali

Answers to these questions about **main ideas:**

1. What were the origins of trade across the Sahara?
2. How did each of the three major kingdoms of West Africa rise and fall?
3. How did the major kingdoms of East Africa gain wealth and power?
4. Which was the most powerful of the rainforest kingdoms?

66 The rich king of Tombouctou has many plates . . . of gold . . . and he keeps a magnificent and well-furnished court . . . Here are a great store [number] of doctors, judges, priests, and other learned men, that are . . . maintained at the king's costs . . . And hither are brought . . . written books out of Barbary [North Africa] which are sold for more money than any other merchandise. 99

This description of Tombouctou, the major city of the Songhai (sông hī′) empire of West Africa, was written by a visitor in 1525. Songhai was only one of many kingdoms that flowered in Africa between A.D. 400 and 1600.

Trade Across the Sahara

In earliest times the people of the grasslands of western Africa lived by hunting animals and gathering fruits and grains. Later, by about 1000 B.C., they began to farm the land. By about 500 B.C., these people had discovered iron, and they did their farm work with iron tools such as axes and hoes.

Farmers could produce a food surplus because of the advanced technology of iron tools. As you have read, when there is a surplus of food, some people are able to do work other than farming. A number of the people in western Africa gave up farming and became traders.

From as early as 300 B.C., the West Africans traded with merchants from Carthage, a city on the Mediterranean coast of northern Africa. When the Roman army destroyed Carthage in 146 B.C., Roman merchants took control of the trade with the West Africans. The Romans were the first to use camels to carry goods across the Sahara.

In time the Roman Empire declined, and trade across the Sahara lost its importance. However, by A.D. 800 Islamic Arabs who had settled in northern Africa made trading across the Sahara an important activity once again.

Cities grew at both ends of the north-south trading routes that crossed the

Sahara. Look at the map below and find the cities on the Saharan trade routes.

The Arab traders from northern Africa brought salt, silk, books, weapons, writing paper, and horses across the desert to the grasslands of western Africa. They traded these goods for the West Africans' gold, ivory, slaves, cotton, and leather. The Arab traders also brought their religion to West Africa. In time many people in this area adopted the Muslim faith.

The West African Kingdoms

The first great kingdom to develop in the grassland area of West Africa was Ghana (gä′nə). Find Ghana on the map below. Ghana began to develop in the early A.D. 400s, but it reached the height of its power around 1050.

Ghana was ruled by a king whom the people thought was divine—that is, chosen by the gods. The king chose all the kingdom's important officials, and he was the final judge in all court cases. Whenever the king appeared in

Map Study

This map has two purposes: to show the major trade routes and to show the locations of major African kingdoms. What direction would the people of Benin have had to travel to reach Algiers on the Mediterranean Sea?

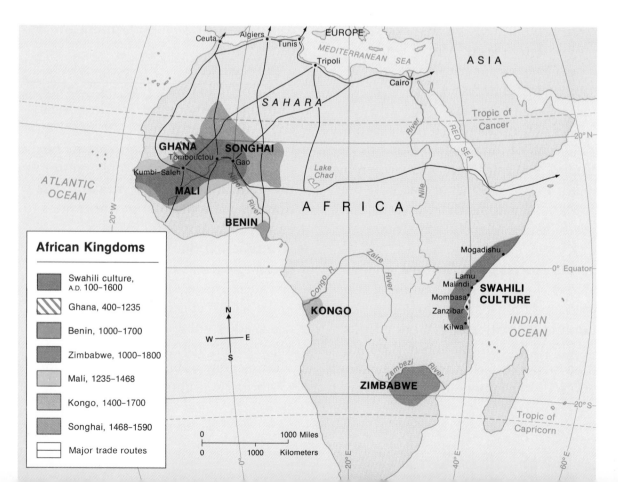

public, he was protected by soldiers with gold swords. The king's horses wore blankets of gold cloth and his dogs had gold or silver collars. An Arab visitor noted that gold could be seen everywhere in Ghana. The people even braided gold threads into their hair.

In the 1000s, Ghana was attacked by armies from neighboring areas. The fighting made trading very difficult, and many traders moved to other parts of West Africa. This loss of trade weakened the power of Ghana. By 1235 another great kingdom, called Mali (mä'lē), had risen in West Africa.

The mansas—rulers—of Mali were Muslims. The greatest ruler of Mali was Mansa Musa (män'sä mü'sä). During his rule the Kingdom of Mali covered an area as large as Western Europe. However, the rulers who followed Mansa Musa were unable to control this huge kingdom. Many provinces rebelled to gain independence.

One province that rebelled against Mali was Songhai, with its capital of Gao (gow). In 1468 Songhai soldiers attacked and captured Tombouctou (tông-bük tü'). Look at the map on page 318. How far did the Songhai soldiers have to travel from Gao to Tombouctou? Within a few years, the rulers of Songhai controlled nearly all of Mali.

The most powerful Songhai leader was Askia the Great, who came to power in 1493. Under his rule the Songhai Empire expanded to cover much of western Africa. Askia encouraged the

This Spanish map, made in 1347, shows the wealthy king of Mali, Mansa Musa. He sits on his throne, awaiting an Arab trader.

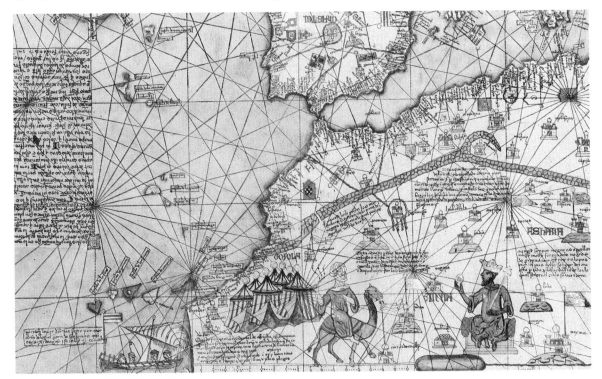

The well-built walls of the Great Zimbabwe have lasted for hundreds of years.

Songhai people to follow the Muslim faith. He also tried to make Tombouctou a center for Islamic studies. Scholars from all over the Arab world were invited to study there.

After Askia's death the Songhai Empire remained powerful. By the late 1500s, much of Europe and North Africa knew about the wealth and power of Songhai. However, this knowledge helped stir up jealousy and greed. In 1590 the king of Morocco sent an army across the Sahara against Songhai. The Moroccan soldiers were armed with guns and easily defeated the soldiers of Songhai, who had only swords and spears. By 1600 the Songhai Empire had disappeared.

The East African Kingdoms

As with the West African kingdoms, trade was important for the growth of the East African kingdoms. Merchants from India and Arabia used seasonal winds called monsoons to help them sail to and from East Africa. The monsoon winds blow steadily across the Indian Ocean toward Africa between October and January. From about April to September, the winds blow the other way—toward India. These winds made sailing between Asia and Africa fairly quick and easy.

The Indian and Arabian merchants wanted East African gold, iron, and ivory. In return, these merchants traded such goods as cotton cloth and porcelain (china). A number of ports grew up on the East African coast to handle this trade. By the 1200s, some of these ports had become powerful kingdoms.

All the people of the port kingdoms shared a way of living. For example, they spoke Swahili, an African language that included many Indian and Arabic words. Most also followed the Muslim religion. Although the people shared the same culture, each port kingdom had its own ruler, laws, and army. In addition, all the port kingdoms competed fiercely for trade.

One of the most powerful of the East African port kingdoms was Kilwa. The map on page 318 shows that Kilwa was the port that was the farthest south and closest to the gold mines of Zimbabwe (sim bä'bwe). The merchants of Kilwa controlled most of the trade in gold.

Zimbabwe did not develop on the coast, as did the port kingdoms of East Africa. Rather, Zimbabwe grew up in the interior of the continent, near the Zambezi River. A group of people called the Shona (shō'nə) founded Zimbabwe sometime between 800 and 1000 near the place where they had discovered gold. In time, Zimbabwe became a rich and powerful kingdom by trading gold to the port kingdoms to the north. One sign of the wealth of Zimbabwe was the huge stone houses that the Shona built. In fact, *Zimbabwe* means "house of stone" in the Shona language.

The Kingdoms of the Rainforest

At the same time the port kingdoms of East Africa were at their height, a number of kingdoms developed on the coastal areas of the rainforests. Among these rainforest kingdoms were Benin and Kongo. Find these kingdoms on the map on page 318. What is similar about their locations?

Benin was the most powerful of the rainforest kingdoms. Its wealth and power came from trading with the grassland kingdoms to the north. Grassland kingdoms such as Songhai traded salt, silk, and weapons in return for gold, slaves, and forest products, such as palm oil.

Kings, called obas, ruled the people of Benin. Obas were religious leaders, and they controlled Benin's religious and political life. Artists of Benin recorded the lives of the obas on bronze plaques. These artists also made bronze sculptures to honor the obas.

The lives of the people of Benin remained much the same well into the 1500s. However, the arrival of European merchants brought great changes to Benin and to many other kingdoms in Africa.

Reviewing the Lesson

Recalling Key Words, People, and Places
1. Tell why it is important to remember:
   a. Mansa Musa
   b. Askia the Great
2. Describe the location of:
   a. Songhai
   b. Kilwa

Remembering Main Ideas
1. What goods were involved in trade across the Sahara?
2. How did the West African kingdoms become powerful and wealthy?
3. What aspect of climate helped the trade between East Africa and India and Arabia?
4. How were the lives of the kings of Benin recorded?

Thinking Things Over
How were the West African kingdoms similar to the East African port kingdoms? How were they different?

Lesson 2   European Influence in Africa

LOOKING AHEAD As you read, look for—

Key words, people, and **places:**

David Livingstone
Henry Morton Stanley
Karl Peters
Pierre de Brazza

Answers to these questions about **main ideas:**

1. Why did Europeans first go to Africa?
2. How did the African slave trade change after Europeans became involved?
3. How did Christianity spread in Africa?
4. Which Europeans explored Africa's interior?
5. What factors influenced the European takeover of Africa?

Imagine you are a Portuguese sailor in the late 1400s. You have been sailing for weeks without sight of land. You finally arrive at your destination—the "gold coast" of West Africa. What are your feelings as you step ashore in this foreign land? What do you expect to see?

Now imagine you live in a village on the West African coast. Visitors to your village have told unbelievable stories about people who live far to the north. What are your feelings as you see strangers coming ashore from a huge wooden ship? What do you think they want? In this lesson you will learn about the arrival of Europeans in Africa.

The Europeans Arrive

The search for new trade routes was one reason for the great voyages of exploration by Europeans. In the 1400s such goods as gold, spices, and silks had to be bought from the Arab and Italian traders who controlled the trade routes from Africa and Asia to Europe. Because the Arab and Italian traders charged high prices for these goods, many people in Europe wanted to find their own trade routes.

The first European country to search for new trade routes was Portugal. Portuguese ships visited the coast of western Africa as early as the 1470s. By the 1490s Portugal carried on a steady trade with Benin and other coastal rainforest kingdoms. The Portuguese exchanged iron goods and guns for the Africans' gold, ivory, and spices.

The Portuguese also found a route around the southern tip of Africa in the 1490s. This route made it possible to visit the port kingdoms of East Africa. Later efforts by the Portuguese to control East African trade led to the destruction of many of the kingdoms.

During the 1500s the English, the Dutch, and the French began to compete with the Portuguese for trade on the coast of western Africa. The obas of Benin closely controlled their kingdom's trade with the Europeans. The obas collected taxes from Europeans for the use of Benin's ports and for goods brought into Benin. Also, the obas forbade Europeans to live in Benin.

Europeans were allowed to visit Benin for a short time, but they had to live on their ships anchored off the coast.

Benin and the other coastal kingdoms had grown rich and powerful through trade with the Arabs. These kingdoms became even richer after they began to trade with Europeans.

The Slave Trade

For nearly three hundred years, the main trade carried on between Africa and Europe was the trade in slaves. The slave trade, under the control of Arab merchants, had been carried on for hundreds of years in Africa. However, under this system, most African slaves were not treated badly and could even gain their freedom if they worked hard for many years. The slave trade changed dramatically when the Europeans became involved.

During the 1500s some European countries set up plantations in the Americas. The American plantations required many workers, and the European plantation owners wanted to find a source of cheap labor. The plantation owners found that source in the slave markets of western Africa.

African slave traders, armed with guns, raided unprotected villages and captured anyone they could find. The captives were marched to the coast and held in fortresses. After the slaves had been bought by a European trader, they were packed inside a dark, filthy ship. The slaves were chained together and barely had room to move. Many of them died on the ten-week voyage to the Americas. Those slaves that survived usually were treated badly on the plantations. Also, they had little hope of ever gaining their freedom.

⦾ Linking Past and Present

How Manioc Became an African Food

Manioc, also called cassava, is the main source of food for many present-day Africans, especially those who live in the rainforest. Note that the roots of the manioc look like sweet potatoes.

Manioc is not native to Africa. Manioc was brought to Africa by the Portuguese in the 1500s. The Portuguese found manioc in their colonies in South America. Manioc grew so well in the hot, wet climate of the African rainforest that within fifty years it had become the main food of many Africans.

Many people profited from the slave trade. Some African rulers, some European shipowners, and some plantation owners became very wealthy. However, their wealth was earned from human misery. People in a number of European countries began to work to end the slave trade. By the early 1800s, the slave trade had been outlawed by some countries. However, the trade in slaves from Africa did not end until the late 1800s.

Christianity in Africa

Trade was not the only reason Europeans traveled to Africa. A number of Europeans wanted to spread the Christian faith to the lands beyond Europe. In fact, some Portuguese explorers said they traveled to distant lands for gold, glory, and God.

Christianity came to the African continent in the A.D. 200s and 300s, when some people in present-day Egypt and Ethiopia became followers. However, Christianity spread no further in Africa until the late 1400s. The Portuguese explorers of that time usually were accompanied by priests. These priests introduced the Roman Catholic faith to many coastal areas of Africa.

In later years Roman Catholic and Protestant missionaries from Europe and North America went to Africa. Protestant missionaries had much success in spreading the Christian faith in southern Africa. One area where Christian missionaries had almost no success was northern Africa. Islam was well established in northern Africa, and the people held fast to that religion.

Europeans Explore Africa's Interior

Although Europeans knew about Africa's coastline and parts of northern Africa, the huge interior of the continent remained a mystery to them for a long time. However, during the 1800s Europeans explored and mapped much of Africa's interior.

Some of the European explorers also were Christian missionaries. The most famous of these was Dr. David Livingstone of Great Britain. On a number of journeys between 1851 and 1873, Livingstone traced the route of the Zambezi River and located Victoria Falls and Lake Tanganyika. He also was the first European to cross the Kalahari Desert.

Henry Morton Stanley was another important British explorer. Stanley explored parts of the interior of Africa. Between 1874 and 1877, for example, he traced the route of the Congo River. A later journey Stanley made to the Congo River area was financed by the Belgian king, Leopold II. On this journey Stanley claimed all the land he explored in the name of Leopold.

Other European explorers followed Stanley's lead and claimed huge areas of Africa for their countries. For example, a German explorer named Karl Peters claimed much of eastern Africa for Germany, and Pierre de Brazza claimed parts of western Africa for France. By making such claims, these explorers helped lay the groundwork for European colonial rule in Africa.

"Dr. Livingstone, I presume." These words were spoken in 1871 by Stanley, sent by an American newspaper to find Livingstone.

Colonial Rule Begins

The European takeover of Africa took only a few years. In the 1870s France, Portugal, and Great Britain had a few small colonies in Africa, mostly along the coasts. By the end of the 1800s, nearly all the continent was under European rule.

Throughout the 1880s and 1890s, countries such as Germany, France, and Great Britain were competing with each other for power. They saw the takeover of areas of Africa and other places as a way to gain such power. In effect, Africa was swallowed up by the European power struggle.

Economic factors also helped to bring about the European takeover of Africa. Most of the European countries wanted new markets for their manufactured goods. Africa looked like an ideal market.

Reviewing the Lesson

Recalling Key Words, People, and Places
Tell the accomplishments of:
1. David Livingstone
2. Pierre de Brazza

Remembering Main Ideas
1. How did the rulers of Benin control their trade with the Europeans?
2. What happened to an African who was sold as a slave to Europeans?
3. Why did Christian missionaries have little success in northern Africa?
4. How did European explorers start the process of colonization in Africa?
5. How did the European power struggle of the late 1800s affect Africa?

Thinking Things Over
Why do you think people such as Livingstone wanted to explore the interior of Africa? Would you have wanted to be an explorer in Africa in those days? Explain your answer.

Lesson 3   African Countries Achieve Independence

LOOKING AHEAD As you read, look for—

Key words, people, and **places:**

segregation
boycott
coup

Kwame Nkrumah

Answers to these questions about **main ideas:**

1. How did colonial rule affect Africa?
2. How did the countries of Africa achieve independence?
3. What challenges faced African countries after independence?

By the end of the 1800s, nearly all the continent of Africa was under control of the European countries of Portugal, France, Great Britain, and Germany. This control led to conditions such as African homelands being divided among three or four countries and deprived many Africans of valuable farmland and livelihood.

Faced with such unjust conditions, many African countries rebelled. For instance, there were revolts in present-day Tanzania in 1888, 1891, and 1905. Rebellion occurred in Ghana in 1900. There were uprisings against the Germans in Namibia in 1904, against the Portuguese in Angola in 1913, and against the French in Tunisia in 1915.

In this lesson, you will learn about the efforts of the African people to gain their independence from European rulers. These efforts eventually did lead to independence for the entire continent of Africa.

Effects of Colonial Rule

The map on page 327 shows colonial rule in Africa in 1914. How many African countries were independent at this time? Some European colonies were well established. For example, the Portuguese had been in Angola for hundreds of years. However, most African colonies were set up after 1880. A few, such as British East Africa, still were trying to attract European settlers in the 1920s and 1930s.

Africa saw many changes during colonial rule. Some of the changes were good. Europeans introduced modern medical services that helped control disease. As a result, death rates fell and life expectancy rose during the years of colonial rule. Many Africans learned to read and write and acquired other skills at schools built by Europeans. Finally, Europeans modernized agriculture, developed mining, and built modern ports, roads, and railways.

However, colonial rule caused many problems. As you have read, the colonial rulers drew the boundaries of their colonies with little thought for where ethnic groups were located. The results added to the hostility Africans felt toward Europeans.

326

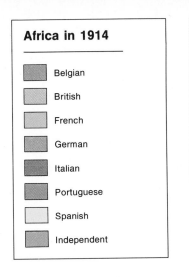

Africa in 1914

- Belgian
- British
- French
- German
- Italian
- Portuguese
- Spanish
- Independent

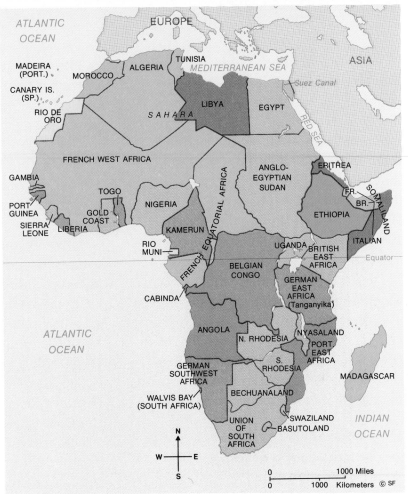

ATLANTIC OCEAN • EUROPE • ASIA • MEDITERRANEAN SEA • Suez Canal • MADEIRA (PORT.) • ALGERIA • TUNISIA • MOROCCO • CANARY IS. (SP.) • LIBYA • EGYPT • RIO DE ORO • SAHARA • RED SEA • FRENCH WEST AFRICA • ANGLO-EGYPTIAN SUDAN • ERITREA • GAMBIA • TOGO • NIGERIA • FR. SOMALILAND • BR. • PORT. GUINEA • GOLD COAST • FRENCH EQUATORIAL AFRICA • KAMERUN • ETHIOPIA • SIERRA LEONE • LIBERIA • UGANDA • ITALIAN • RIO MUNI • BRITISH EAST AFRICA • Equator • BELGIAN CONGO • GERMAN EAST AFRICA (Tanganyika) • CABINDA • ATLANTIC OCEAN • ANGOLA • N. RHODESIA • NYASALAND • PORT. EAST AFRICA • GERMAN SOUTHWEST AFRICA • S. RHODESIA • MADAGASCAR • WALVIS BAY (SOUTH AFRICA) • BECHUANALAND • INDIAN OCEAN • UNION OF SOUTH AFRICA • SWAZILAND • BASUTOLAND • N • W • E • S • 0 1000 Miles • 0 1000 Kilometers © SF

Map Study

Use this map to answer the following questions. Which country controlled the canal between the Mediterranean Sea and the Red Sea in 1914? Which country controlled most of the western part of the Sahara? Did any non-European countries control parts of Africa?

Perhaps the most damaging feature of colonial rule was the **segregation**—the separation of one racial group from another—practiced by most European powers. For example, Europeans took the best farmland for themselves and forced the Africans to live on the poorest land. Also, in most colonies Africans had few civil rights such as the right to vote or have a trial by jury. The result was racial distrust and even hatred.

Achieving Independence

Some Africans fought against European rule from the beginning. For example, the Shona challenged the British settlers in Southern Rhodesia as early as 1896. Not until after World War II, however, did the drive for independence begin to succeed.

327

Many leaders of the independence movement used examples from European and American history, such as the French Revolution and the War for Independence, to show the rightness of their cause. These leaders also noted that India and some other Asian countries had become independent since World War II. If the countries of Asia are free, they argued, Africa also should be free.

To gain support, the leaders of the independence movement staged rallies and organized strikes and boycotts against the colonial governments. A **boycott** occurs when a group refuses to buy or use goods or services produced by a certain company or government.

Jomo Kenyatta, first president of independent Kenya

Some members of the independence movement used violence and terrorism. In Kenya, a part of British East Africa, a secret society called Mau Mau (mou′ mou′) staged attacks on the farms of white settlers in the 1950s. Also in the 1950s, the Algerians fought a bitter war for independence against their French rulers.

Although the threat of violence often was used, most African colonies achieved independence through peaceful means. One of the first colonies to gain independence was the Gold Coast. Its powerful leader, Kwame Nkrumah (kwä′mä en krü′mə), persuaded the British to make the Gold Coast independent in 1957. After independence the Gold Coast was renamed Ghana.

The pressure for independence grew in other countries after Ghana's success. As a British politician noted, "The wind of change is blowing through the continent. Whether we like it or not, this growth of national consciousness is a political fact." By the end of the 1960s, almost all of Africa was independent of European rule.

Challenges After Independence

The people of Africa soon discovered that independence was not the answer to all their problems. Within a few years of breaking with their colonial rulers, many African countries faced new and difficult challenges. Few colonial powers had allowed Africans to participate in government before independence. As a result, African leaders had very little experience in running a government. This lack of experience made their job more difficult.

In some countries civilian leaders were replaced by military officers in coups. A **coup** (kü) is a sudden action, usually involving force, that changes the government of a country. Many of the military officers who carried out coups became dictators—leaders who exercise complete control. For example, Idi Amin (ē′dē ä mēn′), a member of the Ugandan army, took control of the Ugandan government in 1971. For eight years, Amin ruled through force and terror. People who did not agree with Amin were arrested and put in prison. Many of them were tortured, and thousands were murdered.

Ethnic differences continued to be a challenge in many parts of Africa after independence. You read earlier that differences between the Hausa and Ibo groups in Nigeria led to a bitter civil war between 1967 and 1970. This civil war caused much death and destruction. However, the war had some good results. The Hausa, the largest and most powerful ethnic group in Nigeria, finally agreed to share power with the Ibos and the other smaller ethnic groups.

Some countries in Africa still face great economic challenges. Many of these countries have economies based on a single natural resource, crop, or other product. Such economies face great risks. For example, the economy of Zambia is based on copper mining. Falling world prices for copper could ruin Zambia's economy. Also, natural disasters such as crop diseases and droughts can damage and even destroy a single-crop economy.

Natural disasters have created what is perhaps the greatest challenge to the people of Africa—famine. Drought has contributed greatly to African food shortages. A very severe drought struck the desert fringe of Africa in the early 1980s. Thousands of people died of starvation during this time. People from all over the world joined in fund-raising efforts to provide help for the famine victims.

Although the countries of Africa face many challenges, they have made great strides forward during the years of independence. In the next two chapters, you will learn about the countries of Africa today and how these countries are facing new challenges.

Reviewing the Lesson

Recalling Key Words, People, and Places
Identify the key words defined below:
1. the separation of one racial group from another
2. a sudden action, usually involving force, that changes the government of a country

Remembering Main Ideas
1. What problems were caused by colonial rule in Africa?
2. How did the leaders of the African independence movement gain support for their cause?
3. What economic challenges did African countries face in the years after independence?

Thinking Things Over
Leaders of the African independence movement sometimes compared their struggle to the American War for Independence. Do you think this is an accurate comparison? Give reasons for your answer.

329

Forming and Testing a Hypothesis

Imagine that, before you read this chapter, someone had asked you, "Why do you suppose the early African kingdoms did not last beyond 1600?" That is, the person asked you to give a possible explanation for a historical fact. You might have answered, "Europeans were setting sail throughout the world at about that time. The Europeans did colonize Africa. Perhaps the coming of the Europeans to Africa caused the end of the kingdoms."

In giving your answer, you stated a **hypothesis**—a possible explanation for a situation. You develop hypotheses all the time, both in school and out. For example, suppose you have a plant on the windowsill in your room, and you notice the plant seems to be dying. Here are the facts you know about the plant:

- It receives several hours of sunlight a day.
- You water the plant every Sunday and Wednesday. The soil around the plant usually feels damp.

Developing a Hypothesis

What might be wrong with the plant? To form a hypothesis, you look at the facts that you know about the situation. Then you think of possible

explanations. You can then test each hypothesis to find out if it is correct or if it needs to be revised, or changed.

Here is the first hypothesis you form: The soil around the plant usually feels damp, so perhaps the plant is receiving too much water. To test your hypothesis, you stop watering the plant twice a week and instead water it only when the soil feels dry. You watch the plant to see what happens. If the plant becomes healthy again, your hypothesis is correct. If the plant does not improve and even grows more sickly, your hypothesis is wrong.

If your hypothesis is wrong, you need to revise it and test the new hypothesis. You might change your hypothesis to this: The plant receives too much sunlight. You then move the plant to a shadier spot, observe what happens to test the new hypothesis, and decide if that hypothesis is right or wrong.

Let's go back to your hypothesis about the end of the African kingdoms. You could have tested your hypothesis by reading on in the chapter and perhaps by doing further research. If your hypothesis was wrong, you could have developed a new one.

Skills Practice

Try forming and testing a hypothesis yourself. Imagine you have an aquarium in which the water always seems to be cloudy. The aquarium sits in a corner of the room that receives no direct sunlight but is fairly bright. You have a pump and filter in the aquarium, which you bought two years ago. The pump moves the water through the filter. The filter supposedly keeps the water clean. You also remove some of the old water and replace it with fresh water at least once a week.

You go to a pet store and ask how to solve the problem of cloudy water. The store owner tells you that one or more of the following things could be causing the cloudy water.

- You may need a new filter.
- Your aquarium may be getting too much direct sunlight. This light can make small plants grow in the aquarium, causing the water to look cloudy.
- You may need to change more of the water more often.

On a separate sheet of paper, answer the following questions.

1. What facts do you know about the situation?
2. What hypothesis can you form to explain the situation?
3. How will you test this hypothesis? What will you be looking for as you test this hypothesis?
4. Suppose your first hypothesis is incorrect. What new hypothesis will you form to explain the situation and how will you test it?

Chapter 15 Review

Chapter Summary

Lesson 1   Early African Kingdoms—
Ghana, the first great kingdom in the grassland area of West Africa, developed in the early A.D. 400s and thrived for about 800 years. Then a neighboring kingdom in West Africa, Mali, came to power. Songhai conquered the Mali empire and ruled much of West Africa until 1600. In East Africa Kilwa and Zimbabwe became powerful. In the rainforest, the kingdom of Benin reigned until the 1500s.

Lesson 2   European Influence in Africa—Europeans first went to Africa to search for new trade routes. Once controlled by the Europeans, the slave trade caused much misery for Africans who were captured and shipped to the Americas with little hope of ever gaining their freedom. Some Europeans went to Africa as missionaries and explorers. By the end of the 1800s, nearly all of Africa was under European rule.

Lesson 3   African Countries Achieve Independence—Colonial rule in Africa brought both positive and negative changes. Positive changes included modern medical services and schools introduced by the Europeans. Negative changes included the practice of segregation in most colonies. Efforts to gain independence began to succeed after World War II. By the late 1960s, most colonies had achieved independence.

Write your answers on a separate sheet of paper.

Testing Key Words, People, and Places

Part A

Choose the key word from the list that best completes each sentence.

1. A _____ occurs when a group refuses goods or services produced by a company or government.
2. _____ is the separation of one racial group from another.
3. A _____ is a sudden action, usually involving force, that changes a government.
   a. segregation   c. coup
   b. boycott

Part B

1. In a sentence, tell why each person or place is important.
   a. Mansa Musa   **d.** Songhai
   b. Tombouctou   **e.** Zimbabwe
   c. Ghana   **f.** Kwame Nkrumah

Testing Main Ideas

Write the letter of the word or phrase that correctly completes each sentence.

1. By about 500 B.C., farmers in western Africa were able to increase food production because
   a. the Romans gave them camels.
   b. they had discovered iron and used it to make farming tools.
   c. Arab traders gave them guns.

2. The first great kingdom to develop in the grasslands of West Africa was
  a. Ghana.
  b. Benin.
  c. Zimbabwe.

3. The major kingdoms of East Africa gained wealth and power
  a. through trade.
  b. by conquering the Songhai.
  c. by conquering Europe.

4. Europeans first came to Africa
  a. to find slaves.
  b. to establish colonies.
  c. to search for trade routes.

5. Christian missionaries had almost no success in
  a. southern Africa.
  b. northern Africa.
  c. present-day Ethiopia.

6. Stanley claimed land in the Congo River area for
  a. Belgium.
  b. Germany.
  c. France.

7. The European takeover of Africa
  a. took a century to complete.
  b. happened in the 1500s.
  c. took only a few years.

8. The best summary for European rule of Africa is
  a. the health of most Africans improved but ethnic groups and civil rights suffered.
  b. the Africans did not benefit from European rule in any way.
  c. European rule was without problems.

9. Most African colonies achieved independence by
  a. using terrorism.
  b. staging coups.
  c. using peaceful means.

Testing Skills

1. Forming a hypothesis. What might have happened if West Africa did not have gold and ivory to trade? Make a list of the possible changes that might have taken place over the course of history.

2. Making a time line. Make a time line that shows the following events in their correct positions.
  1493—Askia the Great begins to rule Songhai.
  1235—Mali comes to power.
  1590—Morocco uses guns to defeat the Songhai army.
  1468—Tombouctou is captured.
  1600—Songhai empire disappears.

Activities

1. On a map of Africa, show where these ancient kingdoms were located: Ghana, Benin, Mali, Songhai, and Zimbabwe. What present-day nations now occupy these areas?

2. Use the card catalog in the library to find an illustrated book on the African slave trade. Sketch or trace the living quarters on a slave ship.

333

Chapter 16

The Countries of the Dry North Today

The Sahara is the major feature of Africa's dry north. Flying across the Sahara, you would see a seemingly limitless expanse of sand. Only occasionally would you see a patch of green where an oasis sits. The picture shows the landscape of the Sahara.

In this chapter you will learn about the countries of northern Africa and about the desert fringe countries, which together make up the dry north. The lessons in the chapter are listed below.

Lesson 1   The Countries of Northern Africa

Lesson 2   The Countries of the Desert Fringe

Lesson 1   The Countries of Northern Africa

LOOKING AHEAD As you read, look for—

Key words, people, and places:

terrorist
intensive farming

Berber
Tuareg
Bedouin
Muammar el-Qaddafi
Gamal Abdel Nasser

Maghreb
Casablanca
Algiers
Tripoli
Benghazi
Cairo

Answers to these questions about **main ideas:**

1. What are the major characteristics of the land and people of northern Africa?
2. What are the main economic activities in the countries of the Maghreb?
3. How has Libya changed since independence and the discovery of oil?
4. What are the main economic activities in Egypt?
5. How has the Aswan High Dam changed farming in Egypt?

Long ago, Arab travelers thought the scattered settlements along the Mediterranean coast of Morocco, Algeria, and Tunisia were the westernmost point of civilization. They called this land the Maghreb (mä′greb), which means "the west" in Arabic.

The countries of Morocco, Algeria, and Tunisia, together with the countries of Libya and Egypt, form the region of northern Africa. They lie between the Mediterranean Sea and the southern part of the Sahara.

The Land and the People

The chief physical feature of northern Africa is the huge desert known as the Sahara. A hot and dry climate or hot and semi-dry climate covers most of the area. Parts of northern Africa receive less than 10 inches of rain each year. With so little rainfall, much of the area has little or no natural vegetation. One exception to this, however, is the Mediterranean coast lands. They have a warm climate with one dry season. Shrubs and small broadleaf trees grow there.

Many northern Africans are Bedouins, descendants of Arabs who settled in northern Africa beginning in the A.D. 600s. People belonging to smaller ethnic groups, such as the Berbers and the Tuaregs (twär′egz), also live in northern Africa. Many of the people from these smaller ethnic groups live as nomadic herders. Almost all northern Africans are Muslims.

The countries of northern Africa share a common culture which includes the Arabic language and the Islamic religion. For this reason most countries of northern Africa have close ties with one another. They maintain relations with other Islamic countries, such as the Arab countries of Southwest Asia, as well.

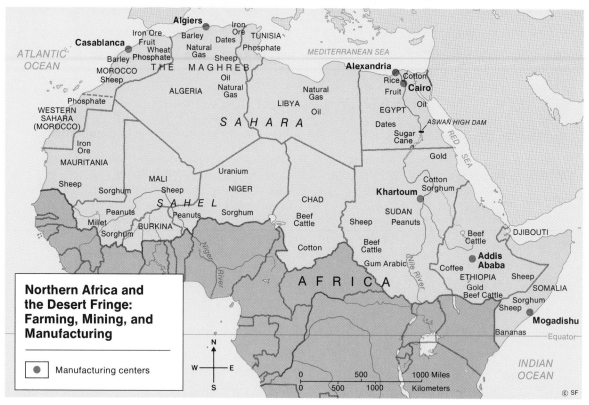

Northern Africa and
the Desert Fringe:
Farming, Mining, and
Manufacturing

● Manufacturing centers

Map Study

Spain gave up control of the area known as Western Sahara in 1976. Both Mauritania and Morocco immediately claimed parts of this land because of its one valuable resource. Find Western Sahara on the map. What mineral is found there? Which country now controls all of this region?

The Maghreb

Morocco, Algeria, and Tunisia are the countries of the Maghreb. These countries gained independence from France in the 1950s and 1960s. Since independence the governments of these countries have been fairly stable.

The map above shows how the people of the Maghreb make a living. The far north, between the Atlas Mountains and the Mediterranean Sea, has a variety of economic activity. Tourism and farming are important there. Look at the map to find the kinds of crops the farmers of the Maghreb grow. Notice

that farther inland, many people graze sheep.

All three countries of the Maghreb have valuable mineral resources, including oil, iron ore, and phosphates. A number of industries, such as oil refining, metal working, and fertilizer production, have grown up around these resources.

The development of industry in the Maghreb has been made easier by the network of roads and dams built by the French during colonial times. The major industrial centers of the Maghreb are Casablanca and Algiers. Find these two cities on the map above.

Libya

The country of Libya lies east of the Maghreb. After achieving independence in 1951, the people of Libya were ruled by a king. However, a military coup led by Colonel Muammar el-Qaddafi (mü ä-mär′ el kä däf′ē) overthrew the king in 1969. At that time Libya became a socialist republic. Qaddafi, as head of the country and "leader of the revolution," exercises almost complete control over the country.

The Sahara covers almost all of Libya, so very little of the land is good for farming. People who live in the desert make a living through nomadic herding. Most of the people of Libya live along the coast or on oases where they are farmers or city dwellers. Tripoli and Benghazi (bengä′zē), Libya's largest cities, are located on the Mediterranean coast.

Libya once was a very poor country. However, since oil was discovered there in the 1950s, Libya has prospered, and today it is one of the richest countries in Africa. Colonel Qaddafi has used some money from the sale of oil to improve Libya. He also has used oil money to build up Libya's army.

Many countries, including the United States, have accused Qaddafi of using money from the sale of oil to support terrorist groups. A **terrorist** is a person who uses deliberate violence against other people for political ends. Qaddafi's policies have caused conflict between Libya and such countries as Chad, Egypt, and the United States.

Oil fields, like the one in the picture, make Libya the wealthiest country in the region.

Egypt

Egypt has the largest population of all the northern African countries. Find Egypt's population in the "Facts About Countries" on pages 546-553. It also is northern Africa's poorest country.

After achieving independence from Great Britain in 1922, Egypt was a monarchy for thirty years. In 1952 a group of army officers led by Colonel Gamal Abdel Nasser overthrew the king. Egypt became a republic, and Nasser was elected as its first president in 1956. Under Nasser, Egypt forged strong ties with most Arab countries and with some communist countries. Throughout his fourteen years as president, Nasser often acted like a dictator. Today the president of Egypt still has a great deal of power.

Someone to Know

Anwar Sadat was an important Egyptian leader who worked for peace. While in the army he joined a group of young officers, led by Gamal Abdel Nasser, who overthrew the king of Egypt in 1952.

Sadat became president of Egypt in 1970. At first Sadat worked for Arab unity and took a strong stand against Israel. He was one of the leaders of the Arab attack on Israel in 1973. However, in the mid-1970s Sadat started to look for a peaceful way to end Arab-Israeli differences.

In 1978, Sadat held meetings with the leaders of the United States and Israel. Out of these meetings came the Camp David Accords—a blueprint for peace.

Many Arabs were unhappy with Sadat. In 1981 he was assassinated by people who disagreed with his policies. However, Sadat's efforts gave people hope that the problems of the Middle East might be settled peacefully.

If you looked down on Egypt from an airplane, you would see a narrow ribbon of water, edged with green, running from the country's southern border north to the Mediterranean Sea. This ribbon is the Nile River valley, one of the most intensively farmed areas in the world. In **intensive farming** a small amount of land is worked to produce a large amount of crops. Look at the map on page 336 to discover what crops are grown in the Nile River valley.

Desert covers much of the rest of Egypt, so most of the people live and work in the Nile River valley. About half the people make a living from farming. However, Egypt has some important industries. Cotton clothing is one of Egypt's major products. Oil refining and making chemicals from oil are two other important industries. Most of Egypt's industrial activity takes place in Cairo and Alexandria, the country's two largest cities. Find these two cities on the map on page 336. How would you describe their locations?

Modernizing Farming in Egypt

For thousands of years, the Nile River in Egypt flooded its banks every August. The waters came rushing from the south, carrying silt—fine particles of earth. When the floods ended in November, a rich topsoil that was good for farming was left on the riverbanks.

The August floods brought life to the desert, but they also brought problems. If the floods were light, not enough food could be grown. If the floods were heavy, whole towns could be destroyed. The Egyptians looked for a way to control the floods and store the Nile's water for the dry season. With water available year-round, Egypt's farmers

338

would be able to plant crops several times a year instead of only once.

In 1960 President Nasser began a project called the Aswan High Dam. He hoped the dam would control the Nile River and produce hydroelectric power for Egypt's cities and villages. The dam took ten years to build and cost more than one billion dollars. Find the Aswan High Dam on the map on page 336. About how far is the dam from the mouth of the Nile River?

The Aswan High Dam has produced some good results. It has controlled the flood waters of the Nile. It stores these waters and releases them a little at a time. As a result, Egypt's farmers can plant several crops a year. In addition, thousands of acres of new farmland have been created through irrigation. The dam has enabled Egypt to double its crop production.

The world's most important waterway—Egypt's Suez Canal

However, the dam has caused some problems. The land along the Nile is not as rich as it was when the yearly floods deposited silt on the land. In addition, the year-round irrigation has left the soil very salty. Farmers must use fertilizers and other chemicals to improve the quality of the soil. These chemicals cost a lot of money.

When the Aswan High Dam was built, most people did not think much about the problems that might result. However, large modernization projects are looked at more closely today to see how they might change the land. In this way people can decide if modernization is worth the cost.

Reviewing the Lesson

Recalling Key Words, People, and Places
1. Identify the key words defined below:
   a. a person who uses violence against other people for political ends
   b. farming in which a small amount of land produces a large amount of crops
2. Tell why it is important to remember:
   a. Muammar el-Qaddafi
   b. Gamal Abdel Nasser
3. Describe the locations of:
   a. Casablanca
   b. Tripoli

Remembering Main Ideas
1. What do the countries of northern Africa share in common?
2. Name two industries that have grown up around mineral resources in the Maghreb.
3. What has made Libya a fairly wealthy country?
4. Where do most people live and work in Egypt?
5. What have been the results of the building of the Aswan High Dam?

Thinking Things Over
How might the lives of the people of northern Africa be different if the Sahara were to be replaced by grassland and rainforest?

Lesson 2   The Countries of the Desert Fringe

 LOOKING AHEAD As you read, look for—

Key words, people, and **places:**

desertification

Khartoum
Addis Ababa
Mogadishu

Answers to these questions about **main ideas:**

1. What are the major characteristics of the land and people of the desert fringe?
2. What are the main economic activities in the Sahel countries and Sudan?
3. How does the location of the Horn of Africa make it important in world affairs?
4. What are the causes and effects of the serious food shortages in the desert fringe?

The people of the desert fringe live on the border of the world's largest desert—the Sahara. They face many challenges. Their greatest challenge comes from the constant threat of drought and the famine it might create.

The desert fringe lies south of northern Africa. The countries of the Sahel make up the western part of the desert fringe. The eastern part of the desert fringe is called the Horn of Africa. Find the countries of Ethiopia, Djibouti (ji-büʹtē), and Somalia on the map on page 292. Why do you think the area these countries cover is called the Horn?

The Land and the People

As in northern Africa, the Sahara dominates the desert fringe. Hot, dry climates occur throughout the area, but the southern parts of Chad, Sudan, and Ethiopia have a hot climate with one dry season. The Ethiopian Highlands have a high mountain climate. As the area's name suggests, desert plant life is the most common form of natural vegetation found in the desert fringe. However, a belt of grassland runs through the southern part of the desert fringe.

The people who live in the northern part of the desert fringe lead different lives from those people who live in the south. Most people in the north are Muslims and make a living through nomadic herding. In the rainier south, most people are subsistence farmers and follow Christian or traditional African religions.

The different ways of life in the north and the south have led to problems. For example, the people who live in northern Sudan have tried to make Islam and Arabic Sudan's official religion and language. However, the people in southern Sudan have fought to keep their own local languages and traditional religions.

The Sahel Countries and Sudan

The countries of the Sahel are Mauritania, Mali (mäʹlē), Burkina Faso, Niger (nī′jər), and Chad. Sudan lies east of the Sahel. Use your finger to trace a line from west to east through these countries on the map on page 292.

The Sahel Countries. The countries of the Sahel are very poor. They depend on economic help from other countries. Most people of the Sahel make their living from the land, either through subsistence farming or through nomadic herding.

The most important resource for the people of the Sahel is water. Rainfall averages only between 5 and 20 inches a year. Also, this rainfall is not dependable. In some years little or no rain falls. You read earlier that low rainfall together with overgrazing and shifting cultivation have caused the desert to spread southward. The spread of the desert is called **desertification.** Some scientists think the Sahara is spreading southward into the Sahel at a rate of about 12 miles a year.

One major body of water, the Niger River, flows through the Sahel. Along the banks of the Niger, farmers raise sorghum (sôr′gəm)—which is used to make syrup and molasses—and peanuts as cash crops. Look at the map on page 336. Compare the number of crops grown in the Sahel countries with the number grown in the Maghreb.

Sudan. The people of Sudan depend on the Nile River in many ways. Most people live along the Nile or one of its tributaries, the White Nile and the Blue Nile. Khartoum (kär tüm′), Sudan's capital and largest city, is located where these two tributaries flow into the Nile.

Planting hardy grasses near the Sahara's edge helps keep the desert from spreading faster.

Much of Sudan's chief economic activity, farming, takes place along the Nile. Sudanese farmers grow two important cash crops—cotton and sorghum. In fact, cotton is Sudan's major export and the base of the country's economy. Sudan also is the world's leading source of gum arabic, a sap taken from a desert bush. People use gum arabic to make products such as candies, medicines, and glue.

Sudan's few industries involve farm products. The two most important industries are food processing and clothing manufacturing. Sudanese leaders have tried to develop more industries. However, Sudan has had to borrow money from foreign countries to finance this development. As a result, Sudan owes money to these countries, and its economy is weak.

341

The Countries of the Horn

Like the Sahel countries, the countries of the Horn—Ethiopia, Djibouti, and Somalia—are very poor. None of these three countries have a yearly GNP per person above $500. In Ethiopia and Somalia, more than three-fourths of the people make a living from farming or nomadic herding. Coffee is an important cash crop in Ethiopia. It is responsible for more than half of Ethiopia's export earnings. Look at the map on page 336 to find the crops grown in Somalia. Notice that no products are shown for Djibouti. Djibouti's economy is based on foreign aid, mostly from France.

The countries of the Horn do not have many industries. The industries they do have mostly involve processing farm products. Addis Ababa is Ethiopia's major industrial center and the country's capital. This city sits high in the Ethiopian Highlands. Mogadishu, Somalia's capital and most important port and industrial center, lies on the Indian Ocean. Mogadishu also serves as a port for some of the landlocked countries west of Somalia.

The countries of the Horn have received much attention in the news in recent years. The Horn guards the entrance to the southern end of the Red Sea. In time of war, those who control the Horn could easily cut off the shipping lane between Europe and Asia.

The Horn is one part of the world where the interests of the United States

Linking Past and Present

When the Sahara Was Wet

Many scientists believe the droughts that have plagued the northern half of Africa recently signal a major change in the climate. This would not be the first time climatic changes have occurred in the area.

Thousands of years ago, the Sahara and the desert fringe had a warm, wet climate. Tassili n'Ajjer—which means "plateau of rivers" in Arabic—in southeastern Algeria provides proof of this.

Huge rock paintings there show giraffes, elephants, bison, antelope, and other large mammals. The natural environment for such animals includes grasslands and forests. The picture on the right shows a rock painting of giraffes.

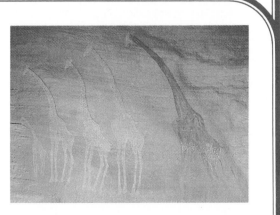

About four thousand years ago, the climate of this area began to get drier and the grasses and trees began to die. In time, the animals were unable to find enough to eat. Those animals that did not die apparently moved south to wetter areas.

and the Soviet Union come into conflict. The Ethiopian government has set up strong political and economic ties with the Soviet Union and other communist countries. Somalia, on the other hand, has allied itself with the United States. The involvement of outside powers in the area has worsened the relations between Ethiopia and Somalia.

Food Shortages in the Desert Fringe

A number of causes have helped create a widespread shortage of food in the desert fringe. First, much of the northern half of Africa has suffered a series of droughts throughout the 1970s and 1980s. The shortage of water during these years has made it difficult for plant and animal life to survive.

To try to survive the droughts, many herders in the desert fringe increased the size of their herds of cattle, sheep, or goats. However, these large herds have overgrazed and helped cause desertification. Shifting cultivation methods also have helped the desert spread. As the Sahara spreads steadily southward, less land is available to use for growing food crops and raising livestock each year.

Government policies also have contributed to the food shortages. In some countries, governments have tried to improve their economies by encouraging farmers to grow cash crops for export. Many farmers have moved from food crops to cash crops in the hope that they might increase their earnings. However, world prices for desert fringe cash crops, such as coffee, cotton, and peanuts, have been very low in recent years. Also, these cash crops do not survive periods of drought as well as food crops. Many farmers have been unsuccessful in their efforts to grow or sell cash crops. Therefore, they have no money to buy the food crops they once grew for themselves.

Nearly all the countries of the desert fringe are experiencing dangerous food shortages. This has had a serious effect on the people of these countries. For example, more than one million Ethiopians died of hunger in 1984. Thousands more fled Ethiopia in search of food and water. The situation also is bad for Ethiopia's neighbors. In some countries, the people have taken to eating the seed for the next year's planting to stay alive.

Reviewing the Lesson

Recalling Key Words, People, and Places
1. What is the spread of the desert called?
2. Describe the locations of:
    a. Khartoum
    b. Addis Ababa
    c. Mogadishu

Remembering Main Ideas
1. How do the people who live in the north of the desert fringe differ from those who live in the south?
2. How do most people in the Sahel and Sudan make a living?
3. Why are foreign countries interested in the Horn of Africa?
4. What effect have food shortages had on the people of the desert fringe?

Thinking Things Over
What, if anything, do you think other countries should do to help the desert fringe countries overcome their problems of drought and famine? Explain your answer.

Using Periodical Indexes to Do Research

If you were preparing a report on a country of northern Africa or the desert fringe, where would you find information? Your library's encyclopedias would be a good place to look for general background information. Magazine articles, however, often have more information on current events. How would you find the magazines and their articles?

Using Periodical Indexes

Your library probably has various periodical indexes. A periodical is a publication, such as a magazine, that is published regularly—every week, every month, or several times a year. A periodical index is a series of books or pamphlets that list subjects you can find in various magazines.

Suppose you want to report on famines in Africa. Your librarian might show you a periodical index called *Children's Magazine Guide.* Looking in the index, you find the following entry.

> **AFRICA–FAMINES**
> Africa Faces Famine.
>   Cur Ev Dec 12 '83 p4-5

This entry means you can find an article titled "Africa Faces Famine" in a magazine called *Current Events.* The article is in the December 12, 1983, issue on pages 4 and 5. (The inside front cover of *Children's Magazine Guide* has a list of abbreviations that are used in the entries.)

Now your librarian can help you find this issue of *Current Events* on the library shelves. What if the library doesn't keep copies of this magazine? *Children's Magazine Guide* also has a section with descriptions of magazines in its index, including addresses. You can write to the magazine's publisher, requesting a back issue.

The *Readers' Guide*

The set of books and pamphlets called the *Readers' Guide to Periodical Literature* is a periodical index that can direct you to articles in many different magazines. Suppose you are reporting on irrigation in Egypt. First, you look up "Egypt" in the alphabetical listing in an issue of the *Readers' Guide.* The issues of the *Reader's Guide* are dated, and you pick an issue based on the dates in which you are interested. Use the most recent issue if you want the most current information. The lines below are part of an entry you might find.

> **Egypt**
>
> *See also*
> Economic assistance, American-
>   Egypt
> Irrigation–Egypt

The first thing the entry tells you is *"See also"* some special topics listed elsewhere in the index. To find information about an article on irrigation in Egypt, you now must look up "Irrigation—Egypt." Under that entry, you find the following.

Irrigation
Egypt
The greening of Egypt. A. Charnock. *World-Press-Rev* 33:54 Ap '86

The Nile Valley. B. Wallach. il map *Focus* 36:16-19 Spr '86

Now look at the entry beginning "The Nile Valley." These lines refer to a specific magazine article. Use the numbered items below to help you understand each part of this entry.

1. "The Nile Valley." (title of the article)
2. "B. Wallach." (author of the article)
3. "il map" (The article has one or more illustrations, including at least one map.)
4. "*Focus*" (the name of the magazine, *Focus*)
5. "36:" (volume number of that issue of *Focus*)
6. "16–19" (The article is found on page numbers 16–19 in the magazine.)
7. "Spr '86" (spring issue of *Focus* in 1986)

The opening pages of each *Readers' Guide* give an explanation of abbreviations used in entries. Samples from that explanation follow:

Ag–August	Spr–Spring
Ann–annual	Summ–Summer
Ap–April	Wint–Winter

Once you have selected an article from the *Readers' Guide,* write down the name of the periodical, the date of the issue, and the page numbers. If the issue is recent, it probably will be on the racks in the library. If it is an older issue, you might need to ask a librarian to find it for you in the library's collection of back issues.

Skills Practice

Suppose you are reporting on Egypt's economy. You look up "Egypt" in the *Readers' Guide* and find the entry below. Answer the questions that follow the entry.

Egypt
Economic policy
Dialogue of the deaf. M.S. Serril. il *Time* 128:31 Ag 18 '86

---

1. What is the name of the magazine in which the article about economic policy appears?
2. What is the date of the issue?
3. Who wrote the article?
4. On what page of the magazine is the article found?
5. Does the article have pictures?

Chapter Summary

Lesson 1   The Countries of Northern Africa—Northern Africa is made up of the huge Sahara desert and the narrow Mediterranean coast lands. The people speak the Arabic language and practice the Islamic religion. In the Maghreb countries, the main economic activities are nomadic herding, tourism, and farming. East of the Maghreb is Libya, where money from oil sales has made that country one of the richest in Africa. Another wealthy African nation is Egypt, whose products include cotton clothing and oil.

Lesson 2   The Countries of the Desert Fringe—The Sahara dominates the desert fringe, although a belt of grassland runs through the southern part of the region. In the Sahel countries, most people are subsistence farmers or nomadic herders. Ethiopia, Djibouti, and Somalia form the Horn of Africa, which guards the entrance to the Red Sea. Drought and low prices for cash crops have caused serious food shortages in the desert fringe.

Write your answers on a separate sheet of paper.

Testing Key Words, People, and Places

Part A

Give the definition of each key word.

1. terrorist
2. intensive farming
3. desertification

Part B

Choose the person or place from the list that best completes each sentence.

1. _____ is a major industrial center of the Maghreb.
2. A military coup led by _____ overthrew Libya's king in 1969.
3. The capital of Ethiopia is _____.
4. _____ was elected as Egypt's first president.
5. Somalia's capital is _____.
6. The capital of Sudan is _____.

   a. Muammar el-Qaddafi
   b. Gamal Abdel Nasser
   c. Algiers
   d. Khartoum
   e. Addis Ababa
   f. Mogadishu

Testing Main Ideas

Choose the best answer for each question.

1. What is the region of northern Africa like?
   a. It is hot and dry all year.
   b. It receives 20 inches of rain yearly.
   c. It is full of blooming vegetation.
2. What do most of the people in the Maghreb do for a living?
   a. They are nomadic herders.
   b. They are tour guides.
   c. They make crafts.
3. What makes Libya one of the richest countries in Africa?
   a. fertile soil
   b. money from oil sales
   c. money from iron mining

4. Where do most of the people in Egypt live and work?
   a. in the desert
   b. in Benghazi
   c. in the Nile River valley

5. What is one positive result of the Aswan High Dam?
   a. The soil along the Nile River is very salty.
   b. The dam has enabled Egypt to double its crop production.
   c. Land along the Nile is less fertile.

6. Which description fits the people in the northern part of the desert fringe?
   a. They are subsistence farmers.
   b. They are nomads.
   c. They are gold miners.

7. What is the most important resource in the Sahel?
   a. water
   b. molasses
   c. oil

8. Which two countries would most likely disagree over their interests in the Horn of Africa?
   a. Canada and the United States
   b. China and Japan
   c. the United States and the Soviet Union

9. Which statement is true?
   a. Increasing the size of the herd helps a herder survive drought.
   b. The Sahara is spreading southward.
   c. Cash crops survive droughts better than food crops.

Testing Skills

1. Using periodical indexes to do research. Answer the following questions about the *Readers' Guide to Periodical Literature.*
   a. What does "il map" tell you about a magazine article?
   b. What does "31–44" mean when it appears in an entry as follows? *Science* 95: 31–44

2. Using latitude and longitude. Listed below are the approximate latitudes and longitudes of five cities. Use the list to answer the questions.
   Addis Ababa   9°N, 38°E
   Benghazi   32°N, 20°E
   Cairo   30°N, 31°E
   Mogadishu   2°N, 45°E
   Tunis   36°N, 10°E
   a. Which city is closest to the Equator?
   b. Which city is farthest north of the Equator?
   c. Is Cairo east or west of Benghazi?
   d. Is Tunis east or west of Benghazi?

Activities

1. Do research to find out what sights a tourist might see while visiting Egypt.

2. Use an encyclopedia to find information about Gamal Abdel Nasser. Then make a time line showing important events in Nasser's life.

Chapter 17

The Countries of Sub-Saharan Africa Today

Sub-Saharan Africa—the land to the south of the Sahara—covers a huge area. It stretches more than 3,500 miles from the grasslands and forests of central Africa to the narrow coastal plain of southern Africa. The picture shows the city of Cape Town, on the coastal plain of southern Africa, with an escarpment known as Table Mountain rising in the background. The vastness of Sub-Saharan Africa helps make it a land of contrast.

In this chapter you will learn about the geography, economics, and governments of the more than thirty countries of Sub-Saharan Africa. The lessons in the chapter are listed below.

Lesson 1   The Western and Central Forest Countries

LOOKING AHEAD As you read, look for—

Key words, people, and **places:**

Jerry Rawlings   Lagos
                    Kinshasa

Answers to these questions about **main ideas:**

1. What are the major characteristics of the land and people of the central forest countries?
2. What are the main economic activities of the western forest countries?
3. What important mineral resources do the central forest countries of Zaire and Angola have?
4. How does Ghana provide an example of how economic problems can affect political stability?

In western and central Africa, the rainforest covers at least part of the land of seventeen countries. On the map on page 292, use your finger to trace a line along the west coast of Africa from Senegal to Angola. Note each country you pass. The Central African Republic, which is not on the west coast, also is considered one of this group of western and central forest countries.

The Land and the People

The western and central forest countries lie on or near the Equator. On the map on page 298, notice that the area around the Equator has hot and wet climates. As the area's name suggests, forest—in the form of rainforest—is the most widespread form of vegetation. Use the map on page 299 to find what kind of natural vegetation covers much of the rest of the area.

Many different ethnic groups live in the western and central forest lands.

Turn back to the map on page 308 and notice how many ethnic groups are clustered in the forest lands of western Africa. These ethnic groups have very different cultures. Nearly every group has its own language, and many groups have different religions. Groups in the far north mostly follow Islam, whereas most southern groups practice either traditional African religions or Christianity.

Most people live near the coasts or along the region's two major rivers, the Congo (Zaire) and the Niger. Nearly all the large cities of the area are ocean ports. Lagos—the capital of Nigeria and its main port city—has more than one million people. Ibadan (ē bä′dän), Nigeria, also has more than a million people. Kinshasa (kēn shä′sä), located on the Congo (Zaire) River, is the capital of Zaire (zä ir′) and the largest city in the area. More than 2,500,000 people live in Kinshasa.

349

The Western Forest Countries

Most people in the western forest countries make a living through subsistence farming. However, some people in the area practice commercial farming. In each area of commercial farming, usually only one cash crop is grown. These cash crops include bananas, coffee, cotton, peanuts, and cacao. Study the map on page 351 to find the crops grown by each country in the western forest area.

The economies of most western forest countries are weak because they depend upon the sale of a single cash crop. For example, Gambia's chief cash crop is peanuts. When world prices for peanuts fall, Gambia's economy weakens. Gambia has been unable to build a strong economy as a result.

Nigeria and Oil. Farm products are the main product of most western forest countries. However, some of these countries have important mineral resources. The Central African Republic has diamonds, Gabon has oil, and Sierra Leone and Ghana have deposits of bauxite. Nigeria has valuable reserves of tin, iron ore, coal, and natural gas. However, Nigeria's most important mineral resource is oil. In fact, oil accounts for close to 95 percent of Nigeria's exports.

Nigeria has more people than any other African country. Because Nigeria depends on the sale of oil, its economy is strong only when the price of oil is high. The weakness of Nigeria's economy appeared in the early 1980s. People in European countries and the

Local women carry their packages near an open-pit mine in Zaire.

United States, Nigeria's chief trading partners, began to use less oil. That meant the demand for oil went down. At the same time, oil was in plentiful supply. When supply is greater than demand, prices fall. As a result, Nigeria's income from oil went down. Nigeria's economic problems continued throughout the 1980s because of changing oil prices.

Development in the Ivory Coast. Unlike most western forest countries, the Ivory Coast has a fairly strong economy. After the Ivory Coast gained independence in 1960, its leaders wanted to develop farms and factories that could produce many goods for export.

These government leaders invited foreign investors to develop the land for the production of cash crops. In a short time, farms in the Ivory Coast were producing cacao, coffee, cotton, and pineapples for export.

The foreign investors were allowed to keep most of the money they made from export sales. However, they had to give some money to the government. The Ivory Coast's government has used this money to build schools, hospitals, roads, and factories. In this way, foreign investment has helped many people in the Ivory Coast.

In recent years the Ivory Coast's economy has been strengthened by the discovery of oil. So many jobs are now available in the Ivory Coast that workers from other countries go there to work.

Zaire and Angola

The majority of the people in the central forest countries of Zaire and Angola make a living from farming.

Map Study

A major industry in Lubumbashi, Zaire, involves changing metal ores into pure metal. Find Lubumbashi on the map. What metals are mined in the area near the city? What metal ores would you think are processed in Lubumbashi? Would you expect to find oil refineries in Lubumbashi?

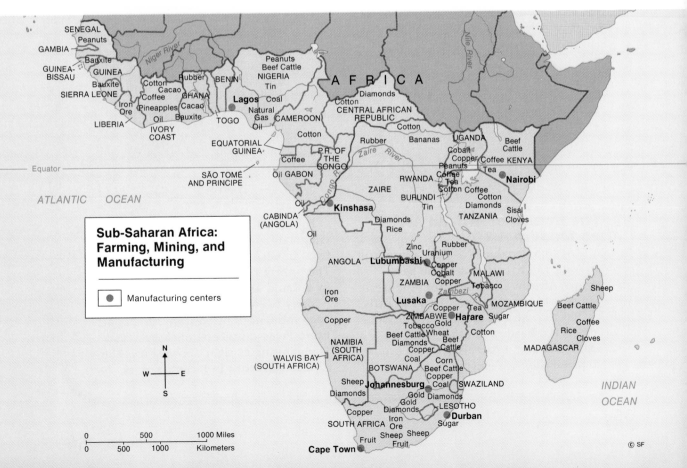

Most people who work the land are subsistence farmers, but these countries do produce some cash crops for export. Look at the map on page 351 and list three cash crops grown in Zaire and Angola.

Both Zaire and Angola are rich in minerals. Zaire has large supplies of cobalt, tin, zinc, and uranium. It is one of the world's leading producers of copper and diamonds. Shaba province, in the southeast of the country, is the most important area for minerals. *Shaba* means "copper" in Swahili. Angola has rich deposits of iron ore and oil. The sale of these two minerals provides a large part of Angola's wealth.

The mineral riches of Zaire and Angola have not been fully developed. In part, this development has been slowed by political problems in these two countries. For example, a civil war has raged in Angola since the 1960s. Since the 1970s, foreign powers have become involved in this struggle. The Soviet Union and Cuba support the Communist Popular Movement, which governs the country. The opposition party, the National Union, is supported by the United States and South Africa.

Linking Past and Present

Mask, Etoumbi region, People's Republic of the Congo. Wood, 14" high. Musée Barbier-Müller, Geneva.

PICASSO, Pablo. *Les Demoiselles d'Avignon* (detail). (1907) Oil on canvas. 8' × 7'8". Collection, The Museum of Modern Art, New York. Acquired through the Lillie P. Bliss Bequest.

The Impact of African Art on Modern Art

Africa has produced a great amount of striking and beautiful art. The best-known African art comes from the western part of the continent. From as early as 300 B.C., African artists were producing carved heads and other objects made of wood. Later artists used bronze to make their art objects.

The Ife and the Benin became especially famous for their art. These groups lived in what is now western Nigeria. The bronze head at left above was made by a Benin artist in the 1500s.

Many twentieth-century artists have been influenced by western African art. Pablo Picasso was one of these artists. The painting at right above shows the African influence in Picasso's work.

Economic and Political Problems

Countries that depend on one product for their wealth often have economic problems when the price of that product falls. In some cases these economic problems lead to political problems. The western forest country of Ghana is an example of this.

Ghana is one of the largest producers of cacao in the world. When world prices for cacao are high, the government and people of Ghana have money to spend. When world prices are low, little money is available. In the early 1960s, world cacao prices were very high. This allowed Kwame Nkrumah, Ghana's president, to begin a number of large building projects. However, world cacao prices dropped eventually, and Ghana was unable to pay for these building projects.

Some people in Ghana began to blame Nkrumah for all their problems. Nkrumah responded by throwing those who opposed him into jail. He also limited the civil rights of many people in Ghana.

In 1966, while Nkrumah was out of the country, a group of army officers took over the government. These officers promised to restore the people's rights and to improve the country's economy. However, they failed to live up to their promise, even when prices for cacao began to rise. Conditions in Ghana were made worse by the corruption—bribery and dishonesty—in government. The people of Ghana were very upset with the government, and they wanted to remove the army officers from power.

In June of 1979, an air force officer named Jerry Rawlings seized power. Although he was from the military, Rawlings said he would soon step down and let civilians rule Ghana. He said he had seized power in order to remove dishonest people from government. Rawlings kept his word. By September of 1979, he had left office and a freely elected civilian government took control.

However, Ghana's problems continued. The price of cacao fell again, and Ghana's economy weakened. Members of the civilian government argued with one another and did little to solve the problems. In 1981, Rawlings took control of the government once again. The economic and political problems of countries such as Ghana make it likely that the military will play a part in government for some time to come.

Reviewing the Lesson

Recalling Key Words, People, and Places
1. What role has Jerry Rawlings played in the government of Ghana?
2. Describe the location of:
   a. Lagos
   b. Kinshasa

Remembering Main Ideas
1. What are the religious differences among ethnic groups in the western and central forest countries?
2. How did the Ivory Coast develop its economy?
3. What is the most important area for minerals in Zaire?
4. What was the cause of political problems in Ghana in the 1960s and 1970s?

Thinking Things Over
Why do you think the military has taken control of government in some countries in the western and central forest area? Explain your answer.

Lesson 2   The Countries of Eastern Africa

LOOKING AHEAD As you read, look for—

Key words, people, and places:

infant mortality
life expectancy
literacy

Kikuyu
Luo
Masai
Turkana
Julius Nyerere

Mombasa
Dar es Salaam
Maputo
Nairobi

Answers to these questions about main ideas:

1. What are the main characteristics of the land and people of eastern Africa?
2. What are the chief economic activities of the east coast countries of eastern Africa?
3. How do most people in the landlocked countries of eastern Africa make a living?
4. What are the two major economic activities in Madagascar?
5. How did President Julius Nyerere plan to develop the economy of Tanzania?

The Great Rift Valley separates eastern Africa from the rest of Africa. Eight countries make up eastern Africa. Three countries lie on Africa's east coast. Four more are landlocked. The eighth country of eastern Africa is an island. Locate the countries of eastern Africa on the map on page 292. Which of these countries is an island? Which coastal country also includes an island?

The Land and the People

Much of eastern Africa consists of high plateau. A narrow belt of coastal plain runs along the Indian Ocean. Eastern Africa is the site of the continent's highest mountains and largest lakes. Most of the area has a hot climate with one dry season, and grassland is the most widely found form of vegetation.

Many east Africans live on the coastal plain or near Lakes Victoria, Tanganyika, and Nyasa. The countries of Rwanda (rü än′də) and Burundi are

the most crowded countries in the area and on the continent. Rich farmland—more than half the land is good for farming—has attracted many people to these countries.

The major cities of eastern Africa are the Indian Ocean port cities. Mombasa in Kenya, Dar es Salaam (där es sə-läm′) in Tanzania, and Maputo in Mozambique (mo zam bēk′) serve as ports for the landlocked countries to the west as well as for their own countries. Nairobi, Kenya's capital, sits high on the plateau in the south of the country. It is eastern Africa's chief business center.

Like western and central Africa, eastern Africa is home to many ethnic groups. As has happened elsewhere in Africa, ethnic groups have had disagreements. For example, the largest ethnic groups in Kenya—the Kikuyu (ki kü′yü), the Luo, the Masai (mä sī′), and the Turkana (tər kä′nä)—mostly live as farmers or herders. They often argue about who owns land or animals. However, Kenya's leaders have tried to get the ethnic groups to think of themselves as Kenyans first and as Kikuyu, Masai, or members of another group second.

In some parts of eastern Africa, ethnic differences have led to bloodshed. As you have read, during the 1970s Uganda was ruled by a dictator, General Idi Amin. Part of Amin's plan was to attack the ethnic groups who opposed him. Even though Amin was removed from power in 1979, violence based on ethnic differences continues to be a problem in eastern Africa.

The East Coast Countries

Three countries of eastern Africa—Kenya, Tanzania, and Mozambique—lie directly on the east coast of the continent. By far the majority of people in the east coast countries make a living from farming. However, many people in these countries make a living from other jobs.

Kenya. Before Europeans settled in the land that is now Kenya, most Africans there made a living through nomadic herding. Even today nomadic herding still is a widespread form of land use. However, commercial farming occurs in western Kenya, where tea and coffee are grown on plantations as cash crops. The climate of this area is very good for growing such crops.

Tourism is a very important economic activity in Kenya. Many people come from all over the world to visit Kenya's wild game parks. These game

By the time a Masai is eight years old, he must begin to care for his family's animals.

parks are huge—one park covers more than 8,000 square miles. Animals such as lions, elephants, antelope, and zebras roam free in these parks.

Tanzania. More than three-fourths of the workers in Tanzania are involved in farming. Most of these people work as subsistence farmers. However, in some parts of the country people grow coffee, cotton, and sisal as cash crops. In addition, cloves are an important export for Tanzania. Zanzibar and Pemba, two islands off the mainland of Tanzania, provide nearly all the world's cloves. Cloves are a spice.

355

Tourists view wildebeest and zebras from the safety of their vehicle. These tourists are at a national park in Kenya.

As in Kenya, tourism is an important economic activity in Tanzania. Tanzania also earns considerable income from the sale of minerals. Diamonds are one of the country's chief exports.

Mozambique. Mozambique is a very poor country. It gains some income from the sale of farm products such as cotton, sugar, and tea. Mozambique also exports bauxite.

Although Mozambique has a communist government, it has close economic ties with noncommunist countries. For example, Mozambique has close ties with South Africa. Many people from Mozambique work in the mines and factories in South Africa.

The Landlocked Countries

The landlocked countries of eastern Africa, from north to south, are Uganda, Rwanda, Burundi, and Malawi (mə lä′wē). Find these countries on the map on page 292.

These countries sit high above sea level; some parts of the countries are well over 7,000 feet high. Most people in these countries make a living through subsistence farming. However, all four countries have some commercial farming. Crops such as coffee, cotton, tea, and peanuts are grown for sale. Look at the map on page 351 and note the crops grown in each of the landlocked countries.

The landlocked countries have little mining or industry. However, cobalt and copper are mined in Uganda. Uganda also makes money by selling electricity to its neighbors. A power station at Owens Falls, near Lake Victoria, generates this electricity.

Madagascar

At 980 miles long and 360 miles wide, Madagascar (mad ə gas′kər) is one of the world's largest islands. It covers about the same amount of land as does the state of Texas. People from present-day Malaysia and Indonesia settled Madagascar about ten thousand years ago. Look at the Atlas map on

By the Way

When you think of diamonds, you probably think about jewelry. However, most of Tanzania's diamonds—in fact, most of the world's diamonds—are not used for jewelry. They are used in manufacturing.

Diamonds are the hardest of all natural minerals. Diamonds are made of carbon that was buried under rock millions of years ago. Heat and pressure turned the carbon into diamonds.

Industries use tools with diamond tips or edges to drill through or grind very hard metals. Powdered diamonds sometimes are used to make knife sharpeners. The man in the picture at the right is cutting diamonds for use by industries.

pages 528-529 to find in which direction these people traveled to reach Madagascar.

Most of Madagascar has a hot climate. However, mountains run the length of the island. In some places these mountains rise above 4,000 feet. Climates in these mountain areas are cooler than elsewhere on the island.

The majority of Madagascans make a living through nomadic herding or subsistence farming. In some places farmers have terraced the mountain slopes. Terracing involves cutting narrow ledges into the mountain slopes to create flat land for farming. Rice, the main food of Madagascans, is the most common crop grown on the terraces. However, some farmers grow coffee, peanuts, and spices for export.

Development in Tanzania

Tanzania, one of the east coast countries, has followed a path to development somewhat different from that followed by most African countries. Most countries have followed the example of the Ivory Coast, seeking foreign investment to help economic development. However, Tanzania's president, Julius Nyerere (ni rer'ē), wanted Tanzanians to develop their resources in their own way. Nyerere did not want the people to use resources to produce more and more exports. Instead, he wanted Tanzanians to produce more things they needed for use at home.

President Nyerere's main goal was to build up the human resources—the people—of Tanzania. He wanted the people to be healthier and better educated. He also wanted all Tanzanians to have more opportunities. Part of Nyerere's plan for getting this done was to build schools and health clinics.

Another part of Nyerere's plan was to establish ujamaa (ü'jä mä') villages. These are villages where people farm together as one large family. *Ujamaa* means "familyhood" in Swahili. Nyerere said the government could supply the people with schools, health clinics, and farming tools. However, it would

A nurse gives a talk on nutrition. The women are at a clinic in an ujamaa village in Tanzania.

Farming in the ujamaa villages has had mixed results. Food production seems to have increased. However, the production of cash crops has fallen. One explanation for this may be that President Nyerere encouraged farmers to switch from cash crops to food crops. Also, prices for cash crops have fallen in the world, and this has discouraged people from growing these crops. In addition, some people did not like the idea of moving to the ujamaa villages.

Despite President Nyerere's efforts to develop Tanzania's economy, the country is still fairly poor. Tanzanians may have to find new ways to develop their economy.

be difficult to offer these things if the people were scattered over the countryside. The ujamaa villages would bring people together so they could take advantage of what the government offered. Nyerere thought the people would benefit and would produce more crops by living and working together.

Tanzanians have been successful in achieving some of their goals. The government has built the health clinics it promised. As a result, **infant mortality,** or deaths among babies one year of age or younger, has dropped. **Life expectancy,** or the average length of time people live, has increased. Better schools have led to an increase in **literacy**—the ability to read and write. About three-fourths of all Tanzanians are literate. Few other African countries can match that figure.

Reviewing the Lesson

Recalling Key Words, People, and Places
1. Identify the key words defined below:
    a. the average length of time people live
    b. the ability to read and write
2. Why is it important to remember Julius Nyerere?
3. Describe the location of:
    a. Dar es Salaam
    b. Nairobi

Remembering Main Ideas
1. What are the major landforms of eastern Africa?
2. What important economic ties does Mozambique have with South Africa?
3. In what ways other than farming and mining does Uganda make money?
4. How do Madagascan farmers make the mountain slopes suitable for farming?
5. What was President Nyerere's main goal in developing the economy of Tanzania?

Thinking Things Over
Which approach to economic development do you think is better: the Ivory Coast's or Tanzania's? Give reasons for your answer.

358

Lesson 3 The Countries of Southern Africa

 LOOKING AHEAD As you read, look for—

Key words, people, and **places:**

protectorate
apartheid
sanction

Khoi-khoi
San
Bantu
Zulu
Boer

Afrikaner
Kenneth Kaunda

Cape Town
Port Elizabeth
Durban
Lusaka
Harare
Bulawayo
The Rand

Answers to these questions about **main ideas:**

1. What are the main characteristics of the land and people of southern Africa?
2. What are the main economic activities in South Africa?
3. What are the main economic activities in Zambia and Zimbabwe?
4. How do most people make a living in Botswana, Lesotho, Swaziland, and Namibia?
5. How does the system of apartheid work?

Southern Africa is an area of contrasts. For example, it has a number of climates and many different kinds of vegetation. Look at the maps on pages 298 and 299 to find where these climates and kinds of vegetation occur.

Perhaps the biggest contrast in southern Africa is between rich and poor countries. Southern Africa covers only one-tenth of Africa's land, and less than one-tenth of Africa's people live there. However, the area accounts for more than one-fifth of Africa's total income. Most of this income is earned by white people in the country of South Africa. Blacks in South Africa are not nearly so well off, and neither are the people of southern Africa's other countries—Zambia, Zimbabwe, Swaziland (swäz′ē land), Lesotho (lə sō′tō), Botswana (bot swä′nə), and Namibia (nä mib′ē ə).

The Land and the People

If you look at the map on pages 32-33, you will see that much of southern

Africa is covered by plateau. Parts of this plateau sit between 4,000 and 6,000 feet above sea level. The plateau slopes down sharply to a narrow coastal plain. Grassland covers most of the plateau, but the western areas of southern Africa have desert vegetation. Look at the map on page 296 and name two deserts in southern Africa.

Before Europeans came to southern Africa, three major African groups lived in the area. The Khoi-khoi and the San (sän) lived in the far south. The Khoi-khoi were farmers and herders, and the San were hunters. Different groups of Bantu people lived in the north of the area. They are called *Bantu* because that is the language they speak. Perhaps the most powerful of the Bantu groups was the Zulu. They farmed the land and herded cattle on the grasslands of the plateau of southern Africa.

The first European settlers in southern Africa were Dutch. These settlers farmed the land around the site of

359

Cape Town. They drove the Khoi-khoi and the San off this land. In time, French and German settlers joined the Dutch in this area. The European settlers became known as Boers (bôrz), a Dutch word that means "farmers."

In the early 1800s, Great Britain took control of the part of southern Africa where the Boers lived. British settlers began to arrive in about 1820. The Boers did not want to share their lands with the British, nor did they want to live under British rule. Therefore, the Boers moved north onto the grasslands of the plateau. Here they came into conflict with the Zulus and other Bantu groups. The Boers and the Bantu groups fought bitter battles for control of the best farming and grazing lands.

Today many southern Africans live on the coastal plain. Three large port cities—Cape Town, Port Elizabeth, and Durban—are located on the coastal plain. Find these cities on the map on page 292. On which oceans do these cities lie?

Important industrial centers have grown up around the cities of Lusaka in Zambia and Harare (hə rä′rē) and Bulawayo (bü lə wä′ō) in Zimbabwe. However, the most densely populated area of southern Africa is the Rand. This is the area around the city of Johannesburg. It is South Africa's major mining and industrial center.

South Africa

Since gaining independence in 1910, South Africa has become wealthy. Its chief economic activities are farming, mining, and manufacturing. South Africa has some very rich farmland. On the southwest and south coastal plain, farmers grow fruit, such as apples and grapes. On the southeast coastal plain, sugar cane is grown on large plantations. Farmers grow corn on the grasslands of the Rand. Ranchers raise sheep and cattle on the Rand and in the drier parts of the coastal plains.

The Rand is the site of most of South Africa's mines and factories. South Africa is the world's leading producer of gold and diamonds. The country's wealth is based mostly on the export of these precious minerals. South Africa also produces other minerals, such as copper, iron ore, and uranium.

South Africa maintains economic ties with most of its neighbors. For example, Botswana, Zambia, and Zimbabwe import and export goods through South African ports. Also, people from Botswana, Lesotho, Malawi, Mozambique, and Swaziland work in many of South Africa's mines and factories.

Zambia and Zimbabwe

Zambia and Zimbabwe are the former British colonies of Northern Rhodesia and Southern Rhodesia. They were named for Cecil Rhodes, a British colonial administrator. Rhodes brought much of southern Africa under British control.

Zambia. Many Zambians make a living through subsistence farming. Very little of Zambia's land is suitable for commercial farming. However, rubber from rubber trees is an important export. The rubber trees are grown on

Gold miners often dig up tons of earth to produce a few pounds of gold. The waste is piled up in mine dumps. These mine dumps sit within the modern city of Johannesburg, South Africa.

large plantations. Zambia's most important product is copper. Like many other African countries that largely depend on one product, Zambia has an unstable economy. Zambia's economy is fairly strong when world copper prices are high. However, it weakens when copper prices fall.

Zambia is landlocked and, therefore, has no port. Its imports and exports must come and go through other countries, such as South Africa.

Since gaining independence in 1964, Zambia has been led by Kenneth Kaunda (koun′də). Kaunda has long been an outspoken supporter of black rights. This often has brought him into conflict with the South African government.

Zimbabwe. Southern Rhodesia became the independent country of Zimbabwe in 1980. White leaders had declared Southern Rhodesia independent in 1965. However, Great Britain refused to recognize independence because the white leaders would not give full civil rights to black Rhodesians. After years of civil war, a settlement was reached in 1978. Blacks were given full civil rights, and independence was recognized in 1980.

Central Zimbabwe has a large area of commercial farming. Farmers grow such cash crops as tobacco and wheat there. Ranchers raise cattle on the grazing lands west of the commercial farming area. Minerals, especially coal and copper, are other important

361

products for Zimbabwe. Zimbabwe has some industries, with clothing and chemicals among the most important.

Zimbabwe's economy does not depend on one product. Therefore, Zimbabwe's economy could become strong. However, much needs to be done before the economy can be said to be developed. One problem is that Zimbabwe is landlocked. Money that might be spent on further developing the economy has to be spent on transporting goods to ports in other countries.

Other Countries of Southern Africa

Botswana, Lesotho, and Swaziland are landlocked and, to some extent, economically dependent on South Africa. Nearly all the trade of these three countries is with South Africa. Also, many workers from these three countries work in South Africa's mines and factories.

Subsistence farming is the main method of making a living in Lesotho and Swaziland. Even though the Kalahari Desert covers a large part of Botswana, farmers grow some crops for export and ranchers raise some cattle. Some important minerals were found in Botswana in the 1960s. Find out what these minerals were by looking back at the map on page 351.

Namibia is a protectorate of South Africa. A **protectorate** is a weak country under the protection and control of a stronger country. South Africa has been unwilling to give Namibia independence because Namibia has some valuable mineral resources.

The System of Apartheid

After South Africa gained independence, white South Africans ruled the country. During the late 1930s, one group of whites—the Afrikaners, as the Boers had become known—took control of the government. They limited the rights of the other South African races: blacks, Asians, and "coloreds"—the Afrikaners' name for people of mixed race. The Afrikaners also introduced Afrikaans, a mixture of Dutch and other European languages, as one of South Africa's official languages.

In the late 1940s, the Afrikaner government passed a series of laws that took away what few rights the other races still enjoyed. Under these laws only white South Africans could vote or run for political office. These laws also introduced the policy of apartheid.

Apartheid involves the complete separation of the races. The word *apartheid* means "separateness" in Afrikaans. Under apartheid it is against the law for whites and other races to live in the same area or attend the same schools. Whites and other races cannot even attend the same movie theater or ride in the same train car. Anyone who disobeys the apartheid laws can be sent to jail.

During the 1950s and 1960s, many people inside and outside South Africa began to call for an end to apartheid. However, people in South Africa who spoke out against the system often were treated harshly. Some people were held in jail for long periods without being charged. During the 1970s

Under apartheid, whites and blacks are kept apart. These people are leaving a train station in Cape Town.

violent clashes between anti-apartheid groups and South African police took place. For example, nearly six hundred people, mostly black South Africans, were killed in anti-apartheid demonstrations in 1976. In 1986, many more black South Africans died in violent clashes when unrest over apartheid increased again. African leaders, including Zulu Chief Gatsha Buthelezi and Archbishop Desmond Tutu, continue to work for change.

Under pressure from leaders of other countries, South Africa's government eased some apartheid laws in the mid-1980s. For example, black South Africans no longer had to carry an identity card when traveling outside their home towns. Now, all South Africans must carry a Uniform Identity Document, regardless of race. However, some people have felt these reforms were not enough. These people have called for sanctions against South Africa to force that country's government to give full civil rights to all its citizens. **Sanctions** are actions by one or more countries that withhold certain benefits from another country. For example, some people have suggested that countries stop trading with South Africa. These people hoped such actions would bring about change in South Africa peacefully.

Reviewing the Lesson

Recalling Key Words, People, and Places
1. What is the system of complete separation of the races in South Africa called?
2. Tell why it is important to remember:
   a. Boers
   b. Kenneth Kaunda
3. Describe the location of:
   a. Durban
   b. Harare

Remembering Main Ideas
1. What three major groups lived in southern Africa before the arrival of Europeans?
2. Where are most of South Africa's mines and factories located?
3. How do the economies of Zambia and Zimbabwe differ from one another?
4. Why has South Africa been reluctant to give Namibia independence?
5. What happens to people in South Africa who disobey apartheid laws?

Thinking Things Over
Do you think one country has the right to impose sanctions on another country in order to bring about change? Explain your answer.

363

Preparing a Social Studies Report

Writing reports is a good way to add to the knowledge you gain from your textbook and to share that knowledge with others. Suppose your teacher asks you to choose a Sub-Saharan country and report on a certain aspect of that country. Assume that you decide to report on the products and trade of Zaire.

First, you need to find information about your topic. Then, you need to take notes on the information you find. Next, you need to organize your information, or put it together in a way that makes sense. Finally, you need to write your report.

Finding and Recording Information

After you have selected your topic—the products and trade of Zaire—you need to find information on the topic. You may want to use magazines, encyclopedias, almanacs (reference books with information on many subjects), and other books. You also might write to Zaire's mission to the United Nations in New York City or to its embassy in Washington, D.C. Address your letter to "The Delegate of Zaire to the United Nations" (or "to the United States"), begin with "Dear Sir or Madam," briefly ask for specific information, and end your letter politely. Be sure to give your complete name and address.

Once you have found the information you need, make notes on index cards. Write only one main idea on each card. Then add whatever details are needed to support that main idea. Write your notes in short phrases, or small groups of words, rather than in complete sentences. Writing short phrases takes less time.

Also write where you found the information. If the information came from a book, write the name of the author or editor, the book title, the publisher, the copyright date, and the page numbers. If the information came from a magazine article, write the name of the writer, the article title, the magazine, its date, and page numbers. Using these note cards will help you when you organize your information.

Organizing Your Report

When you have found enough information for your report, you need to organize your notes. Outlining your topic is an excellent way of organizing your information. A good way to start an outline is to list questions you want your report to answer. Your outline for products and trade of Zaire might look like this:

I. What are Zaire's most important products?

II. What does Zaire export?

III. What does Zaire import?

Now regroup your cards to answer the questions. If you have information that does not fit the outline, either add to the outline or discard the information.

Writing Your Report

Now you are ready to begin writing your report from your outline and note cards. Rewrite your outline questions in sentence form. For instance, your first question could be rewritten based on the card below: "Some of Zaire's most important products are copper, cobalt, and diamonds, all of which come from mines." Then add details from your cards. Continue writing to answer the remaining questions in your outline, using the information on your note cards.

> Zaire's most important products from mining:
>
> copper - most important
> cobalt - 2nd in importance
> diamonds - 3rd in importance
>
> More than half of all Zaire's wealth from mining
>
> Source: Kaplan, Irving, ed.
> Zaire: A Country Study,
> United States Printing Office, 1979.
> (pp. 226-227)

You also should include short opening and closing paragraphs. An opening paragraph introduces the topic. A closing paragraph sums up main ideas.

After you have finished writing, include a bibliography, which is a list of the sources of information you used. Write the last names of authors or editors in alphabetical order for books and articles. The sample note card at the left shows how to list a book in a bibliography. However, do not include the page numbers in your bibliography.

Skills Practice

1. Use information from the sample note card below to write a paragraph telling about the products of Zaire.

> Zaire's most important products from manufacturing:
>
> cement for new buildings and roads
> refined petroleum
> flour (from imported wheat)
> footwear (from rubber, leather, and
>   imported plastic)

2. Suppose you found additional information in the two books described below. Write how you would list the books in your bibliography.
   a. A book published by Franklin Watts, Inc., in 1981, titled *Zaire, Gabon, and the Congo,* written by Gerald Newman.
   b. Elizabeth Campling's book, *Africa in the Twentieth Century.* The book was published in 1980 by David and Charles, Inc.

Chapter Summary

Lesson 1   The Western and Central Forest Countries—These countries, lying on or near the Equator, have hot, wet climates and wide stretches of rainforest. People of many different ethnic groups live in this part of Africa. Economic activities include subsistence farming, commercial farming, and mining. Many countries in this region depend on one product for their wealth. One such country is Ghana, where low prices for cacao have caused economic problems leading to political unrest.

Lesson 2   The Countries of Eastern Africa—Much of eastern Africa is a high plateau with high mountains, large lakes, and rich farmland. The largest ethnic groups live as farmers or herders. All eight countries in the region export such crops as tea, coffee, sugar, and cotton. Tourism is important in Kenya and Tanzania.

Lesson 3   The Countries of Southern Africa—This region of varying climates and vegetation represents one-tenth of Africa's total land area and contains one-fifth of its wealth. Economic activities include commercial farming, subsistence farming, and mining. Manufacturing is centered in South Africa, where a system of apartheid has been in effect since the late 1940s.

Write your answers on a separate sheet of paper.

Testing Key Words, People, and Places

Part A

Give the definition of each key word.

1. infant mortality
2. life expectancy
3. literacy
4. protectorate
5. apartheid
6. sanction

Part B

Match each description with the correct person or place in the list.

1. the president of Tanzania
2. South Africa's major industrial center
3. a member of the Bantu group
4. an ethnic group in Kenya
5. a port in South Africa
6. the head of Ghana's government
7. the president of Zambia
8. a port in Tanzania

   a. Jerry Rawlings
   b. Kikuyu
   c. Julius Nyerere
   d. Zulu
   e. Kenneth Kaunda
   f. Dar es Salaam
   g. Durban
   h. The Rand

Testing Main Ideas

Answer these questions.

1. Where do most people live in the western and central forest region?
2. Why is Nigeria's economy strong only when the price of oil is high?
3. What has been the United States involvement in Angola's civil war?
4. What event took place in Ghana after Jerry Rawlings left office?
5. Which city is eastern Africa's chief business center?

6. What attracts tourists to Kenya?
7. What are two minerals that are mined in Uganda?
8. What is the most common crop grown on the terraces of Madagascar?
9. What was one result of the effort to increase opportunities for the people of Tanzania?
10. What three major African groups lived in southern Africa before the Europeans arrived?
11. On what two exports is most of South Africa's wealth based?
12. Why has Kenneth Kaunda come into conflict with the South African government?
13. To what extent do the economies of Botswana, Lesotho, and Swaziland depend on South Africa?
14. How could South Africa's government be described?

Testing Skills

1. **Preparing a social studies report.** Put the following steps used in preparing a social studies report in the correct order.
   a. Write a closing paragraph.
   b. Organize your notes by writing an outline.
   c. Find information about your topic.
   d. Write a bibliography.
   e. Use index cards to take notes.
   f. Use your outline and your notes to write the report.

2. **Distinguishing fact from opinion.** Write the letter of the sentence that states an opinion.
   a. Nigeria has the largest population of any African country.
   b. Kenya has the best government of all African countries.
   c. Drought is one of the great problems in the desert fringe countries.
   d. Namibia is a protectorate of South Africa.

Activities

1. Use the *Readers' Guide to Periodical Literature* to find and read articles on contemporary African leaders, such as Jerry Rawlings of Ghana, Julius Nyerere of Tanzania, or Nelson Mandela, an imprisoned black leader in South Africa. Then write a summary of the articles in your own words.
2. Write a letter to a friend describing an imaginary visit to one of the countries discussed in the chapter. Check an encyclopedia for information.
3. Use the maps on pages 292 and 296 to find which countries have the following physical features.

   Kalahari Desert   Lake Victoria
   Mt. Kilimanjaro   Mt. Kenya
   Victoria Falls   Congo Basin

   Do research to find a picture of one of the above features. Use the picture to make a drawing or painting of the feature.

Biography   Archbishop Desmond Tutu

When Archbishop Desmond Tutu of South Africa won the Nobel Prize for Peace in 1984, he recalled his humble beginnings. He also remembered that life has not improved for many others in his country. Archbishop Tutu donated his prize money to improve education for young blacks in South Africa. "This award is for you who sit at railway stations selling potatoes," he said when he received the prize.

When Archbishop Tutu was a boy in a gold-mining town near Johannesburg, he too sold potatoes at a railway station. Tutu was born October 7, 1931. His father was a teacher. Tutu himself wanted to be a doctor when he grew up. He could not afford the costs of medical school, however, so he also became a teacher.

As a teacher in South Africa, Tutu became discouraged by what he saw. Tutu taught in the school system for black children. In South Africa blacks and whites are separated under a system called apartheid. Tutu thought the South African government did not allow blacks equal rights.

Like Mohandas Gandhi, whom you will read about in the next unit, Tutu believes strongly that his country needs to change. Also like Gandhi, Tutu opposes violence and hatred. Both men were willing to be jailed for their beliefs.

Archbishop Tutu has become a civil rights leader by speaking out against apartheid. In speeches to blacks, he urges peaceful change. In speeches outside his country, he urges governments to pressure South Africa to share power with blacks.

Tutu became an Anglican priest in 1961 and became the first black man to be appointed head of the large South African Council of Churches in 1978. He also became the first black bishop in Johannesburg in 1984. In 1986 he was elected Archbishop of Cape Town. Tutu has chosen to live with blacks in the poor town of Soweto (sō wet'ō).

Many people do not approve of Archbishop Tutu's ideas about ending apartheid. However, Tutu continues to speak out for what he believes. He hopes for change, but he wants it to be a "peaceful evolution."

Questions to Think About

1. What does Archbishop Tutu, as a civil rights leader, do to bring about change?
2. Why, do you think, does Archbishop Tutu stay in Soweto?

The Suez Canal

In the 1860s, Europeans who wanted to trade with Asia had to sail more than 10,000 miles around Africa. In the 1870s, however, the trip was about 6,000 miles shorter. What had happened? The Suez Canal had been opened in 1869.

As the map shows, the Suez Canal cuts across the Isthmus of Suez. An isthmus (is'məs) is a narrow strip of land with water on both sides, connecting two large areas of land. Which two seas are connected by the Suez Canal? Which two continents are separated by the Suez Canal?

In 1859, a French company, partly owned by Egypt, began building the canal. The Suez Canal Company worked for ten years on the canal.

When the canal was opened, it changed the world. Here, at last, was the long-sought trade route to Asia. By using the canal, European trading ships could make two or three trips in the time that once was needed to make just one trip to Asia. That meant that shipping costs—and prices—dropped.

The Suez Canal helped European nations add to their empires too. For example, the Suez Canal allowed Great Britain easy access to eastern Africa. By the end of the nineteenth century, Britain had added Egypt and much of Africa to its empire.

Today the Suez Canal is one of the most important canals in the world. As you can see from the map on page 72, ships from North America, Europe, and Asia carry great amounts of freight through the Suez Canal. Its location makes the canal a significant link between the United States and the Middle East.

Using Your Geography Skills

1. Look at the map on page 327. How did the Suez Canal help European nations control their empires in eastern Africa?
2. Ships are the least costly way of moving goods such as grain and oil. What might happen to the prices of such goods if ships were not allowed to use the Suez Canal?

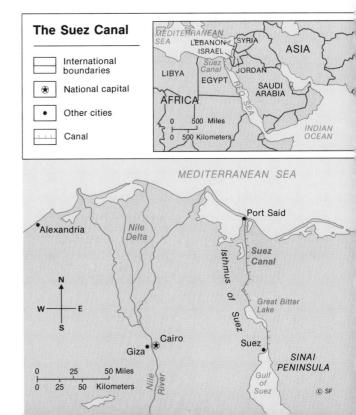

Unit 4   Review

Write your answers on a separate sheet of paper.

Key Words
Use each key word in a sentence.

1. savanna
2. shifting cultivation
3. official language
4. segregation
5. boycott
6. coup
7. intensive farming
8. desertification
9. literacy
10. protectorate
11. apartheid
12. sanction

Main Ideas
Choose the answer that best completes each sentence.

1. The Great Rift Valley stretches north and south through the
   a. northern part of Africa.
   b. eastern part of Africa.
   c. western part of Africa.
2. In the center of Africa near the Equator, the climate is
   a. cool and dry.
   b. hot and dry.
   c. hot and wet.
3. Libya gained wealth from
   a. gold.
   b. oil.
   c. bauxite.
4. Subsistence farmers in Africa
   a. grow enough food to feed their families.
   b. grow enough food to export.
   c. work on plantations.
5. Most of the people in Africa
   a. speak the same language.
   b. live in urban areas.
   c. live in rural areas.
6. Trade across the Sahara began
   a. after the Europeans gained control of the slave trade.
   b. after iron was discovered in western Africa.
   c. after David Livingstone explored Africa's interior.
7. Mansa Musa was a ruler of
   a. Zimbabwe.
   b. Benin.
   c. Mali.
8. Most African colonies were set up
   a. after 1880.
   b. during the 1700s.
   c. during the 1500s.
9. Kwame Nkrumah helped gain independence for
   a. Uganda.
   b. Egypt.
   c. Ghana.
10. The chief physical feature of northern Africa is
    a. the Great Rift Valley.
    b. the Sahara.
    c. rainforest.
11. The Aswan High Dam helped improve intensive farming in
    a. the Maghreb.
    b. Egypt.
    c. South Africa.

12. Before Europeans came to Africa, Zulus lived in
    a. the desert fringe.
    b. eastern Africa.
    c. southern Africa.
13. The Sahara is spreading southward into the countries of
    a. the Sahel.
    b. the Horn of Africa.
    c. Kenya and Tanzania.
14. Tanzania's president is
    a. Kenneth Kaunda.
    b. Jerry Rawlings.
    c. Julius Nyerere.

Skills

1. **Making inferences from a map.** Answer the questions by using the map at right.
    a. What parts of western Africa are most populated, and why?
    b. Make an inference that accounts for the long, narrow strip of heavily populated land in northeastern Africa.
2. **Identifying points of view.** Read each point of view that follows. Then decide whether the point of view might have been held by an African or by a European during Africa's movement to end colonial rule and achieve independence.
    a. Europeans are needed in Africa to run the farms and mines.
    b. Africans should govern themselves, just as people of India, France, and the United States do.

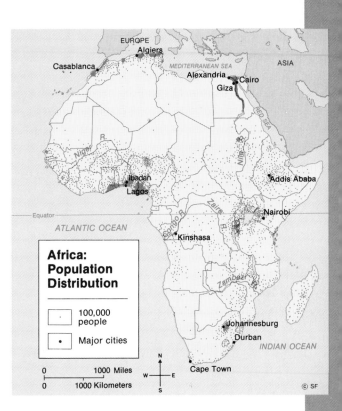

Africa: Population Distribution

· 100,000 people

• Major cities

0   1000 Miles
0   1000 Kilometers

c. Laws that Africans have to obey should be made by Africans.
d. If colonial rule ends, the literacy rate will drop.

Essay
Many African nations have weak economies because they depend on the sale of a single export. Write an essay that tells how such countries can be affected when prices of their exports drop. Use examples from the unit to support your statements.

371

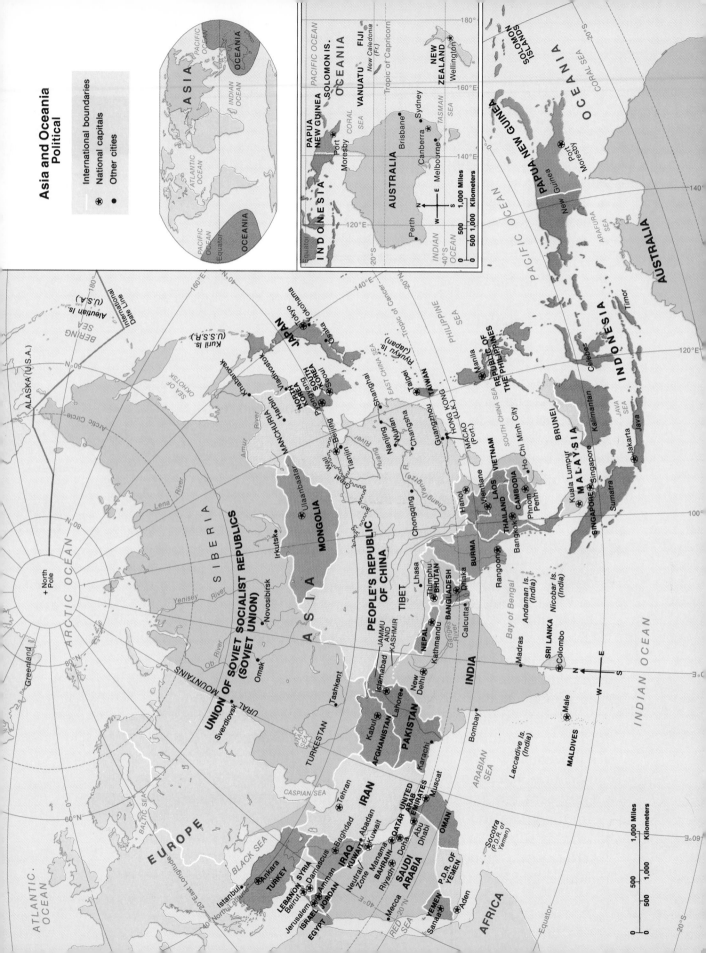

Asia and Oceania
Political

International boundaries
⊛ National capitals
• Other cities

ASIA

OCEANIA

INDIAN OCEAN

ATLANTIC OCEAN

PACIFIC OCEAN

OCEANIA

Equator

PACIFIC OCEAN

PAPUA NEW GUINEA

SOLOMON IS.

OCEANIA

VANUATU

FIJI
New Caledonia (Fr.)

NEW ZEALAND
Wellington

Port Moresby ⊛

CORAL SEA

Tropic of Capricorn

Brisbane •

AUSTRALIA

Canberra •
Sydney •
Melbourne •

TASMAN SEA

Perth •

INDONESIA

INDIAN OCEAN

N
W   E
S

500   1,000   Kilometers
0   500   1,000 Miles

180°
160°E
140°E
120°E
20°S
40°S

PACIFIC OCEAN

OCEANIA

SOLOMON ISLANDS

PAPUA NEW GUINEA

Port Moresby ⊛

New Guinea

ARAFURA SEA

AUSTRALIA

Timor

140°

120°E

100°

CORAL SEA

20°S

ALASKA (U.S.A.)

BERING SEA

Aleutian Is. (U.S.A.)

International Date Line

180°
160°E
140°E

40°N

JAPAN

Tokyo ⊛
Yokohama •
Osaka •

Kuril Is. (U.S.S.R.)

Vladivostok •

Khabarovsk •

SEA OF OKHOTSK

60°N

NORTH KOREA
Pyongyang ⊛

SOUTH KOREA
Seoul ⊛

MANCHURIA

Harbin •

Shanghai •

Ryukyu Is. (Japan)

EAST CHINA SEA

TAIWAN
Taipei ⊛

20°N

PHILIPPINE SEA

REPUBLIC OF THE PHILIPPINES
Manila ⊛

120°E

HONG KONG (U.K.)
Guangzhou •
MACAO (Port.)

BRUNEI

Celebes

INDONESIA

Kalimantan

Java
Jakarta ⊛

JAVA SEA

Sumatra

100°

Arctic Circle

ARCTIC OCEAN

North Pole

Greenland

80°N

SIBERIA

Lena River

Yenisey River

Ob River

Irkutsk •

Novosibirsk •

UNION OF SOVIET SOCIALIST REPUBLICS
(SOVIET UNION)

MONGOLIA
Ulaanbaatar ⊛

Omsk •

Sverdlovsk •

URAL MOUNTAINS

Tashkent •

TURKESTAN

ASIA

ARAL SEA

Amur River

Great Wall

Beijing ⊛
Tianjin •

PEOPLE'S REPUBLIC OF CHINA

Huang River

Nanjing •
Wuhan •
Changsha •

Chang (Yangtze) R.

Chongqing •

TIBET

Lhasa •

Ho Chi Minh City •

VIETNAM
Hanoi ⊛
LAOS
Vientiane ⊛
THAILAND
Bangkok •
CAMBODIA
Phnom Penh ⊛

BURMA
Rangoon ⊛

SOUTH CHINA SEA

MALAYSIA
Kuala Lumpur ⊛
SINGAPORE
Singapore ⊛

60°N

EUROPE

BALTIC SEA

BLACK SEA

CASPIAN SEA

TURKEY
Ankara ⊛
Istanbul •

LEBANON
Beirut ⊛
SYRIA
Damascus ⊛
Amman ⊛
JORDAN
ISRAEL
Jerusalem ⊛

EGYPT

RED SEA

IRAQ
Baghdad ⊛

IRAN
Tehran ⊛
Abadan •

KUWAIT
Kuwait ⊛
Neutral Zone
BAHRAIN
Manama ⊛
QATAR
Doha ⊛
Riyadh ⊛
SAUDI ARABIA

Mecca •

P.D.R. OF YEMEN
Aden ⊛

YEMEN
Sanaa ⊛

UNITED ARAB EMIRATES
Abu Dhabi ⊛
OMAN
Muscat ⊛

Socotra (P.D.R. of Yemen)

AFRICA

ARABIAN SEA

AFGHANISTAN
Kabul ⊛

PAKISTAN
Islamabad ⊛
Lahore •
Karachi •

JAMMU AND KASHMIR

New Delhi ⊛

INDIA

Bombay •

Madras •

NEPAL
Kathmandu ⊛

BHUTAN
Thimphu ⊛

BANGLADESH
Dhaka ⊛
Calcutta •

Ganges River

Bay of Bengal

Andaman Is. (India)

Nicobar Is. (India)

SRI LANKA
Colombo ⊛

Laccadive Is. (India)

MALDIVES
Male ⊛

INDIAN OCEAN

N
W   E
S

0°

20°N

40°N

40°E

RED SEA

Equator

20°S

1,000 Miles

0   500   1,000
Kilometers

60°E

80°E

100°E

20° East Longitude

160° East Longitude

Asia and Oceania

When we talk about Asia, words like *biggest, oldest, tallest,* and *first* are sure to be used. Asia is the biggest continent in area. It has the most people. Its mountains are the highest. In this unit you will learn about the geography and history of Asia and Oceania. You also will learn about the countries and people of the region today.

Before You Go On

Preview the unit. Look back to Unit 2 to find the locations of some early Asian civilizations. In which present-day countries did these civilizations develop?

Study the map. Use the map to name at least eight countries that are islands or groups of islands.

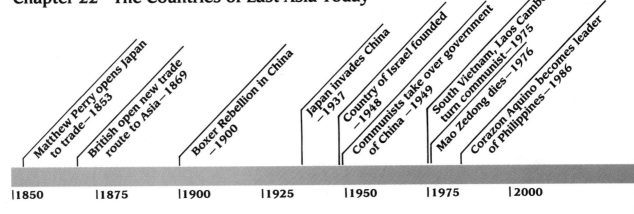

Matthew Perry opens Japan to trade—1853

British open new trade route to Asia—1869

Boxer Rebellion in China —1900

Japan invades China —1937

Country of Israel founded of China—1948

Communists take over government of China —1949

South Vietnam, Laos Cambodia turn communist—1975

Mao Zedong dies—1976

Corazon Aquino becomes leader of Philippines—1986

| 1850 | 1875 | 1900 | 1925 | 1950 | 1975 | 2000 |

373

The Land and People of Asia and Oceania

Asia and Oceania include over one-third of our planet's land surface and more than three-fifths of all the people in the world. The picture above shows Tahiti, one of the islands of Oceania.

As you read this chapter, you will learn about the natural environment of Asia and Oceania. You also will learn how people use their land to make a living. Finally, you will learn about the various people in the region. The lessons in the chapter are listed below.

Lesson 1   The Natural Environment
of Asia and Oceania

Lesson 2   Resources and Land Use
in Asia and Oceania

Lesson 3   The People of Asia and Oceania

Lesson 1 The Natural Environment of Asia and Oceania

📖 **LOOKING AHEAD** As you read, look for—

Key words, people, and **places:**

earthquake   Middle East
volcano   Anatolian Plateau
high island   Arabian Peninsula
low island   North China Plain
                        Melanesia
                        Micronesia
                        Polynesia

Answers to these questions about **main ideas:**

1. What are the five regions of Asia and Oceania?
2. What are the main bodies of water of Asia?
3. What are the main landforms of Asia?
4. What are the climate and vegetation of Asia like?
5. What are the landforms, climate, and natural vegetation regions of Oceania like?

The region of Asia and Oceania covers a vast amount of land that stretches across the Equator into both the Northern and Southern hemispheres. Natural barriers such as long distances, oceans, mountain ranges, and harsh climates have always kept people of the region apart. Because the region has so many natural divisions, we can understand Asia and Oceania better by dividing it into smaller regions. Each region has its own natural environment. Each region includes people with their own unique history and culture.

The Five Regions of Asia and Oceania

The map on page 376 shows the four regions of Asia. You can identify the countries in each region by comparing this map with the map on page 372. Notice that the Soviet Union forms another region that covers the entire northern part of Asia. You learned about this land in Unit 3.

The southwestern part of Asia contains one region, which also is known as the Middle East. This region borders both Africa and Europe. In fact, part of one Southwest Asian country lies in Europe. What is this country?

Zanskar, Tibet, is the world's highest inhabited valley.

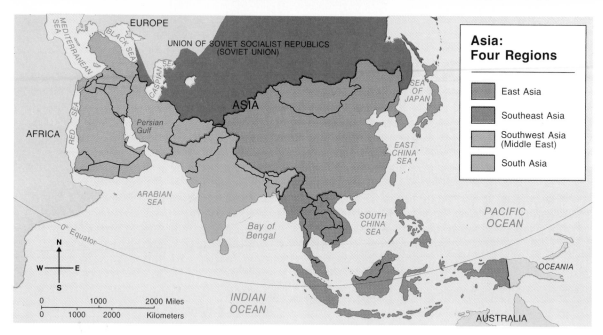

**Asia:
Four Regions**

- East Asia
- Southeast Asia
- Southwest Asia (Middle East)
- South Asia

Map Study

The map shows the four regions of Asia. What are the names of the four regions? What part of the map did you look at to find out? What are the names of the oceans shown on the map? What seas are shown? About how many miles are shown from west to east on the map? What did you use to find out?

A second region, South Asia, lies southeast of the Middle East. One country—India—occupies most of this region. For this reason, South Asia is sometimes called the Indian subcontinent. Use your finger to point to a third region—Southeast Asia. This region includes the southeastern part of the Asian landmass as well as thousands of islands.

The fourth region of Asia is East Asia. This region includes the east coast of Asia and reaches deep into the interior of the continent.

Oceania is a fifth region and is separate from Asia. Experts guess that from 20,000 to 30,000 islands make up Oceania. Nobody knows for certain how many islands make up this region because some islands are so small and

remote. Later you will read about the countries in each of these five regions.

Water Bodies of Asia

Most of Asia's great rivers begin in the Himalayan Mountains or Tibetan Plateau in central Asia. Use the map on page 378 to locate the Indus and Ganges rivers in India. Notice that these rivers flow south toward the Indian Ocean. Trace the path of these rivers with your finger.

The Huang and Yangtze rivers in China and the Mekong River in Southeast Asia also begin in the mountains and plateaus of Asia. (In China the Yangtze is known as the Chang.) Follow each river to see where it empties.

Not all of Asia's rivers start in central Asia. For example, in the Middle East,

376

the Euphrates and Tigris rivers begin in the mountains above the Anatolian Plateau. Into which body of water do the Tigris and Euphrates rivers empty?

The coastal areas of Asia contain many seas, gulfs, straits, and bays. The jagged shape of Asia and the many islands create these bodies of water. Locate the Red Sea between Africa and the Arabian Peninsula. Beginning at the Red Sea and heading east, follow the coastline of Asia with your finger. Name each body of water as your finger points to it. Continue around the continent until you reach the Sea of Japan, which sits between Japan and the eastern coast of Asia.

Asia's Landforms

Asia has more high and rugged mountain ranges than any other continent. The map on page 378 shows the Himalayas, the highest mountains in the world. Asia contains other mountain ranges as well. Find the Caucasus Mountains. Trace with your finger a line eastward from these mountains across Asia. As you move your finger, note the mountain ranges you pass. The highest mountains are in central Asia. Most of the Tibetan Plateau is so high, 16,000 to 20,000 feet above sea level, that it is called "the roof of the world."

High, rugged mountain ranges are caused by forces within the earth's crust. These forces also can cause violent events such as earthquakes and volcanic explosions. An **earthquake** is a violent shaking of the earth caused by sudden movements in the earth's crust. Earthquakes often occur in the mountainous areas of Asia. When they occur in heavily settled areas, many people may die. In 1976, for example, 800,000 people died in an earthquake in northeastern China.

Hot gases, liquids, and solid material sometimes escape, often violently, from inside the earth through surface openings called **volcanoes.** Because most of the earth's active volcanoes are found around the edge of the Pacific Ocean, this area sometimes is called the "ring of fire." Many islands of Oceania are really volcanic mountains.

Plateaus border on mountains in many parts of Asia. These high, level areas are almost always dry. As you have read, air loses its moisture as it rises over mountains. Most Asian plateaus, such as the Plateau of Iran and the Mongolian Plateau, are drier than the mountains around them.

Coastal plains edge the Asian continent. The most important one is the North China Plain, where more than one billion Chinese people live. Narrower coastal plains are located in Japan and India and along the Mediterranean Sea. The lower courses of several of Asia's great rivers flow through plains areas that were once the sites of early civilizations.

Asia's Climate and Vegetation Regions

Asia is so large that it has many kinds of climate. You learned earlier that much of Soviet Asia has cold climates. Parts of central Asia, such as

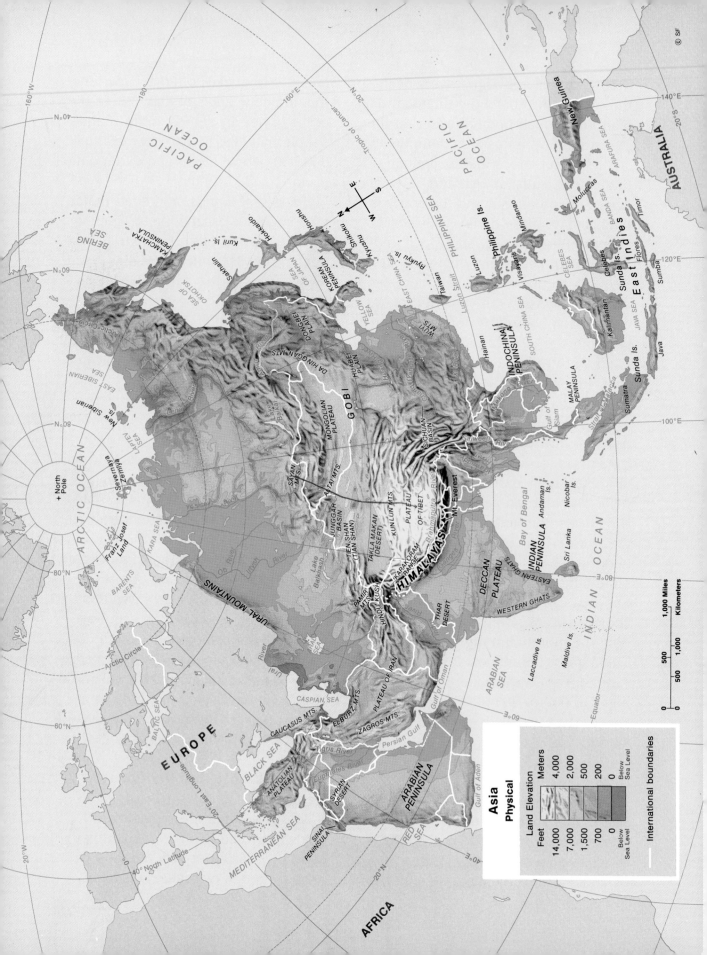

Asia
Physical

Land Elevation

Feet	Meters
14,000	4,000
7,000	2,000
1,500	500
700	200
0	0
Below Sea Level	Below Sea Level

— International boundaries

© SF

1,000 Miles
1,000 Kilometers
500
500

ARCTIC OCEAN
North Pole
PACIFIC OCEAN
BERING SEA
EAST SIBERIAN SEA
LAPTEV SEA
KARA SEA
BARENTS SEA
Franz Josef Land
Severnaya Zemlya
New Siberian Is.
Franz Josef Land
KAMCHATKA PENINSULA
SEA OF OKHOTSK
Sakhalin
Kuril Is.
Hokkaido
Honshu
Shikoku
Kyushu
KOREAN PENINSULA
SEA OF JAPAN
YELLOW SEA
EAST CHINA SEA
Taiwan
Ryukyu Is.
Luzon Strait
PHILIPPINE SEA
Philippine Is.
Luzon
Mindanao
Visayas
SOUTH CHINA SEA
Hainan
Gulf of Siam
INDOCHINA PENINSULA
MALAY PENINSULA
Strait of Malacca
Sumatra
Sunda Is.
Java
JAVA SEA
Kalimantan
CELEBES SEA
Celebes
Sumba
Flores
Timor
BANDA SEA
Moluccas
ARAFURA SEA
New Guinea
AUSTRALIA
East Indies

Tropic of Cancer
URAL MOUNTAINS
ARAL SEA
CASPIAN SEA
BLACK SEA
CAUCASUS MTS.
ELBURZ MTS.
ZAGROS MTS.
ANATOLIAN PLATEAU
MEDITERRANEAN SEA
SINA PENINSULA
RED SEA
SYRIAN DESERT
ARABIAN PENINSULA
Euphrates River
Tigris River
Persian Gulf
Gulf of Oman
Gulf of Aden
ARABIAN SEA
PLATEAU OF IRAN
HINDU KUSH
PAMIR MTS.
THAR DESERT
KARAKORAM RANGE
HIMALAYAS
Mt. Everest
PLATEAU OF TIBET
KUNLUN MTS.
TAKLA MAKAN (DESERT)
TIEN SHAN (TIAN SHAN)
JUNGGAR BASIN
ALTAI MTS.
SAYAN MTS.
Lake Baikal
MONGOLIAN PLATEAU
GOBI
DA HINGGAN MTS.
DONGBEI PLAIN
HUABEI PLAIN
SICHUAN BASIN
WUYI MTS.
Mekong River
Salween River
Brahmaputra River
Ganges River
Indus River
DECCAN PLATEAU
EASTERN GHATS
WESTERN GHATS
INDIAN PENINSULA
Sri Lanka
Bay of Bengal
Andaman Is.
Nicobar Is.
Laccadive Is.
Maldive Is.
INDIAN OCEAN
Equator
Ob River
Irtysh River
Ural River
Lena River

EUROPE
AFRICA

20° East Longitude
40° North Latitude
40°N
80°N
60°N
20°W
0°
160°W
180°
160°E
140°E
120°E
100°E
80°E
60°E
40°E
20°S

Someone to Know

In May, 1953, a Nepalese man named Tenzing Norgay and a New Zealander named Edmund Hillary became the first people to reach the top of Mt. Everest, the highest mountain in the world. Norgay, a member of the Sherpa ethnic group, guided members of a British expedition that included Hillary. The picture shows, from left to right, Norgay and Hillary.

The Sherpas live in the shadow of Mt. Everest. They are used to the thin air of high altitudes and are experienced climbers. Each time a group of mountain climbers has attempted to scale Mt. Everest, a member of the Sherpas has guided them.

the Gobi, have cool, dry climates. However, hot climate types dominate the rest of Asia.

Look back at the climate map on pages 36–37. The map shows that almost all of the Middle East has a hot, dry climate. The map also shows that a hot climate with one dry season occurs along the coasts of South and Southeast Asia. The wet season in these areas may last five months. As much as 50 inches of rain can fall during the wet season. Farther south, in the islands of Southeast Asia, another type of hot climate occurs. Describe this type of climate.

Much of East Asia has a warm climate that is wet all year. However, you will notice on the map that the northern parts of East Asia have cool or cold climates.

Asia's natural vegetation varies with its climate. You can see Asia's natural vegetation regions on the map on pages 38–39. What region of Asia contains rainforests? What is the climate in these areas?

Oceania's Natural Environment

The islands of Oceania sit in the Pacific Ocean. The largest island, Australia, is also a continent. The other islands of Oceania are divided into three groups.

To the north of Australia lies Melanesia (mel′ə nē′zhə). This name comes from Greek words meaning "black island." The first Europeans who visited these islands found very dark-skinned people living there. North of Melanesia are the islands of Micronesia, meaning "little islands." To the east of Australia,

Map Study

Page 378 shows a physical map of Asia. Notice that the names of countries are not shown on a physical map, although international boundaries are shown. How are international boundaries shown? What is the elevation of the Plateau of Tibet? What is the elevation around the Aral Sea?

A group of Australians enjoy the climate and waters off Green Island, Australia.

across the Tasman Sea, is New Zealand. It is part of the vast group of islands known as Polynesia, which means "many islands." Altogether, Melanesia, Micronesia, and Polynesia include close to 30,000 islands.

The kinds of soil and vegetation found on the Pacific Islands are determined by the way in which each island was formed. **High islands,** such as Fiji and Hawaii, were formed by volcanoes. They have fertile soil and many plants. Using the Atlas map on page 545 to find New Zealand. How high are the island's mountains?

The **low islands** usually have poor soil and little vegetation. These islands were formed over thousands of years by tiny sea animals called coral. These animals live in colonies on the tops of underwater mountains. As the coral die, their hard skeletons build up so high that they form islands above the sea.

Much of the island continent of Australia has a hot, dry climate and desert vegetation. Australia is mostly flat, but a string of low mountains runs near the east coast. Climates are wetter and cooler east of the mountains. Vegetation in these areas consists largely of broadleaf forests.

Reviewing the Lesson

Recalling Key Words, People, and Places
1. Identify the key words defined below:
    a. an opening in the earth's surface from which hot gases, liquids, and solid material sometimes escape
    b. land formed over thousands of years by tiny sea animals
2. Tell where each place is located:
    a. Middle East
    b. North China Plain

Remembering Main Ideas
1. Which region of Asia sometimes is called the Indian subcontinent?
2. Where do most of Asia's great rivers begin?
3. Where are the plains areas of Asia located?
4. How does the climate of the Middle East differ from the climate of Southeast Asia?
5. How did the islands of Melanesia, Micronesia, and Polynesia get their names?

Thinking Things Over

China has more people than any other country in the world. What parts of China's natural environment help to support so many people?

Lesson 2   Resources and Land Use in Asia and Oceania

LOOKING AHEAD As you read, look for—

Key words, people, and **places:**

paddy
dike
pesticide

Answers to these questions about **main ideas:**

1. How do Asians farm in areas where many people live close together?
2. What are Asia's major crops and where are they grown?
3. What methods have Asian farmers used to grow more food?
4. What are the areas of mining, fishing, and manufacturing in Asia?
5. How do people use their land in Oceania?

The most valuable natural resource in Asia is farmland. In this lesson you will learn how the land is used for agriculture and about Asia's other natural resources. You also will learn about the products of Asia's mines, forests, and seas.

Farming and Nomadic Herding

In most Asian countries, the majority of people are farmers. They live in small villages near their fields. In fertile, well-watered areas, farm villages are close together. Each family has a small plot of land. In drier areas the villages are farther apart, and farms are bigger. Most subsistence farmers in Asia have only hand tools—a hoe to chop weeds and a scythe (a long, thin blade with a handle) to cut the crop. Some farmers use water buffaloes to plow their fields.

Compare the population distribution map on page 60 with the land use map on pages 64–65. Notice that most people in Asia live where people use the

Nomadic herders gather before their tents in northwestern China.

land for subsistence farming. Farm villages are very close together in these places. On the land use map, find the areas where nomadic herding supports the people. Are these places crowded or do few people live there?

Nomadic herders are always on the move, so they live in tents that are easy to erect and take down. The herders move in search of water and grass for their sheep or goats. In mountainous areas this means moving to the higher slopes in summer and the lower slopes in winter. In desert areas, nomads move from oasis to oasis.

Asian Crops

Asia has such a wide variety of climates that almost every food crop is raised somewhere on the continent. Wheat and rice, however, are the leading food crops.

Wheat does not require as much water as rice, and it thrives in cooler climates. Farmers plant wheat seeds in plowed fields and wait for rain to make the plants grow.

Rice farming is different. Rice is grown in fields called **paddies.** The paddies are surrounded by walls of earth called **dikes.** When the monsoon rains come, the farmers plant their rice seedlings in the soft, wet earth. The dikes keep the paddies filled with water during the growing season. When the plants have finished growing, the farmers drain the fields and let the rice ripen for picking.

In addition to food crops, Asian farmers produce a variety of commercial crops. Cotton grows in the drier

Farmers in China plant rice in fields called rice paddies.

areas, particularly in China and India. Jute, a fiber used for making rope and heavy cloth, is grown on wet lands in India and Bangladesh. Tea bushes grow in hilly areas of India, Sri Lanka, and China. Rubber and oil palm trees are important plantation crops in climates that are hot and wet all year.

Increasing Food Production

The population of Asia is so large that people have to keep thinking of ways to increase the food supply. One way, in dry climate areas, is by irrigating. Wherever water is available nearby, people have devised ways of getting it to the fields. Another way farmers increase food production is by building flat surfaces called terraces on hillsides.

Farmers also can increase the size of their crops by using fertilizer. They save animal and vegetable waste products and plow them back into the soil. Some fertilizers are bought, but these commercial fertilizers are expensive.

In the 1960s, scientists began to develop new kinds of rice and wheat plants. The new wheat was used in India. In ten years, farmers were able to produce twice as much wheat. In Indonesia new rice production increased by more than one third. People called the use of these new food plants a "Green Revolution."

However, problems arose. The new plants did best when they were given large amounts of fertilizer. Farmers had to buy expensive commercial fertilizers.

The new plants also needed irrigation and chemical poisons called pesticides. A **pesticide** wards off attacks by insects. The old plants had not needed artificial fertilizer or extra water, and they also had resisted most plant diseases.

Wealthier farmers benefited from the Green Revolution. Many poorer farmers, however, were not helped. Some poor farmers even lost their land because they could not afford to buy fertilizer, pesticides, or irrigation pumps.

The Green Revolution is not over, however. Scientists are continuing to develop new types of plants. Farmers hope these new plants will increase production without the need for chemical fertilizers and pesticides.

Farmers in Asia build terraces and dikes to trap rain for rice paddies and to prevent soil erosion. These terraces are in the Philippines.

Mining, Fishing, and Manufacturing in Asia

Asia contains many areas with large deposits of minerals. Petroleum is perhaps the most important mineral resource. It is bringing great wealth to some countries in the Middle East. Petroleum also is found in Indonesia and China.

Among other important mineral resources in Asia are tin in Indonesia and Malaysia and coal and iron in India and China. The rainforests of Southeast Asia supply some wood, but, in general, Asia does not have large forest resources. Asia has been settled for so long that most of its valuable forests were cut down long ago.

Fish are a valuable renewable resource. All Asian countries fish off their own shores. Japan has a fishing fleet that ranges widely, even into the Atlantic Ocean.

Manufacturing is a prominent activity in some parts of Asia. Locate these areas by looking at the land use map on pages 64–65. Which region of Asia has the greatest amount of manufacturing and commerce?

All Asian cities are manufacturing centers. Some cities specialize in textiles and clothing, chemical products, or machinery and steel making. In many Asian cities, manufacturing takes place in small factories employing less than fifty people. Many Asian families even do manufacturing in their homes.

Australia and the Pacific Islands

Most of the interior of Australia is very dry. However, farmers can grow wheat and other crops near the eastern coast. In the drier areas, farmers raise sheep and cattle. Australia exports most of its wheat and meat to Japan.

Like the United States, Australia is an industrialized country. It has ample coal, iron ore, and other minerals to support its industries.

Lying over a thousand miles southeast of Australia is New Zealand. This country consists of two main islands and many smaller ones. New Zealand is one of the world's leading farming countries. New Zealand's chief exports are frozen meats, wool, lumber, and dairy products.

Most people on the islands of Polynesia, Micronesia, and Melanesia live by fishing and farming. Another major resource of many of these islands is their natural beauty. Tourists are attracted to this beauty from all over the world.

Reviewing the Lesson

Recalling Key Words, People, and Places
Identify the key words defined below:
1. a wall of earth that holds water in the rice fields
2. a chemical poison that wards off insects

Remembering Main Ideas
1. What tools do most Asians use to farm their land?
2. Describe how rice is grown in Asia.
3. What benefits and problems have resulted from the introduction of new kinds of seeds in Asia?
4. Which region of Asia is a major producer of petroleum?
5. What are the three main sources of income for the Pacific Islanders?

Thinking Things Over
In general, do you think that the Green Revolution has been good or bad for Asia? Explain your answer.

Lesson 3   The People of Asia and Oceania

LOOKING AHEAD As you read, look for—

Key words, people, and **places:**

aborigine   Maori
underpopulated

Answers to these questions about **main ideas:**

1. How is the population of Asia distributed?
2. How has the growth of cities changed the way of life for many Asians?
3. What are some of the major languages and religions of Asia?
4. What is the population of Oceania like?

> Whether he made the world or did not make it,
> He knows whence this creation came, he only
> Who in the highest heaven guards and watches;
> He knows indeed, but then, perhaps he knows not!

This poem comes from the Rig-Veda, the world's oldest book of religious writing. The Aryans, who lived in India's Indus valley, wrote the Rig-Veda in 800 B.C.

As you have read, all the world's major religions began in Asia. Religion is a major part of the culture of Asia's people. In this lesson, you will learn more about how the people of Asia live and more about their cultures.

The Population of Asia

Asia has more people than any other part of the world. The regions of East Asia, South Asia, and Southeast Asia contain more than half the world's people. China alone has more than a billion people, and India has over 800 million. The countries of Indonesia, Japan, Bangladesh, and Pakistan also have very large populations.

The overall population of Asia is unevenly distributed across the continent. The river valleys and coastal plains of Asia are crowded. However, some parts of Asia, such as mountain areas and dry areas, have very few people. Look back at the population distribution map on page 60. With your finger, trace the crowded areas around Asia's southern and eastern coasts. Then, point to the areas where few people live. Some of these areas are in the Middle East, the Himalayas, and the Tibetan Plateau.

The number of people in Asia has grown rapidly since 1900. In some parts of Asia, the growth rate has slowed recently. However, the population of Asia continues to increase. The chart on page 386 tells how demographers think the population of Asia will grow. In what year will the population of South Asia become greater than the population of East Asia?

The Growth of Asian Cities

Fifteen Asian cities have populations of more than 5 million people. These cities are listed on the chart on page 387. How many of these large cities are in China? Asia contains hundreds of other large and medium-sized cities in addition to the cities on the chart. Most of them are growing rapidly.

More than three out of every four people in Asia live in rural areas, even with all the large Asian cities. However, in Japan, South Korea, and most Middle Eastern countries, the majority of the people live in the cities.

Asian cities in developing countries, such as India or Indonesia, are very crowded. People constantly fill the streets. Cars, taxis, trucks, buses, bicycles, hand carts, and animal-drawn carts jam the narrow streets along with the people. Although these cities may have beautiful downtown areas and industrial centers, most of the space is filled with housing. Many people live where they work. In older parts of cities, small shops or workshops often face the street. Living areas connect to the workshops.

Not all Asian cities are the same, however. Cities in highly industrialized Japan have high-speed highways, large factories, and apartment houses that look like those in the United States.

Languages and Religions in Asia

Hundreds of different languages are spoken in Asia. Often people cannot understand someone who lives just a few miles away. Therefore, countries with many languages have adopted one or two national languages. Having a national language can help unify a country, help people make a living, and prevent conflicts among ethnic groups.

National languages usually are taught in schools and used on billboards and street signs. Gradually people learn the national language. In India, for example, most people would speak the language of their village. In addition, they would probably speak Hindi, India's national language. Most Indians also speak English, which is the country's language of business and education. All high schools and universities in India teach English.

The chart below shows population projections for Asia. Projections are estimates. Is population expected to increase or decrease?

Population Projections for Asia for the Years 1990-2025			
Region	**Year**		
	1990	**2000**	**2025**
South Asia	1,170 million	1,386 million	1,816 million
Southeast Asia	440 million	520 million	685 million
East Asia	1,317 million	1,470 million	1,696 million
Southwest Asia (Middle East)	130 million	168 million	270 million
Total Asia (except U.S.S.R.)	**3,057 million**	**3,544 million**	**4,467 million**

Streets in Hong Kong (above) are busy. Look at the chart below to see where Hong Kong ranks among Asian cities in size.

Asia's Largest Cities	
City	**Population**
Shanghai, China	12.0 million
Seoul, South Korea	9.2 million
Calcutta, India	9.1 million
Beijing, China	8.5 million
Tokyo, Japan	8.3 million
Bombay, India	8.2 million
Tianjin, China	7.2 million
Jakarta, Indonesia	6.5 million
Chongqing, China	6.0 million
Hong Kong	5.2 million
Delhi, India	5.2 million
Guangzhou, China	5.2 million
Karachi, Pakistan	5.1 million
Bangkok, Thailand	5.0 million
Tehran, Iran	5.0 million

As you have read, all the major religions of the world got their start in Asia. The Middle East is the home of three major religions—Judaism, Christianity, and Islam. India is the birthplace of Hinduism and Buddhism. Confucianism and Taoism began in China, and Japan is the home of Shintoism.

The map on page 388 shows where Asia's major religions are practiced. Notice that most people in the Middle East practice Islam. Most people in Pakistan, Bangladesh, Malaysia, Indonesia, and the southern part of the Philippines practice Islam also. People who follow the Islamic religion are called Muslims.

387

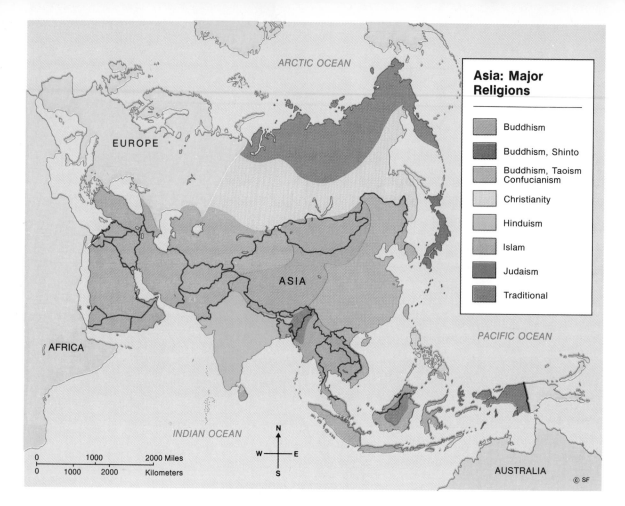

Map Study

The major religions of Asia are shown on the map. Refer to the map on page 372 for the names of the countries shown above. What major religion is practiced in India? In what Asian countries is Buddhism practiced? What is the major religion of Saudi Arabia? What is the major religion in the Philippines?

Buddhism began in India 2,500 years ago. Today Buddhism has little importance in the land of its birth. However, the religion spread to many places in East and Southeast Asia. Find the areas where Buddhism is practiced on the map above. Notice that the map key has three different listings for Buddhism. Buddhism differs in each country where it is practiced because it has mixed with older religious ideas.

Buddhism in China, for example, is mixed with two other ancient systems of thought, Confucianism and Taoism. Confucianism is concerned with order in relations among people. Taoism stresses the importance of being in harmony with nature. In Japan another religion called Shintoism exists alongside Buddhism. Shintoism teaches the Japanese to appreciate the beauty of their land.

People of Australia and Oceania

When Captain James Cook landed on the east coast of Australia in 1770, he called its first inhabitants **aborigines,** which means "originals." Today Australia is a thriving nation of fifteen and a half million people. Only about 100,000 of these people are Aborigines. The majority of Australia's population is of British ancestry.

Life in Australia is much like life in the United States. Both are vast countries with large cities, many farms and ranches, and a great deal of desert land. The government of Australia thinks the country is **underpopulated.** That is, they think that too few people live in the country. Recent governments have encouraged people from other countries to migrate to the land "down under."

Across the Tasman Sea, over 3 million people live in New Zealand. Most are of British descent, but there are also a quarter million Maoris, New Zealand's "originals." Although New Zealand is an important agricultural country, more than four of five New Zealanders now live in urban areas.

The populations of the thousands of smaller islands of Oceania differ a great deal. In general, the high islands have the most people because of their fertile soil. On most islands, the people are natives. However, on a few islands, the majority of people come from other parts of the world. On Fiji, for example, Indians were brought over by the British as workers and now are the largest group on the island.

The original inhabitants of New Zealand, the Maoris, number about 250,000 people.

Reviewing the Lesson

Recalling Key Words, People, and Places
1. Identify the key words defined below:
    a. a member of the original group of a region
    b. having fewer people in a region than the region can support
2. What people are the original inhabitants of New Zealand?

Remembering Main Ideas
1. Which three regions of Asia have the largest populations?
2. Describe what many cities in the developing countries of Asia are like.
3. In which countries is Buddhism practiced today?
4. What is the ancestry of most people in Australia and New Zealand?

Thinking Things Over
Suppose Australia does attract new people from other countries. What problems do you think having a larger population will cause?

Understanding Different Map Projections

In the Skills Workshop for Chapter 8, you saw how the size and shape of land can be distorted on a flat map of the round earth.

Interrupted Projection

In order to make up for distortions that occur on Mercator projections, mapmakers have developed equal-area projections. These maps show true areas of the earth's land. One square inch on such a map is equal to a certain number of square miles on the earth's surface. To draw such a map, however, the mapmaker must distort the shapes of land and water.

Some equal-area projections are interrupted. That means they start and stop again. In interrupted projections, like the one below, the shapes and sizes of most land areas are almost the same as on a globe. The oceans and some land areas, however, are split up.

People who want to study land areas find interrupted-projection maps useful. However, such maps are not good for people who want to travel, because directions and distances

Interrupted Projection (Equal Area)

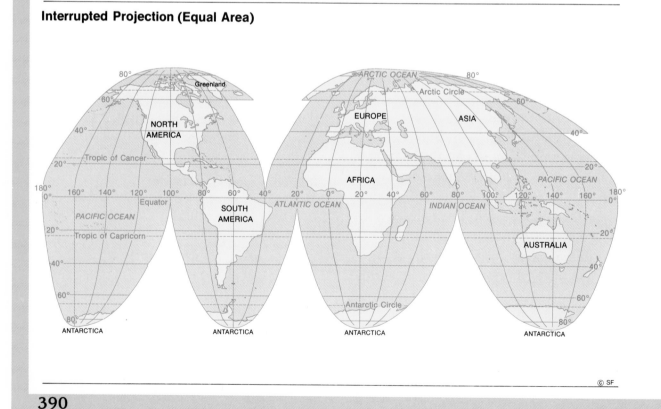

Eckert Projection (Equal Area)

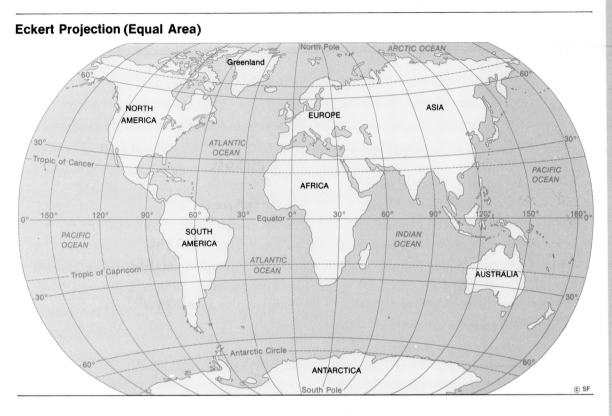

between land areas cannot be shown accurately.

Eckert Projection

The Eckert projection is another equal-area projection. It is not interrupted. This kind of projection has the advantage of showing the sizes of most continents and oceans correctly. The shapes of some land and water areas, however, are distorted. This happens around the edges of the map.

Now compare two equal-area maps shown on these pages. Look at Australia on both maps. On which map does Australia have more nearly the same shape that it has on a globe?

Skills Practice

You learned before that a globe has no distortions. On a globe:

1. All meridians meet at the poles.
2. All parallels are exactly parallel to one another.
3. Parallels vary in length.
4. All meridians are the same length.

Apply these rules to the interrupted-projection map. Number your paper from 1 to 4. If the interrupted-projection map breaks the rule, write *distortion* beside the number of that rule. If the map does not break a rule, write *no distortion*. Then do the same for the Eckert projection map.

Chapter 18 Review

Chapter Summary

Lesson 1   The Natural Environment of Asia and Oceania—Asia and Oceania cover over one-third of the earth's land surface and stretch into the Northern and Southern hemispheres. Most of Asia's great rivers begin in the world's highest mountains, the Himalayas, and flow into the Indian or Pacific oceans. Australia, the world's biggest island, and 20,000 to 30,000 other islands make up the region called Oceania.

Lesson 2   Resources and Land Use in Asia and Oceania—Most of Asia's people are subsistence farmers who work on small, fertile, well-watered plots. Rice and wheat are Asia's major crops. The Green Revolution has increased the amount of food that can be grown on Asian farms. Minerals are an important source of income, especially oil in the Middle East. Australia and New Zealand have a great deal of industry, and many Pacific islands rely on tourism and fishing to make a living.

Lesson 3   The People of Asia and Oceania—Asia has more people than any other part of the world. The river valleys, coastal plains, and cities are the most crowded places in Asia. All the world's major religions began in Asia. The original people of Australia and Oceania are far outnumbered by descendants of European settlers.

Write your answers on a separate sheet of paper.

Testing Key Words, People, and Places

Part A

Choose the key word from the list that best completes each sentence.

1. A _pesticide_ is a chemical that wards off insects and plant diseases.
2. An _earthquake_ is a shaking of the earth.
3. An original inhabitant of a place is called an _aborigine_
4. Asians build a _dike_ to hold water in their rice fields.
5. Australia is _underpopulated_ because it contains fewer people than the land can support.
6. A _high island_ in the Pacific Ocean has fertile soil and many plants.
7. Hot gases, liquids, and solid material can escape through a _volcano_.
8. A _low island_ is formed by the remains of tiny sea animals called coral.
9. A flooded field where rice is grown is called a _paddy_

a. earthquake   f. dike
b. volcano   g. pesticide
c. high island   h. aborigine
d. low island   i. underpopulated
e. paddy

Part B

In a sentence, tell why each person or place is important.

1. Middle East   5. Melanesia
2. Anatolian Plateau 6. Micronesia
3. Arabian Peninsula 7. Polynesia
4. North China Plain 8. Maori

Handwritten answers:
1. The Middle East is important because there there is lots of oil.
2. The source for 2 rivers.
3 - oil
4. High population, for crops
5. This place is important for tourists.
6. Same as 5.
7. Same as 5 and 6.
8. The Native people of New Zealand.

Testing Main Ideas

Answer these questions.

1. From which mountains do all the major rivers of East Asia begin? *Himalayas*
2. What is the climate of the Middle East like? *Hot, dry all year*
3. What is the biggest island in Oceania? *Australia*
4. What is the major crop of Southeast Asia? *rice*
5. What do scientists hope to achieve through the Green Revolution? *bigger crop production*
6. What is the main economic activity on the Indian subcontinent? *Commercial fishing farming*
7. Why do tourists enjoy visiting the islands of Oceania? *beautiful*
8. Which of Asia's four regions has the fewest people? *Middle East*
9. What are five major world religions that began in Asia? *Judism, Buddhism, Christianity, Confucianism Islam,*

Testing Skills

1. **Understanding map projections.** Tell whether each statement describes an interrupted projection map or an Eckert projection map.
   a. The oceans and some land areas are split up. *Interrupted projection map*
   b. The shapes of some land and water areas are distorted, especially around the edges of the map. *Eckert projection map*
   c. The sizes of most land and water areas are shown correctly without breaks. *Eckert projection map*
   d. Directions and distances are not shown accurately. *interrupted projection map*

2. **Making a bar graph.** Construct a bar graph from the following information about the population of cities in East Asia.

Shanghai, China	12.0 million
Seoul, S. Korea	9.2 million
Beijing, China	8.5 million
Tokyo, Japan	8.3 million
Tianjin, China	7.2 million
Chongqing, China	6.0 million
Hong Kong	5.2 million
Guangzhou, China	5.2 million

When you finish your graph, give it a title. How could someone use the information contained in the graph?

Activities

1. Look through current newspapers and magazines and find articles about Asia and Oceania. Locate the places you read about on the map on page 372.
2. Make the following chart. First, pick a region of Asia or a region of Oceania. Then, list all the countries in that region. After each country, list the major landforms, types of climate, mineral resources, and crops. Use the different parts of this book to gather information. You may wish to check almanacs and encyclopedias for further information.
3. Research the way in which a coral island is formed. Discover some places other than the Pacific Ocean where coral islands are located.

Chapter 19

From Past to Present in Asia and Oceania

The Great Wall of China, which you see in the picture, is the longest structure ever built. The Chinese built the wall to protect themselves from invaders. Unfortunately, the wall proved to be a poor defense. Both the wall and China were conquered many times.

As you read this chapter, you will learn about the invasions and great empires of China and the rest of Asia. You also will learn what took place in Asia this century. The lessons in the chapter are listed below.

Lesson 1 **"Golden Ages" in Asia**

Lesson 2 **East Meets West**

Lesson 3 **Asia in the Twentieth Century**

394

Lesson 1 "Golden Ages" in Asia

> 📖 **LOOKING AHEAD** As you read, look for—
>
> **Key words, people, and places:**
>
> | | |
> |---|---|
> | Guptas | Beijing |
> | Mughuls | |
> | Akbar | |
> | Manchus | |
>
> Answers to these questions about **main ideas:**
>
> 1. What events caused the Muslim cities of the Middle East to lose their power?
> 2. How did the Guptas and the Mughuls rule India?
> 3. What were the leading dynasties of China and what did they achieve?

You read earlier about the river valleys in Asia where civilizations first began in Chapter 4. These civilizations were located in Mesopotamia, the Indus Valley, and the valley of the Hwang Ho. From each of these three regions, trade and ideas spread outward. Eventually, three major Asian cultures were formed: the Islamic culture of Southwest Asia, Indian culture, and Chinese culture.

Throughout Asian history, wandering invaders often attacked great empires. The wealth of Asia's cities attracted the invaders like a magnet. Sometimes the invaders stayed to rule. Gradually, however, they took on the manners and ways of life of the people they had conquered. In this way the cultures of Asia blended and changed time and time again. The original cultures of the conquered people never died out.

Islamic Civilization in the Middle East

In the long history of the Middle East, many groups ruled. In order, these groups included the Hittites, Assyrians, Medes, Greeks, Romans, and Persians. Each group grew strong in the countryside. Then, attracted by the wealth, they would sweep into the cities of the river valleys.

As you read earlier, the groups that controlled the Middle East had grown weak from constant warfare in the 600s. Nomadic herders, inspired by the teachings of Muhammad, came out of the desert of Arabia. These Muslim Arabs believed they had a sacred duty to spread the teachings of Muhammad and the religion of Islam.

By 711, the Islamic world had spread beyond Asia to Africa and Europe. This was the beginning of the Middle East's golden age. Centers of Islamic civilization grew up in the cities. Muslim scholars made advances in architecture, mathematics, science, and medicine.

In the 1200s the golden age of the Middle East ended. The Mongols invaded Southwest Asia. You read about the Mongols in Chapter 10. They were the nomadic horsemen from central Asia who also conquered Russia in the

1200s. The Mongols destroyed the cities and irrigation works of Mesopotamia and then left. The Islamic empire never recovered totally from the Mongol invasion.

After the Mongols left the Middle East, another invading group took control of the area. These invaders were the Ottoman Turks. The Turks were Muslims, and they stayed to rule. They ruled the Arab lands until the early 1900s.

The Rulers of India

India's early history, like that of the Middle East, was made up of a series of invasions. Invaders entered India through the mountain passes in the northwest. Invaders then moved southeast across the Indus River and into the rest of India. Trace this path of invasion with your finger on the map on page 378.

The golden age of Indian culture came with the Hindu Guptas between A.D. 320 and 500. The Guptas united India, promoted business and trade, and ruled strongly and fairly. A Chinese traveler gave this description of life under the Guptas.

 . . . The people are many and happy. They do not have to register their household with the police. There is no death penalty. Religious groups have houses of char-

Linking Past and Present

Mecca: Islam's Holy City

All Muslims try to go to Mecca, Saudi Arabia, once in a lifetime. Mecca is Islam's holy city. The city is so sacred that only Muslims are allowed to enter.

Upon arrival in Mecca, Muslims go to the huge Sacred Mosque in the center of town, which you see in the picture. The Kaaba (kä′bə), Islam's most holy shrine, stands in the the Sacred Mosque. *Kaaba* means "square building" in Arabic. The Kaaba is draped in black cloth.

When Muslims pray, they turn toward the direction of Mecca and the Kaaba. Embedded in one corner of the Kaaba and enclosed in a silver ring is the Black Stone. Muslims believe the Black Stone was a gift from God to Abraham. One goal of Muslims who visit Mecca is to touch or kiss the Black Stone.

ity where rooms, couches, bed, food, and drink are supplied to travelers. 🙴

Learning and science grew during Gupta rule. Gupta astronomers knew that the world was round and estimated its size. Gupta mathematicians developed the number symbols we use today. Doctors learned to perform surgery and metal workers made steel. Weavers made cotton cloth and a fine wool known as cashmere.

India grew poor after the end of the Gupta Empire. Then, Muslim invaders came through the mountain passes from the present-day country of Afghanistan. By 1311, they had conquered all of India and established a kingdom with Delhi as the capital. Unlike other invaders, the Muslims did not take on Indian ways. They considered themselves and their religion superior to the Hindus. The Muslims destroyed many Hindu temples.

In the early 1500s, Delhi was conquered by the Mughuls (mu′gůlz), a new group of Muslim horsemen descended from the Mongols. They liked art and poetry and were also skillful builders. The Mughuls also treated the Hindus fairly.

The greatest Mughul ruler was Akbar, who brought peace and prosperity. During his rule, between 1556 and 1605, India was perhaps the best governed and richest country in the world. Akbar's successors, however, lacked his skill at governing. The Mughul's poor government made moving into India fairly easy for the British in 1757.

This Mughul painting was done in the 1500s. It shows the greatest of the Mughul rulers, "Akbar the Builder." Find Akbar in the picture. What evidence of building and trade can you find in the picture?

397

The Dynasties of China

Chinese history has the same pattern as the history of India and the Middle East. A dynasty would come to power and then, after a period of time, invaders would overthrow it and a new dynasty would arise.

You read earlier about the Shang Dynasty in the Hwang Ho Valley. This dynasty ruled until a new group conquered it in 1027 B.C. The conquerors formed the Zhou Dynasty and they ruled for almost 800 years.

About 200 B.C., the Han Dynasty began a 400-year rule. Under Han rule, China grew to include much of its present territory. The Chinese also came into contact with people from many other parts of the world. Traders from Han China carried silk to India and the Caspian Sea, where Romans traded for the silk. The Hans invented paper, recorded their history, and developed a dictionary. The Hans also completed the Great Wall.

Under the Hans, any man of any class could become a government official by passing a difficult test. It required knowledge of more than fifty thousand Chinese characters! This type of examination gave China an educated ruling class, but it also resulted in a society that resisted change.

The Han dynasty ended when invaders broke through the Great Wall. Trade fell off. At last, two dynasties, the Tang and the Song, brought back peace and prosperity. The Tangs ruled from 618 to 907. The Songs controlled China between 960 and 1279. The Tang and Song emperors strengthened the Great Wall to keep out invaders. They encouraged art and literature, and trade grew once again. The ships of Chinese traders probably reached as far as the coast of Africa. Silk and glazed pottery called porcelain were traded. Much later Europeans began to call this porcelain "china."

Under the Tang and Song dynasties, Chinese developed many great inventions. They invented printing and the first mechanical clock. The Chinese learned to make a magnetic compass, an instrument to detect earthquakes, and an adding device called an abacus. They also invented gunpowder, which they used to produce fireworks. The

The world's first mechanical clock was invented in China.

Only the royal family and nobles could enter the walled area of Beijing called the Forbidden City. Today it is open to all.

Chinese people call the Tang and Song periods their golden age.

Disaster struck in the 1200s when Mongols broke through the Great Wall and poured into China. At first they destroyed all they saw, but later they adopted Chinese ways, using Chinese advisers in their court. As India had done more than once, China absorbed its conquerors.

Eventually, in 1368, the Mongols were overthrown, and the Ming dynasty came into power. They built a beautiful capital at Beijing (bā′jing′). The emperor and his court lived a life of luxury within a walled area of Beijing called the Forbidden City. Only members of the royal family could live there.

A new band of nomads, known as the Manchus, captured Beijing in 1644. They took control of the country and extended Chinese territory. At first the Manchus tried to keep their own language and customs, but they soon took on Chinese ways. The Manchus were not bad rulers, but they had little interest in outside contacts. Thus, China was not prepared for the coming meeting with European technology.

Reviewing the Lesson

Recalling Key Words, People, and Places
1. Identify each of these groups:
    a. Guptas
    b. Mughuls
    c. Manchus
2. In what Chinese city was the Forbidden City built?

Remembering Main Ideas
1. How long did the golden age of Islamic civilization last?
2. Describe the route taken by the invaders who conquered India.
3. What were some important inventions during the Tang and Song dynasties?

Thinking Things Over
You learned that the invaders who conquered Asian cities soon took up the cultures of the people they conquered. Why do you think this happened?

399

Lesson 2 East Meets West

LOOKING AHEAD As you read, look for—

Key words, people, and **places:**

treaty   East Indies
             Indochina

Answers to these questions about **main ideas:**

1. Why did the European powers want trade with Asia?
2. In what ways did European merchants help to establish colonialism in Asia?
3. What kind of relationship did China have with Western countries during the 1800s?
4. What steps did Japan take to modernize itself?
5. What was Britain's interest in the Middle East?

While Europe was in the so-called Dark Ages, China, India, and the Middle East were in their golden ages. Yet Europe and Asia were not completely out of contact. China's "Silk Road" carried goods for thousands of miles to the cities of the Middle East. Indian traders reached the Middle East by crossing the mountain passes. Arab traders then carried the goods—and ideas—of Asia from the Middle East to the West. Asia's achievements in mathematics and science were passed on to Europe.

Europe Reaches Out to Asia

By the 1500s Europe was experiencing the Renaissance, a new awakening in learning and the arts. Portuguese navigators such as Dias and Vasco da Gama had found a way to reach Asia around the southern tip of Africa. Europe was reaching out.

Europe also was growing richer. More and more people could afford luxuries, especially the luxuries of Asia. Demand grew for Asia's silk and spices, porcelain and tea.

Meanwhile, weavers in Europe were making cloth that could be sold abroad. Later, with the Industrial Revolution in the late 1700s, all kinds of goods were produced. European factories needed markets for these goods. European merchants sailed to Asian ports to trade.

The first to reach East Asia were the Spanish and Portuguese. Ferdinand Magellan landed in the Philippines in 1521 and claimed the islands for Spain. Portugal secured trading posts from India to Japan. Later, other European countries began to compete with Spain and Portugal for Asian trade. By the 1600s merchants from Britain, France, and the Netherlands had their own trading posts in Asia.

From Trading Posts to Colonies

European merchants arrived in Asia at a time when most Asian countries were weak. Robbers stalked the roads and pirates plundered the coasts. Still, enough opportunities for trade existed for Europeans to form large trading companies. These companies owned

European merchant ships dock at a Chinese waterfront in the 1800s. The merchants had warehouses and offices built for them.

their own ships. They even had their own armies and navies.

In many of the ports of Asia, the merchant companies set up warehouses and offices. These were the beginnings of colonialism in Asia. To protect their goods, merchant companies made **treaties,** or formal agreements, with local rulers. The treaties gave the merchants the right to trade. In return, the company armies would protect the local rulers.

Little by little, European merchants carved up Asia among themselves. British merchant companies gained territorial control in India, Ceylon (now Sri Lanka), Burma, and the Malay peninsula. A Dutch company gained control over the islands of the East Indies (now Indonesia). A French company gained

control of Indochina (now Vietnam, Cambodia, and Laos).

The merchant companies developed plantations on which special crops, such as spices, tea, or coffee, were grown. The merchants sold machine-woven cloth from Europe. It was cheaper than the Asian hand-woven cloth. The companies made money, and the local rulers also increased their wealth. However, living standards in the countryside were very low, and there was unrest.

Over time, the governments of Britain, France, and the Netherlands became concerned that the companies were becoming too powerful. They put an end to company control. The regular armies of the European countries took over for the company armies and European governments made their own

treaties with local rulers. By the early 1800s, most of India, Indochina, and the East Indies had become European colonies.

The European governments built railroads and seaports to aid trade. The British drained a swamp at the southern tip of the Malay peninsula and built the city of Singapore. Missionaries, protected by the colonial powers, set up schools and hospitals and tried to win converts to Christianity.

China Is Opened

After European traders first came to China and Japan, rulers in these countries decided they wanted no part of European culture. They closed their countries to Europeans.

The Japanese government was strong and, therefore, was able to enforce the isolation. In China, however, the government was weak. Merchant vessels from Europe and the United States landed at Chinese ports, and their captains insisted on trading. The Chinese wanted little that was made in the West, so British merchants carried an unwelcome cargo of Indian opium to unload in China.

To stop the opium trade, the Chinese went to war against Britain in 1839. The Opium War lasted three years, but the British won easily. The Chinese found they were no match for the West in battle. The British forced China to agree that Europeans could trade throughout China and that Western merchants would be protected.

After the Opium War, conditions in China did not improve. China lost a war to Japan in 1895 and were forced to give Japan the island of Taiwan. An uprising against foreigners in 1900, known as the Boxer Rebellion, failed, and China was humiliated more than ever. Finally, in 1911 China's last dynasty was overthrown, and a new era began.

Japan Industrializes

Meanwhile the Japanese were having a different kind of experience with the West. In 1853 Matthew Perry, an American naval captain, sailed into Tokyo Bay and demanded that Japan open itself to trade. When he returned six months later, he brought many gifts, and the Japanese could see that Western technology had much to offer.

In the next forty years, Japanese students went to all the leading countries of the West. The Japanese changed their government, laws, army, and school system to be like those of Western countries. New industries were built. Japan was able to defeat China in a war, and in 1905, Japan stunned the world with a military victory over Russia. This victory was the first time, since colonialism began, that an Asian country had defeated a European power in a war. The world now realized that Japan had done the impossible. It had become a modern industrial and military power in only 50 years.

Southwest Asia

By the 1800s the West had lost interest in Southwest Asia. Once trade routes between Europe and Asia had crossed the Middle East. Now, however, European ships carried trade along sea routes. Muslim traders lost their business. The Middle East grew poor.

Britain was most interested in protecting the water route to India and beyond. For centuries, ships had to go around the tip of Africa. After 1869, however, the new Suez Canal greatly shortened the distance. The canal became the pathway between Europe and Asia. As long as the canal was safe, Britain was willing to allow the Ottomans to continue ruling the Middle East.

Britain also had a strong presence in Iran and Afghanistan. It had no wish to rule these lands, but it did not want the Russians to have them. Britain's real interest was India, the "jewel in Britain's crown."

The Suez Canal shortened the sailing distance between Western Europe and India by 6,000 miles. The canal made the middle East an important military location.

Reviewing the Lesson

Recalling Key Words, People, and Places
1. Tell what the word **treaty** means.
2. Tell where each place is located:
   a. East Indies
   b. Indochina

Remembering Main Ideas
1. Which two European powers were the first to begin trade with Asia?
2. Why did European governments take control of Asian trade away from the merchants?
3. Name two rebellions against Western influence in China.
4. What event made Europeans realize that Japan had become a powerful country?
5. How did the Suez Canal reduce traveling time between Europe and Asia?

Thinking Things Over
Why were Europeans able to force Asian countries to trade with them?

Lesson 3   Asia in the Twentieth Century

LOOKING AHEAD As you read, look for—

Key words, people, and **places:**

refugee
militarist

Ho Chi Minh
Sun Yat-sen
Chiang Kai-shek
Mao Zedong

Answers to these questions about **main ideas:**

1. How did the countries of the Middle East achieve independence?
2. What events led to Japan's entry into World War II?
3. How did the countries of South and Southeast Asia achieve independence?
4. What wars took place in China and Korea in the twentieth century?

In the early morning of August 6, 1945, a single bomb fell from an American plane. It dropped on the city of Hiroshima, Japan. The force of this first atomic bomb equaled 20,000 pounds of dynamite. It killed or seriously wounded 160,000 people.

Since that August morning, Asia and the world have changed greatly. Many other changes also have occurred in Asia in this century. You will read about some of these changes in this lesson.

Changes in the Middle East

The Arabs, with the help of the British, ended five hundred years of Turkish rule in the Middle East during World War I. The treaty that ended the war did not grant independence to the region, however. It gave control of the Middle East to Great Britain and France. Only later, after the end of World War II, did Iraq, Syria, Lebanon, and Jordan became independent countries.

One part of the Middle East, called Palestine, had special problems after World War II. Palestine is the old homeland of both Jews and Arabs. In the first century A.D., the Romans exiled Jews from the area and scattered them throughout the Roman world. Eventually, most Palestinians came to think of themselves as Arabs and practiced Islam. However, a few Jews continued to live in Palestine.

In the 1800s a movement called Zionism arose among some Jews in Europe. It favored the return of Jews to Palestine. Before and after World War II, many Jewish people fled from Europe to Palestine. They wanted to escape from the dangers they faced in Europe. Jews also wanted to form their own country.

In 1947 the United Nations agreed to divide Palestine into a Jewish section and an Arab section. Britain agreed to keep the peace between the two groups. However, constant fighting forced Britain to withdraw from the area in 1948. The Jews then formed

Japanese children pledge allegiance to the emperor in 1932.

the country of Israel. Most of the Arab Palestinians fled to neighboring Arab countries where they became refugees. A **refugee** is a person who flees for safety, especially to another country, because of a war or disaster.

The neighboring Arab countries immediately began a war against Israel. Israel won the 1948 war. It also won wars against its Arab neighbors in 1956, 1967, and 1973. Today hard feelings still exist between the Jewish Israelis and their Arab neighbors.

Japan and World War II

By the early 1900s, Japan was the leading country in East Asia. With its industry growing, Japan needed markets and raw materials for its products.

Militarists had gained control of Japan's government. A **militarist** favors a strong military organization or believes that military interests are the most important. The militarists in Japan wanted to control the mineral riches of East Asia and Southeast Asia. Japan also wanted to increase its control over trade. Japan already had taken Taiwan. It then moved into Korea. In addition, Japan took over many Pacific islands.

Japan invaded China in 1937. Soon afterward, in 1939, World War II started in Europe. Japan sided with the Axis powers during the war. In 1941 it bombed the United States naval base in Pearl Harbor, Hawaii. Japan also invaded several Southeast Asian countries governed by European countries.

At first, Japan was successful, but soon the United States, Britain, and China fought back. Other countries in the region, such as Australia and New

Zealand, also fought the Japanese. On August 10, 1945, Japan surrendered, and World War II ended.

Changes in South and Southeast Asia

All the countries of Asia shook off colonial rule after the end of World War II. Some countries gained independence without fighting a war. For example, the United States granted independence to the Philippines on July 4, 1946. Elsewhere, the road to independence was less easy.

India. Britain did not want to give up its colonies in Asia. However, feelings of nationalism in Britain's Asian colonies had grown very strong. Britain knew it would have to fight a long war to keep its colonies. Therefore, Britain choose to grant independence to Burma, Ceylon (Sri Lanka), India, and Malaysia.

At the time of India's independence in 1947, its Muslim population demanded that a separate country for Muslims—Pakistan—be formed. When Pakistan was created, more than 12 million Hindus and Muslims crossed the India-Pakistan border. Another 200,000 people died in the fighting that broke out between the Hindus and the Muslims.

Indonesia. The Dutch fought to keep their colonies in the East Indies, which had brought them great wealth. Finally, in 1949 after four years of fighting, the Dutch gave up their colonies. The country of Indonesia was created from the Dutch East Indies.

Vietnam. The French in Indochina fought even harder to keep their colonies. They agreed to independence for Laos in 1949 and Cambodia in 1953 without fighting. However, they fought for nine years—between 1946 and 1954—to keep Vietnam.

During World War II, many Vietnamese formed a group to fight the invading Japanese. After the war, this group—headed by a communist named Ho Chi Minh (hō′ chē′ min′)—continued to fight for independence. The French wanted to prevent Vietnam from having a communist government. However, in 1954 the French were defeated in the north, and the country was divided. North Vietnam became a communist government headed by Ho Chi Minh. A noncommunist government was set up in South Vietnam.

United States troops land in Vietnam to fight the communists.

After the country was divided, the North Vietnamese tried to conquer the south. The United States then entered Vietnam to keep it from becoming communist. Between 1964 and 1973, almost 9 million Americans went to Vietnam. More than 47,000 American soldiers died there. United States troops finally withdrew from Vietnam in 1973. The South Vietnamese government fell in 1975, and the North Vietnamese took control of all Vietnam.

Changes in China and Korea

The last dynasty in China was overthrown in 1911. One of China's great leaders, Sun Yat-sen (sun' yät'sen'), led the revolution. Sun believed in democracy, but was never able to bring peace and order to China.

When Sun died in 1925, China struggled in a civil war. One side, led by Chiang Kai-shek (chyang' kī'shek'), wanted China to have private ownership of property. The other side, led by Mao Zedong (mou' dzu'dung), wanted a communist state, with the government owning all property.

When the Japanese invaded China, the two forces joined together for a while to fight their common enemy. After the Japanese were defeated, however, the civil war began again. Finally, in 1949 Mao Zedong's forces won. Chiang Kai-shek and his followers fled to Taiwan. Mainland China was renamed the People's Republic of China.

In Korea, at the end of World War II, the Soviet Union established a communist government in the northern part of the country. South Korea, on the other

Dr. Sun Yat-sen led a revolution.

hand, was occupied by soldiers from the United States and allied countries. In 1950 North Korea invaded South Korea. The United Nations formed an army to push the North Koreans back. A treaty ended the Korean War in 1953. Since then, North and South Korea have been uneasy neighbors.

Reviewing the Lesson

Recalling Key Words, People, and Places
1. Identify the key words defined below:
   a. a person who flees for safety, especially to another country
   b. a person who favors a very strong military organization
2. Tell why it is important to remember:
   a. Ho Chi Minh
   b. Sun Yat-sen

Remembering Main Ideas
1. How did the Zionist movement lead to the formation of the country of Israel?
2. Why did Japan try to conquer a large part of Asia?
3. Why did the United States enter the conflict in Vietnam?
4. Where did Chiang Kai-shek's followers go after losing to Mao Zedong?

Thinking Things Over
This lesson might have been titled "Wars and Change in Asia in the Twentieth Century." Why might this have been a good title?

407

Making Inferences from Maps

You have read about such places as the Caspian Sea, Thailand, Taiwan, and Pakistan. If you didn't know where these places were, you could look at a map to find them. People often use maps to find specific information such as the locations of places or ways to go from one place to another. As you have learned, you also can use a map to make inferences about additional information—information that the map does not specifically show.

Inferring Why Changes Have Occurred

Some maps show boundaries between countries. When boundaries change, mapmakers draw new maps to show the changes. By studying and comparing maps, you can see where such changes have occurred. Then you can make inferences about the political events that caused the changes to occur.

You read about the creation of Israel in 1948 and the war Israel fought with neighboring Arab countries. Israel and its Arab neighbors, including Egypt,

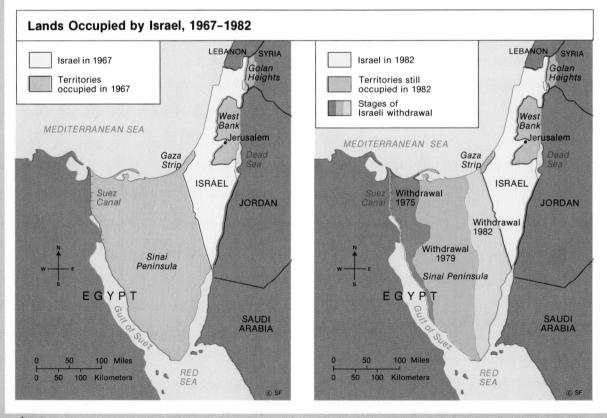

Lands Occupied by Israel, 1967–1982

fought another war in 1967. Then, in 1975, Israel and Egypt began to talk about peace. Some of their talks were held at Camp David in the United States. Egypt and Israel signed a peace treaty called the Camp David Accords in 1979.

Who won the 1967 war between Israel and its neighbors? What did the Camp David Accords call for Israel to do? You don't have to look in a history book to answer these questions. You can use the information on the two maps on page 408 to infer the answers. Here is how to do it.

The left-hand map shows which lands Israel occupied, or took possession of, after the 1967 war. Who won the war? You can infer that Israel did because it came to occupy so much land outside its borders after the war. Israel must have won this land from its Arab neighbors in the war.

What did the Camp David Accords call for Israel to do? Look at the right-hand map on page 408. You can see that Israel slowly withdrew, or drew back, from the Arab lands it had occupied after the 1967 war. The first withdrawal occurred in 1975, before the Camp David Accords. When did the other two withdrawals occur? What can you infer about what Israel agreed to do as part of the Camp David Accords?

Skills Practice

Look again at the two maps on page 408. Use the map, the map labels, and the map key to infer the answers to these questions.

1. In 1973, Egypt and Syria attacked Israel, starting another major war. At first, Egypt drove Israel away from the Suez Canal. However, Israeli troops counterattacked and crossed the canal. In 1974, the United States was able to convince Egypt, Syria, and Israel to stop fighting. In exchange for peace, Israel agreed to give up some of its occupied land the following year. Describe the location of the land that Israel gave back to Egypt.

2. Many people favor forming a new country for Palestinians. One suggested location for such a country is land belonging to Jordan and occupied by Israel. What is the name usually given to this suggested location for a Palestinian country?

3. Israel insists on keeping a part of Syria. The Israelis claim they cannot defend their country if they give up this land. What is the name of this occupied territory? Can you guess a reason why Israel considers this territory important for its defense? (Hint: Think about what the name of this territory means.)

Chapter Summary

Lesson 1 "Golden Ages" in Asia— Each of the three great civilizations of Asia had golden ages. In the Middle East, the Islamic civilization made great advances. The Hindu Guptas united India in South Asia, and China's golden age came under the Tang and Song dynasties.

Lesson 2 East Meets West—European countries developed a strong interest in trade with Asia by the 1500s. Eventually, European countries carved the weak Asian countries into colonies. The Chinese were forced to trade with the West. However, Japan refused to trade with the West for many years.

Lesson 3 Asia in the Twentieth Century—Japan was the leading Asian nation by the early 1900s. Japan's attempt to conquer an empire resulted in a defeat during World War II. The countries of the Middle East finally became independent after World War II. The countries of South and Southeast Asia also became independent after World War II. However, many countries had long struggles to achieve independence.

Write your answers on a separate sheet of paper.

Testing Key Words, People, and Places

Part A

Choose the key word from the list that best answers each question.

1. What is a person who is forced to leave home because of war or other disaster?
2. What is an agreement between two nations called?
3. What is a person who favors a strong army and believes that military interests are the most important?
   a. treaty
   b. refugee
   c. militarist

Part B

Choose the person or place from the list that best completes each sentence.

1. The communist leader of North Vietnam was _____.
2. The man who led China during the Cultural Revolution was _____.
3. The region of _____ includes Vietnam, Cambodia, and Laos.
4. The Netherlands ruled the _____, which later became Indonesia.
5. The _____ were successful leaders during India's golden age.
6. After taking control of China, the _____ became weak and were defeated by European powers.
   a. Guptas   **d.** Indochina
   b. Manchus   **e.** Ho Chi Minh
   c. East Indies **f.** Mao Zedong

Testing Main Ideas

Choose the answer that best completes each sentence.

1. The religion of the Mughuls was
   a. Hinduism.   **c.** Islam.
   b. Christianity.

2. The Islamic civilization of the Middle East declined when it was defeated by the
   a. Chinese.
   b. Mongols.
   c. European colonists.

3. Two great inventions during the golden age of China include
   a. printing and gunpowder.
   b. electricity and the wheel.
   c. iron and steam power.

4. Europe's main interest in Asia was
   a. trade.
   b. slaves.
   c. adventure.

5. In general, the people of China
   a. enjoyed contact with Europeans.
   b. disliked Europeans.
   c. ignored Europeans.

6. By 1905 Japan had become
   a. the leading power in Asia.
   b. the loser in two wars.
   c. an industrial democracy.

7. The Suez Canal made Europeans more interested in the Middle East because the canal
   a. irrigated new farmland.
   b. opened a new trade route.
   c. connected Europe and North America.

8. Japan entered World War II because
   a. Japan was attacked by China.
   b. Japan's leaders didn't like war.
   c. Japan wanted colonies.

Testing Skills

1. Making inferences from maps. Tell what you could infer from the maps that are described below.
   a. A map of South Asia in 1947 shows Pakistan in two parts: East Pakistan and West Pakistan. A map of the same region after 1971 shows the countries of Pakistan and Bangladesh. What do you think occurred in 1971?
   b. A map of New Guinea in 1973 labels the eastern part of the island "New Guinea (Aus.)." After 1976 the map label reads "PAPUA NEW GUINEA." What do you think happened in 1976?

2. Using latitude and longitude. Alice Springs sits in central Australia. Its latitude and longitude are 23°S, 133°E. For each Australian city below, tell which direction you would travel from Alice Springs to reach the city.
   a. Adelaide   34°S, 138°E
   b. Perth   31°S, 115°E
   c. Darwin   12°S, 130°E

Activities

1. Look in the *Readers' Guide to Periodical Literature* for articles about Zionism and the founding of Israel.

2. Read the book *Shogun* (New York: Dell, 1980) by James Clavell. This book tells about an early contact between a European sea captain and the Japanese.

Chapter 20

The Countries of the Middle East and South Asia Today

New and old exist side by side in the countries of the Middle East and South Asia. The wall you see in the center of the picture is the holiest place of the Jews. It is the remaining wall of the Jewish temple destroyed by the Romans. In the background is the Dome of the Rock, a holy mosque of the Muslims.

As you read this chapter, you will learn about the countries of the Middle East and South Asia. You will discover how the long history of these regions continues to influence them today. The lessons in the chapter are listed below.

Lesson 1   The Countries of the Middle East

Lesson 2   India and Its Neighbors

Lesson 1   The Countries of the Middle East

LOOKING AHEAD As you read, look for—

Key words, people, and **places:**

mullah   Bosporus
embargo   West Bank

Answers to these questions about **main ideas:**

1. What types of climates are found in the countries of the Middle East?
2. What occurred when the countries of Turkey, Iran, and Afghanistan tried to make changes?
3. How do the people of Israel make a living?
4. What are some of the conflicts that have taken place in the Arab countries of the Middle East?
5. How has OPEC helped countries in the Middle East become wealthy and powerful?

You have learned that seven thousand years ago the Middle East was the "cradle of civilization." The first city-based cultures began here. Judaism, Christianity, and Islam began here also.

The Middle East includes the countries of Southwest Asia. Europeans gave it this name because of its location. The Middle East sits between the Far East, as East Asia is sometimes called, and Europe. Some people include the Arab countries of North Africa when they talk about the Middle East. You studied about these countries in Unit 4. As you read this lesson, think how the northern African countries are alike and different from the Middle Eastern countries.

Land and People

Arabs live in twelve Middle Eastern countries. Eight of these countries are on the Arabian Peninsula. Use the map on page 372 to name the countries on the Arabian Peninsula. Syria, Jordan, Lebanon, and Iraq, are Arab countries

that are not on the Arabian Peninsula. The people in Arab countries are almost all Muslims.

Three other countries in the Middle East are Muslim, but their people are not Arabs. These countries are Turkey, Iran, and Afghanistan. Finally, one country in the Middle East—Israel—is neither Arab nor Muslim. Most of Israel's people are Jewish. They come from many places in Europe and the Middle East.

All of the Middle East has a climate with limited amounts of rainfall. The hot, dry climate of the Arabian Desert covers most of the region. Areas close to the Mediterranean Sea—in Israel, Lebanon, Syria, and Turkey—have a warm climate with one dry season. Their climate is similar to the climate in other countries near the Mediterranean Sea. Three other climates can be found in the Middle East. Use the climate map on pages 36–37 to name them. Notice that all three climates are dry or semi-dry.

413

When World War I broke out in 1914, Mustafa Kemal (müs tä fä′ kə mäl′) was a young officer in the Ottoman (Turkish) army. He did not want Turkey to side with Germany. However, he served his country bravely throughout the war and became a national hero. After the war Kemal organized a nationalist movement and led a revolt that overturned the government of Turkey.

As president of Turkey, Kemal set about to bring his nation into the twentieth century. He succeeded where rulers in other countries failed. Before his death in 1938, the Turkish parliament honored him by adding to his name, "Ataturk." It means "Father of the Turks."

The Non-Arab Muslim Countries

Turkey, Iran, and Afghanistan are non-Arab countries in which most of the people are Muslims. All three countries have made efforts to change in this century.

Turkey. A strong effort was made to change Turkey in the 1920s. Men and women were encouraged to wear European clothes. Children were made to go to school, and modern industry was started. A new capital city, Ankara, was built on the dry central plateau.

The former capital, Istanbul (once called Constantinople), is Turkey's largest city. It is located on both sides of the Bosporus, the narrow stretch of water between Asia and Europe. Although Turkey belongs to NATO, the Bosporus is open to ships of all nations, including ships from the Soviet Union. Most Turks are Muslims. However, the country has religious freedom.

Iran. After World War I a British company discovered oil in the south of Iran near the Persian Gulf. With new wealth from oil sales, Iran built schools, hospitals, and new industries. For a time, Iran did very well.

Many Iranians, however, did not like the direction their country was taking. Some religious leaders did not like the way Western culture was affecting their

Istanbul, Turkey, is open to ships of all nations.

country. Other people wanted a fairer, more democratic country. They did not like the autocratic way in which Iran was ruled.

In 1979 a revolution led by Muslim religious leaders called **mullahs** forced the head of the country to flee. The mullahs drew up a new constitution, making Iran a Muslim republic. They took many laws from Islam's holy book, the Koran.

The mullahs' goal was to wipe out Western influences. They tried to spread their beliefs, particularly into neighboring Iraq. Iran began a lengthy war with Iraq in 1980.

Afghanistan. Directly east of Iran is the dry and mountainous land of Afghanistan. Its people are subsistence farmers and nomadic herders. Few have been to school. As in Iran, one of Afghanistan's rulers tried to modernize the country in the 1920s. He was forced out of office by Muslims who wanted no changes.

The Soviet Union invaded Afghanistan in 1979, and many Afghans became refugees in Pakistan. Some later returned to their country to fight a guerrilla war against the Soviets.

Israel and the Palestinians

In the previous chapter you learned about the birth of Israel. In the years since 1948, Israel has received Jewish settlers from all over the world. Some live in farming settlements where land and work are shared. Others have become farmers on their own land. Most, however, settled in one of Israel's modern cities, such as Tel Aviv.

The poster shows Ayatollah Khomeini, the chief mullah in Iran after the Islamic revolution.

Israeli agriculture and industry advanced rapidly during the country's early years. Desert areas were irrigated, and trees now grow where hillsides were once bare. Oranges, aircraft, textiles, and cut diamonds are exported.

Most Muslim countries claim that Israelis are foreigners on Arab land. They believe the Palestinian Arabs should have their own country. The Muslim countries also want Israel to give back the land it won in wars with Arab countries. In 1979, Israel gave back some territory it won, but it is unwilling to give back the fertile West Bank of the Jordan River. Many Jewish settlers have moved into this area.

Israelis have irrigated desert areas and planted orange trees.

Meanwhile, the Palestinian Arabs are widely scattered. The majority live in refugee camps or work in the cities of Jordan and Lebanon. Some have formed armed groups which hope to drive Israel out of the Middle East.

The Arab Countries

The Arab countries can be divided into two groups. One group includes the desert kingdoms of the Arabian Peninsula. The second group of Arab countries includes Lebanon, Syria, Iraq, and Jordan.

The Countries of Iraq, Syria, Lebanon, and Jordan. Iraq has two main sources of wealth. One source is the fertile plains between the Tigris and Euphrates rivers. Iraq's other major source of income is from oil. Much of Iraq's wealth is used for defense.

Almost half (46 percent) of the country's money is spent on its army.

Syria has good agricultural land, too. Much of the farmland has been made fertile through irrigation. During the 1970s Syria came close to forming a single nation with Iraq. However, leaders in the two countries changed their minds.

Lebanon, on the Mediterranean Sea, once was a rich country. It was a resort and banking center for all of the Middle East. Then, in the 1970s, it became torn by fighting. Lebanon's Christians are one group in the conflict. The Christians once controlled the government. The Muslim majority is broken into many small groups. These groups fight the Christians and also fight among themselves. Thousands of Palestinian refugees make the situation worse. Every group maintains its own army.

Jordan is a desert country with few resources to support its 2 million people. Jordan lost its best farmland when Israel captured the West Bank.

The Arabian Peninsula. The desert kingdoms of the Arabian Peninsula once were the center of the great Islamic civilization. Arab traders used the seasonal winds which blew near the Arabian Peninsula to trade in East Africa, South Asia, and Southeast Asia.

The Arabian Peninsula is still the center of the Muslim world. Each year thousands of Muslim pilgrims from all over the world come to Mecca, the birthplace of Muhammad, located about fifty miles inland from the Red Sea in Saudi Arabia. Every Muslim hopes to make the trip to Mecca at least once.

In the south of the Arabian Peninsula are the two Yemens. North Yemen receives enough rainfall in its mountains for farming. South Yemen is almost entirely desert. Their position near the entrance to the Red Sea makes them important to the world's navies. South Yemen now has a communist government, and the port in the capital city of Aden is used by Soviet ships.

The Organization of Petroleum Exporting Countries (OPEC)

More than 40 percent of the world's petroleum lies underneath the sands of the Arabian Peninsula. Petroleum has brought great wealth not only to Saudi Arabia, but also the smaller countries of Kuwait, Bahrain, Qatar, and the United Arab Emirates. Oman also has a little oil, but South Yemen and North Yemen have none.

Saudi Arabia took the lead in founding the Organization of Petroleum Exporting Countries (OPEC). Other Middle Eastern countries belonging to OPEC include Kuwait, Qatar, the United Arab Emirates, Iran, and Iraq.

OPEC was formed in 1960 to raise world oil prices. However, OPEC did not have much effect on world oil prices until 1973. In that year, Saudi Arabia and the other Arab members of OPEC declared an oil **embargo.** That is, they cut off all oil to Western Europe and the United States. The Saudis started the embargo because the United States and most Western European countries supported Israel against

Arab countries in a war. The plan worked. The United States convinced Israel to stop fighting early in 1974.

Another effect of the embargo was that oil prices soared. OPEC countries became powerful and wealthy because they were able to control the world's supply of oil. Oil earnings were used to build schools and hospitals, roads, and chemical industries. In 1982, however, the price of oil started to drop. Efforts by OPEC to keep prices high were not successful. Nevertheless, the countries of OPEC continue to enjoy more wealth and power than they have had for centuries.

Reviewing the Lesson

Recalling Key Words, People, and Places
1. Identify the key words defined below:
    a. a Muslim religious leader
    b. a limitation on the flow of goods between countries
2. Tell where each place is located:
    a. Bosporus
    b. West Bank

Remembering Main Ideas
1. Which countries in the Middle East are not Arab countries?
2. Why did Iranians overthrow their ruler in 1979?
3. Name some of the products exported by the country of Israel.
4. What are some of the groups involved in the fighting in Lebanon?
5. How have the countries of OPEC benefited from the money they have earned from oil?

Thinking Things Over
1. Look at the map on page 372. What do you think might happen if Turkey did not let Soviet ships through the Bosporus? Explain your answer.
2. Compare the ethnic groups, religion, and way of life of people in northern Africa with the people of the Middle East.

417

Lesson 2   India and Its Neighbors

LOOKING AHEAD As you read, look for—

Key words, people, and **places:**

monsoon   Singhalese
cottage industry   Tamil

Answers to these questions about **main ideas:**

1. How do the seasonal winds affect the climate of South Asia?
2. How has India developed its economy since independence?
3. In what ways do people make a living in South Asia's three smallest countries?
4. How are the countries of Pakistan and Bangladesh similar and different?
5. How does India's rate of population growth affect its cities?

The countries of South Asia include India, Pakistan, Bangladesh, Sri Lanka, Nepal (nə pôl′), and Bhutan (bü tän′). Find these countries on the map on page 372. Which country is an island? Which two mainland countries are very small in area?

Land and People

South Asia extends from the slopes of the Himalayan Mountains in the north to the island of Sri Lanka in the south. The northern part of the Indian subcontinent contains plains. Plains also run along the eastern coast. Look back at the landform map on pages 32–33. Which two landforms cover most of the southern part of the Indian subcontinent?

The climate for most of South Asia is controlled by the **monsoon,** a seasonal wind that occurs in the Indian Ocean and South Asia. From April through October, the wind blows from the southwest, off the warm Indian Ocean.

The wind carries moisture inland and dumps large amounts of rain. During the rest of the year, the wind comes from the northeast. This wind blows off the dry Plateau of Tibet. Rainfall is rare when the wind blows from the northeast. The monsoon wind produces a large area with a hot or warm climate and one dry season. Look at the climate map on pages 36–37 and find this large area of land affected by the monsoon.

The northwestern part of South Asia does not benefit from the monsoon. This part of South Asia is dry or semidry all year. Compare the map on pages 36–37 with the map on page 372 to find which South Asian country has the driest climate.

India

Since its independence, India has remained a democracy, despite containing many different cultures. Fourteen major languages and one hundred eighty other languages are spoken in various areas.

British colonial rule helped India in some ways. The British built one of the world's best railway networks, as well as dams and irrigation canals. They educated some Indians and introduced India to new technology.

The long British rule also had bad effects, however. India once traded many goods with Africa and Southeast Asia. Handwoven cotton cloth from India was especially valued in these places. Then, the British brought in their own manufactured goods, including cloth. They exchanged these goods for India's raw cotton, spices, and tea. The Indian textile industry almost disappeared.

Since independence, many kinds of industries have been started in India. The country produces almost all the manufactured products it needs. It has good supplies of raw materials. These include iron ore, coal, and manganese for making steel and cotton and jute

for the textile industry. Oil is one of the few resources India must import.

Few of India's factories are large. India contains many **cottage industries,** in which families work either at home or in small workshops. They do most of the work by hand. Many products from India's cottage industries are sold in the United States. Perhaps you have seen handwoven fabric, jewelry, or handcarved wood from India.

Although the government encourages industry, 70 percent of the people in India still make their living by farming. India has some of the world's best soils. These include the deep rich soils in the river valleys of the Brahmaputra, Ganges, and Indus rivers. The soils along the southern coastal plains are good for growing crops also.

Many Indian farms are not very productive, however. Most farmers are subsistence farmers who cannot afford modern equipment, fertilizer, or pesticides. Individual farm plots are small.

British and Indian leaders met in New Delhi, India, in 1947 to discuss India's future. India gained independence the next year.

Bhutan, Nepal, and Sri Lanka

Bhutan, Nepal, and Sri Lanka are South Asia's three smallest countries. Bhutan and Nepal are nestled at the foot of the high Himalayas. Mount Everest, the world's highest peak, is on the border between Nepal and China. Sri Lanka is a beautiful island nation.

Long isolated, both Nepal and Bhutan now can be reached by road or air from India. Most of the Nepalese are Hindu farmers who live in the foothills. Farmers in tiny Bhutan, most of whom are Buddhists, cultivate rice, wheat, barley, and tea. Almost all of Bhutan's trade is with India. India has helped Bhutan pave its roads and establish a postal system.

Sri Lanka's tea plantations in the central hills provide an important export. Graphite, the material used in pencils, is found in these hills as well. Fertile coastal plains produce excellent rice, and the surrounding waters supply many fish.

Unfortunately, the people on the island come from differing backgrounds and are suspicious of each other. The majority are called Singhalese (sing'gə-lēz') and are Buddhists. When tea plantations were started under the British, Tamil (tam'əl) workers came from southern India. The Tamals are Hindu and make up one-fifth of the population. They have now been in Sri Lanka for over two hundred years. Many Tamils feel that northern Sri Lanka should be a separate Tamil nation.

Pakistan and Bangladesh

You have read that Pakistan and Bangladesh once were part of British

Linking Past and Present

The World's Most Beautiful Building

The Taj Mahal (täj' mə häl') in northern India often is called the most beautiful building in the world. The emperor Shah Jahan had it built as a tomb for his wife in the 1600s.

The building, which is made of white marble, rises to a height of 243 feet. At dusk, the sun's reflection turns the white into a soft pink color. Twenty thousand workers needed twenty-two years to build the Taj Mahal. Today thousands of people come each year from all over the world to marvel at its quiet beauty.

India. At the time of independence in 1947, the two countries split. The new Muslim nation of Pakistan included territory on both sides of northern India. In 1971 West Pakistan and East Pakistan separated. East Pakistan became Bangladesh. A common religion was not enough to hold these two very different areas together.

Pakistan varies from semi-dry to very dry. Three-fourths of all the farmland is irrigated. Excellent soils exist in the valley of the Indus River and its tributaries. In most years Pakistan grows enough wheat and cotton to export. However, Pakistan has the same problem as India. Few farmers can afford to buy enough fertilizer.

In Bangladesh, rainfall is good and the Ganges River delta is fertile. In good years, farmers can use the same plot of land to grow three separate crops of rice. However, Bangladesh usually cannot grow enough to feed itself. The reason for the lack of food is that Bangladesh has a huge population for its size. Over 100 million people live in an area smaller than the state of Wisconsin.

India's Growing Population

India also has a problem with its huge population. At its present growth rate of over 2 percent a year, India's population would double between 1990 and 2025. The great port cities of Calcutta, Bombay, and Madras will continue to grow. Delhi, the inland capital, will spread farther into the countryside. Find India on the population distribution map on page 60. How crowded is India compared to other parts of Asia?

India's growing population causes many problems. For example, hundreds of thousands of homeless people live in the cities. Many sleep on sidewalks. Others, only a little more fortunate, build shelters out of any material they can find. India does not have jobs for all the people who need them.

The Green Revolution, which you have read about, has temporarily solved one problem related to India's population. This problem is possible famine. In most years, India now grows enough food to feed its people. However, the Indian government still considers the fast-growing population a serious problem.

Reviewing the Lesson

Recalling Key Words, People, and Places
1. Identify the key words defined below:
    a. a seasonal wind that occurs in the Indian Ocean and South Asia
    b. an industry in which families work either at home or in small workshops
2. Why are the Singhalese and the Tamil important in Sri Lanka?

Remembering Main Ideas
1. Why does it rain heavily in South Asia between April and October?
2. How did colonialism hurt industries in India?
3. How has the longtime isolation of Nepal and Bhutan ended in recent years?
4. What type of climate is found in Pakistan?
5. What kinds of problems are caused by the size of India's population?

Thinking Things Over
As you read in this lesson, fourteen major languages are spoken in India. In a country where different languages are used, how might the people feel united despite their differences?

421

SKILLS WORKSHOP

Evaluating Information

We live at a time when a great deal of information about many subjects is available to us. Some of this information is accurate and useful. Some is not.

When you read, do the following:

- Think about whether the author has given you enough information to suit your purpose.
- Determine whether the information is reliable—that is, can you depend on its accuracy? One way to check reliability is to determine what sources the author used in preparing the material you are reading. Are the sources themselves reliable? You even may want to look at the original sources yourself to make sure the author picked up the information accurately.

Is There Enough Information?

Read the following Indian folk tale about three blind men and an elephant. The story shows the need for having enough information to suit the purpose.

66 One day, three blind men bumped into an elephant.

'I wonder what this is,' said the first man. He put his arms around one of the elephant's legs. 'It's the trunk of a tree,' he said.

'No,' said the second man, as he touched one of the elephant's ears. 'This is a huge fan.'

The third man put his hand on the elephant's trunk. 'This is a very thick hose,' he said. 99

Why did all three men make the wrong decision about what they were encountering? The reason is that each man touched only part of the elephant. None of the men had enough information to make the correct decision.

Is the Information Reliable?

The following quotations include information about the early use of elephants for work and travel in India. Read each quotation and decide how reliable the information is.

66 The earliest evidence for the use of elephants is to be found on seals from Mohenjo-Daro (Indus Valley) about 2500–1500 B.C. The pictures distinctly [clearly] show the outline of a rug covering the [elephant's] back. Coins from the fifth century B.C. in Taxila, Punjab, show elephants; and terra-cotta [clay] toy elephants dating from the fourth century have been found in the same area. 99

66 Quite by chance I heard about a group of . . . jungle people who antedate [came before] the early Aryan invaders who swept over India. . . . These are

elephant people. As far back as any one can remember, they have taken care of elephants. They understand elephants as no one else does. They grow up with elephants, and the elephants with them.

[When I spoke to seventeen-year-old Ashoka, he told me:] 'There are twenty-five of us in our village. We have six elephants to care for; they belong to the government, but we are the *mahouts* [elephant trainers] . . . . We are clearing land and bringing in timber. When the job is done here we will move to another spot.'

. . . Then Ashoka . . . signals in some way to an elephant, steps . . . up on the elephant's back and rides away. **99**

What are the first author's sources of information? The sources are objects dating from thousands of years ago. We can assume that such sources are accurate. The second author's source is the memories and legends (stories from the past) of a group of people. Those memories and legends, like folk tales, may have a certain amount of truth in them, but we cannot be sure. In general, the writings of historians and other experts who study the past are reliable. Legends and fictional (made-up) stories probably are not reliable.

Skills Practice

1. How are the three quotations you read in this lesson different? How are they alike?
2. Which quotation best helped you understand the elephant's place in Indian life today?
3. Did the third quotation provide enough information for you to know how Ashoka feels about elephants? Explain your answer.
4. Would the three quotations taken together give you enough information to prepare a report on the history and modern-day use of elephants in India? If not, where else might you look for such information?
5. Suppose you were assigned to prepare a report on how animals have been used for work and travel throughout history. Which of the following sources of information would be reliable ones for your report? Which might not be reliable? Explain your answers.
   - an encyclopedia article about animals
   - a book of legends about animals and their relationships with people
   - a book on the taming of animals by a well-known archaeologist and historian
   - a fictional story about a brother and sister and their pet elephant living in the Indus Valley in 2000 B.C.

Chapter 20 Review

Chapter Summary

Lesson 1   The Countries of the Middle East—The climate of Middle Eastern countries is generally dry. All Middle Eastern countries but Israel are Muslim. Most of the people in the Middle East—except in the countries of Israel, Turkey, Iran, and Afghanistan—are Arabs. Recent wars in the Middle East have hurt many countries. The discovery of oil has made some countries in the area wealthy.

Lesson 2   India and Its Neighbors—The monsoon winds affect the climate of the Indian subcontinent by bringing moisture to most parts of the region. Most people in South Asia are farmers. However, as the population of the region grows, cities also are growing rapidly.

Write your answers on a separate sheet of paper.

Testing Key Words, People, and Places

Part A

Match each definition with the correct key word in the list.

1. a seasonal wind that occurs in the Indian Ocean and South Asia
2. manufacturing jobs, either in homes or in small workshops
3. a Muslim religious leader or teacher
4. a limitation on the flow of goods between countries

   a. mullah   **c. monsoon**
   b. embargo   **d. cottage industry**

Part B

Match each description with the correct group.

1. The original inhabitants and majority group of Ceylon
2. People who came to Ceylon from southern India and make up about one-fifth of the population

   a. Singhalese   **b.** Tamil

Testing Main Ideas

Choose the best answer for each question.

1. Which description fits most of the people on the Arabian Peninsula?
   a. They are both Arabs and Muslims.
   b. They are Muslims but not Arabs.
   c. They are neither Arabs nor Muslims.
2. Why did Iran's religious leaders lead a revolt?
   a. They wanted to build more industries.
   b. They did not like the way Western culture was affecting Iran.
   c. They wanted the country to have a communist government.
3. Which group of people became refugees when Israel became a country?
   a. Ottoman Turks
   b. Palestinians
   c. Egyptians
4. Where do most of the oil reserves in the Middle East lie?
   a. in the Anatolian Peninsula
   b. in the Arabian Peninsula
   c. in the Tigris-Euphrates Valley

5. What effect do the monsoon winds have on India's climate?
   a. Heavy rains fall in summer.
   b. Little rain falls all year.
   c. Heavy rains fall in winter.
6. How do most people in India make their living?
   a. business and commerce
   b. nomadic herding
   c. farming
7. Which South Asian country is nearest the Himalayan Mountains?
   a. Nepal
   b. Ceylon
   c. Bangladesh
8. Which river irrigates many of the farms in Pakistan?
   a. Ganges
   b. Indus
   c. Mekong
9. How many people live in India?
   a. about 80 million
   b. about 800 million
   c. about 8 billion

Testing Skills

1. **Evaluating information.** For each pair of sources, pick the one that probably is the best source of factual information. Explain your answer.
   a. a biography of an actor or an article in a fan magazine
   b. a book with many statistics or a book with no statistics
   c. an account of the United States Civil War by someone from the South or someone from the North

2. **Using the parts of a textbook.** Tell how you can use each part of this textbook to find information. Describe the kinds of information you can find in each section.
   a. Glossary
   b. Table of contents
   c. Index
   d. Gazetteer
   e. Facts About Countries
   f. Map and Globe Introduction
   g. Atlas
3. **Identifying cause-and-effect relationships.** Tell what effects occurred for each of the causes listed below.
   a. Religious leaders in Iran did not like the way Western culture was changing their country.
   b. OPEC was formed in 1960.
   c. Hindus and Muslims could not get along in colonial India.

Activities

1. Look in the library for articles about the Arab-Israeli conflict in the Middle East. Make sure that you examine articles from the Arab and the Israeli points of view. Summarize the major arguments of each side in the conflict.
2. Imagine that you worked for an international oil company and were sent to Saudi Arabia. What questions would you have about the country? What sources would you examine to find answers to your questions?

425

The Countries of Southeast Asia and Oceania Today

A hundred years ago, Southeast Asia and Oceania seemed like faraway places. They were the kinds of places that most Westerners only saw in the movies or read about in books. Such names as Burma, Bali, and Siam brought forth pictures of a different world. The place you see in the picture, Angkor Wat (än′kər wät′) in Cambodia, is one of those places people dreamed about.

As you read this chapter, you will learn about the countries of Southeast Asia and the Pacific Islands as they exist today. You will learn how these countries changed from faraway places to familiar names. The lessons in the chapter are listed below.

Lesson 1   The Countries of Southeast Asia

Lesson 2   Oceania Today

Lesson 1 The Countries of Southeast Asia

 LOOKING AHEAD As you read, look for—

Key words, people, and **places:**

martial law

Pol Pot
Ferdinand Marcos
Corazon Aquino

Borneo
Java

Answers to these questions about **main ideas:**

1. How were the cultures of Southeast Asia influenced by India and China?
2. How have conflicts hurt the people of mainland Southeast Asia?
3. What are the major economic activities of the island countries of Southeast Asia?
4. How have Southeast Asians been disappointed since achieving self-rule?

Southeast Asia includes the mainland countries of Burma, Thailand, Laos, Cambodia, and Vietnam. The region also includes the island countries of Singapore, Indonesia, the Philippines, and Brunei (brü nī'). One country, Malaysia, is both a mainland and an island country.

Brunei shares Borneo—the world's third-largest island—with Indonesia and Malaysia. Find Brunei on the map on page 372. Then, point with your finger to each of the other nine countries of Southeast Asia.

Land and People

All of Southeast Asia has a hot, tropical climate. The tip of the Malay Peninsula and all the island countries, except the Philippines, are wet all during the year. The rest of the region has one dry season.

Two types of natural vegetation can be found in Southeast Asia. One type, broadleaf deciduous forest, is located away from the coasts on the mainland. Look back at the map on pages 38–39 to find the natural vegetation for Southeast Asia's islands and coastal areas.

Through the centuries, the cultures of Southeast Asia have been greatly influenced by India and China. Learning about these influences can help you understand the people of Southeast Asia.

Indian influence began in the area more than 1500 years ago, when Indian traders entered the area. They spread their culture and the Hindu and Buddhist religions as they sold their products. Today strong traces of Indian culture remain in Thailand, Burma, Cambodia, Malaysia, and Indonesia. People on the Indonesian island of Bali still practice a form of the Hindu religion. Most people on the mainland follow Buddhism.

Indian influences are seen everywhere—in ancient ruins, in ways of cooking, and in music and dance. Indian words also have entered the various languages heard in the region. When India came under Muslim rule,

Singapore is densely populated and very prosperous.

traders brought this new religion and Arabic script to present-day Malaysia and Indonesia.

China's influence in Southeast Asia came from migration. From the hill country of South China, people moved south to reach fertile river valleys. Some arrived thousands of years ago. Others have come in the last hundred years. Today most languages spoken in mainland Southeast Asia are related to Chinese. Ancient Chinese culture still influences how people think and act.

The Mainland Countries

The mainland countries of Southeast Asia once were known as the "world's rice bowl." Surplus crops of rice were grown in the fertile soil of the river valleys in Vietnam, Cambodia, Laos, Thailand, and Burma. Now most of these countries no longer grow enough food for their own needs.

Vietnam. Before the French colonists arrived in Vietnam, most of the people lived on small farms. During the French period, however, life changed. Some people moved to cities to work in factories. Wealthy landowners took over most of the farms.

After the communist victory, the government took control of all farms and industries in the country. People who had left their farms during the war returned. However, Vietnam's farms have not recovered from the war. The country must import much of its food.

Many thousands of people fled from Vietnam after the war. Some of these people—known as the "boat people"—left in small boats to face the dangers of the open sea. Many drowned, but some have been able to start new lives in countries around the world.

Cambodia. For several years after World War II, Cambodia remained peaceful. Then, in 1969, the war in Vietnam spilled into Cambodia. The government, with help from the United States, began a war against Cambodian and Vietnamese communists. The communists won the war in April, 1975. Over 100,000 Cambodians died in the fighting.

The new communist leader of Cambodia was Pol Pot. He changed the name of the country to Kampuchea (kam′pü chē′ə). Pol Pot also tried to change the entire way of life in Cambodia. He wanted all Cambodians to live as farmers in the countryside. The cities were emptied, and people were forced to clear the forests to make more farmland. More than a million people were murdered by Pol Pot's government, and thousands of refugees escaped to neighboring Thailand.

Pol Pot's brutal effort to change Cambodia failed. In 1979 the Vietnamese invaded the country and overthrew his government. The name of the country was changed back to Cambodia.

Laos. Almost all of Laos is covered by heavily wooded mountains. The people are mostly rural and earn their living as subsistence farmers. Laos has no industries.

The isolation of the hill country did not keep Laos out of war during the 1970s. Thai troops, supported by United States planes, fought North Vietnamese soldiers in Laos between 1970 and 1975. The communists took over the country in 1975.

Thailand. Thailand is the richest country on the mainland. It is the only country still exporting large amounts of rice. Thailand also is the only country in the region with a free enterprise, market economy.

About three-fourths of the Thai people are farmers. However, since the 1960s, Thailand's industries have grown. The Thais assemble automobiles and electronic equipment. They also manufacture drugs and textiles.

Burma. Since 1962, Burma has had a socialist government that does not allow private enterprise. The government has turned down offers of foreign aid and keeps most visitors out of the country. Burma also is among the poorest countries in the world, with an average income of less than two hundred dollars a year. Burma is rich in mineral and agricultural resources. It also has an improving educational system.

The Island Countries

Brunei, the Philippines, Indonesia, Malaysia, and Singapore sit in a huge area between the Indian and Pacific oceans. The islands of Indonesia alone stretch for 3,200 miles, longer than the distance between Seattle and Miami.

Except for Brunei, all the island countries have large populations. Indonesia has the world's fifth largest population. In fact, the island of Java in Indonesia is one of the most densely populated places in the world. Look at pages 546–553 and find the populations for the Southeast Asian island countries.

Most people in the region are farmers. Crops include coconuts, coffee, rubber, bananas, sugar cane, peanuts, corn, rice, pineapples, and palm oil. Lumbering also provides income for the island countries. Many of the hardwoods used for furniture, such as teak, mahogany, and ebony, come from the islands' rainforests.

The island countries have many valuable minerals. Malaysia produces over one-third of the world's tin. Nickel, iron, and bauxite also are mined.

Brunei and Indonesia have large oil deposits. In fact, about 90 percent of Brunei's income comes from oil.

Manufacturing is the chief occupation in Singapore. Only 1 percent of the people are farmers. The industries of Singapore include shipbuilding, oil refining, electronics, textiles, and food processing. The other island countries manufacture rubber goods, steel, and chemicals.

Working Toward Stable Governments

When colonialism ended, the people of Southeast Asia hoped for better lives. They felt that self-government would help them economically and give them peace. Instead, war and political unrest have filled the region.

You have read about the wars on the mainland that led to communist governments in Vietnam, Cambodia, and Laos. The other two mainland countries had political problems too. Military coups overthrew the elected governments of both Thailand and Burma.

Communists have created tension in both Indonesia and the Philippines. For example, communists in Indonesia tried to take over the government in 1965. The army defeated the rebels.

Linking Past and Present

Bali: The Island of the Arts

One island—the island of Bali—stands apart from all the rest of the 13,600 Indonesian islands. One way that Bali stands apart is in the religion of its people. They follow a faith called Bali-Hinduism. This religion contains parts of Hinduism and the ancient religions of Bali and Java.

However, the most unusual part of Balinese culture is the importance of art in everyday life. The visual and performing arts practiced in Bali include the dance you see in the picture. A unique orchestra called a gamelan accompanies the dancers. The Balinese also perform ancient Hindu stories using the shadows cast by flat leather puppets. Beautiful wood carvings decorate temples and many homes. Even the colorful clothes worn by the Balinese people are works of fine art.

President Corazon Aquino is welcomed in the city of Davao. She became Philippine president in 1986.

The Philippines had a stable government for many years under Ferdinand Marcos. However, Marcos was very corrupt. He took money intended to help poor people and used it for himself. He also favored his friends, many of whom were wealthy landowners. For many years he ruled under **martial law.** That is, he ruled with the army and took away many of the people's rights.

Protests against the government forced Marcos to hold elections in 1985. Marcos won. However, many people thought that Marcos had won the election by cheating. Protests began again, and he was forced to leave the country in 1986. The losing candidate, Corazon Aquino, took over as president.

Reviewing the Lesson

Recalling Key Words, People, and Places
1. What is the key word that defines military rule?
2. Which country once was ruled by Pol Pot?
3. What island is shared by the countries of Indonesia, Malaysia, and Brunei?

Remembering Main Ideas
1. Which two religions entered Southeast Asia from India?
2. Which country in mainland Southeast Asia has a free enterprise system?
3. How do most people of the island countries make a living?
4. Why did the people of the Philippines protest the rule of Ferdinand Marcos?

Thinking Things Over
Do you think that stable governments can help the economies of Southeast Asian countries? Explain your answer.

Lesson 2   Oceania Today

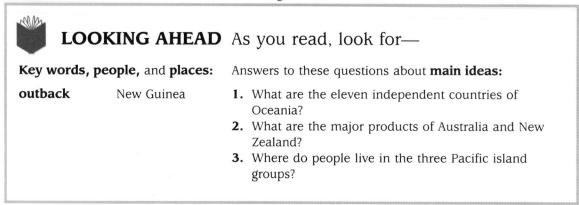

LOOKING AHEAD As you read, look for—

Key words, people, and **places:**

outback   New Guinea

Answers to these questions about **main ideas:**

1. What are the eleven independent countries of Oceania?
2. What are the major products of Australia and New Zealand?
3. Where do people live in the three Pacific island groups?

The large Pacific island nations are Japan, Indonesia, the Philippines, and Taiwan. They lie near the mainland of Asia and are linked to that continent by history, language, religion, and ethnic background. Farther out into the Pacific Ocean are islands, and one island continent, that are not linked to Asia in these ways. They are the islands of Oceania.

Land and People

Look at the map of Oceania on page 434. Notice that all the islands shown on the map—except for Australia and Tasmania—are grouped into Melanesia, Micronesia, or Polynesia. Find the island of New Guinea (gin′ē), which is the world's second-largest island. To which group of islands does New Guinea belong?

In addition to Australia and New Zealand, nine independent countries are found among the thousands of Pacific islands. These countries include Papua New Guinea, Fiji, Tonga, Kiribati (kir′ə bäs), Tuvalu, Nauru (nä ü′rü), Vanuatu (vä′nü ä′tü), the Solomon Islands, and Western Samoa. Point to each of the eleven countries on the map on page 434. Remember that the names of countries are written in all capital letters so that they stand out from other names on the map.

Australia and New Zealand

The British began to settle Australia and New Zealand about two hundred years ago. Since that time, the two countries have had much in common.

Australia. Australia lies about 2,000 miles to the southeast of mainland Asia. British explorers found a vast, largely empty land. Only about 300,000 Aborigines lived on the continent then, occupying a landmass almost as large as the United States. Today only about 100,000 Aborigines are left in Australia.

The land that early European settlers found was mostly flat. Low mountains ran down the east coast, but west of these mountains Europeans found plains and plateaus extending across the continent. Much of the land was very dry, so the earliest settlers lived along the eastern coast. These settlers

432

Bark painting is an old art form in Australia. Aborigine artists first go into the forests to strip sheets of bark from trees. After the bark is trimmed, cured, and dried, it is ready to be painted. The artists make brushes out of strips of bark, green twigs, feathers, or leaf fibers.

One famous type of bark painting is known as X-ray painting. It is generally done in several colors on a plain red background. As you can see at the right, an X-ray painting of an animal, for instance, shows not only its face and legs and coat, but its heart and lungs and other internal organs. This style reflects the belief that life is more than what is visible on the outside.

These Aborigines work on a ranch in Australia. Its ranches are leading exporters of beef and the world's largest exporters of wool. Aborigine ancestors probably were from Southeast Asia. Aborigines have inhabited Australia for 40,000 years.

established the cities of Sydney, Melbourne, and Brisbane.

Australia's dry climate was ideal for sheep herding and cattle grazing. Look back at the map on pages 64–65 to find how Australians use their land. The settlers built large ranches in the interior, which they called the outback. An **outback** is a thinly settled area of a country. Where the climate allowed, wheat farming began. Today wool, meat, dairy products, and wheat remain four of Australia's most important exports.

In addition to farming, Australia has developed many industries and mineral resources. Important minerals include iron ore, coal, copper, lead, zinc, oil, uranium, and natural gas.

During World War II Australia was threatened by Japanese invasion and drew closer to its wartime ally, the United States, whose army and navy were pushing back the Japanese advances. Today, Australians live much as Americans do. Most live in large cities, and most have service jobs.

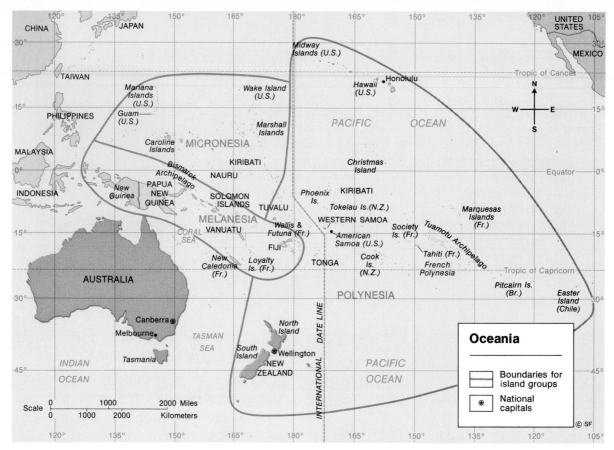

Map Study

Oceania is made up of the continent of Australia plus the islands of the central and south Pacific. These Pacific islands are grouped into main divisions: Micronesia, Melanesia, and what other group? Find *Cook Is. (N.Z.)* on the map above. What does *Is.* stand for? What does *N.Z.* stand for?

New Zealand. A thousand miles to the southeast of Australia lies the island country of New Zealand. It belongs to the island group know as Polynesia. New Zealand consists of two main islands and dozens of much smaller islands. It is a beautiful country with a high standard of living. In 1893 it became the first country to give women the right to vote. New Zealand was also among the first to give its people social security and pensions.

About 85 percent of New Zealand's three million people were born in New Zealand. Four-fifths of all New Zealanders live in cities, although it basically is an agricultural country.

Exports are dominated by dairy products, meat, and wool. However, New Zealand also exports chemicals, paper, processed foods, and textiles. Most of the farm products are shipped halfway around the world to England.

The Pacific Islands

Polynesia stretches from New Zealand in the southwest, to Easter Island in the east, and Hawaii in the north.

434

Many of the Polynesian islands are quite tiny and uninhabited. A few have fairly large populations. Near the center of Polynesia is Western Samoa, where more than 160,000 people live. Tahiti has 85,000 residents. Hawaii, the fiftieth state in the United States, has over 1 million people.

All Polynesian island groups are high islands, formed from underwater volcanoes. Many of them have good soil and ideal farming conditions. Coconuts, bananas, and breadfruit grow on most of the islands. Breadfruit is a fruit that, when cooked, has a texture very much like bread.

West of the Polynesian islands and north of New Zealand and Australia lie the Melanesian islands. They include New Guinea, and many hundreds of much smaller islands. The western half of New Guinea belongs to Indonesia, the eastern half is the independent country of Papau New Guinea. The Melanesian islands were the first Pacific islands to be settled.

Micronesia is made up of many small islands. The largest of these islands is Guam, and it is only thirty miles long and about five miles wide. Many of the Micronesia islands are low islands, formed from coral skeletons. This means that their soil is usually poor, and the islands are thinly populated. Micronesia was the last Pacific Ocean island group to be settled.

Western Samoa is a country of small islands in the Pacific.

Reviewing the Lesson

Recalling Key Words, People, and Places
1. What key word is used to refer to the interior of Australia?
2. What is the world's second-largest island?

Remembering Main Ideas
1. Name the three groups of islands found in Oceania.
2. What are the main agricultural products of Australia?
3. Why are the low islands unable to support large populations?

Thinking Things Over
Many of the original people in the islands of Polynesia have very similar cultures. What does this fact suggest about the original settlement of the Polynesian islands?

435

Interpreting Different Kinds of Literature

When you read, it is important to know what kind of literature you are reading. All literature, or writing, falls into one of two main groups; fiction and nonfiction. Fiction is writing created by an author's imagination. Fiction includes short stories, novels, and other writings that tell about make-believe people and happenings. Nonfiction is factual writing. Nonfiction deals with real people and real events.

Fact or Fiction?

The following quotation is from a book called *The Shadow on the Hills*. It tells of the friendship between a boy, Bodo Schneider, and a hermit, Ebenezer Blitz. Bodo first meets Ebenezer when he is lost one day in a dense fog in the hills of South Australia.

❝ . . . He [Bodo] let out a strange sound that was more cry than gasp. Then he froze where he was. It was a figure, a human figure. It was wearing knee boots and a long cloak made from an old blue blanket . . . But most fearful of all was the face—a huge forehead, wizened [dried-up] cheeks, and fanatical [intense] eyes— entirely surrounded by a vast sea of white hair and a beard that hung down to the chest. The face was framed in it, like an owl peering from a shock [bundle] of white straw . . . ❞

The Shadow on the Hills is an example of fiction. As with any work of fiction, it has characters, plot, and setting. The characters are the people or animals in the story. The plot is what happens to those people or animals. The setting is where and when the story takes place.

The next quotation is from a legend of the Australian Aborigines, "Joongabilbil Brings Fire." It, too, is fiction.

❝ In [past] times, Joongabilbil the Chicken Hawk was a seacoast man, and he was able to make fire by flapping his wings. No one else could make fire in those far-off days; all the people shivered in the cold seasons, and ate their meat raw, for they could not cook it.

Kart-gart, kart-gart, kart-gart: all the womba, the people who lived then, would hear the flapping of Joongabilbil's wings as he rose high, high, high in the sky, then swooped down to set the grass alight [on fire]. The people would rush out to try to catch the fire while it was still burning, but it always went out before they could reach it. ❞

Does this legend have characters? Who are they? What is the setting? What do you think the rest of the plot of the legend might be?

Compare the quotations you have just read with the following, from *Australia*.

❝ The small clans [groups of related families] moved from place to place searching for food and water. The men carried their few possessions—spears . . . and boomerangs. They left behind for future use any simple tools they had made at a site. . .

To start a fire, sometimes Aboriginals rubbed two sticks or stones together. This made sparks for igniting [setting on fire] a mound of dry grass. When possible, wood from small trees was used for fuel. ❞

This quotation is an example of nonfiction. The author's purpose is to give her readers facts about the Aborigines of Australia. Turn to the biography of Mohandas Gandhi that appears at the end of this unit. It, too, is nonfiction.

Another Form of Writing: Poetry

The quotations you have just read are all written in the nonpoetic form of writing called prose. Following is part of the poem "Lyrebirds" (līr′bėrdz′) by Judith Wright.

❝ Over the west side of this mountain,
that's lyrebird country.
I could go down there, they say,
in the early morning,
and I'd see them, I'd hear them.

Ten years, and I have never gone.
I'll never go.
I'll never see the lyrebirds—
the few, the shy, the fabulous,
the dying poets. ❞

Although this poem does not use rhyme, it does have the special rhythm of poetry. It is a lyric poem—that is, a poem in which the author expresses personal feelings about a subject.

Skills Practice

Read the following book descriptions. Tell whether each book is fiction or nonfiction.

1. *Australian Legendary Tales* by Catherine Parker. This is a collection of folk tales from Australia.
2. *Red Earth, Blue Sky: The Australian Outback* by Margaret Rau. Illustrated with photographs, this book describes the land and people of the Australian interior.
3. *Free Spirit: Evonne Goolagong* by D. J. Herda. This is the biography of the tennis star, who is an Aborigine.
4. *Blue Fin* by Colin Thiele. This award-winning book tells of a boy's seafaring adventures off Australia.

Chapter 21 Review

Chapter Summary

Lesson 1   The Countries of Southeast Asia—All of Southeast Asia has been influenced by the cultures of China and India. Recently, most of the mainland countries of Southeast Asia have had major wars. The island countries of Southeast Asia rely on farming. Communists, military coups, and corrupt rulers have hurt the chances of having stable governments in the region.

Lesson 2   Oceania Today—Many islands and groups of islands in Oceania are independent countries. Australia and New Zealand are urban and industrialized. However, farming and ranching are important in both Australia and New Zealand. The Pacific island countries rely on farming, tourism, and fishing.

Write your answers on a separate sheet of paper.

Testing Key Words, People, and Places

Part A
Choose the key word that best completes each sentence.

1. The interior of Australia, used mainly for raising livestock, is called the _____.
2. When normal laws are taken away and the military runs the country, it is called _____.
   a. martial law
   b. outback

Part B
Choose the person or place that best completes each sentence.

1. The communist leader who took over the country of Cambodia in 1975 was
   a. Pol Pot.
   b. Mao Zedong.
   c. Corazon Aquino.
2. Brunei, Malaysia, and Indonesia share the world's third largest island called
   a. Java.
   b. Singapore.
   c. Borneo.
3. The person who became president of the Philippines in 1986 was
   a. Corazon Aquino.
   b. Ho Chi Minh.
   c. Ferdinand Marcos.
4. The island which is shared by Indonesia and an independent country and is the world's second largest island is
   a. Borneo.
   b. New Guinea.
   c. Hong Kong.

Testing Main Ideas
Answer these questions.

1. What type of climate is found throughout Southeast Asia?
2. Which country had the greatest influence on the religions of Southeast Asia?
3. Who are the "boat people" of Vietnam?

4. How do most people in Indonesia and the Philippines make a living?

5. What events caused the people of the Philippines to rise up against their president?

6. Which island in Oceania is also a continent and a country?

7. What are the major exports of the country of New Zealand?

8. Which group of Pacific islands were the first to be settled?

Testing Skills

1. Interpreting different kinds of literature. Read the following book descriptions. Tell whether you think each book or story is fiction or nonfiction.

   a. "The Day Grandfather Tickled a Tiger" by Ruskin Bond. This story tells of a man who tickles a tiger in a zoo because he mistakenly believes the tiger to be tame.

   b. *The Ways of Tigers* by George B. Schaller. This book reports on a study of wildlife in the Kanha National Park in India.

   c. *Hawaiian Myths of Earth, Sea, and Sky* by Vivian L. Thompson. This book retells a number of the myths and legends of the people of Hawaii.

2. Writing letters to obtain information. Write a letter to a tourist office of a country in Oceania. Ask for specific information about a vacation on a Pacific island.

3. Ranking land masses from largest to smallest. Make a bar graph using the information below. Arrange the countries in order based on size, beginning with the largest country first.

Thailand	198,500 square miles
Kiribati	266 square miles
Malaysia	127,316 square miles
Philippines	115,831 square miles
Indonesia	741,101 square miles

Activities

1. Many Australian animals, such as the wombat and the duckbilled platypus, are not found in any other part of the world. Do a research project on a unique Australian animal. Ask your teacher if you may present your report to the class.

2. List several countries in Southeast Asia. Use an almanac to discover the kind of government each of them has. For example, do they have a democratic government or a communist government? Then, make a table, grouping the countries with similar kinds of government.

3. If you can, locate some recordings of Southeast Asian music in your school or local library. Discover how this music is different from or similar to music played in the United States and Europe. Do you like the way this music sounds? Why or why not?

Chapter 22

The Countries of East Asia Today

In this century, no region has changed as much—or as often—as East Asia. The countries of East Asia have changed because of wars they won. They also have changed because of wars they lost. The countries of East Asia have built new industries and have changed the ways their people make a living. The picture shows billboards along a street in China today. As recently as 1976, you would not have seen such advertising in China.

As you read this chapter, you will learn about the many changes that have occurred in East Asia. You also will learn how the countries in this region have grown in importance. The lessons in the chapter are listed below.

Lesson 1   China, Taiwan, and Mongolia

Lesson 2   Japan and Korea

Lesson 1   China, Taiwan, and Mongolia

LOOKING AHEAD As you read, look for—

Key words, people, and **places:**

commune
moderate

Deng Xiaoping

Gobi Desert

Answers to these questions about **main ideas:**

1. What is the climate like in East Asia?
2. How do people make a living in Hong Kong, Taiwan, and Mongolia?
3. What were Mao Zedong's plans for changing China?
4. How has China changed since the death of Mao?

"A man who has committed a mistake and doesn't correct it is committing another mistake." This statement was written by Confucius (kən-fyü′shəs), the most honored teacher and thinker in Chinese history. The Chinese have used the sayings of Confucius to guide their actions for 2,500 years.

When the Chinese communists took over the country in 1949, they set out to correct many mistakes of the past. In doing so, they committed some new mistakes. As you read this lesson, you will learn about the actions taken by the Chinese communists and the new direction the country has taken recently.

Land and People

Southern China has a wet climate and northern China a dry climate. In the warm south, rice grows very well. Wheat and corn are raised in the north. To the west is the high cold land known as Tibet, now a part of China. Few people live in Tibet because of its high mountains and deserts. Eastern China is very crowded.

The Gobi Desert covers most of Mongolia. This high land is dry because moisture is blocked by mountains. Look back at the map on page 378. Trace the mountains surrounding the Gobi Desert. The natural vegetation of Mongolia is mostly desert scrub, but the eastern part of the country contains grasslands. Most of Mongolia's land is used for nomadic herding.

Taiwan has the same warm, wet climate that is found in southern China. Therefore, the people of Taiwan grow the same crops found in southern China.

Hong Kong, Taiwan, and Mongolia

You read about the Opium War that took place in China in 1839. The British forced the Chinese to sign a treaty at the end of the war. The treaty gave the port city of Hong Kong to the British. Since that time, the Crown Colony of Hong Kong has been an important British naval base and trade center.

The colony of Hong Kong has only 409 square miles of area. The 35 square miles of city are crowded but orderly. Hong Kong has a market economy.

Hong Kong is one of the world's most densely populated cities. It produces many products for export around the world.

Its industries make many products for sale in the West. Under the treaty, the British have agreed to turn over this city to China in 1997. China has stated that Hong Kong will be allowed to continue its capitalist ways.

Taiwan, like Hong Kong, produces all kinds of industrial products for export, especially to the United States. When the communists won the civil war in China, the losing government took over Taiwan. Even today, China does not recognize Taiwan's independence.

Mongolia is very different from either Hong Kong or Taiwan. Its people are not Chinese, but Mongols. Mongolia became independent of China in 1911.

The country is larger than Texas but has fewer than two million people. The country has a communist government and is a close ally of the Soviet Union.

The Communists Remake China

In 1949 the communists under Mao Zedong won control of China. Probably in all of China's long history, no government ever changed the way people lived more than the communists did. They ended all private ownership. In the cities, stores and factories became the property of the government.

At first heavy industry was emphasized. Steel mills and factories that built machinery were developed. China

442

has a rich supply of raw materials, and the new government opened mines and oil fields.

In the rural areas, where four-fifths of the people live, both wealthy land-owners and poor peasant farmers had to surrender their property. Many rich landowners even lost their lives. How-ever, most farmers did not own land. They were extremely poor and had nothing to lose by following the gov-ernment plan.

Small fields were combined into large fields. Giant collectives farms called **communes** were formed. A commune included many villages and perhaps fifty thousand people. Each commune was given a production goal, and each commune member was given a specific task. The task might be field work such as planting, weeding, and harvesting. It might include building terraces on a mountainside or planting trees, or it might involve building roads or dams.

The new China relied on the labor of its own people. At first very little ma-chinery was used on farms. The people worked very hard and received very lit-tle. In the evenings they had to attend meetings. There they were told that the ways of the past were over.

In some ways China became better. Heavy industry was developed in China for the first time, and food production increased greatly. Clinics were set up in the communes and the health of the

Linking Past and Present

The Unusual Tomb of Shi Huangdi

The clay soldiers you see in the pic-ture are among 7,500 figures found in an underground tomb. The tomb is near the central Chinese city of Xi'an (shē'än'). Thought to be a model of the universe, the tomb is several miles wide. The Chinese emperor Shi Huangdi, who died in 210 B.C., is buried there. He is the same emperor who began building the Great Wall of China.

Shi Huangdi was a harsh ruler who used force to accomplish his goals. He murdered thousands of people who op-posed him. Many others died building his Great Wall. Shi Huangdi even be-lieved that he could rule a kingdom af-ter he died by using force. Notice that

the clay soldiers are extending open hands. These hands once held weapons. Shi Huangdi planned to use these armed soldiers to conquer a new kingdom in the afterlife.

In 1984 President Ronald Reagan of the United States met with China's most powerful leader, Deng Xiaoping.

people improved. Schools became available for all children.

Communist planners realized, however, that they were in trouble. Despite all the goals and planning, the communes were not producing enough food. Factories were turning out goods that were not well made. People were getting tired of working hard with little pay and few pleasures.

In 1966 Mao and his supporters thought they had the answer. They believed China needed another revolution. This "Cultural Revolution" would overthrow those people who still held on to the ways of the past. For the next ten years China suffered while Mao's new revolution was begun.

Schools closed for four years and teachers were sent to work in the fields. Gangs roamed the countryside smashing ancient monuments. For a while it looked as if China would be torn apart. By now many people did not agree with Mao, but they were afraid to speak out.

China Today

In 1976 Mao died. After a brief struggle, a new group with Deng Xiaoping (dung´ shyou´ping´) as spokesman came into power. They were **moderates** who did not hold extreme views as Mao had. They kept many communist ideas but also allowed some private ownership. In 1988 Deng stepped down and had Zhao Zyiang (jou´ zèr´yäng´) made chief spokesman.

The country still had a communist economy, but the commune system changed. Some commune land was divided among families. They had the responsibility for meeting the government's production goals but could grow food on private plots and sell it.

The new directions made a big difference. Farmers worked harder now that they were working partly for themselves. They produced much more food than before, and many were able to save money. Communes bought small tractors and other farm machinery. The people built new houses, and some

444

This sign on the main street of Beijing urges one-child families.

China has invited foreign companies to help build the country's economy. Japanese, American, and European companies are now trying to work out ways of doing business in China in partnership with the communist Chinese government.

All of this progress is hurt by one of China's main problems, its huge population. Most families used to have at least three or four children, but the government encourages one-child families. Posters such as the one on this page are seen all over China. Families with one child are paid a bonus, and their child receives a free education. Families with two children must pay for the second child's education. Families with three or more children must pay heavy taxes. In this way China is slowing its population growth.

Reviewing the Lesson

Recalling Key Words, People, and Places
1. Identify the key words defined below:
    a. a giant collective farm
    b. a person who holds views that are not extreme
2. Which Chinese political leader led China toward greater economic freedom?
3. Where is the Gobi Desert located?

Remembering Main Ideas
1. What is the main difference between the climate of northern China and southern China?
2. What will happen to the British colony of Hong Kong in 1997?
3. Why did Mao Zedong want China to have a new revolution?
4. What changes were made in Chinese agriculture after Mao's death?

Thinking Things Over
What was life like for the people of rural China during the rule of Mao Zedong? How has life changed since Mao's death?

even bought such luxuries as radios, sewing machines, and bicyles.

City dwellers, too, earned extra money. Small private shops and businesses were allowed. The government would even loan money to someone who wanted to start a private shop. Larger stores and factories still were government-owned, but they were more concerned with quality than they had been previously.

Lesson 2 Japan and Korea

LOOKING AHEAD As you read, look for—

Key words, people, and **places:**

melting pot

Honshu Island
Kyushu Island

Answers to these questions about **main ideas:**

1. How do landforms and climate affect farming in Japan?
2. How do the economies of North and South Korea differ?
3. Where are Japan's main industrial cities located?
4. Why must the Japanese sell their products in other countries?

At the end of World War II the outlook for Japan certainly was not good. The country was defeated and its major cities were heavily bombed. Japan's colonies were gone. Its people were tired out by long years of war. United States soldiers occupied the country. Now, Japan is wealthy. Its people are well educated and healthy. They live comfortable lives. In this lesson you will learn about the present-day country of Japan. You also will learn about the countries of North and South Korea.

Land and People

Japan is a crowded island country. Its 120 million people live in an area smaller than California, and food can be grown on less than one-fifth of this area. About three-fourths of Japan is covered by steep mountains. However, Japan still can grow more rice than it needs. It grows many other food crops too. Such crops as tropical fruits are grown in the south and potatoes and wheat in the north. Obviously, the people have used their land to the fullest.

The four large islands of Japan are mostly mountainous. In most places the mountains drop directly to the sea, and the coastal plain is very narrow. In a few places the coastal plains spread out. These coastal plains are the most important food growing areas.

The rainy climate of Japan provides plenty of water for most crops. However, in some areas irrigation is needed. In southern Japan two or even three crops a year can be grown. In northern Japan cold, snowy winters make only one crop possible.

Fish is an important part of the Japanese diet. The long coastline is dotted with fishing villages. Fishers set off in small boats to catch fish near the shore. From larger ports, fleets of fishing ships roam the world's oceans.

Korea has three climate regions in a small area. You can see these climates by locating the Korean Peninsula on the map on pages 36-37. Notice that the southern tip of the peninsula has a warm climate that is wet all year. What are the other two climates of Korea?

The Two Koreas

The Korean people developed their own culture, but with Chinese influences. After World War II Korea was divided into a communist north and a noncommunist south.

The two countries could benefit from being united again. Most of Korea's minerals are in the mountainous north and most of the good farmland is in the south. South Korea has more than twice the population of North Korea. Both countries have industrialized heavily, but along different paths.

The market economy of South Korea has grown much faster than the command economy of the north. South Korea is now one of the world's leading producers of ships and electronics. Its industrial products are sold abroad to pay for imported raw materials.

Japan

Most Japanese share a common culture. Unlike the United States, Japan is not a **melting pot,** a country in which people of various cultures live together. Instead most Japanese share the same culture. Japan has kept many traditional values. For example, the Japanese value a strong sense of belonging and loyalty to a group. A person remains a member of a group always—whether the group is a family, a class, a work crew, or a team.

Many Japanese farmers have left the land and moved to the cities. In fact, most Japanese are now city-dwellers. They live in apartments and take trains or buses to get to their jobs.

Jobs are available in the cities. Every kind of manufactured product is made, from toothbrushes to TV sets, from

A Japanese fish market is shown below. Japan leads the world in tons of fish caught each year.

By the Way

Because Japan is such a crowded nation, the Japanese have limited space in which to live and work. They must make their lives fit into small places. However, their imaginations are free to roam as far as they wish them to go.

Because the Japanese love nature, they have developed art forms to bring nature into their homes. One form, called bonsai (bon′sī), is the art of growing miniature trees. This art form developed around A.D. 1000. Bonsai artists try to grow tiny trees that look exactly like large trees. Some bonsai plants are as small as 2 inches. Some bonsai artists even grow whole forests of miniature trees in a single tray.

---

cars to computers. Japan makes excellent electronic equipment. For example, the Japanese make computers, TV sets, video recorders, and radar equipment. Also, many people are employed in commerce, shipping, banking, and transportation.

Japan has four main urban industrial areas, all of them located near the sea. The chief industrial area sits on the eastern side of Honshu Island. Tokyo, the capital, is on the island. The port city of Yokohama is nearby. Together these cities form the second-largest urban area in the world. The Tokyo-Yokohama area is a leading trade and manufacturing center. It receives goods from all over the world and sends its manufactured goods around the world. Point to the city of Tokyo on the map on page 372.

The other three leading industrial areas also are trade centers. Nagoya (nä gô′yə) faces the sea and, like Tokyo, is on a broad plain. Osaka is on the quiet waters of the Inland Sea,

protected from the fierce winds that sometimes send waves crashing against ships docked in Yokohama and Nagoya. Kitakyushu (kē′tə kyü′shü), at the northern tip of Kyushu Island, is located near coal deposits. It is Japan's chief steel-making city. It also has the best position for trade with Korea and China.

Finding Markets for Japanese Goods

Japan is not rich in mineral resources. It has a little coal and less iron ore. Japan realized long ago that it would have to import most raw materials for its industry. To pay for these imports, it would have to sell to other countries.

Japan built a colonial empire in the early part of this century to supply both raw materials and markets. Korea, Taiwan, parts of China, and many Pacific Ocean islands were parts of this empire. In World War II Japan attempted to extend its empire farther into China and into all of Southeast Asia. With defeat, the entire empire collapsed. Japan was left with only its home islands. However, its need for raw materials and markets for its products remained.

Japan became a democracy after the war. Its new constitution did not allow Japan to have an army or navy. As Japan rebuilt its economy, having no military was an advantage. The country could then devote more of its energy and money to manufacturing. It did not have to spend money on military forces.

Until recently the Japanese people did not have much buying power. Wages were kept low so that Japanese products could be sold abroad at low prices. Gradually wages have risen, and most people now can afford to buy many products, even luxuries. Now, one of the chief markets for Japanese products is Japan itself.

Of course, Japan still needs to export in order to pay for such imports as petroleum, iron ore, coal, and cotton. Automobiles and electronic products are the leading exports. People around the world think Japan's products are well built.

Today other well-built products are being exported from such places as North and South Korea, Taiwan, Hong Kong, and Singapore. In these places wages are lower than in Japan. So the Japanese must work harder than ever to develop new products and to sell them abroad.

As Japanese trade grew, countries that bought Japanese products, such as

A Japanese factory in Tennessee

the United States, found that their own industries were hurt. They want Japan to limit its trade, but Japan does not want to do this. Instead, Japanese-owned factories, using local workers, are being set up in the United States and other countries. Japan continues to put a great deal of effort into keeping up its way of life.

Reviewing the Lesson

Recalling Key Words, People, and Places
1. What key word defines a place where people of many different cultures live together?
2. Tell where each place is located:
   a. Honshu Island
   b. Kyushu Island

Remembering Main Ideas
1. Where does most of the farming in Japan take place?
2. Why would both North and South Korea benefit from being reunited?
3. Which Japanese port city is sheltered from ocean storms?
4. Why do some countries want Japan to limit the amount of goods it sells?

Thinking Things Over
What might happen to Japan if the United States limited the amount of Japanese goods that could be sold in the United States?

Debating Issues

Do you ever discuss your opinions about a subject with someone who has very different opinions? If so, you have taken part in a kind of debate.

What Happens in a Debate

A debate is a discussion of different sides of an issue. Often a debate begins with the definition of a problem to be solved. Possible solutions to the problem then become issues to be debated. For example, you may feel the need for better communication among the classes in your school. In a discussion with your classmates, you may decide that putting out a school paper is one way to solve the communication problem. In preparation for a debate, you might state your solution this way, "Resolved, that the sixth-graders should put out a school newspaper to keep all students informed of school activities."

That resolution could then be debated. Students who agree that a school paper is a good idea would debate on the affirmative, or yes, side. Those who feel that a paper would take up too much class time or cost too much money would debate on the negative, or no, side. In a formal debate, the same number of speakers talk on each side. The sides take turns talking. Usually a time limit is set for each person's talk.

Preparing for a Debate

To have a good debate, you need to have a good resolution to discuss. A resolution may be a statement that you debate to determine whether it is true or false. An example would be, "Resolved, that communes are not producing enough food in China." Another kind of resolution is a proposed action that you debate to determine whether or not it should be carried out. An example would be, "Resolved, that communes in China should be broken up so that the land can be farmed by individuals." Which kind of resolution is the one about the school paper?

Here are some guidelines for making resolutions:

- Choose a resolution topic that fits with your knowledge and interests.
- Make sure the resolution is one that has no "right" opinion or answer. For example, a resolution that people should be kind to one another is not debatable.
- Limit the resolution to only one idea.
- Word the resolution clearly so that you do not waste time arguing over the meanings of words.

When your resolution is ready, members of the sides that will take part in the debate need to find arguments that support their side. Statistics and other facts can be used. The opinions of experts also can be used, though personal opinions should not be. When doing research for your side of a debate, try to think about what the other side will say. That way, you will be prepared to answer any argument they raise.

Skills Practice

1. Read each resolution below. Tell what kind of resolution each is: a true/false statement or a proposed action.
   - Resolved, that the Chinese are better off today than they were before the communists took over.
   - Resolved, that the United States should put quotas and high tariffs on Japanese goods to protect American products.
2. Choose one of the resolutions given above. Decide which side of the issue—affirmative or negative—you want to take. Give at least four sentences that support your side of the issue.
3. With a few classmates, discuss some issues related to Asia. Decide on one that would make a good topic for a debate. Follow the guidelines in this lesson to write a resolution. Then choose sides. Get together with the other students who are on the same side. Plan what research you need to do. After you have done your research, discuss your findings and decide who is going to talk about what in the debate. Finally, arrange with your teacher for a convenient time to hold your debate in class. Each person's talk should be limited to about five minutes.

Chapter Summary

Lesson 1 China, Taiwan, and Mongolia—China is so vast that it contains several climate regions. Mongolia's climate is very dry, so most land is used for nomadic herding. The British Crown Colony of Hong Kong will became a part of China in 1997. The communists, under Mao Zedong, took over China's government in 1949, and the losing government moved to Taiwan. Mao made many changes, including the "Cultural Revolution." However, upon Mao's death in 1976, China set off in a new direction under more moderate leadership.

Lesson 2 Japan and Korea—Japan is a crowded island country where the coastal plains are the best areas for growing crops. Korea is split into two countries: a communist North Korea and a noncommunist South Korea. As Japan industrialized, its people did not lose their traditional values. However, Japan has been able to change quickly, becoming a democracy and regaining its economic power after World War II. Japan relies on trade with other countries to get the raw materials it needs.

Write your answers on a separate sheet of paper.

Testing Key Words, People, and Places

Part A

Choose the key word from the list that best completes each sentence.

1. A person who does not hold extreme views is a _____.
2. A _____ is a place where people of many different cultures live together.
3. A giant farm in China where the government owns all the land is a _____.

    a. commune   **c. melting pot**
    b. moderate

Part B

Match each description with the correct person or place in the list.

1. the island where the capital of Japan is located
2. Japan's southernmost island, where the country's chief steel-making city is located
3. a moderate Chinese leader who led the country in the 1980s
4. a region of Mongolia

    a. Deng Xiaoping   **c.** Honshu Island
    b. Gobi Desert   **d.** Kyushu Island

Testing Main Ideas

Choose the answer that best completes each sentence.

1. The climate in southern China is
    a. warm and wet.
    b. warm and dry.
    c. cool and dry.
2. The area of the British colony of Hong Kong is
    a. 409 square miles.
    b. 4,900 square miles.
    c. 40,900 square miles.

3. In 1966 Mao and his supporters began a new revolution called the
   a. Green Revolution.
   b. Cultural Revolution.
   c. Industrial Revolution

4. China changed its communes after the death of Mao Zedong by
   a. allowing some private ownership.
   b. removing most communist managers.
   c. building new factories in rural areas.

5. The four large islands of Japan are mostly
   a. plateaus.
   b. plains.
   c. mountains and hills.

6. The economy of North Korea is
   a. a private enterprise system.
   b. a communist economy.
   c. a market economy.

7. All of Japan's main industrial areas are located
   a. on Japan's southern islands.
   b. in the middle of the islands.
   c. near the ocean.

8. Japan's major exports include such products as
   a. automobiles and electronics.
   b. iron ore and oil.
   c. cotton and citrus fruits.

Testing Skills

1. **Debating issues.** Choose to support or oppose each of the following resolutions. Then, write three or four sentences stating your point of view about each.

   a. Resolved, that the British should refuse to return their colony in Hong Kong to the Chinese.
   b. Resolved, that Japanese-owned factories should be encouraged to operate in the United States.

2. **Making circle graphs.** Make three circle graphs using the following statistics about Japan. Remember to give your graphs titles and label them correctly.

   a. More than three-fourths of Japan's people live in cities. Less than one-fourth live in rural areas.
   b. One-tenth of Japan's people are farmers and fishers, about one-third work in manufacturing, and about half are service workers. The rest have other jobs.
   c. The areas of each of Japan's four main islands are listed below.

Honshu	87,805 square miles
Hokkaido	30,144 square miles
Kyushu	14,114 square miles
Shikoku	7,049 square miles

Activities

1. Two books about Chinese history in the 1900s that you might read are: *The People of New China,* edited by Margaret Rau (New York: Julian Messner, 1978); and *China from Manchu to Mao* by John R. Roberson (New York: Atheneum, 1980).

2. Find some statistics about Japanese exports and imports. Make a bar graph or a line graph using these statistics.

Biography — Mohandas K. Gandhi

The people of India gave Mohandas Gandhi (mō′hən däs′ gän′dē) a name that means "Great Soul." In their language this word is "Mahatma" (mə hät′mə).

Mohandas K. Gandhi was born in 1869. He came to be considered a "great soul" because of his beliefs. He believed in truth above all else and in firmness. Gandhi also believed in not using violence to get one's way. Although India was ruled by Great Britain from 1858 to 1947, Gandhi and many other Indians wanted India to rule its own land. Gandhi became a leader in the struggle for Indian independence in 1920. He started programs in which the people did not pay taxes or go to British schools. He also led the people in developing work to make them independent of Great Britain and helped prepare Indians to govern themselves.

Gandhi first saw how Indians were mistreated in another British colony, South Africa. He went to South Africa as a young man to do legal work for one year. He soon saw that Indians living there were discriminated against. He stayed for twenty–one years working for Indian rights.

Back in India after his stay in South Africa, Gandhi continued working to end unfair treatment of all Indian people as well as fighting for India's independence. He was imprisoned for a total of seven years for his opposition to the British, in both the colony of South Africa and in India.

Gandhi wanted people of all faiths to live together in a united India. However, Hindus and Muslims fought each other. When the British finally freed India in 1947, due in part to Gandhi's efforts, they divided it into two countries. India was for the people of the Hindu faith. Pakistan became a country for those of the Muslim faith.

These two groups continued to fight bitterly over the divided India. Gandhi was unhappy with the situation. He decided to fast, or starve himself, to protest the fighting. After his fifth day of fasting, the leaders of the fighting groups agreed to stop fighting. Soon after that, however, a person who opposed Gandhi's teachings shot him to death in the Indian city of New Delhi. Mohandas "Mahatma" Gandhi died in 1948 at the age of seventy-eight.

Questions to Think About

1. What methods did Gandhi use in India's struggle for independence beginning in 1920?
2. People who have struggled for peaceful change have sometimes become the target of violence. Why do you suppose this is so?

Update: The Green Revolution Goes On

When the Green Revolution began, many Asian farmers were disappointed. They could not afford to buy fertilizers or pesticides or irrigation pumps. Was this the only way to increase their production of rice, their most important crop? Today agricultural scientists can answer no—there are better kinds of rice and better ways of farming.

The scientists began their work by collecting samples of different kinds of rice seeds. So far, they have collected samples of almost 100,000 different kinds of rice. Some kinds of rice have short, thick stems that can hold up heavy heads of grain. Other kinds of rice have particularly good flavor. Some kinds of rice grow well in dry climates or in poor soils. Other kinds of rice can resist attacks by insects and diseases, without the use of pesticides.

Scientists use these rice samples to develop new kinds of rice that combine the best qualities of many different kinds of rice. For example, thirteen kinds of rice were combined to develop a kind of rice called IR36. This rice can resist four of the worst rice diseases, and four of the most damaging insects. It grows quickly and does well in poor soils and dry climates.

Scientists also are teaching farmers about less costly ways to fertilize their

Using machines to harvest rice

fields. For example, tiny water plants, which will grow in rice fields, can supply the same nutrients as chemical fertilizers. In China and Vietnam, these water plants are called "green manure."

Using Your Geography Skills

1. Rice is the only grain that can grow in flooded fields. Use the climate map on pages 36–37 to decide why rice is so important to many Asian farmers.
2. Some people think it costs too much to store thousands of kinds of rice seeds for research. What might happen if some kinds of rice were allowed to die out?

Unit 5 Review

Write your answers on a separate sheet of paper.

Key Words

Use each key word in a sentence.

1. earthquake
2. high island
3. paddy
4. pesticide
5. aborigine
6. treaty
7. refugee
8. mullah
9. monsoon
10. martial law
11. outback
12. commune
13. moderate
14. melting pot

Main Ideas

Choose the best answer for each question.

1. How do most of the people of Asia earn a living?
   a. by subsistence farming
   b. by manufacturing
   c. by commercial farming

2. What is the most important food crop in most of Asia?
   a. bananas
   b. manioc
   c. rice

3. What is the goal of Asia's Green Revolution?
   a. to develop the economies of Asian countries
   b. to bring peace and stable governments to Asia
   c. to increase the amount of food grown on Asian farms

4. What is the most important mineral resource of Southwest Asia?
   a. gold
   b. petroleum
   c. tin

5. Where do most of the people of Asia live?
   a. in the fast-growing cities
   b. in the rural areas
   c. in the mountain and desert areas

6. Which religion began in India?
   a. Islam
   b. Hinduism
   c. Judaism

7. What is the ancestry of most people who now live in Australia and New Zealand?
   a. aboriginal
   b. European
   c. Asian

8. How did most of the great civilizations of Asia end?
   a. They were conquered by warlike nomads.
   b. Disease wiped out the leaders of the civilizations.
   c. Crop failures forced people to leave the area.

9. Why did Europeans want to open trade with Asia?
   a. to help Asians have a better life
   b. to educate Asians about democracy
   c. to increase the power and wealth of Europe

456

10. When did European countries realize that Japan had become a world power?
    a. when Japan defeated Russia in 1905
    b. when Japan invaded China in 1937
    c. when Japan bombed Pearl Harbor in 1941

11. When did most Asian countries achieve their independence?
    a. after World War I
    b. after World War II
    c. after the war in Vietnam

12. What happened to most of the Palestinians who once lived in Israel?
    a. They moved to refugee camps.
    b. They became Israelis.
    c. They migrated to the United States.

13. What kind of government do the countries of Indochina have now?
    a. communist
    b. capitalist
    c. democratic

14. Which island group in Oceania has the fewest people?
    a. Polynesia
    b. Micronesia
    c. Melanesia

15. Why must Japan buy from other countries?
    a. It lacks natural resources.
    b. Its technology is not modern.
    c. Its people are mostly farmers.

Skills

1. **Understanding different map projections.** Tell whether the answer to each question is Eckert-projection, interrupted-projection, or both.
    a. What type of a map has each square inch on the map equal to a certain number of square miles?
    b. What type of map splits up some ocean and land areas?
    c. What type of map shows the sizes of land areas correctly but distorts their shapes?

2. **Making a bar graph.** Construct a bar graph using these statistics about the highest mountains on the seven continents.

Asia, Everest	29,028 ft.
Africa, Kilimanjaro	19,340 ft.
N. America, McKinley	20,320 ft.
S. America, Aconcagua	22,834 ft.
Europe, Elbrus	18,510 ft.
Australia, Kosciusko	7,310 ft.
Antarctica, V. Massif	16,864 ft.

Essay

Select either the country of Japan or China. Then, imagine you are a person who was born in 1900. Describe how your life has changed in this century. Use the events in this unit to help you write your essay.

North America and South America
Political

International boundaries
⊛ National capitals
• Other cities

North Pole
ASIA
ARCTIC OCEAN
Arctic Circle
ICELAND
EUROPE
Greenland (DENMARK)
ALASKA (U.S.)
CANADA
Hudson Bay
NORTH AMERICA
Mackenzie R.
Vancouver
Columbia R.
Montreal
Ottawa
St. Lawrence R.
Great Lakes
Toronto
Chicago
New York City
Washington, D.C.
UNITED STATES
Missouri R.
Ohio R.
Mississippi R.
Los Angeles
Bermuda (Br.)
PACIFIC OCEAN
ATLANTIC OCEAN
Tropic of Cancer
Rio Grande
Gulf of Mexico
BAHAMAS
WEST INDIES
Virgin Is. (U.S.) (Br.)
ST. CHRISTOPHER AND NEVIS
ANTIGUA-BARBUDA
Guadeloupe (FRANCE)
DOMINICA
Martinique (FRANCE)
SAINT LUCIA
SAINT VINCENT & THE GRENADINES
BARBADOS
TRINIDAD AND TOBAGO
Havana
CUBA
HAITI
DOM. REP.
Puerto Rico (U.S.)
MEXICO
JAMAICA
Guadalajara
Mexico City
BELIZE
Belmopan
HONDURAS
GUATEMALA
Guatemala
San Salvador
Tegucigalpa
EL SALVADOR
NICARAGUA
Managua
CENTRAL AMERICA
San José
COSTA RICA
Panamá
PANAMA
CARIBBEAN SEA
Neth. Antilles (NETH.)
GRENADA
Caracas
VENEZUELA
Georgetown
Paramaribo
French Guiana (FRANCE)
Panama Canal
COLOMBIA
Bogotá
GUYANA
SURINAME
Orinoco R.
Quito
ECUADOR
Equator
Galápagos Islands (ECUADOR)
Amazon R.
SOUTH AMERICA
BRAZIL
PERU
Lima
Brasília
La Paz
BOLIVIA
Sucre
Rio de Janeiro
Tropic of Capricorn
PARAGUAY
Asunción
São Paulo
Paraná R.
CHILE
Córdoba
ARGENTINA
URUGUAY
Santiago
Buenos Aires
Montevideo
PACIFIC OCEAN
40° South Latitude
N
W E
S
0   500   1000 Miles
0 500 1000 Kilometers
Falkland Islands (Br.)
South Georgia I. (Falkland Is.)
Strait of Magellan
© SF

North America and South America

Countries such as Canada, Costa Rica, Jamaica, and Bolivia are part of the North American and South American continents. Together, nearly 700 million people live in more than thirty countries on these two continents, the Americas.

As you read this unit, you will learn about the land, people, and history of the Americas. You will study many countries to see what they are like today.

Before You Go On

Preview the unit. Read the chapter titles below. Which chapter do you think is mostly about geography?

Study the map. Name the countries that lie between Mexico and South America. What is this region called?

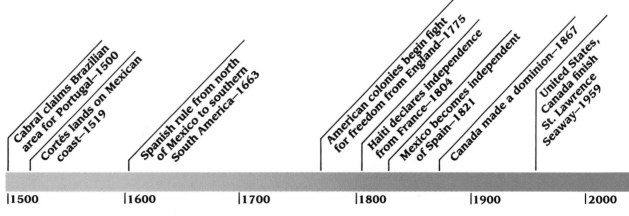

Cabral claims Brazilian area for Portugal–1500

Cortés lands on Mexican coast–1519

Spanish rule from north of Mexico to southern South America–1663

American colonies begin fight for freedom from England–1775

Haiti declares independence from France–1804

Mexico becomes independent of Spain–1821

Canada made a dominion–1867

United States, Canada finish St. Lawrence Seaway–1959

|1500 |1600 |1700 |1800 |1900 |2000

Chapter 23

The Land and the People of North and South America

The Americas are two huge continents that make up about 30 percent of the earth's land. Five of the world's eight largest cities sit on this land. The picture shows the world's most populous city, Mexico City.

As you read this chapter, you will learn about the features, resources, and people of the Americas. The lessons in the chapter are listed below.

Lesson 1   The Natural Environment of North America and South America

Lesson 2   Resources and Land Use in North America and South America

Lesson 3   The People of North America and South America

Lesson 1 The Natural Environment of North America and South America

📖 **LOOKING AHEAD** As you read, look for—

Key words, people, and **places:**

glacier
prairie
basin

Rocky Mountains
Central America

Andes Mountains
Patagonia
Pampas
Great Lakes
Amazon River
Mississippi River

Answers to these questions about **main ideas:**

1. What are some of the major landforms of North America and South America?
2. What are the major bodies of water found in the Americas?
3. How do climate and natural vegetation vary in North America?
4. How do climate and natural vegetation vary in South America?

Imagine you are far above the earth piloting an airplane above the vast continents of North and South America. Below you lie some of the world's most spectacular natural features. Notice the rugged snow-capped mountains towering in ranges over both continents. See the world's largest group of freshwater lakes—the Great Lakes—and the mighty rivers. Don't overlook the rolling plains that seem to stretch on forever. Find the deserts, valleys, and the islands, large and small, dotting the coastal waters. Massive forests blanket large areas too. Did you know that some of these are rainforests? As you would expect, lands that stretch north to south between the two polar regions have varied climates. Together, land and climate make up part of the story of North America and South America.

Landforms of the Americas

The Americas have all four kinds of landforms: mountains, hills, plateaus, and plains. Find the Rocky Mountains on the map on page 462. These mountains make up North America's longest mountain range and contain some of its most majestic peaks. Now look just west of the Rocky Mountains and find the ranges that border the coast. North America's highest peak, Mount McKinley, is here. North American Indians called this mountain *Denali,* meaning "the great one."

Use your finger to trace the mountains all the way south along the west coast of North America from Alaska through Central America. Central America is the narrow strip of land south of Mexico that connects the continents. It is considered part of North America. Note that the coastal mountain chain is nearly unbroken. Name four mountain ranges that you pass through here.

Crossing into South America, you come to a mountain range called the Andes. The Andes Mountains form South America's western backbone.

461

North Pole

ASIA

ARCTIC OCEAN

BEAUFORT SEA

BROOKS RANGE

Mt. McKinley ▲

Bering Strait

Gulf of Alaska

COAST MTS.

ROCKY MOUNTAINS

CASCADES

SIERRA NEVADA

GREAT PLAINS

Columbia R.

Colorado R.

SIERRA MADRE WEST

SIERRA MADRE EAST

Rio Grande

Greenland

Iceland

Arctic Circle

EUROPE

Baffin I.

Hudson Bay

CANADIAN SHIELD

Mackenzie R.

St. Lawrence R.

Newfoundland

ATLANTIC OCEAN

PACIFIC OCEAN

NORTH AMERICA

INTERIOR PLAINS

Mississippi R.

Missouri R.

Ohio R.

APPALACHIAN MTS.

COASTAL PLAIN

Great Lakes

Bermuda Is.

Tropic of Cancer

Gulf of Mexico

Yucatán Peninsula

Bahama Is.

Cuba

Jamaica

WEST INDIES

Hispaniola

Puerto Rico

CARIBBEAN SEA

CENTRAL AMERICA

Panama Canal

Galápagos Islands

Equator

LLANOS

Orinoco R.

GUIANA HIGHLANDS

ANDES MOUNTAINS

AMAZON BASIN

Amazon R.

SOUTH AMERICA

MATO GROSSO PLATEAU

BRAZILIAN HIGHLANDS

PACIFIC OCEAN

ATACAMA DESERT

ANDES MOUNTAINS

GRAN CHACO

Paraná R.

Paraguay R.

PAMPAS

Mt. Aconcagua ▲

Rio de la Plata

PATAGONIA

Falkland Islands

Strait of Magellan

South Georgia I.

Cape Horn

North America and South America
Physical

Land Elevation

Feet		Meters
14,000		4,000
7,000		2,000
1,500		500
700		200
0		0
Below Sea Level		Below Sea Level

—— International boundaries

▲ Mountain peaks

Ice packs

0   500   1000 Miles

0   500   1000 Kilometers

N
W   E
S

© SF

They are the world's longest mountain range and the second tallest after Asia's Himalayas. Find Mount Aconcagua (ä′kông kä′gwə), the highest peak in the Western Hemisphere, on the map on page 462.

Hilly regions border most mountain areas in North America. Note that the Appalachian Mountains in eastern North America have lower elevations than many of the western mountains. Actually, the Appalachians are mostly hills rather than true mountains. The Appalachians formed much earlier in the earth's history than the Rocky Mountains and other high mountains. Over the years, rains and winds have worn down the Appalachian peaks, making them lower and more rounded than the jagged peaks in the western Americas.

Most of the land in the Americas is made up of plateaus and plains. Patagonia in southern South America is a dry, windswept plateau in the shadow of the Andes. Some other plateau areas are nestled between mountains. The vast plains of North America have most of the continent's richest farmland. The Pampas, part of South America's plains region, are important grazing lands. In contrast, the plains around the Amazon River to the north are mostly forested, wet lowland areas.

Bodies of Water in the Americas

Think back again to your overhead view of the Americas. Some of the most impressive features of the American continents are its waters. Enormous Hudson Bay in the north cuts deeply into the land from the Atlantic Ocean. The bay is so close to the North Pole that much of it is frozen for part of the year.

The Great Lakes lie south of Hudson Bay. Glaciers carved out these five lakes thousands of years ago. **Glaciers** are huge ice sheets. They formed over large areas of the Northern Hemisphere when the earth's average temperature was much colder than it is now. Eventually temperatures rose, and most of the glaciers melted. Some of their waters collected in huge depressions scraped out by the ice, forming the Great Lakes.

Your overhead view lets you see great rivers surging through the Americas too. South America's Amazon River is the longest river on the two continents. On the whole earth, only Africa's Nile River is longer. In fact, we often say that the Amazon is the world's largest river, if not the longest. The Amazon's great depth and width allow it to hold more water than any other river on earth. People of Brazil call their Amazon River *O Rio Mar,* which means

Map Study

The map on page 462 shows some of the important physical features of North America and South America. Look at the map key. In what two measures is land elevation expressed? What other information is given in the map key? What do you look at to tell which direction north is on the map? About how many miles is it from North America's northernmost land to the southern tip of South America?

"the river sea." Ocean-going ships can navigate the huge Amazon for about 2,300 miles inland.

Winding south through North America is the Mississippi River. Find the Mississippi on the map on page 462. What tributaries flow into the Mississippi before it empties into the Gulf of Mexico? Name some other rivers on both continents.

Climate and Vegetation of North America

North America has many different climates and a wide variety of natural vegetation. The northernmost areas are ice-covered or cold and dry all year. The southernmost areas of Central America are hot all year, with varying precipitation. Look at the world climate map on pages 36–37 and find the other climate regions of North America. How does Mexico City's climate differ from most of Central America's?

As you would expect, climate influences the natural vegetation of North America. Any area with as many climate regions as North America is going to have many vegetation regions. Find the needleleaf forest region of northern North America on the map on pages 38–39. The evergreen trees that grow

Linking Past and Present

The Moving Continents

Have you ever wondered why the continents are shaped as they are? Many scientists believe that the continents once formed one large landmass, which they call Pangaea (pan jē′ə). Volcanic activity within the earth broke up the landmass into pieces. In time the pieces drifted apart because they rest on huge, slowly moving surfaces called plates under the earth. The pieces of land became the continents we know today.

Look at the map of Pangaea. See how North America and South America fit into each other. Note, too, how the eastern coast of South America fits into the western coast of Africa. Compare Pangaea with the map of the separated continents. In what general direction have North and South America moved from Pangaea?

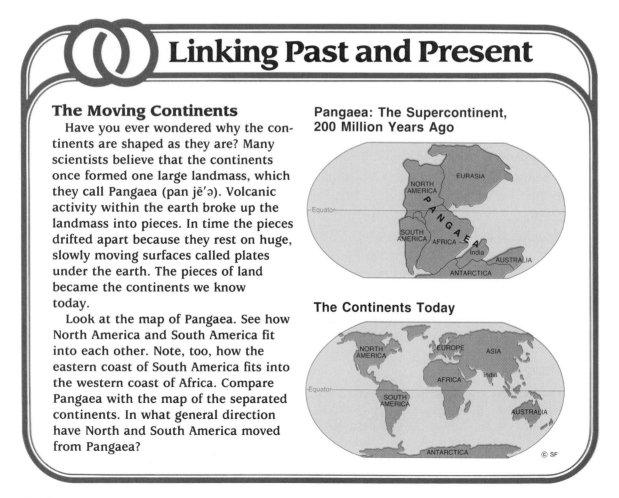

Pangaea: The Supercontinent, 200 Million Years Ago

The Continents Today

here do not lose their leaves in winter. If you can picture grand forests of tall firs and spruce trees, you know what needleleaf forests look like.

Find the desert areas of North America on the vegetation map on pages 38–39. These areas receive so little rain that desert plants have found special ways of surviving. Some plants have roots that reach far underground for water stored deep in the earth. Some cactus plants store water in their roots or trunks for long periods of time. Look for the other major North American vegetation regions on the map. The central **prairies**—large, grassy plains areas—offer rich farmland. What kinds of forests border the grasslands to the east and south?

Climate and Vegetation of South America

South America is almost as varied as North America in its climate and natural vegetation. However, South America does not stretch as close to a polar region as the northern continent does. In fact, a good part of South America lies in the low latitudes and so has a warmer climate than most of North America.

Find the Amazon Basin on the map on page 462. A **basin** is all the land drained by a river and its tributaries. What kind of climate does most of the Amazon Basin have? Use the world climate map on pages 36–37.

Grasslands and deserts make up much of South America's natural vegetation. Find the Atacama (ä′tä kä′mä) Desert on the world climate and

vegetation maps. This long, narrow strip of land in the shadow of the Andes is one of the driest areas on earth. Some places in the Atacama go for years without rain. A cold ocean current in the Pacific produces the cool, dry air that blows over the coast, creating the desert. East of the Andes Mountains, on the leeward side, is another desert area—Patagonia.

Find other climate and natural vegetation regions in South America. Use all three maps to compare both continents. As you do, think of the wide variety of activities and ways of using the land that the natural environments of the Americas must offer.

Reviewing the Lesson

Recalling Key Words, People, and Places
1. Identify the key words defined below:
   a. the term for a grasslands plains area in North America
   b. all the land drained by a river and its tributaries
2. Describe the following features and tell their locations:
   a. Andes Mountains
   b. Great Lakes
   c. Amazon River

Remembering Main Ideas
1. Choose one type of landform—mountain, hill, plateau, or plain—and describe one example of it in North or South America.
2. How did the Great Lakes form?
3. Compare the climate and natural vegetation regions of the northernmost and southernmost areas of North America.
4. Compare the Amazon Basin and Patagonia in South America. How do their climates and natural vegetation vary?

Thinking Things Over
Suppose you were moving from another continent to North or South America. In what climate and landform region would you like to settle? Give reasons for your choice.

Lesson 2   Resources and Land Use in North America and South America

LOOKING AHEAD As you read, look for—

Key words, people, and **places:**

synthetic

Answers to these questions about **main ideas:**

1. What are the major mineral resources and the major ways of using the land in North America?
2. What are the major mineral resources and the major ways of using the land in South America?

Hundreds of years ago, the Zuñi Indians of North America had a poem about corn, an important food for them. Here is part of their poem:

66 Perhaps if we are lucky
Our earth mother
Will wrap herself in a fourfold robe
Of white meal [ground grain],
Full of frost flowers.
A floor of ice will spread over the world,
The forests.
The flesh of our earth mother
Will crack with cold.
Then in the spring, when she is replete [filled] with living waters
All different kinds of corn
In our earth mother
We shall lay to rest. 99

The Zuñi were good farmers. Like other Indians and early settlers of the Americas, they depended on the rich earth to give them food each year. The land of the Americas still is very rich. In fact, farms of the Americas send food all over the world today. The people of the Americas use their land and its plentiful resources in many other ways too. How they do so is part of the story of North and South America.

Resources and Land Use in North America

Look at the map on page 467. Except for the far northern regions, nearly every part of North America is rich in minerals. Find the petroleum (oil) symbols on the map. Where are North America's major oil-producing areas? What other minerals are plentiful in North America, according to the map?

Think of all the uses minerals have. Petroleum, coal, and natural gas are essential fuels. Industries use these minerals in manufacturing as well. For example, petroleum is used to make medicines and synthetic textiles and rubber. **Synthetic** products are made artificially rather than grown naturally or made from natural materials.

Industries use other minerals too. Bauxite (bôk′sīt), for example, is the source of aluminum. Think of ways in which aluminum is used. Lead and zinc are metals used in batteries, among other products. Every mineral is important because people have some use for it and depend on it. Moreover, countries can trade their surplus minerals and buy other needed products.

Mining, shipping, and using minerals are important industries in North America. By developing their mineral resources, the United States and Canada, especially, became industrialized.

Farmland, too, is an extremely valuable resource of the continent. Look at the world land-use map on pages 64–65. Find the large central section of North America used for commercial farming. Notice the huge ranching area just to the west too. On these lands North American farms and ranches raise more wheat, corn, and cattle than any other areas in the world. Name the other food-producing activities in North America shown on the map.

Map Study

Which continent has more coal, North America or South America? Near what body of water are many oil fields found? Where is iron ore found in South America?

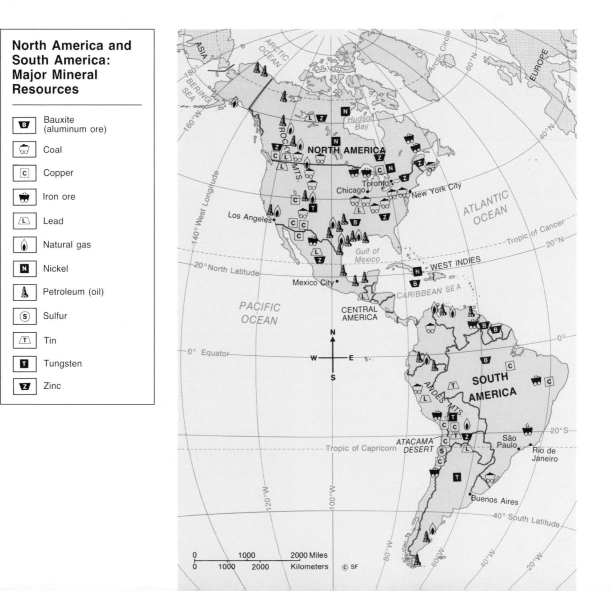

North America and South America: Major Mineral Resources

B	Bauxite (aluminum ore)
⛏	Coal
C	Copper
⛏	Iron ore
L	Lead
◊	Natural gas
N	Nickel
A	Petroleum (oil)
S	Sulfur
T	Tin
T	Tungsten
Z	Zinc

Agricultural technology in North America is highly advanced. Fewer and fewer people are needed to raise more and more farm products.

Much land is used to raise food, yet few people actually raise food for a living in North America. Modern agricultural technology allows very few people to run the machines that are used on large farms. As a result more than 75 percent of North Americans live in or near cities. Find the North American urban areas on the map on pages 64–65. As you might expect, these are the areas where most people live. They are crowded with homes, factories and other buildings, and roads. Name four North American cities shown on the map.

Resources and Land Use in South America

South America, too, has abundant minerals. The copper mines along the western coast are among the richest in the world. Copper has hundreds of everyday uses, notably in pipes and electrical wire. Find the oil-producing areas along the northern coast of South America on the map on page 467. Most of the petroleum here belongs to Venezuela. OPEC-member Venezuela has become wealthy from its oil exports. OPEC, as you have read, is a group of nations that work together in selling oil to other countries. Venezuela and other countries in South America have developed their minerals into manufacturing industries. Brazil, for example, manufactures iron and steel. Did you know that Brazil is a major automobile producer as well? Find the countries of Brazil and Venezuela on the map on page 458.

This woman works in a manufacturing plant in Brazil. The making of iron, steel, and automobiles is an important part of Brazil's economy.

As in North America, most South American land is used to raise food. Turn to the map on pages 64–65 again and note how much of South America is used for ranching. The Pampas are some of the world's best grazing lands. Argentina, especially, has become a leading producer and exporter of beef. Now find the commercial farming areas of South America on the world land-use map. Much of the land used for commercial farming is in Brazil and Argentina, two major crop producers.

People still practice subsistence farming in large areas of South America too. Find this land-use area on the map. In much of the Amazon Basin, in fact, Indians hunt and gather food as they have for centuries. Review the other land-use categories on the map.

Think of how the many ways of using the land and its resources might affect ways of living in both North and South America.

Reviewing the Lesson

Recalling Key Words, People, and Places
Tell what the word **synthetic** means.

Remembering Main Ideas
1. Name four major mineral resources of North America and tell how these minerals are used.
2. How is South America similar to North America in its land use?

Thinking Things Over
South America has quite a bit less urban land-use area than North America. In view of this fact, what statements do you think you could make about life in South America compared with life in North America? Try to come up with three statements.

469

Lesson 3   The People of North America and South America

LOOKING AHEAD As you read, look for—

Key words, people, and places:

immigrant
mestizo
bilingual

Eskimo

Latin America
Buenos Aires
Toronto

Answers to these questions about **main ideas:**

1. Who are the ancestors of today's people of the Americas?
2. How are ways of living both similar and different throughout the Americas?

Ancient Indians of Central America had a myth that they came from the "land of the sun." This land may have been a specific place. Or, it may have been an imaginary land that represented good things to the Indians. In any case, all Indians and later settlers in the Americas came from somewhere—from many different places, in fact. They brought with them a rich variety of traditions. Today their descendants all are Americans. These people and their ways of living make up another part of the story of the Americas.

Ancestors of Today's People

Scientists believe that the first people of the Americas migrated here from Asia. Look at the map on page 467 and note how close the northwestern tip of North America is to Asia. When glaciers covered parts of the Northern Hemisphere thousands of years ago, many scientists believe a land bridge existed between Asia and North America. The bridge gave the ancient Asians a way to get to the Americas.

Native People. The descendants of these first migrating people traveled to the far corners of North America and South America. They became the American Indians and Eskimos. Eskimos are native people who live in the Arctic region.

Over thousands of years, these first Americans adapted their ways of living to the land and climate regions in which they settled. For example, the people of what is now the southwestern United States adapted to the desert conditions. Some of them constructed irrigation systems in order to farm. Farther northeast, Indians lived in the woodlands where they found food and building materials for their homes. In South America the Incas built a powerful empire in the Andes. They made roads, walls, and bridges using the materials they found in the mountains. Indians still live on both American continents. Look at the chart on page 471. In which countries shown are Indians one of the major ethnic groups?

Europeans and Mestizos. As you have read, Europeans explored and then colonized the Americas, beginning in the late 1400s. Today the descendants of Europeans make up the largest

Selected Countries in North America and South America: 1985 Population (Estimated)

Country	Population (estimated)	Major Ethnic Backgrounds
Argentina	30,708,000	European
Canada	25,399,000	European
Guatemala	8,346,000	Indian/Mestizo
Haiti	5,762,000	African
Jamaica	2,266,000	African
Mexico	79,662,000	Mestizo/Indian
Nicaragua	3,232,000	Mestizo/European
Peru	19,698,000	Indian/Mestizo/European
United States	238,631,000	European/African
Uruguay	2,936,000	European

What are the two major ethnic backgrounds in Nicaragua?

group of North Americans. French settlers entered Canada, which still has a heavy French influence, especially in the province of Quebec. English settlers, too, came to Canada and to the United States. In fact, until the middle of the 1800s, most immigrants to the United States came from Great Britain. An **immigrant** is a person who leaves his or her homeland and comes to live in another country.

In the late 1800s and in this century, millions more people from other European countries immigrated to North America. Germans, Italians, Poles, Russians, Czechs, and many other groups left their homelands to make a new life.

Beginning around 1500, Spanish colonizers established a stronghold in much of Latin America, as you have read. Latin America includes Mexico, Central America, islands of the West Indies, and South America. In the years that followed, many Spaniards intermarried with the Indians. Today people of mixed European and Indian ancestry—called **mestizos**—make up a large percentage of the population in many Latin American countries. Other Latin American countries had heavy European immigration, and their present-day populations still are mostly European in background. Argentina is an example. Use the chart on this page to find another country where Europeans are the single major ethnic group.

Africans and Asians. People of African ancestry are another important part of the Americas' population. The first Africans came to the Americas in the early 1600s as slaves. In the next two hundred years, millions more Africans crossed the Atlantic Ocean to North and South America. Today about 12 percent of North America's population is of African ancestry. The percentages are smaller in most South American countries. In some West Indies countries, though, the great majority of the population is of African descent. Haiti and Jamaica are two examples, as you can see from the chart.

The world's most heavily populated continent, Asia, also has contributed to the Americas' ethnic make-up. Guyana and Suriname have had significant immigration from India. In general, Asian-background people are a small but growing minority in the Americas. Today in the United States, for example, Asians are the second-largest immigrant group after Latin Americans.

The Caribbean Sea gets its name from the Carib (kar′ib) Indians. These people once were one of the main Indian groups of the West Indies. The Caribs were fierce fighters. They tried for centuries to stop the Europeans from claiming their lands.

Carib boys had to prove their skill with poison arrows to become full members of the group. The Caribs trained their sons by placing the boys' food high in trees. The young Caribs then had to shoot their food down from the trees if they wanted to eat.

American cultures have grown from this rich mixture of American people. On each continent the people have developed ties. They also have kept some of their cultural identity.

Ways of Living in the Americas

If you describe all the things that make up your way of life, you are describing your culture. People's culture includes different things, such as the language they speak, the religion they practice, and the work they do. In these and other ways, Americans are both alike and different.

Languages. Do you think of Canada and the United States as places where most people speak English? You are right, of course, but there are important exceptions. Languages reflect the history of a country and its ethnic make-up. Canada's Quebec has a large French-speaking population. Also, millions of people in the United States speak Spanish. Some of the French- and Spanish-speaking people in North America speak English also. In other words, they are **bilingual,** meaning they speak two languages.

Latin America varies even more in major languages spoken. Spanish is the official language in most countries. However, Portuguese is the official language in Brazil, which was claimed by the Portuguese in the 1500s. Also, many Indian groups use their own languages throughout Latin America. Paraguay is interesting in that most people have a mixed background of European and Guarani (gwä′rä nē′) Indian. Paraguayans use both Spanish and Guarani as their official languages.

Religion. Religion is another aspect of culture. Like language, religion is a bond that people share with others. However, the Americas are home to many different kinds of religions. Religion is a way that individual Americans keep their own cultural identity.

Christianity, one of the world's major religions, claims the most members by far on both American continents. In fact, many Europeans first came to the New World to practice either Roman Catholic or Protestant Christianity. Modern-day Americans also practice other major religions you have read

472

about. These include Judaism, Islam, Buddhism, and Hinduism.

Work and Lifestyles. Think back to what you have read about world population distribution. Next, recall some general facts about climate, landforms, and land use in the Americas. You probably can make some good predictions about how people live and work in the Americas today.

For example, most North Americans live and work in urban areas. Find the northeastern United States and the Mexico City area on the map on page 60. Notice how crowded the dots are there compared with the rest of the continent. Notice, too, that the majority of South Americans live near the coasts. Most people do not live in regions that have extreme climates or steep mountains. Instead, they often cluster together where they can best use the resources.

Consider a family in the large, bustling port city of Buenos Aires, Argentina's capital, for example. Find Buenos Aires on the map on page 458. Family members may work in shipping or meatpacking, two of the area's important industries. They may live in a modern high-rise building in a crowded part of the city. Think of how different their life might be from that of a ranching family on the pampas. The pampas have few roads and are very thinly populated.

Now consider a Canadian family in Toronto, another large port city, in eastern Canada. This urban family, too, may live in a modern high-rise. Members may work in paper-manufacturing

jobs or, again, in shipping. Find Toronto on the map on page 458. Think of how different the Toronto family's life might be from that of a family of wheat farmers in Saskatchewan. Saskatchewan is a large province, or state, in western Canada. The entire province of Saskatchewan has about one-third the population of Toronto.

All four families are alike even while they are different. They all live on the American continents and they use their resources, just as other Americans do. Both Argentinian families most likely speak Spanish and practice Roman Catholicism. The two Canadian families probably speak English and most likely are either Protestant or Catholic. Two families are urban and two are rural. Both ways of living, and many, many others, are part of the American people's shared and distinct cultures.

Reviewing the Lesson

Recalling Key Words, People, and Places
1. Identify the key words defined below:
    a. a person, usually in Latin America, of mixed Indian and European ancestry
    b. able to speak two languages
2. Describe these places briefly:
    a. Buenos Aires
    b. Saskatchewan

Remembering Main Ideas
1. How did it come to be that descendants of Europeans make up the largest group of North Americans today?
2. What are three languages spoken in the Americas today?

Thinking Things Over
Tell ways in which you think the lives of a Buenos Aires and a Toronto family might be alike. How might the lives of these two urban families be more like each other than like those of rural families in the same country?

Drawing Conclusions from Maps

A conclusion is a decision or judgment that you reach after thinking about the facts that you know. As an example, read the following.

Drawing a Conclusion

On Monday, Jamie went to school early for flute lessons. When he arrived, he noticed that the building seemed warmer than usual. When he opened the door to the band room, he was greeted by a strange smell and smoke. His eyes began to sting. Jamie closed the door and ran back down the hall. He pulled the fire alarm and went outside to wait for help.

Several facts in the paragraph probably helped you draw the same conclusion that Jamie did: there was a fire in the band room. These facts included the warmth of the school building and the smoke and strange smell inside the band room. After thinking about these facts, Jamie drew the conclusion that the band room was on fire.

Jamie's conclusion could have been valid—that is, true. That is, there may have been a fire in the band room. However, his conclusion could have been invalid—that is, not true. Perhaps there was a problem in the school's heating system that caused heat and smoke without a fire being present.

Supporting Your Conclusion

You can use the following strategy to draw conclusions:
- Examine the facts.
- Think about your own experiences.
- Use the facts and your experiences to draw a conclusion.
- Ask yourself if the conclusion makes sense.
- Be able to support your conclusion.

Facts help you draw valid conclusions. The more facts you have, the more accurate your conclusions are likely to be. The facts can come from various sources, including maps. Look at the natural vegetation map of North America on page 475. The map shows you that the northernmost part of Canada is covered by tundra or ice. You could use this fact to help conclude that few people live in northern Canada. Ask yourself how you would support such a conclusion. You might list the following facts, and inferences made from facts, to support the conclusion.

1. Judging from the kind of vegetation and from other facts you have learned, the climate of northern Canada must be quite cold.
2. With that climate and with the kind of natural vegetation that is present, northern Canada probably is not good for farming.
3. In general, few people live in places with extreme climates and poor opportunities for farming.

474

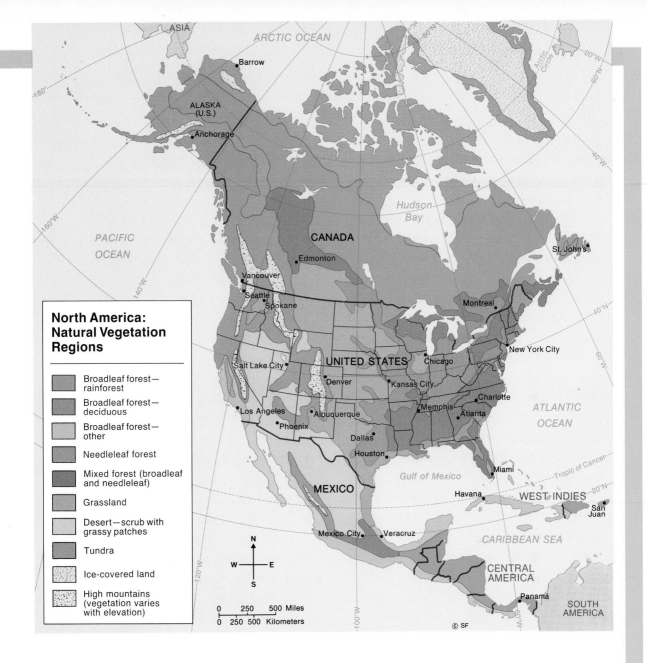

North America: Natural Vegetation Regions

Legend:
- Broadleaf forest—rainforest
- Broadleaf forest—deciduous
- Broadleaf forest—other
- Needleleaf forest
- Mixed forest (broadleaf and needleleaf)
- Grassland
- Desert—scrub with grassy patches
- Tundra
- Ice-covered land
- High mountains (vegetation varies with elevation)

N W E S

0 250 500 Miles
0 250 500 Kilometers

© SF

Skills Practice

List as many facts and inferences as you can think of to support each conclusion listed below. Use the natural vegetation map on this page and the physical and climate maps of North America (page 462 and pages 36–37) to help you.

1. Commercial farming is an important land use in much of the United States.

2. Few people live in the mountain areas of North America.

3. Lumbering is the major land use in most of the northern part of North America.

4. People have difficulty using the land to make a living in the rainforest regions of North America.

Chapter Summary

Lesson 1   The Natural Environment of North America and South America— The two continents have all four kinds of landforms. Bodies of water include Hudson Bay, the Great Lakes, and the Mississippi and Amazon rivers. Climate and vegetation vary in both continents.

Lesson 2   Resources and Land Use in North America and South America— Nearly every part of North America is rich in minerals. Its land produces more wheat, corn, and cattle than any other area in the world. South America also has abundant minerals. Most of its land is used to raise food.

Lesson 3   The People of North America and South America— The first people who spread across the Americas probably came from Asia. Descendants of Europeans make up the largest group of North Americans today. Africans were brought over as slaves, and many Asians immigrated in the late 1800s. Most people on both continents are Christians.

Write your answers on a separate sheet of paper.

Testing Key Words, People, and Places

Part A

Choose the key word from the list that best completes each sentence.

1. A _____ product is made by people.
2. A huge ice sheet is a _____.
3. An _____ is a person who goes to live in another country.
4. A _____ is a large, grassy plain.
5. A person of mixed European and Indian ancestry is called a _____.
6. People who speak two languages are _____.
7. A _____ is all the land drained by a river and its tributaries.

   a. glacier   **e. immigrant**
   b. prairie   **f. mestizo**
   c. basin   **g. bilingual**
   d. synthetic

Part B

Match each description with the correct place in the list.

1. the longest river in the Americas
2. a mountain range in western North America
3. five large lakes between Canada and the United States
4. a mountain range of South America

   a. Rocky Mountains
   b. Andes Mountains
   c. Great Lakes
   d. Amazon River

Testing Main Ideas

Choose the answer that best completes each sentence.

1. Most of the land in the Americas is made up of
   a. plateaus and plains.
   b. hills and mountains.
   c. desert lands.

2. Two great river systems in the Americas are the
   a. Mississippi and Amazon.
   b. Pampas and Mestizo.
   c. Atchison and Topeka.
3. North and South American climate and vegetation
   a. are exactly the same.
   b. vary quite a bit.
   c. are exactly the opposite of each other.

Testing Skills

1. Drawing conclusions from a map.
   Look at the map of selected minerals found in South America and answer *yes* or *no* as to whether you can draw the following conclusions based on the map.
   a. Most of the mines operating in South America are on the western coast.
   b. There are no minerals to be found presently in central South America.
   c. Petroleum is found only in the northern section of South America.
   d. Copper is presently mined in western, eastern, and central South America.
2. Distinguishing fact from opinion.
   Write the letter of the sentence that states an opinion.
   a. Peru is a beautiful country.
   b. Venezuela produces much oil.
   c. Quebec has a large French-speaking population.

Activities

1. Read *Mexico: Giant of the South* by Eileen L. Smith (Dillon Press, 1983) and report to the class on what new things you learned about Mexico.
2. Find information about oil drilling in an encyclopedia and make an outline of the topic.

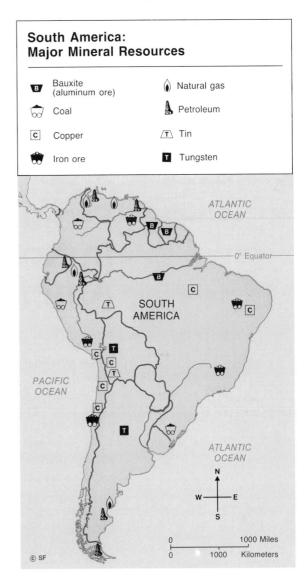

South America: Major Mineral Resources

Chapter 24

From Past to Present in North and South America

The Americas always have been a New World. First, Indians migrated here from Asia. Europeans came later. Still later, Americans worked to make new nations. The picture shows early Quebec, one of the oldest cities in Canada.

In this chapter you will see how Indians built American civilizations and how Europeans conquered them. Also, you will learn how Americans freed themselves from European rule. The lessons in the chapter are listed below.

Lesson 1   Indian Civilizations

Lesson 2   European Influence in the Americas

Lesson 3   The Road to Independence

Lesson 1   Indian Civilizations

LOOKING AHEAD As you read, look for—

Key words, people, and **places:**

tribute

Olmec
Maya
Aztec
Inca

Yucatán Peninsula
Tenochtitlán

Answers to these questions about **main ideas:**

1. What were some general characteristics of early American Indian civilizations in Mexico, Central America, and South America?
2. What were some accomplishments of the Olmec, Mayan, and Aztec civilizations?
3. What was the Inca civilization like?

Early Indians in Mexico and Central America worshiped a god called Quetzalcoatl (ket säl′kô ä′tl), the "plumed serpent." According to Indian legend, Quetzalcoatl discovered maize (corn). This discovery gave them their life, the Indians believed. They farmed maize successfully, giving thanks to their god.

Throughout the Americas, Indians could and did live on other foods and by ways other than farming. They hunted, gathered, and fished for their food, as people had done for thousands of years. As you have read, though, farming led some groups to form villages. From these villages grew some of the world's complex early civilizations in Mesopotamia and other places. A similar thing happened on the American continents.

From Villages to Civilizations

About seven or eight thousand years ago, people in present-day Mexico and Central America began to grow plants such as corn, beans, squash, and peppers. Over time, knowledge of farming spread throughout the Americas. By two thousand years ago, many American Indians practiced farming and lived in villages. In parts of Mexico, Central America, and South America, especially, village cultures grew complex. Led by kings, chiefs, or priests, some villages became cities.

From the cities grew civilizations. Most of the civilizations in these parts of the Americas used writing systems, and all of them had mathematics. Almost all of the civilizations had city centers with temples atop stone pyramids. Leaders ruled the cities through their armies. These Indians built the cities as centers for religion, government, and trade.

Near the cities, farmers grew food to feed the people. Craft workers made beautiful jewelry and other objects from gold, silver, and copper. Other workers made brilliantly colored clothing from wool and cotton. Traders carried these goods far and wide. Through trade, and sometimes war, each of the civilizations spread its influence over wide areas.

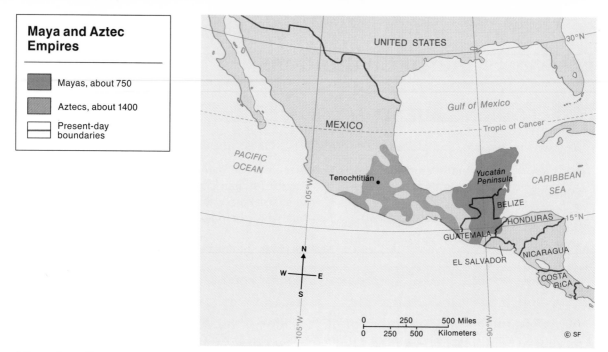

Maya and Aztec Empires

- Mayas, about 750
- Aztecs, about 1400
- Present-day boundaries

Map Study

This map shows the areas controlled by the Mayas and the Aztecs. According to the map key, by about what year did the Mayas control the area of the Yucatán Peninsula? By about what year did the Aztec Empire flourish? What present-day country did the Aztecs occupy?

From Olmecs to Aztecs

The earliest civilization in Mexico was that of the Olmecs. Perhaps as early as 2000 B.C., these people built cities in the highlands of central Mexico. Later they spread north to the lowland areas bordering the Gulf of Mexico. Rubber trees grew here, and the name *Olmec* is an Indian word for "rubber people." Archaeologists have found many remains of Olmec life.

The Olmecs were the first American Indians to build stone pyramids as religious centers. They were skilled traders and had a hieroglyphic writing system. One of their stone writing slabs has been dated at around 300 B.C. and may be among the oldest examples of writing in the Americas. Olmec cities had disappeared by A.D. 200; the reasons are not clear. The great Mayan (mī′ən) civilization developed next.

Mayas. The Mayas lived on the Yucatán (yü′kə tan′) Peninsula in Mexico. Also, their lands spread into Central America—into present-day Belize, Guatemala, and a small corner of Honduras. Find the Maya lands on the map above.

Mayan farmers slashed and burned jungle brush and trees to grow corn and other crops. They also built large, complex canal systems to water farmlands. The farmers lived in villages outside of grand cities. In fact, the farmers and other workers built the huge

480

pyramids and temples of the cities. They built roads through the Mayan lands too.

The Mayas centered their life on religion. They believed in many gods and tried hard to please the gods. Mayan priests made up an educated upper class. They controlled society tightly. The priests even told the farmers when to plant. They developed Mayan writing and a highly accurate calendar. Like our calendar, the Mayan one had a 365-day year.

Mayan civilization collapsed around the year 800. As with the Olmecs, the reasons why are not clear. Mayan population dropped, and many Mayan cities were abandoned. Some Mayas survived and a second Mayan civilization arose, but it was ruled by people from Central Mexico.

Aztecs. The Aztecs were a third major Indian civilization in North America. The Aztecs migrated into Mexico from the north in the 1300s. Learning from other settled people, they built cities and then conquered a large empire. Find the Aztec Empire on the map on page 480. Where was it located in relation to the Maya lands?

The Aztecs ruled about 10 million people from their capital at Tenochtitlán (tā nôch′tē tlän′), where Mexico City is today. Tenochtitlán was a beautiful city that the Aztecs built on an island in the middle of a lake. They filled in some of the lake and built roads, bridges, and canals through the

Linking Past and Present

Mayan Ruins

Historians still wonder why so much of Mayan civilization disappeared around 800. Did disease or famine kill off people suddenly? Did large numbers of Mayas leave to search for better farmland? Some scholars think the Mayas may have revolted against their priests. Perhaps thousands of people died in such fighting. Or perhaps other Indians wiped out large numbers of Mayas. In any case, many of their buildings, such as this temple on top of a pyramid, still stand.

You can visit ruins such as these in the Yucatán Peninsula of Mexico or the jungles of Guatemala.

city. The Indians even used the lake's bottom soil to make more farmland. They piled the soil on rafts above the water.

The city was huge, with at least 100,000 people by the late 1400s. Massive pyramids, public buildings, and palaces clothed the city. Huge markets sold food and other products.

Aztec military strength made all this wealth possible. The armies went out every year to collect tribute from around the empire. **Tribute** is money, goods, or other payment that conquered people are forced to pay their rulers. Often this tribute included human victims who were sacrificed by the thousands to the Aztec gods. The Aztecs believed the gods wanted human sacrifices. Once during a temple dedication, the Aztecs sacrificed 20,000 people to honor the temple's god.

Other Indian groups hated the Aztecs. No one could challenge Aztec strength, however, for many years. It was Spanish conquerors with guns who finally put down this Indian civilization in the 1500s.

The Incas of South America

Far to the south of Mexico, another great Indian civilization developed—that of the Incas of South America. In the 1400s Inca lands stretched along the Pacific coast and through the Andes. They included most of present-day Ecuador and Peru and parts of Bolivia, Chile, and Argentina. Find this general area on the map on page 458.

The Incas were great engineers who built cities, roads, irrigation systems, dams, and bridges throughout the Andes. The bridges were built over rivers and canyons. Incan craft workers made art objects from gold and silver. Weavers produced beautiful textiles.

The Incan civilization was very advanced, as were the civilizations of the Mayas and Aztecs. Their astronomy, architecture, and engineering, for instance, truly were far ahead of their time.

Incan farmers terraced the steep sides of the Andes to get more farmland. They gave over all their crops to the government, which in turn provided food for the people. In fact, everything about Incan life was carefully ordered. Their "god-ruler" had absolute power. An Incan ruler once said, "In my kingdom, no bird flies, no leaf quivers if I do not will it." This great civilization also was conquered by the Spanish in the 1500s.

Reviewing the Lesson

Recalling Key Words, People, and Places
1. What does the word **tribute** mean?
2. Tell the importance of each Indian culture:
   a. Maya
   b. Inca
3. Tell where these places are located:
   a. Yucatán Peninsula
   b. Tenochtitlán

Remembering Main Ideas
1. How did Indian civilizations develop in the Americas?
2. What was the role of the priests in Mayan civilization?
3. What are some examples of the Incas' engineering skills?

Thinking Things Over
The Indian civilizations you have read about all had undemocratic governments. Why do you think these governments were able to rule successfully over so many people for so long?

Lesson 2   European Influence in the Americas

LOOKING AHEAD As you read, look for—

Key words, people, and places:

viceroyalty
hacienda

Pedro Cabral
Montezuma
Francisco Pizarro
Atahualpa

Answers to these questions about **main ideas:**

1. How did Portugal and Spain come to control large areas of the Americas?
2. How did Spain run its empire in the Americas?
3. Why were the British and French interested in North America?

If you had asked a Spanish conquistador why he came to the New World in the 1500s, he might have answered, "for God, gold, and glory." The Spanish were interested in spreading the Christian faith. Also, they wanted to plunder the riches of the Americas. Finally, they desired fame and power for themselves and Spain. Conquering an empire would give them this.

The Spanish were not alone. As you have read, various western European powers wanted new, direct routes to Asia to increase their trading wealth. When they found the New World instead, they began to build new empires in the Americas.

Portugal and Spain Move into the Americas

Portugal and Spain were the first European nations to gain empires in the Americas. The Portuguese, you may remember, already had found a route to India by sailing around Africa. Therefore, they were less interested in sailing west to find other routes. In 1500, however, Pedro Cabral sailed to what is today Brazil. The explorer claimed the area for Portugal.

Spain claimed a much larger section of the New World. By the 1600s Spanish territory stretched from the present-day United States to Chile and Argentina. Find the Spanish territory on the map on page 484.

How did the Spanish gain this vast territory? In 1519 Spanish conquistador Hernando Cortés landed on the coast of Mexico with a small army. Hearing about the wealth of the Aztec Empire, he set out for Tenochtitlán. The Aztec leader Montezuma (mon′tə zü′mə) first thought Cortés was a god. Later, under threat of death, he gave over the Aztec Empire to the Spanish.

The Aztecs rebelled against their leader's action, however, and fought the Spanish. Not until 1521 did the Spanish, with their guns and thousands of non-Aztec Indian allies, finally conquer the Aztecs. At that time, the Spanish destroyed most of Tenochtitlán and built a new capital—the site of modern Mexico City.

483

Within ten years all of central Mexico came into Spanish hands. Remaining Indian areas in Central and South America also were conquered and looted of their wealth. In 1532, for example, the conquistador Francisco Pizarro (pi zär′ō) led a surprise attack against the Incas, whom he had gathered for a "meeting." The Spanish captured and then killed the Inca leader Atahualpa (ä′tä wäl′pä). Within a short time, the entire Inca Empire fell to the Spanish.

The effects of conquest on the Indians were great. Their civilizations were destroyed. Millions of Indians died of diseases brought to the Americas by the Europeans. Others died in war. In fact, out of about 25 million Indians, perhaps only about half survived the conquest.

The Spanish Empire in the Americas

The Spanish monarchy controlled its New World colonies tightly. It appointed managers called viceroys to oversee large districts called **viceroyalties.** Find the Spanish viceroyalties on the map at the right.

The main job of the colonial governments was to make sure Spain got as much wealth as possible from the Americas. Thousands of Indians mined gold and silver that was sent to Spain. Other Indians were put to work on **haciendas,** which were large estates used for cattle ranching or raising sugar or tobacco. So many Indians died from the hard labor that the Spanish looked to Africa for more workers. A huge

slave trade began, bringing millions of Africans to the Americas.

During the years of colonial rule—the early 1500s to the early 1800s—Spanish culture grew throughout much of Latin America. Spanish became the official language and Roman Catholicism the official religion in all Spanish colonies. The surviving Indians adapted to the new ways, but they also managed to keep their own cultures alive.

Map Study

According to the map below, which groups of Europeans possessed land in North America in the mid-1600s? in South America?

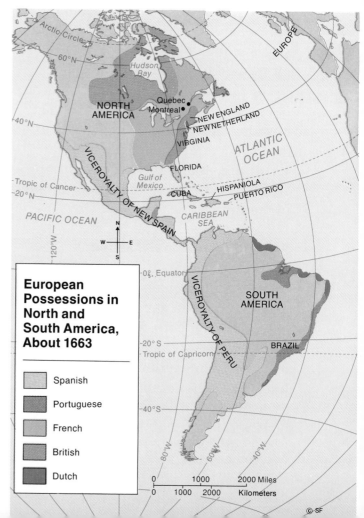

European Possessions in North and South America, About 1663

- Spanish
- Portuguese
- French
- British
- Dutch

The British and French in North America

Other countries looked on with envy as Spain gathered its wealth from the New World. As you have read, French and British explorers tried for years to find a Northwest Passage through North America. While searching, they claimed large parts of the continent for Great Britain and France. Look at the map on page 484. Find the British and French claims.

Both countries competed for the valuable fur trade in northern North America. They both tried to make the Indians their allies in this competition. Eventually, the competition led to the French and Indian War of 1756–1763. The British won the war and became the major power in northern North America as a result.

Meanwhile, people from France and Great Britain spread their culture to North America. British culture became more widespread because so many more British than French settlers set up colonies in the New World. Find New England and Virginia on the map on page 484. These colonies were the beginnings of the United States.

French culture remained strong in parts of eastern Canada, as it still does today. Find Quebec on the map. Both Quebec and Montreal were founded by the French, who kept their culture and language even though France lost its North American claim in 1763.

The Indians in northern North America were not made to work for their conquerors, as Indians in Latin America were. Still, they lost their lands as

Indians in the New World were put to work for Europeans.

more and more settlers came to North America. The European conquest of the Americas changed Indian life forever on both continents. More changes were to come for all people—native and newcomer—as Europeans tried to hold on to the New World.

Reviewing the Lesson

Recalling Key Words, People, and Places
1. Identify the key words defined below:
   a. a Spanish colonial district in the Americas
   b. a large estate in Spanish colonial America, used for cattle ranching or farming
2. Tell why the following people were important:
   a. Montezuma
   b. Francisco Pizarro

Remembering Main Ideas
1. How did the Spanish go about taking over the Indian areas in the Americas?
2. What was the main job of Spain's colonial government in the Americas?
3. How did the British gain greater influence in North America than the French?

Thinking Things Over
Why do you suppose the Europeans thought they had a right to claim and settle the Americas as they did?

Lesson 3 The Road to Independence

LOOKING AHEAD As you read, look for—

Key words, people, and **places:**

creole   Toussaint l'Ouverture
caudillo   Miguel Hidalgo
confederation   Simón Bolívar
dominion   John Macdonald

Answers to these questions about **main ideas:**

1. How did Haiti, Mexico, and several South American countries gain their independence from Europe?
2. What were some results of independence in many countries in Latin America?
3. How did Canada become independent?

In the late 1700s, a Spanish viceroy in the Americas told his subjects that "you have been born to be silent and to obey—and neither to discuss nor hold opinions on . . . government." The viceroy probably did not realize the force of changes that were about to sweep through the American empires of Spain and other European nations as well.

As you have read, liberal ideas were gaining power in Western Europe and the Americas in the late 1700s. Increasing numbers of people wanted fairness from their governments. Even more, they wanted freedom for themselves. British colonists proved this in 1775 when they began their successful revolution and formed the United States of America.

Within a short time, Latin American nations were fighting for their independence too. Meanwhile, European countries were weakened as a result of fighting each other. This fact made it harder for them to rule their colonies tightly.

Revolutions in Latin America

Between 1804 and 1824, much of Latin America became free of European rule. Let's look at what happened.

Haiti. The first successful revolution in Latin America took place in Haiti (hā′tē) in 1804. Haiti was a French colony on the island of Hispaniola in the Caribbean Sea. Find Haiti on the map on page 458. Haiti was one of the few French-held areas in Latin America. Sugar, coffee, and cotton plantations made Haiti one of the richest French colonies in the 1700s. Few Spanish settled there, and Spain allowed the French to take over Haiti in 1697.

African slaves made up most of Haiti's population. The slaves had miserable lives. They did not have enough to eat, and they were forced to work long, hard days in the hot sun. An ex-slave named Toussaint l'Ouverture (tü san′ lü ver tyr′) wanted to help his people. L'Ouverture trained an army of runaway slaves and led them against the French in 1791.

486

Haiti declared its independence in 1804, after its people staged the first successful revolution in Latin America.

The slaves won battle after battle under l'Ouverture. Eventually, the leader won control of the government of Haiti. In 1799, however, the French emperor Napoleon Bonaparte sent an army to Haiti to regain control. L'Ouverture was captured and returned to France, where he died in prison. However, the Haitian revolution continued until early in 1803, when the slaves finally defeated the French. Haiti declared its independence the next year.

Mexico. In the early 1800s, a creole priest named Miguel Hidalgo (mē gel′ ēdh äl′gō) lived in Mexico. A **creole** is a person of French or Spanish ancestry born in Latin America. Hidalgo wanted to improve the lives of the Indians and mestizos. These people lived very poorly under Spanish rule. Hidalgo knew about the ideals of the American and French revolutions. Accordingly, he wanted Mexico to be free of Spain.

In September 1810, Hidalgo acted. He gave a rousing speech and called all creoles, Indians, and mestizos to join him in a fight against Spanish rule. Soon thousands of Mexicans were marching through the country, battling Spanish troops. They did well at first, but disorder set in after a while. Government troops were able to capture Hidalgo, and he was executed in 1811. For the next ten years, however, other Mexicans continued the fight. In 1821 they defeated the Spanish, and Mexico became independent.

South America. A wealthy creole landowner in Venezuela became one of South America's leaders for independence. As a young man, Simón Bolívar (sē mōn′ bō lē′vär) had dreamed of freeing South America from Spain. His dream came partly true in 1821. After twenty years of struggle, Venezuela, Colombia, and Ecuador fought their way free of Spanish rule with Bolívar's help. Argentina and Chile had had successful revolutions too. Spain's final hold on South America broke when Peru and Bolivia became free in the early 1820s. Meanwhile, Brazil became free from Portugal in 1822. Portugal supported the independence of its colony, and very little fighting actually was involved.

Results of Independence in Latin America

Unfortunately, independence created its own problems in many places in Latin America. The people were unused to self-government. Disagreements arose over how to run the new countries. Often caudillos—local warlords—stepped in and took power. **Caudillo** is a Spanish word meaning

"dictator." Some of the caudillos headed both the army and the government. In many of the new nations, too, a few rich people still owned most of the land and wealth. Meanwhile, most Latin Americans were poor and uneducated.

The governments of many Latin American countries have worked hard to solve these problems. Even though they have not always succeeded, they have brought peace and productivity to many areas.

Canada's Independence

Canada's road to independence was far more peaceful than that of most Latin American nations. Great Britain had won much of Canada from France in 1763. The population was split between English- and French-speaking

Linking Past and Present

Independence Days

Did you know that Americans besides ourselves celebrate independence days each year? On September 15, for example, Mexicans remember Father Hidalgo's cry for freedom and his march through the country. The president of Mexico rings a bell and repeats Hidalgo's speech to start off the celebration. The next day, Mexican Independence Day, the people celebrate with fiestas, or festivals, with dancing, parades, and feasting. How do people in the United States celebrate our Independence Day?

Canada Day is July 1. On this national holiday, Canadians celebrate the British North America Act, which gave them

self-government. They have parades, speeches, and other events to mark the day. You can see members of the Canadian armed services marching in a Canada Day celebration above.

John Macdonald (speaking) served as Canada's first prime minister. He helped Canada become a strong, self-governing country.

people. There had often been trouble between these two groups. Hoping to keep peace, however, Britain divided the colony into French Canada and English Canada.

Neither group of Canadians liked being ruled by a distant nation, however. As a result, they both began independence movements in the 1830s. Britain, not wanting another colonial war, granted Canada extensive self-government in 1847. Over the next several years, Canadians worked to unify their large colony and increase their self-government.

Canadian leader John Macdonald helped join areas of eastern Canada into a confederation. A **confederation** is a group of provinces under one central government. Provinces are one of the main divisions of a country, similar to states. The provinces were Quebec, Ontario, Nova Scotia, and New Brunswick. Confederation was made possible by the British North America Act of 1867, which Macdonald helped shape. Under this act, Canada became a **dominion,** or self-governing country. In foreign affairs Canada still had ties to

Britain. In every other respect, however, Canada was free.

Macdonald led Canada for many years as its first prime minister, or head of government. Under his leadership Canada formed strong democratic principles and expanded its borders to the Pacific Ocean.

Reviewing the Lesson

Recalling Key Words, People, and Places

1. Identify the key words defined below:
   a. a person of Spanish descent born in Latin America
   b. a group of provinces or states under one central government
2. Tell why the following people were important:
   a. Toussaint l'Ouverture
   b. John Macdonald

Remembering Main Ideas

1. How were the revolutions in Haiti and Mexico both alike and different?
2. What problems did Latin America face after its revolutions?
3. How did the British North America Act affect Canada?

Thinking Things Over

Leaders were important in bringing independence to Latin America and Canada. What qualities do you think leaders needed to carry out such a great and difficult task? What problems do you think they faced?

489

Solving Problems and Making Decisions

People everywhere have problems to solve. They need to make decisions about the best way to solve those problems. Some decisions are fairly easy to make. Others are much harder. How do people make decisions to solve problems? One way is to use a decision tree.

Using a Decision Tree

The trunk of a decision tree shows the problem that needs to be solved. The goal at the top of the tree tells what one hopes to achieve by making a decision. In between the problem and the goal are possible solutions and possible good and bad results of each solution. You can use a decision tree to consider all the possibilities carefully in order to make the wisest decision.

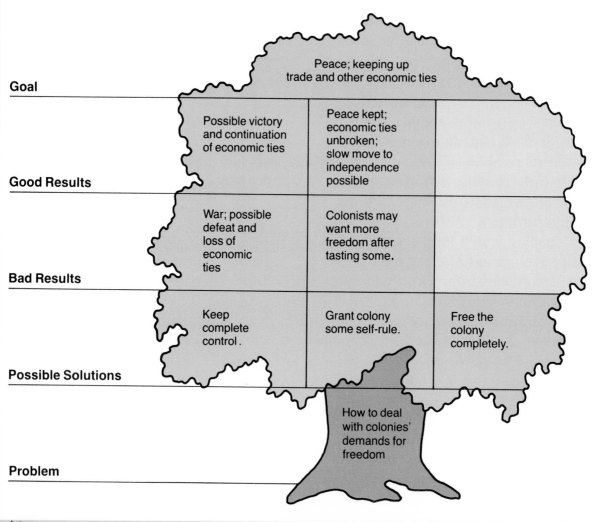

	Goal	Peace; keeping up trade and other economic ties	
Good Results	Possible victory and continuation of economic ties	Peace kept; economic ties unbroken; slow move to independence possible	
Bad Results	War; possible defeat and loss of economic ties	Colonists may want more freedom after tasting some.	
Possible Solutions	Keep complete control.	Grant colony some self-rule.	Free the colony completely.
Problem		How to deal with colonies' demands for freedom	

The decision tree on page 490 deals with a problem faced by many European countries in the 1700s and 1800s. These countries had to decide how to treat their colonies' demands for freedom. This problem is stated on the trunk of the decision tree.

What goal did the rulers have? Most rulers probably wanted peace since wars with rebellious colonies cost lives and money. Also, colonies provided their ruling countries with great wealth. Most rulers wanted to keep up trade and other economic ties with their colonies.

The first possible solution on the decision tree is to try to keep complete control of the colony. Look above this solution for possible bad and good results. One bad result is that a war probably would have to be fought, costing lives and money. This war might end in defeat for the ruling country, which would probably break all economic and political ties with the colony.

However, if the ruling country won the war, the colony would remain within the empire—at least for a while. The wealth of the colony would continue to help make the ruling country rich.

Now look at the second possible solution on the decision tree. What possible bad result of this solution is given? What possible good results are given?

Skills Practice

1. Look at the third possible solution on the decision tree. What might be some bad results of this solution? What good things might result? On a separate sheet of paper, copy the decision tree and fill in the third column.

2. Tell which solution on the decision tree you think is the best. Give reasons for your answer.

3. A conclusion is a decision or judgment you reach after thinking about the facts you know. Read the following facts. Then decide which conclusion—a, b, or c—is probably correct.

- By 1822 Venezuela, Colombia, Ecuador, Argentina, and Chile had won their independence after fighting Spain.
- Portugal supported Brazil's desire for independence and granted it in 1822.
- To avoid another colonial war, Great Britain granted Canada some self-rule; Canada became a self-governing country in 1867.

   a. Fighting against a rebellious colony is the surest way to keep the colony under control.

   b. One way or the other, most colonies in North America and South America gained their freedom.

   c. Brazil would have won its independence much earlier if it had fought against Portugal.

491

Chapter Summary

Lesson 1 Indian Civilizations—In Mexico the Olmecs built cities perhaps as early as 2000 B.C. The Mayan civilization flourished on the Yucatán Peninsula by about A.D. 250. The Aztecs came into Mexico in the 1300s and soon ruled 10 million people. To the south, the Inca empire stretched along the Pacific coast and into present-day Bolivia and Argentina.

Lesson 2 European Influence in the Americas—The Spanish conquered many Indian communities in the Americas. The Portuguese settled the area of Brazil. The British settled along the Atlantic coast, and the French settled in Canada.

Lesson 3 The Road to Independence—The British colonies revolted against Europe in 1775. Soon Haiti also revolted, then Mexico in 1810, and much of the rest of Latin America by the 1820s. In 1822 Portugal gave Brazil its independence. Great Britain granted Canada self-government in 1867.

Write your answers on a separate sheet of paper.

Testing Key Words, People, and Places

Part A

Give the definition of each key word.

1. tribute
2. viceroyalty
3. hacienda
4. creole
5. caudillo
6. confederation
7. dominion

Part B

Match each description with the correct person or place in the list.

1. Portuguese captain who discovered Brazil in 1500
2. Aztec emperor who was defeated by Cortés
3. place where the Mayan civilization flourished until 800
4. conqueror of the Inca Empire in 1532
5. Inca emperor who was killed by Pizarro
6. Montezuma's capital city
7. Venezuelan who led the revolt against the Spanish in South America
8. leader in the Canadian movement who became the dominion's first prime minister
9. creole priest who started the revolution in Mexico

   a. Cabral   f. Atahualpa
   b. Bolívar   g. Pizarro
   c. Macdonald h. Hidalgo
   d. Montezuma i. Yucatán
   e. Tenochtitlán   Peninsula

Testing Main Ideas

Choose the answer that best completes each sentence.

1. The Mayan civilization suddenly disappeared because of
   a. the slashing and burning of jungle brush and trees.
   b. immigration of its people to other lands.
   c. unclear reasons.

2. The Inca Empire included most of what is present-day
   a. Peru.
   b. Brazil.
   c. Argentina.
3. For more than 300 years, Brazil was ruled by the
   a. French.
   b. Portuguese.
   c. Spanish.
4. Not until 1821 did Mexico achieve
   a. independence from Spain.
   b. self-government on haciendas.
   c. independence from Portugal.
5. Joining Macdonald's confederation in the 1860s were Canadians of
   a. English and Dutch ancestry.
   b. Portuguese and Spanish ancestry.
   c. French and English ancestry.
6. In Canada a prime minister is a
   a. leading member of the church.
   b. head of government.
   c. general of the army.

Testing Skills

1. **Solving problems and making decisions.** Apply what you have learned about solving problems and making decisions.
   a. In the 1700s and 1800s, Latin American countries were struggling for independence. Imagine living in one of those countries. Start a decision tree. The problem your country faces is that it is ruled by a foreign country. Your goal is to achieve fairness in government.
   b. Put two possible solutions to your problem on the tree.
   c. Put a possible bad result and a possible good result of each of your solutions on the tree.
   d. Choose the better solution, and tell why you did.
2. **Making a time line.** Make a time line that begins with A.D. 1500 at the left and ends with A.D. 1540 at the right. Put the events listed below in order on your time line.
   a. Cortés lands in Mexico and marches to the Aztec capital of Tenochtitlán, 1519
   b. Cabral sails to Brazil and claims the area for Portugal, 1500
   c. Pizarro attacks and captures Atahualpa and the Incas, 1532
   d. Spanish and Indian allies finally conquer Aztecs, 1521

Activities

1. Find photographs of Mayan ruins. Make a model of one of the structures you find. Try to reconstruct the ruin as it might have looked when the Mayas built it. You might use clay, cardboard, building blocks, or any other material that will stand up well.
2. In a book on Canadian history, find pictures of the various Canadian flags, from the Union Jack of the British Empire to the Commonwealth flag to the Maple Leaf flag of today. Draw and color pictures of these flags.

Chapter 25

Countries of North America Today

Immigration from other lands, fights for freedom and independence, and belief in democracy have given the countries of North America a great deal in common. However, differences do exist among these countries today. For example, Canada and the United States largely use modern technology in their farms and factories. Other countries of North America use traditional as well as modern technology. The workers in the picture are using hand methods to make shoes in a factory in Mexico.

This chapter will give you an idea of what it would be like to live in North American countries other than the United States. The lessons in the chapter are listed below.

Lesson 1   Canada and Mexico

Lesson 2   Central America and the West Indies

Lesson 1   Canada and Mexico

LOOKING AHEAD As you read, look for—

Key words, people, and **places:**

ejido   Rio Grande
                St. Lawrence Seaway
                Mexico City

Answers to these questions about **main ideas:**

1. In what way are Canada and Mexico alike and different?
2. What things make Canada a rich country?
3. What are some ways the people in Mexico make their living?
4. How has oil wealth affected Mexico?

Canada, Mexico, and the United States are close and friendly neighbors in North America. To the south, the Rio Grande—spanned by a number of bridges—marks the boundary between Mexico and the United States. To the north, the Great Lakes help form the long border between Canada and the United States.

Land and People

As you have learned, Canada's colonial history was linked with Great Britain and France. Mexico's was linked with Spain. Today, Spanish is the official language of Mexico. Both English and French are official languages in Canada. The earlier French influence makes the Roman Catholic religion nearly as strong as Protestant Christian religions in Canada. Spanish influence accounts for the mostly Roman Catholic population of present-day Mexico.

Located in relatively high latitudes, Canada is a country with a mostly cold climate. It is the world's second largest country in land area. Compared with its area, however, Canada's population is small. Its average population density is only 6 or 7 persons per square mile.

Most Canadians live in cities or on farms in the comparatively warmer, southern part of the country—near the border with the United States. Farther north, fishers, foresters, and miners make up much of the thinly scattered population. The Eskimos fish and hunt in the far north, along the coasts of the Arctic Ocean and the Hudson Bay.

Mexico, by contrast, is a mostly low-latitude country. Low elevations have warm temperatures the year round. It is only a fifth as large as Canada, yet its population is three times larger. As you might guess, its average population density is very high—more than 94 people per square mile.

More than half of Mexico's millions live crowded into the mild, highland climate region at the southern end of the Mexican Plateau. Mexico City is in this region.

The very dry northern half of Mexico, which borders the United States, is mostly sparsely populated. Mexico's rugged and mountainous landscape makes highways and railroads difficult to build. Landforms have created natural barriers among Mexico's population regions throughout its history.

Growth and Potential in Canada

Canada is one of the world's wealthy industrial nations. If you moved to Canada, you would live just about the same way you do in the United States. Canada is a democratic country in which the people elect a parliament much like that of Great Britain. It has commercial farms and manufacturing cities similar to those in the United States and Western Europe.

Toronto, Montreal, Hamilton, and other Canadian cities are all part of the densely populated region around the Great Lakes and the St. Lawrence River. They are part of the most important urban-industrial region in North America, together with the United States cities of the Northeast and Great Lakes.

Factories in Canada's St. Lawrence-Great Lakes region manufacture heavy goods like steel, cars, and machinery. They also produce many more lighter goods, including flour, textiles, computers, and plastics. The biggest manufacturing output, however, is in wood and paper products. Canada's immense northern forests supply the pulp for this industry. Canada leads the world in the production of newsprint, the kind of paper used by newspapers.

Canada has reached its high level of industrial strength only within the last fifty years or so. In 1959 Canada and the United States finished their joint project of the St. Lawrence Seaway.

Map Study

The map shows the Great Lakes-St. Lawrence River region. What ocean is shown in the east? What other water bodies are shown on the map? With your finger, trace an all-water route from the ocean as far west as you can. What is the name of the body of water at that point?

Great Lakes-St. Lawrence River Region

International boundary
State and provincial boundaries
Canal

Workers prepare salmon in a cannery in Vancouver, British Columbia.

Since then, ocean ships have been able to travel all the way to Canada's Great Lakes manufacturing cities. They opened the inland cities to world trade and so helped Canada's industries grow even faster than before.

The western plains have always made Canada a strong agricultural country. Shipments of wheat grown on the plains travel down the St. Lawrence Seaway each year. Canada is one of the world's leading exporters of wheat. Cattle and sheep ranching are just as important as wheat farming for people living on the Canadian plains.

Canada is extremely rich in mineral resources. Since the 1950s, oil discoveries in the western plains have added drills and refineries to the fields and ranches there. In the Canadian north and western mountains are deposits of coal, iron, nickel, zinc, silver, gold, and many more riches. Many still wait to be taken from the earth. Canadians are moving quickly, however, to develop

these resources. Today mining is growing faster than any other part of Canada's economy. It might be growing even faster if the cold climate did not slow down road building and discourage people from moving into the sparsely settled wilderness to seek their fortunes.

Life and Work in Mexico

More than half of Mexico's people—about 65 percent—live in cities. Mexico's population is growing rapidly, and many people are moving to cities to look for jobs. They are coming from the **ejidos,** which are small farms formed from the plantations of colonial times. The small land plots of the ejidos can no longer meet all the needs of the growing numbers of people. Mexico City, with more than 18 million people now, has grown to be the world's largest city.

Some of Mexico's new urban dwellers are poor and jobless. While there are many factories and industries in the cities, they do not need thousands of new workers each year. Many discouraged job seekers have left Mexico to live in the United States.

Mexico has a sizable iron and steel industry. Its factories make cars, chemicals, and electrical goods. Mexico also manufactures cement, fertilizers, home appliances, paper, and processed foods. It has many businesses that produce clothing, footwear, and other items that workers make by hand. Ever since its revolution in 1917, Mexico's government has promoted the growth of manufacturing and has

497

Mexico's beaches attract many tourists.

created various programs to help its workers.

A number of Mexico's rural workers have jobs on haciendas owned by wealthy Mexicans. Modern haciendas are large commercial farms. They grow coffee, cotton, sugar, fruit, and other crops for export to the United States and other countries. Other rural workers have jobs on big cattle ranches.

Mexico's Excitement and Challenges from the Past

The 1970s were exciting times in Mexico. Gold, silver, copper, sulfur, and other minerals have brought wealth to Mexicans since colonial times. In the 1970s, Mexico began to mine its huge oil deposits along its eastern coast. As you may recall, world oil prices were very high during the 1970s and were expected to continue climbing.

The democratic government of Mexico borrowed money from banks in the United States and other foreign countries. It used the money to explore and drill its new-found oil riches. Mexico's income soared. Its future looked bright.

Oil prices fell abruptly in 1983, however, and Mexico's income dropped with them. Today, Mexico's leaders must try to repay a foreign debt of more than $100 billion.

Mexico's government is trying various ways to repay its debt. For instance, it encourages a large tourist trade, which adds to the country's income. Mexico also is increasing its trade with Japan and Western Europe. The country further is increasing trade with other Latin American countries. Indeed, Mexico continues to work toward the goal of improving the lives of its people.

Reviewing the Lesson

Recalling Key Words, People, and Places
1. Tell what the word **ejido** means.
2. Tell at least one important fact about:
   a. Rio Grande
   b. St. Lawrence Seaway
   c. Mexico City

Remembering Main Ideas
1. How does Mexico's average population density compare with Canada's?
2. What is the fastest growing economic activity in Canada and what difficulties must it overcome?
3. Why are Mexico's cities growing rapidly in population?
4. Why did Mexico borrow large sums of money during the 1970s?

Thinking Things Over
Suppose that the world price of oil suddenly became very high again and then continued climbing. Do you think Mexico's income would soar again? Do you think Mexico's bright outlook of the 1970s would return? Tell why or why not.

498

Lesson 2   Central America and the West Indies

📖 **LOOKING AHEAD** As you read, look for—

Key words, people, and **places:**

illiterate   Fidel Castro
junta   Sandinistas
            contras

Answers to these questions about **main ideas:**

1. What languages and cultures are found in Central America and the West Indies today?
2. What sources of income do Central Americans have?
3. What are the products of the West Indies nations?
4. What political pattern marks the history of Central America and the West Indies?

As you have learned, Central America is the narrow strip of land at the southernmost tip of the North American continent. The West Indies are made up of the islands that lie in the Caribbean Sea, between the Gulf of Mexico and the Atlantic Ocean.

Land and People

Because of their location in the low latitudes, Central America and the West Indies islands have very warm temperatures the year round. Most of the region also receives abundant rainfall. The highland regions in Central America are drier and more temperate. The people generally find them more comfortable places to live than the hot steamy lowlands. In the islands, winds and breezes off the water often moderate the climate also. They create the balmy tropical weather found along many island beaches.

Central America. Guatemala, Belize, Honduras, El Salvador, Nicaragua, Costa Rica, and Panama make up the seven small countries of Central America. They have been separate independent nations since 1838. Locate the Central American countries on the map on page 458.

If you traveled through Central America, you would find that most of the people speak Spanish—the language of their earlier colonial rulers. In Belize, however, you could speak English, since it is a former British colony. The majority of the people in Belize are blacks, the descendants of Africans brought to work as slaves on colonial plantations.

In Guatemala, you would frequently hear Indian languages. Although the country's official language is Spanish, more than half the population is Indian. Guatemalans descended from the ancient Mayans still speak the old language and follow many of their traditional customs.

People of Indian and mestizo ancestry make up the majority of the people in Central America. Only Costa Rica has a large number of people directly descended from original Spanish settlers. As in other regions with Spanish colonial backgrounds, the Roman Catholic religion remains a strong cultural influence.

Independent Nations of the West Indies

Nation	Area in Square Miles	Population	Year of Independence
Antigua and Barbuda	171	74,000	1981
Bahamas	5,386	231,000	1973
Barbados	161	253,000	1966
Cuba	44,400	9,000,000	1898
Dominica	290	79,000	1978
Dominican Republic	18,900	5,000,000	1821
Grenada	133	111,000	1974
Haiti	10,800	5,500,000	1804
Jamaica	4,240	2,200,000	1962
St. Christopher and Nevis	100	44,000	1983
St. Lucia	238	120,000	1979
St. Vincent	150	116,000	1979
Trinidad and Tobago	1,930	1,200,000	1962

Thirteen independent island nations are found in the West Indies. Which nation is the largest both in area and in population?

Populations are growing rapidly in most Central American countries. Yet population densities vary greatly. El Salvador and Guatemala are the most crowded. El Salvador's average population density is more than 600 people per square mile. Guatemala's is more than 180. Nicaragua, on the other hand, has a low density—only about 50 people per square mile. Nicaragua is also the largest country in Central America.

The West Indies. Thirteen independent island nations plus a number of islands belonging to the United States or European countries make up the West Indies. Use the chart at the top of this page to find the names of the thirteen nations. Which nations have been independent only since 1970 or later?

Now locate the islands of the West Indies on the map on page 458. To what country do Puerto Rico and the Virgin Islands belong? Near which state in the United States does the island nation of the Bahamas lie?

People and cultures of the West Indies are much more mixed than they are in Central America. Most of the original Indians of the islands died during the days of European colonization. Unlike Central America, therefore, the West Indies have few traces of American Indian culture today. The people of Cuba, the Dominican Republic, and Puerto Rico are largely Spanish and African in culture and descent. Throughout the other islands, however, you would meet people who speak English, French, Dutch, and East Indian languages. In most of these places, you would also find music, food, clothing, and many other customs that were inherited from the people's originally African backgrounds.

500

Economies in Central America

The countries of Central America tend to be poor. They generally have very few industries, partly because most of the natural resources needed to develop strong industries are not to be found in their lands. A number of countries have some deposits of gold, silver, copper, and a few other minerals.

Clothing and textiles, prepared foods, and wooden items are the most important products of the region's limited industries. Timber for wood products is the most widespread resource in every country. Most countries also have some refining industries that make gasoline, chemicals, and other petroleum products. They import the crude oil used in these refineries. The countries also import the few cars, machines, and other modern factory-made goods that their people have.

Farming and stock raising control the economies and the lives of most of the people throughout Central America. About two out of every three persons in Central America live in rural areas. Many are subsistence farm families. They live mostly on the corn, beans, wheat, and vegetables they grow on small plots. They are very poor and many are **illiterate**—that is, they do not know how to read or write.

Many other rural Central Americans work the plantations and cattle ranches owned by a few wealthy people. The plantations produce sugar cane, cacao, cotton, and citrus fruit for sale to other countries. Bananas and coffee grown on plantations, however, bring in the most income from exports.

Cattle ranching, especially along the Pacific coast, is also very important and growing more so. Central Americans are clearing many of their mountain forest areas, not only for the wood, but to make room for more cattle grazing. Most of the beef is exported. Much of it goes to the United States. You probably have eaten some of it in hamburgers sold at fast-food restaurants.

Central American cities are smaller than the major cities in other parts of the Americas. Guatemala City is the largest, with about 700 thousand people. Urban populations are growing, however, as poor farmers arrive to look for better lives and jobs in the modest industries.

Since independence, most Central American countries have continually struggled for stable governments. Costa Rica is the only country that has had a long history of stable democracy. The peace and relative prosperity of Costa Rica contrast sharply with other countries in Central America.

West Indies Nations

Nations of the West Indies have had their share of dictators, unstable governments, and revolutions. On the whole, however, their governments have been more lasting than those of Central America. During the 1950s, a military leader named Fidel Castro led a revolution to overthrow a harsh dictator in Cuba. In 1959 he won the revolution and eventually set up the first communist government in the

The West Indies depend on the export of farm crops such as sugar cane. The United States is the leading importer of these products.

Americas. Cuba is still a communist nation and has close ties with the Soviet Union.

The living conditions and the economies of West Indies nations are very similar to those of Central America. Poverty is widespread. Even though good farmland is scarce, the biggest portion of West Indian incomes comes from the export of farm crops. Sugar cane has always been the most important crop. Other farm exports include coffee, coconuts, and bananas. Many places have traditionally depended on only one kind of export. When world prices for that product are low, the people face especially hard times. Many West Indies nations are deeply in debt today because of the low prices they receive for their farm exports. The United States is the biggest customer for West Indies exports. Cuba, however, sells to communist countries. The United States does not trade with Cuba.

Jamaica has mined and exported bauxite for many years. There is some petroleum in Cuba and the islands off South America. Cuba also mines nickel and manganese. In the main, though, minerals are as scarce in the West Indies as in Central America. Heavy debts and scarce mineral resources make it difficult for the countries to build modern industries.

The tropical climate and lovely scenery provide the West Indies with a valuable resource, however. Tourists from the United States and Europe vacation in the West Indies all year round. The money they spend while they are there is a large and important addition to incomes in the West Indies.

Political Struggles and Civil Wars

Unlike the rest of Latin America, Costa Rica has a large middle class. A large part of its population is neither rich nor poor. Instead of working on plantations or subsistence plots, middle-class families own enough land to grow coffee and other crops to give them a secure living. The country's relatively contented population has helped Costa Rica achieve its largely stable democracy.

As you have just read, the story is much different in other parts of Central America and the West Indies. For more than a hundred years, a few wealthy landowners have controlled the governments in Central American countries. They have usually behaved selfishly and done little to improve the lives of the many poor people.

Time and again, someone promising to change ruling attitudes has urged the people to fight against the government in power. Often the rebel leaders have been soldiers or guerrillas. Rebel winners have often set up dictatorships or juntas. A **junta** is a small group of military leaders who govern with the help of their army after a revolution or coup.

The rebellions and conflicts have continued during the 1980s especially in Nicaragua. In 1979 a group of Nicaraguan guerrillas who called themselves the Sandinistas (The Sandinista National Liberation Front) started a civil war. They overthrew a line of corrupt presidents from the same family that had ruled the country for more than forty years. The Sandinista victors set up a new government and held it in place with the army. They soon broke their promise to hold a free election and let the people decide who should rule. They also formed a friendship with Cuba and the Soviet Union.

Just two years after the Sandinistas gained control, other Nicaraguans began forming guerrilla bands. Calling themselves "contras," they began a fight to overthrow the Sandinistas. (*Contra* means "against.")

Although the countries of the West Indies face a number of problems, they are trying to solve them while remaining independent. The countries are working to become less dependent on exports, tourism, and foreign aid.

Reviewing the Lesson

Recalling Key Words, People, and Places
1. Identify the key words defined below:
   a. unable to read or write
   b. a small group of military leaders who govern with the help of their army after a revolution or coup
2. Tell why the following are important:
   a. Fidel Castro
   b. Sandinistas
   c. contras

Remembering Main Ideas
1. How do the populations of Guatemala and Costa Rica differ from most of the rest of Central America?
2. What three kinds of rural work do people do in Central America?
3. What advantage does a tropical climate give to West Indies nations?
4. Why did political struggles and civil wars arise in parts of Central America and the West Indies?

Thinking Things Over
In addition to buying Central American and West Indies products, the United States has always given money and other aid to help the countries feed their people and try to build industries. Do you think the United States therefore should have some influence in the politics and governments of this region? If so, what influence should it have? If not, why not?

Practicing Persuasive Writing

Think about the letters you have written. You may have written to thank family members or friends for gifts or to tell them about things you have done or plan to do. You may have written business letters to ask for information about a product. However, have you ever written a letter to try to persuade someone to agree with you about something? Follow the steps Lisa took to write a persuasive letter.

Planning

Before you actually write a letter, you need to plan what you want to say. Lisa's assignment was to write a letter persuading a classmate to visit a region of Canada, Mexico, Central America, or the Caribbean. Lisa chose the Caribbean because she was interested in visiting that area herself. She knew it would be easier to write a persuasive letter about a place that she would like to visit. Next, Lisa listed three possible places to write about. She thought that the entire Caribbean would be too broad a topic. She also listed some features she wanted to be sure to include in her letter.

Places	Features
Haiti	Tourist spots
Puerto Rico	Climate
Jamaica	Interesting landforms and water bodies
	Educational value

Lisa decided to write about Puerto Rico. Because she did not know a great deal about Puerto Rico, she needed to do some research first. She used her social studies text for reference. She also used the library to find additional sources of information on Puerto Rico.

Writing

Once she had the information she needed, Lisa wrote a rough draft of her letter. Her only concern at this point was getting her ideas on paper. She did not worry too much about spelling, punctuation, or capitalization.

As she wrote, Lisa tried to use words that would convince her reader to want to visit Puerto Rico. She used a thesaurus, a kind of dictionary, to replace ordinary words such as *nice* with less ordinary words such as *pleasant.* Since she was writing the letter to a classmate, she also made sure to include things that would be of interest to someone her own age.

Revising

Revising, or changing, is the most important step in writing. This is the stage when you can rethink what you want to say and get reactions from others.

Lisa's teacher said it was all right to get opinions from other people, so Lisa shared her rough draft with a classmate. Because the class was learning Spanish, the classmate suggested that Lisa include something about Puerto Rico's language. The classmate also suggested that Lisa use more interesting synonyms. (A synonym is a word that means the same or nearly the same thing as another word.)

After Lisa made her changes, she checked her letter for mistakes in spelling, punctuation, and capitalization. Then Lisa made a final, neat copy of her letter.

Skills Practice

1. Find the spelling, punctuation, and capitalization errors in the paragraph from Lisa's letter below. Then rewrite the paragraph, making the needed corrections.

> A visit to puerto rico are also educational. What better biology lesson than snorkeling in clear waters! What better history lesson than walking through old fortrisses! Finally, the bustling cities festivals and carnivals show how the past reaches into the present.

2. Choose a region of Canada, Mexico, Central America, or the Caribbean (other than Puerto Rico). Then follow the steps in this lesson to write a letter persuading a classmate to visit that place.

Chapter Summary

Lesson 1   Canada and Mexico—
Canada's colonial history was linked with Great Britain and France, Mexico's with Spain. Canada's population is relatively small, Mexico's is large. Canada is one of the world's wealthy industrial nations, with a strong agricultural and mining economy. Mexico has huge oil deposits, a sizable iron and steel industry, and many large commercial farms.

Lesson 2   Central America and the Caribbean—The countries of Central America have been independent nations since 1838. The Catholic religion is a strong influence throughout the region. In the Caribbean, thirteen independent island nations share the region with island possessions of the United States and Europe. Spanish, English, African, and French cultures are intermixed. Economies in Central America and the Caribbean are slow.

Write your answers on a separate sheet of paper.

Testing Key Words, People, and Places

Part A
Choose the key word from the list that best answers each question.

1. People who cannot read or write are called what?
2. What is a military government that rules a country by force?

3. What is a small community farm in Mexico?
   a. ejido
   b. illiterate
   c. junta

Part B
Choose the person or place from the list that best completes each sentence.

1. The _____ is the river between the United States and Mexico.
2. The _____ was opened in 1959.
3. _____ is Mexico's largest city.
4. Since 1959 Cuba has been ruled by _____.
   a. Rio Grande   **c.** Fidel Castro
   b. Mexico City   **d.** St. Lawrence Seaway

Testing Main Ideas

Choose the answer that best completes each sentence.

1. In Canada people speak
   a. English only.
   b. English and French.
   c. Spanish.
2. Most Canadians live
   a. in the far north.
   b. in the southern part of the country.
   c. near Hudson Bay.
3. The St. Lawrence Seaway was
   a. built to provide water transportation in Mexico.
   b. a joint project of Canada and the United States.
   c. built by Great Britain.

4. Mexico's population is
   a. largely rural.
   b. decreasing.
   c. growing rapidly.
5. Mexico's income dropped abruptly in 1983 when
   a. oil prices fell.
   b. hurricanes hit the coast.
   c. a drought struck the farmlands.
6. Most people in Central America speak
   a. English.
   b. French.
   c. Spanish.
7. The largest portion of Caribbean income comes from
   a. oil revenue.
   b. export of farm crops.
   c. tourism.
8. Fidel Castro led a revolution to overthrow a harsh dictatorship in
   a. Nicaragua.
   b. Mexico.
   c. Cuba.

Testing Skills

1. Practicing persuasive writing.
   Should the United States grant aid to impoverished Central American and Caribbean countries? Write a paper stating your views. Follow the steps of writing a persuasive paper:
   a. Plan what you want to write about.
   b. Research your topic.
   c. Write a rough draft.
   d. Revise your paper.

2. Using and making charts. Make a chart for the list of selected Caribbean nations below. Include the names of the nations in alphabetical order, populations, and areas. (The number in parentheses is each nation's area, given in square miles.) Make up a title and headings for your chart.
Jamaica: 2,200,000 (4,240)
Barbados: 253,000 (161)
Cuba: 9,000,000 (44,400)
Haiti: 5,500,000 (10,800)
Antigua and Barbuda: 74,000 (171)
   a. Which nation in your chart has the largest population?
   b. Which nation has the smallest population?
   c. Which two nations have almost the same land area?
   d. Which of those two nations is more crowded?

Activities
1. Select a country of Central America. Then consult an encyclopedia and write a brief account of its history.
2. As a class project, write a letter asking for brochures and a map of Canada to:
   Canadian Consulate General
   Public Affairs
   310 S. Michigan
   Chicago, Illinois 60604
When you receive the materials, plan an imaginary vacation in Canada. Include historic sites you could visit.

Chapter 26

Countries of South America Today

Once the capital of Brazil, Rio de Janeiro spreads out around one of the world's finest harbors. It is an old and beautiful city. The statue of Jesus on the mountains overlooking the city shows the strong Roman Catholic heritage of the area. Prosperous and educated people have made the city a center of culture and a place that tourists from around the world enjoy visiting year around. New industries fill the city's people with even greater and brighter hopes for the future.

In this chapter you will learn about progress that Brazil and other South American countries have made or hope to make. You will compare and contrast people and lifestyles in four major regions. The lessons in the chapter are listed below.

Lesson 1 The Andean and Northern Countries

Lesson 2 The Silver River Countries and Brazil

Lesson 1   The Andean and Northern Countries

LOOKING AHEAD As you read, look for—

Key words, people, and **places:**

altiplano   Guianas
llanos   Orinoco River
                  Guiana Highlands
                  Lake Maracaibo
                  Ciudad Guayana

Answers to these questions about **main ideas:**

1. In what landscapes do most people of Andean and northern South America live?
2. How are the economies and people of the Andean countries alike and different?
3. What are some major crops and minerals of the northern countries?
4. How has Venezuela handled its oil wealth and economy?

A metal forest of oil derricks sits above shallow gulf waters. Modern skyscrapers rise in growing cities. Ore boats are loaded with copper and tin. Indians using hand tools grow potatoes in high mountain plots. All of these scenes help make up the cultural landscape of the Andean and northern countries of South America.

Land and People

You traced the long, continuous chain of the Andes Mountains that stretches along the west coast of South America in your study of Chapter 23. The highest and widest portions of these majestic mountains run through Ecuador, Peru, Bolivia, and Chile. These four countries make up Andean South America.

Curving north and east from the Andean countries are the northern countries of Colombia, Venezuela, and the three Guianas. Among the Guianas, Guyana and Suriname are independent nations. French Guiana is an overseas province of France.

Except for Chile, the largest part of the population of the Andean countries lives in the mountains and high plateaus and valleys. About eight in ten Bolivians live on the **altiplano,** a plateau on the eastern side of the Andes. Almost half the people in Bolivia, Peru, and Ecuador are Indians. Most of the remaining people are mestizos. Although Spanish is the official language, people of Spanish descent make up only a small part of the population.

Chile, by contrast, has only a very small Indian population. Its people are mainly mestizos and people of Spanish descent. They live mostly on the narrow plain along the Pacific coast.

Hills, rugged highlands, and plateaus of the northern Andes spread over the northern part of Colombia and reach into Venezuela. Rugged landscapes create many isolated villages. The people of both countries are mostly mestizos or people of Spanish descent. The mestizos live largely in highland rural areas while the people of Spanish descent live in the cities. Venezuela's capital of

509

Angel Falls, the world's highest waterfall, is in Venezuela's Guiana Highlands. The misty waters spray down a steep cliff for more than half a mile.

The entire Guiana Highlands are one of nature's most breathtaking treasures. Rainforests filled with unknown plants cover valley floors. Jaguars, deer, short-legged tapirs, and capybaras—the world's largest rodents, almost 4 feet long—wander among the trees. Flat-topped mountains rise around the forests. Across their smooth-rocked surfaces, giant sink-holes suddenly open to depths of 1,000 feet.

As tourism and industry develop the Guiana Highlands, their eerie beauty becomes better known, and one of the world's last frontiers begins to vanish.

Caracas and Colombia's capital of Bogotá are both built in highland regions.

The Orinoco River and its tributaries thread through eastern Colombia and southern Venezuela. They form a grassy plains region known as the **llanos.** For Venezuelans, the llanos are an important frontier. People are moving to the llanos to start farms and cattle ranches. A rugged region known as the Guiana Highlands covers most of Venezuela's south and reaches into the Guianas.

In the Guianas, the people cluster along the coastal lowlands. Since Europeans other than Spaniards or the Portuguese colonized the Guianas, cultures there differ from the rest of South America. The people are descended from immigrants of East Indians, Africans, and Southeast Asians, as well as Europeans.

Living in the Andean Countries

Like the rest of the continent, the Andean countries have rich minerals stored in the earth. Industries that make use of these riches, however, have been slow to develop. Difficulties in building roads and railways over mountains, unstable governments, and large numbers of illiterate people have stood in the way for many years. The Andean countries make use of their minerals by selling them to other nations around the world.

Chile, with the world's largest copper deposits, is the leading copper exporter. It also exports ore from its massive iron deposits. Bolivia is a major world exporter of tin to other countries. Peru exports copper and iron. Ecuador has developed its major oil resources for export income.

The wide gap between rich and poor stands out in Andean South America. The many Indians and mestizos live as subsistence farmers. Some governments have seen to it that these people own their own land, but the farmers still face land shortages and infertile mountain soils. With government help, some are moving to lower land regions and using modern farming practices. Still the Andean countries must import much of their needed food.

Chile is one of the most urban countries in South America. It also has a sizable middle class that sets it apart from the other Andean countries. Its middle-class workers find jobs in the country's mines and in such urban industries as papermaking, food processing, steelmaking, and automobile and truck manufacturing.

The Northern Countries

The countries to the north face the Caribbean Sea and the Atlantic Ocean. All have major coastal cities through which imports and exports flow. Colombia's cities of Barranquilla and Cartagena are both large and bustling Caribbean seaports.

Colombia. Gold, platinum, and emeralds are among the iron, coal, and other minerals that Colombia exports through Cartagena. Oil, Colombia's second most important export, is also an important natural resource.

Almost half the population of Peru is made up of Indians.

Colombia's coffee, however, is its most valuable and best-known export. Small farmers and large plantation owners harvest high-quality crops in mountain areas. Like other countries that depend on a single source of wealth, Colombia suffers when world coffee prices fall. Colombians, therefore, are trying hard to strengthen their mining and petroleum industries. New textile factories, steel mills, and refining centers have helped. Still Colombia's cities, including Bogotá, are crowded with poor jobless people who are migrating from rural areas.

Venezuela. Compared with most of Latin America, Venezuela is a prosperous country with a long history of democratic government. Coffee grown in the highlands along with sugar, bananas, and other tropical crops from the coastal lowlands are important products. The country has gone far with irrigation projects and other steps to improve farming and ranching in the dry llanos.

Venezuela has mined huge iron ore deposits along the Orinoco River near the Guiana Highlands for almost fifty years. Since the 1960s, it has used coal from the same area to manufacture steel in a mill it built in the new city of Ciudad Guayana.

Oil wealth, however, plays the leading role in shaping Venezuela's economy. Venezuela ranks fifth among the world's largest oil-producing countries. It took the lead in forming OPEC in 1960.

With the help of foreign industrial countries, Venezuela began drilling rich

511

This Indian child in Venezuela (left) lives much as his ancestors did, although the country has rich oil deposits under Lake Maracaibo (right).

oil deposits under the waters of Lake Maracaibo in the early 1900s. It now has its own new and modern refineries so that it can export finished petroleum products along with crude oil.

The Guianas. Guyana and Suriname are both important world suppliers of bauxite. They also produce wood, rice, sugar, and shrimp for export. Overall, the Guianas—especially French Guiana—are quite poor. Failure of the mixed peoples to work together creates many problems for growth and stable governments.

Oil Wealth and Growth in Venezuela

High oil prices of the 1970s made Venezuela's income four times greater than it had been before. The small, traditionally wealthy class took much of the sudden new riches. The government, however, insisted that more than

half the money be used to speed up the development projects already underway in other parts of the economy. It put up modern buildings and skyscrapers in Caracas. It began new roads and highways through the llanos and built schools and hospitals the people needed. Many Venezuelans eagerly trained to fill new jobs that the building of these projects opened.

Venezuela also borrowed a great deal of money from foreign banks to help pay for its growth plans. It put much money into a new hydroelectric dam near Ciudad Guayana. The dam was needed to power a new aluminum industry there. The government put up buildings and even whole new towns in the area even though there was no one to live in them yet.

Venezuelans spent much of the 1970s' oil money on foreign goods. Some of the country's leaders worried

Many people live in cities such as Caracas, Venezuela (left), but others are moving to the llanos (right) to farm and ranch.

about spending so much in this way. The government official who had helped found OPEC once said, "The income from oil has discouraged us from trying to . . . [arrive] at solutions through hard work. That is why we have a line of ships at our harbors, loaded with [imported] goods; we think we can solve our problems by buying outside."

When oil prices fell in 1983, Venezuela's boom ended. After a long history of no foreign debts, Venezuela suddenly became a developing country with trouble paying its bills. Its debt of $21 billion is much smaller than Mexico's $100 billion, but it is still hurting the country. Venezuela's leaders are working with foreign banks to gain more time for repaying what the country owes. In the meantime, they have had to slow down or end many of their plans for greater development.

Reviewing the Lesson

Recalling Key Words, People, and Places
1. Identify the key words defined below:
   a. a plateau, as on the eastern side of the Andes
   b. a grassy plains region, as in Colombia and Venezuela
2. Tell how each of the following is important to Venezuela:
   a. Orinoco River
   b. Lake Maracaibo
   c. Ciudad Guayana

Remembering Main Ideas
1. How do the Guianas differ from the rest of South America?
2. Tell two important ways in which Chile differs from the other Andean countries.
3. What are the two most important exports of Colombia?
4. What were some projects on which Venezuela spent some of its oil riches?

Thinking Things Over
Although Venezuela has poor people it is trying to help, class differences are not as sharp as elsewhere in Latin America. Many Venezuelans are middle class. Why do you think Venezuela has a large middle class? What do you think lies ahead for all the people of Venezuela?

Lesson 2   The Silver River Countries and Brazil

LOOKING AHEAD As you read, look for—

Key words, people, and **places:**

mulatto   Brazilian Highlands
estancia   Gran Chaco
gaucho   Rio de la Plata
                     Buenos Aires
                     Brasília
                     São Paulo
                     Rio de Janeiro

Answers to these questions about **main ideas:**

1. What population patterns stand out in the Silver River countries and Brazil?
2. In what ways do the Silver River countries depend on the pampa?
3. What economic plans is Brazil developing?
4. How is Brazil handling its need for energy resources?

Brazil and the Silver River countries cover more than twice as much land area as the Andean and northern countries. Except for the mountains in western Argentina, they all lie east of the Andes.

Land and People

Brazil is the land of the Amazon River Basin and its huge, tropical rainforest. Brazil is by far the largest country in South America and the fifth largest in the entire world. The steamy Amazon Basin covers about a third of the country. Low mountains, hills, and gentle plateaus with pleasant climate conditions make up Brazil's south. Called the Brazilian Highlands, the south is still thinly settled, and the Amazon Basin has even fewer people.

Most of Brazil's people crowd into the small plains and highland regions closest to the Atlantic Coast. For years Brazil's cultural, political, and economic life all took place in these areas. The pattern is changing, however. The Brazilian government is following a number of plans to develop its huge, empty Amazon forest and its western highland regions.

Portuguese-speaking, Brazilians are mostly of European descent. About one in five of them is a **mulatto,** a person of mixed African and European descent. The few remaining Brazilian Indians live mostly in the Amazon Basin.

Uruguay, Paraguay, and Argentina are the lands of the fertile pampas and bleak, barren Patagonia—which covers southern Argentina. (The pampas are a grasslands region in Argentina and Uruguay.) A wilderness called the Gran Chaco crosses Paraguay and northern Argentina. Its tall grasses and thick forests differ sharply from the seemingly endless pampas that border it. The major rivers that course through all three countries meet and empty into an arm of the sea called the Rio de la Plata. *Rio de la Plata* is Spanish for "river of silver." The Rio de la Plata gives the countries their "silver river" name.

People of the Silver River countries fall into two main groups. Spanish-speaking descendants of immigrants from Spain and Italy live in Argentina

514

and Uruguay. As you learned in an earlier chapter, mestizos who prefer the Indian Guarani to the Spanish language live in Paraguay. Paraguay joins the Andean countries of Peru, Ecuador, and Bolivia in having a very strong Indian cultural heritage.

The Agricultural Silver River Countries

The pampas are a great natural blessing for the Silver River countries. Huge fields of wheat, corn, and flax sprawl over the treeless plain. In Argentina large ranches called **estancias** produce large herds of cattle. The famous South American cowhands called **gauchos** work the stock with their dogs and riding horses. In isolated Patagonia, ranchers brave the cold and bleak surroundings to raise sheep for wool and meat.

Argentina's portion of the Andes contains copper, zinc, iron, silver, and other metals. Compared with its agriculture, however, Argentina's mining industry is not highly developed. The country makes greater use of the modest oil and natural gas deposits in southern Patagonia. The oil and gas is used to power the country's industries in the cities.

Well over three-fourths of Argentina's population lives in cities. Beautiful Buenos Aires, with 3 million people, is the capital and largest city. Buenos Aires—along with six or seven other major cities—processes the meat, hides, grain, and wool from Argentina's agriculture. The country's income from exporting agricultural products is its most important source of wealth. Argentine urban industries also make cars, machines, chemicals, and steel.

Despite its many possibilities for a very strong economy, Argentina could not function without the money it borrows from foreign countries. It now has a huge debt to repay.

An Argentinian gaucho rides the pampas.

515

The nation restored democracy in 1985. For years, however, juntas and dictatorships upset the nation and denied citizens' rights. Many wealthy Argentines invested their money in the industries of other countries. They felt it was too risky to put their money into Argentina's own industries under the country's unstable leadership.

Uruguay's largely urban population and history of junta governments are much like Argentina's. Uruguay lacks Argentina's supply of mineral wealth, though. It's agricultural export economy is strong, and Uruguay will probably continue to rely on the pampas in the future.

Paraguay is a traditionally very poor country. Its military government has restricted people's freedoms and abused small Indian groups among its population. More than half the people live in rural areas. They farm and ranch on the pampas and take forest resources from the Gran Chaco. The country is now building several hydroelectric dams on its rivers. Paraguay may greatly improve its future by selling electricity from the dams to neighboring countries.

Brazil—South America's Giant

Although its leaders have sometimes ruled in undemocratic ways, Brazil has had stable government since 1930. Brazil of the 1980s is a very wealthy country compared with the rest of Latin America. It is one of the world's most promising developing nations. Its economy rests on a wide variety of both agricultural and industrial products.

The huge Brazilian Highlands are a treasure chest. The region's soils and grazing lands are rich. Nearly a third of all the world's iron ore is deposited there. Manganese, low-grade coal, and other minerals add to the wealth.

The nation began to develop its unsettled highlands during the 1950s and 1960s. It even built a new capital city there. Find Brasília on the map on page 458. Gradually, more and more Brazilians are moving to the highland region from eastern cities and crowded coastal plains. They are opening new farms and ranches. Many are taking government jobs or finding work in more new cities that are growing there.

Brazil's agriculture produces more cattle and beef than even Argentina's. It is a world leader in its cacao, cotton, and soybean crops. For a very long time, Brazil has been the world's number-one coffee grower. Its best coffee plantations are in the highlands near São Paulo. With more than 15 million people, São Paulo is the largest urban area in South America and the third largest in the world.

Brazil's manufacturing industries are only about twenty years old. In 1970 Brazil began a drive to break its own Latin American pattern of exporting agricultural goods and raw minerals to gain income. It borrowed huge sums of money from foreign countries to develop steelmaking that used the iron, coal, and manganese from the Brazilian Highlands. It built factories that make cars, machinery, textiles, electrical goods, chemicals, and other modern industrial products. São Paulo,

Rio de Janeiro, and the region just north of Rio de Janeiro are now major industrial centers.

City workers and wealthy land and business owners are excited with the new jobs and growing wealth. Nearly half of Brazil's population, however, is made up of poor rural workers. These people have been left out of the economic boom. Many have migrated to huge slums outside Rio de Janeiro and other Brazilian cities. As yet there is no place for them in Brazil's economy.

The nation must find ways to provide for its large rural population, which is still growing. The rural population problem and a foreign debt even larger than Mexico's have slowed down Brazil's drive for development during the mid-1980s.

Meeting Energy Needs — Brazilian Style

In today's energy-minded world, Brazil's plan for meeting its power needs has attracted much attention. The country has only a little oil, and the poor-quality coal of the highlands cannot fulfill its needs. So Brazil looks to water power and to energy from wood and alcohol.

Brazil is working with Paraguay to build the world's largest hydroelectric power plant. It will stand near a dam on the river bordering both countries. By 1993 Brazil may be second only to the United States in hydroelectricity.

Wood from the northern forests provides some heat and power for Brazilian industry. Steel mills are already beginning to use charcoal, which is made from wood, in place of coal. Many scientists, however, are worried that cutting the rainforests will destroy the land.

Fuels burned in Brazil's 10 million or so autos are unique. Most cars use a mixture of alcohol and gasoline. Some run on pure alcohol. Large sugar-cane crops provide the raw material for making alcohol fuels. The government is encouraging farmers to turn more of their lands into sugar-cane production.

In addition, scientists are working on ways to use vegetable rather than petroleum oils in the nation's diesel trucks. Brazil hopes to stop importing foreign oil for motor fuels altogether by 1993.

Reviewing the Lesson

Recalling Key Words, People, and Places

1. Identify the key words defined below:
   a. a person of mixed African and European descent
   b. a large ranch producing large herds of cattle
   c. a South American cowhand
2. Tell where these places are located:
   a. Gran Chaco
   b. Buenos Aires
   c. São Paulo

Remembering Main Ideas

1. How did the Silver River countries get their name?
2. How does Uruguay's possibility for growth differ from Argentina's?
3. Describe Brazil's economic activities of the 1970s.
4. Why are wood resources important to Brazil?

Thinking Things Over

Growing more sugar cane for fuel resources means that Brazil's farmlands produce fewer food crops. How might this affect Brazil's people and economic growth?

Making Predictions from Maps and Tables

Would you like to have a crystal ball to see into the future? Where do you think you will be living in ten years? What kind of work will you be doing in twenty years?

Demographers and Demography

Some people study population figures to answer questions about the future. You learned in Unit 1 that such people are called demographers. The work they do is called demography.

Demographers collect information about people's ages, birth and death rates, ethnic backgrounds, and migration patterns. Some of this information comes from censuses. A census is an official count of the people in a country or other area.

Making Demographic Predictions

With this information, demographers can examine what has happened in the past. They use their knowledge of past events to make predictions about what will happen in the future.

For example, demographers have found that the death rate tends to decrease as a country becomes industrialized. Knowing this, demographers can predict that the population will increase more in developing countries than it will

increase in countries that already are industrialized. They know this because population growth is based on the number of births minus the number of deaths. If the number of deaths goes down, the total number of people probably will go up.

Look at the map below. It shows how the population of South America is distributed. The table on the next page shows the current population

Population of Eight South American Countries	1984	Estimated 1990	Percent of Increase
Argentina	30,097,000	32,900,000	9%
Bolivia	6,037,000	7,300,000	21%
Brazil	134,380,000	150,400,000	12%
Chile	11,655,000	13,100,000	12%
Colombia	28,248,000	31,800,000	13%
Ecuador	9,091,000	10,900,000	20%
Paraguay	3,623,000	4,200,000	16%
Peru	19,157,000	22,300,000	16%

of selected countries in South America. The table also shows what demographers estimate the populations of these countries will be in 1990. Most of the countries of South America are developing. South America has one of the highest rates of population growth in the world. Knowing these facts, which continent would you predict will have the highest population growth rate in the next ten years: Europe or South America? Explain your answer.

Skills Practice

1. Tell whether the following predictions about population growth in South America are likely to be true or false. Give a reason for each of your answers. Use the table above and the map on page 518 to help you. Also keep in mind what you have learned about urban population growth and about the landforms, climate, and resources of South America.

a. Bolivia will experience the fastest population growth.

b. Chile will be only thinly populated.

c. Santiago, Buenos Aires, and Rio de Janeiro will continue to be small cities.

d. The central part of Brazil will be less populated than the coastal areas.

e. Argentina, Paraguay, and Peru all will grow at about the same rate.

2. Choose one country in South America. Draw a map that shows what you think the population distribution of that country will be in 1990. Make each dot on your map equal 100,000 people. Be sure the total number of dots adds up to about the estimated 1990 population for that country.

Chapter Summary

Lesson 1   The Andean and Northern Countries—Contrasts of bustling industry and poverty are found in the Andean countries: Ecuador, Peru, Bolivia, and Chile. The same is true of the northern countries of Colombia, Venezuela, and the three Guianas. Most of the people live in the mountains, except in Chile. The entire region is rich in minerals.

Lesson 2   The Silver River Countries and Brazil—Uruguay, Paraguay, and Argentina are the Silver River countries. These are the lands of the fertile pampa, which produces much of the continent's wheat and cattle. All three countries depend largely on their farm products for export income. As in so many of its neighbors, the Silver River countries and Brazil have immense family wealth side by side with poverty.

Write your answers on a separate sheet of paper.

Testing Key Words, People, and Places

Part A

Match each definition with the correct key word in the list.

1. a name used for famous cowhands of South America
2. a grassy plains region, such as the area formed by the Orinoco River and its tributaries in eastern Colombia and southern Venezuela
3. a large estate producing large herds of cattle in countries such as Argentina
4. a person of mixed African and European descent
5. a high plateau located on the eastern side of the Andes Mountains

   a. altiplano   **d. estancia**
   b. llanos   **e. gaucho**
   c. mulatto

Part B

Choose the place from the list that correctly completes each sentence.

1. The _____ is a wilderness in Paraguay and northern Argentina.
2. The three small countries in northern South America are called the _____.
3. Venezuela mines iron ore near the _____ River.
4. The capital of Brazil is _____.
5. _____ is South America's largest city.
6. In the 1960s Venezuela built the city of _____ to manufacture steel in the Guiana Highlands.
7. The rivers of Paraguay, Uruguay, and Argentina empty into an arm of the sea called the _____.
8. The city of _____, especially its northern section, is part of a major industrial center in Brazil.

   a. Guianas   **e.** Rio de la Plata
   b. Orinoco   **f.** Brasília
   c. Ciudad Guayana **g.** São Paulo
   d. Gran Chaco   **h.** Rio de Janeiro

Testing Main Ideas

Choose the answer that best completes each sentence.

1. The mountain range that stretches down the western coast of South America is the
   a. Andes.
   b. Inca.
   c. Sierra Madre.
2. Eight out of ten Bolivians live on the
   a. Gran Chaco.
   b. antiplano.
   c. Amazon.
3. The official language of Brazil is
   a. Spanish.
   b. Portuguese.
   c. English.
4. Colombia's most valuable product for export is
   a. oil
   b. emeralds.
   c. coffee.
5. Venezuela's economy boomed in the 1970s when
   a. the llanos were irrigated.
   b. tourism was introduced.
   c. oil prices skyrocketed.
6. Chile is the world's largest exporter of
   a. coffee.
   b. copper.
   c. gold.
7. Most of Brazil's people live near
   a. the Amazon River.
   b. the Atlantic Ocean.
   c. the Brazilian Highlands.
8. The government of Paraguay is
   a. a democracy.
   b. a monarchy.
   c. a military dictatorship.

Testing Skills

1. **Making predictions from maps and tables.** Suppose you look at the table below showing population estimates for some countries of South America for the years 1995 and 2000. Assuming population growth rates stay approximately the same, what figures would you project for the year 2025? Could you make the same predictions by looking at a population distribution map?

Country	Year 1995	Year 2000
Argentina	35,100,000	37,200,000
Brazil	165,100,000	179,500,000
Chile	14,000,000	14,900,000
Peru	25,100,000	28,000,000
Venezuela	24,200,000	27,200,000

2. **Drawing conclusions.** How do you think Chile's abundance of copper is both helping and hindering the country and its people?

Activities

1. Research the coffee industry. How did Brazil and Colombia become major producers?
2. Read *Secret of the Andes* by Ann Nolan Clark (Penguin, 1976) for a picture of life in the Andean countries.

Biography Simón Bolívar

Simón Bolívar was one of South America's greatest leaders. He is sometimes called "the George Washington of South America" because he helped lead the fight for freedom from Spanish rule in South America.

Bolívar was born in 1783 in Caracas (kə rä′kəs), Venezuela. His parents died when he was a young boy. Bolívar inherited a large fortune. An uncle took responsibility for Bolívar's education. Some people believe that the tutor whom Bolívar's uncle chose for him influenced the young boy's ideas about democracy. A belief in freedom and democracy was becoming popular throughout the world after the American and French revolutions.

Bolívar traveled throughout Europe and met people who were excited about the ideals of democracy. When he returned to Venezuela in 1810, Bolívar joined a group of patriots and began a struggle that would last many years. In 1811 they declared Venezuela's independence from Spain. Bolívar led three revolts against the Spanish during the next five years but could not push them out of Venezuela.

In 1819 Bolívar's army freed present-day Colombia from the Spanish, and he became president of a united republic including Colombia, Venezuela, and present-day Ecuador. By 1822 he completely drove the Spanish from Venezuela and Ecuador. Bolívar hoped to model these nations upon the government of the United States.

By 1825 Bolívar helped push the Spanish out of Peru. The last of the Spanish had been forced completely out of South America. Part of Peru was made into a separate nation named Bolivia in honor of Bolívar.

From 1826 to 1830, Bolívar struggled to maintain this united republic. One by one, however, the countries he had helped to free withdrew from the republic. By 1828 Bolívar ruled only Colombia. He resigned in 1830 and died that same year. In his message of farewell, Bolívar said, "You should all labor for the boundless benefit of union. My last wishes are for the happiness of our homeland."

Questions to Think About

1. Bolívar lost his fortune in the fight for freedom. What, do you think, did he gain?
2. Bolívar said, "You should all labor for the boundless benefit of union." Name at least one benefit that might result from a union.

The Challenge of the Amazon Basin

When some people think of the Amazon Basin, they picture a huge open zoo of rare birds and animals. Other people see the Amazon Basin as a bottomless treasure chest of valuable minerals. Many scientists, however, warn that the resources of the Amazon Basin must be developed carefully. Otherwise, they could be used up within about forty years.

Everyone agrees that the Amazon Basin can add to Brazil's wealth. For example, miners have found rich reserves of iron, gold, tin, and bauxite. In addition, tributaries of the Amazon River are being dammed to make electricity, which can be used by new factories. Also, the rainforests of the Amazon Basin contain millions of valuable trees, such as mahogany and rosewood. Once the trees are cut for lumber, the land can be used for farming and grazing.

Clearing the rainforests can prove damaging to the land, however. Although rainforests look rich, the soil is often poor. Nutrients in the rain are soaked up by the vegetation before they can soak into the soil. When the land is cleared of vegetation, many nutrients are lost. Unless the soil is fertilized regularly, it wears out. Also, wind, rain, and bulldozers often erode the

soil, revealing a layer of clay. In the sun, the clay layer bakes to a bricklike hardness.

Many scientists are working with Brazil's government to avoid such problems. For example, a Brazilian law says that large developers must leave one-half of their land in its natural state. Scientists are studying the birds, animals, and plants to develop guidelines on the best size and shape of these nature preserves.

Using Your Geography Skills

1. Use the scale on the map on page 462 to give one reason why Brazil finds it hard to enforce its many laws protecting the Amazon Basin.
2. How do you think the interest in developing the Amazon Basin is related to Brazil's growing population?

Write your answers on a separate sheet of paper.

Key Words
Use each key word in a sentence.
1. prairie
2. basin
3. synthetic
4. immigrant
5. mestizo
6. bilingual
7. tribute
8. hacienda
9. dominion
10. ejido
11. illiterate
12. altiplano
13. llanos
14. mulatto

Main Ideas
Choose the answer that best completes each sentence.

1. The mountains that form South America's western backbone are
   a. the Appalachians.
   b. the Andes.
   c. the Alps.
2. Because South America lies in the low latitudes, it has
   a. much snow.
   b. huge needleleaf forests.
   c. a warm climate.
3. Nearly every part of North America is rich in
   a. money.
   b. minerals.
   c. mesquite.
4. About 2000 B.C., the earliest civilization in Mexico
   a. was the Olmecs.
   b. disappeared.
   c. immigrated south.
5. In the 1500s, the Spanish conquered all the Indians in Mexico and
   a. North America.
   b. Central and South America.
   c. Spain and France.
6. In the 1800s, newly won independence in Latin America created many
   a. armies.
   b. problems.
   c. plantations.
7. Located in relatively high latitudes, Canada has a
   a. dry climate.
   b. poor source of minerals.
   c. cold climate.
8. Guatemala, El Salvador, and Panama are countries of
   a. Central America.
   b. South America.
   c. North America.
9. The Caribbean nations export most of their products to
   a. Cuba.
   b. the United States.
   c. Argentina.
10. Ecuador, Peru, Bolivia, and Chile are called
    a. the Andean countries.
    b. the Silver River countries.
    c. the United Republics.
11. The Orinoco River and its tributaries flow through
    a. Peru and Ecuador.
    b. Colombia and Venezuela.
    c. Brazil.

12. The Silver River countries are Argentina, Paraguay, and
   a. Bolivia.
   b. Uruguay.
   c. Peru.
13. Paraguay hopes to improve its economy by
   a. increasing agricultural production.
   b. improving its railroads and highways.
   c. selling electricity to its neighbors.

Skills

1. **Distinguishing fact from opinion.** Write the letters of the sentences that state opinions.
   a. The llanos are made up largely of grassy plains.
   b. The llanos will soon be an important Venezuelan frontier.
   c. There was an oil boom in Venezuela in the 1970s.
   d. Venezuela, despite its huge debt, is one of South America's most progressive countries.
2. **Drawing conclusions from a map.** The orange areas on the map at right indicate countries in South America that have been classified as "hungry countries."
   a. What are these five countries?
   b. From what you have read in this unit, why do you think these countries have inadequate food supplies?

Hunger Levels in South America

Well-fed countries

Hungry countries

Adequately-fed countries

Information not available

Essay

Imagine you live in Suriname or Guyana. Write an essay describing how life has changed there since independence.

525

Resource Section: Contents

The **Resource Section** includes a variety of information to aid your Social Studies learning. Here you will find maps, tables of facts, and more.

Atlas 528

The **Atlas** includes the following maps:

Facts About Countries 546

This section includes the flag, capital, area, population, languages, and products of each country.

Gazetteer 554

The **Gazetteer** is a geographical dictionary. Here you will find the latitude/longitude locations and brief descriptions of the places in *Our World Yesterday and Today*. Page references also are included.

Glossary 564

The **Glossary** gives the pronunciations, parts of speech, and definitions of the key words in the text. Page references also are included.

Index 570

The **Index** lists page references for people, places, and topics to help you locate information in the book.

The World: Political

ARCTIC OCEAN

180°
160°W
140° West Longitude
80°W
60°W
40°W

Arctic Circle
80°N
Alaska (U.S.)

Greenland (DENMARK)

60°N

CANADA

ATLANTIC OCEAN

NORTH AMERICA

Aleutian Islands

40°North Latitude

UNITED STATES

Azores (PORT.)

PACIFIC OCEAN

Midway Islands (U.S.)

Bermuda (U.K.)

MEXICO

CUBA

BAHAMAS

Tropic of Cancer

Hawaii (U.S.)

20°N

DOMINICAN REPUBLIC
Puerto Rico (U.S.)
ST. CHRISTOPHER AND NEVIS
ANTIGUA-BARBUDA
HAITI
DOMINICA
JAMAICA
ST. VINCENT AND
THE GRENADINES
BELIZE
Virgin Is. (U.S.-U.K.)
ST. LUCIA
GUATEMALA
HONDURAS
ST. LUCIA
BARBADOS
EL SALVADOR
NICARAGUA
GRENADA
TRINIDAD AND TOBAGO

CAPE VERDE

COSTA RICA
VENEZUELA
GUYANA
PANAMA
SURINAME
COLOMBIA
FR. GUIANA (FRANCE)

KIRIBATI

P
O
L
Y
N
E
S
I
A

0°
Equator

Galapagos Islands (ECUADOR)

ECUADOR

PERU

SOUTH AMERICA

BRAZIL

WESTERN SAMOA
American Samoa (U.S.)

BOLIVIA

TONGA

French

20°S

Polynesia (FRANCE)

Tropic of Capricorn

PARAGUAY

Easter Island (CHILE)

CHILE

URUGUAY

PACIFIC OCEAN

ARGENTINA

40°S

Falkland Islands (U.K.)

South Georgia (Falkland Is.)

60°S

Antarctic Circle

80°S

ANTARCTICA

180°
160°W
140°W
120°W
100°W
80°W
60°W
40°W

Central America and the Caribbean

30°N

Gulf of California

UNITED STATES

Gulf of Mexico

Tropic of Cancer

NORTH AMERICA

BAHAMAS

ATLANTIC OCEAN

20°N

MEXICO

CUBA

DOMINICAN REPUBLIC
Puerto Rico (U.S.)
Virgin Is. (U.S.)
HAITI
ANTIGUA-BARBUDA
Guadeloupe (Fr.)
JAMAICA
DOMINICA
ST. CHRISTOPHER AND NEVIS
Martinique (Fr.)
West Indies
ST. LUCIA
BELIZE
ST. VINCENT AND
THE GRENADINES
BARBADOS

CARIBBEAN SEA

HONDURAS
GUATEMALA
GRENADA
EL SALVADOR
NICARAGUA
TRINIDAD AND TOBAGO

PACIFIC OCEAN

Central America

Panama Canal

VENEZUELA

10°N

GUYANA

COSTA RICA

528

PANAMA
COLOMBIA
SOUTH AMERICA
SURINAME

0   500 Miles
0   500 Kilometers

110°W 100°W 90°W 80°W 70°W 60°W 50°W

N W E S

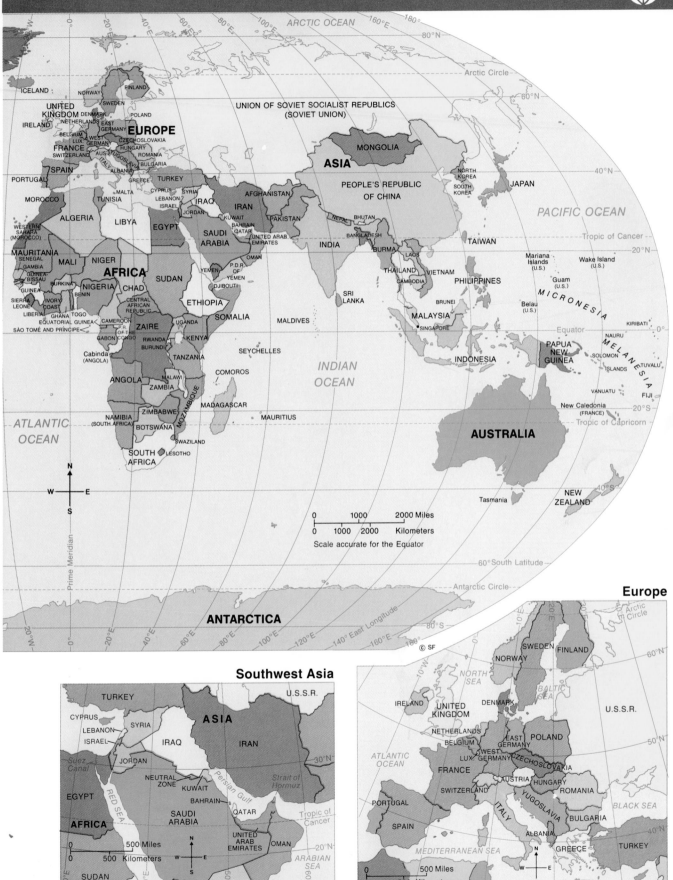

The World: Physical

ARCTIC OCEAN

GREENLAND

Arctic Circle Yukon R.

BERING
60°N
SEA

Gulf of
Alaska

Hudson
Bay

ALEUTIAN IS.

ROCKY MOUNTAINS

**NORTH
AMERICA**

Great Lakes

St. Lawrence R.

APPALACHIAN MTS.

40°North Latitude

PACIFIC
OCEAN

ATLANTIC
OCEAN

Mississippi R.

Rio Grande

Gulf of
Mexico

Tropic of Cancer

20°N

HAWAIIAN
ISLANDS

WEST
INDIES

CARIBBEAN SEA

0°   Equator

GUIANA
HIGHLANDS

Amazon R.

ANDES

**SOUTH
AMERICA**

*BRAZILIAN
HIGHLANDS*

20°S

ATACAMA
DESERT

MOUNTAINS

Tropic of Capricorn

Parana R.

PACIFIC
OCEAN

40°S

60°S

Antarctic Circle

80°S

ANTARCTICA

Land Elevation

Feet		Meters
10,000		3,000
5,000		1,500
2,000		600
500		150
0		0
Below
Sea Level		Below
Sea Level

Ice-covered land

International
boundaries

0   500   1000   1500 Miles

0   500 1000 1500   Kilometers

Scale accurate for the Equator

530

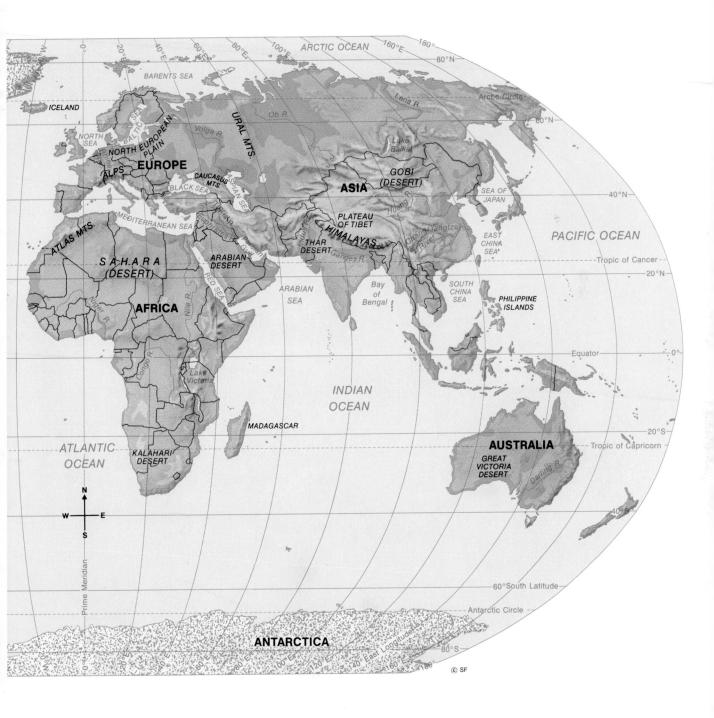

ARCTIC OCEAN

BARENTS SEA

ICELAND

NORTH
SEA

BALTIC
SEA

URAL MTS.

Ob R.

Lena R.

Arctic Circle

80°N

60°N

40°N

Volga R.

NORTH EUROPEAN
PLAIN

EUROPE

ALPS

CAUCASUS
MTS.

BLACK SEA

CASPIAN SEA

MEDITERRANEAN SEA

Lake
Baikal

ASIA

GOBI
(DESERT)

SEA OF
JAPAN

PACIFIC OCEAN

ATLAS MTS.

S A H A R A
(DESERT)

ARABIAN
DESERT

RED SEA

Nile R.

Niger R.

AFRICA

Congo R.

Lake
Victoria

Tigris

Euphrates R.

Indus R.

Ganges R.

PLATEAU
OF TIBET

THAR
DESERT

HIMALAYAS

Huang R.

Chang (Yangtze)
River

EAST
CHINA
SEA

Tropic of Cancer

20°N

ARABIAN
SEA

Bay
of
Bengal

SOUTH
CHINA
SEA

PHILIPPINE
ISLANDS

Equator

0°

INDIAN
OCEAN

MADAGASCAR

ATLANTIC
OCEAN

KALAHARI
DESERT

20°S

AUSTRALIA

GREAT
VICTORIA
DESERT

Darling R.

Tropic of Capricorn

N
W   E
S

40°S

Prime Meridian

20°E

40°E

60°E

80°E

100°E

120°E

140°East Longitude

160°E

180°

60°South Latitude

Antarctic Circle

ANTARCTICA

80°S

© SF

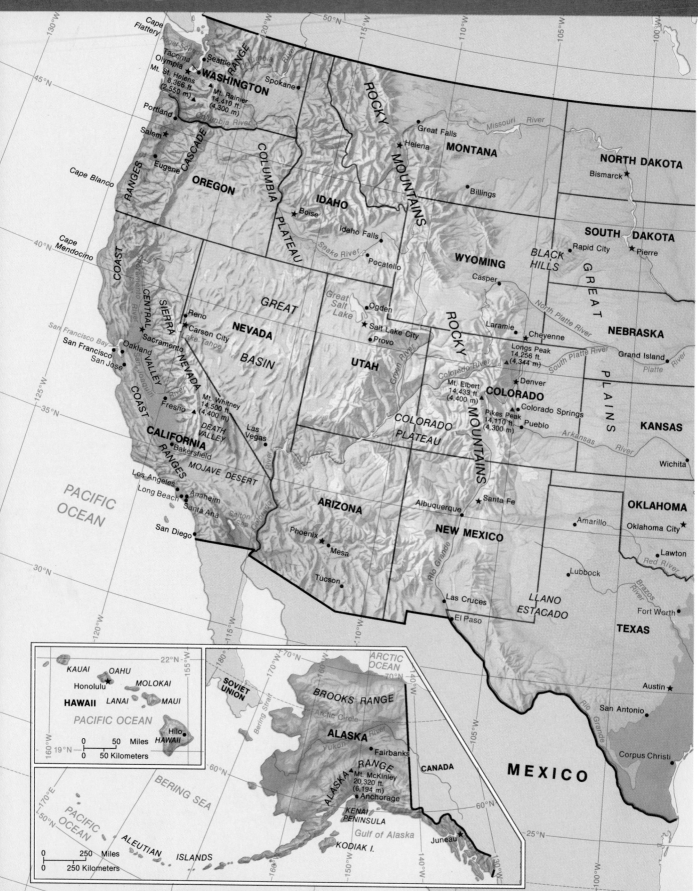

CANADA

Grand Forks
Fargo
Duluth

MINNESOTA
St. Paul ★
Minneapolis ★

Sioux Falls

WISCONSIN
Green Bay

MICHIGAN

Lake Superior

Lake Huron

Lake Michigan

Madison ★
Milwaukee

Grand
Rapids
Lansing ★

IOWA
Cedar
Rapids
Des Moines ★
Davenport
Rockford
Chicago
Gary

Omaha
Lincoln ★

Peoria

CENTRAL

ILLINOIS
Springfield ★

Fort Wayne

INDIANA
Indianapolis ★

OHIO
Toledo   Cleveland   Akron
Wheeling
Columbus ★

Cincinnati

PLAINS

Kansas
City ★
Topeka
Kansas
City
St.
Louis
Jefferson
City

MISSOURI
Springfield

OZARK PLATEAU

Louisville
Frankfort ★
Lexington

KENTUCKY

**WEST
VIRGINIA**
Huntington
Charleston ★

Pittsburgh

PENNSYLVANIA
Harrisburg ★
Philadelphia

**NEW
YORK**
Buffalo   Rochester   Syracuse
Albany ★

**ADIRONDACK
MTS**

MAINE
Augusta ★
Lewiston
Portland

Burlington
VT Montpelier ★
NH Concord ★
Manchester
Boston ★ Cape Cod
MA
Worcester
CT **RI** Providence ★
Hartford ★
Bridgeport
New York City
Jersey City   **LONG ISLAND**
Newark
Trenton ★
NEW JERSEY
Wilmington
DELAWARE
Dover ★

**WASHINGTON,
D.C.** ✪
Baltimore
Annapolis ★
MARYLAND
**DELMARVA
PENINSULA**
Chesapeake Bay

**ATLANTIC
OCEAN**

40°N

VIRGINIA
Richmond ★
Newport News
Norfolk

APPALACHIAN
Mt. Mitchell
6,684 ft.
(2,030 m)
BLUE RIDGE MTS
PIEDMONT
Winston-Salem
Greensboro
Raleigh ★
NORTH CAROLINA
Charlotte

Cape Hatteras

35° North Latitude

Tulsa

ARKANSAS
Fort
Smith
Little Rock ★
Pine Bluff

Memphis

Nashville ★

TENNESSEE
Knoxville

Huntsville

MISSISSIPPI
Jackson ★
Meridian

Birmingham

ALABAMA
Montgomery ★

Columbus

GEORGIA
Atlanta ★
Macon

Greenville
SOUTH CAROLINA
Columbia ★
Charleston

PIEDMONT
COASTAL   PLAIN
Cape Fear

Savannah

Dallas

Shreveport

LOUISIANA

COASTAL   PLAIN
Baton
Rouge ★
New Orleans
Biloxi   Mobile

Houston

Jacksonville

Tallahassee ★

FLORIDA
Cape
Canaveral

**FLORIDA
PENINSULA**
Tampa
St. Petersburg

Lake
Okeechobee
Fort Lauderdale
Miami

Gulf of Mexico

Mississippi
Delta

20°N

ATLANTIC OCEAN

**PUERTO RICO
(U.S.)**   San Juan

N
W   E
S

0   100 Miles
0   100 Kilometers

Tropic of Cancer

CUBA

Straits of Florida

Florida Keys

Mississippi River

Missouri River

Illinois River

Ohio River

Tennessee River

Alabama River

Hudson River

St. Lawrence River

Bay of Fundy

Lake Ontario
Lake Erie

Detroit

0   100   200 Miles
0   100   200   Kilometers

The United States:
Physical–Political

Land Elevation

Feet	Meters
10,000	3,000
7,000	2,000
3,000	1,000
700	200
(Sea Level) 0	0 (Sea Level)
Below Sea Level	Below Sea Level

International boundaries

State boundaries

✪   National capital

★   State capitals

50°N

65°W

70°N

75°W

80°W

85°W

90°W

95°W

70°West Longitude

533

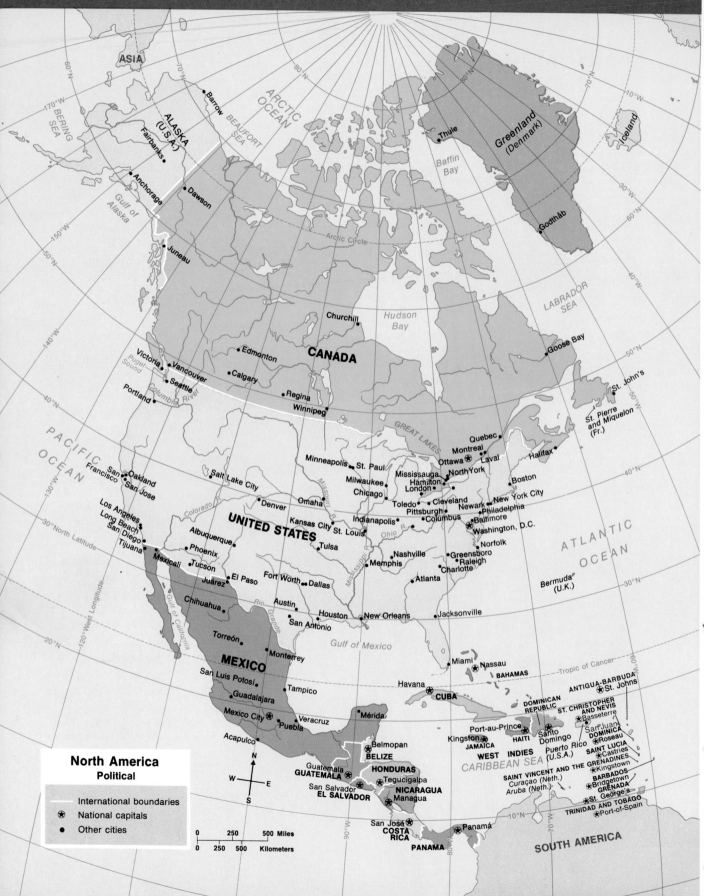

ASIA

ARCTIC OCEAN

BEAUFORT SEA

BERING SEA

•Barrow

ALASKA (U.S.A.)
•Fairbanks

•Anchorage
Gulf of Alaska
•Dawson

•Juneau

Arctic Circle

Thule•

Greenland (Denmark)

Baffin Bay

Iceland

•Churchill

Hudson Bay

LABRADOR SEA

CANADA

•Edmonton

Victoria•
Puget Sound
•Vancouver
•Calgary
Seattle•
Columbia River
•Regina
Portland•
•Winnipeg

•Goose Bay

Godthåb•

GREAT LAKES

•St. John's

St. Pierre and Miquelon (Fr.)

PACIFIC OCEAN

San Francisco•
•Oakland
•San Jose

Salt Lake City•

Minneapolis• •St. Paul
Milwaukee•
Chicago•

Quebec•
Montreal•
Ottawa⊛ •Laval
North York•
Mississauga•
Hamilton•
London•

Halifax•

Boston•

Los Angeles•
Long Beach•
San Diego•
Tijuana•

Denver•
•Omaha
UNITED STATES
Kansas City• •St. Louis
Indianapolis•
Toledo•
Pittsburgh•
Cleveland•
Columbus•
Newark• •New York City
Baltimore•
Philadelphia•
Washington, D.C.⊛

Mexicali•
Tucson•
Albuquerque•
Phoenix•
Tulsa•

Norfolk•

30°North Latitude

Juárez•
El Paso•
Fort Worth• •Dallas

Memphis•

Nashville•

Greensboro•
Raleigh•

ATLANTIC OCEAN

Chihuahua•

Austin•

Charlotte•

Atlanta•

Bermuda (U.K.)

120°West Longitude

Torreón•

San Antonio•

Houston•
New Orleans•

Jacksonville•

MEXICO

Monterrey•

San Luis Potosí•

Gulf of Mexico

Miami•
•Nassau
Tropic of Cancer

Guadalajara•

Tampico•

BAHAMAS

Mexico City⊛
•Puebla

Veracruz•

Havana•
CUBA

ANTIGUA-BARBUDA
⊛St. Johns

Acapulco•

•Mérida

DOMINICAN REPUBLIC
ST. CHRISTOPHER AND NEVIS
⊛Basseterre

•Belmopan
⊛BELIZE

Port-au-Prince•
Kingston•
JAMAICA
HAITI⊛ ⊛Santo Domingo
San Juan•
Puerto Rico (U.S.A.)

DOMINICA
⊛Roseau
SAINT LUCIA
⊛Castries

North America
Political

Guatemala•
⊛GUATEMALA
HONDURAS•
⊛Tegucigalpa

WEST INDIES
CARIBBEAN SEA

SAINT VINCENT AND THE GRENADINES
⊛Kingstown
BARBADOS

International boundaries
⊛ National capitals
• Other cities

San Salvador⊛
EL SALVADOR

NICARAGUA
⊛Managua

Curaçao (Neth.)
Aruba (Neth.)

⊛Bridgetown
GRENADA

⊛St. George's
TRINIDAD AND TOBAGO
⊛Port-of-Spain

N
W E
S

0   250   500 Miles
0 250 500 Kilometers

San José⊛
COSTA RICA

•Panamá⊛

PANAMA

SOUTH AMERICA

NORTH AMERICA

CARIBBEAN SEA

CENTRAL
AMERICA

10° North Latitude

Barranquilla
Cartagena

Maracaibo
Valencia

Caracas

Ciudad Guyana

VENEZUELA

Georgetown

Coco Is.
(Costa Rica)

Medellín

GUYANA
Paramaribo
Cayenne

ATLANTIC

OCEAN

Bogotá

Cali

SURINAME

FRENCH
GUIANA
(Fr.)

COLOMBIA

Equator

Galápagos Is.
(Ecuador)

Quito

ECUADOR

Belém

Guayaquil

Iquitos

Manaus

Amazon R.

PACIFIC

OCEAN

Trujillo

PERU

BRAZIL

Recife

10° South Latitude

10°S

Callao
Lima

Cuzco

Salvador

Arequipa

La Paz

BOLIVIA

Brasília

Sucre

20°S

Belo Horizonte

Tropic of Capricorn

PARAGUAY

São Paulo

Rio de Janeiro

Antofagasta

Santos

Asunción

30°S

Tucumán

Pôrto Alegre

Córdoba

Rosario

URUGUAY

Valparaíso
Santiago

Buenos Aires
La Plata

Montevideo

CHILE

Concepción

ARGENTINA

Bahía Blanca

40°S

N

W   E

S

South America
Political

International boundaries

National capitals

Other cities

Falkland Is.
(U.K.)

50°S

Punta Arenas

0   200   400   600 Miles

0   200   400   600
Kilometers

NORTH AMERICA

CENTRAL
AMERICA

CARIBBEAN   SEA

GUAJIRA PENINSULA

Lake Maracaibo

Coco Is.

LLANOS

Orinoco R.

Angel Falls

GUIANA HIGHLANDS

ATLANTIC
OCEAN

10° North Latitude

10°N

Equator 0°

0°

Galápagos Is.

Río Negro

Marajó I.

Amazon R.

Cape São
Roque

Gulf of Guayaquil

▲ Mt. Chimborazo

A M A Z O N

B A S I N

Aguja Point

ANDES

Mt. Huascarán ▲

Madeira R.

Tapajós R.

Xingu R.

Paraná R.

São Francisco R.

10° South Latitude

10°S

MOUNTAINS

MATO GROSSO PLATEAU

PACIFIC

OCEAN

Lake Titicaca

▲ Mt. Ancohuma

BRAZILIAN

HIGHLANDS

20°S

ATACAMA DESERT

ANDES

20°S

GRAN CHACO

Tropic of Capricorn

Iguaçu Falls

Cape Frio

N

W   E

S

MOUNTAINS

30°S

Mt. Aconcagua ▲

PAMPAS

Río de la Plata

30°S

Salado R.

Uruguay R.

Colorado R.

Blanca Bay

PATAGONIA

San Matías Gulf

South America

Physical

40°S

Chiloé I.

40°S

Gulf of San Jorge

Land Elevation

Feet		Meters
14,000		4,000
7,000		2,000
1,500		500
700		200
0		0
Below Sea Level		Below Sea Level

▲ Mountain peaks

200   400   600 Miles

Strait of Magellan

Falkland Is.

50°S

0   200 400 600   Kilometers

Strait of Magellan

Tierra del Fuego

White lines represent
international boundaries

Cape Horn

60°S

Europe
Political

— International boundaries
⊛ National capitals
• Other cities

ARCTIC OCEAN

ICELAND
⊛ Reykjavik

NORWEGIAN SEA

ATLANTIC OCEAN

Arctic Circle

FINLAND

SWEDEN

NORWAY
• Bergen

Helsinki ⊛
• Leningrad

⊛ Oslo
⊛ Stockholm

• Moscow

Faeroe Is.
(Den.)

Shetland Is.
(U.K.)

Hebrides Is.
(U.K.)

Orkney Is.
(U.K.)

SCOTLAND
• Glasgow

Orust I.—
(Sweden)

NORTHERN
IRELAND • Belfast

Dublin ⊛
REPUBLIC
OF
IRELAND

UNITED KINGDOM

WALES

• Manchester
ENGLAND

• London

NORTH
SEA

DENMARK ⊛ Copenhagen

BALTIC SEA

UNION OF
SOVIET SOCIALIST REPUBLICS
(SOVIET UNION)

NETHERLANDS
The Hague • ⊛ Amsterdam

• Hamburg

Elbe

East Berlin ⊛

⊛ Warsaw

Volga River

Essen • • Dortmund
Brussels ⊛ • Dusseldorf
BELGIUM • Bonn
LUXEMBOURG
Luxembourg ⊛

EAST
GERMANY

Oder River

POLAND

Vistula

WEST
GERMANY

⊛ Prague

Dnieper River

⊛ Paris

Seine River

Rhine River

CZECHOSLOVAKIA

Dniester River

River

Loire River

• Munich

Danube

Vienna ⊛

Dniester River

FRANCE

Zurich •
Bern ⊛
SWITZERLAND

LIECHTENSTEIN
• Vaduz

AUSTRIA

⊛ Budapest
HUNGARY

ROMANIA

BLACK
SEA

• Bordeaux

Gironde River

Milan •
• Turin

Po River
• Genoa

Belgrade ⊛

Bucharest ⊛
Danube River

PORTUGAL

Ebro River

• Monaco
Marseille • MONACO

SAN MARINO
⊛ San Marino

YUGOSLAVIA

BULGARIA
Sofia •

Istanbul •

Madrid ⊛

Tagus River

⊛ Andorra la Vella
ANDORRA
• Barcelona

Corsica
(Fr.)

ITALY

⊛ VATICAN CITY ⊛ Rome

ALBANIA
Tirana •

TURKEY

40°N

⊛ Lisbon

SPAIN

Sardinia
(It.)

• Naples

GREECE

ASIA

Guadalquivir River

• Córdoba

Balearic Is.
(Sp.)

Athens ⊛

Nicosia ⊛

Gibraltar (U.K.)

• Palermo

Sicily
(It.)

N
W   E
S

Crete
(Gr.)

CYPRUS

MALTA ⊛ Valletta

MEDITERRANEAN SEA

AFRICA

0   200   400 Miles
0   200   400   Kilometers

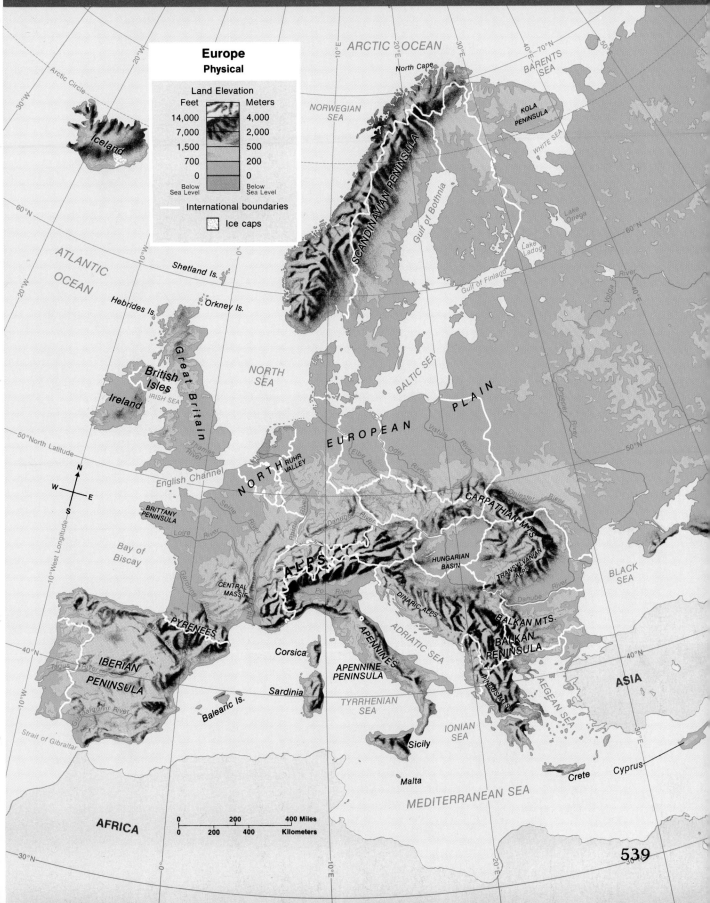

Europe
Physical

Land Elevation

Feet		Meters
14,000		4,000
7,000		2,000
1,500		500
700		200
0		0
Below Sea Level		Below Sea Level

International boundaries

Ice caps

ARCTIC OCEAN

North Cape

NORWEGIAN SEA

BARENTS SEA

KOLA PENINSULA

WHITE SEA

SCANDINAVIAN PENINSULA

Gulf of Bothnia

Lake Onega

Lake Ladoga

Gulf of Finland

Arctic Circle

ATLANTIC OCEAN

Shetland Is.

Hebrides Is.

Orkney Is.

British Isles

Ireland

IRISH SEA

Great Britain

NORTH SEA

BALTIC SEA

NORTH EUROPEAN PLAIN

Vistula River

Dnieper River

Volga River

50°North Latitude

Thames River

English Channel

RUHR VALLEY

Elbe River

Oder River

CARPATHIAN MTS.

Dniester River

BRITTANY PENINSULA

Seine River

Rhine River

Danube River

Bay of Biscay

Loire River

HUNGARIAN BASIN

TRANSYLVANIAN ALPS

BLACK SEA

Garonne River

CENTRAL MASSIF

ALPS

Po River

DINARIC ALPS

Danube River

PYRENEES

IBERIAN PENINSULA

Corsica

APENNINES

ADRIATIC SEA

BALKAN MTS.

BALKAN PENINSULA

Tagus River

APENNINE PENINSULA

PINDUS MTS.

AEGEAN SEA

ASIA

Guadalquivir River

Balearic Is.

Sardinia

TYRRHENIAN SEA

IONIAN SEA

Strait of Gibraltar

Sicily

Crete

Cyprus

Malta

MEDITERRANEAN SEA

AFRICA

N
W E
S

0	200	400 Miles
0	200	400

Kilometers

539

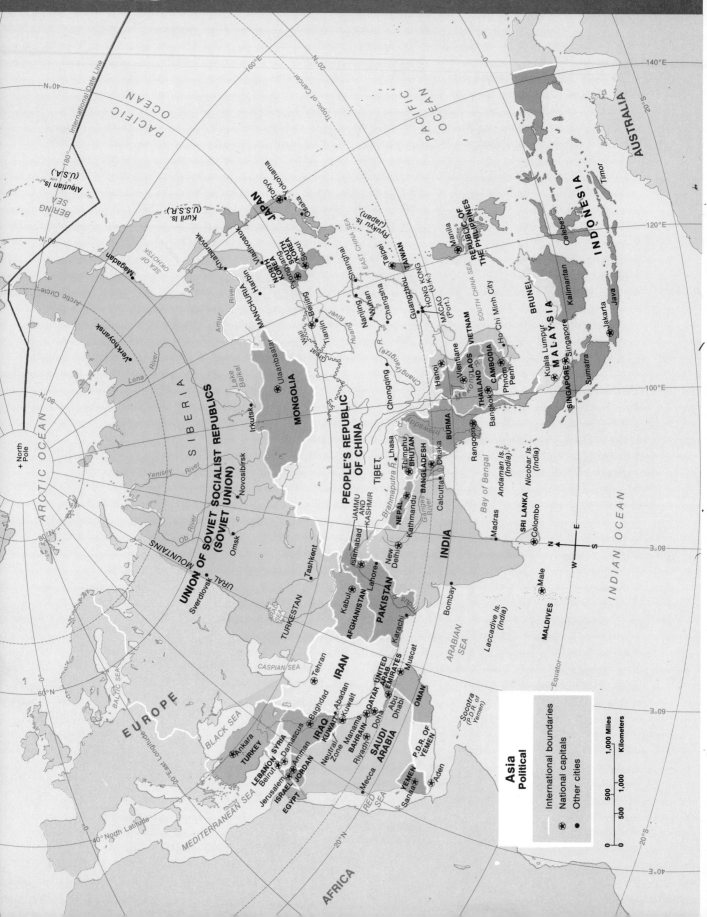

Asia
Political

International boundaries
National capitals ⊛
Other cities ●

1,000 Miles
1,000 Kilometers
500
500
0

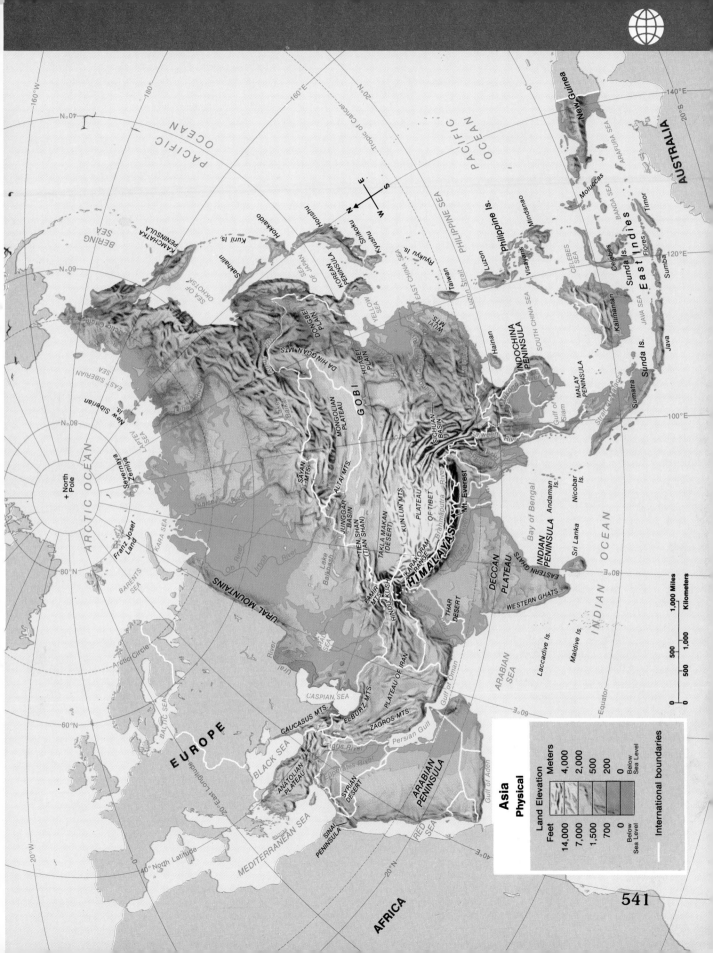

Asia
Physical

Land Elevation

Feet	Meters
14,000	4,000
7,000	2,000
1,500	500
700	200
0	0
Below Sea Level	Below Sea Level

International boundaries

1,000 Miles

1,000 Kilometers

500

500

0

ARCTIC OCEAN

+ North Pole

PACIFIC OCEAN

INDIAN OCEAN

EUROPE

AFRICA

AUSTRALIA

BERING SEA

KAMCHATKA PENINSULA

SEA OF OKHOTSK

Sakhalin

Kuril Is.

Hokkaido

Honshu

Shikoku

Kyushu

SEA OF JAPAN

KOREAN PENINSULA

YELLOW SEA

EAST CHINA SEA

Ryukyu Is.

Taiwan

Luzon Strait

PHILIPPINE SEA

Philippine Is.

Luzon

Mindanao

Visayans

South CHINA SEA

Hainan

Gulf of Siam

MALAY PENINSULA

INDOCHINA PENINSULA

WU-I MTS

Sumatra

Strait of Malacca

Sunda Is.

Kalimantan

Celebes

CELEBES SEA

JAVA SEA

Java

Sumba

Flores

Timor

BANDA SEA

Moluccas

ARAFURA SEA

New Guinea

East Indies

Sunda Is.

GOBI

DA HINGGAN MTS

DONGBEI PLAIN

HUABEI PLAIN

MONGOLIAN PLATEAU

ALTAI MTS.

SAYAN MTS.

Lena

Baikal

JUNGGAR BASIN

TIEN SHAN (CIAN SHAN)

TAKLA MAKAN (DESERT)

KUNLUN MTS.

PLATEAU OF TIBET

SICHUAN BASIN

Salween River

KARAKORAM RANGE

HIMALAYAS

Mt. Everest

Brahmaputra River

Huang River

PAMIR MTS.

HINDU KUSH

Indus

Ganges

THAR DESERT

DECCAN PLATEAU

EASTERN GHATS

WESTERN GHATS

INDIAN PENINSULA

Bay of Bengal

Andaman Is.

Nicobar Is.

Sri Lanka

Laccadive Is.

Maldive Is.

ARABIAN SEA

Equator

Ob River

Irtysh River

Lake Balkhash

Aral Sea

URAL MOUNTAINS

Ural River

CASPIAN SEA

CAUCASUS MTS.

ELBURZ MTS.

ZAGROS MTS.

PLATEAU OF IRAN

Gulf of Oman

Persian Gulf

ARABIAN PENINSULA

Tigris River

Euphrates River

SYRIAN DESERT

ANATOLIAN PLATEAU

BLACK SEA

MEDITERRANEAN SEA

BALTIC SEA

SINAI PENINSULA

RED SEA

Gulf of Aden

BARENTS SEA

KARA SEA

LAPTEV SEA

EAST SIBERIAN SEA

New Siberian Is.

Severnaya Zemlya

Franz Josef Land

Yenisey

Lena

20° East Longitude

40° North Latitude

20°N

40°N

60°N

80°N

160°W

180°

160°E

140°E

120°E

100°E

80°E

60°E

Tropic of Cancer

Arctic Circle

20°S

Kyzyl Kum

Tarim

N E S W

ATLAS

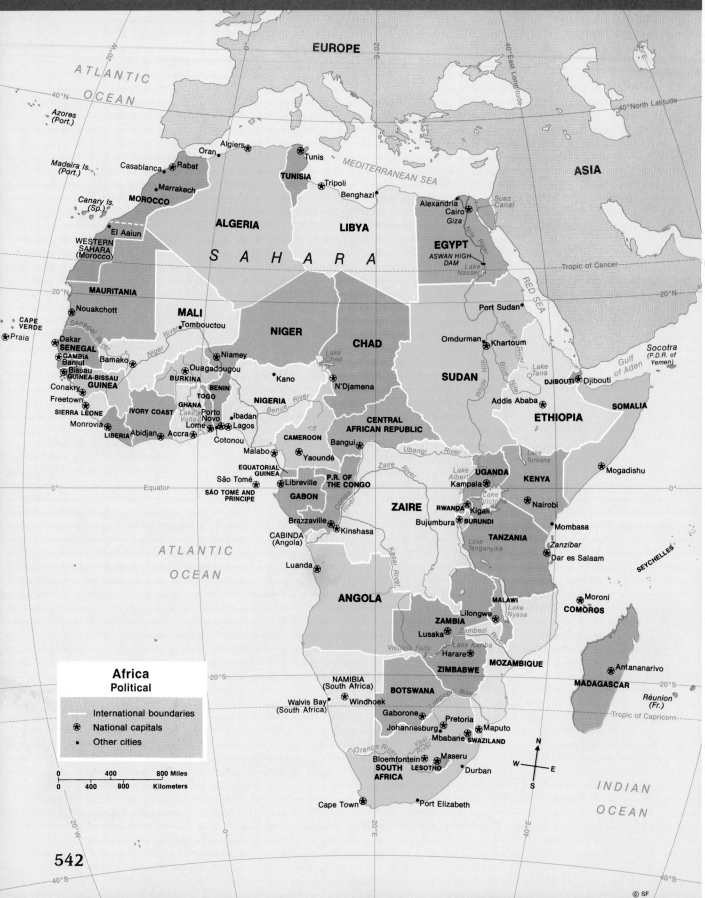

ATLANTIC OCEAN

EUROPE

ASIA

MEDITERRANEAN SEA

Azores (Port.)

Madeira Is. (Port.)

Canary Is. (Sp.)

Oran •Algiers •Tunis
Casablanca •Rabat   TUNISIA   •Tripoli
•Marrakech   Benghazi•
MOROCCO

El Aaiun•
WESTERN SAHARA (Morocco)   ALGERIA   LIBYA

S A H A R A

Alexandria•
Cairo•
Giza

EGYPT

Suez Canal

ASWAN HIGH DAM
Lake Nasser

Tropic of Cancer

MAURITANIA

Nouakchott•   MALI
Senegal River   •Tombouctou   NIGER   CHAD

CAPE VERDE
•Praia

Dakar•   SENEGAL
GAMBIA•Banjul
Bissau•
GUINEA-BISSAU

Niger River

•Niamey
Bamako•   BURKINA
•Ouagadougou
BENIN
TOGO

Kano•

Lake Chad

N'Djamena•

Port Sudan•

Omdurman• Khartoum•

SUDAN

Atbara River

RED SEA

Lake Tana

Socotra (P.D.R. of Yemen)

Gulf of Aden

Conakry•
Freetown•   GUINEA
SIERRA LEONE
Monrovia•   IVORY COAST
LIBERIA   Abidjan•   Accra•

GHANA
Porto Novo
Lomé• Lagos•
Cotonou•

•Ibadan   NIGERIA

Benue River

DJIBOUTI•Djibouti

Addis Ababa•

SOMALIA

ETHIOPIA

Malabo•   CAMEROON
EQUATORIAL GUINEA   •Yaoundé
São Tomé•
SÃO TOMÉ AND PRINCIPE
Libreville•   GABON

Lake Volta

CENTRAL AFRICAN REPUBLIC

Bangui•

Ubangi River

P.R. OF THE CONGO

Zaire River

Lake Albert   UGANDA
Kampala•
Lake Turkana

•Mogadishu

Equator

Brazzaville•
CABINDA (Angola)   •Kinshasa

ZAIRE

Congo River

RWANDA •Kigali
Bujumbura• •BURUNDI

Lake Victoria

KENYA
•Nairobi

•Mombasa

ATLANTIC OCEAN

Luanda•

Kasai River

ANGOLA

Lake Tanganyika

TANZANIA

Zanzibar•
Dar es Salaam•

SEYCHELLES

•Moroni
COMOROS

MALAWI
Lilongwe•
Lake Nyasa

ZAMBIA
Lusaka•   Zambezi River
Victoria Falls   Lake Kariba
Harare•

ZIMBABWE   MOZAMBIQUE

•Antananarivo

MADAGASCAR

Réunion (Fr.)

Tropic of Capricorn

NAMIBIA (South Africa)
Walvis Bay (South Africa)   •Windhoek

BOTSWANA   Limpopo River
Gaborone•
Johannesburg• Pretoria•
•Maputo
Mbabane•SWAZILAND

Africa
Political

— International boundaries
⊛ National capitals
• Other cities

| 0 | 400 | 800 Miles |
| 0 | 400 | 800 Kilometers |

Orange River   Vaal River   Maseru•
Bloemfontein•   LESOTHO
SOUTH AFRICA

•Durban

N
W   E
S

Cape Town•   •Port Elizabeth

INDIAN OCEAN

© SF

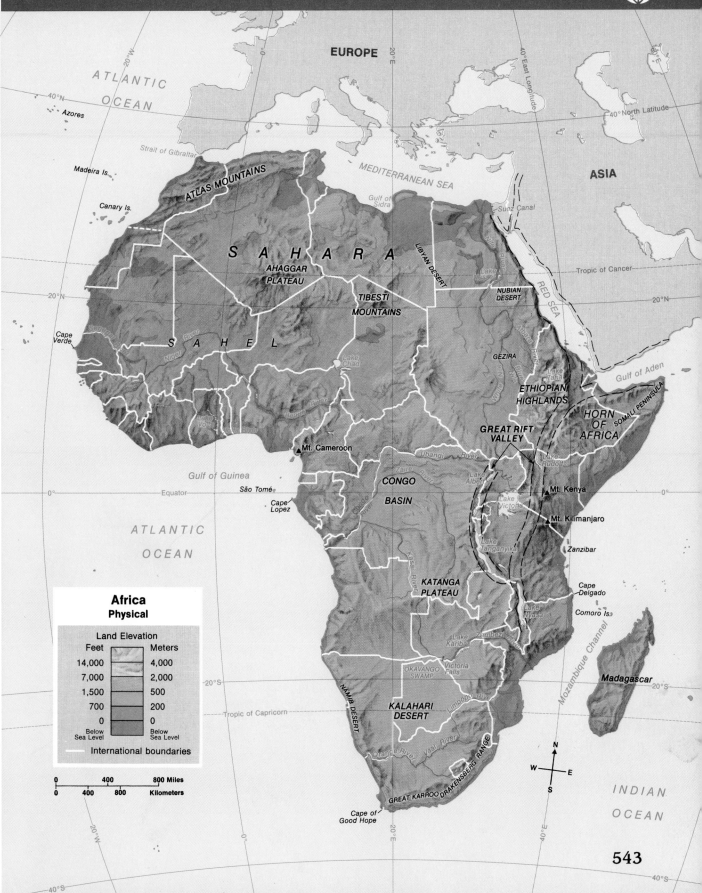

ATLANTIC OCEAN

EUROPE

40°N

Azores

ATLAS MOUNTAINS

Madeira Is.

Strait of Gibraltar

Canary Is.

Cape Verde

S A H A R A

AHAGGAR PLATEAU

TIBESTI MOUNTAINS

20°N

Niger River

S A H E L

Lake Chad

MEDITERRANEAN SEA

20°E

Gulf of Sidra

LIBYAN DESERT

40°East Longitude

ASIA

Suez Canal

Tropic of Cancer

Nile River

NUBIAN DESERT

RED SEA

Gulf of Aden

40°North Latitude

8°E

20°N

GEZIRA

Lake Tana

Atbara River

ETHIOPIAN HIGHLANDS

SOMALI PENINSULA

HORN OF AFRICA

Mt. Cameroon

Gulf of Guinea

São Tomé

Cape Lopez

Equator

ATLANTIC OCEAN

Benue River

Volta River

Ubangi River

CONGO BASIN

Zaire River

Congo River

Kasai River

GREAT RIFT VALLEY

White Nile

Lake Albert

Lake Victoria

Lake Rudolf

Mt. Kenya

Mt. Kilimanjaro

Zanzibar

Lake Tanganyika

0°

KATANGA PLATEAU

Lake Nyasa

Cape Delgado

Comoro Is.

Africa
Physical

Land Elevation

Feet		Meters
14,000		4,000
7,000		2,000
1,500		500
700		200
0		0
Below Sea Level		Below Sea Level

International boundaries

Lake Kariba

Zambezi River

Victoria Falls

OKAVANGO SWAMP

20°S

NAMIB DESERT

KALAHARI DESERT

Tropic of Capricorn

Limpopo River

Mozambique Channel

Madagascar

20°S

0 400 800 Miles

0 400 800 Kilometers

Orange River

Vaal River

GREAT KARROO

DRAKENSBERG RANGE

N

W E

S

INDIAN OCEAN

Cape of Good Hope

20°W

0°

20°E

3.0

40°S

© SF

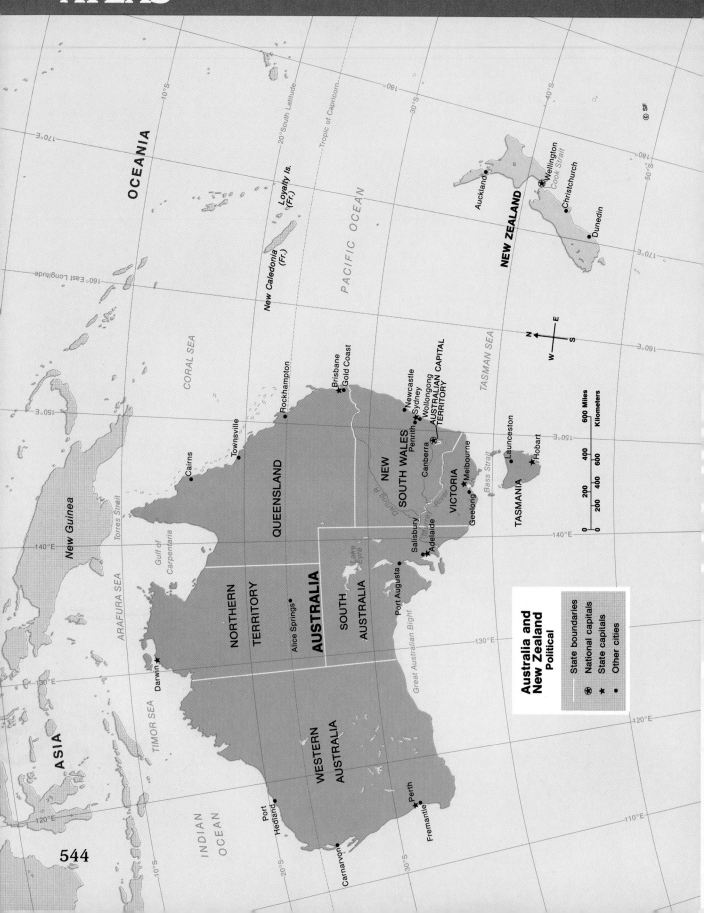

ASIA

New Guinea

OCEANIA

PACIFIC OCEAN

NEW ZEALAND

Auckland

Wellington
Christchurch

Dunedin

Cook Strait

TASMAN SEA

CORAL SEA

New Caledonia (Fr.)

Loyalty Is. (Fr.)

Tropic of Capricorn

20°South Latitude

160° East Longitude

180

Brisbane
Gold Coast

Rockhampton

Newcastle
Sydney
Penrith Wollongong
Canberra AUSTRALIAN CAPITAL TERRITORY

NEW
SOUTH WALES

Townsville

Cairns

QUEENSLAND

ARAFURA SEA

Gulf of
Carpentaria

Torres Strait

TIMOR SEA

Darwin

NORTHERN
TERRITORY

Alice Springs

AUSTRALIA

SOUTH
AUSTRALIA

WESTERN
AUSTRALIA

Perth
Fremantle

Port
Hedland

Carnarvon

INDIAN
OCEAN

Great Australian Bight

Port Augusta

Salisbury
Adelaide

Lake
Eyre

Darling R.

Murray River

VICTORIA

Melbourne
Geelong

Launceston

TASMANIA

Hobart

Bass Strait

Australia and
New Zealand
Political

State boundaries
National capitals
State capitals
Other cities

600 Miles
Kilometers
400
200
0
200
400
600

© SF

544

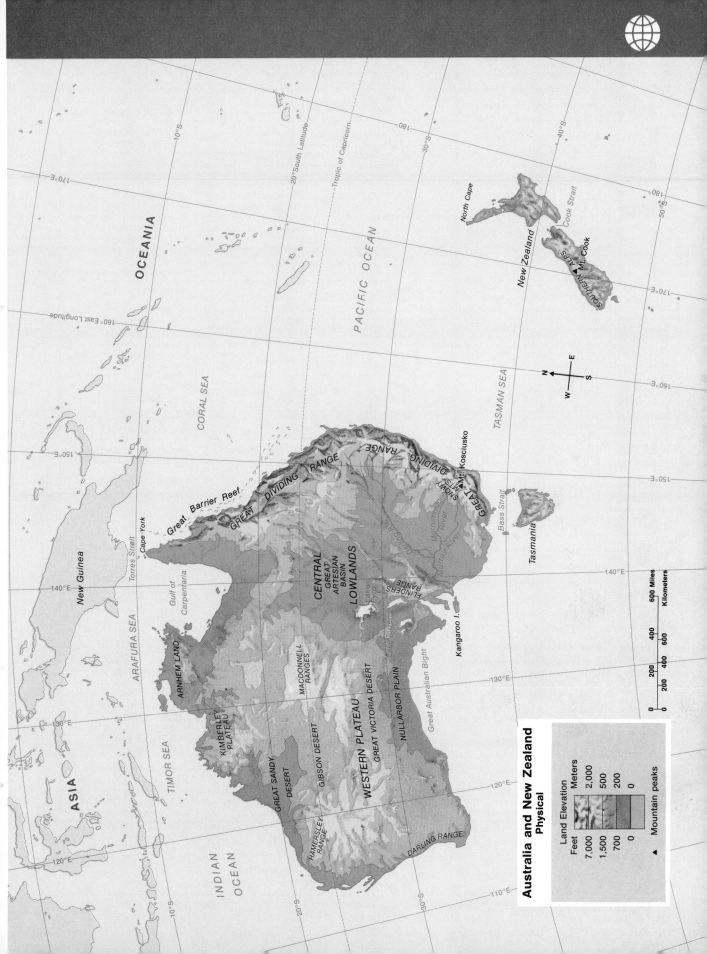

Australia and New Zealand
Physical

Land Elevation

Feet	Meters
7,000	2,000
1,500	500
700	200
0	0

▲ Mountain peaks

ASIA

OCEANIA

New Guinea

INDIAN OCEAN

TIMOR SEA

ARAFURA SEA

Torres Strait

Cape York

Gulf of Carpentaria

CORAL SEA

PACIFIC OCEAN

Great Barrier Reef

ARNHEM LAND

KIMBERLEY PLATEAU

GREAT SANDY DESERT

HAMERSLEY RANGE

GIBSON DESERT

MACDONNELL RANGES

WESTERN PLATEAU

GREAT VICTORIA DESERT

GREAT DIVIDING RANGE

CENTRAL LOWLANDS

GREAT ARTESIAN BASIN

FLINDERS RANGE

Lake Eyre

Lake Torrens

NULLARBOR PLAIN

Great Australian Bight

Kangaroo I.

DARLING RANGE

Darling River

Murray River

Murrumbidgee R.

SNOWY MTS.

GREAT DIVIDING RANGE

▲ Mt. Kosciusko

Bass Strait

Tasmania

TASMAN SEA

North Cape

Cook Strait

New Zealand

SOUTHERN ALPS

▲ Mt. Cook

110°E
120°E
130°E
140°E
150°E
160°E
170°E
180°

10°S
20°S
30°S
40°S
50°S

20° South Latitude

Tropic of Capricorn

160° East Longitude

N
E
S
W

0	200	400	600 Miles
0	200	400	600 Kilometers

Flag	Country or Dependency	Capital	Area	Population	Major or Official Languages	Important Products
	Afghanistan	Kabul	250,000 (mi²) 647,497 (km²)	19,000,000	Pushtu, Dari Persian	carpets, natural gas, fruit, salt, coal, wheat
	Albania	Tirana	11,099 28,748	3,000,000	Albanian	minerals, metals, olives, cereals, tobacco, lumber
	Algeria	Algiers	919,591 2,381,741	23,000,000	Arabic, French	wheat, barley, petroleum, wine, fruit, iron ore
	Andorra	Andorra la Vella	175 453	47,000	French, Spanish	livestock, tobacco, cereals, potatoes, iron ore
	Angola	Luanda	481,351 1,246,700	8,000,000	Bantu languages, Portuguese	coffee, diamonds, cotton, oil, fish, iron ore
	Anguilla (UK)	The Valley	35 91	8,000	English	fruit, vegetables, lobsters, fish, salt
	Antigua and Barbuda	St. Johns	171 442	83,000	English	cotton, clothing, rum, molasses, sugar, bananas
	Argentina	Buenos Aires	1,068,297 2,766,889	31,000,000	Spanish	meat, wool, hides, wheat, corn, fruit, vegetables
	Australia	Canberra	2,967,895 7,686,848	16,000,000	English	wheat, wool, livestock, metal ores, coal, bauxite
	Austria	Vienna	32,374 83,849	8,000,000	German	lumber, metal products, paper, textiles, food
	Azores (PO)	Ponta Delgada	902 2,335	280,000	Portuguese	farm products, fish, fruit, grains
	Bahamas	Nassau	5,380 13,935	232,000	English	pharmaceuticals, salt, fish, lobsters, rum
	Bahrain	Manama	254 659	400,000	Arabic, English, French	petroleum products, fish, aluminum processing
	Bangladesh	Dhaka	55,598 143,998	104,000,000	Bengali, English	jute goods, tea, fish, leather, seafood, hides
	Barbados	Bridgetown	166 431	280,000	English	clothing, molasses, rum, sugar, fish, lime
	Belgium	Brussels	11,781 30,513	10,000,000	Dutch, French	precious stones, iron and steel products
	Belize	Belmopan	8,867 22,965	161,000	English, Spanish	molasses, rice, lumber, livestock, fish, fruit
	Benin	Porto-Novo	43,483 112,622	4,000,000	French, others	palm oil, cotton, cocoa beans, fish, iron ore
	Bermuda (UK)	Hamilton	20 53	60,000	English	perfumes, petroleum products, pharmaceuticals
	Bhutan	Thimphu	18,147 47,000	1,000,000	Dzongkha, Nepali	lumber, fruit, coal, vegetables, cement
	Bolivia	La Paz, Sucre	424,163 1,098,581	7,000,000	Spanish, Quechua, Aymara	petroleum, tin, gold, lead, zinc, coffee
	Botswana	Gaborone	231,804 600,372	1,000,000	English, Setswana	livestock, diamonds, copper, nickel, salt
	Brazil	Brasília	3,286,473 8,511,965	140,000,000	Portuguese	iron ore, steel, motor vehicles, coffee, sugar
	Brunei	Bandar Seri Begawan	2,226 5,765	221,000	Malay, English, Chinese	petroleum, rubber, lumber, rice, pepper, bananas

(UK) United Kingdom   (PO) Portugal

Flag	Country or Dependency	Capital	Area	Population	Major or Official Languages	Important Products
	Bulgaria	Sofia	42,823 (mi²) 110,912 (km²)	9,000,000	Bulgarian	farm products, minerals, machinery, equipment
	Burkina Faso	Ouaga-dougou	105,869 274,200	8,000,000	French, others	livestock, cotton, peanuts, sesame, grains
	Burma	Rangoon	261,216 676,552	37,000,000	Burmese	teak, rice, sugar, precious stones, rubber
	Burundi	Bujumbura	10,747 27,834	5,000,000	Kirundi, French	cotton, hides, tea, coffee, bananas, grain
	Cambodia	Phnom Penh	69,898 181,035	6,000,000	Khmer	fish, rubber, paper, timber, rice, sugar
	Cameroon	Yaoundé	183,568 475,442	10,000,000	English, French, others	cotton, coffee, cocoa beans, tea, rubber
	Canada	Ottawa	3,851,791 9,976,139	27,000,000	English, French	motor vehicles, machinery, lumber, metal ores
	Canary Islands (SP)	Las Palmas	2,808 7,273	1,000,000	Spanish	fish, fruit, grains, wine, vegetables, sugar
	Cape Verde	Praia	1,557 4,033	356,000	Portuguese	fish, shellfish, salt, bananas, coffee, sugar
	Cayman Islands (UK)	Georgetown	100 259	20,000	English	turtle products, fish, lobsters
	Central African Republic	Bangui	240,534 622,984	3,000,000	French, Sango	coffee, diamonds, cocoa beans, lumber, cotton
	Chad	N'Djamena	495,752 1,284,000	5,000,000	French, Arabic, others	livestock, cotton, rice, animal products, fish
	Chile	Santiago	292,256 756,945	12,000,000	Spanish	paper, lumber, copper, iron, nitrates, fish
	China	Beijing	3,705,390 9,596,961	1,000,000,000	Mandarin Chinese, others	farm products, petroleum, minerals, metals
	Colombia	Bogotá	439,735 1,138,914	30,000,000	Spanish	petroleum, coffee, sugar, cotton, textiles
	Comoros	Moroni	719 1,862	469,000	Arabic, French	vanilla, copra, cloves, perfume essences, sugar
	Congo	Brazzaville	132,046 342,000	2,000,000	French, Lingala, Kokongo	lumber, petroleum, cocoa beans, palm oil, sugar
	Cook Islands (NZ)	Avarua	93 241	21,000	English	citrus, clothing, canned fruit, vegetables
	Costa Rica	San José	19,575 50,700	3,000,000	Spanish	livestock, sugar, cocoa beans, coffee, palm oil
	Cuba	Havana	44,218 114,524	10,000,000	Spanish	sugar, rice, citrus, tobacco, nickel, fish
	Cyprus	Nicosia	3,572 9,251	700,000	Greek, Turkish	cereals, citrus, grapes, potatoes, copper, cement
	Czechoslo-vakia	Prague	49,370 127,869	16,000,000	Czech, Slovak, Hungarian	iron and steel, machinery, beer, wheat, potatoes
	Denmark	Copenhagen	16,629 43,069	5,000,000	Danish	machinery, textiles, dairy products, clothing
	Djibouti	Djibouti	8,494 22,000	481,000	Arabic, French, Afar, Somali	salt, livestock, hides
	Dominica	Roseau	290 751	88,000	English, French patois	cocoa beans, lime juice, bananas, pumice, fruit

(SP) Spain   (NZ) New Zealand   (UK) United Kingdom

Flag	Country or Dependency	Capital	Area	Population	Major or Official Languages	Important Products
	Dominican Republic	Santo Domingo	18,816 (mi²) 48,734 (km²)	7,000,000	Spanish	coffee, tobacco, bauxite, nickel, sugar, cocoa
	Ecuador	Quito	109,483 283,561	10,000,000	Spanish, Quechua	bananas, coffee, cocoa beans, fish, petroleum
	Egypt	Cairo	386,659 1,001,449	48,000,000	Arabic	cotton, textiles, chemicals, rice, petrochemicals
	El Salvador	San Salvador	8,124 21,041	6,000,000	Spanish	cotton, coffee, sugar, livestock, lumber, rice
	Equatorial Guinea	Malabo	10,830 28,051	282,000	Spanish, Fang, Bubi	lumber, coffee, cocoa beans, bananas, fish
	Ethiopia	Addis Ababa	471,776 1,221,900	36,000,000	Amharic, others	hides, coffee, oilseeds, fruits, vegetables, metals
	Falkland Islands (UK)	Stanley	4,700 12,173	3,000	English	wool, hides, whales
	Fiji	Suva	7,056 18,274	700,000	Fijian, Hindi, English	copra, sugar, gold, lumber, bananas, ginger
	Finland	Helsinki	130,128 337,032	5,000,000	Finnish, Swedish	lumber, paper, manufactured goods, glassware
	France	Paris	211,207 547,026	55,000,000	French	machinery, clothing, farm products, textiles
	French Guiana (FR)	Cayenne	35,135 91,000	82,000	French, Creole	shrimp, rice, lumber, gold, bauxite, sugar
	French Polynesia (FR)	Papeete	1,544 4,014	166,000	French, Polynesian languages	coconuts, citrus, bananas, sugar, vanilla, pearls
	Gabon	Libreville	103,346 267,667	1,000,000	French, Bantu languages	coffee, petroleum, lumber, manganese, iron ore, gold
	Gambia	Banjul	4,361 11,295	751,000	English, others	fish, peanuts, cotton, grains, livestock
	Germany, East	East Berlin	41,767 108,178	17,000,000	German	machinery, precision instruments, textiles
	Germany, West	Bonn	95,976 248,577	60,000,000	German	manufactured goods, chemicals, motor vehicles
	Ghana	Accra	92,099 238,537	14,000,000	English, others	lumber, petroleum, gold, manganese, cocoa beans
	Greece	Athens	50,944 131,944	10,000,000	Greek	textiles, minerals, fish, fruit, cotton, tobacco
	Greenland (DE)	Godthab	840,000 2,175,600	54,000	Danish, Greenlande	metallic ore, fish, fish products, seals
	Grenada	St. George's	133 344	116,000	English	cocoa beans, citrus, fish, nutmeg, bananas, sugar
	Guadeloupe (FR)	Basse-Terre	687 1,779	335,000	French, Creole	fruits, vegetables, sugar, vanilla, cocoa beans, fish
	Guam (US)	Agana	212 549	115,000	Chamorro, English	palm oil, fish, copra, citrus, bananas, sugar
	Guatemala	Guatemala	42,042 108,889	9,000,000	Spanish, Indian languages	cotton, sugar, livestock, bananas, coffee, lumber
	Guinea	Conakry	94,925 245,857	6,000,000	French, Fulani, others	bauxite, fruit, coffee, iron ore, rice, bananas
	Guinea-Bissau	Bissau	13,948 36,125	640,000	Portuguese	peanuts, palm oil, fish, shrimp, lumber, coconuts
	Guyana	Georgetown	83,000 214,969	1,000,000	English, Hindi, Urdu	bauxite, aluminum, sugar, rice, shrimp, coffee

(FR) France   (DE) Denmark   (US) United States   (UK) United Kingdom

Flag	Country or Dependency	Capital	Area	Population	Major or Official Languages	Important Products
	Haiti	Port-au-Prince	10,714 (mi²) 27,750 (km²)	7,000,000	French, Creole	coffee, sugar, rice, textiles, bauxite
	Honduras	Tegucigalpa	43,277 112,088	5,000,000	Spanish, Indian languages	bananas, coffee, sugar, lumber, livestock
	Hong Kong (UK)	Victoria	403 1,045	6,000,000	Chinese, English	textiles, clothing, electronic goods, cameras, shoes
	Hungary	Budapest	35,919 93,030	11,000,000	Hungarian	consumer goods, tools, machinery, wheat, fruit
	Iceland	Reykjavik	39,768 103,000	245,000	Icelandic	fish, livestock, dairy products, chemicals
	India	New Delhi	1,269,339 3,287,590	767,000,000	Hindi, others	clothing, textiles, jute, machinery, cars, steel
	Indonesia	Jakarta	788,421 2,042,012	164,000,000	Bahasa Indonesia, others	petroleum, tin, lumber, rubber, tea, rice
	Iran	Tehran	636,293 1,648,000	45,000,000	Persian, Kurdish, Azerbaijani	wheat, petroleum, livestock, textiles, cement
	Iraq	Baghdad	167,925 434,924	16,000,000	Arabic, Kurdish	petroleum, cement, livestock, cotton, textiles
	Ireland	Dublin	27,136 70,283	4,000,000	Irish, English	chemicals, dairy products, textiles, machinery
	Israel	Jerusalem	8,019 20,770	4,000,000	Hebrew, Arabic	citrus, chemicals, clothing, machinery, food products
	Italy	Rome	116,303 301,225	58,000,000	Italian	clothing, shoes, textiles, machinery, foods, cars
	Ivory Coast	Abidjan	124,503 322,463	10,000,000	French, others	lumber, coffee, cocoa beans, sugar, cotton
	Jamaica	Kingston	4,244 10,991	2,000,000	English	bauxite, bananas, sugar, citrus, rum, cocoa beans
	Japan	Tokyo	143,750 372,313	121,000,000	Japanese	cars, metal products, textiles, electronics
	Jordan	Amman	37,737 97,740	4,000,000	Arabic	phosphates, fruits, olives, copper, sulfur
	Kenya	Nairobi	244,960 582,646	20,000,000	Swahili, Bantu languages, English	livestock, coffee, tea, hides, cement, sugar
	Kiribati	Bairiki	281 728	68,000	English, Gilbertese	copra, fish, mother-of-pearl, phosphates
	Korea, North	Pyongyang	46,540 120,538	21,000,000	Korean	chemicals, minerals, rice, wheat, cement
	Korea, South	Seoul	38,025 98,484	42,000,000	Korean	machinery, steel, clothing, footwear
	Kuwait	Kuwait	6,880 17,818	2,000,000	Arabic, English	petroleum, shrimp, fertilizer
	Laos	Vientiane	91,429 236,800	4,000,000	Lao	lumber, tin, coffee, textiles, fruits, rice
	Lebanon	Beirut	4,015 10,400	3,000,000	Arabic, French	textiles, fruits, lumber, jewelry, cotton, tobacco
	Lesotho	Maseru	11,720 30,355	2,000,000	English, Sesotho	livestock, diamonds, hides, wool, wheat
	Liberia	Monrovia	43,000 111,800	2,000,000	English, others	lumber, iron ore, gold, cocoa beans, coffee, fish
	Libya	Tripoli	679,359 1,759,540	4,000,000	Arabic	petroleum, olives, dates, barley, citrus fruit

(UK) United Kingdom

Flag	Country or Dependency	Capital	Area	Population	Major or Official Languages	Important Products
	Liechtenstein	Vaduz	61 (mi²) 157 (km²)	27,000	German	chemicals, metal products machinery, optical lenses
	Luxembourg	Luxembourg	998 2,586	367,000	Luxembourgish, German, French	chemicals, steel, oats, barley, potatoes, wheat
	Macao (PO)	Macao	6 16	320,000	Chinese, Portuguese	manufactured goods, fish, electronic goods, clothing
	Madagascar	Antananarivo	226,657 587,041	10,000,000	Malagasy, French	chromium, graphite, cloves, cotton, coffee
	Malawi	Lilongwe	45,747 118,484	8,000,000	English, Chichewa	fish, tobacco, peanuts, fertilizer, textiles
	Malaysia	Kuala Lumpur	127,316 329,749	16,000,000	Malay, Chinese, Tamil, English	petroleum, lumber, tin, rubber, palm oil, textiles
	Maldives	Male	115 298	177,000	Divehi	coconuts, fish, millet, breadfruit, vegetables
	Mali	Bamako	478,764 1,240,000	8,000,000	French, others	fish, livestock, cotton, peanuts, textiles, rice
	Malta	Valletta	122 316	360,000	Maltese, English	manufactured goods, ships, textiles, fruits
	Marshall Islands (US)	Majuro	70 183	31,000	English, others	copra, tortoise shell, mother-of-pearl, fish
	Martinique (FR)	Fort-de-France	425 1,102	329,000	French, Creole	bananas, rum, sugar, pineapples, vegetables
	Mauritania	Nouakchott	397,953 1,030,700	2,000,000	Arabic, French	copper, iron ore, dates, cereals, vegetables
	Mauritius	Port Louis	790 2,045	1,000,000	English, others	molasses, sugar, tea, iron ore, rice, fish
	Mexico	Mexico City	761,601 1,972,547	80,000,000	Spanish, Indian languages	cotton, petroleum, corn, livestock, coffee, minerals
	Micronesia (US)	Kolonia	280 726	80,000	English, others	copra, fish, handicrafts
	Monaco	Monaco-Ville	.73 1.90	26,000	French, Monégasque	industrial products, chemicals, perfume
	Mongolia	Ulaanbaatar	604,247 1,565,000	2,000,000	Mongolian	livestock, wheat, oats, footwear, minerals
	Montserrat (UK)	Plymouth	40 104	14,000	English	cotton, mangoes, citrus, livestock, potatoes
	Morocco	Rabat	172,413 446,550	25,000,000	Arabic, Berber, French, Spanish	phosphates, citrus, carpets, chemicals
	Mozambique	Maputo	309,494 801,590	14,000,000	Portuguese, Bantu languages	cotton, cashew nuts, sugar, copra, tea
	Namibia (SA)	Windhoek	318,259 824,292	1,000,000	Afrikaans, English, others	sheepskins, diamonds, uranium, copper, lead
	Nauru	Yaren	8 21	8,000	Nauruan, English	phosphates
	Nepal	Katmandu	54,362 140,797	17,000,000	Nepali, Newari	rice, lumber, grain, sugar, jute, cotton
	Netherlands	Amsterdam, The Hague	16,041 41,548	14,000,000	Dutch	manufactured goods, foods, flower bulbs
	Netherlands Antilles (NE)	Willemstad	383 993	152,000	Dutch	oil refining, phosphates, livestock

(SA) South Africa   (NE) Netherlands

Flag	Country or Dependency	Capital	Area	Population	Major or Official Languages	Important Products
	New Caledonia (FR)	Nouméa	7,358 (mi²) 19,058 (km²)	148,000	French, Melanesian languages	nickel, coffee, copra, chrome, iron, cobalt
	New Zealand	Wellington	103,736 268,676	3,000,000	English, Maori	lumber, dairy products, wool, manufactured goods
	Nicaragua	Managua	50,193 130,000	3,000,000	Spanish, Indian languages	coffee, cotton, sugar, chemicals, livestock
	Niger	Niamey	489,189 1,267,000	6,000,000	French, Hausa, others	coal, iron, uranium, peanuts, livestock
	Nigeria	Lagos	356,667 923,768	91,000,000	English, others	petroleum, lumber, tin, cotton, palm oil
	Northern Marianas (US)	Saipan	185 480	18,000	Chamorro, English	copra, livestock, fish, fruits, vegetables
	Norway	Oslo	125,182 324,219	4,000,000	Norwegian, Lapp	petroleum, lumber, fish, ships, chemicals
	Oman	Muscat	105,000 271,950	1,000,000	Arabic	petroleum, fish, asbestos, dates
	Pakistan	Islamabad	310,402 809,943	103,000,000	Urdu, English, others	cotton, rice, fish, sugar, leather
	Palau (US)	Koror	191 494	16,000	English, others	bauxite, yams, copra, fruits, fish, handicrafts
	Panama	Panama City	29,761 77,082	2,000,000	Spanish, English	bananas, sugar, rice, coffee, lumber, corn
	Papua New Guinea	Port Moresby	178,259 461,691	4,000,000	Melanesian languages, English	cocoa beans, copra, lumber, copper, rubber
	Paraguay	Asunción	157,047 406,752	4,000,000	Spanish, Guarani	livestock, tobacco, cotton, oilseeds, lumber
	Peru	Lima	496,222 1,285,216	21,000,000	Spanish, Quechua, Aymara	coffee, cotton, sugar, fish, copper, silver
	Philippines	Manila	115,830 300,000	57,000,000	Pilipino, English, others	lumber, sugar, textiles, coconuts, tobacco
	Poland	Warsaw	120,725 312,677	38,000,000	Polish	machinery, textiles, coal, iron, steel
	Portugal	Lisbon	35,552 92,082	10,000,000	Portuguese	cork, fish, wine, olives, textiles
	Puerto Rico (US)	San Juan	3,435 8,897	3,000,000	Spanish, English	chemicals, clothing, fish, electronic goods, sugar
	Qatar	Doha	4,247 11,000	300,000	Arabic	petroleum, fish, steel
	Réunion (FR)	Saint-Denis	969 2,510	571,000	French, Creole	sugar, beans, vanilla, molasses, rum, bananas
	Romania	Bucharest	91,699 237,500	23,000,000	Romanian, Hungarian, others	lumber, petroleum, coal, machinery, minerals
	Rwanda	Kigali	10,169 26,338	6,000,000	Kinyarwundu, French	coffee, tea, beans, potatoes, livestock
	St. Christopher and Nevis	Basseterre	100 258	50,000	English	molasses, sugar, cotton, salt, fish, spices
	St. Helena (UK)	Jamestown	47 122	5,000	English	fruits, vegetables, handicrafts
	St. Lucia	Castries	238 619	130,000	English, French patois	bananas, coconuts, fish, cocoa beans, spices
	St. Vincent and the Grenadines	Kingstown	150 390	138,000	English	bananas, arrowroot, copra, nutmeg, sugar

Flag	Country or Dependency	Capital	Area	Population	Major or Official Languages	Important Products
	Samoa, American (US)	Pago Pago	76 (mi²) 198 (km²)	34,000	Samoan, English	tuna, pet food, fish meal, handicrafts
	Samoa, Western	Apia	1,093 2,831	163,000	Samoan, English	copra, cocoa beans, lumber, bananas
	San Marino	San Marino	23 61	21,000	Italian	lime, building stone, wheat, textiles, wine
	São Tomé and Príncipe	São Tomé	372 964	106,000	Portuguese	copra, palm oil, cocoa beans, lumber, bananas
	Saudi Arabia	Riyadh	829,996 2,149,690	11,000,000	Arabic	petroleum, cement, dates, chemicals, livestock
	Senegal	Dakar	75,750 196,192	7,000,000	French, Wolof, others	phosphates, fertilizer, peanut oil, cotton, fish
	Seychelles	Victoria	108 280	69,000	English, French	copra, vanilla, fish, livestock, cinnamon
	Sierra Leone	Freetown	27,699 71,740	4,000,000	English, Mende, others	coffee, cocoa beans, fish, ginger, peanuts, sugar
	Singapore	Singapore	224 581	3,000,000	English, Chinese, Malay, Tamil	manufactured goods, fish, electronic goods, textiles
	Solomon Islands	Honiara	10,983 28,446	273,000	Melanesian languages, English	lumber, fish, copra, rice, palm oil, spices
	Somalia	Mogadishu	246,199 637,657	6,000,000	Somali	spices, iron ore, livestock, bananas, peanuts
	South Africa	Capetown, Pretoria	471,443 1,221,037	33,000,000	Afrikaans, English, Bantu languages	gold, diamonds, uranium, wool, fruits, chrome
	Spain	Madrid	194,896 504,782	39,000,000	Spanish, Catalan, Galician, Basque	footwear, fruit, vegetables, cars, clothing
	Sri Lanka	Colombo	25,332 65,610	17,000,000	Sinhala, Tamil, English	rubber, tea, graphite petroleum, spices, fish
	Sudan	Khartoum	967,495 2,505,813	22,000,000	Arabic, others	livestock, peanuts, copper, cotton, sesame seeds
	Suriname	Paramaribo	63,251 163,820	460,000	Dutch, Surinamese, English	aluminum, bauxite, citrus, lumber, shrimp, sugar
	Swaziland	Mbabane	6,704 17,363	671,000	English, Siswati	coal, iron ore, citrus, cotton, livestock, sugar
	Sweden	Stockholm	173,731 449,964	8,000,000	Swedish	lumber, motor vehicles, machinery, iron and steel
	Switzerland	Bern	15,941 41,288	6,000,000	German, French, Italian	precision instruments, dairy products, chemicals
	Syria	Damascus	71,498 185,180	11,000,000	Arabic	clothing, fruits, vegetables, cotton, petroleum
	Taiwan	Taipei	13,885 35,961	20,000,000	Mandarin Chinese	electrical machinery, footwear, textiles, citrus
	Tanzania	Dar es Salaam	364,898 945,087	22,000,000	Swahili, Bantu languages, English	diamonds, cashews, sisal, cloves, coffee, tea
	Thailand	Bangkok	198,456 514,000	54,000,000	Thai, Chinese	rubber, tapioca, tin, rice, textiles, lumber
	Togo	Lomé	21,925 56,785	3,000,000	Ewe, Mina, others	coffee, cocoa beans, rice, phosphates, cotton, iron
	Tonga	Nuku'alofa	290 751	107,000	Tongan, English	coconuts, bananas, vanilla, pineapples, papayas, fish

Flag	Country or Dependency	Capital	Area	Population	Major or Official Languages	Important Products
	Trinidad and Tobago	Port-of-Spain	1,981 (mi²) 5,130 (km²)	1,000,000	English, Hindi	ammonia, fertilizer, petroleum, sugar, rice
	Tunisia	Tunis	63,379 164,152	7,000,000	Arabic, French	textiles, phosphates, olive oil, fertilizers
	Turkey	Ankara	301,381 780,576	52,000,000	Turkish	fruits, textiles, foods, livestock, cotton, nuts
	Turks and Caicos (UK)	Grand Turk	166 430	8,000	English	salt, crayfish, conch shells, fish
	Tuvalu	Funafuti	10 26	8,000	Tuvaluan, English	bananas, handicrafts, copra, postage stamps
	Uganda	Kampala	91,343 236,880	15,000,000	English, Swahili, others	cotton, coffee, tea, tobacco, sugar, textiles
	Union of Soviet Socialist Republics	Moscow	8,649,490 22,402,200	281,000,000	Russian, Ukrainian, others	petroleum, machinery, lumber, grains, cotton
	United Arab Emirates	Abu Dhabi	32,278 83,600	1,000,000	Arabic, others	petroleum, fish, pearls, dates, tobacco, fruits
	United Kingdom	London	92,247 244,100	56,000,000	English, Welsh, Gaelic	chemicals, foods, iron and steel, motor vehicles
	United States of America	Washington, D.C.	3,615,105 9,363,123	240,000,000	English	aircraft, chemicals, machinery, grain, fruits
	Uruguay	Montevideo	68,037 176,215	3,000,000	Spanish	livestock, wool, leather, textiles, wheat, rice
	Vanuatu	Port-Vila	5,700 14,763	138,000	Bislama, English, French	fish, copra, cocoa beans, livestock
	Vatican City	Vatican City	.17 .44	1,000	Italian, Latin	coins, postage stamps
	Venezuela	Caracas	352,143 912,050	18,000,000	Spanish	petroleum, iron ore, coffee, cocoa beans
	Vietnam	Hanoi	127,242 329,556	60,000,000	Vietnamese	coal, minerals, fruits, vegetables, rice, rubber
	Virgin Islands (UK)	Road Town	59 153	12,000	English	fruits, vegetables, livestock, coconuts
	Virgin Islands (US)	Charlotte Amalie	133 344	107,000	English	manufacturing, petroleum refining, fruits, sugar
	Yemen, North	Sanaa	75,289 195,000	6,000,000	Arabic	coffee, cotton, wheat, hides, fruits, vegetables
	Yemen, South	Aden	128,559 332,968	2,000,000	Arabic	fish, salt, petroleum products, dates, cotton
	Yugoslavia	Belgrade	98,766 255,804	23,000,000	Serbo-Croatian, Slovene, others	processed foods, lumber, chemicals, shoes, fruits
	Zaire	Kinshasa	905,563 2,345,409	33,000,000	French, Bantu languages	copper, diamonds, cobalt, petroleum, coffee
	Zambia	Lusaka	290,584 752,614	7,000,000	English, Bantu languages	cobalt, lead, zinc, cotton, chemicals
	Zimbabwe	Harare	150,803 390,580	9,000,000	English, Shona, Sindebele	cotton, fruits, sugar, copper, chrome, nickel

Gazetteer

Aconcagua (33°S/70°W), a mountain in the Andes range of South America; the highest peak in the Western Hemisphere. p. 463

Addis Ababa (9°N/39°E), the capital city and major industrial center of Ethiopia; located in central Ethiopia. p. 342

Adriatic Sea, a sea in Europe between Italy and Yugoslavia and Greece. p. 266

Aegean Sea, a sea to the east of Greece. p. 138

Africa, a continent that lies between the Atlantic Ocean on the east and the Indian Ocean on the west. The Mediterranean Sea separates Africa from Europe. It makes up 20 percent of the world's land and contains 53 countries. p. 29

Alexandria (31°N/30°E), a port city in Egypt at the mouth of the Nile on the Mediterranean Sea. Founded by Alexander the Great, it was the greatest city of the Hellenistic Age. Today it is the second largest city in Egypt. p. 142

Algiers (37°N/3°E), the capital of Algeria and one of the major industrial cities of the Mahgreb; located on the Mediterranean coast. p. 336

Alps, the highest mountains in Europe. They extend from eastern France through Switzerland, southern West Germany, Austria, and northern Italy. p. 210

Altiplano, a high plateau in Bolivia on the eastern side of the Andes Mountains. p. 509

Amazon River, a river in South America; the longest in the Western Hemisphere and second longest in the world. The Amazon winds mostly through Brazil. p. 463

Amsterdam (52N°/5°E), the capital of the Netherlands and Europe's busiest port. p. 251

Anatolian Plateau, a plateau in central Turkey. p. 377

For information about individual countries, see Facts About Countries on pages 546–553.

Andes, a mountain range in South America that runs north and south near the Pacific coast. It is the world's longest mountain range and second tallest after the Himalayas. p. 461

Angel Falls (6°N/62°W), the world's highest waterfall; located in the Guiana highlands of Venezuela. p. 510

Angkor Wat, archaeological ruins in Cambodia. p. 426

Ankara (40°N/33°E), the capital city of Turkey; located on Turkey's central plateau. p. 414

Antarctica, a continent that makes up 9 percent of the world's land. Most of it is covered by a huge ice cap up to a mile thick. p. 30

Apennines, a mountain range in Europe that runs down the center of the Apennine Peninsula, which contains Italy. p. 210

Appalachian Mountains, a mountain range in the eastern part of the United States. p. 463

Arabian Peninsula, a peninsula located between the Mediterranean Sea, the Red Sea, and the Indian Ocean; part of the Middle East. p. 168

Arctic Ocean, one of the four oceans of the world; located in the Northern Hemisphere north of 75°N. p. 34

Asia, the largest of the seven continents. Asia has the most inhabitants of any continent and is the site of the oldest civilizations. p. 29

Aswan (24°N/33°E), a city on the Nile in southern Egypt; site of the Aswan High Dam. p. 339

Aswan High Dam (24°N/33°E), a dam built on the Nile just above the city of Aswan; built to control floods and produce hydroelectric power. p. 339

Atacama Desert, a long, narrow desert in Chile. p. 465

Athens (38°N/24°E), the capital city of Greece. It began as a city-state that flourished during the golden age of ancient Greece. p. 135

Atlantic Ocean, one of the four oceans of the world; borders the continents of Africa, Europe, North America, and South America. p. 34

Atlas Mountains, a mountain range in Morocco and the longest mountain range in Africa. p. 295

Australia, a continent in the Southern Hemisphere surrounded by the Pacific and Indian Oceans. Australia is the largest island in Oceania. p. 30

Austrian Empire, a former empire in Europe that included parts of Germany, Italy, Austria, and Hungary. It became the Austro-Hungarian Empire and was dissolved after World War II. p. 228

Babylon (32°N/45°E), an ancient city in southern Mesopotamia; home to the Babylonian civilization. p. 107

Bali (8°S/115°E), an island in Indonesia. p. 427

Balkans, the area around the Balkan mountains in Europe. Present-day Balkan countries include Greece, Bulgaria, Yugoslavia, Romania, and Albania. p. 228

Baltic Sea, the sea between Poland and Scandinavia. p. 212

Bangkok (14°N/100°E), the capital of Thailand. p. 387

Barbary, a region of north Africa. p. 317

Barranquilla (11°N/75°W), a port city in Colombia on the Caribbean Sea. p. 511

Beijing (40°N/116°E), the capital city of China; located near the northeastern coast. p. 399

Benghazi (32°N/20°E), a city in Libya on the Mediterranean coast. p. 337

Benin, a precolonial West African kingdom located in what is now Nigeria. p. 321

Berlin (53°N/13°E), a divided city in East Germany. East Berlin is the capital of East Germany. West Berlin is part of West Germany. p. 261

Birmingham (52°N/2°W), a city in England and one of Great Britain's major manufacturing centers. p. 244

Black Sea, an inland sea between Europe and Asia. p. 212

Blue Nile, a main branch of the Nile River rising in Ethiopia. p. 341

Bogotá (5°N/74°W), the capital of Colombia. p. 510

Bombay (19°N/73°E), a port city on the western coast of India. p. 421

Borneo (0°/114°E), an island in Southeast Asia; includes the country of Brunei and parts of the countries of Indonesia and Malaysia. p. 427

Bosporus (41°N/29°E), a narrow stretch of water between Asia and Europe; connects the Black Sea with the Mediterranean Sea. p. 414

Brahmaputra, a river in Asia that runs through Tibet, China, India, and Bangladesh. p. 419

Brasília, the capital of Brazil; built during the late 1950s. p. 516

Brazilian Highlands, an area of low mountains, hills, and plateaus in southern Brazil. p. 514

Brazzaville (4°S/15°E), the capital of the People's Republic of the Congo. p. 310

Brisbane (27°S/153°E), a city on the eastern coast of Australia. p. 433

British Isles, a group of islands off the western coast of Europe; includes Great Britain and Ireland. p. 243

Buenos Aires (34°S/58°W), the capital city of Argentina. p. 515

Bulawayo (20°S/29°E), a city in the southern part of Zimbabwe; serves as an important industrial center. p. 360

Byzantine Empire, the eastern portion of the Roman Empire, originally made up of Asia Minor, the Levant, Egypt, and the Balkans. p. 155

Cairo (30°N/31°E), the capital and largest city of Egypt; located in the eastern part of Egypt on the Nile River. p. 338

Calcutta (23°N/88°E), a port city on the eastern coast of India. p. 421

Gazetteer

Cape Town (34°S/18°E), a port city on the southwestern coast of South Africa. p. 360

Caracas (10°N/67°W), the capital of Venezuela. p. 510

Caribbean Sea, a sea that lies east of Central America between the Gulf of Mexico and South America. p. 499

Carpathian Mountains, a mountain range extending across Romania and Czechoslovakia. p. 212

Cartagena (10°N/76°W), a port city in Colombia on the Caribbean Sea. p. 511

Carthage, an ancient Phoenician colony located near present-day Tunis in Tunisia. p. 151

Casablanca (34°N/8°W), a city in Morocco; located on the Atlantic coast. It serves as a major industrial center in the Maghreb. p. 336

Caspian Sea, an inland salt lake between Europe and Asia; the world's largest lake. p. 213

Caucasus Mountains, a mountain range in the Soviet Union and Turkey that provides part of the division between Europe and Asia. p. 29

Central America, a narrow strip of land south of Mexico that connects North and South America. p. 461

Chhatara, a farming village in northern India near Delhi. p. 82

Chiang Mai (19°N/99°W), the second-largest city in Thailand. p. 86

Chongqing (30°N/107°E), a city in China. p. 387

Ciudad Guayana (8°N/63°W), a city in eastern Venezuela. p. 511

Congo River, a river in central Africa that flows through Zaire and empties into the Atlantic Ocean. p. 297

Crete (35°N/24°E), an island south of Greece in the Mediterranean Sea; site of the ancient Minoan civilization. p. 130

Danube River, a river in central Europe; the second longest river in Europe. p. 210

Dar es Salaam (7°S/39°E), the capital city of Tanzania and a major east African port on the Indian Ocean. p. 354

Delhi (29°N/77°E), the capital city of India; formerly the capital of the Gupta Empire. p. 83

Denali (63°N/151°W), the highest mountain peak in North America; also known as Mount McKinley. p. 461

Dnieper River, a river in the Soviet Union that empties into the Black Sea. p. 212

Don River, a river in the Soviet Union west of the Urals; empties into the Sea of Azov. p. 212

Drakensberg Mountains, an escarpment in southern Africa rising 10,000 feet above the coastal plain. p. 295

Dublin (53°N/6°W), the capital and largest city of Ireland; located on the mouth of the Liffey River. p. 246

Durban (30°S/31°E), a port city on the eastern coast of South Africa. p. 360

East Indies, a former Dutch colony now known as Indonesia. p. 401

Easter Island (27°S/109°W), an island in Polynesia. p. 434

Ethiopian Highlands, a region in Ethiopia, it has a mountain climate. p. 340

Euphrates River, a river in Southwest Asia that empties into the Persian Gulf. It defines the western edge of Mesopotamia in what is now Iraq. p. 103

Eurasia, the land mass divided into Europe and Asia. It stretches from the Atlantic on the west to the Pacific on the east. The United States could fit into this land mass five times. p. 29

Europe, the western part of Eurasia; considered a separate continent because of the landforms and water bodies that separate it from Asia. p. 29

Fertile Triangle, an area of rich farmland in the Soviet Union defined by Leningrad, Odessa and Novosibirsk. p. 216

Fiji (18°S/175°E), an island in the Pacific Ocean formed by volcanos. p. 380

Florence (44°N/11°E), a city in Central Italy. p. 254

Ganges, a river in Asia that flows from the Himalayan mountains to the Indian Ocean through India and Bangladesh. p. 376

Geneva (46°N/6°E), a city in Switzerland. p. 175

Genoa (44°N/10°E), a port city in northern Italy and the birthplace of Christopher Columbus. p. 254

Giza (30°N/31°E), a city in Egypt located across the Nile from Cairo; the site of the Great Pyramids. p. 11

Gobi Desert, a high desert that covers most of Mongolia. p. 441

Gran Chaco, a wilderness region in Paraguay and northern Argentina. p. 514

Great Lakes, a group of five lakes south of the Hudson Bay in North America and the world's largest group of freshwater lakes. p. 461

Great Rift Valley, one of the longest and deepest valley systems in the world. The valley extends about 4,000 miles from Lake Nyasa in southeastern Africa north into Southwest Asia. It includes the Red Sea and Lake Tanganyika. p. 295

Guam (13°N/144°E), the largest of the Micronesian Islands. p. 435

Guangzhou (23°N/113E), a city in China. p. 387

Guiana Highlands, a rugged region in southern Venezuela. p. 510

Guianas, an area of land in northern South America that makes up Guyana, Suriname, and French Guiana. p. 509

Gulf of Mexico, the body of water between mainland North America and the West Indies. p. 464

Hamburg (54°N/10°E), the second largest city in West Germany, located on the Elbe River about seventy miles from the North Sea. p. 89

Hamilton (43°N/80°W), a city in the Great Lakes region of Canada; located on Lake Ontario. p. 496

Harare (18°S/31°E), the capital of Zimbabwe; serves as a center for industry and transportation. p. 360

Hawaii, one of the fifty United States; made up of a group of islands in the Pacific Ocean. p. 380

Hebrides, a group of islands off the coast of Scotland. p. 243

Himalayas, a mountain range in central Asia which includes the 200 highest peaks in the world. p. 31

Hiroshima (34°N/132E), a city in Japan devastated in World War II by the first atomic bomb. p. 404

Hispaniola (19°N/71°W), an island in the Caribbean Sea. It contains the countries of Haiti and Santo Domingo. p. 486

Hong Kong (22°N/115°E), a port city on an island off the southeastern coast of China. p. 441

Honshu Island, the largest of the four main islands that make up Japan. p. 448

Horn of Africa, a region in northeastern Africa containing the countries of Ethiopia, Djibouti, and Somalia. p. 340

Huang, a river in China that begins in the Plateau of Tibet and empties into the Yellow Sea. p. 118

Hudson Bay, a bay off the Atlantic Ocean in Canada. p. 463

Hungarian Basin, a plains region in Hungary; contains the best cropland in Eastern Europe. p. 215

Gazetteer

Ibadan (7°N/3°E), a city in southwestern Nigeria. p. 349

Iberian Peninsula, a peninsula in Europe bordered by the Mediterranean Sea and the Atlantic Ocean. It contains the countries of Spain and Portugal. p. 210

Indian Ocean, one of the four oceans in the world; located in the Eastern Hemisphere bordering Africa, Asia, and Australia. p. 34

Indian Subcontinent, a part of South Asia mostly comprised of the country of India. p. 376

Indochina, a former French colony in Southeast Asia; now the countries of Cambodia, Laos, and Vietnam. p. 401

Indus River, a river that flows mostly through Pakistan and empties into the Indian Ocean. p. 116

Istanbul (41°N/29°E), a city in Turkey and the former capital of the Ottoman Empire; located on both sides of the Bosporus. p. 414

Jakarta (6°S/107°E), the capital of Indonesia. p. 387

Japan Current, a warm ocean current that runs along the eastern coast of Japan. p. 45

Java (7°S/110°E), an island in Indonesia. p. 429

Jerusalem (32°N/35°E), the capital of Israel and holy city for Jews, Christians, and Muslims. p. 156

Johannesburg (26°S/28°E), a city in South Africa and a major South African mining and industrial center. p. 305

Jordan River, a river flowing through Jordan and Israel. p. 415

Kalahari Desert, a desert that covers a large part of Botswana in southern Africa. p. 362

Karachi (25°N/69°E), the capital of Pakistan. p. 387

Khartoum (16°N/33°E), the capital and largest city of Sudan; located where the White Nile and the Blue Nile flow into the Nile River. p. 341

Kiev (50°N/30°E), a city in the Soviet Union near the Dnieper River. It was the site of the first Russian kingdom. p. 229

Kilwa (9°S/39°E), a precolonial port kingdom in East Africa. p. 321

Kinshasha (4°S/15°E), the capital and largest city of Zaire; located on the Congo (Zaire) River near the border between Zaire and the People's Republic of the Congo. p. 349

Kitakyushu (34°N/130°E), a city in Japan on the northern tip of Kyushu Island. It is Japan's chief steel producer. p. 448

Kongo, an African Kingdom that lasted from the 1400s to the beginning of the 1700s; contained parts of what is now Zaire and Angola. p. 321

Korean Peninsula, a peninsula between the East China Sea and the Sea of Japan; contains the countries of North and South Korea. p. 446

Kounzoulou, a village on the Congo River in the People's Republic of the Congo; located about 150 miles north of Brazzaville. p. 309

Kush, an early civilization of Africa in what is now Sudan. p. 114

Kyushu, the southernmost of the four main islands of Japan. p. 448

Lagos (6°N/3°E), the capital of Nigeria; located on the southwest coast. p. 305

Lake Maracaibo (9°N/71°W), a lake in northwestern Venezuela; contains rich oil deposits. p. 512

Lake Nyasa (12°S/34°E), a lake in southeastern Africa. p. 297

Lake Superior (48°N/88°W), one of the five Great Lakes of North America and the largest freshwater lake in the world. p. 34

Lake Tanganyika (6°S/30°E), a lake in eastern Africa; borders Tanzania on the east and Zaire on the west. It is the longest freshwater lake in the world. p. 297

Lake Victoria (2°S/32°E), a lake in eastern Africa. The northern half lies in Uganda and the southern half lies in Tanzania. p. 297

Latin America, an area of land that includes Mexico, Central America, South America, and the West Indies. p. 471

Lena River, a river in the Soviet Union east of the Ural Mountains. p. 212

Leningrad (60°N/30°E), a city in the Soviet Union that forms a point of the Fertile Triangle; the second largest city in the Soviet Union. p. 216

Liverpool (53°N/3°W), a city in England. p. 195

London (51°N/0°W), the capital of the United Kingdom and a major banking, trade, and education center; one of the largest cities in the world. p. 244

Low Countries, the countries of Belgium, the Netherlands, and Luxembourg, so-called because of their low elevation. p. 251

Lubumbashi (12°S/27°E), a city in Zaire and a center for mining, manufacturing, and commerce. p. 305

Lusaka (15°S/28°E), the capital of Zambia. p. 360

Macedonia, a region north of ancient Greece, most of which lies in present-day Yugoslavia; home of Alexander the Great. p. 140

Madagascar (20°S/47°E), an island off the eastern coast of southern Africa and one of the largest islands in the world. p. 356

Madras (13°N/80°E), a port city in India. p. 421

Maghreb, a region in northwestern Africa that includes Morocco, Algeria, and Tunisia. Major industrial centers in the Maghreb are Casablanca and Algiers. p. 335

Manchester (53°N/2°W), a city in England and a leading manufacturing center. p. 244

Maputo (27°S/32°E), a port city on the Indian Ocean in Mozambique; one of the major cities of east Africa. p. 354

Mecca (21°N/40°E), the holiest city of the Islamic faith; located in Saudi Arabia. It was an ancient trading center and the birthplace of Muhammad, founder of Islam. p. 168

Medina (24°N/40°E), a city in Saudi Arabia. p. 168

Mediterranean Sea, a nearly landlocked body of salt water that separates Europe and Africa. p. 253

Mekong River, a river in Indochina that begins in the Himalayan Mountains. p. 376

Melanesia, a group of islands in the Pacific Ocean north of Australia. p. 379

Melbourne (38°S/145°E), a city on the east coast of Australia. p. 433

Meroe, an ancient city in Kush and a famous iron-working center. p. 114

Mesopotamia, an area of land between the Tigris and Euphrates rivers in what is now Iraq. Site of the ancient civilizations of the Sumerians and the Babylonians. p. 103

Mexico City (19°N/99°W), the capital of Mexico and one of the world's ten largest cities. p. 62

Miami (25°N/80°W), a city in the United States on the southern tip of Florida. p. 429

Micronesia, a group of islands in the Pacific Ocean north of Melanesia. p. 379

Middle East, a region of Asia located in the southwestern part of the continent. The Middle East borders both Europe and Africa. p. 375

Milan (45°N/9°E), a city in northern Italy and Italy's major banking center. p. 254

Mississippi River, the longest river in North America; flows through the United States from north to south and empties into the Gulf of Mexico. p. 464

Mogadishu (2°N/45°E), the capital and most important port and industrial center of Somalia; located on the Indian Ocean. p. 342

Mombasa (4°N/40°E), a port city on the southeastern coast of Kenya, located on the Indian Ocean. p. 354

Gazetteer

Mongolian Plateau, a large plateau region in central Asia that covers much of Mongolia. p. 377

Montreal (45°N/74°W), a city in Canada on the northern side of the St. Lawrence River. p. 485

Moscow (56°N/38°E), the capital and largest city of the Soviet Union. p. 277

Mount Everest (28°N/87°E), the highest mountain peak in the world; located in the Himalayas in the country of Nepal. p. 420

Mount Kenya (0°/37°E), a mountain in central Kenya; rises 17,058 feet above sea level. p. 295

Mount Kilimanjaro (3°S/37°E), a mountain in Tanzania near the Kenyan border; rises 19,340 feet above sea level. p. 295

Mount McKinley (63°N/151°W), the highest peak in North America; also called Denali. p. 461

Mycenae, a city in ancient Greece. p. 131

Nagoya (35°N/137°E), a city in Japan on the island of Honshu. p. 448

Nairobi (1°S/37°E), the capital of Kenya. p. 310

Naples (41°N/14°E), a port in southern Italy that exports food products. It is a former city-state of Italy. p. 254

New Brunswick, a province in eastern Canada. p. 489

New England, a region in the northeastern section of the United States; formerly a group of English colonies. p. 485

New Guinea (5°S/140°E), an island in the Pacific Ocean north of Australia. The western half is part of Indonesia and the eastern half is the country of Papua New Guinea. p. 432

New World, the European term for North and South America. p. 185

Niger River, a river in western Africa; flows into the Atlantic Ocean. p. 297

Nile River, the longest river in the world, measuring 4,145 miles from its source near Lake Victoria in Africa to its mouth on the Mediterranean Sea. p. 34

North America, a continent that stretches from the Arctic Ocean in the north to the Caribbean Sea in the south; bordered by the Atlantic Ocean on the east and the Pacific Ocean on the west. It contains the countries of Canada, the United States, and Mexico. p. 29

North Atlantic Drift, a huge ocean current that brings warm water from the tropics to the western European coast. p. 210

North China Plain, a large coastal plain in China; home to more than one billion people. p. 377

North European Plain, a plain that stretches over 1,000 miles between the Ural Mountains and the western coast of France. It is the world's largest plain and contains Europe's best farmland. p. 31

North Sea, a body of water that lies between Scandinavia and Great Britain. It has become a major source of oil. p. 215

Northern Ireland, six counties of Ireland that did not unite with the other Irish counties in independence but chose to stay a part of Great Britain. p. 244

Nova Scotia, a province in eastern Canada. p. 489

Novosibirsk (55°N/83°E), a city and manufacturing and transportation center in the Soviet Union. p. 216

Ob River, a river in the Soviet Union east of the Ural mountains. p. 212

Oceania, an area containing more than 20,000 islands in the Pacific Ocean. p. 376

Odessa (46°N/31°E), a city in the Soviet Union on the Black Sea. p. 216

Ontario, a province in Canada. p. 489

Orinoco River, a river in South America that winds through eastern Colombia and southern Venezuela. p. 510

Orkneys, a group of islands off the northern coast of Scotland. p. 243

Osaka (35°N/135°E), a port city in Japan facing the Inland Sea. p. 448

Ottoman Empire, a former empire centered in present-day Turkey. p. 228

Pacific Ocean, one of the four oceans of the world; bordered on the east by North and South America and on the west by Asia and Australia. p. 34

Pampas, a part of South America's plains region. p. 463

Paris (49°N/2°E), the capital and largest city of France; serves as a manufacturing center. p. 250

Patagonia, a dry plateau in southern Argentina. p. 463

Pearl Harbor (21°N/158°W), a harbor in the Hawaiian Islands; site of Japan's attack against the United States in 1941. p. 236

Peloponnesis, the area which is now southern Greece. p. 139

Pemba (5°S/40°E), an island off the coast of Tanzania that, along with Zanzibar, provides nearly all the world's cloves. p. 355

Persia, an ancient country much of which is now Iran. p. 142

Persian Gulf, a body of water that lies between the Arabian Peninsula and Iran. p. 414

Philadelphia (40°N/75°W), a city in Pennsylvania on the east coast of the United States. p. 22

Plateau of Tibet, the world's highest plateau, rising 20,000 feet above sea level in western China. p. 31

Polynesia, a vast group of islands of the central Pacific Ocean. They include New Zealand, Easter Island, Hawaii, Western Samoa, and Tahiti. p. 380

Port Elizabeth (34°S/26°E), a major port city on the southeastern coast of South Africa. p. 360

Prussia, a former German state in Western Europe. In the early 1800s its ruler, Otto von Bismarck, led the other German states into unification. p. 226

Pyrenees, a mountain range that separates Spain from France. p. 210

Quebec, a province in eastern Canada and an early French colony. p. 471

Rand, The, an area surrounding the city of Johannesburg, South Africa; South Africa's major mining and industrial center. p. 360

Red Sea, a sea that forms the northeastern boundary of Africa; part of the Great Rift Valley between Africa and the Arabian Sea. p. 297

Rhine River, a river in West Germany. p. 210

Rhone River, a river in southern France. p. 210

Rio de Janeiro (22°S/42°W), a port city on the southeastern coast of Brazil. p. 508

Rio de la Plata, an arm of the Atlantic extending into South America between Uruguay and Argentina. p. 514

Rio Grande, a river in North America that marks the boundary between the United States and Mexico. p. 495

Rocky Mountains, the longest mountain range in North America. p. 461

Roman Empire, an ancient empire centered in Rome that at its height stretched from Great Britain to Mesopotamia. p. 152

Rome (42°N/13°E), the capital of Italy and the city from which the Roman Empire expanded. p. 151

Rotterdam (52°N/4°E), a city in the Netherlands and one of Europe's busiest ports. p. 251

Ruhr Valley, an industrial region in West Germany that includes the industrial cities of Dortmund, Dusseldorf, and Essen. p. 249

Gazetteer

Sahara, one of the hottest deserts in the world; stretches across the northern part of Africa. The greatest distance from east to west is about 3,200 miles. p. 335

Sahel, the western part of the desert fringe of the Sahara; made up of the countries of Mauritania, Mali, Burkina, Niger, and Chad. p. 300

St. Lawrence River, a river that, with the Great Lakes, forms part of the northeastern border between Canada and the United States. p. 496

St. Lawrence Seaway, an inland waterway along the St. Lawrence River; connects the Great Lakes and the Atlantic Ocean. p. 496

San Tan Bong, a village in northern Thailand. p. 85

São Paulo (24°S/47°W), a city in southeastern Brazil and the largest urban area in South America. p. 516

Sardinia (40°N/9°E), an island off Italy's western coast. One of the Italian states of the 1800s, it took the lead in the movement to unify Italy. p. 226

Saskatchewan, a province in western Canada. p. 473

Scandinavia, a region in northern Europe including Norway, Sweden, Finland, Denmark, and Iceland. p. 243

Scandinavian Peninsula, a peninsula in Europe that includes Norway and Sweden. p. 210

Scotland, a formerly independent country that now makes up the northern third of Great Britain. p. 244

Sea of Japan, the sea between Japan and the eastern coast of Asia. p. 377

Seattle (48°N/122°W), a city in Washington in the United States. p. 429

Seoul (38°N/127°E), the capital city of South Korea. p. 74

Serbia, formerly a small country in the Balkans and now a state in Yugoslavia. p. 229

Shaba, a province in southeast Zaire that is an important source of minerals. Shaba means "copper" in Swahili. p. 352

Shanghai (31°N/127°E), a city in southern China. p. 387

Shetlands, a group of islands off the coast of Scotland. p. 243

Siberia, a region of the Soviet Union that is thinly populated and cold for a large part of the year. p. 212

Sicily (37°N/14°E), an island south of Italy in the Mediterranean Sea. Part of the former Kingdom of the Two Sicilies. p. 226

Silver River Countries, Argentina, Uruguay, and Paraguay. p. 514

Songhai, an empire in precolonial western Africa. p. 319

South America, a continent bordered by the Atlantic Ocean on the east and the Pacific Ocean on the west. p. 30

Sparta (37°N/22°E), a city in Greece and a city-state in ancient Greece. p. 139

Strait of Gibraltar (36°N/6°W), a narrow strip of water that connects the Mediterranean Sea and the Atlantic Ocean. p. 34

Sub-Saharan Africa, Africa south of the Sahara desert. p. 348

Suez Canal (29°N/32°E), a canal in Egypt connecting the Mediterranean Sea and the Red Sea. p. 403

Sumer, the earliest known Mesopotamian civilization which developed in southeastern Mesopotamia near the Persian Gulf. p. 105

Sydney (34°S/151°E), a city on the eastern coast of Australia. p. 433

Tahiti (17°S/149°W), an island in Oceania. p. 374

Taiwan (23°N/121°E), an island off mainland China. p. 442

Tasman Sea, the sea between Australia and New Zealand. p. 380

Tasmania (42°S/147°E), an island in Oceania. p. 432

Tel Aviv (32°N/35°E), a city in Israel on the Mediterranean coast. p. 415

Tenochtitlán, the capital of the Aztec Empire; now the site of Mexico City. p. 481

Thar, a desert in India. p. 46

Thebes, an ancient Greek city-state. p. 132

Tianjin (39°N/117°E), a city in China. p. 387

Tibet, a former country in the Himalayan Mountains and now part of China. p. 441

Tibetan Plateau, a plateau in central Asia where many of Asia's great rivers begin. It is called the roof of the world because most of it is over 16,000 feet above sea level. p. 376

Tigris River, a river in Southwest Asia that empties into the Persian Gulf; forms the eastern boundary of ancient Mesopotamia in what is now Iraq. p. 103

Tokyo (36°N/140°E), the capital of Japan; located on the east side of Honshu Island. p. 448

Tombouctou (16°N/3°W), a city in Mali; the major city of the Songhai empire of West Africa. p. 317

Toronto (44°N/79°W), a port city in Canada; located on the northern shore of Lake Ontario. p. 473

Tripoli (33°N/13°E), the capital of Libya; located on the coast of the Mediterranean Sea. p. 337

Tropics, an area between 23½° north and south latitudes. p. 38

Troy, an ancient city-state located on the eastern coast of the Aegean Sea. p. 132

Tunis (37°N/10°E), the capital of Tunisia. p. 11

Turin (45°N/8°E), an industrial city in northern Italy. p. 254

Ural Mountains, a mountain range in the Soviet Union that forms the northern boundary between Europe and Asia. p. 29

Venice (45°N/12°E), a city in Italy. p. 254

Victoria Falls (18°S/26°E), a waterfall in the Zambezi River on the boundary between Zambia and Zimbabwe in southern Africa. p. 297

Vienna (48°N/16°E), the capital and largest city of Austria. Considered by some to be the capital of western European music. p. 251

Wales, a former country that is now part of the United Kingdom; makes up the southwestern part of Great Britain. p. 244

West Berlin (53°N/13°E), the part of Berlin controlled by West Germany. It is 100 miles inside the East German border. p. 261

West Siberian Plain, a vast plain east of the Ural Mountains. p. 212

White Nile, the name of the longest branch of the Nile River as it flows through Sudan. p. 341

Yangtze River, a river that flows through China. p. 376

Yenisey River, a river in the Soviet Union east of the Ural Mountains. p. 212

Yokohama (36°N/140°E), a city in Japan near Tokyo on the east side of Honshu Island. p. 448

Yucatán Peninsula, a peninsula in southern Mexico that extends between the Gulf of Mexico and the Caribbean Sea. p. 480

Zaire River, a river formerly known as the Congo River; flows into the Atlantic Ocean. p. 349

Zambezi River, a river in the southern part of eastern Africa. p. 297

Zanzibar (6°S/39°E), an island in the Indian Ocean off the coast of Tanzania. p. 355

Zimbabwe, a major kingdom of East Africa founded sometime between A.D. 800 and 1000. p. 321

Glossary

Full Pronunciation Key

The pronunciation of each word is shown just after the word, in this way: **ab bre vi ate** (ə brē′vē āt). The letters and signs used are pronounced as in the words below. The mark ′ is placed after a syllable with a primary, or heavy, accent, as in the example above. The mark ′ after a syllable shows a secondary, or lighter, accent, as in **ab bre vi a tion** (ə brē′vē ā′shən).

a	hat, cap	f	fat, if	n	no, in
ā	age, face	g	go, bag	ng	long, bring
ä	father, far	h	he, how	o	hot, rock
b	bad, rob	i	it, pin	ō	open, go
ch	child, much	ī	ice, five	ô	order, all
d	did, red	j	jam, enjoy	oi	oil, voice
e	let, best	k	kind, seek	ou	house, out
ē	equal, be	l	land, coal	p	paper, cup
ėr	term, learn	m	me, am	r	run, try

u	cup, butter	s	say, yes
u̇	full, put	sh	she, rush
ü	rule, move	t	tell, it
v	very, save	th	thin, both
w	will, woman	ẋH	then, smooth
y	young, yet		
z	zero, breeze		
zh	measure, seizure		
ə	represents:		

ə represents:
a in about
e in taken
i in pencil
o in lemon
u in circus

The pronunciation key is from the *Thorndike-Barnhart* Dictionary Series.

---

aborigine (ab′ə rij′ə nē), *noun*, one of the first or original inhabitants of a region. p. 389

absolute monarchy, a government ruled by a king or queen, where the monarch—king or queen—has total control over the government. p. 176

altiplano (äl′ti plä′nō), *noun*, a plateau, as on the eastern side of the Andes Mountains. p. 509

altitude (al′tə tüd), *noun*, height above the earth's surface; elevation. p. 45

ancestor worship, the practice of honoring dead family members. p. 119

apartheid (ə pärt′hāt), *noun*, the complete separation of the races, especially as practiced by law in South Africa. p. 362

archaeologist (är′kē ol′ə jist), *noun*, a scientist who studies the people, customs, and life of ancient times. p. 103

aristocracy (ar′ə stok′rə sē), *noun*, an upper class of people. From about 800 to 600 B.C., the Greeks were ruled by upper-class families known as the aristocracy. p. 133

assassinate (ə sas′n āt), *verb*, to kill for political reasons. p. 232

autocrat (ô′tə krat), *noun*, a person who governs by himself or herself, without the consent of anyone else. p. 225

barbarian (bär ber′ē ən), *noun*, (in ancient Greece) a person who did not speak Greek. p. 133

basin (bā′sn), *noun*, all the land drained by a river and its tributaries. p. 465

bilingual (bī ling′gwəl), *adjective*, able to speak another language as well or almost as well as one's own. p. 472

boycott (boi′kot), *noun*, an organized refusal to buy or use goods or services produced by a certain company or government. p. 328

caste system, a system, practiced by Hindus, that divides people into groups based on the caste (social class) of their parents. p. 84

cataract (kat′ə rakt′), *noun*, a large, steep waterfall. p. 297

caudillo (kô de′lyō), *noun*, a dictator in a Spanish-speaking country. p. 488

citizen (sit′ə zən), *noun*, a member of a community, state, or nation who has certain rights and responsibilities. p. 133

city-state, a city with its surrounding land, which acts like a nation. Athens and Sparta were two city-states in ancient Greece. p. 133

civilization (siv′ə lə zā′shən), *noun*, an advanced culture, usually based on city living. p. 103

climate (klī′mit), *noun*, the kind of weather a place has over a long period of time. p. 35

collective (kə lek′tiv), *noun*, a farm, factory, or other organization worked by a large group of people and, in communist countries, owned and directed by the government. p. 264

colony (kol′ə nē), *noun*, a place controlled by a distant government. p. 110

command economy, a system in which the government decides how the economy of the country is to be run. p. 262

commercial farming, farming that produces crops for sale. p. 63

commune (kom′yün), *noun*, a collective farm in communist China. p. 443

communism (kom′yə niz′əm), *noun*, a philosophy that holds that the only way to bring about socialism is through violent revolution; socialism. p. 231

confederation (kən fed′ə rā′shən), *noun*, a group of provinces or states under one central government. p. 489

conquistador (kon kwis′tə dôr), *noun*, a Spanish conqueror of the 1500s. p. 188

constitution (kon′stə tü′shən), *noun*, a set of rules used in governing a nation. p. 179

cooperative (kō op′ər ə tiv), *noun*, an apartment building owned and run by the people who live in it. p. 282

cottage industry, an industry in which families work either at home or in small workshops. p. 419

coup (kü), *noun*, a sudden action, usually involving force, that changes the government of a country. p. 329

creole (krē′ōl), *noun*, a person of French or Spanish ancestry born in Latin America. p. 487

crusade (krü sād′), *noun*, a war fought over religion. Several Crusades occurred in the Middle Ages. p. 166

culture (kul′chər), *noun*, the total way of life that people in a society share. p. 79

cuneiform (kyü nē′ə fôrm), *noun*, a writing system developed by the Sumerians consisting of thousands of small pictures, each standing for a different word. p. 106

custom (cus′təm), *noun*, a common way of doing something among a group of people. p. 81

deciduous (di sij′ü əs), *adjective*, shedding leaves each year. p. 40

deity (dē′ə tē), *noun*, a god or goddess worshiped by people. p. 126

democracy (di mok′rə sē), *noun*, a form of government run by the citizens who live under it. p. 135

demographer (di mog′rə fər), *noun*, person who studies human populations. p. 59

depression (di presh′ən), *noun*, a period of low economic activity, during which businesses and banks may close, and people may lose their jobs and their savings. p. 235

desertification (di zėr′ti fi kā′shən), *noun*, the spread of a desert. Some scientists think the Sahara is spreading southward at a rate of about 12 miles a year. p. 341

dictator (dik′tā tər), *noun*, a leader who rules with absolute authority. p. 255

dike (dīk), *noun*, a wall made of earth or another material, designed to keep water in or out of a place. p. 382

direct democracy, a form of government in which political decisions are made by the people themselves. p. 247

dominion (də min′yən), *noun*, a self-governing territory or country. p. 489

drought (drout), *noun*, a long period without rain. p. 307

earthquake (erth′kwāk′), *noun*, a violent shaking of the earth caused by sudden movements in the earth's crust. p. 377

ejido (ā hē′dō), *noun*, a small farm in Mexico, once part of a plantation. p. 497

elevation (el′ə vā′shən), *noun*, height above sea level. p. 30

embargo (em bär′gō), *noun*, an official limitation on the flow of goods between countries. p. 417

empire (em′pīr), *noun*, a group of lands under one ruler or government. p. 107

erosion (i rō′zhən), *noun*, the wearing away of land by water, wind, or ice. p. 212

escarpment (e skarp′mənt), *noun*, a steep slope, usually at the edge of a plateau; a cliff. p. 295

estancia (e stän′syä), *noun*, a large ranch or estate in Latin America. p. 515

ethnic group, a group whose members share the same cultural or racial background. p. 218

exile (ek′sīl), *verb*, to force someone to leave his or her country or home. p. 230

export (ek′spôrt), *noun*, a good that one country sells to another country. p. 72

extended family, a family made up of various relatives in addition to parents and children. p. 83

Glossary

famine (fam'ən), *noun*, starvation. p. 307

feudalism (fyŭ'dl iz'əm), *noun*, a system in medieval Europe in which a number of powerful nobles, also known as lords, controlled their own areas of land. The lords divided their land among lesser nobles in return for military service and money. p. 165

gaucho (gou'chō), *noun*, a cowhand of southern South America. p. 515

general secretary, the head of the Communist party in a communist country. p. 276

genocide (jen'ə sīd), *noun*, the deliberate killing of a cultural or racial group. p. 236

glacier (glā'shər), *noun*, a huge sheet of ice. Glaciers formed over large areas of the Northern Hemisphere when the earth's average temperature was much colder than it is now. p. 463

gross national product (GNP), the value of all goods and services produced by a country in a given year. p. 67

guerrilla (gə ril'ə), *noun*, a member of a band of fighters who are not part of a regular army. p. 268

guild (gild), *noun*, (in the Middle Ages) an organization of craft workers that controlled the quality of goods produced and trained young workers in the crafts. p. 167

hacienda (hä sē en'də), *noun*, (in Spanish colonial America) a large estate used for cattle ranching or farming. p. 484

hieroglyph (hī'ər ə glif), *noun*, a small picture or sign that stands for a word. The writing system of the ancient Egyptians used hieroglyphs. p. 113

high island, an island formed from mountains that rise above sea level; the mountains may be active volcanoes. p. 380

hypothesis (hī poth'ə sis), *noun*, something assumed because it seems likely to be a true explanation. p. 330

illiterate (i lit'ər it), *adjective*, unable to read or write. p. 501

immigrant (im'ə grənt), *noun*, a person who leaves his or her homeland and comes to live in another country. p. 471

imperialism (im pir'ē ə liz'əm), *noun*, the control of a country's political and economic life by another country. p. 197

import (im'port), *noun*, a good that one country buys from another country. p. 72

infant mortality, the rate of death among babies one year of age or younger. p. 358

intensive farming, a kind of farming in which a small amount of land is worked to produce a large amount of crops. p. 338

junta (jun'tə), *noun*, a small group of military leaders who govern with the help of their army after a revolution or coup. p. 503

kaiser (kī'zər), *noun*, the title given to the German emperor. p. 227

knight (nīt), *noun*, (in the Middle Ages) a warrior from the class of lesser nobles. p. 165

landform (land'form'), *noun*, a surface feature of the earth. The major kinds of landforms are mountains, hills, plateaus, and plains. p. 30

language family, a group of languages that have a common ancestor. p. 217

latitude (lat'ə tüd), *noun*, location north or south of the Equator. p. 43

leeward (lē'wərd), *adjective*, on the side away from the wind. p. 47

liberalism (lib'ər ə liz'əm), *noun*, a philosophy of government based on the ideas of John Locke, an English philosopher of the 1600s. Locke said all human beings were created free and equal, with certain rights. p. 190

life expectancy, the average length of time people live. p. 358

limited monarchy, a government ruled by a king or queen, where the monarch's power is limited by law and custom. p. 176

literacy (lit'ər ə sē), *noun*, the ability to read and write. p. 358

llanos (lä'nōz), *noun*, a grassy plains region, as in Colombia and Venezuela. p. 510

longitude (lon'jə tüd), *noun*, location east or west of the Prime Meridian. p. 74

low island, an island made of coral skeletons that have built up on underwater mountains. p. 380

map projection, any flat map that shows parallels and meridians. p. 198

market economy, a system in which businesses have the freedom to produce what they choose and to sell their products for whatever price they can get in the marketplace. p. 264

martial law, rule by the military, usually carried out in time of war or other trouble and involving the elimination of certain rights. p. 431

medieval (mē′dē ē′vəl), *adjective*, a word that refers to the Middle Ages, the period of European history from about A.D. 500 to 1350. p. 163

melting pot, a city or country in which people of various cultures live together. p. 447

meridian (mə rid′ē ən), *noun*, an imaginary line running halfway around the earth, from pole to pole. Meridians mark longitude. p. 74

mestizo (me stē′zō), *noun*, a person of mixed ancestry, especially a person of Spanish and American Indian ancestry in Latin America. p. 471

migration (mī grā′shən), *noun*, the movement of people from one place to another. p. 59

militarist (mil′ə tər ist), *noun*, a person who favors a very strong military organization or believes that military interests are most important. p. 405

military alliance, a joining together of countries that agree to support one another in case of war. p. 232

mineral (min′ər əl), *noun*, a nonliving substance obtained through mining, or digging in the earth. p. 49

missionary (mish′ə ner′ē), *noun*, a person sent by a church to teach others about the religious beliefs of the church. p. 308

moderate (mod′ər it), *noun*, a person who holds views that are not extreme. p. 444

monarchy (mon′ər kē), *noun*, a government ruled by a king or queen. p. 176

monastery (mon′ə ster′ē), *noun*, one or more buildings in which a group of people, especially monks, live according to certain rules and religious vows. p. 88

monotheism (mon′ə thē iz′əm), *noun*, the belief in only one God. p. 111

monsoon (mon sün′), *noun*, a seasonal wind that occurs in the Indian Ocean and South Asia. p. 418

mores (môr′āz), *noun, plural*, norms that establish what is morally right or wrong to do in a society. p. 81

mulatto (mə lat′ō), *noun*, a person of mixed black and white ancestry. p. 514

mullah (mul′ə), *noun*, a Muslim religious leader. p. 415

nation (nā′shən), *noun*, a large group of people who live in a specific territory under one government. p. 176

nationalism (nash′ə nə liz′əm), *noun*, the idea that people who are united by a common language, history, and tradition should form their own country. Nationalism is also the strong feeling of loyalty that people have toward their country. p. 225

natural environment, the physical setting of a place. Landforms, climate, natural vegetation, and natural resources are the four main parts of the natural environment of a place. p. 209

natural resource, anything in, on, or above the earth that people use to meet their needs. p. 48

natural vegetation, plant life that is native to a region and grows without the help of people. p. 36

neutrality (nü tral′ə tē), *noun*, the policy of a country that does not take sides in conflicts among other countries. p. 250

norm (nôrm), *noun*, a standard of behavior, or rule by which members of a society are supposed to live. p. 81

nuclear family, a family that includes only parents and their children. p. 91

oasis (ō ā′sis), *noun*, a fertile place in a desert where there is water and some vegetation. p. 299

ocean current, a flow of water through the ocean. p. 45

official language, the language of business and government in a country. p. 307

oligarchy (ol′ə gär′kē), *noun*, a government ruled entirely by a few people. p. 278

outback (out′bak′), *noun*, a thinly settled area or back country, especially in Australia. p. 433

Glossary

paddy (pad′ē), *noun*, a field of rice. p. 382

parallel (par′ə lel), *noun*, an imaginary line running from east to west around the earth. Parallels mark latitude. p. 74

parliament (par′lə ment), *noun*, an assembly that is the highest lawmaking body in some countries. p. 247

patrician (pə trish′ən), *noun*, (in ancient Rome) a rich landowner. p. 150

peasant (pez′nt), *noun*, (in the Middle Ages) one of the farmers who lived in and around the villages of a noble's land. p. 165

peninsula (pə nin′sə lə), *noun*, land surrounded by water on all sides but one. p. 210

permafrost (pėr′mə frôst′), *noun*, a layer of permanently frozen soil below the land surface. p. 213

pesticide (pes′tə sīd), *noun*, a chemical poison that wards off attacks by insects on plants. p. 383

pharaoh (fer′ō), *noun*, a king of ancient Egypt. Egyptians believed that each pharaoh was a living god on earth. p. 112

philosopher (fə los′ə fər), *noun*, a person who studies everything having to do with nature and human beings. p. 137

plantation (plan tā′shən), *noun*, a large farm on which a crop such as cotton or coffee is grown for sale. p. 304

plebeian (pli bē′ən), *noun*, (in ancient Rome) one of the ordinary people. p. 150

polder (pōl′dər), *noun*, land that once was under the sea but has been recovered for use. p. 251

pollution (pə lü′shən), *noun*, the dirtying of any part of the air, water, or soil. p. 52

population distribution, the way people are spread out over the earth. p. 59

prairie (prer′ē), *noun*, a large, grassy plains area. p. 465

precipitation (pri sip′ə tā′shən), *noun*, moisture that falls to the ground as rain or snow or in some other form. p. 35

premier (pri mir′), *noun*, (in communist countries) the chairman of the executive branch of the government. p. 277

prime minister, the executive leader of a government that has a parliament. p. 247

prophet (prof′it), *noun*, a religious leader who claims to be God's messenger. p. 168

protectorate (prə tek′tər it), *noun*, a weak country under the protection and control of a stronger country. p. 362

rainforest (rān′fôr ist), *noun*, a very dense forest that grows in hot areas of heavy rainfall. p. 38

reform (ri fôrm′), *verb*, to improve by removing faults. p. 174

refugee (ref′yə jē′), *noun*, a person who flees for safety, especially to another country, because of persecution, war, or disaster. p. 405

reincarnation (rē′in kär nā′shən), *noun*, the rebirth of the soul in a new body, a philosophy in which Hindus and Buddhists believe. p. 84

renaissance (ren′ə säns′), *noun*, a period of new or heightened interest in something, such as art or learning. The Renaissance began in Italy in the 1300s. p. 172

representative democracy, a form of government in which citizens elect people to make political decisions for them. p. 247

republic (ri pub′lik), *noun*, a government in which the citizens elect representatives to lead them. p. 150

revolution (rev′ə lü′shən), *noun*, a major change that makes a difference in the lives of many people. Political revolutions often involve the overthrow of a government and the replacement of it with another. p. 190

rural area, a country area made up of farms, villages, and small towns. p. 60

sanction (sangk′shən), *noun*, an action by one or more countries that withholds certain benefits from another country. p. 363

savanna (sə van′ə), *noun*, a tropical grassland with scattered trees. p. 299

scrub (skrub), *noun*, a kind of vegetation that grows in some deserts. Scrub includes patches of hardy grass, small shrubs, and cactuses. p. 40

segregation (seg′rə gā′shən), *noun*, the forced separation of one racial group from another. p. 327

senate (sen′it), *noun*, a governing or lawmaking assembly. In ancient Rome, the senate was made up of members elected by wealthy landowners. p. 150

serf (sėrf), *noun*, (in the Middle Ages) one of the poorest peasants. A serf rented land from a lord and had to work for the lord. A serf could not leave the land. p. 165

shifting cultivation, a kind of farming in which farmers farm a plot of land until the soil loses fertility, then shift to another plot until the first plot regains fertility. p. 304

socialism (sō′shə liz′əm), *noun*, a theory that holds that the government should control production and distribution of goods and services. p. 230

society (sə sī′ə tē), *noun*, a group of people who have common goals. p. 79

soviet (sō′vē et), *noun*, a council formed by revolutionaries to take over parts of the government during the Russian Revolution; a legislative body in the Soviet Union today. p. 234

specialization (spesh′əl i zā′shən), *noun*, an economic system in which each person does only one kind of job. p. 104

standard of living, the quality of life as measured by available food, clothing, housing, medical care, education, and so on. p. 247

standard time, a system of time that divides the world into twenty-four regions, one for each hour of the day. p. 92

steppe (step), *noun*, a treeless region of short grasses. p. 213

strike (strīk), *verb*, to stop work (at a business, factory, etc.) in an attempt to try to get such benefits as better wages and working conditions. p. 280

subsistence farming, farming that produces only about enough for farmers and their families to meet their basic needs. p. 63

suburb (sub′ėrb′), *noun*, a city or town near a larger city. p. 60

synthetic (sin thet′ik), *adjective*, artificially made rather than grown naturally or made from natural materials. p. 466

tariff (tar′if), *noun*, a tax that a country charges on imports or exports. p. 252

technology (tek nol′ə jē), *noun*, the knowledge, skills, tools, and methods people use to meet their needs. p. 50

terrorist (ter′ər ist), *noun*, a person who uses deliberate violence against other people for political ends. p. 337

time zone, one of the twenty-four regions of the world established by the standard time system. There is one time zone for each hour of the day. p. 92

totalitarian (tō tal′ə ter′ē ən), *adjective*, having to do with a government controlled by one group or leader who permits no opposition and tries to control the lives of the people. p. 235

tradition (trə dish′ən), *noun*, a belief or custom handed down from generation to generation. p. 217

treaty (trē′tē), *noun*, a formal agreement, especially between countries. p. 401

tribe (trīb), *noun*, a group of people related by common ancestors and a common way of life. p. 127

tribute (trib′yüt), *noun*, money, goods, or other payment that conquered people are forced to pay their rulers. p. 482

tropics (trop′iks), *noun*, the area between these two parallels—the Tropic of Cancer (north of the Equator), and the Tropic of Capricorn (south of the Equator). p. 38

tsar (zär), *noun*, the title given to the Russian emperor. p. 230

tundra (tun′drə), *noun*, an area where mosses and short, hardy grasses grow in a cold and dry climate. p. 42

underpopulated (un′dər pop′yə lāt ed), *adjective*, having fewer people in a region than the region can support. p. 389

urban area, a central city surrounded by smaller cities and towns. p. 60

value (val′yü), *noun*, an object, idea, or belief that a culture considers very important. p. 81

veto (vē′tō), *verb*, to overturn or reject a law passed by a lawmaking body. p. 150

viceroyalty (vīs′roi′əl tē), *noun*, (in Spanish colonial America) a large district run by a viceroy, a manager appointed by the Spanish monarch. p. 484

volcano (vol kā′nō), *noun*, an opening in the earth's crust, through which hot gases, liquids, and solid material sometimes escape. p. 377

weather (weŧH′ər), *noun*, the daily condition of the air. p. 35

windward (wind′wərd), *adjective*, on the side toward the wind. p. 47

Index

---

* = glossary word; *c.* = chart, diagram, graph,
or table; *m.* = map; *p.* = picture

Index

Index

Index

Acknowledgments

Quoted Material

UNIT 2 **114** Howard Carter and A. C. Mace, THE DISCOVERY OF THE TOMB OF TUTANKHAMEN. New York: Dover Publications, 1977, pp. 98, 99. **139** Thucydides, THE HISTORY OF THE PELOPONNESIAN WAR, edited by Sir Richard Livingstone. New York: Oxford University Press, 1966. **149** H. A. Guerber, THE MYTHS OF GREECE AND ROME, rev. ed. London: London House and Maxwell, 1938, pp. 82, 83. **159** (left) Chelsea Quinn Yarbro, LOCADIO'S APPRENTICE. New York: Harper & Row, Publishers, 1984, pp. 177-179. **159** (right) Pliny the Younger, LETTER TO TACITUS. A.D. 79.

UNIT 3 **226** George M. Trevelyan, GARIBALDI'S DEFENCE OF THE ROMAN REPUBLIC, 1848-9. Westport, Connecticut: Greenwood Press, 1971, p. 231. **231** From the preface by Karl Marx and Friedrich Engels, MANIFESTO OF THE COMMUNIST PARTY. San Francisco: China Books & Periodicals, Inc., 1965.

UNIT 4 **293** John Gunther, INSIDE AFRICA. New York: Harper & Brothers, 1955, p. xxi. **294** C. P. Kirby, EAST AFRICA: KENYA, UGANDA AND TANZANIA. New York: David White, 1968, p. 7. **301** John Gunther, INSIDE AFRICA. New York: Harper & Brothers, 1955, p. 553. **306** Kathleen Arnott, AFRICAN MYTHS AND LEGENDS. New York: Henry Z. Walck, Inc., 1962, pp. 32-33. **317** Margaret Shinnie, ANCIENT AFRICAN KINGDOMS. New York: St. Martin's Press, Inc. 1965.

UNIT 5 **396-397** J. Legge, trans. and ed., "The Travels of Fa-Hsien," in CHINESE LITERATURE. London: Cooperative Publishing Co., 1900, p. 230. **422** P. D. C. Davis and A. A. Dent, ANIMALS THAT CHANGED THE WORLD, New York: Crowell-Collier Press, 1968, p. 81 (Based on the work of F. E. Zeuner, A HISTORY OF DOMESTICATED ANIMALS. **422-423** From MOTHER INDIA'S CHILDREN: MEETING TODAY'S GENERATION IN INDIA by Edward Rice. Copyright © 1971 by Edward Rice. Reprinted by permission of Pantheon Books, a Division of Random House, Inc. **436** (left) Colin Thiele, THE SHADOW ON THE HILLS, New York: Harper & Row, Publishers, 1977, pp. 18-19. **436** (right) Aboriginal Legends collected by Daisy Bates, retold by Barbara Ker Wilson, TALES TOLD TO KABBARLI, New York: Crown Publishers, Inc., 1972, p. 25. **437** (left) Emilie U. Lepthien, AUSTRALIA, Enchantment of the World series. Chicago: Childrens Press, 1982, pp. 20, 21. **437** From "Lyrebirds" from COLLECTED POEMS 1942-70 by Judith Wright. Reprinted by permission of Angus & Robertson Publishers.

UNIT 6 **466** Margot Astrov, ed., AMERICAN INDIAN PROSE AND POETRY. New York: Capricorn Books, 1962, p. 233. **490** The Decision-Tree device used on page 490 was developed by Roger LaRaus and Richard C. Remy. The device is used in this text with their permission.

Illustrations

The abbreviations indicate position of pictures when more than one picture is on a page. *Bk* is background, *t* is top, *b* is bottom, *l* is left, *r* is right, and *c* is center. Unless otherwise acknowledged, all photos are the property of Scott, Foresman and Company.

INTRODUCTION **1** © Copyright by RAND MCNALLY & COMPANY, R.L.86PG13. **4** Environmental Research Institute of Michigan **12** George Rodger/Magnum Photos **19** The National Maritime Museum, London

UNIT 1 **26** Courtesy of Christian Scientist Publishing Society **28** Earth Satellite Corp./GEOPIC **32** S. Vidler/Leo deWys **33** Gordon Wiltsie 1985/Bruce Coleman Inc. **34** Robert Frerck/Odyssey Productions, Chicago **35** Paolo Koch/Photo Researchers **40** Giorgio Gualco/Bruce Coleman Inc. **41(l)** George D. Dodge/Bruce Coleman Inc. **41(r)** Brian & Cherry Alexander **42** Kryn Taconis/Magnum Photos **44(l)** Stacy Pick/Stock Boston **44(r)** Tom Walker/Stock Boston **47** Loren McIntyre **48** Robert Frerck/Odyssey Productions, Chicago **49** Milt & Joan Mann/Cameramann International **51** Hiroji Kubota/Magnum Photos **52(l)** Joseph A. DiChello **52(r)** Baron Wolman **55** Georgiann Flowers **58** Joseph F. Viesti **61** Courtesy of Parke-Davis Division of Warner-Lambert Company **67** Farrell Greman/Photo Researchers **69** Milt & Joan Mann/Cameramann International **70** William J. Megna **71** Michael Salas/The Image Bank **73** Al Satterwhite/The Image Bank **79** Brian & Cherry Alexander **80** Milt & Joan Mann/Cameramann International **81** S. Vidler/Leo deWys **82** Jacques Jangoux/Peter Arnold, Inc. **83** Milt & Joan Mann/Cameramann International **84** M. Friedel/G & J Images/The Image Bank **89** Christa Armstrong/Photo Researchers **96** J.L.Atlan/Sygma

UNIT 2 **100(l)** Hirmer Fotoarchiv/Iraq Museum, Bagdad **100(c)** Robert Harding Picture Library Ltd., London/Egyptian Museum, Cairo. Photo by B. L. Kenett © George Rainbird Ltd. **100(r)** Scala/Art Resource/Museo Nazionale de Villa Giula, Rome. **102** Courtesy of the Trustees of the British Museum **105** G. Gerster/Rapho/Photo Researchers **106** © Copyrighted by the University Museum, University of Pennsylvania **109** Hirmer Fotoarchiv **110(bk)** Giraudon/The Louvre, Paris **111** Jorg. P. Anders/Staatliche Museen Preussischeu/Gemaldegalerie, Kulterbesitz, West Berlin **114** George Holton/Photo Researchers **115** Lepsius, Denkmake . . . 1860 **118** Ladies Preparing Newly Woven Silk (detail) Attr. To: Emperor Hui-Tsung (1082-1135) Northern Sung Dynasty, early 12th century. Handscroll; ink and colors and gold on silk 37 x 145.3 cm. Chinese and Japanese Special Fund. Courtesy, Museum of Fine Arts, Boston **124** Rene Burri/Magnum Photos **128** George Holton/Photo Researchers **130** Leo deWys **131** Scala/Art Resource NY/Heraklion Museo, Crete **132** Antikenmuseum SMPK Berlin. Foto: J. Geske-Heiden **134** Walter S. Clark Jr./Photo Researchers **136(t)** Connie Geocaris/Click/Chicago Ltd. **136(b)** Giorgio Nimarallah/Art Resource NY/Museo Nazionale, Athens **137** Scala/Art Resource NY/Museo Nazionale, Naples **138** Bolden/Focus On Sports **140** Scala Art Resource NY/National Museum, Naples **148** M. Bertinetti/Photo Researchers **153** Porterfield-Chickering/Photo Researchers **156(l)** David Luttrell **156(r)** © 1984 Jose Azel/Contact Press Images/Woodfin Camp **157** "The Calling of the Apostles Peter and Andrew" Duccio d. Buoninsegna, Samuel H. Kress Collection, National Gallery of Art, Washington, D.C. **162** Scala/Art Resource NY/Galleria dell Accademia, Florence **165** Ms. Harley/The jousts of St. Ingilbert, French, 14th century. Courtesy of the Trustees of the British Library **167** Bibliotheque Nationale/MS5062 Fol.145R **170** Freer Gallery of Art/Smithsonian **171** Istanbul University Library **172** Scala/Art Resource NY/Mona Lisa.Leonardo da Vinci, Louvre, Paris **173** Art Resources NY/Hunters in the Snow, Peter Brueghel, Kunsthistorishes Museum, Vienna **174** Milt & Joan Mann/Cameramann International **175** Scala/Art Resource NY/Martin Luther by Cranach. Nurnberg, German National Museo **177** Musee de Versailles/Service de Documentation Photographique de la Reunion des Musees Nationaux **178(t)** Giraudon Art Resource NY/Archives Nationales, Paris **178(b)** Granger Collection, New York City **179** Mansell Collection **184** John Carter Brown Library, Providence, R.I./Brown University **185** Granger Collection, New York City **187** Scala/Art Resource NY/Uffizi, Florence **189** From Vallard Atlass-1546 MM29/Huntington Library, San Marino, Ca. **192(l)** From Storia Del Resorgimento E Dell' Unita' D'Italin **192(r)** De Hogues/Gamma-Liaison **193** Giraudon/Art Resource NY/Painting by Demachy. Carnavolet, Paris **195** The Bettmann Archive **197** Photo Science Museum, London **202** From the Art Collection of the Folger Shakespeare Library